Doug Bollig 2002

Close Listening

Close Listening

POETRY *and the* PERFORMED WORD

Edited by Charles Bernstein

NEW YORK   OXFORD
OXFORD UNIVERSITY PRESS
1998

Oxford University Press

Oxford   New York
Athens   Auckland   Bangkok   Bogota   Bombay
Buenos Aires   Calcutta   Cape Town   Dar es Salaam
Delhi   Florence   Hong Kong   Istanbul   Karachi
Kuala Lumpur   Madras   Madrid   Melbourne
Mexico City   Nairobi   Paris   Singapore
Taipei   Tokyo   Toronto   Warsaw

and associated companies in
Berlin   Ibadan

Library of Congress Cataloging-in-Publication Data
Close listening : poetry and the performed word /
edited by Charles Bernstein
p.   cm.
Includes bibliographical references.
ISBN 0-19-510991-0; ISBN 0-19-510992-9
1. Poetics.   2. American poetry—History and criticism.
3. English poetry—History and criticism.   I. Bernstein, Charles,
1950–   .
PN 1042.C46 1998
808.1—dc21   97-32636

9 8 7 6 5 4 3 2 1

Printed in the United States of America
on acid-free paper

Acknowledgments

Grateful acknowledgment is made to David Antin, Clark Coolidge, Eugen Gomringer, Ana Hatherly, Maurice Lemaitre (through the Bismuth-Lemaitre Foundation), Jackson Mac Low, Karen Mac Cormack, Maggie O'Sullivan, Joan Retallack, Sonia Sanchez, and Rosmarie Waldrop for permission to reproduce their work. Thanks also to Georges Borchardt, Inc., for permission to quote from W. S. Merwin; to New Directions Publishing Corporation for permission to quote from Denise Levertov, Susan Howe, and Gary Snyder; to the University of California Press for permission to quote from Robert Creeley; and to Wesleyan University Press for permission to quote from Joan Retallack.

Contents

Contributors

BRUCE ANDREWS lives in New York City, where he performs as Musical Director for Sally Silvers & Dancers and teaches political economy at Fordham University. Recent books include *Paradise & Method: Poetics & Practice* (essays on poetics from Northwestern) and *Ex Why Zee* (poems and performance scores from Roof).

CHARLES BERNSTEIN is the editor of *The Politics of Poetic Form: Poetry and Public Policy* and, with Bruce Andrews, *The L=A=N=G=U=A=G=E Book*. His most recent books are *Republics of Reality: Poems 1975–1995* and *A Poetics*. Bernstein is David Gray Professor of Poetry and Letters, Poetics Program, SUNY-Buffalo.

MARIA DAMON teaches literature at the University of Minnesota. She is the author of *The Dark End of the Street: Margins in American Vanguard Poetry* (University of Minnesota Press, 1993) and a member of the National Writers' Union.

JOHANNA DRUCKER has been publishing her own visual and concrete works since the early 1970s. Her scholarly work includes *The Visible Word: Experimental Typography and Modern Art* (1994) and *The Alphabetic Labyrinth* (1995). Currently a professor at Yale, she will be joining the faculty at SUNY-Purchase in the Fall of 1998.

SUSAN HOWE's most recent books of poems are *Frame Structures* and *The Nonconformist Memorial*. She is the author of two books of essays, *The Birth-mark: Unsettling the Wilderness in American Literary History* and *My Emily Dickinson*. Howe is a professor of English at SUNY-Buffalo.

STEVE McCAFFERY is Associate Professor of English, Temple University, and author of more than twenty books of poetry and prose including *North of Intention: Critical Writings 1974–1986, The Black Debt,* and *The Cheat of Words*. He is coeditor with Jed Rasula of *Imagining Language: Three Millennia of Conjecture on the Written and Spoken Sign.*

PETER MIDDLETON is a poet and a Senior Lecturer in English at the University of Southampton in the U.K. His most recent book is *The Inward Gaze: Masculinity and Subjectivity in Modern Culture* (Routledge). He has recently published articles on Lorine Niedecker and on contemporary British poetry.

BOB PERELMAN has written nine books of poetry, including *Virtual Reality* and *Captive Audience,* and two critical books, *The Marginalization of Poetry* and *The Trouble With Genius,* and has edited two collections of talks, *Writing/Talks* and *Talks (Hills 6/7).* He teaches at the University of Pennsylvania.

MARJORIE PERLOFF's most recent books are *Wittgenstein's Ladder: Poetic Language and the Strangeness of the Ordinary* and *Poetry On & Off the Page: Essays for Emergent Occasions.* She is Sadie Dernham Patek Professor of Humanities at Stanford University.

NICK PIOMBINO is a poet, essayist, and psychoanalyst who lives in New York. His books include *Poems, The Boundary of Blur: Essays* and *Light Street.* His work has been anthologized in *The L=A=N=G=U=A=G=E Book, In the American Tree, The Politics of Poetic Form,* and *From the Other Side of the Century.*

PETER QUARTERMAIN is the author of *Disjunctive Poetics: From Gertrude Stein and Louis Zukofsky to Susan Howe,* and editor, with Richard Caddel, of the anthology, OTHER *British and Irish Poetry 1970–1995.* He lives in Vancouver and teaches at the University of British Columbia.

JED RASULA teaches English at Queen's University in Ontario. He is the author of *The American Poetry Wax Museum* and *Tabula Rasula,* a book of poems and calligrams. The essay included here is part of a work in progress, *Seeing Double,* another part of which is "Poetry's Voice Over" in *Sound States,* edited by Adalaide Morris.

SUSAN M. SCHULTZ teaches in the department of English at the University of Hawai'i-Manoa. She edited *The Tribe of John: Ashbery and Contemporary Poetry.* Her book of poems, *Aleatory Allegories,* is forthcoming, and she edits a journal of experimental writing from the Pacific, *Tinfish.*

RON SILLIMAN works as a market analyst in the computer services industry. He lives in the Valley Forge region of Philadelphia. Among his twenty-one books are *The New Sentence, In the American Tree, Ketjak, Tjanting, The Age of Huts,* and several volumes that contain portions of the long poem *The Alphabet.*

SUSAN STEWART's most recent book is *The Forest.* Stewart is also the author of *Crimes of Writing* and *On Longing.* She teaches poetry and poetics at the University of Pennsylvania, where she is Regan Professor of English.

DENNIS TEDLOCK is McNulty Professor of English and Research Professor of Anthropology at SUNY-Buffalo. His books include *Finding the Center: Narrative Poetry of the Zuni Indians* and *Breath on the Mirror: Mythic Voices and Visions of the Living Maya.* He was awarded the PEN Translation Prize in Poetry for *Popol Vuh: The Mayan Book of the Dawn of Life.*

LORENZO THOMAS, associate professor of English at the University of Houston—Downtown, has contributed essays to the *African American Encyclopedia, American Literary Scholarship,* and *Oxford Companion to African American Literature.* His collections of poetry include *The Bathers* and *There Are Witnesses.*

Close Listening

Introduction

CHARLES BERNSTEIN

I sing and I play the flute for myself.
For no man except me understands my language.
As little as they understand the nightingale
do the people understand what my song says.

PEIRE CARDENAL

No one listens to poetry. The ocean
Does not mean to be listened to. A drop
Or crash of water. It means
Nothing.

JACK SPICER

Close Listening: Poetry and the Performed Word brings together seventeen essays, written especially for this volume, on poetry readings, the sound of poetry, and the visual performance of poetry. While the performance of poetry is as old as poetry itself, critical attention to modern and contemporary poetry performance has been negligible, despite the crucial importance of performance to the practice of the poetry of this century. This collection opens many new avenues for the critical discussion of the sound and performance of poetry, paying special attention to innovative work. More important, the essays collected here offer original and wide-ranging elucidations of how twentieth-century poetry has been practiced as a performance art.

While this book is grounded in contemporary poetry, its project extends well beyond the contemporary in its considerations of the history of the modern poetry reading, oral poetries, and the lyric in our own culture and other cultures, and in its attempt to rethink prosody in the light of the performance and sounding of poetry. This is a wide-ranging subject and one that I believe the essays here will fundamentally transform. At one end of the spectrum are philosophical and critical approaches to the contribution of sound to meaning: the way poets, and especially twentieth-century innovative poets, work with sound as material, where sound is neither arbitrary nor secondary but constitutive. At the other end of the spectrum is the critical interpretation of the performance style of individual poets. Such approaches are intended to encourage "close listenings," not only to the printed text of poems but also to tapes and performances (and so to encourage far greater use of sound recordings, which will, hopefully, foment greater production of such recordings by publishers).

Close listenings may contradict "readings" of poems that are based exclusively on the printed text and that ignore the poet's own performances, the "total" sound of the work, and the relation of sound to semantics. Certainly, discussion of sound as a material and materializing dimension of poetry also calls into play such developments as sound poetry, performance poetry, radio plays and radio "space," movie soundtracks, poetry/music collaborations, and other audioworks, an area of investigation taken up by Steve McCaffery's essay in this volume and which is the subject of a new, related collection, *Sound States: Acoustical Technologies and Modern and Postmodern Writing,* edited by Adalaide Morris. Beyond that, this book is a call for a non-Euclidean (or complex) prosody for the many poems for which traditional prosody does not apply. Certainly, this might be one way to frame the contributions here of Marjorie Perloff, who looks at what comes after "free verse," and Bruce Andrews, whose poetics of "informalism" advocates the continuing radicalism of "constructivist noise." In her essay, Susan Stewart provides both a historical and theoretical context for—and alternative to—these accounts by "sounding" the lyric as a form of feeling, with particular reference to song and the spoken, rhythm and meter; her subject is the promise of aurality. Susan Howe sounds the limits of this subject in her evocation of sound as embedded in a sensorium of memory, smell, rhythm, song, and recitation. She charts this theater of lost history, where poetry makes its home, in terms of the vampirish transformations of photos, microfilm, and news clippings—which is to say, memory's hold—all the while accenting the voyage of her family's voice from Ireland to America.

Any account of poetry readings must also give an account of the sound of poetry; the first part of this collection sets the stage for the specific discussion of performance in the subsequent sections. In part III, Peter Middleton tackles the difficult and elusive subject of the history of the modern poetry reading. His essay suggests that the question of the origins of the poetry reading might better be inverted—not, When did modern poetry readings begin? but When did poetry cease to be presented primarily through performance? That is, When (if ever) did silent reading take precedence over live performance? As it is, Middleton concludes not that poetry readings are something that happens to poems but that poems sometimes happen as readings. My own discussion here, while placing the other contributions in context, focuses primarily on the acoustic dimensions of the poetry reading.

Since the 1950s, the poetry reading has become one of the most important sites for the dissemination of poetic works in North America, yet studies of the distinctive features of the poem-in-performance have been rare (even full-length studies of a poet's work routinely ignore the audiotext), and readings—no matter how well attended—are rarely reviewed by newspapers or magazines (though they are the frequent subject of light, generally misinformed, "feature" stories on the perennial "revival" of poetry).[1] A large archive of audio and video documents, dating back to an early recording of Tennyson's almost inaudible voice, awaits serious study and interpretation. In these essays, we have tried to integrate the modern history of poetry into a more general history of performance art and philosophical and linguistic approaches to the acoustic dimension of language. The absence of such a history has had the effect of eliding the significance of the modernist poetry traditions for postwar performance art. At the same time, the performative dimension of poetry has significant relation to text-based visual and conceptual art, as well as visual poetry, which extend the performative (and material) dimension of the literary text into visual space.

The newly emerging field of performance studies and theory provides a useful context for this study. By considering examples of "total" performances in other cultures, performance theorists have reoriented the discussion of the relation of theater, audience, and text. While much of the discussion of postmodern performance art has been focused on this and related contexts, there has been considerably less focus on the implications for poetry performance. Particularly helpful for "close listening" is Erving Goffman's *Frame Analysis,* especially his conception of how the cued frame through which a situation (or work) is viewed necessarily puts other features out of frame, into what he calls the "disattend track." Focusing attention on a poem's content or form typically involves putting the audiotext as well as the typography—the sound and look of the poem—into the disattend track. Indeed, the drift of much literary criticism of the two decades has been away from the auditory and performative aspects of the poem, partly because of the prevalent notion that the sound structure of language is relatively arbitrary, a view that is often contested in this book. Such elements as the visual appearance of the text or the sound of the work in performance may be extralexical but they are not extrasemantic. When textual elements that are conventionally framed out as nonsemantic are acknowledged as significant, the result is a proliferation of possible frames of interpretation. Then it becomes a question of whether we see these frames or strata as commensurate with each other, leading to a "total image complex" of the poem, to use Veronica Forrest-Thomson's term; or whether we see these strata as incommensurate with each other, contradictory, leading to a reading of the poem as untotalizable. Here "strata" might usefully be thought of also as the kind of layers one finds in a palimpsest.

In a sense, this collection presents a complex, multilayered response to a quite simple, and common, response to a poetry reading, as when one says: "I understand the work better hearing the poet read it. I would never have been able to figure out that the poems would sound that way." (This is not to discount the significance of performances by poets that seem "bad" for one reason or another or may make one like the work less than on the page, nor to distract from the significance of the performance of a poem by someone other than its author.) Insofar as poetry performance is countenanced as a topic of discussion, the subject is often assumed to be exemplified by such high-octane examples as Vachel Lindsay's notorious "Congo" ("MUMBO JUMBO in the CONNNG-GO"), or Carl Sandberg's melodramatic presentation style ("in the tooooombs, the coooool tooooooombs"), or Allen Ginsberg's near-chanting of "Howl," or more recently the "rap" and "slam" poetry discussed in part III by Maria Damon. But the unanticipatably slow tempo of Wallace Stevens's performance tells us much about his sense of the poem's rhythms and philosophical sensuousness, just as John Ashbery's near monotone suggests a dreamier dimension than the text sometimes reveals. The intense emotional impact of Robert Creeley's pauses at line breaks gives an affective interpretation to what otherwise reads as a highly formal sense of fragmented line breaks—the breaks suggest emotional pitch and distress in a way audible in the recordings but not necessarily on the page. The recordings of Gertrude Stein make clear both the bell-like resonance of her voice and her sense of shifting rhythms against modulating repetitions and the shapeliness of her sound-sense; while, hearing Langston Hughes, one immediately picks up not only on the specific blues echoes in the work but how he modulated shifts into and out of these rhythms. Having heard these poets read, we change our hearing and reading of their works on the page as well.

As Middleton notes in his essay in this volume, there are a number of factors involved in the dramatically increased significance of the poetry reading in the postwar period in North America and the United Kingdom. At the outset, though, let me put forward one explanation. During the past forty years, more and more poets have used forms whose sound patterns are *made up*—that is, their poems do not follow received or prefabricated forms. It is for these poets that the poetry reading has taken on so much significance. For the sound shapes of the poems of such practitioners are often most immediately and viscerally heard in performance (taped or live), even if the attuned reader might be able to hear something comparable in her or his own (prior) reading of the text. *The poetry reading is a public tuning.* (Think of how public readings in the 1950s by Creeley, Ginsberg, Olson, and Kerouac established—in a primary way—not only the sound of their work but also the possibilities for related work. Bob Perelman's discussion of the poet's talk in part II explores more recent versions of a practice largely established by these poets.) The proliferation of poetry readings has allowed a spinning out into the world of a new series of acoustic modalities, which have had an enormous impact in informing the reading of contemporary poetry. These performances set up new conventions that are internalized and applied to further reading of the poetic texts. They are the acoustic grounding of innovative practice—our collective sounding board.

To be heard, poetry needs to be sounded—whether in a process of active, or interactive, reading of a work or by the poet in performance. Unsounded poetry remains inert marks on a page, waiting to be called into use by saying, or hearing, the words aloud. The poetry reading provides a focal point for this process in that its existence is uniquely tied to the reading aloud of the text; it is an emblem of the necessity for such reading out loud and in public. Nor is the process of transforming soundless words on a page into performed language unique to the poetry reading. To give just one example, Jerome Rothenberg points to the ancient Jewish tradition of reading and incanting the Torah—turning a script without vowels into a fully voiced sounding.[2] Public recitation also brings to mind a number of sermonic traditions, from subdued preachment to gospel call-and-response. And if the poetry reading provides unscripted elements for the performer, it also provides special possibilities for the listener, from direct response to the work, ranging from laughter to derision; to the pleasure of getting lost in language that surges forward, allowing the mind to wander in the presence of words.

When the audiotape archive of a poet's performance is acknowledged as a significant, rather than incidental, part of her or his work, a number of important textual and critical issues emerge. What is the status of discrepancies among performed and published versions of poems, and, moreover, between interpretations based on the text versus interpretations based on the performance? Amiri Baraka is one of the most dynamic poetry performers of the postwar period. For Baraka, making the words dance in performance means taking the poems off the page, out of the realm of ideas, and into action. In some of his most vibrantly performed poems, such as "Afro-American Lyric," the text can seem secondary, as if, as William Harris seems to suggest in his discussion of the poem, the text—with its inventive typography—has become merely a score for the performance.[3] Surely, it is always possible for some poems to seem thinner on the page than in performance, *and vice versa*. But I don't think this is the case for Baraka, whose work is always exploring the dialectic of performance and text, theory and practice, the literary and the oral—a dialectic that will involve clashes more than harmony. Performance, in the sense of doing, is an underlying formal aesthetic as much as it is a political issue in Baraka's work.[4] The shape of his performances are iconic—they signify. In this sense the printed text of "Afro-American Lyric" works to spur the (silent, atomized) reader *into* performance—it insists on action; the page's apparent textual "lack" is the motor of its form.

The text of "Afro-American Lyric" brings to mind the language of Marxist political pamphlets, foregrounding the poem's untransformed didacticism. Hearing Baraka read this poem on a tape of his July 26, 1978 performance at the Naropa Institute, however, gives a distinctly different impression. Baraka sounds the syllables of "simple shit" ("Seeeeeeeeeee-immmmmmmmmmmm pull" in the text), interweaving and syncopating them with "exploiting class, owning class, bourgeois class, reactionary class," turning the text's diatribe into a cross between a sound poem and a scat jazz improvisation. He makes playful yet dissonant music from the apparently refractory words of Marxist analysis, bringing out the uncontained phonic plenitude inside and between the words. This is no mere embellishment of the poem but a restaging of its meaning ("Class Struggle in Music," as Baraka titles a later poem). Baraka's recitations invoke a range of performance rhetorics from hortatory to accusatory: typically, he will segue from his own intoning of a song tune to a more neutrally inflected phrase, then plunge into a percussively grating sound. (Notable in this context is Lorenzo Thomas's synoptic account, in part III of this collection, of the prehistory of the performance styles of the Black Arts Movement, including, of course, Baraka's. Thomas starts with nineteenth-century recitations, going on to give accounts of the Harlem Renaissance and Projective Verse, in the process considering questions of the vernacular, dialect, public art, orality, and community/nationality.)

What's the relation of Baraka's performance—or of any poem performed by its author—to the original text? One goal I have for this book is to overthrow the common presumption that the text of a poem—that is, the written document—is primary and that the recitation or performance of a poem by the poet is secondary and fundamentally inconsequential to the "poem itself." In the conventional view, recitation has something of the status of interpretation—it provides a possible gloss of the immutable original. One problem with this perspective, most persuasively argued by Jerome McGann in *Black Riders, The Textual Condition,* and *A Critique of Modern Textual Criticism,* is that there is often no one original written version of a poem. Even leaving aside the status of the manuscript, there often exist various and discrepant printings—I should like to say textual performances—in magazines and books, with changes in wording but also in spacing, font, paper, and, moreover, contexts of readership; making for a plurality of versions, none of which can claim sole authority. I would call these multifoliate versions *performances* of the poem; and I would add the poet's own performance of the work in a poetry reading, or readings, to the list of variants that together, plurally, constitute and reconstitute the work. This, then, is clearly not to say that all performances of a poem have equal authority. An actor's rendition, like a type designer's "original" setting of a classic, will not have the same kind of authority as a poet's own reading or the first printing of the work. But the performance of the poet, just as the visualization of the poem in its initial printings, forever marks the poem's entry into the world; and not only its meaning, its existence.

A poem understood as a performative event and not merely as a textual entity refuses the originality of the written document in favor of "the plural event" of the work, to use a phrase of Andrew Benjamin's. That is, the work is not identical to any one graphical or performative realization of it, nor can it be equated with a totalized unity of these versions or manifestations. The poem, viewed in terms of its multiple performances, or mutual intertranslatability, has a fundamentally plural existence. This is most dramatically enunciated when instances of the work are contradictory or incommensurable, but it is also the case when versions are commensurate. To speak of the poem in performance is, then, to overthrow the idea of the poem as a fixed, stable, finite linguistic object; it is to deny the poem its self-presence and its unity. Thus, while performance emphasizes the material presence of the poem, and of the performer, it at the same time denies the unitary presence of the poem, which is to say its metaphysical unity.

Indulge me now as I translate some remarks by Benjamin on psychoanalysis and translation into the topic at hand:

> The question of presence, the plurality within being present, is of fundamental significance for poetry. The presence of the text (the written document) within the performance but equally the presence of the performance inside the text means that there are, at any one moment in time, two irreducible modes of being present. As presence becomes the site of irreducibility, this will mean that presence can no longer be absolutely present to itself. The anoriginal marks the possibility of the poem being either potentially or actually plural, which will mean that the poem will always lack an essential unity. (Within the context of poetry, what could be said to be lacking is an already given semantic and interpretive finitude, if not singularity, of the poem.) It is thus that there is no unity to be recovered, no task of thinking of the origin as such, since the origin, now the anorigin, is already that which resists the move to a synthetic unity. Any unity will be an aftereffect. Such aftereffects are comprised of given publications, performances, interpretations, or readings. The poem—that which is anoriginally plural—cannot be known as such because it cannot exist *as such*.[5]

The relation of a poem to variations created in a poetry reading has not, so far as I know, received attention. Variations created in performing "oral" poetry is, however, a subject of Gregory Nagy's *Poetry and Performance,* where, speaking of both the Homeric epics and troubadour poetry, he writes, "to perform the song . . . is to recompose it, to change it, to *move* it."[6] Indeed, Nagy's "poetics of variation" is suggested by two variant epithets for the nightingale in the *Odyssey*—where the nightingale can be understood as a metaphor for the performer of poetry: "patterning many different ways" (49–50) and also "with many resoundings" (39). Nagy quotes Alfred Lord's study of Homer, *The Singer of Tales:* "Our real difficulty arises from the fact that, unlike the oral poet, we are not accustomed to thinking in terms of fluidity. We find it difficult to grasp something that is *multiform*. It seems ideal to us to construct an ideal text or to seek an *original,* and we remain dissatisfied with an ever-changing phenomenon. I believe that once we know the facts of oral composition we must cease to find an *original* of any traditional song. From an oral point of view each performance is *original.*"[7]

The poetry reading, considered along with typographic, holographic, and contextual variants, modulates and deepens what McGann calls the "textual condition." The poetry reading extends the patterning of poetry into another dimension, adding another semantic layer to the poem's multi-formity. The effect is to create a space of authorial resistance to textual authority. For while writing is normally—if reductively and counterproduc-tively[8]—viewed as stabilizing and fixing oral poetic traditions, authorial po-etry readings are best understood as destabilizing, by making more fluid and pluriform, an aural (post-written) poetic practice. And here the double sense of reading is acutely relevant. For in realizing, by supplementing, the semantic possibilities of the poem in a reading, the poet encourages readers to perform the poem on their own, a performance that is allowed greater latitude depending on how reading-centered the poem is—that is, how much the poem allows for the active participation of the reader (in both senses) in the constitution of the poem's meaning.

I am proposing that we look at the poetry reading not as a secondary exten-sion of "prior" written texts but as its own medium. What, then, are the characteristics specific to this medium and what can it do that other live performance media—instrumental music, song and opera, theater—cannot? The answer may be found in what seems to many the profoundly anti-performative nature of the poetry reading: the poetry reading as radically "poor theater," in Jerzy Grotowski's sense. If that is true, it may show how what some find as the most problematic aspect of the poetry reading may turn out to be its essence: that is, its lack of spectacle, drama, and dynamic range, as exemplified especially in a certain minimal—anti-expressivist—mode of reading. I'm tempted to label this mode *anti-performative* to sug-gest a kind of rhetorical (in the stylistic sense of "antirhetorical") strategy and not to suggest it is any less a performance choice than the most "theatri-cal" reading. (John Cage's poetry readings are a good example of this mode.) In an age of spectacle and high drama, the anti-expressivist poetry reading stands out as an oasis of low technology that is among the least spectaclized events in our public culture. Explicit value is placed almost ex-clusively on the acoustic production of a single unaccompanied speaking voice, with all other theatrical elements being placed, in most cases, out of frame. The solo voice so starkly framed can come to seem virtually disem-bodied in an uncanny, even hypnotic, way. Such poetry readings share the intimacy of radio or of small-ensemble or chamber music. In contrast to theater, where the visual spectacle creates a perceived distance separating viewers from viewed, the emphasis on sound in the poetry reading has the opposite effect—it physically connects the speaker and listener, moving to overcome the self-consciousness of the performance context. Indeed, the anti-expressivist mode of reading works to defeat the theatricality of the performance situation, to allow the listener to enter into a concave acoustic space rather than be pushed back from it, as in a more propulsive reading mode (which creates a convex acoustic space). When a poem has an auditory rather than a visual source (the heard performance rather than the read text), our perspective on, or of, the work shifts. Rather than looking at the poem—at the words on a page—we may enter into it, perhaps to get lost, perhaps to lose ourselves, our (nonmetrical) "footing" with one another. According to Charles Lock, "the absence or presence of perspective marks the crucial difference between 'pictorial' and 'symbolic' signs, both of which are 'visual.' "[9] For a text is the only visual sign system that, as Lock puts it, is "entirely free of perspective" (418). Like a text, auditory phenomena do not permit perspective but they do have an auditory version of perspective, *location,* and that is a constitutive element of the medium of the poetry reading.

This formalist approach to the poetry reading may explain the common dislike, among poets, of actors' readings of poems: for this registers not a dislike of vocalization but of a style of acting that frames the performance in terms of character, personality, setting, gesture, development, or drama, even though these may be extrinsic to the text at hand. That is, the "acting" takes precedence over letting the words speak for themselves (or worse, eloquence compromises, not to say eclipses, the ragged music of the poem). The project of the poetry reading, from this formalist perspective, is to find the sound in the words, not in any extrinsic scenario or supplemental accompaniment. Without in any way wishing to undermine the more extravagantly theatrical style of reading, I would point to this more monovalent, minimally inflected, and in any case unaugmented, mode as touching on the essence of the medium. For poetry cannot, and need not, compete with music in terms of acoustic complexity or rhythmic force, or with theater in terms of spectacle. What is unique, and in its own way exhilarating, about the performance of poetry is that it does what it does within the limits of language alone.

(Let me note here Peter Quartermain's essay in this volume and in particular to his caution that the poet's voicing of a poem should not be allowed to eliminate ambiguous voicings in the text; nor should the author's performance of a poem be absolutely privileged over that of other readers and performers.)

The (unaccompanied) performance of poetry has as its upper limit music, as realized in what has come to be called sound poetry, and its lower limit silence, as realized in what has come to be called visual poetry. Visual poetry gets us to look at works as well as read them, while sound poetry gets us to hear as well as listen. Curiously, these two limits intersect, as when a visual poem is performed as a sound poem or a sound poem is scored as a visual poem (a phenomenon that is relevant to the explorations, in this volume, of Johanna Drucker, Dennis Tedlock, and Steve McCaffery). For the most part, however, this book focuses on the poetry reading in the ordinary sense, since it seems to me that this mode of reading is most critically neglected—or perhaps just taken for granted, if not derided. Even those sympathetic to performed poetry will remark that most poets can't read their work, as if such a sentiment suggests a defect with the medium of poetry readings. One might say that most of the poems published in books or magazines are dull without that observation reflecting on poetry as a medium. Perhaps it makes most sense to say that if you don't like a poet's reading it is because you don't like the poetry, to pick up on an observation of Aldon Nielsen on a recent internet discussion list. There are no poets whose work I admire whose readings have failed to engage me, to enrich my hearing of the work. That is not to say, however, that some readings don't trouble or complicate my understanding or appreciation. For related reasons, I am quite interested in audio recording of poetry readings. If, as I am suggesting, poetry readings foreground the audible acoustic text of the poem—what I want to call the audiotext of the poem, specifically extending Garrett Stewart's term *phonotext*—then audio reproduction is ideally suited to the medium. (Video, it seems to me, is often less engaging for poetry, since the typically depleted visual resources—static shots of a person at a podium—are no match for the sound track and tend to flatten out the affective dimension of the live performance. For me, the most energetic and formally engaging cinematic extension of the poetry reading are a series of films made from the mid-1970s to mid-1980s by Henry Hills, especially *Plagiarism, Radio Adios,* and *Money.*)

What is the relation of sound to meaning? Any consideration of the poetry reading must give special significance to this question, since poetry readings are acoustic performances that foreground the audiotext of the poem. One way of approaching this issue is to emphasize the oral dimension of poetry, the origins of the sounds of language in speech. And of course many poets do wish to identify their performance with just such an orality, even to the extent of stressing a "return" to a more "vital" cultural past, before the advent of writing. But I am interested in a broader range of performance practice than is suggested by orality; in fact, some of the most interesting poetry-reading styles—from Jackson Mac Low to Stein to T. S. Eliot—defy orality in very specific ways: Eliot through his eerily depersonalized vocal style (emanating from the mouth more than the diaphragm); Stein with her all-over, modulating or cubist resonances; and Mac Low with his immaculate enunciation of constructed word patterns. Orality can be understood as a stylistic or even ideological marker of a reading style; in contrast, the audiotext might more usefully be understood as aural—what the ear hears.

By *aurality* I mean to emphasize the sounding of the *writing,* and to make a sharp contrast with *orality* and its emphasis on breath, voice, and speech —an emphasis that tends to valorize speech over writing, voice over sound, listening over hearing, and indeed, orality over aurality. *Aurality precedes orality,* just as language precedes speech. Aurality is connected to the body—what the mouth and tongue and vocal chords enact—not the presence of the poet; it is proprioceptive, in Charles Olson's sense. The poetry reading enacts the poem not the poet; it materializes the text not the author; it performs the work not the one who composed it. In short, the significant fact of the poetry reading is less the presence of the poet than the presence of the poem. My insistence on aurality is not intended to valorize the material ear over the metaphysical mouth but to find a term that averts the identification of orality with speech. Aurality is meant to invoke a performative sense of "phonotext" or audiotext and might better be spelled *a/orality.* (Both Susan Schultz and Dennis Tedlock, in their essays, explore aspects of this issue.)

The audiotext, in the sense of the poet's acoustic performance, is a semantically denser field of linguistic activity than can be charted by means of meter, assonance, alliteration, rhyme, and the like (although these remain underlying elements of this denser linguistic field). Thinking in terms of the performance of the poem reframes many of the issues labored over by prosodists examining the written text of poems, often syllable by syllable, phoneme by phoneme, accent by accent, foot by foot, stress by stress, beat by beat, measure by measure. The poem performed conforms even less to analysis of syllable and stress than the poem as read. Many prosodists have insisted that the (musical) phrase provides a more useful way of understanding poetry's sound patterns than do accentual systems, whether quantitative or syllabic, that break poetry into metrical feet. Consideration of the performed word supports that view, although the concept of phrasing and of musicality is much expanded when one moves from the metrical to the acoustic, beyond "free verse" to sound shapes. For one thing, the dynamics charted by accentual prosodies have a much diminished place in the sound environment of a poetry reading, where intonations, pitch, tempos, accents (in the other sense of pronunciation), grain or timbre of voice, nonverbal face and body expressions or movements, as well as more conventional prosodic features such as assonance, alliteration, and rhyme, take on a significant role. But more importantly, regularizing systems of prosodic analysis break down before the sonic profusion of a reading: it's as if "chaotic" sound patterns are being measured by grid-oriented coordinates whose reliance on context-independent ratios is inadequate. The poetry reading is always at the edge of semantic excess, even if any given reader stays on this side of the border. In fact, one of the primary techniques of poetry performance is the disruption of rationalizable patterns of sound through the intervallic irruption of acoustic elements not recuperable by monologic analysis. While these irruptions may be highly artful, they may also fall into the body's rhythms—gasps, stutters, hiccups, burps, coughs, slurs, microrepetitions, oscillations in volume, "incorrect" pronunciations, and so on—that is, if you take these elements to be semantic features of the performed poem, as I propose, and not as extraneous interruption.[10]

Prosody is too dynamic a subject to be restricted to conventionally metrical verse. Yet many accounts of poetry continue to reduce questions of poetic rhythm to meter or regularized stress, as if nonmetrical poetry, especially the more radically innovative poetry of this century, were not *more* rhythmically and acoustically rich than its so-called formalist counterparts. In the acoustic space of performed poetry, I would emphasize *distress* and asymmetry, as much as accentual patter: dissonance and irregularity, rupture and silence constitute a rhythmic force (or *aversion of force*) in the sounded poem.[11] Such counterrhythmic elements create, according to Giorgio Agamben, "a mismatch, a disconnection between the metrical and syntactic elements, between sounding rhythm and meaning, such that (contrary to the received opinion that sees in poetry the locus of an accomplished and perfect fit between sound and meaning) poetry lives, instead, only in their inner disagreement. In the very moment when verse affirms its own identity by breaking a syntactic link, it is irresistibly drawn into bending over into the next line to lay hold of what it has thrown out of itself."[12]

If studies of prosody foundered in the early twentieth century on the inability to reconcile the musicality of poetry with strictly metrical classifications, then recitation usefully transforms the object of study from meter to rhythm, to use the distinction made by Henri Meschonnic, for whom meter is asocial and without meaning, while rhythm is grounded in the historicity of the poem and implies a sociality.[13] The issue is not the written—the text—versus the oral, but the embodied acoustic performance—the aurality of the work—versus an abstract or external idealization that is based on a projection of time as a "smooth" space, which is unilinear, homogenous, and incremental. The new prosody requires an engagement not with abstract time but with duration and its microtones, discontinuities, striations, and disfluencies. Traditional metrics, with its metronomic beats, remains a fundamentally Euclidean system that is unsuited to a full measuring of the complex prosodies of the twentieth century or, moreover, much older poetry (including that discussed in Tedlock's contribution to this book).

In performance, meter is eclipsed by isochrony—the unwritten tempo (rhythmic, cyclical, overlapping) whose beat is audible in the performance as distinct from the text. In *Free Verse: An Essay on Prosody,* Charles Hartman quotes Karl Shapiro's comment that isochrony "equalizes unequal accentual elements by varying the *time* of feet, whether in the ear or in the recitation."[14] Hartman goes on to argue that "equivalence" has "only secondary bearing on English verse" (38); to which I would say: *exactly the same secondary bearing as performance!* Insofar as the performed word is granted a reciprocal status to the text, isochrony becomes a dominant prosodic element, not just in the poetry reading but also in the silent reading (I would now say silent recitation) of the poem, as well as in the composition of poem—whether "by ear" (in Charles Olson's phrase) or by sentence (in Ron Silliman's). In short, recitation rests on temporal rather than syllabic or accentual measure, which themselves may become secondary. This greatly expands the sense of isochrony from slight variations of nonstressed syllables to larger acoustic and lettristic units, and indeed the sort of isochronic practice I have in mind would allow for the equivalence of temporally unequal units. For this complex or "fuzzy" prosody of sound shapes, such polyrhythmic equivalencies are created by performed pauses, syncopations, emphasis, as well as shifts in tempo and pitch; just as on the page equivalencies are indicated by visual organization (lines irrespective of tempo), by nonmetrical counting (of syllables or words), and the like. The page's enjambment and syntactic scissoring become performance's isochronic disruption of syntactic flow, creating a contra-sense rhythm (or anti-rhythm) that is abetted by breaking, pausing (temporal caesura), and other techniques that go against the flow of speech rhythms. Isochrony may also be used to create a stereo or holographic effect, for example in the intense overlapping phrasal units in Leslie Scalapino's readings.

PERForMANCE readily allows FOR stressING ("promotING") unstressED syllaBLEs, INcluding prepOsitions, artiCLEs, aNd conjunctIONS—creaTING syncOPAted rHyThms, whiCH, onCE hEArd are THen caRRied over by readERS iNTo theIr oWN reAding of tHe teXT. (Let me stress that, as with many features I am discussing in the context of performance, it is often possible to hear such rhythmic and arhythmic patterns in the process of close listening to the written text of the poem, as in Stein's aptly titled prose-format poem *How to Write*. Gerard Manley Hopkins's marvelously delirious attempts to visually mark such patterns in his texts is discussed in Jed Rasula's essay in this volume.) Performance also underscores (or should I say underwrites?) a prosodic movement of which I am particularly fond, in which the poem suggests a certain rhythmic pattern over the course of perhaps, a few lines, then segues into an incommensurable pattern, sometimes shuttling between the two, sometimes adding a third or fourth pattern: the prior pattern continues on underneath as a sort of sonic afterimage, creating a densely layered, or braided, or chordal, texture. The complex or fuzzy prosodics of such sprung rhythm produces the acoustic equivalent of a moiré pattern.

Performance also allows for the maximum inflection of different, possibly dissonant, voices: a multivocality that foregrounds the dialogic dimension of poetry. Hannah Weiner's performance of her *Clairvoyant Journal* is an exhilarating example—three competing voices of one "self" collide with one another in an electric ensemble consisting of Weiner, Peggy DeCoursey, and Sharon Matlin in a tape published by New Wilderness Audiographics in 1976. But I am equally interested in the possibility of slippage among tones, dictions, accents, and registers in polyvocal performances in which different voices are evoked using performative cues rather than alphabetic ones. The potential here is to create rhythms and voicings that are not only supplemental to the written text but also at odds with it.

Such poetry is more usefully described as polymetrical or plurimetrical than as "free"; still, our technical vocabulary strains at accounting for more than a small portion of the acoustic activity of the sounded poem and there are a number of performative features that are only available in readings (in both senses) since they are not (readily) scorable in the lexical text. Ernest Robson, going steps further than Hopkins, developed an elaborate and eccentric system for scoring pitch and stress in the written texts of his poems.[15] Among the most resourceful attempts to designate acoustic features of performed poetry has been Erskine Peters's, in his work-in-progress *Afro-Poetics in the United States*. Peters, together with an associate at the University of Notre Dame, J. Sherman, has developed a "special font to document the sounds, rhythms, and melodies of the Afro-poetic tradition."[16] The sixty characters in Peters's system designate such acoustic figures as accelerated line pacing, accented long and short stretches, blue noting, bopping, calibrated stagger, call-response, chant, crypting, deliberate stutter, echo toning, extreme unaccented, falsetto, field hollering, gliding or glissando, glottal shake, guttural stress, humming, moan, ostinato, pegging, pitch alteration (heightened and lowered), quoting, riff, rushing, scatting, slurring (three versions), sonorous chant stretching, sonorous inhaling, sonorous moaning, sonorous tremor, spiking, syllabic quaver, tremolo, and ululating rhythm.

One reason that Hopkins figures so prominently in this book is that he initiates, within the English tradition, a complex prosody that requires performance to sound it out. With rational metrics, the "competent" reader could be presumed to be able to determine the poem's sound based on well-established principles. With complex prosody and poylmetricality, however, the performance establishes the sound of the poem in a way not necessarily, or not easily, deducible from the text.

Despite these many examples, many poetry performances tend to submit to, rather than prosodically contest, the anesthetized speech rhythms of official verse culture. Indeed, one of the effects of chatty introductions before each poem is to acoustically cue the performer's talking voice so that it frames the subsequent performance. David Antin radically extends and transforms such talk to become the main event of his performances, or "talk pieces," which remain among the postwar period's most provocative critiques of—and useful interventions within—the poetry reading. Conversely, when a poet makes no incidental remarks, it may be to allow the sound of the poem to have its full sway. Clark Coolidge is a particularly adept practitioner of this style, and his remarkable extensions and riffs on speech rhythms are all the more resonant on account of it.

What makes sound patterns expressive? Beats me. But a rose by any other name would no longer rhyme with *doze* or *shows* or *clothes,* unless the other name was *pose* or *glows*. A rose by any other name wouldn't be the same—wouldn't arouse the same associations, its sound iconicity might be close but no pajamas. Sound enacts meaning as much as designates something meant.

The relation of sound to meaning is something like the relation of the soul (or mind) to the body. They are aspects of each other, neither prior, neither independent. To imagine that a meaning might be the same despite a change of words is something like imagining that I'd still be me in a new body. (So disagreements on this matter are theological as much as metaphysical—they cannot be reduced to factual disputes.) It won't come as a big surprise to most people that a poet is investing so much in sound—no doubt we've been seduced into confusing the shell for the husk, or is it the pea for the nut?

J. H. Prynne, in "Stars, Tigers and the Shape of Words," makes the argument quite well, though it does bear repeating, since repetition is never interesting for what is the same but for what is different: While verbal language may be described as a series of differential sound values, and while it makes sense to say that it is these differences that allow for meaning, it does not follow that the only meaning these sounds have lies in their difference from other sounds. Positive meanings adhere to sound in a number of ways. To speak of the positive, rather than merely negative or differential, meaning of sound does not rely on what might be called "pure" sound symbolism—the perception that particular sounds and dynamic features of sounds (as in pitch, constellations of sound, intonation, amplitude, timbre) have intrinsic meaning; though there is much that is appealing in this view, as Walter Benjamin shows in his "Doctrine of the Similar." The claim that certain sound vibrations have an inhering or immutable meaning is the perhaps mystical nodal point of a constellation of iconic attributes of language. Other points in this constellation cluster around the purely extrinsic meanings that adhere to sounds and dynamic features of sounds, either based on historical associations, which over time get hard-wired into some words or sounds; or, more intricately, based on the oral range made possible by a specific dietary pattern that alters the body's sounding board (dentation, palette, vocal chords, breath). Each language's specific morphology allows many possibilities for iconicity—from the physical size or number of characters in a word, to the number of syllables or patterns of syllables in a word, to associations with timbre or intonation or patterning. Iconicity refers to the ability of language to *present,* rather than represent or designate, its meaning. Here meaning is not something that accompanies the word but is performed by it. One of the primary features of poetry as a medium is to foreground the various iconic features of language—to perform the verbalness of language. The poetry reading, as much as the page, is the site for such performance.

Iconicity can also provide a way of hearing poetry readings, where the iconic focus shifts from an individual word to the chosen mode of performance; for example, the stress and tempo. I have already given an iconic reading of Baraka's performance style. John Ashbery's relatively monovalent, uninflected reading style—he is surely one of the masters of the anti-expressivist mode—is marked by an absence of isochronicity, a correlate to the fluidity and marked absence of parataxis in his texts. The cutting out of this rhythmic dynamic is iconically significant.

It is certainly not my intention to reinvent the wheel, just to let it spin words into acts. Any consideration of the relation of sound to poetry needs to point to the pioneering work of linguists such as Charles Sanders Peirce, Roman Jakobson, Linda Waugh, George Lakoff, and many others. In a recent treatment of this topic, *What Makes Sound Patterns Expressive,* Reuven Tsur quite usefully emphasizes a distinction between the perception of speech sounds (the "speech mode" of listening) and material sounds (the "nonspeech mode").[17] He argues that there is a marked cognitive difference in the way a listener hears a material sound—say a flapping flag or the pouring rain—and the way she or he hears human speech. Speech triggers a specific cognitive mode of interpretation in a way that material sound does not. This is something like the distinction Roland Barthes makes, in an essay called "Listening," between hearing (physiological) and listening (psychological).[18] According to Tsur, and following Jakobson, the "poetic function" of language is a third type: it involves *hearing* what we are *listening* to. That is, poetry creates something of the conditions of hearing (not just listening to) a foreign language—we hear it as language, not music or noise; yet we cannot immediately process its meaning. Another way of saying this is that the poetic function—what Tsur calls "the poetic mode of speech perception"—rematerializes language, returns it from "speech" back to "sound"; or rather, the poetic mode synthesizes the speech mode of perception and the nonspeech mode of perception. I want to project this frame of reference onto Barthes's evocative speculations on rhythm in "Listening." Barthes uses Sigmund Freud's famous discussion of the child's game of *fort/ da,* in which the child tosses out and pulls back a spool attached to a thread, as an example of a primal rhythmic oscillation of presence and absence, miming the presence and absence of the mother at the same time as it makes palpable the structure of the linguistic sign. It's as if when I say, "You're here"/"You're not," the sounds are present but *you* are not. In the poetic mode of listening, there is an oscillation (or temporal overlap) between the materially present sound (hearing: the nonspeech mode) and the absent meaning (listening: the speech mode): this is a satisfaction of all reading aloud, as when we read stories and poems to children. The poetry reading allows for a particularly marked extension of this pleasure, especially when the performance seizes the opportunity to make rhythmic oscillations between its opaque soundings and its transparent references. No doubt this helps to explain the uncanny power of a great sound poem like Kurt Schwitters's "Merz Sonata," with its exquisite passages of child-like entoning, which evoked tears from its first hearers. But it also a quality inherent in the structure—the medium—of the poetry reading itself, and it can be found in its most ordinary forms. In this way, the poetry reading occupies a formal space akin to song, but one in which the musicality, or sound-grounding, of the language is produced strictly within the range of speech-mode perception. It is the transformation of language to sound, rather than the setting of language in sound, that distinguishes song from recitation.

As a matter of habituated fact, the distinction between speech perception and sound perception seems well established. I do hear the beat of a hammer, the lapping of water, or the bleat of a sheep in a way that is cognitively discontinuous with the way I listen to human speech. With the speech in which I am most at home, I automatically translate streams of sounds into streams of words with a rapidity and certainty that makes the sounds transparent—a conjuring trick that is slowed by variant accents and arrested by foreign tongues. But this transparency effect of language may be less an intrinsic property of speech than a sign of our opaqueness to the transhuman world, which also speaks, if we could learn (again) to listen, as writers from Henry David Thoreau in *Walden* to, most recently, David Abram in *The Spell of the Sensuous* have argued. "It is animate earth that speaks; human speech is but a part of that vaster discourse" (Abram, 179). Yet language is not just a part of the "animate earth": its sounds also echo the music of the *nonanimate* earth. Speech-mode perception, as an habituated response to language, may indeed preemptively cut off our response to non-human sounds—organic and machinic—at the same time as it dematerializes human language, muting its sonic roots in the earth as well as the world. Yet while Abram argues that our alienation from the sensuous is partly to be blamed on alphabetic writing, I would emphasize—against such self-proclaimed "oralist" perspectives—that our insistent separation of human and nonhuman sounds is not the result of writing (alphabetic or otherwise) but of human language itself.[19] Alphabetic aurality is not cut off from the earth but is a material embodiment of it.

In attributing the transparency effect of language to speech-mode perception, I am eliding two prominent developmental models that provide powerful accounts of how and when language works to differentiate its users from their sensorial surroundings. In *Revolution of Poetic Language,* Julia Kristeva writes of infancy as an absorption in a preverbal "chora" that is (tellingly) a "rhythmic space" that "precedes evidence, verisimilitude, spatiality, and temporality" and indeed "figuration."[20] Kristeva goes on to theorize the subsequent development of a symbolic order in which a "subject" emerges from the chora when the child is able to differentiate herself from her surrounds. For Kristeva, the chora—which she associates with radically poetic language—is anterior to "sign and syntax," anterior to the linguistic order of language: "Indifferent to language, enigmatic and feminine, this space underlying the written is rhythmic, unfettered, irreducible to its intelligible verbal translation; it is musical, anterior to judgment, but restrained by a single guarantee: syntax" (29). Abram and Walter Ong write not of the development of individual subjects but of human culture, charting the alienation that alphabetic writing inaugurates in previously oral cultures in terms of the loss of the "presence" of the word, for Ong, and the loss of language's interconnectivity with the more-than-human world, for Abram. Yet both of these accounts rely on unilinear, progressivist models of development. The implication is that one stage of human consciousness replaces or supersedes the next and that something like "poetic" language is needed to put us back in touch with—to return us to, or retune us with—the previous stage.

The problem is that writing does not eclipse orality nor does the symbolic law supersede the amorphousness of the "semiotic," any more than objectivity replaces subjectivity (or vice versa). We don't return to anything—turning (tuning) is enough. The power of symbolic—of the ego or the alphabet—does not come in Faustian trade for the virtually Edenic space of undifferentiated connectivity. Moreover, this originary myth is literally delusional, for it leads us away from the concrete material situation of our connectivity through the alphabet, through aurality, through the "symbolic." Better than to speak of the preverbal, we might speak of the omniverbal. Rather than referring to the presymbolic, we might say *asymbolic* or *heterosymbolic*. Instead of projecting a preliterate stage we might say *analphabetic* or *heteroliterate:* for aren't the petroglyphs and megaliths—those earliest human inscriptions made on or with rocks—already writing, already "symbolic"?[21] As if the first human "babbling" were not already language, always social, a toll as well as a tool! We go "From amniotic fluid to / semiotic / fluidlessness," where the semiotic is drenched in the symbolic and the symbolic absorbed within the semiotic.[22] As Nick Piombino observes in his discussion of D. W. Winnicott in this volume, *language is also a transitional object.*

If "orality" or the "semiotic," aurality or logic, are stages, they are stages not on a path toward or away from immanence or transcendence but rather stages for performance: *modalities* of reason; *prisms* not prisons. Or let me put this in a different way: Perhaps the first writing was not produced by humans but rather *recognized* by humans. That is, it's possible that the human inscriptions on the petroglyphs frame or acknowledge the glyphs already present on the rock face (Lock, 415–16). Then we might speak of the book of nature, which we read as we read geologic markers or the rings around tree ("can't see me!").

Poetry characterized as presymbolic (and praised or condemned as primitive, infantile or childlike, nonsensical, meaningless) would more accurately be characterized as postsymbolic (and thus described as paratactic, complex or chaotic, procreative, hyperreferential); just as such works, when they aver rationality, are not irrational. Rather, such works affirm the bases of reason against a dehumanizing fixation on the rigidly monologic and rationalistic. The problem is being stuck in any one modality of language— not being able to move in, around, and about the precincts of language. I am not antisymbolic any more than I am pro-"semiotic." Rather I am interpolated in their folds, knowing one through the other, and hearing the echo of each in the next. This is what I mean to evoke by "a/orality"—sound language, language grounded in its embodiments.

Human consciousness has as much a sedimentary as a developmental disposition; stages don't so much replace each other as infiltrate or interpenetrate—I want to say *perform*—each other. Consciousness is a compost heap, to borrow a term from Jed Rasula. Neither the symbolic stage nor the rise of literacy marks language's de-absorption in the world. Language itself, speech itself, is a technology, a tool, that, from the first cultures to the first responses to the cry of a baby, allows us to make our way on the earth by making a world of it. The iconic sound shape of language beats the path.

Iconicity recognizes the ability of language to present its meaning rather than to represent or designate it. The meaning is not something that accompanies the words but is performed by them. Performance has the potential to foreground the inexorable and "counterlogical" verbalness of poetry— "thickening the medium" by increasing "the disparity between itself and its referents."[23] When sound ceases to follow sense, when, that is, it *makes* sense of sound, then we touch on the matter of language.[24] This is the burden of poetry; this is why poetry matters.

It is precisely because sound is an arational or nonlogical feature of language that it is so significant for poetry—for sound registers the sheer physicality of language, a physicality that must be the grounding of reason exactly insofar as it eludes rationality. Sound is language's flesh, its opacity as meaning marks its material embeddedness in the world of things. Sound brings writing back from its metaphysical and symbolic functions to where it is at home, in performance.

Sound, like poetry "itself," can never be completely recuperated as ideas, as content, as narrative, as extralexical meaning. The tension between sound and logic reflects the physical resistance in the medium of poetry. Rime's reason—the truth of sound—is that meaning is rooted in the arationality of sound, as well as in the body's multiple capacities for signification. Language is extralexical, goes beyond sense, and nothing shows this better than verbal performance, which, like the soundless performance of the body, exceeds what seems necessary to establish the substantive content of the poem—what it is saying, its metaphors and allusions.

In sounding language, we sound the width and breadth and depth of human consciousness—we find our bottom and our top, we find the scope of our ken. In sounding language we ground ourselves as sentient, material beings, obtruding into the world with the same obdurate thingness as rocks or soil or flesh. We sing the body of language, relishing the vowels and consonants in every possible sequence. We stutter tunes with no melodies, only words.

And yet sound, while the primary focus of my considerations here, is only one iconically expressive medium of the performing body, and I specifically want to leave room for the apprehension, by nonacoustic means, of some of the features I have attributed to sound. I am thinking of a conversation I had with the English poet and performer Aaron Williamson, who is deaf, in which he noted that he is able to experience many of the physicalizing features I have discussed in terms of sound. Rhythm is an obvious but crucial example: Williamson pointed out that he could feel the rhythm of the poet's performance while reading and looking at (something akin to *listening* and *hearing*) the poet's lips.

Poetry readings, like reading aloud (and this is something most explicitly marked in sound poetry), are a performance of the carnality of language—its material, sensuous embodiment. But this bodily grounding of language is not a cause for celebration any more than it is a reason for repression: it is a condition of human being and a fundamental material for poetry; call it language's *animalady*. Yet, in the present cultural context of the late twentieth century, this animalady loses its force as concrete experience when reified as (represented) speech or sentimentalized as (a return to) orality. The most resonant possibilities for poetry as a medium can be realized only when the performance of language moves from human speech to animate, but transhuman, sound: that is, when we stop listening and begin to hear; which is to say, stop decoding and begin to get a nose for the sheer noise of language.

Beyond all of these formal dimensions of the audiotext and the performed word, a primary significance of the poetry reading rests with its social character. Readings are the central social activity of poetry. They rival publishing as the most significant method of distribution for poetic works. They are as important as books and magazines in bringing poets into contact with one another, in forming generational and cross-generational, cultural and cross-cultural, links, affinities, alliances, communities, scenes, networks, exchanges, and the like. While San Francisco and New York remain the centers of poetic activity in the United States, dozens of cities across the country, and in Canada, Australia, New Zealand, and Great Britain, have active local reading series that serve to galvanize local poetry activity. The range of such activity is so great as to be difficult to document, since the written record is so much poorer than that of publications. This absence of documentation, together with the tendency among critics and scholars to value the written over the performed text, has resulted in a remarkable lack of attention given to the poetry reading as a medium in its own right, a medium that has had a profound impact on twentieth-century poetry, and in particular the poetry of the second half of the century.

The reading is the site in which the audience of poetry constitutes and reconstitutes itself. It makes itself visible to itself. And while the most attention had been paid to those moments when the poetry reading has been a means for poetry to cross over to a wider audience—as in the antiwar and other politically oriented readings of the 1960s or in some of the performance poetry of the present moment—the fundamental, social significance of the reading, it seems to me, has to do with infrastructure not spectacle. For this reason I would turn around the familiar criticism that everyone at a poetry reading is a poet to say that this is just what is vital about a reading series, even the essence of the poetry reading. For poetry is constituted dialogically through recognition and exchange with an audience of peers, where the poet is not performing to invisible readers or listeners but actively exchanging work with other performers and participants. This is not to say that reading series geared to a more "general" public or to students are not valuable. Of course they are. But such events resemble nonpoetry performances in that their value is dissemination to an unknown audience more than creation and exchange. They are not the foundries of poetry that a more introverted reading series can be. Poetry, oddly romanticized as the activity of isolated individuals writing monological lyrics, is among the most social and socially responsive—dialogic—of contemporary art forms. The poetry reading is an ongoing convention of poetry, by poetry, for poetry. In this sense, the reading remains one of the most participatory forms in American cultural life. Indeed, the value of the poetry reading as a social and cultural form can be partly measured by its resistance, up to this point, to reification or commodification. *It is a measure of its significance that it is ignored.* That is, the (cultural) invisibility of the poetry reading is what makes its audibility so audacious. Its relative absence as an institution makes the poetry reading the ideal site for the presence of language—for listening and being heard, for hearing and for being listened to.

All the essays published here were written especially for this collection; each pushes the putative subject into new and often unexpectedly pertinent directions. This book grows out of a series of conversations between and among many of the contributors. In 1993, Dennis Tedlock and I taught a graduate seminar called "Language and Performance," in which we addressed many of the issues under consideration here. I am also grateful to many of the participants of that and other Poetics Program seminars at SUNY-Buffalo. Full citations for works mentioned in this introduction can be found in the appended bibliography, which also provides a selected list of recommended readings; thanks especially to Peter Middleton, Steve McCaffery, Peter Quartermain, Marjorie Perloff, and Lorenzo Thomas for numerous suggestions. A call from Elda Rotor of Oxford University Press initially prompted this collection; her commitment to the project has been exceptional.

NOTES

The first epigraph, by Peire Cardenal, is from "Song 56" (early 13th century), quoted in Gregory Nagy, *Poetry as Performance: Homer and Beyond* (Cambridge: Cambridge University Press, 1996); tr. Nagy, based on W. Pfeffer's *The Change of Philomel: The Nightingale in Medieval Literarture.* The second epigraph is from Jack

Spicer's "Thing Language" in *Language* in *The Collected Books of Jack Spicer* (Los Angeles: Black Sparrow, 1975), p. 217.

1. There are only two collections that I have been able to locate that address the poetry reading: *Poets on Stage: The Some Symposium on Poetry Readings,* ed. Alan Ziegler, Larry Zirlin, and Harry Greenberg (1978) and *The Poetry Reading: A Contemporary Compendium on Language and Performance,* ed. Stephen Vincent and Ellen Zweig (1981). The accounts of poetry readings in these pioneering collections are largely anecdotal. Also notable are the annual reports for 1981 and 1982 of San Francisco's 80 Langton Street Residency Program, assembled by Renny Pritikin, Barrett Watten, and Judy Moran, which provided a number of sustained accounts, by different writers, of a series of talks and readings and performances at the space. More recently, the Poetics Lists, an electronic discussion group archived at the Electronic Poetry Center (http://wings.buffalo.edu/epc) often features accounts of readings and conferences (including lists of those in attendance at readings and even the occasional fashion report). In contrast, reflecting standard academic practice, there is no mention of Wallace Stevens's recorded poetry performance in a recent book on the poet by Anca Rosu, but there is some irony in this given the book's auspicious title, *The Metaphysics of Sound in Wallace Stevens* (Tuscaloosa: University of Alabama Press, 1995), which only goes to show that metaphysics tends to displace physics.

2. See Jerome Rothenberg, "The Poetics of Performance," in Vincent and Zweig, 123. See also David Abram, *The Spell of the Sensuous* (New York: Pantheon, 1996), pp. 241–50.

3. William Harris, *The Poetry and Poetics of Amiri Baraka: The Jazz Aesthetic* (Columbia: University of Missouri Press, 1985), pp. 109–10; Harris extracts portions of the text, from which I quote below. See also Harris's interview with Baraka, where the poet agrees that his poem is a score and says he is principally interested in performance—"[the text] is less important to me" (147). Harris briefly discusses Baraka's performances on pp. 59–60. See especially his discussion of the relation of music and dance to Baraka's work, starting on p. 106.

4. See Nathaniel Mackey, "Other: From Noun to Verb," in *Discrepant Engagement: Dissonance, Cross-Culturality, and Experimental Writing* (Cambridge: Cambridge University Press, 1993).

5. The passage is based on Andrew Benjamin, "Translating Origins: Psychoanalysis and Philosophy," in *Rethinking Translation: Discourse, Subjectivity, Ideology,* ed. Lawrence Venuti (London: Routledge, 1992), p. 24; all the references to poetry are my substitutions made to Benjamin's "original"; I have also elided a few phrases. See also Benjamin's *The Plural Event: Descartes, Hegel, Heidegger.*

6. Nagy, 16. Nagy specifically sites McGann's work on "the textual condition."

7. Nagy, 9; his emphasis. Quoted from Alfred Lord, *The Singer of Tales* (Cambridge, Mass.: Harvard University Press, 1960), p. 100. Dennis Tedlock's contribution to this collection is relevant here.

8. This qualification is in response to a comment by Dennis Tedlock on this passage. Tedlock emphasizes that writing is also a performance and as such readily open to variation and revision. I am also grateful to other suggestions by Tedlock, which I have incorporated into the essay.

9. Charles Lock, "Petroglyphs In and Out of Perspective," *Semiotica,* vol. 100, nos. 2–4 (1994), p. 418.

10. I am well aware that prosodists can mask and analyze a performed poem in ways that will illustrate their particular theory (including quite conventional

ones)—just as I have. This is no more than proper in such semantically dynamic terrain.

11. The science of dysprosody is still in its infancy, although it is likely to dominate technical studies of unidentified poetic phenomena (UPPs) in the coming millennia. The Dysprosody Movement was founded by Carlo Amberio in 1950. A translation of its main theoretical document, *The Dyssemia of Dystressed Syllables,* from a previously undisclosed language into trochaic hexameter "blink" verse—a form Amberio believes to come closest to the counterintuitive thought patterns of unspoken American English—has long been forthcoming from the Center for the Advancement of Dysraphic Studies (CADS). (Blink verse, invented by Amberio, involves a fractal patterning of internal rhymes.)

12. Giorgio Agamben, in "The Idea of Prose," in *The Idea of Prose,* tr. Michael Sullivan and Sam Whitsitt (Albany: State University of New York Press, 1995), p. 40. Agamben's specific subject here is enjambment. Thanks to Carla Billitteri for bringing this essay to my attention.

13. Henri Meschonnic, *Critique du rythme: anthropologie historique du langage* (Lagrasse: Verdier, 1982).

14. Charles O. Hartman, *Free Verse: An Essay on Prosody* (Princeton: Princeton University Press, 1980). Shapiro is quoted from "English Prosody and Modern Poetry," *ELH,* vol. 14 (June 1947), p. 81. This is a good place to thank George Lakoff for pointing me in several useful directions.

15. See Ernest Robson's *I Only Work Here* (1975) and *Transwhichics* (1970), both from his own Primary Press in Parker Ford, Pennsylvania. On Robson, see Bruce Andrews's "The Politics of Scoring" in *Paradise and Method: Poetics & Practice* (Evanston: Northwestern University Press, 1996), pp. 176–77.

16. I am grateful to Professor Peters for providing me with relevant sections of his manuscript. In a chapter entitled "African-American Prosody: The Sermon as a Foundational Model," he provides detailed descriptions for each of the prosodic terms he employs.

17. Reuven Tsur, *What Makes Sound Patterns Expressive?: The Poetic Mode of Speech Perception* (Durham, N.C.: Duke University Press, 1992). See pp. 11–14.

18. Roland Barthes, "Listening," in *The Responsibility of Forms,* tr. Richard Howard (New York: Hill and Wang, 1985).

19. Dennis Tedlock comments: "But there is nothing intrinsic to the alphabet that makes its effects on perception inevitable. Such writing has been used in many places and periods without any notion that it is an adequate or sufficient notation of the sounds of speech. What is rather at issue is the projection of phonemics (with its linear system of differences) back onto speech and its installation as the very foundation of a flattened (and 'scientific') conception of language. Yet we can recognize that the sounds coming from the next room are those of a person speaking *without being able to distinguish any phonemes!*" (Personal communication, September 1, 1996.)

20. Julia Kristeva, *The Revolution in Poetic Language,* tr. Margaret Waller (New York: Columbia University Press, 1984), pp. 25–27.

21. In his article on petroglyphs, already cited, Lock critiques the term *prehistoric:* "Better, surely, to speak of 'ahistoric' . . . and then note that 'ahistoric' also serves well for 'illiterate'; by the word 'ahistoric' we might avoid the pejorative, and the Darwinian tendency" (407). Here I yet again switch frames from human history to human development.

22. The lines are from "Blow-Me-Down Etude," in my collection, *Rough Trades* (Los Angeles: Sun & Moon Press, 1991), p. 104.

23. William K. Wimsatt, "On the Relation of Rhyme to Reason" in *The Verbal Icon: Studies in the Meaning of Poetry* (Lexington: University of Kentucky Press, 1954), p. 217. Wimsatt is referring to poetry as text not to the performance of poetry.

24. See Agamben, "The Idea of Matter," p. 37.

PART I

Sound's Measures

I

Letter on Sound

SUSAN STEWART

*T*his is the letter I promised on sound in lyric. In classical practice, and classical criticism, the relation between music and lyric is paramount—non-narrative and nondramatic poetic genres were intended to be sung, chanted, or recited to musical accompaniment.[1] *Lyra,* a musical instrument; *mele,* air or melody. These are commonplaces of the history of lyric poetry and when we regard a poem's structure, regardless of the language in which it is composed, we speak of such features as counterpoint, harmony, syncopation, stress, duration, and timbre as if the ways in which sound is measured in music and lyric were analogous.

But lyric is not music—it bears a history of a relation to music—and, as a practice of writing, it has no sound—that is, unless we are listening to a spontaneous composition of lyric, we are always *recalling* sound with only some regard to an originating auditory experience.[2] The sound recalled in lyric is not abstract, not a succession of tones without prior referents; rather the sound recalled is the sound of human speech. What is the nature of this recalling? It is not like reading a score or script with an orientation toward performance, for we are absorbed in the temporality of the poem's form and have no need to prepare ourselves for, or orient ourselves toward, a repetition of the poem—in fact to produce such a repetition would not necessarily require reading the poem at all.[3] It is not like looking at an imitation of an utterance, as in looking at a painting of sound—Munch's screaming figure or the "mouthing" of *The Oath of the Horatiae*—for the poem itself is an utterance, an expression of a person, which we apprehend in turn as the expression of a person. And it is not like an exercise in historical linguistics where we try to reconstitute a context of original utterance, for we are interested in *what* the poem says and we attend to *how* the poem says as part of this semantic orientation in reception.

Because we cannot reconstitute these auditory conditions of the poem's production, our recalling will always have a dimension of imagination. Such remembering in fact requires neither auditory prompting nor the presence of a text at all. Just as we have the capacity to compose or remember a visual field or sequence of musical phrases without external stimuli, so can we "hear" a poem when a text is not present by calling it to mind. In turn, we will bring to a text our memories of speech experience, including what we may know of the intended speaker's speech experience, but such "voicing" will be in the service of, provide the vehicle for, the apprehension of the poem as a whole.

Whenever a poetic values metaphor, or the supersensible dimension of poetry more generally, sound as the material manifestation of the work will be less emphasized; often sound will be held in diminished estimation as a mere "prop" or frame for poetic thought. Consider Kant's elevation of poetry over music in the "Analytic of the Sublime":

> Poetry holds the first rank among all the arts. It expands the mind by giving freedom to the imagination and by offering, from among the boundless multiplicity of possible forms accordant with a given concept, to whose bounds it is restricted, that one which couples with the presentation of the concept a wealth of thought to which no verbal expression is completely adequate, and by thus rising aesthetically to ideas. It invigorates the mind by letting it feel its faculty—free, spontaneous, and independent of determination by nature—of regarding and estimating nature as phenomenon in the light of aspects which nature of itself does not afford us in experience, either for sense or understanding, and of employing it accordingly in behalf of, and as a sort of schema for, the supersensible.

In contrast, music, "the art of tone," "speaks by means of mere sensations without concepts, and so does not, like poetry, leave behind it any food for reflection." Kant does emphasize, however, that the transience of music lends it "intenser effect."[4] Hegel's *The Philosophy of Fine Art* promotes a similar view of the relation between the sensible and the thought in poetry:

> Mind, in short, here determines this content for its own sake and apart from all else into the content of idea; to express such idea it no doubt avails itself of sound, but employs it merely as a sign without independent worth or substance. Thus viewed, the sound here may be just as well reproduced by the mere letter, for the audible, like the visible, is here reduced to a mere indication of mind. For this reason, the true medium of poetical representation is the poetical imagination and the intellectual presentation itself; and inasmuch as this element is common to all types of art it follows that poetry is a common thread through them all, and is developed independently in each. Poetry is, in short, the universal art of the mind, which has become essentially free, and which is not fettered in its realization to an externally sensuous material.[5]

Yet as Kant's position gives us a clue that the intensity of affect in music might lend something of its emotional force to the sonorous dimension of the poetic, so does Hegel's position stray so far from the reception of particular instances of the poetic that poetry threatens to disappear entirely on its trajectory toward the universal. Neoclassical theories making sound a mode of ornament can make meaning seem ornamental as well: "When Alexander strives some rock's vast weight to throw / The line too labors, and the words move slow"—is Alexander then the example of the sound or the sound the example of Alexander? Although Pope has complained only a few lines earlier about the "sure returns of still expected rhymes" there is such ease to his own perfect rhymes that one wonders if self-parody is really the point.[6]

Conversely, avant-garde materialism in twentieth-century poetics (the symbolist ideal of fusing meaning and sound as expressed in Verlaine's "Art Poétique," Marinetti's "bruitisme," Dada sound poems) with its pursuit of pure sound finds itself readily encapsulated into prior generic conventions—either "nonsense" discourse or experimental music. A sound poem such as Hugo Ball's

> gadji beri bimba
> glandridi lauli lonni cadori
> gadjama bim beri glassala
> glandridi glassala tuffm i zimbrabim
> blassa galassasa tuffm i zimbrabim . . .

reverses the conventional priority of meaning over sound. Ball wrote in his autobiography, *Flight out of Time,* "I have invented a new genre of poems, 'Verse ohne Worte,' [poems without words] or Lautgedichte [sound poems], in which the balance of the vowels is weighed and distributed solely according to the values of the beginning sequence . . . we must give up writing secondhand: that is, accepting words (to say nothing of sentences) that are not newly invented for our own use."[7] Significantly, the improvisatory aspect of such a poem makes it a challenge to memory; memory relies upon the "placing" or contextualization of language in relation to other language, and "pure" sounds are indeed pure of such context—they are harder to call to mind than musical sequences, for musical sequences are themselves coded in relation to expectations of musical sequence. Ball's demand that language be "newly invented" depends upon the novelty and surprise produced by the unpredictability of the sequence. A claim is made for the "pure" incantatory experience of the sound poem, but the theory nevertheless is used as a frame for the sound. Further, since we have prior speech experience of these sounds as discernible phones, if not as discernible words, we "hear" them phonetically. The few repetitions in the work and the sequence of sounds in time compel us to hear aural connections, as in the sequence of first "words" of the "lines"—gad*ji*, gad*jama*—which are heard as deploying suffix variations, or the way *bl*assa and *gal*assasa appear as prefix variations, or the repetitions of gl*andridi,* gl*assala,* and the "phrase" *tuffm i zimbrabim,* or the variations in "a" and "i" endings, which seem to echo Latinate noun and pronoun endings for gender and number. In other words, we produce phonemes whenever we can, even if the lexical level remains opaque, here defined only by the intervals between clusters of syllables rather than by prior reference. A student of historical linguistics coming upon this poem would know that it is closer to Italian, French, and Japanese than to English because of its emphasis on syllabics. The mind is a grammar-making device and it is difficult to turn it off, even though Ball has not provided a syntactical framework of the kind maintained in Dodgson's "Jabberwocky," where the connective words remain in the standard lexicon. We would conclude that Ball is performing a poem because he has framed his performance, he has spoken in "lines," and "the work" has a beginning—if it does not have closure, it nevertheless does *stop*. Sounds follow other sounds and so appear in a *relation* to those sounds preceding and following them. Play within the determinations of such a relation will always be in tension with any "pure" arbitrariness.

There are, then, a number of complex conditions under which we can say that "sound" is and is not an aspect of lyric. When lyric is disseminated through written form, speech is represented through alphabetical letters and diacritical marks and symbols; as systems of differentiated marks, these forms of representation stand for the differentiation of phones in sound production. Most features of spoken intonation, pitch, stress, and intensity must be supplied by the reader. There is no reason to emphasize the idiolectal quality of speech in this regard—phonetic patterns are learned at an early age for one's own primary language and can be discerned for other languages whether or not one actually "knows" the language or not;[8] this is why a parrot will repeat phrases without what we might call a "parrot" accent, for the parrot is producing a string of phones, but human beings who learn languages after puberty will bring the inflection of that language or those languages they have first learned (Deese, 117). As readers take up the sequence of written symbols, they thereby supply the rhythm that characterizes their experience of the language. For English speakers the linguistic principle of isochronism, which breaks utterances into segments correlated to the pulses of breathing, will not be based on the syllable (as it is in French, Japanese, and "gadji beri"); rather, the unit of utterance will generally include a stressed syllable and a number of unstressed syllables; this interval, from stress to stress rather than from syllable to syllable, has of course had a profound effect on English metrics. Because the stress generally falls on form words, rather than grammatical and structural elements, stress will underscore the structure of the grammar.[9] In speech, stress can determine emphasis in ways that remain indeterminate to writing without the addition of supplemental discourse or diacritical marks: Did Isolt say hello to *Tristan*? Did Isolt say *hello* to Tristan? In a poem the acoustical "space" of the form, the context wherein the stress is reconstructed, becomes the work itself—the consequent phrase or sentence or stanza or form from title or first line to closure—and all the knowledge one brings to the poem.[10] This process from sound production to inscription to reading to sound reception is pocked with anachronisms that in themselves are productive of historical meaning. Spelling, for example, always lags behind pronunciation;[11] off-rhyming can be taken as exact rhyming and vice versa; poetry itself is often cited as an index to past pronunciation of the language. The sounds of a poem are not heard within the room of the poem, but they are heard within a memory of hearing that is the total auditory experience of the listener in response to what knowledge of the poem is extant at a given moment.

Musical conventions proper have been applied to our sense of lyric's "musicality" and yet do not overlap with lyric's meter even within the domain of spoken lyric. It is not that some speech is organized rhythmically and other speech is not. Victor Zuckerkandl has suggested that "whereas melody and harmony are essentially musical phenomena, native to the world of tone and not to be found elsewhere (the adjectives derived from these terms can be applied only metaphorically outside the realm of music), rhythm is a truly universal phenomenon . . . rhythm is one manifestation of the reign of law throughout the universe."[12] Speech arrives in rhythmical form and our experience of it cannot be separated from our knowledge of its rhythmical structure. Zuckerkandl's writings on music provide a number of valuable insights regarding these issues. He points to the important distinction between rhythm and meter. Rhythm is described after the fact as the particular structure or order of tones in time. Although Zuckerkandl does not explicitly define rhythm as a historical and actual phenomenon, his emphasis on rhythm as the "living" dimension of music helps us see the tension between the organic and experiential unfolding of rhythm and the "time" of meter—that fixed and ideal measurement by which we say we are "keeping time." Zuckerkandl in fact uses poetry as his example of an art form that uses both rhythm and meter and nevertheless constantly asserts the priority of rhythm over meter: "A poem is a rhythmic construction . . . We could beat time to a poem if the syllables in it were all of equal length or departed from a basic unit in accordance with simple numerical proportions . . . 'Time' and rhythm here appear even to exclude each other: rhythm resists regular time: 'time' appears to suffocate rhythm." He points out that

> except for the special case of dance music, which is obliged to conform to the bodily movement it supports, musical rhythm in general is of the nature of the poetic rhythm; free rhythm in the sense that it is not constrained to keep time. There is one notable exception, Western music of the second millennium of our era—our music. It alone has imposed the shackles of time, of meter, upon itself, and indeed at the same moment when it was preparing to take the momentous step into polyphony. So long as only a single voice is involved, it is free to give each of its steps whatever duration it pleases. But if several voices, voices saying different things, are to proceed side by side and together, their motions must, for better or worse, be regulated by some time standard. (Zuckerkandl, 158–59)

In lyric, then, we find the continuance of a prepolyphonic emphasis on the individual voice and the tension between rhythm and meter. A key dimension of this tension is its productivity: "musical meter is not born in the beats at all, but in the empty intervals between the beats, in the places where 'time merely elapses,'" writes Zuckerkandl. "The mere lapse of time here effects something; it is felt as an event, strictly speaking as a wave. In the macroscopic picture something else happens; to the wave, intensification is added. As wave and intensification the lapse of time sustains and nourishes the rhythmic life of music. The function of time here is, then, no longer that of the empty vessel, which contains the tones, or the bowling alley down which the tones roll; on the contrary, time intervenes, is directly active, in the musical context" (Zuckerkandl, 181). Meter augments, extends, and organizes our hearing of speech rhythm in such a way as to intensify our experience—we hear the sound of sound and become aware of the sound of meaning in consequence. "Meter . . . draws boundary lines, interrupts, and separates. Rhythm is the unbroken continuity of a flux, such a continuity as the wave most graphically represents . . . Meter is the repetition of the identical; rhythm is return of the similar" (169–70). The sound of the poem emerges from this dynamic tension between the unfolding temporality of the utterance and the recursive temporality of the fixed aspects of the form. There is something of this in the multiple senses of the word itself—for sound as the most material and "superficial" dimension of speech is also sound as the measure, the depth, the "sounding" of the material, as when we ask if something "sounds good"—that is, good enough to act upon, bearing the integrity of a completed form. Because lyric maintains the convention of the individual speaking voice, a convention under which rhythm continues to have priority over the mechanical imposition of meter no matter how strongly organized the metrical dimension of the poem, it will not, in the Western tradition, be synonymous with music.

Another complexity of the relation between lyric and musicality is that the dynamic tension between sound and semantic can at once both extend and diminish meaning. David I. Masson's entry on "sound" in the Princeton *Encyclopedia of Poetry and Poetics,* for example, delineates fifteen forms of "sound manipulation" that affirm the relation between sound and meaning in individual poems: structural emphasis (rhetorical addition to the formally required sound structure); underpinning (subtle reinforcement of the verse structure through features like Milton's use of line-end consonance and assonance in blank verse); counterpoising (sounds employed in opposition to the verse structure, as in imperfect rhymes used in line endings in combination with internal rhymes); rubricating emphasis or words or images (his examples come from Tudor echo effects, as in Surrey's "The turtle to her make hath tolde her tale" where *turtle, to, tolde,* and *tale* are in effect underlined by the sound); tagging (punctuation of syntax by words or sounds); correlation (indirect support of argument by related echoes);

implication (interconnection of sound, meaning and feeling); diagramming (abstract pattern symbolizing sense—as in the relation between "leaping" syllables and "leaping" fire in Dryden's "He wades the Streets, and streight he reaches cross"); sound representation (onomatopoeia); illustrative mime (mouth movements recall motion or shape); illustrative painting (articulations, sounds and patterns correspond synaesthetically to appearances and nonacoustic sensations); passionate emphasis (emotional outburst); mood evocation (choice of tone colors resembling the usual sounds expressed in a given emotion); expressive mime (mouth movements ape the expression of emotion, as in the spitting effects necessary for pronouncing Adam's expulsion of the serpent in these lines from Milton: "Out of my sight, thou Serpent, that name best / Befits thee with him leagu'd, thy self as false / And hateful"); expressive painting (sounds, articulations correspond to feelings or impressions, as in Crabbe's "And the dull wheel hums doleful through the day"); ebullience (pure exuberance or pleasure in sound); embellishment (superficial musicality, as in Surrey's application of a rubricating emphasis above); incantation (musical or magical use of sound) (*Encyclopedia of Poetry and Poetics*, 785–86). Such a taxonomy is helpful for understanding the effects of particular sounds in individual poems. Yet who is to say that Yeats's "That dolphin-torn, that gong-tormented sea" is an example of incantation, as it is for Masson, rather than embellishment or ebullience? Surely the most effective alignments of sound and meaning will use a number of these techniques. Further, the relation between sound and meaning "created" by such lines is dependent upon a prior expectation of a profound relation between sound and meaning, an expectation brought to the reading of poetry more generally. When Riding and Graves wittily suggest there is an arbitrary, rather than onomatopoeic, relation between sound and meaning in Tennyson's "The moan of doves in immemorial elms / And murmuring of innumerable bees" by pointing to how the sounds produced in a line of different meaning ("More ordure never will renew our midden's pure manure") [13] hardly produce a similar onomatopoeic effect, they miss the point. Sounds in poems are never heard outside of an expectation of meaning, and sounds in nature will be framed for human listeners by human expectations. Robert Frost, in "The Oven Bird," reminds us vividly that we hear even bird songs in terms of human phonemes—the robin's "cheer, cheer, cheer," the nighthawk's "sp-e-e-d," the nuthatch's "yank, yank," or Thoreau's suggestion that the song sparrow sings "Maids, maids, maids, hang up your teakettle—ettle—ettle." When Frost writes of this bird who "knows in singing not to sing" but rather to frame questions, we silently "hear" the song of the oven bird: "teacher teacher."

Such features of sound manipulation in poetry as counterpoising, tagging, echo effects, diagramming, and the "ornamental" devices of rubrication and embellishment can, as Dillon emphasizes, make the relation between sound and meaning particularly textured and complex. Yet they also point to the possibilities of severing the relation between sound and meaning. At the heart of such a diremption is the ineluctable fact of the arbitrary nature of language forms. Long before de Saussure, folk forms often pointed to this dilemma. Think of the legend of Tom Tit Tot or Rumpelstiltsken: human beings will not be able to reproduce themselves (to name or claim their own offspring) until they use their intelligence to tease out a completely arbitrary name for the source of their suffering; only language can reveal to them the hidden term. Ballads often stage the separation of sound and meaning to create anticipation in the unfolding of narrative. For example, a series of nonsensical sounds are used to both arrest and move forward the incremental repetitions of this version of the "Wife in Wethers Skin," collected in North Carolina in 1962:

> (chant) There was an old man who lived in the West
> (sung) Dandoo
> (chant) There was an old man who lived in the West
> (sung) To my clash a-my klingo
> (chant) There was an old man who lived in the West
> (chant) He married him a wife which he thought the best
> (sung) Lingarum, lingorum smikaroarum, kerrymingorum
> (sung) To my clash a-my klingo.[14]

This is a particularly rich example, for the ballad tetrameter is followed exactly in the first three chanted narrative lines, but the narrative development is halted until the fourth narrative line where the meter is abandoned. In the fourth line the only way to get a four beat measure is to switch from ballad meter into pure accentual verse. In this, the song merges ballad form and the particular pattern of repeated lines common to blues form. Meanwhile, the nonsense syllables, which, because they are sung, would be expected to be in the more regular meter are not in any particular meter at all until the four-beat final sung line "To my clash a-my klingo." The listener hears three chanted lines before the narrative starts and three sung lines before the meter starts. Such juxtaposition of song and speech is typical of other forms as well, such as the cante-fable. In the cante-fable, song sections often include set pieces, riddles, dialogue, sayings, imitations of animal sounds, or magical utterances; the speech sections will stage the scene and explain the narrative. In ballad and song burdens, mood and place may as well be set by an incantatory, evocative, repetition: "Down by the greenwood side" or "Down by the green, by the burnie-o."[15] In the rubato-parlando style of dramatic recitative found in much of Eastern European and Anglo-American balladry where the last words of the song are uttered as speech, speech marks the return to the threshold of reality; in consequence, singing is associated with the incantatory, the sacred and the imaginary.

The trajectories of speech and song are both opposed and complementary in such forms. The sounds of speech rhythmically proceed forward in time according to conventions of articulation and interval. The sounds of song are organized both melodically and harmonically, that is in both linear and recursive fashion, and use fixed repetitive patterns of stress, tone, and duration. Speech disappears into the function of its situation; it can be repeated as fixed text or reported in an approximation. Song, by virtue of its measure, is fixed and repeatable, although it is, like all utterances, subject to transformation.[16] It is the tension between the unfolding semantic pressure of speech and the asemantic pulse of measure that defines the possibilities of lyric art. As Wimsatt wrote in *The Verbal Icon:* "Verse in general, and more particularly rhyme, make their special contribution to poetic structure in virtue of a studiously and accurately semantic character. They impose upon the logical pattern of expressed argument a kind of fixative counter-pattern of alogical implication." [17] Telling as telling slant makes lyric capable of evoking not only meaning, but as well the conditions under which meaning is formed by human speakers. There is an axiological consequence to this account of lyric. Lyric which mechanically emphasizes the fulfillment of metrical expectations will result in mere "tub-thumping," as Robert Lowell described the fourteeners of Golding's translation of Ovid's *Metamorphoses:* "Even if one is careful not to tub-thump, as one reads Golding's huge, looping 'fourteeners,' for 'sense and syntax' as Pound advises, even then one trips, often the form seems like some arbitrary and wayward hurdle, rather than the very backbone of what is being said." [18] John Thompson, in a discussion of this passage in his work on *The Founding of English Meter,* suggests that the early Elizabethans may not have had the same difficulty in keeping poulter's measure from overwhelming the grammatical and logical structure of the language. But he also explains that whenever there are balanced contours in evenly spaced rhythm units that dominate the grammatical units of the language, "singsong" will result.[19] If such a reification of the metric results in an overwhelmed semantic, similarly a semantic organized without consideration of metrical counterpatterning will be absorbed into mere rhetoric; any poetry produced under conditions that suppress the recursive and patterned dimensions of form cannot hope to move the reader or listener beyond the expectations of speech absorbed into the time of everyday life.

When Wimsatt mentions "a counterpattern of alogical implication," we might well ask what it is to which the metrical pattern is counter and what is so alogical about meter's implications. The pattern of *logical* implication in speech will be oriented toward the future; given a set of conditions and elements, a certain consequence will follow. Speech in a poem, like speech in the face-to-face communication of everyday life, is articulated in time. But unlike speech oriented toward conversational functions, speech in a poem is not absorbed in time. Essentialist arguments that negate any purported differences between "ordinary" and "poetic" language always already cheat in this regard, for attending to ordinary language in order to emphasize its inherently "poetic" qualities is synonymous with poeisis in the first place, and imagining "ordinary" functions for poetic utterances ("I'd like to go out tonight, but I'm feeling half in love with easeful death") is inseparable from the fabrication of fictive contexts. Once one is involved in such self-conscious making, there is no return to the contingencies of mere "function," let alone nature. Attention to the material elements of form in both its production and reception moves counter to that temporal absorption; indeed, attention to the material elements of form threatens to halt reception and to dominate the semantic dimension. This threat demands a certain complex form of apprehension wherein the logical implication, the implication of the reason, is put into play with the recursive and repetitive trajectory of the meter. Here is the *compulsion* of meter to return, to reenact, to transform and imitate. A tension ensues between the intentional and volitional dimensions of both sound-production and listening and the involuntary dimension of hearing—the unregulated openness of the ear to the world and the infinite nuance of the unsaid. Meter, and song as its vehicle, is the repository of emotion as *compositio* is the repository of the reason. Meter disrupts the absorptive dominance of time and makes time manifest as the dimension of interval.[20] In lyric, interval loses its "natural stance"; just as the phonemic dimension of sound only comes into existence as a system of differences, so the rests and caesuras, the line and stanza breaks of lyric are "sounded" or measured. Through lyric the human voice both reenacts the conditions of its emergence from silence and wrests that silence into the intersubjective domain of made and shaped things.

"Keeping time" in poetry, unlike keeping time in postpolyphonal Western music, does not involve a reduction of sound to the interstices of a metrical grid; keeping time in poetry is exercised through the single voice manipulating duration in such a way as to produce both expectation and surprise. The posture of reception is that of listening—an orientation of hearing within a finite auditory space. Producing and receiving sounds under these conditions involves mastery over relations of proximity and distance and presence and absence. In this is the profound relation between lyric and the ontology of persons. Through the young child's play with absence and presence, the game Freud terms *fort/da* wherein the nurturer's disappearance is supplanted with an imitation, a rhythm, he or she masters desire and produces pleasure under conditions no longer external to his or her agency. This rhythm suffuses the production of speech in general, yet is heightened in the difference/no difference relations of rhyme, line, stanza, and refrain we find in lyric. In Lacan's discussion of the *invocatory* drive, the propulsion to make one's self seen and heard, the outward-return movement of all drives—the oral as the urge to incorporate; the anal as the urge to retain; the scopic as the urge to organize the visual field—is recapitulated. Lacan is careful to specify that this movement is not a matter of "a reciprocity," for the pure activity of the drive is not "balanced" by the narcissistic field of love;[21] what goes out overwhelms what comes back—what goes out is constant and inescapable, whereas what comes back is contingent and determined. Here we find the incommensurable relation between production and reception as a "nonreciprocal" production in its own right.

This incommensurability is not a barrier to some recuperable originary meaning; it is in itself the "mishearing" or "misrecognition" under which the material element of the sign acquires an untotalizable semantic dimension. Poets who have worried the relation between sound and sense (the slant and off-rhymes of Emily Dickinson and Wilfred Owen, the use of cacaphony or "noise" in Hart Crane, the coining of neologisms in Paul Celan and Cesar Vallejo) have provided a vivid commentary on the alienation that can arise between speakers on the one hand and between human beings and nature on the other. It is significant that these are also poets for whom the stance of the "natural person," or any enthusiasm in the presentation of the self, is unbearable.

Gerard Manley Hopkins's writings on poetics, informed by his deep knowledge of classical literature and his skills as a musician and draftsman, constantly return to the relation between sound, meter, and emotion. In his lecture notes on "Rhythm and the Other Structural Parts of Rhetoric—Verse," Hopkins defined verse as a "figure of spoken sound": "verse is speech having a marked figure, order of sounds independent of meaning and such as can be shifted from one word or words to others without changing . . ." (House, 267). He creates a taxonomy of possible kinds of verse by "the kinds of resemblance possible between syllables: musical pitch or tonic accent; length or time or quantity so called; stress or emphatic accent; likeness or sameness of letters, vowels or consonants initial or final; holding, break and circumflexion, slurs, glides, slides etc." He contrasts quantification of syllables (as in classical verse) with lettering (early English alliteration), the first "running" and the second "intermittent," explaining that stress is between these two, with English verse characterized by a strong stress and weak pitch (House, 268–69). In further notes, he explains that "all poetry is not verse but all poetry is either verse or falls under this or some still further development of what verse is, speech wholly or partially repeating some kind of figure which is over and above meaning, at least the grammatical, historical and logical meaning" (House, 289). Yet what seems to be here a technical definition of the relation between syllabification and metrical systems, and a separation of the material and semantic aspects of poetry, is for Hopkins part of a complex metaphysic he has borrowed from Parmenides and combined with Christian, particularly Ignatian, theology. In Hopkins's notes on Parmenides he particularly singles out the ways

> the phenomenal world (and the distinction between men or subjects and the things without them) is unimportant in Parmenides: the contrast between the one and the many is the brink, limbus, lapping, run-and-mingle or two principles which meet in the scape of everything—probably Being, under its modification or siding of particular oneness or Being, and Not-being, under its siding of the Many. The two may be called two degrees of siding in the scale of Being. Foreshortening and equivalency will explain all possible difference. The inscape will be the proportion of the mixture. (House, 130)

It is in these notes on Parmenides that we find the earliest evidence of Hopkins's use of what were to become key terms in his work: "inscape" and "instress." Although he uses these words almost colloquially and does not provide a rigorous or even speculative definition of them, he usually implies by *inscape* the characteristic shape or pattern of a phenomenon; he describes in his journal the ways in which fine "stems" of a cloud could change into ribs or coral: "Unless you refresh the mind from time to time you cannot always remember or believe how deep the inscape of things is" (House, 204–5). *Instress* is the identifying impression a thing can communicate and is associated with emotion; as a "stress within" it is a force binding something or a person into a unit.[22] Being and not-being, the one and the many, the constantly changing aspect of things—"the brink, limbus, lapping, run-and-mingle," which induces in the perceiver an emotional response.[23] This way of seeing the phenomenal world cannot be separated in Hopkins's thought and practice from the running and intermittent aspects of English speech as deployed in the poem; by torquing the relation between stress and pitch, deploying sprung rhythm as the reawakened tension between pure accentual and accentual syllabic traditions, Hopkins is able to invent a mode of poetic utterance that will serve his philosophy of perception and representation.

Consider, for example, two uses of the term *siding,* which appears first in the Parmenides discussion quoted above. In a journal entry of June 13, 1871, he writes: "A beautiful instance of inscape sided on the slide, that is/ successive sidings of one inscape, is seen in the behaviour of the flag flower from the shut bud to the full blowing: each term you can distinguish is beautiful in itself and of course if the whole 'behaviour' were gathered up and so stalled it would have a beauty of all the higher degree" (House, 211). A second example comes from the discussion of the definition of verse in the lecture notes on rhythm: "[The figure of spoken sound] must be repeated at least once, that is/ the figure must occur at least twice, so that it may be defined/ Spoken sound having a repeated figure. (It is not necessary that any whole should be repeated bodily; it may be *sided off,* as in the metres of a chorus, but then *some* common measure, namely the length of a< or – or strength of a beat etc., recurs)" (Hopkins's emphasis; House, 267). In addition to the "siding" of the metrical scheme, caesura can break up the rhythm into "sense-words of different lengths from sound-words"; alliteration and *skothending* (the Icelandic practice of ending with the same consonant, but after a different vowel) can break up the run of the sense with intermittent sound; open sounds can be transformed by *vowelling on* (assonance) or *vowelling off* (changing the vowel down some "scale or strain or keeping"). Hopkins made lists of words of similar sound, listening for semantic connections between them, as in "drill, trill, thrill, nostril, nese-thirl," "Common idea piercing. To *drill,* in sense of discipline, is to wear down, work upon. Cf. to *bore* in slang sense, wear, grind. So *tire* connected with *tero*" ("Early Diaries," in House, 1–11). In the end there is no difference between "sense" and "sound" words as words "tone up" or vary the impli-

cations of sound and meaning. Hopkins pointedly remarks that "these various means of breaking the sameness of rhythm and especially caesura do
not break the unity of the verse but the contrary; they make it organic and
what is organic is one" (House, 283–84).

As a figure of *spoken* sound, the poem produces effects of transformation in sound; it does not fix or reify the terms of utterance; it becomes in
itself a living, breathing thing. The technique is the emotional stress of the
otherwise inherent qualities of speech: "Emotional intonation," he notes,
"especially when not closely bound to the particular words will sometimes
light up notes on unemphatic syllables and not follow the verbal stresses
and pitches" (House, 270). In a New Year's Day letter to Robert Bridges in
1885, Hopkins describes the alexandrine: "[T]here is according to my experience, an insuperable tendency to the Alexandrine, so far, I mean, as this,
that there is a break after the third foot cutting the line into equal halves
. . . I have found that this metre is smooth, natural and easy to work in
broken dialogue . . . In passionate passages I employ sprung rhythm in it
with good effect." [24] In April he suggested that in regard to alexandrines
"as the feeling rises the rhythm becomes freer and more sprung" (Abbott,
212). The emotional resources of meter are paramount for Hopkins; he is
able to use the rhythms of speech as a kind of backdrop against which the
emotions play their changes in stress and emphasis. In his lecture notes on
rhythm he explained how the syllabic, lexical, and "emotion" levels of the
poem could be in dynamic tension:

> We may think of words as heavy bodies, as indoor or out of door objects
> of nature or man's art. Now every visible palpable body has a centre of
> gravity round which it is in balance and a centre of illumination or *highspot*
> or *quickspot* up to which it is lighted and down from which it is shaded.
> The centre of gravity is like the accent of stress, the highspot like the accent
> of pitch, for pitch is like light and colour stress like weight and as in some
> things as air and water the centre of gravity is either unnoticeable or
> changeable so there may be languages in a fluid state in which there is light
> difference of weight or stress between syllables or what there is changes
> and again as it is only glazed bodies that shew the highspot well so there
> may be languages in which the pitch is unnoticeable. English is of this
> kind, the accent of stress strong, that of pitch weak . . . Emotional intona-
> tion, especially when not closely bound to particular words will sometimes
> light up notes on unemphatic syllables and not follow the verbal stresses
> and pitches. (House, 269–70)

Consider the tension between the standard reading of the stress at closure
of "Spelt from Sibyl's Leaves," Hopkins's meditation on doomsday—
"*thoughts* against *thoughts* in *groans grind*"—against the mounted stress Hopkins marks for the line—"*thoughts against* thoughts *in* groans *grind*." It is as
if, at the end of this sonnet, Hopkins were stripping the gears of sound.

"Spelt from Sibyl's Leaves," begun at the end of 1884 and completed
in 1886, is a transitional poem, produced in a period of pessimism that
would result in Hopkins's "Terrible Sonnets" of 1885: "To seem the

stranger," "I wake and feel the fell of dark," "No worst there is none," "Carrion Comfort," "Patience, hard thing," and "My own heart." Because these poems existed only in manuscript at the time of Hopkins's death and were never dated or prepared for publication by Hopkins, we do not know the order in which he wrote them. They seem to have been composed between January and August of that year.[25] A great deal has been written about these sonnets. They mark the end of Hopkins's intense involvement with describing external nature; they appear during a period of despair regarding his situation as a teacher and examiner in classics at the Royal University, an English Catholic posted in Ireland. His health was poor, his eyesight was failing him: he wrote in his journal, "being unwell I was quite downcast: nature in all her parcels and faculties gaped and fell apart, *fatiscebat,* like a clod cleaving and holding only by strings of root" (House, 236).[26]

The 1885 sonnets and "Spelt from Sibyl's Leaves" are of a piece with Hopkins's reading of Ignatius's instructions for meditating on sin and hell. The role of sound here becomes foregrounded in such a way as to obviate any distinction between the form and theme of the poetry. As an "experiment"—although such a word hardly begins to approach the stakes involved for Hopkins—these poems make a formidable contribution to our understanding of the possibilities of sound in lyric. But they as well, and foremost, work through the capacity of sound in the sonnet—the "son" taking place in a confined room—to express a mental despair. Norman White's biography of Hopkins quotes a 1933 book by Denis Meadows, *Obedient Men,* which describes the Jesuit novitiate's exercise on hell, a composition of place required under Ignatius's *Spiritual Exercises* of 1541: "We must take each of the senses in turn. First, says St. Ignatius, you see the fire, and the souls as though in bodies of fire. With your ears you hear the wailing, howling, and blasphemy of the lost ones. You smell the sulphur, smoke and putrescence of hell. Then you taste in imagination the bitterness of tears, sadness, and conscience ever remorseful, ever unabsolved, yet ever in rebellion. Last of all, you feel the fire touching and burning even an immaterial entity like the soul" (White, 179–80). The use of the term "exercise" indicates, then, a method of self-transformation, or unmaking and remaking the self. In Hopkins's own commentary on Ignatius's prescription, he wrote, "Sight does not shock like hearing, sounds cannot so disgust as smell, smell is not so bitter as proper bitterness, which is in taste . . . [S]till bitterness of taste is not so cruel as the pain that can be touched and felt. Seeing is believing but touch is the truth the saying goes."[27] The function of the "exercise" was not to distance one's self and so acquire an encompassing view of hell, but rather to experience, and engage, the sufferings of the damned.

After the "lonely began" of "To seem the stranger," "I wake and feel the fell of dark, not day" introduces the onset of hell's night—where light, the instrument of reason, should be, touch discovers the animal pelt of the darkness. But because "fell" also means "a blow," it is symptomatic of originary suffering and sin: Adam's curse, the murder of Abel, the "long night" of Job 7:4. Hopkins continues to link bitterness and orality in "Bitter would have me taste: my taste was me; / Bones built in me, flesh filled, blood brimmed the curse." When in the last stanza Hopkins ends the first line "I see," he again interrupts the continuity of sight—the line break turns into a kind of trick, for the line continues "[I see] / The lost are like this." In his sermons, Hopkins associated sight with continuous apprehension and hearing with intermittent apprehension.[28] Sight is, however, intermittent in hell and linked to the invisibility of sin. In his commentary on the "Meditation on Hell," Hopkins writes of the sinner's "imprisonment in darkness . . . for darkness is the phenomenon of foiled action in the sense of sight . . . But this constraint and this blindness or darkness will be most painful when it is the main stress or energy of the whole being that is thus balked" (Devlin, 137). Hence this thwarted, balked stress or energy of being is expressed in a continuous, and continuously painful, form of utterance which is the sonnet itself. "I wake and feel" uses sound pairs—"feel the fell," "sights saw," "ways went," "longer light," "cries countless," "alas away," "gall heartburn," "deep decree," "bitter taste," "bones built," "flesh filled," "blood brimmed," "selfyeast of spirit," "a dull dough," "lost like," "sweating selves"—which are also semantic pairs: nouns are often followed or preceded by participles functioning as adjectives. In this way a quality of an object is put into a dynamic relation with it, transforming it as that quality adheres to, or becomes part of, its structure and so continuing the "siding" process Hopkins had pursued since his early studies of Parmenides. But here this "siding" is not a joyful insight into the transformative dimensions of nature: the singularity and futility ("cries like dead letters sent") of mortal entities is brought to an abrupt halt, a final judgment: "but worse." What does it mean for Hopkins to say that his "cries" are "like dead letters sent / To dearest him that lives alas! away"? Whether "dearest him" is God, or Christ, or Robert Bridges, or some other interlocutor, he is not present—neither within the range of the speaker's cries, nor available as the recipient of a letter. There is no "delivery" from torment; here the tautological consequences of sin are expressed as a tautology of the poet speaking to and for himself; "my taste was me," "selfyeast of spirit a dull dough sours."

Hopkins wrote to Bridges in May 1885, "I have after long silence written two sonnets, which I am touching; if ever anything was written in blood one of these was" (Abbott, 219). Robert Bridges himself later concluded that the poem "written in blood" might have been "Carrion Comfort," but what also is emphasized here is that Hopkins is "touching" two sonnets. Although we have no way of knowing which two sonnets or which sonnet "written in blood" Hopkins had in mind, "I wake and feel" and "No worst there is none" may be the "two," for "No worst," can be read as a complex "response" or echo to "I wake and feel." The last words "but worse" are answered, "No worst, there is none." Issues of sequence are complicated in auditory ways, for if we here have an "answer" or echo, "no worst" will return to the earliest sounds of speech, like pains experienced retrospectively once the knowledge of pain has begun. In the opening lines of "No worst" we find that word pairs are set up not via a truncated echoing effect, but rather in a reverse fashion, so that the first instance is extended: no/ none, pangs/forepangs, comforter/comforting, lull/lingering. These balked phrases, interspersed with repetitions ("Pitched past pitch of grief") and clotted spondees ("My cries heave, herds-long"; "huddle in a main, a chief / Woe, world-sorrow"; "on an age-old anvil wince and sing / Then lull, then leave off"), produce an effect of *stuttering;* the involuntary hesitations, rapid repetitions of speech elements, sputtering and violent explosions of breath following a halt characteristic of that speech disorder are all here. They diminish by the close of the octave: "Let me be fell." At this moment the stuttering is overcome and the speaker *is* "the fell," the animal pelt and mantle of darkness, the blow of awakened consciousness from which the rhetorical grandeur of the sestet next proceeds with its admonition regarding the scale of our "small durance" "under a comfort serves in a whirlwind." The body as a hollow instrument nevertheless can barely breathe as it struggles into speech. In this sonnet Hopkins does not assume the invocatory drive, but rather expresses the conditions under which that drive is externalized. To read this sonnet is to listen to sound unborn being born. Nevertheless the final line with its deliberate and theologically bankrupt oversimplification "Life death does end and each day dies with sleep," marks the closure of abstract human time—the closure is like a false bottom; it will offer no consolation; hell itself gives testament to the incapacity of death to end life.

"Carrion Comfort" is the transition to "Patience, hard thing" the consoling and resolved last sonnet, which is likely to have been based on Ignatius's spiritual exercise (VIII) on patience. In "Carrion Comfort" the exact repetition of "not" ("Not, I'll not carrion comfort, Despair, not feast on thee; / Not untwist . . . not choose not to be") produces a pattern of negatives and positives ensuing from double negatives—"turns of tempest." The poem has a great deal of the hysterical mixture of sounds one finds in extreme situations—"cry," "wish," "fan," "frantic," "coil," "laugh," "cheer." Utterances are spoken and quoted at once: "cry *I can no more*. I can," "(my God!) my God." The God who is both the addressee of the exclamation and the object of the verb ("I wretch lay wrestling with . . . my God") appears then in the second person and the third person and so throws light (itself described negatively as "now done darkness") back upon the question "Cheer whom though? The hero whose heaven-handling flung me, fóot tród / Me? or me that fought him?" Here Hopkins uses interpolated utterance (as he had in the famous "fancy, come faster" of "The Wreck of the Deutschland") to express an agonized self-consciousness. The self who acts is part of the mortal fallen world and the self who speaks carries a painful knowledge of the conditions under which he speaks, a knowledge that is

inherently tautological: "We hear our hearts grate on themselves; it kills /
To bruise them dearer," Hopkins writes in "Patience, hard thing," thus repeating the "thoughts against thoughts in groans grind" of "Spelt from Sibyl's Leaves." Hopkins had written in his *Sermons* (Devlin, 122–23) [29] of how
"nothing else in nature comes near this unspeakable stress of pitch, distinctiveness, and selving, this self-being of my own," but the signs of pitch and
stress that mark the individuality of being are now, in a negative analogy to
poetic expression, the material cries of a material being condemned to suffering by insight as well as experience.[30]

Hopkins's 1885 sonnets return us to the origins of the invocatory drive,
but in doing so they underscore the relation of sound production to a
heightened consciousness of reception in aurality. Like the reception of visual phenomena, the reception of sound might be framed as a *feeling;* we
receive light and sound waves as we receive a touch, a pressure. Yet when
we hear, we hear the sound *of something;* the continuity of sight does not
provide an analogue to this attribution of source or cause in sound reception. And we do not pinpoint sound in space. We see properly only what is
before us, but sound can envelop us; we might, as we move or change,
have varying experiences of sound's intensity, but it will not readily "fit" an
epistemology of spatiality, horizon, or location.[31] The tormented "groans"
and "cries within cries" heaving in the 1885 sonnets resound in a claustrophobic space and yet are locationless. The "something" to which we attribute these sounds is a self "pitched past pitch" by the anxiety of his own
capacity for self-reference. The poems are a radically vivid expression of the
"silence" of lyric sound; rather than assume the presence of speech and
reception, they struggle with our presumptions of speech and reception;
their theological matrix only heightens the torment of Hopkins's insights
into the human ends of poeisis.

What saved Hopkins, or at least saved the poetry of Hopkins for reception, was that there *was* a recipient to the "dead letter"—Bridges, who so
patiently brought the work into history. For Hopkins, in the midst of a
theological crisis regarding the reality of his perceptions and the impossibil-
ity of ascribing a divine source to mortal apprehension, there was ultimately
little salvation in poetry itself. But Bridges's commitment to Hopkins's letters is, in closing, significant for the analogy I want to make between the
silence of the poem and the recalled aurality of its reception. There is a limit
to the metaphor of presence in lyric. When we attend a poetry reading or
hear a poem read aloud by its author in a recording or some other context,
we may confuse the speech in the poem with the speech of the person and
we may confuse the person who speaks with either the person who speaks
in the poem or the person who speaks at the reading. It is not that such
information is not useful and interesting; however it will be information
that will be both too particular (specific to an occasion) and too general
(theatrical and repeatable in its exaggeration of "significant" features). As a

consequence the "poet" "him- or herself" runs the risk of becoming an artifact of the poem, and the poem itself becomes an artifact of performance.

This was the letter I promised on sound; I propose that the sound of poetry is heard in the way a promise is heard. A promise is an action made in speech, not in the sense of something scripted or repeatable, but something that "happens," that "occurs" as an event and can be continually called upon, called to mind, in the unfolding present. When I promised, I created an expectation, an obligation, and a necessary condition for closure. Whether we are in the presence of each other or not, the promise exists. Whether you, the one who receives the promise, continue to exist or not, the promise exists. Others may discontinue making and fulfilling promises, the word *promise* might disappear, you or others may no longer remember, or deserve, or make sense of that promise—nevertheless the promise exists. As Austin wrote, in *How to Do Things with Words,* promises and other "commissives" are not intentions, although intending itself is a commissive— "declarations of intention differ from undertakings," especially if they are framed by the expression *I intend.*[32] The promise can be, must be, fulfilled in time; a "broken promise" cannot be mended—it can only be regretted or used to establish new grounds of demand or indifference. When we consider the historical path of lyric poetry, we find an ongoing process of exploration of the dynamic between an "I" (the speaker) and a "you" (the addressee). Poetry can, it is true, involve a speaker speaking to himself or herself as another, and it can involve an apostrophe to the wind or to a crowd. But personification is *voiced* in poetry—that is, voice takes place not as a presence, but as the condition under which the person appears. The realization of expression depends upon the *bind,* the implicit tie of intelligibility between speaker and listener, which links their efforts toward closure. Through lyric we return literally to the breath and pulse of speech rhythm in tension with those formal structures we have available to us for making time manifest. In this way lyric, no matter how joyous or comic, expresses that seriousness, the good faith in intelligibility, under which language proceeds and by means of which we recognize each other as speakers.

NOTES

1. See James William Johnson, "Lyric," *Encyclopedia of Poetry and Poetics,* ed. Alex Preminger (Princeton: Princeton University Press, 1965), p. 460.

2. Francis Berry, *Poetry and the Physical Voice* (London: Routledge and Kegan Paul, 1962), p. 7, argues against Susanne K. Langer's contention in *Feeling and Form* (London: Routledge and Kegan Paul, 1953), pp. 277–79, that "the treatment of poetry as physical sound comparable to music 'rests on an' utter misconception" and that " 'the voice of a speaker tends to intrude on the created world.' " But Berry goes on to write an entire book on "poetic voice" that largely considers voice in metaphorical terms, making arguments about duration, for example, that are unsustainable with regard to written text. We cannot credibly say that "it takes less time

to say Marvell's 'Had we but World enough, and Time . . . ' than to say Crashaw's 'Love, thou art Absolute sole Lord' " (Berry, 9; the example is borrowed by Berry from Eliot's essay on the metaphysicals), for we have world enough and time to read or remember them at any speed we like. Berry's suggestion in conclusion that "the best we can hope for, when the poem is said aloud, is a voice which approaches [in this instance, Thomas] Gray's as nearly as possible," when we have no access to the voice of Gray and it is not clear what it would mean to have such access in the first place, dissolves the reception of poetry into an absurd exercise in ventriloquism.

3. For a distinction between structural and performative accounts of prosody, see John Hollander, "The Music of Poetry," *Journal of Aesthetics and Art Criticism,* vol. 15, no. 2 (December 1956), pp. 232–44.

4. Immanuel Kant, *The Critique of Judgment,* tr. James Creed Meredith (Oxford: Clarendon, 1982), bk. 2, sec. 325, "Deduction of Pure Aesthetic Judgments," pp. 191–93.

5. G. W. F. Hegel, *The Philosophy of Fine Art,* tr. F. P. B. Osmaston, 4 vols. (New York: Hacker Art Books, 1975), vol. 1, p. 120.

6. Dillon points out that the commonest rhyme vowel in English was and is *a/ai* and that Pope "seems especially addicted to it," using it for 25 percent of the perfect rhymes in *Windsor Forest.* "Sound in Poetry," *Encyclopedia of Poetry and Poetics,* p. 788.

7. Hugo Ball, *Flight out of Time: A Dada Diary,* ed. John Elderfield, tr. Ann Raimes (New York: Viking Press, 1974), pp. 70–71. This passage is discussed in Richard Huelsenbeck, *Memoirs of a Dada Drummer,* ed. Hans J. Kleinschmidt, tr. Joachim Neugroschel (New York: Viking Press, 1969), pp. 60–61, although the translation differs in several minor respects. (I have provided the Elderfield translation here.) Huelsenbeck himself critiques the sound poem by saying, "[T]he dissection of words into sounds is contrary to the purpose of language and applies musical principles to an independent realm whose symbolism is aimed at a logical comprehension of one's environment . . . Language, more than any other form of art, hinges on a comprehension of life- and reality-contents . . . the value of language depends on comprehensibility rather than musicality"(62). The transcription of this poem in various texts is inexact, for as Ball describes his "performance" (he wore a special costume with a huge coat collar that permitted winglike movements of his arms and a high, blue-and-white-striped witch doctor's hat) he "began" with these syllables, but then proceeded between separate "texts" on three music stands, with "Labadas Gesang an die Wolken" [Labada's Song to the Clouds] on the right and the "Elefantenkarawane" [Elephant Caravan] on the left and then improvised a liturgical singing for his conclusion. Hans Richter's *Dada: Art and Anti-Art* (New York: McGraw Hill, 1965), p. 42, transcribes the opening sound poem as

> gadjiberi bimba glandridi laula lonni cadori
> gadjaina gramma berida bimbala glandri galassassa laulitalomini
> gadji beri bin glassa glassala laula lonni cadorsi sassala bim
> Gadjama tuffm i zimzalla binban gligia wowolimai bin beri ban.

8. There are, however, concrete variations in sound production, which can be seen along a spectrum of differences from individual utterance to particular languages at particular historical moments. James Deese writes of vowels: "Vowels are . . . difficult to characterize in terms of their physical characteristics . . . [They] are traditionally identified by their formants. Formants are narrow bands of frequencies,

narrow enough to sound something like musical sounds. They are produced by the shape of the mouth/throat cavity. That cavity provides a resonating chamber for the output of the vocal cords . . . as we change the shape of the mouth we change the frequency of the harmonics that resonate to the output of vocal cords. In general, vowels for particular speakers can be identified with particular formant frequencies. But among different speakers—children, women, as well as different men—it is impossible to characterize any given vowel by the formants that compose it, or by any relation among these formants." *Psycholinguistics* (Boston: Allyn & Bacon, 1970), p. 10.

9. Raymond Chapman, *Linguistics and Literature* (Totowa, N.J.: Littlefield, Adams), p. 86. For a concrete example of how the bias against emphasizing structural words affects English metrics, note the argument Saintsbury makes for a trochaic reading of Browning's epilogue to Asolando, "At the midnight, in the silent of the sleep-time": "Perhaps those who propose this [an English Ionic reading] have been a little bribed by conscious or unconscious desire to prevent 'accenting' *in* and *of;* but no more need be said on this point. The trochees, or their sufficient equivalents, will run very well without any violent INN or OVV." In George Saintsbury, *Historical Manual of English Prosody* (London: Macmillan, 1914), p. 285n. Saintsbury's book remains invaluable for its historical perspective on issues of meter.

10. In his "Summa Lyrica," Allen Grossman takes the consequences of stress even further and emphasizes the tension in English metrics between stress and syllabics: "Syllable count and linear order in general, represent the care which keeps world in being. Stress strokes the line into sense; stress is the evidence of the presence of the interpreter internal to the poem. In stress, the person implied by the poem becomes a countenance which can be recognized. Prosodic stress in English poetry is an arrangement of the stress characteristics of the natural language, in such a way as to explore the possible conformity of the meaning of speakers in natural situations to meaning about meaning and about speakers. Stress both in the natural language and in the context of the poem points diacritically to the meaning-bearing element in the word. Where there is dispute about stress the reader need only accept as an obligation the semantic consequences of any given stressing . . . Stress is the inscription of the subjective or meaning-intending volition of the speaker (this is for the reader). We may dispute about stress. Syllable count, by contrast, is by its nature at the other extreme of intersubjectivity. It has the character of the 'objective' and we do not dispute about it, only correct one another with the understanding that the solution to the counting problem will be univocal. Stress is the point of presence of the hermeneutic issue in the substance of the hermeneutic object itself." Allen Grossman, "Summa Lyrica," in *The Sighted Singer: Two Works on Poetry for Readers and Writers,* with Mark Halliday (Baltimore: Johns Hopkins University Press, 1992), p. 373.

11. See Ferdinand de Saussure, *Course in General Linguistics,* ed. Charles Bally, Albert Sechehaye, and Albert Reidlinger; tr. Wade Baskin (New York: McGraw-Hill, 1966), p. 28: "Spelling always lags behind pronunciation. The *l* in French is today changing to *y;* speakers say *eveyer, mouyer* just as they say *essuyer* 'wipe,' *nettoyer* 'clean'; but the written forms of these words are still *eveiller* 'awaken,' *mouiller* 'soak'. Another reason for discrepancy between spelling and pronunciation is this: if an alphabet is borrowed from another language, its resources may not be appropriate for their new function; expedients will have to be found (e.g. the use of two letters to designate a single sound) . . . During the Middle Ages English had a closed *e*

(e.g. *sed*) and an open *e* (e.g. *led*); since the alphabet failed to provide distinct symbols for the two sounds, the spellings *seed* and *lead* were devised." Following de Saussure's argument we can conclude that written versions of lyric will always inscribe an earlier pronunciation than that in operation at the moment of the lyric's production.

12. Victor Zuckerkandl, *Sound and Symbol: Music and the External World,* tr. Willard R. Trask, Bollingen Series 44 (Princeton: Princeton University Press, 1956), pp. 157–58.

13. See Laura Riding and Robert Graves, *A Survey of Modernist Poetry* (Edinburgh: R. and R. Clark, 1928; reprint, Folcraft Library, 1971), p. 37. Another problem with their example is that they have not employed the stress patterns of the grammar in the same fashion as Tennyson did. All the sound-pattern words in the Tennyson lines (moan, doves, immemorial elms / murmuring, innumerable bees) are stressed form words, with the connectives remaining unstressed. Riding and Graves make some of the sound-pattern words stressed and others unstressed and disperse the sound pattern over connective and form words. If we make up a "nonsense" verse maintaining Tennyson's relation between stress and grammar, and at the same time use Riding and Graves's most parodic nouns, their case still holds, but rather more weakly: "The more ordure momentarily gone / renews more of midden's manure." As with Hugo Ball's poem, examples of arbitrariness are doomed to be symbolic once our attention has been drawn to them.

14. Roger D. Abrahams and George Foss, *Anglo-American Folksong Style* (Englewood Cliffs, N.J.: Prentice-Hall, 1968), p. 167. Among poets, Thomas Hardy is perhaps most adept at using techniques from song style. In the poem "During Wind and Rain" he uses the purely "emotional" refrain "Ah, no; the years O!" (changed in the last stanza to "Ah, no; the years, the years") to lend particular weight to the slowly building drama of the exclamatory last lines of each stanza: "How the sick leaves reel down in throngs!" "See, the white storm-birds wing across!" "And the rotten rose is ript from the wall." "Down their carved names the rain-drop ploughs." In this way the last lines of the stanzas, which seem to be as well "mere" ejaculations of feeling, create a kind of trellis of meaning for the rest of the poem, showing the deep dimension of time emerging out of what might be called the "ordinary" or everyday narratives described in the lines preceding the refrain lines.

15. See Abrahams and Foss, 66: "Burdens do not always contribute to the meaning of a song; they often simply function as an additional incantatory device. This is especially evident in the songs which use flower and herb burdens like 'Savory sage, rosemary and thyme' and ones in which the repeated lines are nonsensical, introduced mainly for the sound patterns which they establish . . . Burdens . . . consequently often crop up in places in which their effect is nullified by a *non sequitur* feeling or by one of lack of appropriateness." They mention that "Twa Sisters"— a horrifying story—has the usual burden in North America of "Bow and balance to me."

16. When songs move from oral to written form, changes also ensue. Consider the case of "The Gypsy Laddie" (Child Ballad 200). In version C the Scottish word "glaumerie" or deception of sight by means of a charm is still used:

She came tripping down the stair,
And all her maids before her;
As soon as they saw her weel-faurd face
They coost their glamourye owre her.

In version G, the language becomes:

> The Earl of Castle's lady came down,
> With the waiting-maid beside her;
> As soon as her fair face they saw,
> They called their grandmother over.

See discussion and further examples in W. Edson Richmond, "Some Effects of Scribal and Typographical Error on Oral Tradition," in *The Critics and the Ballad* (Carbondale: Southern Illinois University Press; 1961), pp. 225–35.

17. W. K. Wimsatt, *The Verbal Icon* (Lexington: University Press of Kentucky, 1954), p. 153.

18. Robert Lowell, "The Muses Won't Help Twice," *Kenyon Review,* vol. 17 (Spring 1955), p. 319. See also Ezra Pound, *The ABC of Reading* (New York: New Directions, 1960).

19. John Thompson, *The Founding of English Meter* (New York: Columbia University Press, 1966), p. 35 n. 1. Gerard Manley Hopkins's writings on meter provide the following catalogue of ways in which "monotony in rhythm is prevented":

(i)   by the mere change of the words, like fresh water flowing through a fountain or over a waterfall, each gallon taking on the same shape as those before it—

(ii) by caesura, the breaking of the feet, or in other words the breaking up of the rhythm into sense-words of different lengths from the sound-words. When the caesura is fixed by rule we have rhythmic counterpoint. By counterpoint I mean the carrying on of two figures at once, especially if they are alike in kind but very unlike or opposite in species.

(iii) by the tonic accent of the words, esp. in French

(iv) by the emphatic accent of the words

(v)   smoothness or break of vowel sound

(vi) all intermittent elements of verse, as alliteration, rhyme. It should be understood that these various means of breaking the sameness of rhythm and especially caesura do not break the unity of the verse but the contrary; they make it organic and what is organic is one.

From "Lecture Notes: "Rhythm and the Other Structural Parts of Rhetoric—Verse," in *The Journals and Papers of Gerard Manley Hopkins* ed. Humphry House, completed by Graham Storey (London: Oxford University Press, 1959), p. 280. Hopkins also mentions issues of singing without words, whistling, or humming, which he explains is in Greek τερετίζειν, "to go *lala* or *ta ra*," p. 268.

20. If in the West reason is associated with the logic of prose and emotion with the outpouring of song, the terms can be more complexly organized in other cultures. Steven Feld's studies of the connections between birdsong, the expression of emotions and singing in Kaluli culture suggest that "men's emotions are irrational, their weeping and anger uncontrolled and unpredictably spontaneous; women's weeping expression is melodic, textured, controlled, reflective and sustained. But men hold rights to song performance, more valued than weeping performance." Steven Feld, *Sound and Sentiment: Birds, Weeping, Poetics and Song in Kaluli Expression* (Philadelphia: University of Pennsylvania Press, 1982), p. 88.

21. Jacques Lacan, *The Four Fundamental Concepts of Psycho-Analysis,* ed. Jacques-Alain Miller, tr. Alan Sheridan (New York: W. W. Norton,), pp. 180, 200.

22. See discussion of these terms in Catherine Phillip's introduction to *Gerard Manley Hopkins,* Oxford Authors Series, ed. Catherine Phillips (Oxford: Oxford University Press, 1986), p. xx.

23. J. Hillis Miller's essay, "The Univocal Chiming," in *Hopkins: A Collection of Critical Essays,* ed. Geoffrey H. Hartman (Englewood Cliffs, N.J.: Prentice-Hall, 1966), pp. 89–116, pays particular attention to the themes of likeness and unlikeness linking the philosophy of Parmenides, the theology of Dun Scotus, and Hopkins's rhyming practices. He suggests that, as a Platonist or realist, Hopkins "proposes the existence of inalterable types at definite intervals, intervals which have a mathematical relation providing for a grand system of harmony" (91).

24. *The Letters of Gerard Manley Hopkins to Robert Bridges,* ed. Claude Colleer Abbott (London: Oxford University Press, 1955), p. 203.

25. As a priest, Hopkins was under particular strictures in this regard. As he wrote to Bridges in 1884, "[A]ll that we Jesuits publish (even anonymously) must be seen by censors and this is a barrier which I do not know how anything of mine on a large scale would ever pass" (12 November postscript to 11 November letter, Abbott, 200). In 1876 he had gone through a difficult process of rejection as *The Wreck of the Deutschland* was first accepted, and then rejected, by his friend Henry Coleridge, the editor of the Jesuit journal *The Month.* Coleridge had asked Hopkins to take out the accents and Hopkins complied, but the poem never appeared (Norman White, *Hopkins: A Literary Biography* [Oxford: Clarendon Press, 1992], pp. 258–59). Hopkins's friend Robert Bridges became the archivist of his work; he sent his work to Bridges frequently, and Bridges's careful attention to the manuscripts and transcripts of the poems enabled editions of Hopkins's work to appear posthumously. In a letter on September 1, 1885 (Abbott, 221), Hopkins wrote: "I shall shortly have some sonnets to send you, five or more. Four [written above 'Three,' canceled] of these came like inspirations unbidden and against my will," but he never sent the poems to Bridges or any other correspondent. See also Paul Mariani, *A Commentary on the Complete Poems of Gerard Manley Hopkins* (Ithaca: Cornell University Press, 1970), p. 210. Mariani suggests, following Jean-Georges Ritz, a logical order to the poems following "the classical descent and ascent of the Ignatian exercises": "To seem the stranger," "I wake and feel the fell of dark," "No worst there is none," "Carrion Comfort," "Patience, hard thing."

26. Norman White's biography cites Hopkins's contemporaries as countering his picture of himself as overworked. Hopkins described the terrible headaches he suffered during this time as "accompanied by the visual images of blocks which had to be fitted together," apparently an allegory of his struggle with poetry (386).

27. "Meditation on Hell," in *Gerard Manley Hopkins,* ed. Catherine Phillips, Oxford Authors Series (Oxford: Oxford University Press, 1986), pp. 292–95. See also Daniel A. Harris's discussion of the role of the senses in the 1885 sonnets in *Inspirations Unbidden: The 'Terrible Sonnets' of Gerard Manley Hopkins* (Berkeley: University of California Press, 1982), especially pp. 56–67. Harris links the sonnets to a crisis in Hopkins's theology regarding the Incarnation and provides an astute reading of the role of the senses in many of the poems.

28. *The Sermons and Devotional Writings of Gerard Manley Hopkins,* ed. Christopher Devlin, S. J., (London: Oxford University Press, 1959), p. 175. Discussed as well in Harris, 62.

29. See also the discussion in Mariani, 224.

30. Geoffrey Hartman describes the "vocative" aspect of Hopkins's style: "This holds for sound, grammar, figures of speech, and actual performance. Tell and toll become cognates . . . We find cries within cries as in: "Not / I'll not / carrion comfort, / Despair / not feast on thee," writing "[language's] end as its origin is to move, persuade, possess. Hopkins leads us back to an aural situation (or its simulacrum) where meaning and invocation coincide. Everything depends on the right 'pitch,' or verbal cast" (6–8). Although Hartman uses one of the 1885 sonnets as an example of this point, it is the facility of the vocative in the majority of Hopkins's work that makes the breakdown of the vocative in these late sonnets so tragic and immediate. In *Hopkins: A Collection of Critical Essays*. See also Hartman's reading of "The Windhover," in "The Dialectic of Sense-Perception," in the same volume (117–30).

31. See G. N. A. Vesey, "Sound," in *The Encyclopedia of Philosophy*, vol. 7, ed. Paul Edwards (New York: Macmillan, 1967), pp. 500–1, and Susanne K. Langer, *Mind: An Essay on Human Feeling*, vol. 2 (Baltimore: Johns Hopkins University Press, 1972), p. 134: "[S]ound, to our ears, is diffuse, like smell, or relatively massive, impinging without any precise spatial articulation. Such detail as it may convey is temporal. The crash of dishes sliding off an unbalanced tray, or the rustling of a mouse fleeing through dry leaves, has certainly more audible structure than an explosion, but it is the progress of an event through time that it conveys, not spatial form."

32. J. L. Austin, *How to Do Things with Words*, ed. J. O. Urmson (New York: Oxford University Press, 1962), p. 157.

2

The Aural Ellipsis and the Nature of Listening in Contemporary Poetry

NICK PIOMBINO

> Hearing is the sense most
> favored by attention; it holds the
> frontier, so to speak, at the point
> where seeing fails.

PAUL VALÉRY, *Analects*

I

I would like to term certain effects of indeterminacy in writing, reading, and listening to contemporary poetry, especially in relation to the use of sounds as apparently detached from everyday meanings, the "aural ellipsis." This term alludes to Walter Benjamin's concept of the "aura" as well as to some unusual notions concerning listening discussed by Roman Jakobson and Krystyna Pomorska:

> Over the centuries, the science of language has more than once addressed the question of ellipsis, which manifests itself at different verbal levels: sounds, syntax and narration. One must admit that for the most part these questions, too, have been elaborated only episodically and fragmentarily. A technique which today receives even less consideration is that of elliptical perception, by which the listener fills in (again on all linguistic levels) whatever had been omitted by him as listener. We have also failed to appreciate properly the subjectivism of the hearer who fills in the elliptic gaps creatively.[1]

The listener tends to "fill in" or weave into any elliptical speech act certain elements of his or her internal experience. This new formulation, at that point existing only within, as Jakobson and Pomorska term it, "the subjectivism" of the listener, functions momentarily as a "transitional object" or area of potential space between the listener and the speaker (I will discuss in detail the psychoanalytic concept of the "transitional object" and its application to contemporary poetry in section 2).

The effect of the "aural ellipsis" in poetry allows that, at certain points, the poem may exist within an indeterminate site of significant verbal experience that is simultaneously physical and mental, objective and subjective, heard aloud and read silently, emanating from a specific self yet also from a nonspecific site of identity, coming toward comprehensibility and disintegrating into incoherence. This analysis or representation, we may find on close examination, frequently corresponds to specific moments of everyday experience far more accurately than the fictions of perception proffered under official categories of self/identity determination and factual authentication. Another function of the aural ellipsis in poetry may be to manifest and model an emerging paradigm shift in the combining and layering of languages as the world moves rapidly toward global forms of communication. It is possible that the emergence of the "aural ellipsis" in poetry presages the coming of ever more widely shared forms of language by subliminally teaching us how to intuitively apprehend at least the rough outlines of meanings, both manifest and latent, of verbal constructs, by means of detecting, tracking and decoding their rhythmic presentations alone. This may be achieved in part by further developing, in listening to contemporary poetry, the everyday practice of evaluating the connotations of utterances by means of sensing the speaker's speech rhythms, whether halting, uneven or tonally nuanced, as, for example, with irony, humor, or sarcasm.

When reading or listening to the words of a poem with an open form of attention, it does appear possible, at times, for the reader to decipher subliminal levels of significance that follow latent streams running apparently parallel to the explicit content, or to sound out encoded message content by tracking meanings primarily through the apprehension of patterns of rhythms and sounds. This effect seems particularly palpable in such works as the avant-garde classic *Trilce* by César Vallejo:

> 999 CALORIES.
> Rumbbb . . . Trraprrrr rrack . . . chaz
> Serpentinic "u" engiraffed
> to the drums of the biscuitmaker [. . .]
> Who like the ices. But no.
> Who like what's going neither more nor less.
> Who like the happy medium.[2]

A clear concern with related issues can be found in as early an American poet as Emily Dickinson:

I felt a Cleaving in my Mind—
As if my Brain had split—
I tried to match it—Seam by Seam—
But could not make them fit.

The thought behind, I strove to join
Unto the thought before—
But Sequence ravelled out of Sound
Like Balls—upon a Floor.[3]

My earliest awareness of the existence of the aural ellipsis came in read-ing, for the first time in the middle to late 1960s, certain works of such poets as Jackson Mac Low, Robert Creeley, Bernadette Mayer, John Ash-bery, and Clark Coolidge, as well as the writing and early performance works of Vito Acconci, the essays and "nonsite" sculptures of Robert Smithson, and the films of Michelangelo Antonioni and Jean-Luc Godard. In the key early works of all of these artists great attention is paid to formal elements that effectively permit these works to be experienced by the reader or viewer as "holding environments" (a term I discuss below), a possibility greatly enhanced by the use of found and invented forms of language and innovative conceptions of the relationships among perception, language, and reality. In contrast, these works are not so improvisatory as to lack significant content, unity, and structure. The relationship or balance be-tween elements of recognizable content and structure and those of semantic and structural innovation create good conditions for the presence of the aural ellipsis. Uses of abstract-expressionist, surrealist, and other innovative techniques foregrounding the juxtaposition of words and images, paradox, ambiguity, and enigma, encourage readers or viewers to bring into aware-ness and project their own experiences, conscious and unconscious, onto the works, enhancing their usefulness as transitional objects.

2

In a much discussed review of John Ashbery's *Selected Poems* published in *Sulfur* in 1987, Sven Birkerts wrote: "John Ashbery's *Selected Poems*: that for-lorn codex, garden of branching paths, termite tree of the late Millennium . . . The assignment was to review it, and I find I cannot. To review is to have read and to be looking back. I have read *at*, toward, near, but never with that cinching tug of understanding. I have moved my eyes and felt the slow dispersion of my sense of self. I have been flung back into the bore-dom and rage of childhood, when the whole world seemed to rear up against me, not to be had or understood."[4] What interests me in this is not only Birkerts's evident tone-deafness to Ashbery's remarkable poetic music, but also the fact that Birkerts frequently has many valuable insights to offer and that there may be one buried in this otherwise dismissive diatribe. Note that Birkerts describes with great feeling, and some poetic evocativeness, the experience of being transported back into childhood. He is perhaps unconsciously alluding here to the child's whole ambivalent experience around symbiosis, the necessary early psychological stage of merging with maternal and paternal figures that can introduce (among many other crucial experiences) feelings of helplessness and depression. He quotes the following passage of one of Ashbery's poems, "We Hesitate":

> Once they come home there is no cursing.
> Fires disturb the evening. No one can hear the story
> Or sometimes people just forget
> . . . Like a child.

Birkerts goes on to say "I could go over this a hundred times and it would mean nothing more that it does on a first reading" (146).

Since I have poor Birkerts here involuntarily on a figurative psychoanalytic couch, I might speculate that he is in a state of "resistance." If this conjecture is correct, the resistance probably is connected with the kind of anxiety Birkerts described earlier as the "slow dispersion of my sense of self." In psychoanalysis we observe that the reason that people frequently "resist" change in living, and in analysis, is that it can be painful to revive the memories that must be elicited and connected with on a feeling level if one is to ultimately understand the past and move on. Why "dispersion . . . of self"? Because this is exactly the feeling one has in a state of merging. Does the Ashbery text in fact encourage an experience of merging? I feel that it does. I might even agree with Birkerts that, in a certain important psychological sense, "Ashbery's poetry works backward along the evolutionary spiral, undoing" (Birkerts, 148). Where I completely disagree with Birkerts is when he asserts that "this is an enterprise that repudiates sense and mocks our faith in the sufficiency of our language structures" (148).

Birkerts's failure to follow up his own carefully documented responses to Ashbery's poetry to a point where he might have connected with it more fully can be taken as an exemplary case of a kind of flight from what I believe to be a paradigm shift not only in the style of much valuable poetry being written today, but also in its functions on many planes—social, psychological, linguistic, philosophical, artistic, and cultural. Apparently, what Birkerts wants from his experience of contemporary poetry is the traditional critical opportunity to use close intellectual reading of poetry as a way of interpreting it and ultimately finding that most satisfying of rational experiences, closure. This is primarily an intellectual process. But much effective creative work today, particularly in the field of poetry, cannot be appreciated and enjoyed by reorganizing it conceptually. Perhaps this is because many, if not most, of the innovative artists and poets of our time are less interested in their works being interpreted as representing or reflecting specific ideas and ideologies, than in having their art work provide something analogous to what the British psychoanalyst D. W. Winnicott called a "holding environment," a context that makes available to poets and other artists and to their readers, listeners or viewers freely juxtaposed modes of paying close attention to external and internal experience. This opening or freeing of forms of focusing in turn makes possible an intensified collaborative sharing (between a poet and listeners at a reading, for example) in the effort of organizing otherwise anomalous, disparate and incommunicable perceptions into patterns of meaning that can be further articulated, refined, and better understood, in an ongoing process. To understand what Winnicott meant by a holding environment we must first examine his concept of the "transitional object":

> I have introduced the terms 'transitional objects' and 'transitional phenomena' for designation of the intermediate area of experience, between the thumb and the teddy bear, between the oral eroticism and the true object-relationship, between primary creative activity and projection of what has already been introjected . . . By this definition an infant's babbling and the way in which an older child goes over a repertory of songs and tunes while preparing for sleep come within the intermediate area as transitional phenomena, along with the use made of objects that are not part of the infant's body yet are not fully recognized as belonging to external reality.[5]

Note that Winnicott here includes sounds, both audible and imagined, as transitional objects.

Winnicott's discovery of the transitional object resolves, or takes to a new level, an issue in Freudian psychoanalysis that seems to have left Freud in an unclear state as to the reasons why art exists. He could only explain it as a kind of "sublimation" or substitute for the sexual instinct. For him, the artist was a neurotic person who felt the need to substitute fantasies for reality. Winnicott's understanding of what he termed "transitional objects" comes out of his work as a pediatrician as much as his work as a psychoanalyst, as well as from his participation in the work of a school of psychoanalysts known as the "object relations" school, which includes Melanie Klein, W. R. D. Fairbairn, and Harry Guntrip. In his theoretical work, as well as his technical recommendations to child psychoanalysts, Winnicott greatly furthers our understanding of the continuity between the needs of the child and the needs of the adult in creating, as he called them, "illusions." A sense of how to apprehend this continuity is exactly what is missing in Birkerts's understanding of Ashbery's poetry. Winnicott's insights not only provide us with a better understanding of the healthy uses of artistic products but also the important and necessary function of art in creating holding environments and "transitional objects" for life long use. Winnicott says of the transitional object (his emphasis): *"Of the transitional object it can be said that it is a matter of agreement between us and the baby that we will never ask the question: 'Did you conceive of this or was it presented to you from without?' The important point is that no decision on this point is expected. The question is not to be formulated"* (Winnicott, 12). This quality of the indefinite origin of the transitional object for the infant is reflected in the psychological and aesthetic functions of indeterminacy and ambiguity in the art object or in the poem that is appreciated and enjoyed by the adult. Winnicott also states: "It is assumed here that the task of reality-acceptance is never completed, that no human is free from the strain of relating inner and outer reality, and that relief from this strain is provided by an intermediate area of experience . . . which is not challenged (arts, religion, etc.). This intermediate area is in direct continuity with the play area of the child who is 'lost' in play" (13). When Winnicott speaks of an "intermediate area" or a "third area," what he is speaking about is an area that is neither strictly subjective or objective: "The place where cultural experience is located is the *potential space* between the individual and the environment (originally the object). The same can be said of playing. Cultural experience begins with creative living first manifested in play" (100). The discovery of the transitional object revealed some of the key social and psychological functions of the contemporary art object in extending psychological development throughout life.

For Winnicott, the experience he calls holding is one provided for an infant by a "good enough" parental "facilitating environment." During this time the infant is gradually introduced into reality or the "objective" world by means of the parents allowing for the infant's, and later the child's, total dependence, gradually shifting into partial dependence, and finally independence. For the child to develop this independence the parental figures must be capable, however, of tolerating the infant's need for feeling a degree of omnipotence, and to permit and empathize with the need on the part of the infant and later the child, for the use of "magical" transitional objects as an intermediate protection and support during the transition from the merged, omnipotent state, to the more vulnerable and self-reliant independent state. The transitional object facilitates a means by which the child and the parent can paradoxically (and often unconsciously) hold on to each other and let go of each other at the same time. Similarly, the contemporary poem that functions as a mode of providing a holding environment makes it possible for the reader to imaginatively hold on to the poem and to let go of it at the same time, thereby enhancing the listener's associative filling-in of elliptical gaps (the aural ellipsis).

Winnicott's application of his discovery of the transitional object identifies, names, and authenticates an area of human experience that is simultaneously physical and mental and not exclusively either, and that does not rely on any notion of "spirit," as does, for example, the concept of the "talisman." The need for knowledge, concepts, and principles to enunciate the intersections or boundaries among language, consciousness, objects, and other less apprehensible and specifiable areas of experience has long been struggled with in philosophy and phenomenology by such figures as Plato, Pascal, Hegel, Kant, Moore, Wittgenstein, Husserl, and others. Aspects of the philosophical and literary theories of Walter Benjamin seem to me complementary to Winnicott's ideas; in particular, his concept of the "aura" and his use of the Paris arcades as physical evidence for his theories about society form important parallels. Benjamin seemed very concerned about finding correlatives in the physical world, types of evidence, for his literary theories. Although there is not sufficient space in this context to explore this at length, a few citations from Benjamin might be enough to suggest a useful connection between the relatively recent work of this important critical theorist and the important "object relations" psychoanalytic theorist, Winnicott, in specifying an area of poetics that in the past could only be adequately encompassed by employing concepts more closely related to religion and mysticism.

In discussing the role of architecture in the life of the private citizen under Louis-Phillipe, Benjamin writes: "The private citizen who in the office took reality into account, required of the interior that it should support him in his illusions . . . From this sprang the phantasmagorias of the interior. This represented the universe for the private citizen. In it he assembled the distant in space and time. His drawing-room was a box in the world-theatre . . . The interior was the place of refuge of Art."[6] What interests me here is Benjamin's focus on the fact that the need for illusion by the "private citizen" had become regularized in relation to the use of everyday objects. He was able to effectively demonstrate this by his explication of the relation of the place of illusion to the functions and forms of everyday decor in the eighteenth century. This understanding of the process of psychological transformation of everyday objects of human habitation into a stage set for illusion or play is akin to the way Winnicott understood the human tendency to transform sounds, language, and things into psychological environments for human transition and growth. Benjamin's profound insights into the functions of the "aura" at times come very close to apprehending and characterizing the area of experience that Winnicott later identified and named "the transitional object": " 'Perceptibility,' as Novalis puts it, 'is a kind of attentiveness.' The perceptibility he has in mind is none other than that of the aura. Experience of the aura thus rests on the transposition of a response common in human relationships to the relationship between the inanimate or natural object and man. The person we look at, or who feels he is being looked at, looks at us in turn. To perceive the aura of an object we look at means to invest it with the ability to look at us in return" (Benjamin, 148).

Benjamin's acute sensitivity to the human propensity to transpose human qualities into natural objects by means of attentiveness to their auras is uncannily close to Winnicott's conception of the transitional object. Like Winnicott, Benjamin describes the aura as existing in an intermediate state which is both human and nonhuman, subjective and objective. Benjamin attributed to Baudelaire particular insight into this phenomenon, twice quoting the following lines from "Correspondances," from *Fleurs du Mal:* "Man wends his way through forests of symbols / Which look at him with their familiar glances" (Benjamin, 140, 149).[7]

Benjamin's apprehension of the "aura" and Winnicott's elucidation of the "transitional object" provide contemporary conceptual frameworks for grasping an aspect of human experience that previously was essentially the province of religion and mysticism. For thousands of years, shamans in tribal cultures have been chanting at least partially improvised, frequently fragmented, elliptical phrases, often when the shaman was in an altered state, as an important aspect of healing rituals.[8] The American Shakers wrote over ten thousand spontaneous hymns in the course of a few decades of prayer meetings. The use of otherwise meaningless syllables of sound (like *Om*) figures importantly in Buddhism and other religions.

"The Spirit is the Conscious Ear" wrote Dickinson (poem 733, p. 359). While for many, notions of the mystical or spiritual are no longer adequate concepts for evoking certain otherwise unnamable yet powerfully influential effects of the sounds of words in poetry, terms like *the transitional object* or, in this context, *the aural ellipsis* can underline how from birth to death particular poetic uses of spoken or sung ellliptical language seem to inspire in us some needed access to otherwise inaccessible and incommunicable realms of experience.

3

In an unguarded moment of reverie I find that I am not only listening to the Debussy *Images* for piano but I am simultaneously listening for something that is further to be heard. I think of Rilke:

> Voices, voices. Listen, my heart, as hitherto only
> saints have listened, so that the mighty call
> lifted them from the earth; but they kept on kneeling,
> these impossible ones, and paid no attention—
> so hard they were listening.[9]

I encounter this theme frequently in the works of contemporary artists. The poet and filmmaker Abigail Child puts it like this:

> Listen! provocatively
> that's your spirit
> that's your fucking consciousness.[10]

Charles Bernstein's poem "Substance Abuse" contains a passage that focuses on the key issue of freedom and improvisation in poetic listening. As is frequently the case in his work, the boundaries between critical writing, poetics, personal self disclosure, and poetic revelation are blurred and many of the issues surrounding what I am terming the aural ellipsis are discussed *and* evoked:

> Nothing tires a vision more than sundry attacks
> in the manner of enclosure. My thoughts toss

trippingly on the tongue—an immense excuse
for proportion [perforation]. What I am saying
here will only come out in joinings:
but to loosen the mind, limber it for
bounding. What does ear contain
that norming senses lack? A resolution
in the air.[11]

The stillness within Lynne Dreyer's call for listening is poignant and resonant:

It was the voice. It was the
voices of people I had known
before. It was my own voice. I
wanted to watch you. The
children are cruel. They find
nothing changed. They find
silence.
　　Yet something increased in
sound. You sat down and for
the first time in your entire life
you listened and heard some-
thing that had nothing to do with you.[12]

In certain readings of poetry I am hearing something parallel but otherwise mysteriously inaccessible, compared to what I am listening to when
listening *to* becomes listening *for*. I can frequently perceive this effect of aural
ellipsis when the poetic text accommodates itself comfortably to what I
sense to be the actuality of everyday, nondeliberate thought, or what I call
"average thought." Jakobson writes: "Quite fragmentary in the most relaxed
thinking, inner language may be only partial even in deliberate cogitation.
'Sentences,' says Egger, 'may be condensed. These words . . . have full
meaning only for the individual who conceives them . . . Synthetic expressions such as 'Wretch—! Another—! Never—!' are sufficient, even without
explanatory context, when we're talking to ourselves."[13] Everyday, nonpur-
posive thought weaves its way through memories, assertions, emotions, reflections, observations, generalizations, comparisons, ellisions almost instan-
taneously and frequently with very elliptical uses of language.

Many of the poems of Paul Celan might well illustrate the powerful
poetic use of the aural ellipsis. In the poem "And with the Book from Ta-
russa," which begins with an epigram from Marina Tsvetayeva—"All poets
are Jews"—Celan writes:

. . . Of the woods
Untrodden, of the
thought they grew from, as sound
and half-sound and changed sound and terminal sound, Scythian
　　rhymes . . .

. . .—into the realm,
the widest of
realms, into
the great internal rhyme
beyond
the zone of mute nations, into yourself
language-scale, word-scale, home-
scale of exile.[14]

It appears that Celan is defining here with great poetic precision what I
have been describing as the aural ellipsis and the development of an international language of thought and sound, "the great internal rhyme / beyond /
the zone of mute nations." With this internal access, words and languages
can become a shared "zone," on one accessible scale, where all "exiles" can
discover a common "home."

Works of poetry that can be characterized as effective mediums for the
aural ellipsis tend to be works that permit listeners and readers to discover
and determine many of the structural elements of the poem for themselves,
rather than foreground the narrative or didactic elements that provide the
illusion of purpose, realism, or verisimilitude. There is a distinction that can
be made between written works that can be appreciated by means of ordinary silent reading and those in which each word should be heard read
aloud or individually sounded out aloud in the mind. With the latter works
readers are encouraged to experience the poem by sounding it out internally
in a process of concentrated, yet freely imaginative listening and reading
rather than only hearing it as something closer to grammatically conventional speech that can be fully explicated. It is in this sense that the aural/
oral ellipsis encourages listening to poetry as a holding environment within
which the gaps among thought, language, and sensory experience must be
bridged by the listener. Rather than only being asked to observe and comprehend a pattern of thinking, here listeners and readers, by means of a
process of close, but freely imaginative, listening, are encouraged to actively
participate in it.

Certainly, of all the poetry written today, Jackson Mac Low's work best
exemplifies, particularly in its consistency of perspective and literary innovation, the presence of the aural ellipsis. My first readings of the poems from
The Pronouns, in 1966–1967, provided my earliest definitive experience of
poems wherein the rhythmical, aural, and visual functions of words within
the poem were equivalent in significance and aesthetic impact to any literal
meanings those words might have had at the time of reading them. This
equivalence was extended to the rhythmic structure of the lines and to the
movements of the eyes in rhythmically reading the words on the page. I felt
that I was recognizing here directly that there was a gap or aporia in the
senses among hearing (which includes mental, imagined hearing as much as
actual physical hearing), seeing, and touching in everyday life. Here, coordinated or combined sensory experiences replace perceptions that are simply

disparate or discrete. The precision of this effect seems to have at least partly resulted from Mac Low's system of recycling his literary source material, which involves the use of randomizing methods, techniques that he has been evolving and experimenting with throughout his career, and masterfully employs in such recent books of poems as *Bloomsday.* [15]

In November 1967 I learned that Mac Low had extended this system of equivalences into the sphere of political action, when I met him for the first time at a demonstration sponsored by the War Resisters League at the Whitehall Street Induction Center. I found an equivalence between the way Mac Low accentuated the transformation of identity in both the subjective and objective realms, in this case, the poetic and the political. In *The Pronouns* the pronoun itself, as a part of language, becomes an allegorical element of the sociopolitical dynamics of the dances. Mac Low has to date continued to be intensely interested in the performance aspect of his poetry, a fact made abundantly clear in his innumerable poetic and music performances that have remained a crucial aspect in the development of his poetic work for over forty years.[16] As he put it in his "Reflections on the Occasion of the DANCE SCOPE issue" (dated 8/29/74): "Since 1954 I have made many pieces—simultaneities for voices &/or instruments, poems, plays, musical works—which call for active creative collaboration of performers and/or audience. My reasons for liking this type of composition has not changed much since I wrote the statement . . . 'An "anarchist" does not believe, as some have wrongly put it, in social chaos. He or she believes in a society where there is no frozen power structure, where all persons may make significant initiatory choices in matters affecting their own lives. In such a society coercion is at a minimum & lethal violence is practically nonexistent.' " [17]

The aural ellipsis, then, in *The Pronouns* is that area of the listening/reading experience that provides a holding environment in which to immerse oneself and participate in the complex, transformative interrelationship between self and other: he = she = they = you = all = I = it = we = one = thou = ye = this = those = these = that = somebody = someone = anyone, and so on, as each of these pronouns replaces the previous one in a collection of poems employing lines all in imperative form to be used as instructions for the dancers. The result is partly one of static/moving simultaneous connectedness with the *whole* of experience, compared with the limited perspective available from the standpoint of the specific identity of the writer or the reader alone. At this boundary, hearing and seeing, looking and listening are interrelated and are paradoxically, dynamically in tension with one another. Since the reading must take place in time, its music or its performance will trace a trajectory of its own that may or may not be equivalent to one or another of the senses—thus another sense, or mode of perception, is evoked. Hearing Mac Low perform these works, of course, makes these effects all the more accessible and apparent.

It is not only the concept of identity that is being displaced, in this and other works by Mac Low, but it is in the presumption (the sometimes necessary illusion) that identity is, in actuality, completely separate from anything else. We are becoming what our perceptions make of us, and in the aural, elliptical holding environment of the poem we can locate an orientation to experience within which we can let go of the specificity of the self and all of its officially documented narratives to enter into a world peopled by unexpected definitions, determinations and relationships:

> You are alone & start out by being a wire,
> & you seem to have a purpose,
> going about, as you do, being a unit.

> Soon you're doing things to make a meal,
> & then you're doing something as in the West,
> as if you were "awaking yesterday when the skin's
>   a little feeble":
> you blacken something
> while you write with a bad pen,
> & smoke,
> letting potatoes go bad
> before you match a few parcels.

> Being earth,
> you harbor poison between cotton or go from
> breathing to a common form,
> testing different things,
> touching them,
> sponging them,
> going under them,
> numbering them,
> wheeling them,
> schooling them,
> getting them.

> You end up by giving enough of anything to anyone.
>   (from "4th Dance—Being a Brother to
>   Someone—11–17 February 1964," 17)

One of Mac Low's central concerns is to find ways to write that bypass the limitations of the self. Another innovative and influential poet deeply concerned with displacing the central role of the poet's identity in the process of writing poetry, particularly by placing close attentions to the rhythms and sounds of language, is Jack Spicer. In his *Vancouver Lectures* Jack Spicer refers to Cocteau's film *Orpheus* in which the poet (as Orpheus) appears to be receiving his lines from a car radio. Spicer wrote about the process of writing poetry as receiving a kind of "dictation," transmission or "message from Mars."[18] Perhaps another way to understand Spicer's concerns is to recognize that the poet's role has changed in contemporary life. While at one time the poet's central role was to declaim his or her beliefs, experiences, wisdom, and ideas eloquently or adamantly through lyrics and narrations in a kind of public speech or song-making, for many poets these notions of a poet's essential role are no longer completely apt. Frequently, the poet seems to view his or her expressive function more as a medium or a "conduit" as Barrett Watten has phrased it.[19] The poet is a researcher who must listen closely to the sounds and voices of actuality to discover where the poetry may exist within it. In an interview with Joan Retallack, in response to a quote from Theodor Adorno ("The greatness of works of art lies solely in their power to let those things be heard which ideology conceals"), John Cage said: "something that you just quoted leads in another direction as though there were a subject. As though it was about something. Which could be the emotions. Ideology would conceal by relationships. And those things being heard would be, so to speak, speaking the mysterious language of the unknown! *(laughs)* Which music could be imagined as being able to do. *(laughs)*."[20]

4

One of the clearest contexts in which to identify the efficacy of the poetic aural ellipsis is in the poet's use of found language. The poem of found language provides for both the poet utilizing it and the listener or reader deciphering it a holding environment in which the poet's identity, beliefs, and personal ideology are not usually obvious as a central aspect of the content. The poetic impact in such cases arises mostly from juxtapositions, both between the words of the poem and between the words and the poem's formal devices as well as the listener or reader's efforts to close the elliptical gaps between the words, ideas and fragments of narrative in the poem. A passage from a recent poem of Joan Retallack may serve as an example:

> erratums for the tummy La La tin *erratum* neuter past *errare* all history
> lies behind before Poetique Terrible delete as/like Duchamp as Fred
> Astaire to read epit ess pref b iv b neut p pple sundry errats' distended
> verse to wander err erratic nudging **ers** root erratum rrroneus erroar The
> World's a Book 'Tis falsely writ . . . et . . . cet . . . era[21]

Drawing from the content as well as the form of errata slips, Retallack deftly performs the alchemical magic of the found-language artist, at the same time uncovering the potential transformative energy implicit in the recognition of all error and distortion, be it typographical, spoken, philosophical, or perceptual. This energy is released by means of a similar access route to the unconscious discussed by Freud in *The Psychopathology of Everyday Life*. Retallack transforms the scraps of language usually hardly glanced at into poetry that contains rhythmically complex music, wit, philosophical sweep, visual grace, presented in a linguistic environment of dynamic compression. Retallack's method of drawing attention to each letter by means of using the reader's natural tendency to notice printed errors, to sound them out internally and to associate to them freely, partly in order to detect the unconscious meaning in these parapraxes, or slips of speech, is clear in this passage. Although the reference is not mentioned in a list of source included with the text, I detect some echoes of *Finnegans Wake,* by James Joyce, which would certainly be one of the earliest examples of the intentional and frequent employment of the aural ellipsis, and certainly one of its literary origins.[22] Although the lines are drawn from various sources, this in no way limits either the ideas or the vibrant lyricism of the language. *Errata suite,* by utilizing words as they appear to us in the inchoate flux of everyday experience, very much including the experience of silent and spoken reading, as well as associative thinking, creates a kind of music that challenges us to listen to the entire complexity of experience in its full density. This is, of course, difficult poetry to read aloud and to hear read aloud. But the process is valuable because it creates an opportunity to transform what might otherwise remain incommunicable internal experiences into concrete, albeit fluid forms of external expression. This is what Jakobson means when he writes, "The principal vehicle for the displacements of the equilibrium [of language] are the elliptical and expressive aspects of language. The changes that attempt to reestablish the destroyed equilibrium in the system of language play an essential role in the passage from the old order to the new" (Jakobson, 179). At poetry readings where such poems as *Errata suite* are read aloud, and listened to conscientiously, both poet and listeners are working together collaboratively to expand the boundaries of spoken and written language.

Another poet who has been central in opening up the exploration of elliptical techniques in poetry is Clark Coolidge. His book *Space,* published in 1970, is a classic in the masterful use of an aural elliptical form of writing and has been broadly influential. It was in reading and rereading this work along with Ashbery's *The Tennis Court Oath,* Mayer's *Story,* Mac Low's *The Pronouns* and Berrigan's *The Sonnets* that I first sensed that a new type of poetry had emerged, one that freely employed linguistic constructs in both a visual and an aural form to evoke and evolve novel metalanguages. The most evident aspect of these new metalanguages for me was that in rereading the poems they seemed to transform themselves right before your eyes, kaleidoscopically refusing to stay in one place, or to be seen from one perspective, and were extremely rich in aural associations. As with the greatest traditionally written poems, returning to them one again and again rediscovers a new poem, only in the case of these works this effect is greatly intensified. The poem "THESE" from *Space* illustrates Coolidge's deceptive simplicity of language and the deft lyricism that persists through the demanding absence of ordinary meaning:

Bers phone the the.
Give showed mail ing.
The on won so.
Ly fetch wonders note.
It's a gim, a de.
On the know, the on, the don't.
Back how's is backs.
To one it, it irons.
Ops a ed, a are any this.
    Don.

    Trucks one.[23]

The reader is encouraged to try sounding out these words internally or aloud. A few minutes of relaxed experimentation should make it obvious that it is nearly impossible to focus on listening to these words without attempting to fill in the gaps. Although the end result of the experiment will probably not lead to a grammatically clear sequence of statements, specific and identifiable sound images will emerge. The poem provides a sound and visual structure for innumerable possible variations. It is in this sense that this work is so apt as a holding environment within which the reader may cocreate his or her own version of the poem while sounding it out within the aural ellipses of the given text. To read and particularly to hear this type of work read by the poet encourages the listener or reader to participate actively in the performative aspect of the work. The reader or listener is invited to become a participant in the creation of the poem's overall aesthetic context and its meaning.

It is no surprise, as was the case in one of the earliest, if not *the* earliest practitioners of the aural ellipsis, Gertrude Stein, that poets interested in such techniques would be interested in creating works for performance. Fiona Templeton, who is now best known for her on-site performance work in such pieces as *You—The City,*[24] which worked on the novel premise of being presented to an audience of one (each audience member made a separate appointment and the piece took place on site in Times Square), published her work *London* in 1984. Fiona Templeton was born and raised in Scotland and then lived for several years in London before moving to New York. In this work her writing teems with echoes of her native uses of language and, in its inventive constructions, evolves a rich metalanguage of its own:

Come miss eagle be ladies barking come model by lick
not end hey I burn primary came well hip bone went be
heart be oval be fig madly hermit lamp shakes a curt
comb out prior and we win if cull be a coin mere fit
yell do mere sit red we gate else John come on me
pages me came man's came combs down in me in deer
hurt chit be he plastic great Marx and fish well silks in [25]

In this work, as in Coolidge's above, each word resounds tellingly with every other word in the piece, not just in a linear sense, but on every plane, in any order or direction you might read it. At the same time, because of the density of the sound and visual images, the passage can echo and reflect innumerable facets of the settings and the actions being evoked. Every reading is unique, densely layered, and the possibilities for reading the work aloud greatly enriched, as the structure as well as the vocabulary allow for many alternative readings on the part of the performer, as well as an imaginative, though demanding opportunity for interpretive and creative participation on the part of the listener. As in Coolidge's poem, Templeton's piece uses mostly simple words of one or two syllables that maximize and intensify the rhythmic continuity as well as the overall rhythmic, sonic, and musical structure of the piece.

Other poets who have used found and invented language to create innovative poetry that elicits unique forms of listening include Frank Kuenstler, Armand Schwerner, Hannah Weiner, Don Byrd, Ray DiPalma, Marshall Reese, Madeline Gins, Bruce Andrews, Tina Darragh, P. Inman, Douglas Messerli, Rod Smith, Mark Wallace, Kim Rosenfield, and Robert Fitterman. The poetically sophisticated use of found language by some of the most distinguished experimental contemporary poets suggests that an important function of contemporary poetry is to present readers and listeners with the sites and materials of the poem so as to invite them to coparticipate in its creation. In this sense, the writing of contemporary poetry has a tendency to become a more and more collaborative process, with the creative functions of writers and readers becoming less and less distinguishable from one another, and, in a sense, even from poets and listeners, or writers and critics. These texts point the way to telling us how poems are created and how to listen closely to our reponses in order to discover the experiential sites of the poem's constituent materials.

The found poem accentuates the physicality of the poem in both its written and heard forms. Hearing the aural ellipses within the poem of found or invented language is also like discovering, by means of internal soundings, openings in an otherwise impenetrable mass. Also, the found poem, like the recent scientific discovery that a meteorite uncovered long ago may contain evidence of previous life on Mars, is a kind of proof that poetic life is "out there," that it objectively exists and is embedded in everyday life. It is a piece of evidence that is also a site of language as poetry *in situ*. As in the case of the Martian meteorite, the section of found poetry often looks and feels like a hefty "chunk" of the raw material from which the poetic substance might be mined, in part by sounding out, by listening to where the raw poetic element within the substance might exist. In that sense, the aural ellipsis is the place where the tuning of the mind to the poetic wavelength takes place. And, in fact, for the time that your poetic receiving "radio" remains on that wavelength it seems that it might emanate—at least in small quantities—from many other proximate sites. As you look out at the universe from the vantage point of the aural ellipsis it appears that disparate elements available in many kinds of places, times, and categories might be placed in each other's proximity to see if a spark of consciousness across the gap might engender the sounds and flash of poetry. By highlighting the possibilities of the poetic process within found material, the poem also accentuates its potential for the listener to experience it as a transitional object because the found material itself has both subjective and objective aspects.

The increased interest on the part of poets and readers in poetic constructions that can serve as transitional objects is an indication that the field of poetry and the culture with which it is engaged are going through a transitional period. As with individuals, transitional periods of culture are characterized by the intensification of conflict around issues of identity and an intensified search via experimentation for new structures. An example in human development is adolescence. Experimentation with values, behaviors, and identities makes possible the discovery of modes of living around which new senses of identity can be crystallized. The same process holds during social and cultural transitions, periods like ours characterized by conflict, the dissolution of old forms, experimentation, and the search for new forms. This includes the creation of new structures, partly by means of incorporating within them a synthesis of the useful parts of existing structures.

The environment of the found poem frequently elicits experiences of sensory overlap or synesthesia where close listening and reading give way to a combinatory apprehension of meanings, associations, and perceptions by all of the senses. One of the reasons that poetry readings are so important in the evolution of contemporary poetry is that the full effect of the poem cannot be experienced until it is heard aloud, preferably in a group context where responses can be shared and discussed among the listeners and often with the poet herself. Since frequently the value of contemporary poetry is not so much in unraveling the thematic aspects of the poem but in offering a holding environment for the evocation and cocreation of innovative modes of language and communication, the poetry reading is one of the key contexts for contemporary poetry to be shared and understood, and for its effects to be disseminated. In this sense, much contemporary poetry is akin to music in that it is one thing to read the musical notations to oneself but it is quite another to hear the music performed. The performance of poetry as a public event formalizes the poem as an artistic object every bit as much as its publication. Just as photography helped to free painting from its traditional function of graphically depicting external reality, the invention of recording techniques has transformed the poetry reading itself into a potential publication event. The aural or video recording of a reading is just as significant as a permanent document of a poem as a printed version. Recording techniques have helped to free poets to become more interested in experimenting with sound just as painters were helped by photography to be free to experiment with image, color, and form.

While this is true for the oral performance of any type of poetry, it is particularly crucial in the type of poetry I am characterizing as embodying the aural ellipsis, because it is in hearing the poem read aloud, particularly in the voice of the poet who wrote it, that the listener has the best opportunity to understand the poet's specific intentions in selecting the sounds of the poem, as well as finding the most apropos, rhythmic interweaving of his or her own inner stream of thinking and language into that listening. Reading the poem later, the listener then has the opportunity of comparing the poet's manner of visualizing the poem as written text vis-à-vis the poet and listener's combined realization of the poem read aloud. Listening, of course, always includes the thoughts, feelings, and associations to the poem of the listener.

The complex nature of the relationship between thinking and listening is at the heart of the experience of listening to poetry. The aural ellipses of the contemporary poem ensure that there will be spaces for invention on the part of the listener, and that the reading of the poem will not only be the public presentation of ideas, but will function as a medium for what is otherwise incommunicable between one mind and another. This is all the more important in contemporary life where there is so much talking and so little listening. Not only is listening becoming a lost art, but there are fewer and fewer opportunities to learn how to listen. Listening to nearly any television or radio talk show will prove this in a few minutes. At the same time, this avoidance is understandable, given that we live in a world that pounds everyone constantly with excruciating emotional trauma, much of it frequently presented in the media in an almost unbearably blaring and glaring manner. It should be no surprise to anyone that under these circumstances the failure to communicate, or the wish to find ways of avoiding communication, are pandemic. In such an environment, a key survival skill is the ability to sometimes turn off the external environment—to not listen. There is so much to communicate and so little time and energy available to listen in an atmosphere of constant trauma and anxiety.

Working their way through the poem of found language, or any poem offering the open spaces of the aural ellipsis, persistent readers and listeners have no choice but to take the time to listen to each word as if they were hearing and following the meandering, intuitive steps of Benjamin's Baudelairean *flaneurs* finding their ways through the Paris boulevards and arcades. Listeners to such poems must learn to mentally and emotionally weave and bob, to be comfortable hearing and reading both randomly and stealthily, to discover, as if by accident, previously inaccessible areas of language and thought. At times risky or potentially subversive, at other times offering a sense of integration, purpose, and insight, the aural ellipses of the contemporary poem invite listeners to respond with their own inner resonances, to take the poem to its immediate and relative subjective and objective realization. The result is nothing less than a radical transformation in the architectonic topology of the text/sound relationship.

Epilogue

Listening is living in time. It is allowing time for the events of living to register themselves in us. "Stop to listen."

I am interested in the way insignificance transforms itself or is transformed into significance or vice versa, the way specificity is changed into the general and the other way around. Inside an old language we may no longer understand something can be hidden. The smallest fragment of part of the thing we are looking for . . . language itself is the translation. I wanted to speak in an unknown tongue . . . in my wildest dreams. But, even now, so soon after, I can't remember which way it went, it was so long ago . . . I'm not asleep . . . whichever way I am going.

Something is wrapped around me like a shell . . . I wanted to smash things too . . . I had to figure the story out from so few clues . . . then I wanted to break off the shell so I could see outside of it . . . I couldn't just sit still . . . It was as if I had to get a glimpse . . . someway to see outside . . .

Tapping on the frame I can hear the sound of of it . . . I listen for the slightest movement . . . I jump at the chance . . .

NOTES

1. Roman Jakobson, *On Language,* ed. Linda R. Waugh and Monique Monville-Burston (Cambridge: Harvard University Press, 1995), p. 172

2. César Vallejo, *Trilce,* tr. David Smith (New York: Grossman Publishers, 1973), poem 32, p. 97.

3. Emily Dickinson, *The Complete Poems,* ed. Thomas H. Johnson (Boston: Little, Brown, 1960), poem 937, pp. 439–40. Another poem of Dickinson's which demonstrates her concerns with sound and creation is poem 1048, pp. 478–79:

> Reportless Subjects, to the Quick
> Continual addressed—
> But foreign as the Dialect
> Of Danes, unto the rest.

> Reportless Measures, to the Ear
> Susceptive—stimulus—
> But like an Oriental Tale
> To others, fabulous—

4. Sven Birkerts, untitled review of John Ashbery's *Selected Poems,* in *Sulfur,* no. 19 (spring 1987), p. 142.

5. D. W. Winnicott, *Playing and Reality* (New York: Tavistock, 1989), p. 2

6. Walter Benjamin, *Charles Baudelaire: A Lyric Poet in the Era of High Capitalism,* tr. Harry Zohn (London: Verso, 1983), pp. 167–68.

7. Cf. Charles Baudelaire, *The Complete Verse,* tr. Francis Scarfe (London: Anvil Press, 1986), p. 61. The first stanza of poem 4 ("Correspondances") reads as follows:

> La Nature est un temple où de vivants piliers
> Laissent parfois sortir de confuses paroles;

L'homme y passe à travers des forêts de symboles
Qui l'observent avec des regards familiers.

"Nature is a temple, in which living pillars sometimes utter a babel of words; man-kind traverses it through forests of symbols that watch him with knowing eyes."

8. Henry Munn offers the following example of a Mazatec (Mexican) shaman's "free associative" recitation: "Thirteen superior whirlwinds. Thirteen whirlwinds of the atmosphere. Thirteen clowns, says. Thirteen personalities, says. Thirteen white lights, says. Thirteen mountains of points, says. Thirteen old hawks, says. Thirteen white hawks, says. Thirteen personalities, says. Thirteen mountains, says. Thirteen clowns, says. Thirteen peaks, says. Thirteen stars of the morning." "The Mushrooms of Language," by Henry Munn, in *Hallucinogens and Shamanism,* ed. Michael J. Harner (New York: Oxford University Press, 1973), p. 109.

9. Rainer Maria Rilke, *Duino Elegies,* tr. C. F. McIntyre (Berkeley: University of California Press, 1968), p. 7.

10. Abigail Child, *Scatter Matrix* (New York: Roof, 1996), p. 51.

11. Charles Bernstein, *Islets/Irritations* (New York: Jordan Davies, 1983), p. 81.

12. Lynne Dreyer, *The White Museum* (New York: Roof, 1986), p. 101.

13. Victor Egger, *La Parole intérieure* (Alcan, 1904), p. 70, qtd. in Jakobson, p. 98.

14. Paul Celan, *Speech Grille,* tr. Joachim Neugroschel (New York: E. P. Dutton, 1971), p. 209.

15. Jackson Mac Low, *Bloomsday* (New York: Roof, 1984).

16. Hear Jackson Mac Low, *Open Secrets* (CD) (New York: Experimental Intermedia Foundation, 1993)

17. Jackson Mac Low, *The Pronouns: A Collection of Forty Dances for the Dancers, 3 February–22 March 1964* (Barrytown, N.Y.: Station Hill Press, 1979), p. 74.

18. Jack Spicer, *Vancouver Lectures,* excerpted in *Caterpillar,* no. 12 (July 1970), pp. 177–78: "The third stage, I think, comes when you get some idea that there is a difference between you and the outside of you which is writing poetry . . . then you start seeing whether you can clear your mind away . . . and here the analogy of the medium comes in, which Yeats started out, and which Cocteau in his *Orphée*—both the play and the picture—used a car radio for, but which essentially is the same thing. But essentially you are something which is being transmitted into . . . It's as if a Martian comes into a room with children's blocks . . . and he tries to convey a message . . . Now the third step in dictated poetry is to try to keep all of yourself that is possible outside the poem."

19. Barrett Watten, *Conduit* (San Francisco: Gaz, 1988), passim.

20. John Cage, *Musicage: Cage Muses on Words Art and Music,* ed. Joan Retallack (Hanover, N.H.: Wesleyan University Press, 1996), p. 176.

21. Joan Retallack, *Errata suite* (Washington, D.C.: Edge Books, 1993), p. 15.

22. In an unpublished letter to me from Marshall McLuhan, dated November 22, 1966, he offers some advice regarding my request for material for the "ear": "Here . . . is prescription for *ear* with 'dearth of material': *Finnegans Wake* by James Joyce. Has to be read aloud. He says everything I am saying and more, much more."

23. Clark Coolidge, *Space* (New York: Harper & Row, 1970), p. 89.

24. Fiona Templeton, *You, the City* (New York: Roof, 1990).

25. Fiona Templeton, *London* (Washington, D.C.: Sun & Moon Press, 1984), p. 29.

3

Praxis

A Political Economy of Noise and Informalism

BRUCE ANDREWS

*L*anguage praxis, the task, remains veiled. What parallels can we draw (abstractly, even ventriloquially) between theorizing about change and theorizing aesthetically about radical art — here, keyed to the question of sound in contemporary writing?

Both Theodor Adorno's music writings — especially his 1961 "Vers une musique informelle," in *Quasi una fantasia* (New York: Verso, 1994) and Jacques Attali's *Noise: The Political Economy of Music* (Minneapolis: University of Minnesota Press, 1985) theorize the social claims of music in different past periods as well as in the future. After the heyday and then crisis of tonal, thematic music in an era of Representation, the radical freedom of the early twentieth century is not sustained (even serial music domesticates it). A trend toward a formalist, systematizing (nonthematic) composition flowers in the pointillist nominalism and material or procedural (even aleatory) fetishism of the postwar avant-gardes — in an era of Repetition. Future hope, in an era of Composition, is held out for a revived radicalism of constructivist noise or athematic "informal music," all accompanied by progressive social claims.

And the parallels for praxis with sound in language? Sound is traditionally domesticated in the melodiousness and semantic underlining of representational writing (grounded in the lyric subject's voice or imagist observation). More recent and apparently less conservative art has sometimes foregrounded the sound dimension, but at the same time risked gutting it of its social charge, either in simplifying rhetorics or drastic systematizing. The challenge for Noise and Informalism in writing is to simultaneously cut the ties that bind sound to traditions of lyric harmony and speech or autonomous, inward-absorbing form *and,* through drastic and emancipated construction, to highlight what we can call its "social tone" or its "semantic music" — *in praxis*.

The emancipation of sound is held back by the great weight of heritage. Pregiven tradition stuns as unmistakability, covering up its tracks as myth. Established modes: those shock absorbers and seals of approval. Sublimating sound matter into helpfully nudging pointers, traditional norms desubstantialize, offering up a guided tour of genteel, personally agreeable and regularizing reinforcements. Sound has become functional: presentational enactments at the service of a representational ideal, with subheadquarters in Identity and Image. The smoothed, comforting harmony affirms, locks in, and eternalizes. Its restorational hygiene offers ideological solace. Yet equilibrium is fraudulent as long as so much smoothness dishonors the larger incompatibilities nested inside the society outside.

Typically, words' referential pointing is doubly enhanced: first, by their conventional formal harnessing, and next by "codic doubling" (the use of sound as normalizing, reinforcing enactment). Wild sound yields to the individualizing of the lyric subject, with its literary variants of the easily graspable line, the uninterrupted upper-voice melody. More than just preconditions, certain sound patterns help confirm lyricism, offering an image of the subject's triumph over the given, overlooking whatever threatens to slip out from under its control. If representations of subject voice replace the triad of diatonic music, they achieve closure by the accuracy or fullness of their revelations or by epiphany of tantalizing insight rendered imagistically. Inwardness disappears the otherness of its objects. This is a spatializing subjectivism, rejecting the frenetic task of an *in-time* writing, like sovereign disposition's usual moneyed power over the sound object.

Still, taken-for-granted assumptions of speech and lyric spontaneity seem shabbier and shabbier when framed against the social wave of crimes against spontaneity, against the sham afterlife of protected "free speech," with subjectivity squeezed down to mere commodity object status within games of oneuppersonship. All that tends to get registered, at very low volume levels, is the puny place of any single voice barely emanating out from inside its harmonious upholstery.

Freedom, liberated from preexisting forms, could champion sensual appearance without succumbing to conventional legality or resorting to this brand of sugariness. Restrictive norms that would wish to settle the destiny of harmonic motives or themes (or, in our parallels, of Image and Identity) confront an insatiability about sound. In doing so, they come to learn their own chintzy artificiality and damage. If musical dissonance offers an index of the lack of freedom faced by the unreconciled subject, a parallel sonic dissonance in free and "unfitting" verse may operate similarly. To take the full measure of sense in sound would celebrate nonidentity, perhaps even obliviousness of self, or at least disrupt the cozy traces of personalization.

To honor time as the heart of the centrifugal tendencies that dishevel the identity of the subject and the stability of the traditions we take for granted. To jettison the deceptively calm and uniform surface. To disrupt clarity. To shake down — nominalize — the units. To discredit overall (representation-reinforcing) consonance. Once we do, this opens up bigger intervals, for maximal registral and rhythmic and colorist variety. And it points ahead.

Dissonance expands the possible range of what can bear momentum and drive it forward — to make incompletions (or frictions) that solicit a resolution in the future. Instead of information, this is deformation — a universalizing of tension, stoking chaos, by denser (and freer) articulation.

Here is catastrophe in music and sound, as nominalism shocks system. A traditional form meltdown, in the wake of the free-floating. An atomization that threatens to make it impossible for any pleasingly meaningful whole to be contracted. The givenness of norms and materials (the relations of literary production) becomes deformed by the forces of production (new sounds, techniques, the foregrounding of dissonance).

Here is a Revolution of the Word with an infinitesimalism, via micrological method and a cubist dismantling of the surface. We start with a more decentralized system, with an already perforated surface and nominalist dissociation, leaving the tiniest capillaries unobligated by form. The easily graspable voice dissolves into small recurrent motifs: the ones that were themselves supposed to have dissolved into mere stage props for the homogeneous voice. Now they are just building blocks of noise.

Noise as wayward, unregimented sound. Or seemingly meaningless, random fluctuations in data — not the "managed data" that defines information. Too irregular, or pumped up with excess timbral richness, its overtones untameable in harmonic terms, undercutting expectations of determinate pitch (or, in our case, of a representational determinacy and bolstering). A free play that the equivocal, undefinitive quality of sound units in language makes possible — as long as they are not recruited as doubling echoes, indentured to stable systems of stable meaning. Noise as chaos.

Informal construction liberates sound on behalf of a more distantiating praxis, a microtechnique of restiveness. Successions of intervals of emotional expressiveness or social resonance are freer: productive and self-differentiating enough to liquidate the given, to scrap any appeal to obligatory stylistic norms or schemata that have acquired the job of enforcement.

Impulse explodes whatever shape has been consolidated, but larger architectures get to be made plausible — and comprehended by — their own tiny structuring. The sensuous articulation builds a whole out of what will only retrospectively make sense as details.

Parataxis, with its discrete sequence of motivic atoms creates too many gaps "in the argument" to allow a rationalizing (or modernizing) of, by, and *for* the individual. It undercuts any single dynamizing teleology or resolution (in a full conversational "turn" or the clicking shut of imagistic epiphany). Instead, outward holistic form is constantly revoked — as it gets simultaneously, microscopically built.

And the mediating work can operate on the sound dimension much more centrally, rather than treating it merely as a spin-off of representational continuities — as in music, with free atonality's highlighting of color, rhythm, and timbre, not just harmonic pitch structuring. What is *substantial* in sound is both a foregrounded (abstract) materiality and a socially semantic penumbra or kinesthetic "feel" or texture. And while the former may be susceptible to a deductive/inferential structure that robs it of particularity, the latter can be constructed down to the last detail. Rhythmic figuration, intervallic combustion, timbral shifts, and tiny melodic shapes can make an *informalist order* of sound in writing, going well beyond the simpler *buttoning-down* of overall reference.

This is a celebration of transition, of *perpetuum mobile:* beyond the austerity of dissociation, toward larger (and more lushly socially evocative) units of material, to make expectations of self-sufficing preset form impossible. With its anti-soothing constructivity, every discrete particle can become a link — pointing sideways, forward, backward, even upside-down — to start to acquire drive-like possibilities, theme-like force. The active relationship of details in constant intervening alteration gives the work its concrete sound shape: spontaneous reverb, maximal explosiveness of concretely unschematic connectives, colliding textures and motions of heterogeneous instants, constellations setting free the unratified and the nonprefab, shaking down their own provisional architecture: *the inexhaustible*. Faced with this breakdown of traditional form and this nominalizing of sound material, praxis can embrace it — not to make the isolated sound into an absolute, but as an emancipatory constructivism.

A recuperative alternative would set up external structures sturdy enough to discipline the freed-up material. (Examples in writing would identify a minor facet of radical — or radicalized — modernism of the post-1945 period, and a major one in so-called avant-garde or experimental writing starting with the 1960s. Variants: minimalist, aleatory, proceduralist, concrete, conceptualist, grid-like or tabular.) Here, sound becomes deductive within an imposing organization, sovereign planning, commanded collectivization, mathematical necessity. Detailing the structure all the way down to its smallest cellular differences risks obliterating the finite. Unlike looser, more fluid kinds of coalescence, the dissociated units — words, rather than phrases, for instance — lose any specific (melodic) contour. The extra sense (made possible by sound) now derives from the general drilling the particular units, from subsumption (resulting in whiplash). The sounds are desubjectivized, just as they are in systematic (serial and postserial) music, where interval succession creates cohesion without regard for melodic shape or tonal connotation.

Systematic structuring, with its immanent and logical ordering of whole and parts, may make disappearing acts out of the local materials. It leads to a tyranny of form over material, over contingency. Events become exemplars, victimized by the grid of quantity, the hygiene of the natural, as if sound (merely) articulates or finishes the form. (Sound, as structure's fin-ishing school?) This leaves us with a desubstantialized formalism, with the meaning expected to derive from an all-pervasive technical structure. The brutal stiffing of all social semblance and artifice in sound, the final marching orders of integral form's pure rationality gives us over to a sound-irrelevant anti-mimesis.

But no hull is dependable. Unless it becomes embarrassingly domi-neering. Rather than a submersion within itself of systematic procedures with their swagger of overdefiniteness, a less formal or informal writing can become a figuration of irreconcilability. Its logic is less deductive (or metaphoric) — with particularities no longer mere consequents — but in-stead more paratactic or metonymic, its details graspable without any gener-ality hankering to buckle their significance directly and peremptorily onto them. Emancipated from schema, individual associations (in sound) act as hecklers against systemic or robotic indenture. Copula rules. No fixed mode safety net, no uniforms.

Now, in Adorno's terms, an internal (or aestheticizing) focus outbids an external (or social) one. It makes possible an internal drama, as different from a series of stimulating pictures. Here is that windowless monad that does not address or blink in the direction of the social. These keep getting in each other's way: the outward tug of reference and the internal structural logic (with its affinity for rhetorical blankness). In writing — just as in film or dance — the raw material almost automatically carries a semantic charge and mimetic force. (The sound features of language, in contrast, if they steer clear of opportunities for revealing their social significance, i.e., *mimesis,* might be perfect candidates for such abstract systematizing.) The refrac-tory is a mask. Could we recommend it? The problem is that the preference for internality threatens to create a self-absorbed, tautologizing blindness with artwork functioning as a desocietalized "in-itself." Worse, overarching procedures (or chance or systematic word grids) encourage automatisms, neutralized positivist set-ups or false fronts for shut-ins.

The more systematized the writing, the more it risks turning into a sleek hypostatizing of means, a correct (and corrective) command structure, a determinacy of fate, in which tautology, redundancy, or homogeneity make individuation superfluous. Spectacle and fetish cling to the entirety of words. And so does an avoidance of unimposed time — (and Reading = Time). As if a static spatializing composes words that are not meant to be read. It makes a critical (negative/Brechtian) form of distancing praxis, or ironic rupture, all the more unlikely. As celebrants of abstraction, the mate-rials are being ritualized to the point of losing any specific weight, any need or opportunity to devote to the deciphering of sense "on your own time" in reading.

But infatuation with the sound material — its pure factuality as an end-in-itself — is no better an alternative. Isn't "mere sonority" just as likely to become fetishized and transfixed in space? And isn't that what cheap "sound effects" offer: hyperassonance, hyperrepetition, cornball rhyme, singsong rhythm, the visual page scoring of loudmouth ALL CAPS performance? Mere stimuli — as the culinary, as an anti-reading and a withdrawal of its "free time." But the currency is counterfeit.

The nonidentical, the qualitatively different: these are social tokens of use value, more respectfully treated by *collage,* a principle at odds with any total infiltrating formalist construction. Montage embraces a freedom to rove over maximally various stocks of material. And the pull or magnetizing of closure ceases to operate at the overall level; it resists the obviousness of both Image and Identity. Here, no overall functional hierarchy is calling the shots. Juxtaposition of the parts cannot just be illustrative, a mechanical *display* of the details of subsumption — (e.g., the subsumption of rhythm by the insistent, booming, burlesquing beat). Instead, the microstructuring makes stability a localized event, not a generalized one — with representational pulls more granularized, yet polyglot: associative irregularities, interwoven and overlapping, chafing and collision, anti-proximities and semanticizing glitches. An altercation, a *counter-contagion*.

Musically, just as tone color, rhythm, texture, and phrasing can replace pitch as a means to create resolution, a parallel emphasis on writing could set aside representational euphony as a focus. Sounds are not fated to help bolster a linear argument or confirm an epiphany. There may be no climax, no argumentative coda or recapitulation — (or need for the reader to serve as the absorbed target of this recapitulation). No, the writing can put forward its own version of quasi-cadences, or elliptical chords that do not quite resolve into a tonal harmony. The task for praxis is to figure out a way to be emphatically open in its temporality, intrinsically developing — yet without centers, fundamental "grounds," and master keys. With such a free informalism, we cannot predict where the sound is going. And we therefore stay *inside* the text — partly by avoiding big cadential goal achievements on behalf of clichés, those clicks of the obvious that resound with an associative pull by the status quo outside. (Oral performances — based on the absorptiveness of image, story, or personality — are often prone to undercut this remarkable temporal freedom.)

Sways and surges can stitch polyrhythmic suspensions (not just tension and resolution) to make an *extensive* anti-epiphany. If new material is constantly being whipped up, or self-animated, a sense of forward momentum may emerge: semiotic mobility, an inner yielding; untamed, prerationalized microscopic crackling liasons that perk up dynamism even without the usual complacencies of surface continuity. An organic ideal of intimate direct contact between the widely disparate materials is called for: a successive camaraderie of great spans, a seamless merging, a way to handle transitions even with apparent non sequitur (which refers to width of interval, this time in a kind of "semantic atonality").

Still, praxis needs something more complex than stringing large blocks (or singularities) of resonating stuff together, something freer than transitions that no longer mediate but simply register the defeat or sacrifice of individual events. Otherwise, it risks losing the forward propulsion of sound-reinforced "songs and tales," trading it for a serial of interesting instants without *relation*.

One version of that risk is word sounds centered within themselves, in total isolation and arbitrariness of sense. The highly differentiated units of pure nominalism, set alongside each other, can end up in a pointillism or an undifferentiated developmentless swarm. Or: disjointed pastiche, chance successions of ephemeral fragments, a mounted display of spatialized commas and disjunctures. As if: montage = fetishistic still lifes; parataxis = medley.

What is needed instead are more sensuous anti-mechanical dissolutions, homeopathically penetrating the material to its core. The individual units are not imaginative enough. Beyond a deployment of mutually alienated and disinterested sounds, this calls for an increase in chances for them to intermingle, merge, and dissociate. (Yet even density of texture by itself can become cloying, an echo chamber effect not unlike "white noise" — as we sometimes hear in crowdedly multivoice work in performance or on tape. Sometimes a more spread-out sonic fabric will be more disruptive.) The concrete: the sum of determinations.

This revives a spontaneity of the moment with a semantic rhythmics — (embracing notions like the rate of change or rhythm of meaning, within an often labile tempo, with semantic accelerandi and ritardandi). (Performance offers another opportunity for registering this, although often its commitment to "breaking through the fourth wall" ends up in charismatic absorptions of the audience into its fixed shapes and closures.) Instead of the crude naked juxtapositions or bold thematic gestures that might more easily yield a finality of shape, we can call for something subtler: elusive filigree, detail perfected within a dynamic syntax to the point where any clear-cut recognizably finite form is virtually ruled out. A free or athematic sound "prose" of permanent transition and motivic fragmentation, a "becoming" of constant subdividing and particularizing where even disruption comes to seem developmental because of the flurry of tangible connection. Everything is incessant flow, polylogic.

The task for praxis is to bind these centrifugal forces together: jerry-rigging the disparate, layering the thickets of the incommensurable. Qualities of the basic shape — fluency, contrasts, variety, logic and unity — are allowed to develop out of *relationship between units*. The material's friction is revived, as independent details help articulate a mesh of contradictions.

Linkage operates with multiple combinations in many directions. A force field without guarantees; full circumference of sound units made available for a near-infinite play of interpenetration, of rich webs of mutually cross-referential (and anti-foundational) atoms; a juxtacomposed rhythmic (and timbral and colorist) irregularity with most everything capable of pushing up against most everything else.

To read (even the tiniest of) the sounding units as socially relevant is to acknowledge how preshaped they are. This recasts their initial profile as material (and often ornamentally euphonious) "things of their own," casting some doubt on these redeemable vouchers of the affirmative and consonant. Even local shape self-liquidates — or turns itself inside out discovering that it too has a "meaningful" social underlayer and framing capability. Social framing serves as shock, dissonance as testimony, negation, noise. Don't get unexcited!

By means of Noise: to disrupt the flow of communiation, to create extreme libidinalized density, to approach "white noise" — mixing so many audible frequencies together that no perceivable definite pitch is observed. (And perhaps we can imagine a white noise of rhythm, timbre, lexicon.) Noise — as freely composed dissonance, and untimely mimesis of shock. To reject the untouchability of auratic beauty. To disturb automatism, to estrange and displace, to burst the binding of current usage.

Here, new forces of production (noise) having shaken up the older aestheticized relations of production (conventions of harmoniousness or lyric voicing, for example) can intimate new methods of configuration — even ones that actively subvert their own ground. Yet the mimetic claims of such a dense tangle are not based on the authority of narrative or causal sequences of represented insights. Contagion as negation may give us a better feel for this manic relationism.

All this would allow us to counterpose a new type of mimesis to aesthetic rationality. Mimesis feeds off the "content" side of sound (and questions the autonomous "pure music" side of sound in writing). Rational construction, on the other hand, plays off the inward and abstract "music" side of sound in writing — even if it sometimes seems capable of pointing beyond that monadic inwardness with its temporal dynamic force.

We can break the rationalizers' mimetic taboo — through freely disposed relation, resonance chambers of the divergent, multiply shifting and pointing: a self-analytical noise that can develop its possibilities of social framing within itself (on behalf of the reader/listener) rather than impose some externalized social willfulness. Informalism as the construction of reading (that is, listening) opportunities and their spontaneous self-interpreting. And noise, in reading, is risk. Its incessant soliciting of a second significance, an added social layer or stage set, can be Grand Guignol — or the catastrophe of involuntary memory.

Yet this is a choreography of *possible reading,* not insistent advocacy. The formal (sound) interior need not cater to the (unsound) outside. Like a layered feast with multiple servers, the outside has already catered virtually everything inside. And today even the smooth (inwardly constellated) sound of a work has become show biz.

Traditionally rhetoric is associated with an extroverted sensual theatrics, hypostatized contours, mesmerized tableaus, extensivity and stasis. (And language in performance often operates in this way, shrinking the wide-open possibilities of *sotto voce* sound in reading.) It threatens to turn sounds into signals, hyped up as broad gesticulating "sound effects," monument façades and decor, as if formulaic sounds are taking bows for the work. Poise and prized enfoldment of details can give way to a search for big striking willful gestures, for outsize intensity, for repetition that revokes time or by the catchy insistent beat that empties it out. Expansive sound (as rhetoric) may go beyond formalism — beyond "music" and into "content" — but does so with clumsily direct and decorative lunges at representation.

Are small units only miniature pictures? Little repetitive stagings to help orient the reader? Listener as closure? Gesture, by overtly anticipating reader response, can easily get manipulative — all the more so because of its static, spatializing proclivities. (The staginess of sound in much performance poetry provides an archive.) Gestural theatrics recapitulate the reader response in advance, guaranteeing coda-like success. And in a fashion made even more pushy and showy by claims to emanate "authentically, naturally" from the loudspeaker of the romanticizable self — (in either its genteel-confessional or streety rebel extremes). (Irony just adds another layer of make-believe to the product.)

The reduction of sound to such *signals* may help with a project of sub-group boosterism or identity politics empowerment. But it may also abandon a project of decoding a larger antagonistic social outside. For that, we need to look again at the social subtext of sound — at how it is repressed and how praxis might excavate it.

The subject has occupied the status of core unit: the motif, the minimally affirmative event, *out of which* a coherent (consonant and diatonic) discourse would unfold. (Or at least that used to be the hope; don't hold your breath.) With sound, this makes for a neoromanticism of pleasant heart-warming "dulcet tones," a vanity of the suspicious and the ephemeral. Thematic (or *motivational*) work with such a subject involves forging connections between the smallest "personally mappable" sound units. These singular teleologies — the dynamics of tonality or imagist possession or lyrically "making the case for the subject") — could perhaps acquire a certain critical edge just from the growing phoniness of individual autonomy within society. Because every part, or aspect, can accomplish something more (or different) than servicing and upholstering the whole. Besides, the motivation of what follows and what does not follow from one moment to the next is partially supplied from outside.

The nonthematic work of formal systematizing — working with non-referential or chance-organized units, for example — tends to evacuate the subject position. With sound, it empties out the "touch" of personal resonances. Purist autonomy, with its tact of avoidance, in other words, can create so much distance *on its own* that praxis atrophies. (The athematic work of informalism would retain the personalized texturing but arrange to enhance its social insinuation, to rehistoricize.)

Now, to speak of the sociality of worldly sounds suggests that the material embodies a sedimented content — even where the lyric equivalents of the intervallic axis have lost their binding power, where less personalizable rhythm and timbre come to the forefront, where we face the complete play of aural signification. (In music, nominalism may suggest an anti-form. Nominalism — in sound within writing — cuts deeper, but also does not strip the individual items of their social significance. It makes possible an informality.)

The key is to stop treating sound as if it were a natural phenomenon, to let the social *interrupt* all ubiquitous immediacy (of emptier — or full because formalized — sounds). After all, any mechanically total aesthetic organization will be contaminated by social significance, some of which adheres to the differentials of sound and gives them a decodable *outward vocation* — (something akin to presence). The subsumptions of structure will be a dilution, counteracting the social vectors of individual language cells. Informalist construction, instead, offers a recognition of the opportunities for emancipating the dissonance of social tone. It makes it impossible for the whole to be merely the sum of its parts, for it acknowledges that the parts occupy an additional *plane* of intersecting waywardness. It spurs on a disheveling, by multiple axes.

A different kind of rhetoricizing of these individual elements will have to be rescued, so that all this autonomy of a work's outer skin can be slashed, so that reading can activate the impermanent absences *with* the fragile presences, can reconcile the poles of material and construction — *within* the social.

Music's inner coherence — the interrelationship of parts to each other and to the whole — is endangered by overwhelming extramusical associations or commonplaces. In writing, though, everything embued with signification — and much that is not — is automatically intertextual. But everything need not have a demonstrable "social tone" or sense. If so, we might have to discombobulate inner coherence in order to highlight it — via stringencies of the vertical and the simultaneous (in conjunction with events succeeding each other). For only the Other — the deviate, the alien — may offer the kind of resistance that defeats stasis (and, we might mention, equilibrium) and lets time constitute itself. For this, we should probably look to a social subtext of sound or noise — to uncork the full restiveness of qualitative difference (even when these are caught up in the same quantified exchangeability of the commodity world that they might seem to resist).

Certain types of formal arrangement might purify the individual sounds of much of their social flair — sometimes by randomizing, at other times simply by ignoring these social vectors. But then they are likely to lack the kind of resistance (fostered by social tone) that allows them to create their own shape. Teeny firings of sound relation may motivate shapes without engendering any overall shape. The form-creating dynamism (the full experiential time) of such relations may still be stunted by the absence of sufficient friction (which possibly only careful attention to a social dimension could supply).

Individual impulses need substantiality before unifying them can generate much dynamism. Here, in a classicist way, to cling to an opposition between autonomy and semblance — and to prioritize the unabsorbing, windowless monad as the premier vehicle of social "work" — would be defeatist. It ignores the near language-like qualities of the musics of writing that contradict their seeming autonomy. For this is what gives them an outwardly blinking and scanning and surfing involvement with a body politic or political economy of sense. And helps us experience a synchronic (or concentric) semantic saturation of sound by the social.

Subjective expressionism often conflicted with constructivity, with integral form, and failed to secure itself. But constructivity with an abstract (nonreferential) material, like musical pitch or sound, differs from one at grips with language (which is so much of a differential, referential web). With sound, beyond the arbitrary and beyond lexical meaning, what is at issue is the possibility of a social equivalent to motivic thematic work in music. (*Motif:* as the smallest composing unit — for the subject: tiny personalized possessions, either observational, revelational, or argumentative — and *Theme:* the larger connections, bringing forward the notion of what is contextually well-motivated.)

To make *drastic* constellations out of the immediately referential elements of language can counteract their naturally mimetic pull and allow for a greater "absoluteness" or abstraction. To radically constellate the *less* mimetic elements (like sound) can pull them in the opposite direction: foregrounding their social charge, perhaps making possible an incipient social mimesis or allegory. Somatic integrity is restored to the musical object by a rejection of its imagistic claims. Social substance might be restored to the sound unit by a rejection of its claims to material self-sufficiency. This suggests that we highlight sounds of a social character — that is, sounds which are only *relatively* autonomous — socially supplying enough qualitative difference to set up relations and combustibility that point outward, mimetically. And the more socially charged the sonic choreography, the easier it is to avoid a ruthless violence of stance (the treatment of sound as abstract, desocialized entities at our immediate disposal).

The social charge occurs first with single items or words, which in language as opposed to music offer an unavoidable social dimension, with nominalized relevance — to some degree in the sound, although mostly in lexical reference. In terms of their sonic-semantic role, these bare articles will be more abstract than the gestalts we make for them. (In the same way, making them mere components of an overarching structure can reduce the individual semantic vectors of words as well as small-scale gestalts, making both of them more abstract as well as more fated, less free.)

If personally motivated material is worked into an internal dynamism, with its units appearing to follow deductively from each other, it too is more likely to create an airtight seal around the whole. Here again, language has opportunities for going beyond a showcase of bare particles or single notes through *relations:* of sound, of referential meaning, and of the gap between the two as a scale embodied in each particle. For these two familiar facets can be composed so that they end up casting a mutually sceptical glance at each other. Freedom here becomes the badge of succession, of the forward motion of an intrinsic otherness. It goes beyond repetition and reflex by drawing on a logic of semantic consequences in sound: to make freedom more than a limited negative determinant, to make it a force of coagulation and affinity. So that something closer to a totalizing perspective could emerge directly out of the impulse of particularity. Unity would be an active work on getting things to synthesize, a motivic-thematic thoroughness at work with atomisms of surface texture and color — as *sites of commentary,* as situations in which sound could account for its own preconditions. *Praxis versus.* Auratic illusions of harmony and reconcilement would now face social contradiction. Easy fiction — and fiction is defined by social stance — disappears within a maximizing of interrelationships between units with high social friction coefficients.

Praxis disconfirms and de-eternalizes: as, in action, productive precipitating critique. And only a multiplicity of associations and swerves equips a constellation to interpretively mediate a social outside (or many social outsides). Such informal composition therefore involves less *communication* (the making dissimilar — or fixed — of the similar), and more *counter-communication* (the making similar — or fluid — of the dissimilar). Pilings on and simultaneity (of social tone) become, for example, one basis of expansive succession. It helps chart the music of *degrees* of semantic suture or "buttoning down," of a topographical terrain of representation.

For the social profile of a sound element is not independently defined or given authority apart from how we operate it. Just as analytic instrumentation can define time by articulating the resolution of tensions, an instrumentation of socially semantic sound helps define something similar: noise as informalist construction with the *raw materials* of social regulation.

Individual sound complexes are social atoms whose (political) significance emerges from interplay, a mix of dislocation and collegiality of incompatibles. Relational work demands this abrasion of mutually qualifying parts. Instead of deconstruction (the wielding of scepticism to embarrass, to refuse the face of belief), we are closer to critical theory's search for crystallized extremes and excesses in opposition: to map a totality embodying internal immanent conflict. The interior is made up of relations: an ensemble choreography of already socially inflected phrases, syllables, lexical mementos, and the like. Since collectivity is a priori, even if wearing masks, our work is inside out.

Antagonistic social experiences would be faced inside, in particular interior events. *In relation* — these serve as a cryptogram of the external social complexions of meaning. These are social dimensions (of a collective subjectivity) brought out of the individual units by valorizing their expectations of readability (and thus, temporality). These negations — by framing and "developing variation" — unfold in the reading process, no longer satisfied with the threats to a deciphering and grazing reading time imposed by the fixed schemas and boosterism of conventional performance. By taking advantage of (hypertextual) opportunities of rearrangement (remaneuvering, collision, osmosis, mutual interruption), it transforms its superficially pure (anti-social) material into eloquent oratory on social conditions, into a pattern of the (collective) subject's own reaction. This is to make progressively more appropriate the subjectively recharged material: by contextualizing it. To heal this polar opposition of material and subject in a praxis of sound: by a constructivist resocializing and "opening out" of the material, and a constructivist contextualizing of the subject.

Such informalist noise refuses any projective resolution of social contradiction. It performs this failure, eliciting a contrast with social openness. Indexed by internal contradictoriness, it offers a social model of surprise and the unforeseen, of unconstrained freedom and self-reflexivity and conceivable coherence. In sound — *among other arenas* — equipped with an unrepressive intersubjectivity, to bring the tensions to a head.

4

After Free Verse
The New Nonlinear Poetries

MARJORIE PERLOFF

*W*hat is generally called *free verse* is now more than a century old. It was in 1886 that Gustave Kahn's Paris *La Vogue* published Rimbaud's "Marine" and "Mouvement" (both written in the early 1870s), translations of some of Whitman's *Leaves of Grass* by Jules Laforgue, ten of Laforgue's own free-verse poems, and further experiments by Jean Moréas, Paul Adam, and Gustave Kahn himself.[1] On the other side of the Channel, *vers libre* was soon picked up by the Imagists: in the March 1913 issue of *Poetry,* Pound put forward his famous Imagist manifesto, whose third principle was "As regarding rhythm: to compose in the sequence of the musical phrase, not in sequence of a metronome."[2]

Even as he made this pronouncement, however, Pound remarked that "*vers libre* has become as prolix and as verbose as any of the flaccid varieties that preceded it . . . The actual language and phrasing is often as bad as that of our elders without even the excuse that the words are shovelled in to fill a metric pattern or to complete the noise of a rhyme-sound" (*Encyclopedia,* 3). And his friend T. S. Eliot, who was to declare in "The Music of Poetry" (1942) that "no verse is free for the man who wants to do a good job,"[3] observed in his 1917 "Reflections on *Vers Libre*," that "there is only good verse, bad verse, and chaos." How to avoid this chaos? "The most interesting verse which has yet been written in our language has been done either by taking a very simple form, like iambic pentameter, and constantly withdrawing from it, or taking no form at all, and constantly approximating to a very simple one. It is this contrast between fixity and flux, this unperceived evasion of monotony, which is the very life of verse." And in a formulation that was to become a kind of First Rule in poetry manuals, Eliot declares, "the ghost of some simple metre should lurk behind the arras in even the 'freest' verse; to advance menacingly as we doze, and withdraw as we rouse. Or, freedom is only truly freedom when it appears against the background of an artificial limitation."[4]

Eliot's formulation, which was, of course, based on his own practice, still governs most discussions of free verse. As recently as 1993, in a book called *The Ghost of Meter,* Annie Finch treats contemporary free verse as essentially a fruitful quarrel with meter, especially iambic pentameter, and tries to show how in the lyric of poets as diverse as Charles Wright and Audre Lorde, "anger at the pentameter and exhilaration at claiming its authority engender much poetic energy."[5] Derek Attridge's *Poetic Rhythm: An Introduction* (1995) characterizes free verse by citing poems like Adrienne Rich's "Night Watch," which "derives its rhythmic quality from its existence on the borders of regular verse."[6] And in recent years the New Formalists have gone further, arguing that "free verse" has been no more than a temporary aberration, given that, in the words of Timothy Steele, "poetry was always, before the modern period, associated with meter."[7] As I was writing this essay, I happened upon Helen Vendler's review, in the *London Review of Books* (4 July 1996), of the Library of America's new *Collected Poems of Robert Frost.* Citing Frost's dismissal of free verse in the lines, "Let chaos storm! / Let cloud shapes swarm! / I wait for form," Vendler declares: "There used to be a critical orthodoxy (still prevalent in a few backwaters) that anyone practicing rhymed and metered verse was a reactionary and no Modernist; we now understand, having seen many later writers (Merrill, Lowell) alternating metered and free verse, that both forms and free verse are neutrally available to all" (6).

The implication of this claim for "neutral availability" is that verse forms, whether free or otherwise, are independent of history as well as of national and cultural context and that metrical choice is a question of individual predilection. And further: that free verse is some kind of end point, an instance of writing degree zero from which the only reasonable "advance" can be, as Steele suggests, a return to "normal" metrical forms. At the risk of allying myself with those "backwater" forces Vendler refers to so dismissively, I want to argue here that there are indeed other possibilities and that verse, like the materials used in any art medium, and like the clothes we wear and the furnishings in our houses, is subject to historical change as well as cultural and political constraint. But before I consider the large-scale transformations "free verse" is now undergoing in America (and, for that matter, in the poetry of most other nations as well), some definitions and clarifications are in order.

What *is* free verse anyway? However varied its definitions, there is general agreement on two points: (1) the *sine qua non* of free verse is *lineation.* When the lines run all the way to the right margin, the result is prose, however "poetic." The basic unit of free verse is thus the line. But (2), unlike metrical or strong-stress or syllabic or quantitative verse, free verse is, in Donald Wesling's words, "distinguished . . . by the lack of a structuring grid based on counting of linguistic units and/or position of linguistic features" (*Encyclopedia,* 425). As Derek Attridge explains:

> Free verse is the introduction into the continuous flow of prose language, which has breaks determined entirely by syntax and sense, of another kind of break, shown on the page by the start of a new line, and often indicated in a reading of the poem by a slight pause. When we read prose, we ignore the fact that every now and then the line ends, and we have to shift our eyes to the beginning of the next line. We know that if the same text were printed in a different typeface, the sentences would be broken up differently with no alteration in the meaning. But in free verse, *the line on the page has an integrity and function of its own.* This has important consequences for the movement and hence the meaning of the words. (5, my emphasis)

The implication of free-verse writing, Attridge adds sensibly, is that poetry "need not be based on the production of controlled numbers of beats by the disposition of stressed and unstressed syllables." A more accurate name, Attridge suggests, would be "*nonmetrical verse,* which, as a negative definition, has the advantage of implying that this kind of verse does not have a fixed identity of its own, whereas 'free verse' misleadingly suggests a single type of poetry" (167–68). But the adjective *nonmetrical* is somewhat misleading, given that the item counted may be the number of primary stresses (no matter how many syllables per line), as in Old English and much of Middle English poetry, the number of syllables per line, regardless of the number of stresses, as in the syllabics of Marianne Moore, or the number of long vowels per line, as in classical quantitative verse, and so on. Charles O. Hartman's definition is thus more accurate: "*the prosody of free verse is rhythmic organization by other than numerical modes.*"[8] Free verse retains the linear *turn* inherent in the etymology of the word *verse* (Latin, *versus*), but there is no regularly recurring counted entity.[9]

Once we try to go beyond these basics, there is little unanimity on the features of free verse. For Donald Wesling, free verse has its roots in the oral forms of ancient cultures—Sumerian, Akkadian, Egyptian, Sanskrit, and Hebrew—none of which have meter (*Encyclopedia,* 425). The speech base of free verse is also accepted by Northrop Frye, who defines it as "the associative rhythm"—that is, the rhythm of ordinary speech, with its short, repetitive, irregular, often asyntactic phrasal units—"strongly influenced by verse," which is to say, by lineation.[10] And Robert Pinsky observes that "the line in contemporary practice seems to fall roughly into two overlapping kinds: a rhetorical indicator for the inflections of speech . . . and a formal principle varyingly intersecting the inflection of speech."[11]

But "inflection of speech" doesn't in fact distinguish free verse from its metrical counterparts. On the one hand, there are those like Derek Attridge who argue that *all* verse is speech-based;[12] on the other, those who hold that free verse is distinguished primarily by its visual form, its typographical layout, and that indeed the line break creates verbal and phrasal units quite unlike those of speech.[13] But the link between free verse and visual formation is by no means essential. For the majority of free-verse poems—say those one finds in any issue of *Poetry* or *American Poetry Review*—retain the justified left margin, some form of stanzaic structure, and lines of similar length, so as to produce visual columns not all that different from their metrical counterparts.

If, then, free verse cannot be definitively distinguished, whether aurally, visually (or, for that matter, syntactically),[14] from, say, blank verse, this is not to say that there isn't what we might call a free-verse culture that occupies a particular place in twentieth-century literary history. In his monumental *Critique du rythme* (1982), Henri Meschonnic works from the premise that "the aim [of prosodic theory] is not to produce a conceptual synthesis of rhythm, an abstract, universal category, an *a priori* form. Rather, an organized understanding of historical subjects."[15] As he explains:

> It is not a question of opposing form to an absence of form. Because the *informe* [formless] is still form. If we want to provide a proper base for the critique of rhythm, we must pass from imperious abstractions to the historicity of language. Where freedom is no more a choice than it is an absence of constraint, but the search of its own historicity.
>
> In this sense the poet is not free. He is not free in confronting the alexandrine, any more than in confronting free verse. *Not free of being ventriloquized by a tradition*. . . One doesn't choose what one writes, nor to write. No more than one chooses to be born into one's language, there and then.[16]

The so-called freedom of free verse must be understood in this context. When Pound declares in Canto 81, "To break the pentameter, that was the first heave," he is speaking to a particular situation in late-Victorian "genteel" verse, when meter stood for a particular collective attitude, a social and cultural restriction on the "freedom" of the subject. Vladimir Mayakovsky, coming out of an entirely different tradition, but in the same time period, makes a similar gesture when he declared in 1926, "Trochees and iambs have never been necessary to me. I don't know them and don't want to know them. Iambs impede the forward movement of poetry" (cited in Meschonnic, 528).

Such statements, Meschonnic points out, are neither true nor untrue; rather, they must be understood as part of the drive toward rupture characteristic of the early-twentieth-century avant-garde. And the form Pound's own prosody took—the "ideogrammizing of Western verse," in Meschonnic's words—had everything to do with the revolution in mass print culture, a revolution that bred what Meschonnic calls the "theatre of the page." "If we were to talk about practices rather than intentions," he says, "every page of poetry would represent a conception of poetry" (303). Blank spaces, for example, would become just as important as the words themselves in composing a particular construct (304–5). Thus, the structuralist argument that lineation in and of itself guarantees that a text will be read and interpreted as a poem[17] is based on two misconceptions. First, it ignores the active role that white space (silence) plays in the visual and aural reception of the poem: the line, after all, is anchored in a larger visual field, a field by no means invariable. Secondly, and more important, the response to lineation must itself be historicized. In a contemporary context of one-liners on the TV screen and the computer monitor, as well as lineated ads, greeting-cards, and catalogue entries, the reader/viewer has become quite accustomed to reading "in lines." Indeed, surfing the Internet is largely a scanning process in which the line is rapidly replacing the paragraph as the unit to be accessed.[18]

How lineation as device signifies thus depends on many factors, historical, cultural, and national. The history of free verse in English remains to be written: when it is, it will be clear that the dominant example has been, not that of Ezra Pound, whose ideographic page has only recently become an influential model, but that of William Carlos Williams, whose verse signature is still a powerful presence. But since my concern in this essay is with the current situation in poetry, I shall confine myself to the postwar era, using as my example two representative anthologies, both of them cutting-edge at their respective postwar moments. The first is *Naked Poetry: Recent American Poetry in Open Forms,* edited by Stephen Berg and Robert Mezey for Bobbs Merrill in 1969 (but including poems from the early fifties on down); the second, *Out of Everywhere: Linguistically Innovative Poetry by Women in North America & the UK,* edited by Maggie O'Sullivan for Reality Street in London in 1996.[19]

An Echo Repeating No Sound

In their foreword to *Naked Poetry,* Stephen Berg and Robert Mezey tell us that they had a hard time finding "a satisfactory name for the kinds of poetry we were gathering and talking about": "Some people said 'Free Verse' and others said 'Organic Poetry' . . . and we finally came up with Open Forms, which isn't bad but isn't all that good either. And we took a phrase from Jiménez for a title which expresses what we feel about the qualities of this poetry as no technical label could do. *But what does it matter what you call it?* Here is a book of nineteen American poets whose poems don't rhyme (usually) and don't move on feet of more or less equal duration (usually)" (xi, my emphasis). The assumption here is that there *is* an "it," alternately known as *free verse, organic poetry, open form,* or whatever, but that this "it" cannot be defined "technically," which is to say, materially. And indeed the editors quickly go on to add that "Everything we thought to ask about [the poets'] formal qualities has come to seem more and more irrelevant, and we find we are much more interested in what they say, in their dreams, visions, and prophecies. Their poems take shape from the shapes of their emotions, the shapes their minds make in thought, and certainly don't need interpreters" (xi). Not "form," then, but "content" is what matters. Still, the choice of free verse is central because "We began with the firm conviction that the strongest and most alive poetry in America had abandoned or at least broken the grip of traditional meters and had set out, once again, into 'the wilderness of unopened life' " (xi).

This is a perfectly representative sixties statement about poetry. It takes off from Charles Olson's "Projective Verse" (1950), with its strong dismissal of "closed" verse and concomitant adoption of the line as coming "from the breath, from the breathing of the man who writes, at the moment that he writes." It is the "LINE" that speaks for the "HEART," even as the syllable does for the "HEAD": "the LINE that's the baby that gets, as the poem is getting made, the attention."[20] Interestingly, Berg and Mezey, who were by no means disciples of Olson, here give a curious twist to the famous Olson credo that "FORM IS NEVER MORE THAN THE EXTENSION OF CONTENT."[21] Whereas Olson demanded that form take its cue from the semantic structure of a given poem, Berg and Mezey take the aphorism one step further, dismissing "formal qualities" as more or less "irrelevant," entirely secondary to "what [the poets] say, in their dreams, visions, and prophecies." Indeed, if poems "take shape from the shapes of their emotions," from "the wilderness of unopened life," then "free verse" is effective insofar as it tracks the actual movement of thought and feeling, refusing to interfere with its free flow, to inhibit its natural motion. Or so, at least, the poem must appear to be doing, no matter how much "craft" has gone into it.

Naked Poetry includes nineteen American poets, born between 1905 and 1935, the largest cluster of them born between 1926 and 1930. In chronological order, they are Kenneth Rexroth, Theodore Roethke, Kenneth Patchen, William Stafford, Weldon Kees, John Berryman, Robert Lowell, Denise Levertov, Robert Bly, Robert Creeley, Allen Ginsberg, Galway Kinnell, W. S. Merwin, James Wright, Philip Levine, Sylvia Plath, Gary Snyder, Stephen Berg, and Robert Mezey. Despite the paucity of women (two out of the nineteen) and the absence (characteristic for 1969) of minority poets as well as poets writing outside the United States,[22] the editors have clearly made an effort to transcend schools and regional affiliations by including representatives of Beat (Ginsberg, Snyder), Black Mountain (Creeley, Levertov), Deep Image (Bly, Kinnell, Wright), Northwest (Roethke, Stafford), and East Coast establishment (Lowell, Berryman, Merwin, Plath) poetry.

So what do the poems in this anthology look and sound like? Consider the following five poems (or parts of poems), for which I have supplied scansions:[23]

A héadless squírrel,‖some blóod →
oózing fròm the unévenlỳ →
chéwed-ôff néck

líes in raínsweêt gráss
neár the wóodshêd dóor.
Dówn the drívewâ

the fírst írisès →
have ópened sînce dáwn,
ethéreàl,‖their máuve →

álmôst a trànspárent gráy,
their dárk véins
brúise-blúe.

                              (Denise Levertov, "A Day Begins," 140)

The sún séts in the cóld withoût friénds
Withoût repróaches after áll it has dóne for ús
It góes dówn belíeving in nóthing
Whén it has góne I héar the stréam rúnning áfter ìt
Ìt has bróught its flúte‖ìt is a lóng wáy
            (W. S. Merwin, "Dusk in Winter," 255)

In the dépths of the Gréyhoûnd Términàl
sítting dúmbly on a bággage trúck ‖lóoking at the ský‖wàiting for
    the Lôs Àngelès Expréss to depárt
wórrying aboút etérnitỳ óver the Póst Ôffice roóf in the níght-tîme
    réd dówntôwn heáven,
stáring through my éyeglàsses I réalìzed shúddering these thoúghts
    were nót etérnitỳ,‖nór the póvertỳ of our líves,‖írritàble
    bággage clérks,
nór the míllions of wéeping rélatìves surroúnding the búses wáving
    gôodbýe,
nór óther míllions of the poór rúshing aroúnd from cíty to cíty to
    sée their lóved ônes . . .
        (Allen Ginsberg, "In the Baggage Room at Greyhound," 194–95)

Dówn válley a smóke hâze
Thrée dâys héat, áfter fíve dâys ráin
Pítch glóws ôn the fír-cônes
Acróss rócks and méadôws
Swárms of néw fliés.

I cánnot remémber thíngs I ónce reád
A féw friénds,‖but théy are in cíties.
Drínking cóld snów-wâter from a tín cúp
Loóking dówn for míles
Through hígh stíll aír.
        (Gary Snyder, "Mid-August at Sourdough Mountain Lookout," 330)

The íce tícks séawârd líke a clóck.
A Négro toásts →
whéat-sêeds óver the cóke-fûmes →
of a púnctured bárrel.
Chémical aír →
swêeps ín from Nêw Jérsey,
and smélls of cóffee.

Acróss the ríver,
lédges òf subúrban fáctoriès tán →
in the súlphûr-yéllow sún →
of the únfôrgívable lándscâpe.
                    (Robert Lowell, "The Mouth of the Hudson," 110–11)

The five poets cited are by no means alike: the conventional wisdom would be to oppose the "raw" Allen Ginsberg to the "cooked" Robert Lowell, or the Black Mountain–based Denise Levertov to the more mainstream *New Yorker* favorite, W. S. Merwin, and so on. Indeed, there are real prosodic differences in the above examples. Certainly Ginsberg's strophes, made up of two or more lines, characterized by their emphatic, predominantly trochaic and dactylic rhythm, each strophe emphatically end-stopped, are a far cry from Levertov's minimal, lightly stressed (two to three stresses per line), frequently enjambed lines, arranged in open tercets. For Ginsberg, repetition, whether clausal or phrasal, is the central sonic and syntactic device; for Levertov, whose poem charts minute differences of perception, repetition is studiously avoided. Again, Levertov's "A Day Begins" differs from Snyder's "Mid-August," whose two five-line stanzas are notable for their monosyllabic base (seven of the poem's fifty-seven words are monosyllables), which ensures strong stress on almost every word in a loosely trochaic sequence. Unlike Levertov, Snyder does not run on his lines; neither, for that matter, does Merwin, whose lines are evenly paced to the point of intentional monotony, the avoidance of secondary and tertiary stresses heightening the epiphany of the final line in which two sentences are unexpectedly run together, culminating in the pyrrhic-spondee pattern of "it is (a) lóng wáy." And finally in Lowell, whose free verse most closely follows Eliot's prescription that the ghost of meter must lurk behind the arras, the frequent enjambment (as if to say, look, I am writing free verse, using open form!) is offset by the underlying iambic rhythm, as in "The íce tícks séawârd líke a clóck" and "A négro toásts," as well as by the repetition of identical stress contours, as in the two-stress lines "and smélls of cóffee," "Acróss the ríver."

But despite all these differences—and who would mistake the sound and look of a Ginsberg poem for that of a Lowell or Levertov one?—there is a period style, a dominant rhythmic-visual contour that distinguishes the lyric of *Naked Poetry* from that of a recent anthology like *Out of Everywhere*. Consider the following features:

(1) The free verse, in its variability (both of stress and of syllable count) and its avoidance of obtrusive patterns of recurrence, tracks the speaking voice (in conjunction with the moving eye) of a perceptive, feeling subject, trying to come to terms with what seems to be an alien, or at least incomprehensible world. Thus Levertov's "A Day Begins" follows the motion of the eye, taking in the frightening sight of the bloody headless squirrel, its location being specified only in the second tercet and in turn juxtaposed to the next thing seen, "the first irises" [that] "have opened since dawn," the poem moving, in the final line, to the "bruise-blue" conjunction between these seeming dissimilars. The same temporal tracking characterizes Merwin's "Dusk in Winter": in line 1, the sun is seen setting, in lines 2–3, the poet responds to the resulting "cold"; in lines 4–5, the sense of loss gives way to renewal as the stream is metaphorically perceived as "running after" the sun, its sound like flute song. In Ginsberg's "In the Baggage Room," the first line sets the scene, "in the depths of the Greyhound Terminal," and each subsequent strophe adds an element of perception or cognition. In Snyder's "Mid-August at Sourdough Mountain Lookout," the patient description of the valley in the first stanza triggers the step-by-step withdrawal into the self in the second. And Lowell's eleven-line conclusion to "The Mouth of the Hudson" focuses on the bleakest and ugliest items in sight as representation of the interior "unforgivable landscape" that is the poet's own.

(2) Free verse is organized by the power of the Image, by a construct of images as concrete and specific as possible, that serve as objective correlative for inner states of mind. Surely it is not coincidental that the origins of free verse coincide with French *symbolisme* and Anglo-American Imagism. From William Carlos Williams's "As the cat" and "The Lotus Tree in Flower" to Snyder's "Mid-August at Sourdough Mountain Lookout" and Levertov's "A Day Begins," the free-verse line presents what are often unmediated images, as they appear in the mind's eye of the poet: "A headless squirrel, some blood / oozing from the unevenly / chewed-off neck" (Levertov), "The sun sets in the cold without friend" (Merwin), "In the depths of the Greyhound Terminal / sitting dumbly on a baggage truck looking at the sky" (Ginsberg), "Down valley a smoke haze" (Snyder), "The ice ticks seaward like a clock" (Lowell)—perception, discovery, reaction: free verse is the form par excellence that strives toward mimesis of individual *feeling,* as that feeling is generated by sights, sounds, smells, and memories.

(3) Although free verse is speech-based, although it tracks the movement of the breath itself, syntax is regulated, which is to say that the free-verse "I" generally speaks in complete sentences: "the first irises / have opened since dawn," "When it has gone I hear the stream running after it," "staring through my eyeglasses I realized shuddering these thoughts were not eternity," "I cannot remember things I once read," "Chemical air / sweeps in from New Jersey, / and smells of coffee." If, these poems seem to say, there is no metrical recurrence, no rhyme or stanzaic structure, syn-

tax must act as clarifier and binder, bringing units together and establishing their relationships.

(4) A corollary of regulated syntax is that the free-verse poem *flows;* it is, in more ways than one, *linear.* Again, the stage for this linear movement was already set in a poem like Williams's "As the Cat," which moves, slowly but surely, "into the pit / of the empty / flowerpot." Even Ginsberg's complicated patterns of repetition (of word, phrase, clause) move toward the closure of "Farewell ye Greyhound where I suffered so much, / hurt my knee and scraped my hand and built my pectoral muscles big as vagina." In Levertov's "A Day Begins" the perception of death (the view of the blood-soaked squirrel) modulates into one of renewal (the opening irises), the epiphany coming in the final line with the compound "bruise-blue," tying the two together. Merwin's "Dusk in Winter" moves from its quiet, anapestic opening, "The sún séts in the cóld withoût friénds," to the markedly divided final line with its two "it" clauses ("It has," "It is") and concluding spondee, "lóng wáy." In Lowell's "The Mouth of the Hudson" every image from the ticking ice to the "sulphur-yellow sun" sets the stage for the reference to the "unforgivable landscape" of the last line. And even Snyder's "Mid-August," which does not push toward such neat closure, moves fluidly from line to line, culminating in the three strong stresses of "hígh stíll aír."

(5) As a corollary of feature 4, the rhythm of continuity of which I have been speaking depends upon the unobtrusiveness of sound structure in free verse, as if to say that what is said must not be obscured by the actual saying. In this sense, free verse is the antithesis of such of its precursors as Gerard Manley Hopkins's sprung rhythm, with its highly figured lines like "I caught this morning morning's minion, king- / dom of daylight's dauphin, dapple-dawn-drawn Falcon, in his riding." Not that the free-verse passages cited above aren't very much "worked," organized as they are by internal sound patterning, repetition of stress groups, and the counterpoint that arises from the isolation-by-line of units that otherwise form part of a larger sequence. In Levertov's poem, for example, "oózing from the unévenly / chewed-off neck," produces a sonic disturbance by means of the "uneven" line break and the jagged rhythm (only two full stresses in eight syllables) of the line "oózing from the unévenly." Or again, end stopping and strong stressing on monosyllabic units produces special effects as in Snyder's "Pitch glóws ôn the fír-cônes," where "cones" picks up the long *o* sound of "glows" and has an eye-rhyme with "on." At the same time, Snyder is wary of the sound taking over: hence the casual quiet lines like "I cannot remember things I once read."

(6) Finally—and this accords with the unobtrusiveness of sound—the free-verse lyric before us is remarkable for its lack of visual interest. Levertov's open tercets, Snyder's five-line stanzas, Ginsberg's strophes, Merwin's minimal linear units, and Lowell's loose verse paragraphs—none of these does much to exploit the white space of the page or to utilize the material aspects of typography. Except for Ginsberg's Whitmanesque long lines, all the examples above have columns of verse centered on the page,

with justified left margins, and only minimally jagged right margins, line lengths being variable only within limits.[24] The look of the poem is thus neither more nor less prominent than in metrical verse.

Interestingly, the six features I have discussed here, all of them, of course, closely related, turn up in the poets' own statements of poetics included in *Naked Poetry*. "The responsibility of the writer," says William Stafford, "is not restricted to intermittent requirements of sound repetition or variation: the writer or speaker enters a constant, never-ending flow and variation of gloriously seething changes of sound" (82). "Page arrangement," Ginsberg observes of "Wichita Vortex Sutra," "notates the thought-stops, breath-stops, runs of inspiration, changes of mind, startings and stoppings of the car" (222). "Organic poetry," writes Levertov in her well known "Some Notes on Organic Form," "is a method of apperception": "first there must be an experience, a sequence or constellation of perceptions of sufficient interest, felt by the poet intensely enough to demand of him [sic] their equivalence in words: he is brought to speech" (141). And Merwin seems to speak for all the poets in the anthology when he says: "In an age when time and technique encroach hourly, or appear to, on the source itself of poetry, it seems as though what is needed for any particular nebulous unwritten hope that may become a poem is not a manipulable, more or less predictably recurring pattern, but *an unduplicatable resonance,* something that would be like an echo except that it is repeating no sound. Something that always belonged to it: its sense and its information before it entered words" (270–71, my emphasis).

An unduplicatable resonance: from its inception, this is what most free verse has striven to be. "For me," says Snyder, "every poem is unique . . . A scary chaos fills the heart as 'spir'itual breath–in'spir'ation; and is breathed out into the thing-world as a poem" (357).

But there is one (and I think only one) exception to this poetics in the Mezey-Berg anthology, and it marks a useful transition to the poetry in *Out of Everywhere*. That exception is the poetry of Robert Creeley. Although Creeley's own "Notes apropos 'Free Verse'" make much of Olson's field composition and the use of breath, it also contains the following statement: "I am myself hopeful that linguistic studies will bring to contemporary criticism a vocabulary and method more sensitive to the basic *activity* of poetry . . . Too, I would like to see a more viable attention paid to syntactic environment, to what I can call crudely 'grammartology'" (185). And he talks about his own interest in "a balance of *four,* a four square circumstance, be it walls of a room or legs of a table . . . an intensive variation on 'foursquare' patterns such as [Charlie Parker's] 'I've Got Rhythm'" (186–87).

The "foursquare" jazz-based pattern Creeley talks of here may turn up as a four-line stanza (e.g., "A Form of Women," "A Sight") but also as the number of words per line, as in part 4 of the sequence called "Anger":

Face me, →
in the dark,
my face. See me.

It is the cry →
I hear all →
my life, my own →

voice, my →
eye locked in →
self sight, not →

the world what →
ever it is
but the close →

breathing beside →
me I reach out →
for, feel as →

warmth in →
my hands then →
returned. The rage →

is what I →
want, what →
I cannot give →

to myself, of →
myself, in →
the world.

      (182–83)

To call such poetry "free verse" is not quite accurate, for something is certainly being counted in these little block-like stanzas, even if it is neither stress nor syllable but word. The pattern is 2–3–4, 4–3–4, 2–3–3, 3–3–3, 4–4–3, 2–3–4, 3–2–4, 4–3–2, the final stanza reversing the word count of the first. So short are the line units and so heavily enjambed (twenty of twenty-four lines) as well as broken by caesuras (see lines 3, 18), so basic the vocabulary, made up as it is of prepositions, pronouns, and function words, that each word takes on its own aura and receives its own stress, as in:

voíce, mý
eýe lócked ín
sélf síght, nót

And the stresses are further emphasized by the internal rhyme ("my / eye," also echoing "cry" "my" in the preceding tercet), overriding the line break, and the pulling of "sight" in two directions: one toward "self" via alliteration and the second toward "not" via consonance.

Indeed, although Creeley's tercets superficially resemble Levertov's, the features of free verse I listed above hardly apply. This poem does not present us with a mimesis of speech, tracking the process of perception. The first-person pronoun ("I" / "my" / "me" / "myself") is used twelve times in the space of seventy-five words, and yet that "I" is less a speaking voice than a particle that passively submits to external manipulation:

is what I
want, what
I cannot give

where "want" and "what," separated by a single letter occlude the *I*'s halting presence. Again, monosyllabic lines like "is what I" refer neither to sun and stream, as in Merwin's poem nor to rocks and meadows, as in Snyder's. There is no image complex to control the flow of speech; indeed the shift from line to line is by no means linear: "See me" does not follow from "Face me." The normal syntagmatic chain is broken, the first tercet, for example, calling attention to the play of signifiers in "face me" / "my face" rather than to that which is signified. And when we come to line 4, "It is the cry," the normal flow of free verse is impeded because the unspecified pronoun "It" returns us to previous tercet as we try to make out what "it" might refer to. Or again, in line 7, "voice, my" means differently *within* the line than in the larger structure of "my own / voice, my eye locked in / self sight."

The syntactic ambiguity of lines like "for, feel as" and "want, what," coupled with the insistent word-stress, produces a rhythm of extreme weight and fragmentation—a kind of aphasic stutter—that is both heard and seen on the page. Each word, to cite Gertrude Stein, is as important as every other word. Sound becomes obtrusive ("me I reach out") as does the creation of paragrams, formed by cutting up complete sentences or clauses. Thus, although at first glance, the look of Creeley's poem on the page is not all that different from, say, the Snyder counterpart, the consistent detachment of words from their larger phrasal or clausal environment—a practice that goes way beyond what is known as enjambment—creates a very different physical image.

Post-Linears and Multi-Mensionals

If the unit of free verse is, as all theorists agree, the line, then the unit of Creeley's poem might more properly be described as what the Russian Futurists called "the word as such." Indeed, just as early free-verse poets called metrical form into question ("To break the pentameter, that was the first heave"), what is now being called into question is the line itself. As Bruce Andrews puts it in his and Charles Bernstein's symposium "L=A=N=G=U=A=G=E Lines":[25]

1. Lines linear outline, clear boundaries' effect, notice the package from its perimeter, consistency, evenness, seemingly internal contours which end up packaging the insides so that they can react or point or be subordinated to a homogenized unit, to what's outside . . . Boundary as dividing—'you

step over that line & you're asking for trouble' . . . Territorial markers and
confinements, ghost towns, congested metropolis on a grid . . .
3. Better, constant crease & flux, a radical discontinuity as a lack, jeopar-
dizes before & after, stop & start, a dynamic in fragments, suggesting an
unmappable space, no coordinates, troubling us to locate ourselves in formal terms. (177)

Who would have thought that fewer than forty years after Olson celebrated
the "LINE" as the embodiment of the breath, the signifier of the heart, the
line would be perceived as a boundary, a confining border, a form of packaging? "When making a line," writes Bernstein in the mock-Romantic blank
verse poem "Of Time and the Line" that concludes the symposium, "better
be double sure / what you're lining in & what you're lining / out & which
side of the line you're on" (216). Similarly, Johanna Drucker talks of "Refusing to stay 'in line,' creating instead, a visual field in which all lines are
tangential to the whole" (181). Peter Inman refers to Olson's sense of the
line as unit of poet's breath "too anthropomorphized." "The general organi-
zational push to my stuff," says Inman, "becomes page-specific I tend to
write in pages . . . not in stories or poems" (204). And Susan Howe remarks that in *The Liberties*, she wanted to "abstract" the "ghosts" of Stella
and Cordelia from " 'masculine' linguistic configuration." "First," says
Howe, "I was a painter, so for me, words shimmer. Each has an aura" (209).
And as an example of a "splintered sketch of sound," Howe produces a
page from *The Liberties* (210).

ENGELANDTS MEMORIAEL

Tragicum Theatrum Actorum

Similar (not identical)

unsigned portraits of

Laud Charles I Fairfax

Holland Hamilton Capel

Cromwell

Figure 4.1 Susan Howe, from Eikon Basilike, Out of Everywhere, *12–13*

Howe's own long verbal-visual sequence *Eikon Basilike* (see figure 4.1), which is the opening selection in Maggie O'Sullivan's new anthology *Out of Everywhere,* forms an interesting bridge to what Wendy Mulford calls, in her "After. Word," the "multi- and non-linear" writing of younger women poets in the United States, United Kingdom, and Canada. Howe's use of cut-ups and found text (or invention of a found text, since her version of the *Bibliography of the King's Book or, Eikon Basilike* is a complex refiguring of the ostensible forgery of Charles I's own writings) [26] come out of the Concrete Poetry movement, but her typographical devices (mirror images of lines, overprints, broken fonts) are designed to question the authority of the historical document, even as she selects certain passages and, so to speak, overstresses them, as in the lineated text "ENGELANDTS MEMORIAEL," where every word has the "aura" Howe speaks of in her statement on the line:

Laúd Chárles Í Faírfax

in which even the number "I" (as in Charles the First) is given a full stress.[27]

According to conventional criteria, the material forms used by the thirty poets in *Out of Everywhere* [28] can be classified as "verse" (e.g., Rae Armantrout, Nicole Brossard, Wendy Mulford, Melanie Neilson, Marjorie Welish) "prose" (e.g., Tina Darragh, Carla Harryman, Leslie Scalapino, Rosmarie Waldrop), or some variant on concrete poetry (e.g., Paula Claire, Kathleen Fraser, Susan Howe, Maggie O'Sullivan, Joan Retallack, Diane Ward). The collection also contains short plays or scenes by Lyn Hejinian, Caroline Bergvall, and Fiona Templeton. But such classifications obscure what is also a common impulse. Consider the following examples:

Although you are thin you always seemed to be in front of my eyes, putting back in the body the roads my thoughts might have taken. As if forward and backward meant no more than right and left, and the earth could just as easily reverse its spin. So that we made each other the present of a stage where time would not pass, and only space would age, encompassing all 200,000 dramatic situations, but over the rest of the proceedings, the increase of entropy and unemployment. Meanwhile we juggled details of our feelings into an exaggeration which took the place of explanation, and consequences remained in the kind of repose that, like a dancer's, already holds the leap toward inside turning out.

Figure 4.2 Rosmarie Waldrop, from "The Perplexing Habit of Falling" (1993), Out of Everywhere, *125*

That line's running-board basics

sidereal on all fours

preen

exploitation of perfect timing

renew

maximum syncopation

temperature tantrums clever yes

but mongrel

statistics are with us.

Head up in arms

pieces of time at regular intervals

if the ring fits answer the phone

non-commital background

indications assume no one's perfect

telepathy

soft patience or landslide afloat

the birds not flying pinpoint

a simile swerving away.

Figure 4.3 Karen Mac Cormack, "Multi-Mentional" (1995), Out of Everywhere, *74*

POPPY THANE. PENDLE DUST. BOLDO SACHET GAUDLES
GIVE GINGER. GIVE INK. SMUDGE JEEDELA LEAVINGS,
TWITCH **JULCE.** WORSEN. WRIST DRIP. SKINDA. JANDLE.

UDDER DIADEMS INTERLUCE.
ICYCLE OPALINE RONDA.

CRIMINAL   CRAB RATTLES ON THE LUTE.
CONSTITUENTS   BLINDINGLY RAZOR-GUT.
                              SHOOKER — GREENEY CRIMSON
                              NEAPTIDE COMMON PEAKS IN THE
                              SWIFT PULLERY. TWAIL,
                              HOYA METHODS: SAXA ANGLAISE
SKEWERED **SKULL** INULA.

Figure 4.4 Maggie O'Sullivan, "A Lesson from the Cockerel" (1988), Out of
Everywhere, *74*

need to give latitude which is often silence and/or

Virginia said she likes the word *breach*

whydon'tfliesdielikeflies

[........*To speke of wo that is in mariage*..........
Men may devyne and glosen up and doun
But wel I woot expres withoute lye]

142
........] *all this I see*
........]*plainly*] *now*

at this point Paul

mentioned that
                                    sunbeams are
extracted from
cucumbers in
Gulliver's Travels

Figure 4.5 Joan Retallack, from AFTERRIMAGES *(1995),* Out of
Everywhere, 23

In *Rational Geomancy,* Steve McCaffery and bp Nichol remind us that in standard prose as well as in the "visually continuous poem (Milton's *Paradise Lost* for instance) the page has no optical significance . . . Being to a large extent a working out of information through duration, prose structures tend to be temporal rather than visual . . . In extended prose or poetry the page becomes an obstacle to be overcome. [Whereas in poetry] the left-hand margin is always a starting point, the right-hand margin a terminal, neither of which is determined by the randomness of page size but rather by the inner necessity of the compositional process" (61).

It is this "inner necessity" that may be noted in the four examples above. Whether ostensibly "prose" (Rosmarie Waldrop) or "verse" (Karen Mac Cormack), these poems are first and foremost page-based: they are *designed* for the eye rather than merely reproduced and reproducable, as I found when I tried to type them up leaving the original spacing and layout intact. In these visual constructs, the flow of the line as the individual's breath as well as of the simulation of the eye's movement from image to image, observation to observation, is inhibited by any number of "Stop" signs. This is the case even in Waldrop's prose passage, which opens with the sentence: "Although you are thin you always seemed to be in front of my eyes, putting back in the body the roads my thoughts might have taken." Syntactically, this sentence is normal enough, but the reader/listener must stop to consider what the conditional clause can possibly mean here. What does being "thin" have to do with inhibiting one's partner's "thoughts," except that the two words alliterate? And does one really "put" those "thoughts" back into the body, as if one is stuffing an envelope? Robert Frost's famous poem "The Road Not Taken," which is alluded to in Waldrop's sentence, moralizes its landscape, turning the two divergent, but quite similar, roads into emblems of the futility of the choice-making process. But in the section from Waldrop's *Lawn of the Excluded Middle, paysage moralisé* gives way to a curious collapsing of the distinctions between mind and body, space and time, inside and outside. On this new "stage," "only space would age" (notice the rhyme) and "exaggeration . . . took the place of explanation." What looks like prose is in fact highly figured: take the "increase of entropy and unemployment" which characterizes these proceedings. Denotatively, the words are unrelated, although both refer to states of negativity. But visually and aurally, the second is almost an anagram of the first, the only unshared letters being *r, u,* and *m.* The dancer's "leap toward inside turning out" of the last line thus enacts the verbal play we have been witnessing—a play in which "you" and "I," "juggl[ing] the details of our feelings," find momentary rest as the voiced stop *(t)* culminates in the silence of the blank space.

If Waldrop's "sentences" are thus more properly "nonsentences," the lines in Karen Mac Cormack's "Multi-Mentional" open like an accordion and close down again, putting pressure on isolated centered words like "preen," "renew," and "telepathy." The relation of space to time, which is central to Waldrop's text, is intricately reconceived here. "Multi-Mentional" signifies "multidimensional" but also the "multi" things "mentioned" or worth mentioning in discourse about space-time. On the one hand, we have the "line's running-board basics," those reliable "straight-line" ledges beneath the car door that help the passengers to "get out." What with "perfect timing," "maximum syncopation," and "pieces of time at regular intervals," linear motion should not be impeded. But the "line's running-board basics" are countered by a motion that is "sidereal on all fours." Does planetary influence control our ordinary moves and why are they on "all fours"? And why are the statistics we should rely on "mongrel"? No use, in any case "preen[ing]" in this situation, a situation in which tantrums are ominously "temperature tantrums" (is something going to explode?) even as being "up in arms," gives way to a case of "Head up in arms," which sounds like a military or calisthenic routine. How, Mac Cormack asks, delimit word meanings? "If the ring fits answer the phone" initially sounds absurd only because we are looking for a finger, but the adage actually makes good sense. If the ring fits (if you recognize the ring as being that of your phone), answer it. Or has the caller already been recognized by "telepathy"? In Mac Cormack's "multi-mentional" world, "patience" is "soft" (which implies there's a hard patience as well), landslides "float," and the location of birds in flight can never be "pinpoint[ed]," any more than "similes" (*a* is like *b*) can measure the "multi-mentional."

The progress from line to line here is thus reversed and spatialized (another "multi-mentional"): "renew," for example, points back to "preen," which has all its letters except the *w*. The heavily endstopped "témperature tántrums cléver yés" jumps ahead to "telepathy." Indeed, going into reverse seems to be the mode of operation in Mac Cormack's poem. Secondary stressing, so central to the poetry of Ginsberg or Snyder (e.g., "Pítch glóws ón the fír-cônes"), as the representation of an actual voice contour, the flow of speech, is avoided as is ellision so that each morpheme receives attention, as in the guttural "Thát líne's rúnning-bóard's básics," which is almost a tongue-twister. Sounds cannot coalesce into rhythmic units, as they do in Snyder's "Sourdough Mountain," for then their "multi-mentional" quality would be lost. Which is to say that in the ear as on the page, the language act becomes central. "Word order = world order" (McCaffery and Nichol, 99).

Maggie O'Sullivan's medievalizing moral tale "A Lesson from a Cockerel" performs similar operations on the catalogue poem. From Pound to Zukofsky to Ginsberg, cataloguing has been a popular poetic device, but here the list is so to speak blown apart by spatial design: the first three lines in capital letters are followed by a rectangular box containing, in a row, the words "CRIMINAL" and "CONSTITUENTS," with a word column along the right margin, and the line "SKEWERED **SKULL** INULA" (reminiscent of Pound's "Spring / Too long / Gongula"),[29] placed beneath the bottom border. The catalogued items, many of them archaic or obscure, like "boldo" and "inula," both of them bitter alkaloid plant extracts used as drugs, and the many neologisms like **"JULCE"** and **"SHOOKER,"** are part of an elaborate roll-call of exotic narcotics, a kind of postmodern "Ode on Melancholy," in which the address to the **"POPPY** THANE" or opium lord becomes a drumcall heightened by its Anglo-Saxon and pseudo-Anglo-Saxon ("SAXA ANGLAISE") word particles—"pendle dust," "wrist drip," "neaptide common peaks," **SWIFT PULLERY.**TWAIL." Lines like "GIVE GINGER, | | GIVE INK,| | SMUDGE JEEDELA LEAVINGS" exploit the rhythm, alliteration, and assonance of the football cheer or political chant, but the caption inside the empty box marks all this chanting as "CRIMINAL / CONSTITUENTS," and label the "frame" as so much "SKEWERED **SKULL**"

Is "A Lesson from the Cockerel" free verse? Yes, if we mean by free verse the absence of meter, stress, syllable count, or quantity. But, strictly speaking, O'Sullivan's verse units are closer to the Old English alliterative line, as in

PÓPPY THÁNE, ‖PÉNDLE DÚST

or to such Poundian variations on that line as "líons lóggy ‖ with Círce's tisáne" (Canto 39), than to nonnumerical linear verse, and, in any case, the visual layout calls attention to itself as what looks like a computer printout, a set of headlines, a sheet of advertising copy coming through the fax machine. As in Mac Cormack's poem, secondary sound features (rhyme, assonance, consonance, alliteration) take precedence over the recurrence of stresses. Phrases like "UDDER DIADEMS INTERLUCE" or "CRAB RATTLES ON THE LUTE" perform at a sonic level before their semantics are fully grasped. The visual/vocal dimension of the words is more prominent than their actual referents. And this too is a time-honored tradition in poetry, however far free-verse poetry, the poetry of the Voice and the Image, has gotten away from it.

Not images, but "afterrimages," as Joan Retallack's sequence by that title makes clear. "We tend to think," says Retallack in the frontispiece of her book, "of afterimages as aberrations. In fact all images are after. That is the terror they hold for us." "I do not know which to prefer," writes Wallace Stevens in "Thirteen Ways of Looking at a Blackbird," "The beauty of inflections / Or the beauty of innuendoes, / the blackbird whistling / or just after." In Retallack's scheme of things, this becomes "*After* whistling or just — — —": in our fin-de-siècle world, every image, event, speech, or citation can be construed as an "afterthought" or "aftershock" of something that has always already occurred.

One form of "afterrimage" Retallack uses is found text: the poem before us draws on Chaucer (the opening of "The Wife of Bath's Tale") and Swift (book 3 of *Gulliver's Travels*) among other "literary" sources; it begins in medias res with someone's advice that there is a "need to give latitude which is often silence," followed by the typographical convention of "and/ or." In keeping with this choice, no given line follows from the preceding one, at least not in any normal sequence, the text incorporating reportage, question, number, iambic pentameter citation (lines 4–6), and narrative fragment. The last six lines recall Creeley's strategy of counting words rather than feet, stresses, or syllables. The pattern is 4 (at center), 2–2 (left and lowered right), and then a 2–2–2 tercet. And now, come the "afterrimages," chosen, Retallack tells us, by chance operation: thirteen characters or spaces from line 8, six from line 10, two from line 12. These tiny morphemic particles are living proof of what a difference a single letter can make. The ellipsis preceding *"all this I see"* becomes the mere stutter of *all th;* "point" loses its *p,* only to regain it from the capital *P* of "Paul" that follows; the loss opens up the text so that we think of "joint" or "anoint," the latter certainly being appropriate for Saint Paul. And the afterimage of "sunbeams," the meaningless vocalization *nb,* is a witty comment on the activities of Swift's Laputa. Not only, the poem implies, can sunbeams not be extracted from cucumbers, the word "sunbeams" doesn't break down neatly into *sun* + *beams* or even into neatly arranged vowels and consonants, but into the difficult-to-pronounce *nb* (as in *nota bene*), followed by an exhalation of breath, or visual blank which is, so to speak, "silence and/or." The final stop (*b*) is the voiced equivalent of the preceding *p*. Retallack's is thus an artifactual, wholly composed meditation on what can and cannot be "extracted from" language.

Susan Howe, I noted above, has referred to her typographical experiments as "abstractions" from "masculine linguistic formations," and many of the poets in *Out of Everywhere* would concur that such deconstruction has been central to their work. But it is also the case that their poems have many counterparts in the work of Clark Coolidge and Steve McCaffery, Charles Bernstein and Bob Perelman, Bruce Andrews and Christian Bök, and my own sense is that the transformation that has taken place in verse may well be more generational than it is gendered. We have, in any case, a poetics of nonlinearity or postlinearity that marks, not a return to the "old forms," because there is never a complete return, no matter how strongly one period style looks back to another, but a kind of "afterrimage" of earlier soundings, whether Anglo-Saxon *keenings,* formally balanced eighteenth-century prose, or Wittgensteinian aphoristic fragment. The new poems are, in most cases, as visual as they are verbal; they must be *seen* as well as heard, which means that at poetry readings, their scores must be performed, activated. Poetry, in this scheme of things, becomes what McCaffery has called "an experience in language rather than a representation by it." [30]

I have no name for this new form of sounding and perhaps its namelessness goes with the territory: the new exploratory poetry (which is, after all, frequently "prose") does not want to be labeled or categorized. What can be said, however, is that the "free verse" aesthetic, which has dominated our century, is no longer operative Take a seemingly minor feature of free verse like enjambment. To run over a line means that the line is a limit, even as the caesura can only exist within line limits. To do away with that limit is to reorganize sound configurations according to different principles. I conclude with a passage from Caroline Bergvall's "Of Boundaries and Emblems":

> By Evening We're Inconsolable. Having Reached This Far, Bent Over Tables Of Effervescence Within The Claustrophobic Bounds Of The Yellow Foreground: Art Has Kept Us High And Separate, Hard In Pointed Isolation, Forever Moved By The Gestures Of Its Positions And The Looseness Of Even That: Now Vexed And Irritated, Still Plotting Endless Similitudes: We Trip Over Things: Strain To Extricate Ourselves From Closing Borders:
>
> (*Out of Everywhere,* 206)

Is this prose or some kind of kind of alphabet game, using majuscules and justified margins? The question is falsely posed: whether "verse" or "prose," Bergvall's is first and foremost a performance, an activation, both visual and aural, of a verbal text, whose every stress, "Hard in Pointed Isolation," seems to reverberate. No wonder those "Closing Borders" in the last line above are followed by a colon: a signature, as it were, of things to come.

NOTES

1. See the entry on "Vers Libre" by Clive Scott, *New Princeton Encyclopedia of Poetry and Poetics,* ed. Alex Preminger and T. V. F. Brogan (Princeton: Princeton University Press, 1993), pp. 1344–45. This book is subsequently cited in the text as *Encyclopedia.*

2. Ezra Pound, "A Few Don'ts," *Poetry,* vol. 1, no. 6 (March 1913); rpt. in "A Retrospect," *Literary Essays of Ezra Pound,* ed. T. S. Eliot (London: Faber & Faber, 1954), p. 3. See also the entries on "Free Verse" by Donald Wesling and Eniko Bollobás and on Imagism by Stanley F. Coffman in *Encyclopedia.*

3. T. S. Eliot, "The Music of Poetry" (1942), in *On Poetry and Poets* (New York: Farrar, Straus, 1957), p. 31.

4. Eliot, "Reflections on 'Vers Libre'" (1917), *To Criticize the Critic and other Writings* (New York: Farrar, Straus, 1965), pp. 183–89. The citations are from pp. 189, 185, 187 respectively, but the whole essay should be read carefully.

5. Annie Finch, *The Ghost of Meter: Culture and Prosody in American Free Verse* (Ann Arbor: University of Michigan Press, 1993), p. 139. For Wright, Finch maintains, "the connotations of iambic pentameter remain positive" (134); for Lorde, "both iambic pentameter and dactylic rhythms carry abundant stores of wordless energy" (135).

6. Derek Attridge, *Poetic Rhythm: An Introduction* (Cambridge: Cambridge University Press, 1995), p. 172.

7. Timothy Steele, *Missing Measures: Modern Poetry and the Revolt against Meter* (Fayetteville: University of Arkansas Press, 1990), p. 10.

8. Charles O. Hartman, *Free Verse: An Essay on Prosody* (Princeton: Princeton University Press, 1980), pp. 24–25.

9. In *Rational Geomancy: The Kids of the Book-Machine. The Collected Research Reports of the Toronto Research Group, 1973–1982* (Vancouver: Talon Books, 1982), Steve McCaffery and bp Nichol have this entry on "Verse & Prose": '*verse*—from the Indo-European root 'wert': to turn, from this root derives the medieval Latin 'versus' literally to turn a furrow, in subsequent usage the furrow became the written line by analogy . . . *prose*—deriving from the same Indo-European root—is a contraction of the Latin "proversus" contracted thru 'prorsus' to 'prosus': literally the term forward, as adjectivally in 'prosa oratio'—a speech going straight ahead without turns" (106).

10. Northrop Frye, *The Well-Tempered Critic* (Bloomington: Indiana University Press, 1963), p. 21. Cf. Frye, "Verse and Prose," *Encyclopedia,* 885.

11. Robert Pinsky, Commentary, in "Symposium on the Line," ed. Rory Holscher and Robert Schultz, *Epoch,* vol. 29 (winter 1980), p. 212. The symposium is subsequently cited as *Epoch.*

12. Derek Attridge, for example, defines *rhythm* as "the continuous motion that pushes spoken language forward in more or less regular waves, as the musculature of the speech organs tightens and relaxes, as energy pulsates through the words we speak and hear, as the brain marshals multiple stimuli into ordered patterns" (1).

13. A classic account of this position is Eleonor Berry's in "Visual Form in Free Verse," *Visible Language,* vol. 23, no. 1 (Winter 1989), pp. 89–111. I have discussed the visual form of Williams's and Oppen's lyric in *The Dance of the Intellect* (1985; rpt., Evanston: Northwestern University Press, 1996), chaps. 4, 5. For statements by poets who stress the visual component, see for example, Margaret Atwood, *Epoch,* 172: "The line, then, is a visual indication of an aural unit and serves to mark the

cadence of the poem." Cf. Allen Ginsberg, *Epoch,* 189, George MacBeth, 203, Josephine Miles, 207. In their introduction to their collection *The Line in Poetry* (Urbana: University of Illinois Press, 1988), Robert Frank and Henry Sayre state that "the line—its status as a 'unit of measure,' what determines its length, the effects which can be achieved at its 'turn'—has come to be the focus of . . . concern" (ix). But the portfolio called "L = A = N = G = U = A = G = E Lines," edited by Bruce Andrews and Charles Bernstein, that concludes *The Line in Poetry* (see pp. 177–216) actually calls this statement into question, as does my essay "Lucent and Inescapable Rhythms: Metrical Choice and Historical Formation," pp. 13–40. I shall come back to the "Language" essays below.

14. See Hartman, chaps. 7, 8 passim; Donald Wesling, "Sprung Rhythm and the Figure of Grammar," *The New Poetries: Poetic Form Since Coleridge and Wordsworth* (Lewisburg, Pa.: Bucknell University Press, 1985), pp. 113–44; Jonathan Holden, "The Free Verse Line," Sayre and Frank, 1–12. "The most fundamental rhythmical unit in verse," writes Holden, "is *not* the line but the syntactical unit" (6).

15. Meschonnic, *Critique du rythme: anthropologie historique du langage* (Paris: Verdier, 1982), p. 21. All translations are mine.

16. Meschonnic, 593, 595, my emphasis. A similar argument is made by Anthony Easthope in *Poetry as Discourse* (London: Methuen, 1983). For Easthope, all verse forms—from the feudal medieval ballad to the courtly sonnet to the transparency of the "ordered" eighteenth-century heroic couplet—are ideologically charged: blank verse, for instance, has to serve as *the* bourgeois subjective verse form for the Romantic period, a form that gives way to free verse when the transcendental ego is replaced by the dispersal of the subject and the dominance of signifier over signified. Easthope's analysis is overly schematic, and he seems to accept the common wisdom that free verse is the end point of prosody. But his basic premise—that verse forms are not just arbitrary or "neutrally available" to everyone at any time—is important.

17. See, on this point, Jonathan Culler, *Structuralist Poetics: Structuralism, Linguistics, and the Study of Literature* (Ithaca: Cornell University Press, 1975), pp. 161–64. Culler borrows from Gerard Genette the example of a lineated version of "banal journalistic prose" ("Yesterday / on the A 7 / an automobile / travelling at sixty miles per hour / crashed into a plane tree. / Its four occupants were / killed") to show that lineation transforms reader expectation and interpretation.

18. Consider, for example, the airline menu on "easy SABRE" that gives commands like "Return to the first line." Or again, consider the following protest poem by Wilma Elizabeth McDaniel, the so-called Gravy Poet of the San Joaquin Valley, cited in an article by Peter H. King in the *Los Angeles Times* (11 August 1996, p. A1): "You can put your trust in gravy / the way it stretches out / the sausage / the way it stretches out / the dreams." Earlier in the century, such versifying would have demanded meter and rhyme; now even polemic jingles are as likely as not to be in free verse.

19. *Out of Everywhere* has an afterword by Wendy Mulford.

20. Charles Olson, "Projective Verse," *Selected Writings,* ed. Robert Creeley (New York: New Directions, 1966), pp. 18–19. Donald Allen, who reprints "Projective Verse" in his *New American Poetry* (New York: Grove Press, 1960), obviously has Olson's rejection of "closed verse" in mind when he writes that the poets in his anthology "have shown one common characteristic: a total rejection of all those qualities typical of academic verse" (xi), the most obvious of those "qualities" being, of course, metrical form.

21. Olson, 16. Here and elsewhere, Olson attributes this aphorism to Robert Creeley, and the attribution has stuck, although Creeley never gave a systematic account of the proposition.

22. The editors do claim that they had wanted to include LeRoi Jones and Michael Harper but were constrained "because of cost and space" (xii). As for the U.S. focus, "We decided to keep it American because we knew nothing much new has happened in English poetry since Lawrence laid down his pen and died" (xii). It is true that English and American poetics were probably furthest apart in the 50s and 60s, when "the Movement" dominated in Britain. But note that it never even occurs to the editors to include Canadian poets or poets of other English-speaking countries; their chauvinism is characteristic of the U.S.-centered imperialist ethos of the sixties.

23. The notation used here is the standard one adopted by George Trager and Henry Lee Smith Jr. in *An Outline of English Structure* (Washington, D.C.: American Council of Learned Societies, 1957). Trager and Smith identify four degrees of stress in English: primary (ˊ), secondary (ˆ) as in a compound noun like "bláck-bîrd," tertiary (ˋ), as in the first syllable of "ēlevátor"; and weak or unstressed ( ), as in the second syllable of "elevator." A double bar (‖) is used to indicate a caesura, and I use a right arrow (→) to indicate that the line is run over.

24. The count of syllables per line here is Levertov: 2–8, Merwin: 9–13, Snyder: 4–10, Lowell: 3–10. Ginsberg's strophes are visually even more unified because of the run over lines.

25. Bruce Andrews and Charles Bernstein, "L=A=N=G=U=A=G=E Lines," in Frank and Sayre, 177–216.

26. See Susan Howe, "Making the Ghost Walk About Again and Again," *A Bibliography of the King's Book or, Eikon Basilike* (Providence, R.I.: Paradigm Press, 1989), unpaginated. This preface is reproduced in Susan Howe *The Nonconformist's Memorial* (New York: New Directions, 1993), pp. 47–50. The poetic sequence itself follows (pp. 51–82) but the page design is not quite that of the original, largely because of page size.

27. In *Poetic Rhythm* (p. 171), Derek Attridge describes an extract from Howe's *Pythagorean Silence*, part 3, as follows: "Susan Howe's poetry illustrates the potential that free verse possesses to fragment and dislocate the normal sequentiality of language, beyond even the techniques deployed by Pound and Williams. This extract . . . uses the disposition of words on the page in combination with disruptions of syntax to suggest bursts of utterance interspersed with silences. The morsels of language demand maximal attention . . . [These lines] indicate something of the resonating power phrases can have when the connectivity provided by syntax, phrasing, rhythm, and visual linearity is partly—though only partly—broken." It is interesting that although Attridge puts his finger on exactly what makes Howe's verse quite unlike the earlier model, he still categorizes it as "free verse," as if there could be no other name for Howe's obviously very "different" page layout.

28. They are in order of appearance (but not chronology or nationality) Susan Howe, Joan Retallack, Tina Darragh, Paula Claire, Diane Ward, Carla Harryman, Lyn Hejinian, Maggie O'Sullivan, Melanie Neilson, Denise Riley, Rae Armantrout, Catriona Strang, Nicole Brossard, Wendy Mulford, Rosmarie Waldrop, Deanna Ferguson, Hannah Weiner, Carlyle Reedy, Geraldine Monk, Karen Mac Cormack, Kathleen Fraser, Lisa Robertson, Marjorie Welish, Barbara Guest, Grace Lake, Caroline Bergvall, Fiona Templeton, Fanny Howe, Bernadette Mayer, and Leslie Scalapino.

29. Ezra Pound, "Papyrus," *Personae: The Shorter Poems, A Revised Edition,* ed. Lea Baechler and A. Walton Litz (New York: New Directions, 1990), p. 115.

30. Steve McCaffery, "Diminished Reference and the Model Reader," *North of Intention: Critical Writings, 1973–1986* (New York: Roof Books, 1986), p. 21. McCaffery's discussion of the Klein worm (pp. 20–21) as emblem of a poetry "without walls," in which "milieu and constellation replace syntax," is also very helpful.

5

Ether Either

SUSAN HOWE

Poetical Labors, Domestic Sorrows

" '[Shelley] was extremely fond of his child,' says Mr. Peacock, 'and would walk up and down a room with it in his arms for a long time together, singing to it a monotonous melody of his own making, which ran on the repetition of a word of his own coining. His song was—"Yáhmani, yáhmani, yáhmani, yáhmani!" It did not please me, but, what was more important, it pleased the child, and lulled it when it was fretful. Shelley was extremely fond of his children. He was preeminently an affectionate father. But to this his first-born there were accompaniments which did not please him. The child had a wet nurse whom he did not like, and was much looked after by his wife's sister, whom he intensely disliked. I have often thought that, if Harriet had nursed her own child, and if this sister had not lived with them, the thread of their married life would have not been so readily broken.' " [1]

Rumor is a story passing from one person to one person without an aboriginal authorized relation. "Where are you going to, my pretty maid? I'm going a milking, sir, she said, sir, she said, sir, she said." Verbal reverberations keep us safe as possible in rapid print outline that is their interest. It is strange how the dead appear in dreams where another space provides our living space as well. Another language, another way of speaking so quietly always there in the shape of memories, thoughts, feelings, which are extramarginal, outside of primary consciousness, yet must be classed as some sort of unawakened finite infinite articulation. Documents resemble people talking in sleep. To exist is one thing, to be perceived another. I can spread historical information words and words we can never touch hovering around subconscious life where enunciation is born in distinction from what it enunciates when nothing rests in air when what is knowledge? Demosthenes with his mouthful of pebbles had to talk without choking him-

.Y, OCTOBER 10, 1938

Beacon Hill Authoress
Back on Transylvania

HOME FROM IRELAND

Mrs. Mark Howe of Beacon Hill, who arrived from Ireland yesterday on the Anchor liner Transylvania with her daughter, Susan Howe, 16 months.

Figure 5.1

self or allowing the pebbles to drop from his mouth who ever saw him who ever saw him bite? Never the nurse of the child, the wife of the wild, the soon to be abandoned rumor. What is your fortune, my pretty maid? My face is my fortune, sir, she said. Approaching poetry all things seem to touch so they are

Yáhmani, yáhmani, yáhmani, yáhmani

"HOME FROM IRELAND: Mrs. Mark Howe of Beacon Hill, who arrived from Ireland yesterday on the Anchor Liner *Transylvania* with her daughter Susan Howe, 16 months. Carrying gold bullion valued at $14,000,000 and more than 900 passengers of which number 163 debarked here, the Anchor

Liner *Transylvania,* Captain David W. Bone, docked in East Boston yesterday afternoon, completing an exceptionally rough crossing from Glasgow, Dublin, and Cobh. Extra guards were at the pier as a precautionary measure while the ship was in port with the shipment of gold consigned to a New York bank. Mrs. Howe is known professionally as Mary Manning and is an authoress. She said that all Europe bears the odor of death, that the young people there are destined to be so much cannon fodder, that she fears the worst is yet to come in Europe."[2]

The newspaper is a negative copy halfway between fact and correspondence it ranges beside invisible day will bear the stroke of a hammer and not break all representation. Newspapers shore up past facts not memories not involuntary memory: cities, states, phantom states, borders, blood, native soil, trade, the arms industry, moving in hearsay of assured monopoly capital. To embark on a theory of possession external acts are necessary a common language for readers of one system in rapid print outline no shelf life without storing noise. Little Polly Flinders, sits among the cinders, warming her pretty little toes. Chance brings numberless strange things to pass before the ascendancy of nominalism Achilles outstrips the tortoise duration is the double of itself. Henri Bergson says the life in the body will be gone if we can only jump the interval of time separating an actual event from what it merely represents. Time (take Zeno's flying arrow) sets out in a past we place ourselves in. Words breathe they are quick. Fear, according to Herbert Spencer, when strong, expresses itself in cries, in efforts to escape, in palpitations, in tremblings. My mother has our passports ready luggage aboard the ship

we are likeness or copies we stand for anything any unknown field relative to direction though the gray years tether we cannot not be kept out. In pre perception I forget the manuscript of characters bequeathed or long awaited, carried mediately immediately distant apart always *either,* not yet actual information no, vice versa.

Proximate and Remote

On Sunday afternoon, August 16, 1868, Lieutenant Governor William Dorsheimer, a member of the New York Survey Commission, took Frederick Law Olmsted for a drive around the city of Buffalo, port of entry and county seat of Erie County. They were scouting for a suitable location for a park. Rapid growth in the bleak industrial city situated at the eastern extremity of Lake Erie on the western corner of New York State at the border of Canada had already shut from sight whatever impressive views of the lake and the Niagara River its citizens once enjoyed if they ever did. Olmsted now stopped off on his way to Chicago where he was designing a residential suburb in order to investigate this lesser project. A municipal system in the form of small parks and squares connected by wide roads and driveways already encircled the city; he didn't see anything suitable for a larger public gathering place until they came to a rise crossed by a creek three and a half miles from City Hall in what was still rolling farmland. "Here is your park almost ready made," the landscape architect is rumored to have said looking back at the view of the downtown area. These days the Scajacuada Parkway, or Route 198, rudely interrupts his nineteenth-century Rousseauian nature-house-community theory, especially at rush hour. Nevertheless, this particular public gathering place maintains an aura of unaccommodating emptiness different from other more passively liberating parks or artificial enclosures planned by Olmsted, Vaux and Company for Boston, Brooklyn, New Haven, and Manhattan, if only in the way the tree-tops echo the as yet unpastured insurrection of clouds and sky

    so openly and secretly

Once I read when Olmsted was a child he took long solitary walks as a remedy for homesickness and particularly enjoyed the edges of woods almost depths of the mighty forest but some say open "grounds" peopled with animals. "What" asks nothing in authentic sense but that substance be defined in this life enlightened by knowledge, strengthened by exercise, I can tell you no one living remembers.

On Sunday afternoon September 22, 1996, I visited the Buffalo and Erie County Historical Society. When I asked to see a copy of the Sunday, December 7, 1941, edition of the *Buffalo Courier Express,* the librarian handed me a small brown cardboard box containing a spool of dated microfilm. A microphotograph is a type of photography in which an original document is reproduced in a size too small to be read by the naked eye, so here the human mind can understand far from it. Film in the form of a strip fifteen or thirty-five millimeters wide bearing a photographic record on a reduced scale for storage or transmission in a small space is enlarged to be read on a reading machine combining a light source and screen together in compact cabinet. What else is to be done with a mass of records when millions of pages of newspapers and magazines are published as throwaways? V-mail during World War II is an example of special wartime application. Do you remember the little child I was? Do you suppose an arrow can ever be motionless all the time it is moving between every sign and its object? Wisdom is comprehension of magnitudes, smallnesses, conditions, acts, places, times, forms. Intervention and isolation have already ranged themselves still war comes home. Now the real question is how far to wind a spool of microfilm and in which direction. But this is not a newsreel it's our American something.

On the night of December 6, 1941, a shrieking wind whipped across the wide open spaces of the Municipal Airport now called Buffalo International;

we lived on Park Street then. Further downtown the wind, as its sole caprice, tripped off a burglar alarm at 68 Peabody. The *Courier Express* says gusts howling and swirling at velocities of fifty to sixty miles an hour herald cold. If I heard you and you remembered hearing. Love hovers telepathically listen flesh instant. A choice which entails a concealed consequence is as to that consequence no choice even if thought has the character of signs. The front page of the Sunday, December 7, 1941, edition, restless with signs and portents, shows the unrelenting movement of all occasions toward some collective boundary of confusion photographs can only frame cut arrange flatten. Even research recorded in advance feels the implacable windows slam. Light snow and strong unclosing winds have already come without sleep over the sea reluctant neither known nor nearer knowing oh truth cohere. London reports another axis raider sunk but the German ship isn't identified while advancing Russian tank units find Nazi troops frozen to death at their posts. 125,000 troops are massed in Indochina, more on the way. American-built Tomahawk fighter planes help the RAF's biggest victory in the Libyan Desert. Early today Japan indicates that she stands on the verge of abandoning efforts to achieve settlement of the Pacific crisis by diplomatic negotiations at Washington. A supreme crisis is at hand. White bird featherless flew from Paradise. "Along came Lord Landless rode away horseless" because the higher anyone falls from the more fatal the fall. Roosevelt dispatches a personal message to Emperor Hirohito in a final attempt to avert the conflict. "The importance of the present step can be measured by the awe and veneration in which the Mikado is held by his 100,000,000 subjects. He is considered descended from the Sun Goddess Amaterasu in a line unbroken from ages eternal . . ." "PILOT KILLED IN PLUNGE OF PURSUIT PLANE." A funeral bird begins to cry a robin to collect little branches. Cloudy in Buffalo 25 degrees above zero in Moscow the temperature 25 below. Tomorrow is today in Tokyo. Either this day or that day the President's patience is at an end a White House Spokesman tells the press. One news item on the front page doesn't concern war or weather: "WILL REVEALS BERGSON CATHOLICISM CONVERT" is how the anonymously authored *Courier Express* headline puts it.

Vitalism

On October 10, 1938, uncannily resembling fictional interlopers from Bram Stoker's *Dracula*, published June 1897, my mother and I arrive in east Boston on the *Transylvania* after a rough crossing between Europe and the United States. The cargo Count Dracula ships from Transylvania to London in the hold of the *Demeter* consists of wooden boxes invoiced as "clay" really filled with mold, yes, he intends to scatter these graves of him all across England. When Jonathan Harker, Quincey Morris, Arthur Holmwood, Lord Godalming, Dr. Seward, and Dr. (Professor) Van Helsing, track eight of the boxes to the dining room of a rented house in Fenchurch Street, Piccadilly, Dracula surprises the men snooping. Jonathan Harker slashes at the vampire's cloth cloak where the heart should be with his great Kukri knife only gold coins and a bundle of banknotes cascade from the wound. Grabbing a fistful of money from the floor Dracula escapes by leaping through a window. Disappearance in language is always deceptive and a ninth box is missing. Is the ninth box more lordly than the rest? The count's pursuers hear the sound of shivering glass the "ting" of sovereigns hitting flagstone. Even if he takes the form of a bat or wolf or mist he cannot cross running water of his own volition so he goes home in the hold of the *Czarina Catherine* his trackers do track him east across the channel (lapping waves, rushing water, creaking masts) bribery can accomplish anything. A character whose adventures are related to me may speak and act in his last earth box his rage is spread across centuries even God cannot find his heart the history of a voice the history of a people, no, he has learned the English intonation. Disregard Jonathan Harker's note-epigraph to the novel Bram (Abraham) Stoker first titled *The Un-dead;* the count and the money are no longer, never have been, the author's property. Supposedly crumbled to dust and passed from sight archaism crosses to Boston Harbor a feedback process (*quid pro quo*) biological from textual separation. The *Transylvania's* gold bullion valued at $14,000,000 will be deposited in a New York bank for the general circulation of capital. Clothed in a separate but related cannibal costume Captain David W. Bone can act fictional Dracula's jackal when he needs to feed.

The Web

"The first time I ever saw Henry Irving was at the Theatre Royal, Dublin, on the evening of Wednesday, August 28, 1867. Miss Herbert had brought the St. James' Company on tour, playing some of the Old Comedies and Miss Braddon's new drama founded on her novel, *Lady Audley's Secret.* The piece chosen for this particular night was *The Rivals* in which Irving played Captain Absolute."[3]

Bram (Abraham) Stoker (1847–1912) was the offspring of middle-class Protestant Irish parents: his father was a clerk at Dublin Castle, his mother, who came from an Irish military family, worked as a social reformer, advocating women's rights for the poor, and serving as a volunteer at workhouses. Stoker attended Trinity College, Dublin, where he studied science and pure mathematics, became president of the Philosophical and Historical Societies, and in 1870 joined Edward Dowden, a well-known Shakespearean scholar and Trinity's professor of English literature, in mounting a passionate defence of Walt Whitman's *Leaves of Grass,* then considered an offence to morals and good taste. After graduating with a degree in pure mathematics he followed in his father's footsteps by accepting a secure position as a civil service clerk. While diligently filling the pedestrian role of Inspector of Petty Sessions, Stoker worked part-time as a freelance journalist, writing stories, editorials, news items, most of them unsigned, for the *Irish Echo, The Halfpenny Press, The Shamrock,* and other short-lived newspapers and periodicals in Ireland.

John Henry Brodribb (1838–1905), born and brought up in Cornwall, chose his stage name Irving in honor of Washington Irving's *The Sketchbook.* Although John Henry started working in and around provincial English and Scottish theatres when he was twelve, he suffered from a debilitating stammer. In order to progress from stage manager to actor Brodribb/Irving conquered his speech impediment, but in the opinion of many he never spoke Victorian or Elizabethan stage English correctly. Caricaturists were fond of imitating his shortened *a*'s and hard *o*'s. "In *Macbeth,* 'trammel up the consequence' became 'tram-mele up-p the cunsequence . . .' In *The Bells* his Mathias was heard to say 'Tack the rup from mey neck' for 'Take the rope from my neck.' "[4] Henry James, also a stammerer, noted disapprovingly: "His voice is apparently wholly unavailable for purposes of declamation . . . You can play hopscotch on one foot, but you cannot cut with one blade of a pair of scissors, and you cannot play Shakespeare by being simply picturesque" (Belford, 71). Maybe this is why the actor, known for his "sardonic, grotesque, fantastic humor," specialized in playing villains and was also a brilliant make-up artist.

In 1871 Irving returned to Dublin, this time in a melodrama adapted from Erckmann-Chatrian's *Le Juif polonais.* The London production had turned the provincial actor into a star. Partly in an effort to explain Irving's new "romantic" acting style, its appeal to himself and others, the future author of *Dracula* began to write regular unpaid theater criticism for the *Dublin Evening Mail.* For the next five years Stoker's unsigned reviews appeared without a byline under the heading "Public Entertainments." Joseph Sheridan Le Fanu, the author of *Carmilla* (1872), was a joint proprietor of the *Evening Mail,* a Protestant bastion of Tory Unionism, until his death in 1873.

In 1877, when "the Garrick of his age" returned to Ireland, this time to play *Hamlet* at Dublin's Theatre Royal, Bram Stoker was the most highly regarded drama critic in the city. His thoughtful review of Irving's "mystic" performance pleased the actor who invited him to dinner in his suite at the Shelbourne Hotel. The two men talked all night and dined again the next evening. On this second occassion Irving recited a familiar dramatic monologue, Thomas Hood's *The Dream of Eugene Aram,* to the assembled party of twelve male dinner guests. More than thirty years later Stoker recalled the event. "[S]uch was Irving's commanding force, so great was the magnetism of his genius, so profound was the sense of his dominance, that I sat spellbound. Outwardly I was as of stone; nought quick in me but receptivity and imagination . . . [H]ere was incarnate power, incarnate passion, so close to one that one could meet it eye to eye, within touch of one's outstretched hand . . ." After finishing his emotional performance Irving collapsed, half-fainting. "As to its effect I had no adequate words. I can only say that after a few seconds of stony silence following his collapse I burst out into something like a violent fit of hysterics . . . In those moments of our mutual emotion he too had found a friend and knew it. Soul had looked into soul! From that hour began a friendship as profound, as close, as lasting as can be between two men" (Stoker, 29–31, 33). Within a year Irving offered the Inspector of Petty Sessions a position as acting and business manager of London's Lyceum Theatre. Stoker quit his job at Dublin Castle (forfeiting his pension rights), completed his first book *The Duties of Petty Sessions Clerks,* and married Florence Bascombe at St Ann's Protestant Church on Dawson Street in the space of a month. Florence, the third of five unmarried daughters in a family of seven children, came from yet another Anglo-Irish military family. The couple had been secretly engaged for some time. Oscar Wilde also shared some sort of unannounced understanding with this *"exquisitely pretty girl . . .* just seventeen with the *most perfectly beautiful face I ever saw and not a sixpence of money"* (Belford, 85). The newlyweds (she was nineteen he was thirty-one) left Dublin immediately after the wedding ceremony, as Stoker was scheduled to start working in Birmingham the same day. They probably sailed on the mailboat from Kingstown (now Dun Laoghaire) to Holyhead, then traveled by train eastward to Birmingham where Irving was performing, and so became either colonialist immigrants or queer exiles.[5] "Irving was staying at the Plough and Harrow, that delightful little hotel at Edgbaston, and he was mightily surprised when he found that I had a wife—*the* wife—with me" (Stoker, 61).

Born in 1905, the same year Henry Irving died, Mary Manning was fifty-eight years younger than Bram Stoker, but her Protestant middle-class Dublin family provided her with strikingly similar though more extreme "models of respectability and penury."[6] Her father and uncles actively served in the Irish military; her maternal aunt, Louie Bennett, was a suffragette, social reformer, and organized the first women's labor union in Ireland. By 1920 my grandmother was a widow, the Easter Rebellion of 1916 was long over but not the chaotic civil war years, 1919–1922. She couldn't afford to send her son to university let alone two daughters. In 1921 the eldest child, sixteen-year-old Mary (not perfectly beautiful and not a sixpence of money), was on her own. By 1935 when she met my father, she had already crossed the Irish Sea several times, though never to the European continent, and crossed the Atlantic Ocean both ways twice (third class). Economic survival tactics during a time of war, counterrevolution, the traumatic birth of a nation, meant, for her and many other daughters, setting out somewhere as a poor relation. Even after my parents hastily married (three months from meeting to wedding was and probably is quick for Proper Bostonians, even liberal ones if there are any left), even well into her eighties Mummy kept leaving in order to arrive either one place or another as the first step in a never-ending process somewhere. Her three daughters became aware of Ireland and New England either concurrently or as the obverse and reverse of the same thing once. Throughout their married life her restlessness seems to have puzzled my father. As a liberal law professor he had problems with the nature of randomness and she could never be reached by appealing to pure abstraction (if abstraction is a form or a deed). "Your mother doesn't know what truth is," he noted more than once.

How do sounds speak to memory? I have brought you out of the land of Egypt and I have broken your bonds. Not true in music where the mind is chained to the vehicle of moving sound. Certain writers hear with their eyes are concerned in their poems and their prose with irregularities and dissipations with monsters of mutation. Dracula exists for Van Helsing as a continuum of changing forms. Here he is in façade language walking on stilts half-mouthed and mincing as the French *a* with the open mouth or as *ah* in the English system of pronunciation. Mummy says when we boarded the *Transylvania* that October at Cobh pronounced Cove, ocean liners couldn't enter the harbor so they anchored beyond the Quay pronounced Key, somewhere in sea-fog. Boarding passengers were rowed out and climbed a rope ladder to get on deck. I was hardly talking had only learned to walk so I suppose a stranger took me up.

Three of Bram Stoker's brothers went to medical school instead of university; so did my grandfather. Thomas and Richard joined the Indian Medical Service, George worked overseas as a surgeon during the wars in Turkey and the Balkans, John Fitzmaurice Manning went to Africa where he worked as a doctor. According to Mummy, so it may not be true, Stoker's nephew Frank was a dentist in Dublin when she was growing up. She remembers *his* three daughters were brilliant tennis players. One was so tall people called her a giant. Frank was a friend of her father's; they were sent to him for problems with teeth. Irish dentistry is or was notoriously bad, and Dr. Stoker was wildly liberal when it came to tooth extraction, so she dreaded visits to his office on Westland Row—a grim, perpetually sunless street, in those days anyway, ending at the railway station. Dracula has systems of transport under control, but his opponents send and receive messages in the space of seconds using telegraphy, so he can't win, but see

Seamus Deane in *A Short History of Irish Literature.*[7] According to Thomas Richards, author of *The Imperial Archive: Knowledge and the Fantasy of Empire,* "Dr. Van Helsing defeats Dracula by studying the functions of Dracula's form." The professor's investigation "preserves all the assumptions of the positive knowledge of form, maintaining the presumed integrity of the world through what can be called an imperialism of particulars."[8] Thank goodness we have Jennifer Wicke's "Vampiric Typewriting: Dracula and Its Media" to remind us how, "in her consumptive possession: Mina [Murray Harker] essentially becomes the detective in the final segment of the story."[9]

In 1897, Mina Harker, fictional fiancée-wife-mother-diarist-lady-copyist-quasi-vampire, types out a mess of material, the forms and collected papers for Stoker's Narrative. Mina (a stenographer in search of an author) takes notes, writes in shorthand, transcribes journals, phonograph recordings, letters; she collects newspaper clippings and maps. Possessing a sharp eye and ear, she assumes, without self-consciousness the poses and motions of the others. For seven years Mina Murray Harker acts Bram (Abraham) Stoker's entire company of characters. Sometimes she speaks in her own voice, sometimes she ranges and arranges myriad polyglot accents and intonations. Her art lies in accuracy. In fact, without Mina's careful attention to particulars, there would be no fiction. Is there a mirror? Perhaps she lost herself through writing and now is old as my mother, if the ear of the mother is shared.

"To do things 'unlightedly' is accordingly to do them without neatness or completeness—and to accept that doom is simply to accept the doom of the slovenly. Our national use of vocal sound, in men and women alike, *is* slovenly—an absolutely inexpert daub of unapplied tone."[10] This is the gist of Henry James's graduation address to the women of Bryn Mawr College, June 8, 1905, the year Henry Irving died and my mother was born. He titled it "The Question of Our Speech." After the war, in June 1947, Mummy, my sister Fanny, and I visited Dublin. This time we crossed the ocean by air. My Irish friends and relations still do imitations of our American accents. In their comic version, Sukey and Fanny (two bratty contemporary American primitives, graceless and slovenly) whine in nasal tones when we aren't chewing gum or devouring comics. Our voices are the shrillest part—the way we pronounce r̠s, Amu̠u̠rrca, pa̠arrrk, wa̠aturrr. Those long nasal a̠s; Baaa-st-n, ḥaarr-br. The horribly dropped *s* in Yes to form a sort of neighing iYe̠a. I can underline letters and use **bold** and *itals* for emphasis, but a person cannot be two places at once, such marks are only acted charades. During our first family meal at 35 Wellington Place, when, tired and bewildered after the flight from Boston to Dublin (two days two planes via Gander in Newfoundland then via Shannon), at the soup course (I wasn't familiar with soup courses) a small drop of liquid, splashing between my spoon and my mouth besmeared the Irish linen table cloth, the grown-ups thankfully didn't notice, or pretended not to; except Diana, a twelve-year-old first cousin seated next to me, who whispered, perfectly matter-of-factly, "you clumsy elephant."

No absentees vie with Mummy's archetypical ancestor. Our first Captain Absolute treads the parallel ether. Familiar with black curtains, he makes appearances from time to time, both true and not true, architect and artist, indeterminate, free. Eminently given to hospitality he scarcely ever breaks bread without some guest at his table yet nonetheless real he loves to thread whatever strange concealments bind him on the mother's side to a commonplace level of life, a particular law, some spiritual record of cloudless passage, things as they *really* are.

New Historicist and Postcolonialist scholars are currently reconsidering Bram Stoker as a colonialist (in Ireland) reemerged as a new immigrant (in England), while Queer Theorists are "analyzing its [*Dracula*] homoerotic desperation, unconscious desire and deeply buried trauma." Talia Shaffer claims she is the first critical investigator to realize that Stoker began writing *Dracula* "one month after his friend, rival, and compatriot Oscar Wilde was convicted of sodomy" (Shaffer, 381). David Glover expresses caution: "The fact that Stoker and Oscar Wilde were rivals for the hand of Florence Balcombe raises questions concerning Stoker's own sexuality and the precise nature of this rivalry, but these are topics for conjecture rather than conclusive analysis" (Glover, 3). He says his book is "an attempt to track the movements of fantasy across a career in writing, to follow its forced march and unexpected detours into the strange territories that abutted on Stoker's crumbling Liberal domain" (21). Glover concentrates on Stoker's treatment of "the Woman Question" in chapter 3, but the Stokers were married for thirty-four years and had a son, Irving Noel Thornley. Florence Balcombe Stoker is mentioned only twice in the body of the text and twice in footnotes on page 162. In the first footnote he writes: "On Florence Stoker's collection, see David J. Skal, *Hollywood Gothic: The Tangled Web of Dracula from Novel to Stage to Screen* (New York: W.W. Norton, 1990), p. 180." Skal's book is currently missing from Lockwood Memorial Library and I am writing for a deadline. I don't yet know if Florence Stoker is a spider or fly. She could be either.

L lingers longest in *walk talk folk half.* A word I always pronounced the Anglo-Irish way, was and is ēi′ther. As my mother's daughter that is a slip I never made because nothing in the medium of utterance could be more slovenly unless it would be to call curtains drapes. To advance with the moving reality you must place yourself between two consecutive vowels *i* icily delicate infinitely small almost *ai* in French words such as main, pain, no, not quite so indeterminate. Not if ē/ther *or* ī'ther is in ink.

A philosophy of forms can change all properties at once in the way most waves move in the way we study sequence as if Idealism is a force foreign to science or deep as being drowned. Shelley never abandons the fiery part of what we call sky. I will never be able to explain why manuscripts are so underestimated in all academic disciplines even including linguistics and semiology. Zeno's arrow again. The philosophers of the Eleatic school see only pure illusion in spatial movement and change in general. In another ideology the very progenitors which are primal truth bracket double-slash signals.

While you are all going about your usual errands beyond the sea I am explaining how a single woman can speak Jacobean, long weekends, nothing but a chair or two to indicate setting, no great house, no help from scenery and costume, only a wall left.

"In yesterday's reach and to-morrow's, / Out of sight though they lie of to-day, / There have been and there yet shall be sorrows / That smite not and bite not in play."[11] When Algernon Swinburne gave a recitation of his poem "Dolores," he created such an ecstatic effect, several of his listeners fell to their knees.

My American grandfather always regarded himself as a liberal. His was a liberalism trimly hedged by "knowledge-producing institutions"—Thomas Richard's term for British organizations and collections united in the service of state and Empire (Richards, 4), such as the Boston Atheneum, the Saturday Club, the Tavern Club, the Examiner Club, the Boston Museum of Fine Arts, the Boston Symphony Orchestra, the Isabella Stuart Gardiner Museum, the Atlantic Monthly Company, and Harvard University. He served on innumerable boards, penned innumerable resolutions, minutes for meetings, obituaries, editorials, biographical memoirs, after-dinner speeches. Books of reference were his mania, especially the *Oxford English Dictionary* along with *The Oxford Companion to English Literature*. His hobby was collecting quotations. Correspondence and after-dinner speeches were littered with apt citations often delivered in Latin or Greek. Between the public duties of a citizen and the private conversations of gentlemen he clung to the touchstone of manners: manners being a matter of vocal habits in a nation, i.e., speaking American English correctly. During the war years his admiration for Winston Churchill was unbounded, possibly because of Churchill's equation of knowledge with national security, although after reading *The Imperial Archive* and *Mummies and Liberals,* I persist in believing Winston Churchill's verbal self-command enthralled one whose vocal presence was so wonderfully mishapen. Mark Antony DeWolfe Howe was a stutterer; so was his brother Wallace.

GRANDPA: (fast) hk hk hk (slow), (gasped vowels) a-a-a-a-a-fast)^ ^k (clogged reiterated consonants) recite or khhhhkk hk hk kh kkk— hkhkhhck hchh in bad moments h^exp)exp kbhhhkk Booth di (desperately fast) k k kaaaagoch a(slower) keehckk kh moments (slower times—ut slow) disorder. Or the old actors did

as if words before they are spoken imagine another echo as if a child were to deliver a long harangue some phonetic chiaroscuro of disorder. Or the way if a match is scraped fire results.

The family was mortified by these consistently repeated episodes of immediacy versus constraint. Time and again they waited for whatever tortuous narrative strategy might illustrate a happy ending was possible, the sentence could go on. One result of anxious familial scrutiny was the formidable emphasis his three children placed, not only on speaking correctly, but on moving speech, on audience response. During the 1940s Uncle Quincy became a newscaster for CBS, Aunt Helen toured the United States performing monologues in the manner of Ruth Draper, while my father prided himself on being able to lecture to large classes in perfect sentences never using notes.

Seven years after Dracula's multiple knifing by Jonathan Harker (English) and Quincey Morris (American), Mina gives birth to a son. "It is an added joy to Mina and to me [Harker writes speaking for his wife] that our boy's birthday is the same day as that on which Quincey Morris died. His mother holds, I know, the secret belief that some of our brave friend's spirit has passed into him. His bundle of names links all our little band of men together; but we call him Quincey."[12] After Henry Irving's death Bram Stoker returned to writing journalism. He worked for several newspapers in London and New York. Winston Churchill, then undersecretary for the colonies, agreed to an interview, "because you are the author of *Dracula*" (Belford, 311). In October 1938 many of our fellow passengers aboard the *Transylvania* are sorrowful and frightened, they speak other languages, my mother says she can hear sobbing at night and lapping water level with where we lie confined, enclosed, self-enclosing, always moving throughout this time you know nothing of now, I never dreamt it was too late.

The two hemispheres contain a fixed aspect of reality in arrested form. When souls are separated the atmosphere becomes electrical anxiety. You can't touch a thread of the fabric without seeing more immediate dispatch of copy and so far the only arranging to be accomplished in one sitting is both sides of the Atlantic.

If I shut my eyes the point of view gets elbowed out.

Do something to amuse us, dear? Mrs. Green as Mrs. Malaprop, Sara Allgood as Maura in *Riders to the Sea,* or later as O'Casey's Juno. Leave the body to take possession. Carmilla did this so did Millarca. Retrospective random memory not the stray subliminal bits the details.

In *Personal Reminiscences* Bram Stoker listed some of the items sold at Christies at the sale of Irving's curios. Among them was a knitted green silk purse with steel rings found in Edmund Kean's pocket after his death. The purse had been a gift from Robert Browning. "In addition to this purse [Irving] had a malacca cane which had come from Garrick, to Kean; the sword and sandals worn by him as Lucius Brutus; a gold medal presented to him in 1827; his Richard III sword and boots; the Circassian daggar presented to him by Lord Byron" (Stoker, 98). Stoker died on April 20, 1912 (the week of the sinking of the *Titanic*). A year later Sotheby's sold off his books, presentation copies, and original manuscripts including the "Dracula Notes," seventeen volumes by or about Walt Whitman, the death mask and hands of Abraham Lincoln, a portrait study of Kean as Sir Giles Overreach in Philip Massinger's *A New Way to Pay Old Debts,* and a book of Winston Churchill's illustrations inscribed: "To Bram Stoker, October 31, 1899. Another Gentleman who belongs to both sides of the Atlantic" (Stoker, 325–26).

In 1968, a year after my father's death, Mary Manning Howe, now a United States citizen, reimmigrated to Dublin where she became a columnist and theater critic for the *Irish Times* and wrote a comic novel called *The Last Chronicles of Ballyfungus.* During the 1970s she and Shelagh Richards (another Irish actress and director) visited Romania, a popular Irish tourist spot at the time. It was rumored to be sunny, and hotels in East Europe were affordable under a Communist regime. While there, they decided to go on a day trip to Dracula's Castle. It turned out to be harder to reach than they had imagined and the transportation was expensive, but they set off anyway. When they arrived after a long and arduous journey the place was deserted. A sign said "Closed for Repairs."

6 October, close to midnight — Poised on the brink of the World Wide Web I am a widow almost as old as Juno or Mummy when Daddy died. As a Liberal who believes in progress I am creeping into computer literacy but only experimentally, for Prose. For Poetry I am superstitiously addicted to a gray Smith Corona XE5100. I cannot change form and flourish without it. The Smith Corona printwheel with the font called Presidential 12 has been discontinued. It is still possible to obtain H 2100 Correctable Film Ribbons and H 21050 Lift-Off Tapes; but the Electronic Revolution has the resources of science on its side and the company is bankrupt. I await the coming day when, walking into OfficeMax in search of one more XE5100 transfusion, I discover all Smith-Corona products are missing.

Spare Time

One summer during the war, or just after, we stayed with friends of my parents at their family compound, Seven Gates Farm, in Martha's Vineyard. My mother directed some scenes from *A Midsummer Night's Dream*. Not the whole play, because the only players were children; three Parkmans, maybe a couple of Parkman cousins, Fanny, and myself. I played Titania but still know the Fairy's first speech by heart so could have been two characters at once. Imagine rushing on from one side of a sea garden labyrinth to speak with Puck, only here in print when Titania enters a few speeches later from the same side to meet Oberon, the Fairy gives them their cue, as if space traversed were interchangeable with motion itself. The soul does move without body, the body moves but does not move alone. *Dream* has been called a masque of missing mothers. If figures no one did see or can see are truly so, how do I distinguish either from ether? In the ordinary way of muliple memories it all comes down to a question of confusion.

So long as you hear so long as you stay within earshot.

"*Puck.* 'But room fairy! Here comes Oberon. *Fai.* And here my mistress. Would that he were gone!' *Enter* OBERON, *the King of the Fairies, at one door, with his* Train; *and* TITANIA, *the Queen, at another, with hers.*" [13] Momentarily rendering the Fairy King stage-Irish, Poppy Parkman (PUCK) offended our adult audience by calling her sister Debby (OBERON) "O'Brien." What lack of tone standard in a seven-year-old could manifest itself by sweeping *e* from the presence of *Ob* only to restore it later where the second *o* should be. O *must* be double. For years Poppy's verbal accident served as a byword in our family for American civilization run wild.

One might as well be chattering at screech owls.

Oberon comes onstage arguing. "Ill met by moonlight, Proud Titania". He only begs her little changeling boy to be his henchman. "Set your heart at rest, / The fairy land buys not the child of me, she angrily replies. The editor of the Arden edition says that love in relation to marriage is the dramatist's subject. Removed to Europe so infinitely foreign; our fathers help to plan the Normandy invasion. Restoring concepts of democracy they arrange legal retribution for inexpiable crimes. Later, at Potsdam, thinking is another kind of action. "Yáhmani, yáhmani, yáhmani, yáhmani!"—Someone is crying out In childhood all land is common to imagination without officials for public speech merely to see is to know. Navigation used to be a matter of the eyes. Forgotten or barely considered at the centers of power local sailors know their local coasts like a book. Before June 1637, in the Massachusetts Bay Colony, able-bodied people preferred to walk an old Indian trail called the Shore Path. Some wandering mariners have no memorial in original Republic Abstract. Much of the fairy lore in Shakespeare's own childhood doesn't come from books at all but barefoot and in poor attire from popular belief from oral tradition. Two ideas resemble each other. A piece of a sentence left unfinished can act as witness to the question proposed by a suspended ending. A dividing instant the other side is what will happen. Children pass from imaginary to antique fable through liquid imagery before the perceived structure of the world breaks into blackboard subtitles.

"8 Octobris [1600] / Thomas Fyssher. / Entred for his copie vnder the handes of Master Rodes / and the Wardens A booke called A mydsommer nightes Dreame. vj^{dn} (Brooks, xxi). A canoe blows over water skimming it like a seabird. Such fragile conveyances. I went over the water water went over me. Imagination wants material to work with; costumes, curtains, footlights turned on, a prompt book ready at every wing. There are the words and there is the air.

My head is so cold, give me something to cover it with. Give me something to eat, I am so hungry.

Miscellanea

George Cooke (1756–1830) one of England's greatest tragedians of the latter part of the eighteenth century was also an alcoholic, and by the turn of the century had lost his preeminent position on the English stage. In 1810 he was brought to America by Thomas Cooper, an American actor and producer, and died here ten months later. He was buried in Saint Paul's Churchyard in New York without a stone to mark the spot. Cooke's English successor, Edmund Kean, made two successful tours of America in 1820 and 1825. On the first tour he moved Cooke's remains to a more prominent place in the churchyard and had a cenotaph erected to his memory. Kean kept as a relic one of Cooke's toe bones, compelling all visitors to worship it.[14]

"During our Museum visit Mr. Fortescue took us into the King's Library and led us to a glass-case in which was enshrined the extremely rare first edition of *Hamlet*. He unlocked the case, took out the precious volume, and, with great solemnity, placed it in Swinburne's hands. I shall never forget the look of rapturous awe on the poet's face as he turned the pages of the priceless book. He spoke no word. His wonder and reverence were too deep even for the customary 'Ah-h-h!' He simply gazed—silent and transfixed. Then with a look of thanks in which I could see a trace of emotion, and with the inevitable bow he handed back the treasure to Mr. Fortescue."[15]

NOTES

1. *Shelley Memorials: From Authentic Sources . . . To Which Is Added, an Essay on Christianity, by Percy Bysshe Shelley, Now First Printed,* ed. Shelley and Jane Gibson, (Boston: Ticknor & Fields, 1859), p. 71.

2. Cutting from Boston newspaper, October 10, 1938, pasted in Mary Manning Howe's photograph album.

3. Bram Stoker, *Personal Reminiscences of Henry Irving,* vol. 1 (London: William Heinemann, 1906), p. 1. This is the first paragraph of the two-volume memoir, written a year after Irving's death.

4. Barbara Belford, *Bram Stoker: A Biography of the Author of Dracula* (New York, Alfred A. Knopf, 1996), p. 71.

5. Talia Shaffer, in " 'A Wilde Desire Took Me': The Homoerotic History of *Dracula,*" *ELH,* vol. 61 (1994), p. 387. Talia Shaffer here points out that in *Personal Reminiscences* Stoker mentions his wife only twice. One of these references tells of Irving's shock at Stoker's marriage.

6. David Glover, *Vampires, Mummies, and Liberals: Bram Stoker and the Politics of Popular Fiction* (Durham, N.C.: Duke University Press, 1996), p. 9.

7. Seamus Deane, *A Short History of Irish Literature* (Notre Dame, Ind.: University of Notre Dame Press, 1986), p. 110–11.

8. Thomas Richards, *The Imperial Archive: Knowledge and the Fantasy of Empire* (London: Verso, 1993), p. 63.

9. Jennifer Wicke, "Vampiric Typewriting: Dracula and Its Media," *ELH,* vol. 59 (1992), p. 486.

10. Henry James, "The Question of Our Speech" in *The Question of Our Speech, The Lesson of Balzac: Two Lectures* (Boston: Houghton, Mifflin, 1905), pp. 24–25.

11. Algernon Charles Swinburne, "Delores," in *The Complete Works of Algernon Charles Swinburne,* ed. Edmund Gosse and Thomas James Wise (New York: Russell & Russell, 1925), p. 284.

12. Bram Stoker, *Dracula* (London: Penguin Books, 1993), p. 485.

13. William Shakespeare, *A Midsummer Night's Dream,* ed. Harold F. Brooks (London: Methuen, 1979), p. 30.

14. Frederick Marryat, *A Diary in America, with Remarks on Its Institutions,* ed., with notes and introduction by Sydney Jackman (New York: Alfred A. Knopf, 1962), p. 93 n. (Not a direct quote.)

15. Clara Watts-Dunton, *The Home Life of Swinburne* (London: A. M. Philpot, 1922), p. 228.

PART II

Performing Words

6

Visual Performance of the Poetic Text

JOHANNA DRUCKER

Visual Performance in Poetic Work

The idea of performance in poetry is conventionally associated with a real-time event in which a live or recorded reading provides effective dimensions to a poetic work through the immediate experiences that constitute an event. But a visual performance of a poetic work on a page or canvas, as a projection or sculpture, installation or score, also has the qualities of an enactment, of a staged and realized event in which the material means are an integral feature of the work. Performance in this sense includes all of the elements that make the work an instantiation of a text, make it specific, unique, and dramatic because of the visual character through which the work comes into being. The specific quality of presence in such a work depends upon visual means—typefaces, format, spatial distribution of the elements on the page or through the book, physical form, or space. These visual means perform the work as a poem that can't be translated into any other form.

Such a material, visual performance of a poetic work has no necessary temporal, spatial, or social relation to the author or artist. Written work is always at a remove from the writer, cast into an autonomous form, not dependent of the presence of the author as a performance. In fact, there is every possibility of hiding, eclipsing, effacing, or disguising the writer through writing. One of the great virtues of the print form has been its capacity to conceal gender and other aspects of physically apparent identity—all those characteristics that contribute to the auratic whole of the poet as persona in a real-life performance. So the visual performance of a work, rather than being about the presence of the author/reader, is about the presence of a poem.

The strongest link between visual and sound performance is their mutual emphasis upon material as a primary, rather than incidental or secondary, consideration. But where the visual material has a presence, that is, is in a condition of being a poem while remote from an author spatially and temporally, sound poetry consists of a presencing, a bringing into being in a spatial and temporal location of the performance. While a recording of a sound poem obviates certain literal aspects of this limitation, it does not alter the basic distinction between the way visual and verbal/vocal signs exist materially. The foregrounding of the performative aspects of material over and above the linear, normative logic of conventional linguistic formulations is a shared feature of visual and sound poetry—and certain correspondences can be drawn between the idea of a "field" of page and a field of vocalization. Visual poetry and sound poetry also share the quality of being untranslatable (even more than other poetry) because of their emphatic insistence on the bond between material form and performance.

In the course of the twentieth century, visual performances of poetic works have taken many forms—from early experiments with figured verse, orchestral scoring, painted and collaged works that characterize the early decades, to works in which compositional strategies and process provide the motivation for the visual form, as in work of the later decades. The use of collage practices has proved flexible and adaptable to a multitude of sensibilities, as has the elaborate painting or calligraphy of poetic language, and changes in available technology have also had their impact as photographic manipulations, electronically generated image texts, and videographics have become familiar tools for poetic practice. But I am not not concerned here with mapping a history of experiments in visual poetry across the vast heterogeneous field of twentieth-century poetics. Instead, I want to concentrate on a handful of representative works in order to point out the variety of ways in which visual performativity has been enacted.

Strategies for Visual Performance in Early-Twentieth-Century Poetics

Any discussion of early-twentieth-century visual poetry necessarily begins with a reference to earlier precedents—figured poems and iconic verse stretching back into antiquity, the oft-cited Lewis Carroll poem in the shape of a mouse's tail in *Alice in Wonderland* (first published in 1864), and Stéphane Mallarmé's enigmatic masterwork, *Un Coup de dès,* which was first rendered according to his typographic specifications in a 1914 edition. The aesthetic arenas in which visual experimentation takes on a developed form in the first half of the century include Italian Futurism, Russian Futurism, German and Swiss Dada, English Vorticism, Dutch De Stijl, Anglo-American modernism, and, to a lesser degree, French modern poetry and visual arts associated with Cubism and then Surrealism.[1] In other words, there was a visual component to almost every area of modern poetry, though this is not meant to imply that visual poetry dominated any of these fields (in only a few cases did the visual quality of poetic texts come to be a signature feature of the aesthetic movement such as in Futurism and Dada).[2]

Without too much difficulty, however, one could expand the study of visual poetics to the work of almost every poet who has put words on a page. The long lines of printer/poet Walt Whitman, the terse and elaborately scored poetic forms of Emily Dickinson, the distinct visual choices evident in the work of William Butler Yeats and William Morris—all of these have been subject to serious critical investigation.[3] Though long ignored, the visual aspects of modern poetics are increasingly well understood and appreciated, though in this article particular attention will be paid to instances of work that cannot suffer any translation into alternative visual or typographic form without sacrificing their integrity as works.

In spite of the many poets involved in these activities, the strategies for engaging visual aspects in the performance of a poetic work are finite. These include the use of visual elements in order to create an image—either a simple iconic form or a more elaborate pictorial structure, those that create a score or script (sometimes meant for verbal interpretation and sometimes as a performance in its own right), those that use visual means for expressive effect through collage, calligraphy, and paint, and those that stretch the conventions of traditional poetic verse form. Before considering these in turn, it's necessary to consider the singular contribution of Mallarmé.

The Spatialized Constellationary Figure of Thought: Mallarmé

The concept of visual abstraction, of a poem whose form would resemble thought, came into visual poetics through a single work of the late-nineteenth-century French Symbolist poet Stéphane Mallarmé. Mallarmé's contribution resided in its enigmatic power, refusal of closed meaning, and its elusive visual and verbal configurations. The 1914 publication of *Un Coup de dès* in a format corresponding to his original notes (the work first appeared in print in 1896 in a modified form) made this work available in the context of Dada and Futurist interest in typographic experiment. The influence of Symbolist poetics on Futurism was well marked, and the verbal mimicry and onomatopoeic qualities of Filippo Marinetti's work in particular demonstrated this affinity. But the visual qualities of *Un Coup de dès* differentiated it from any other visual poem of the period.

When Mallarmé's poem is considered as a whole, the distribution of words on the spreads (each pair of facing pages in a book) that comprise the work, and the marked differentiation of elements through the use of subtle but obvious distinctions in size and between italic and roman fonts, amount to a nonspecific visual figure. There is no shape to which the image refers in any iconic sense, though the themes of shipwreck and the idea of the constellation are both aspects of the way the spatialization of the whole can be understood. The ability of the visual performance of the work to push against the constraints of a fixed referential field of meaning combines with the phrase-by-phrase abstraction of the text to produce a work that is without parallel in its effects of distillation and resonance. While much of twentieth-century poetic activity owes a debt to Mallarméan poetics (and not merely visual poetics—though in this tradition Mallarmé is always a lurking reference), few poets actually attempted to extend the specific implications of Mallarmé's abstract visual and vocal form. It is above all *space*— with all the abstract, metaphysical associations of the French term *éspace*— that structures Mallarmé's text, not form or image. It is this spatial and conceptual abstraction—rather than any direct imitation of visual form— that resonates through later twentieth-century French poetry in the work of such writers as Maurice Blanchot, Claude Royet-Journoud, or Anne-Marie Albiach. By its historical priority and its uncompromising radicality, *Un Coup de dès* remains a critical reference for modern visual poetics.

Figural, Iconic, and Pictorial Work

The most obvious and established tradition of visual poetry is that of the shaped or iconic work. In the early twentieth century this form was given its modern cast in the vernacular language and quotidian image structures of Guillaume Apollinaire. Along with the lesser known Pierre Albert Birot, editor of the Paris journal *SIC* (*Sons-idées-couleurs*) published between 1916 and 1919), Apollinaire made shaped works with strong iconic referents (a poem in the form of a house, a rose, a still life, and so on) that were essentially pictorial in character. The anglophone counterpart to this work found its greatest degree of development in the works of e. e. cummings, which, like Apollinaire's *Calligrammes,* are instances of the performative potential of this particular visual form.[4] In such work, the textual values are read against the visual imprint of a shape whose referential frame inflects the entire text. When a verbal work resembles a schematic pictorial image, the verbal terms are always read in relation to that image as a referent. Snippets of text placed around a watch-face at the locations of the hours, for instance, in Apollinaire's "La Montre" ("The Watch"), gives them a specific twist ("la main" or "hand" occupies the place on the watch-face reserved for the numeral five, and so on). In an even more dynamic instance, "Il pleut" ("It's Raining"), the visual effect does more than merely emphasize the theme, it actually forces the reader to perform the reading according to a movement identical with the action of the rain—eyes running down the page following the rivulets of running letters on the page. This is a clearcut instance of visual performance, though one might readily subsume the discussion of the visual properties of these works—calligrammes and ideograms—under the general influence of the interest in synesthesia, and a desire to reinforce the properties of one medium with the properties of another.[5]

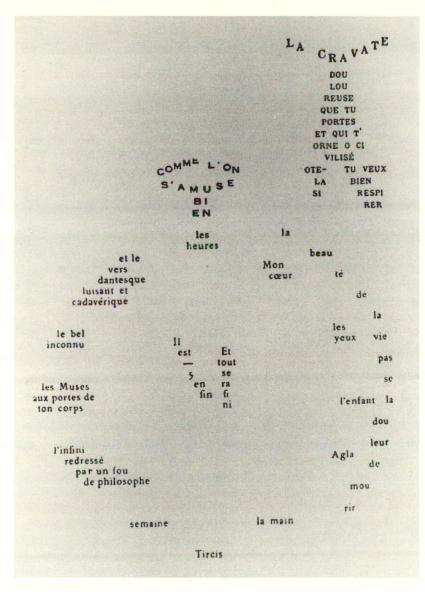

Figure 6.1 Guillaume Apollinaire, "La Montre," Calligrammes, Paris, 1918

The iconically referential poem-in-the-shape-of is not always so dynamic: its visual character is circumscribed by the image, which becomes an insistent framework for the reading of the poem. This is slightly different, however, from using the conventions of pictorial composition as a way of positioning elements of a visual poem in relation to each other on a page.

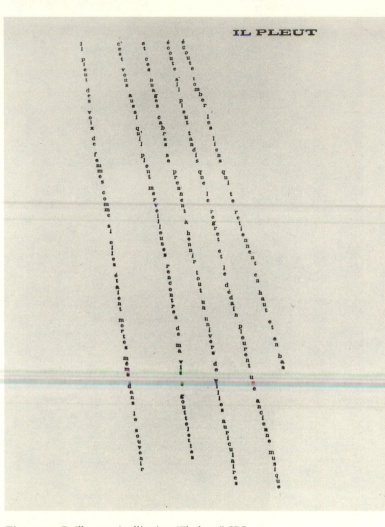

Figure 6.2 Guillaume Apollinaire, "Il pleut," SIC, 1916

There are several poems by Italian Futurist Filippo Marinetti, for instance, where he relies upon such conventions to structure a work.[6] "Bataille à neuf étages: Mont Altissimo" ("Battle at Nine Levels: Mount Altissimo") and "La Nuit, dans son lit, elle relisait . . ." ("At night, in her bed, she re-reads") are two such works.[7] Marinetti observes the spatial schema of representational painting: the foreground is at the bottom of a page, middle ground above, and the background is in the uppermost position as the words "rise" toward the top of the sheet. This arrangement is at odds with the conventions of top-to-bottom left-to-right reading practice, stressing the fact that here the verbal meaning is being made in relation to visual norms.

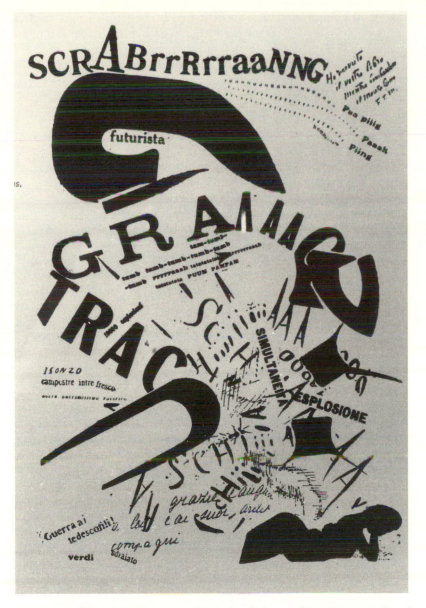

Figure 63 Filippo Marinetti, "At night, in her bed . . . ," Les Mots en liberté futuristes, Milan, 1919

In "At night . . ." the verbal material is onomatopoeic language, representing sounds, explosions, battle noises as if in the interior space of the woman's mental imagining. The poem doesn't represent the letter, but the reconceived and represented form of its contents—or even, perhaps, of the context of its composition. The work is highly theatrical; it is a staging or restaging of an ephemeral sound event that is given visual form as a pictorial image. There is no iconic form to which the image is reduced, though the title and the visual materials serve to circumscribe the referential field. There are many other instances of pictorially based visual poetics within Italian Futurism, each of which has its own particular characteristics, but all of which demonstrate the potential of poetics shaped in accord with such conventions.

Orchestral Verse: Dramatic Script and Musical Score

The idea that the poetic page can be constructed along the same lines as a musical score is an idea that has been rediscovered periodically and made use of by poets in various ways. The best known instance of such a strategy in the early twentieth century is the 1916 work of simultaneous poetry, "L'Amiral cherche une maison à louer" ("The admiral is looking for a house to rent"), written by Richard Huelsenbeck, Marcel Janco, and Tristan Tzara. It appeared in print in the pages of *Cabaret Voltaire* (Zurich, 1916), where its visual form clearly reveals its derivation from a combination of musical and dramatic formats: the work proceeds linearly, as in a score, and down the page, with the dramatis personae indicated in the left margin as in a performance script. Simultaneity is indicated by the placement of the three individual lines of text, each meant to be pronounced at the same moment as the others, and gaps in the vocalization are indicated by spaces between words, as in the progression of notes along a musical staff. But the most elaborate example of this orchestral verse exists in the little-known work of Ilia Zdanevich.

Zdanevich, known professionally as Iliazd, was a poet/printer who had participated in various avant-garde activites in St. Petersburg, Moscow, and Tiflis in the 1910s.[8] He integrated linguistic and typographic experiments in his own unique version of *zaum,* the transmental language created by various poets within the Russian avant-garde as a radical extension of poetic possibility in which the suggestive potential of language is realized through immediate effect rather than according to the norms of words and syntax. *Zaum* poems, particularly those of Iliazd's fellow *zaumniks* Alexei Krutchenyk and Velimir Khlebnikov, derived their chief impetus from convictions about the emotional and essential value of sound.[9] But Iliazd's concept of poetics always included a visual dimension and the five dramas that he wrote and printed between 1916 and 1923 are unique in the field of *zaum* works—first because of their length and sustained engagement and second because of the typographic elaboration that they received. Iliazd had worked in a print shop in his native Tiflis in the late 1910s, and his acquaintance with the technology of letterpress printing informed his typographic design and interwove this knowledge with his poetic practice.

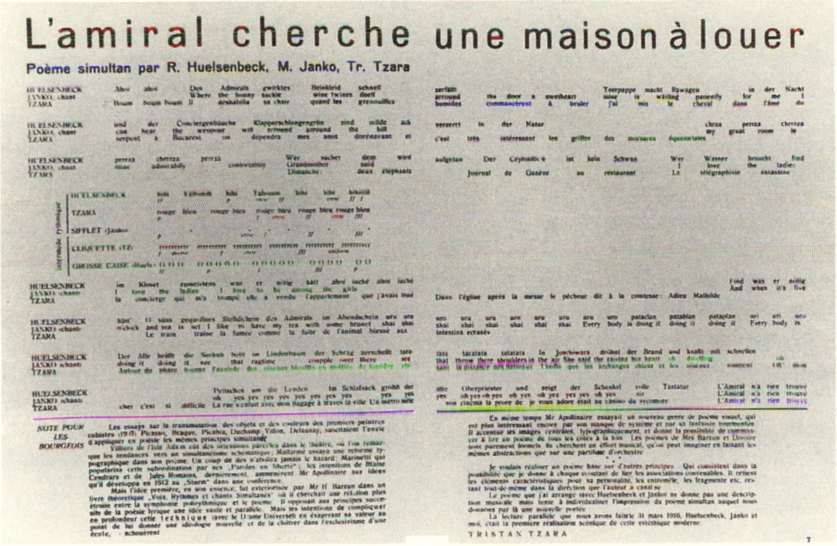

Figure 6.4 Richard Huelsenbeck, Tristan Tzara, Marcel Janco, "L'amiral cherche une maison à louer," Cabaret Voltaire, Zurich, 1916

Iliazd was clearly convinced that the page is a space of performance. He realized that actual live, staged performances of his esoteric works might be few and far between but that the book was an arena with its own theatricality. There is a clear progression in Iliazd's series of five plays. The earliest, *Janko, King of the Albanians,* most clearly resembled a script, with certain mild innovations in setting lines of speech against each other to indicate a chorus of simultaneous voices or assigning a place value to a particular character in a set sequence.[10] The last of the five plays, *Ledentu as Beacon,* exploited typographic possibilities for which there would be no performed oral equivalent: one cannot make letters into huge, page-sized characters out of typographic ornaments and expect that this has a specific correlation to a verbal rendering.[11] The visual quality of the typographic work had become a performance in its own right, meant to impact the eye through the expressive effect of the page.

This concept of orchestrating verbal language through visual means became a mainstay of experimental poetics in the twentieth century (in the work of Kurt Schwitters, Henri Chopin, John Cage, and Jackson Mac Low among many others)—in some cases working as a record of a performed piece, in some cases as its point of departure. Some of this work, such as Schwitters's *Ursonate,* was sound poetry which, like *zaum,* was propelled by a conviction about the effective power of verbal material.[12] Other scored works, like "L'Amiral," noted above, also contained conventional words and phrases, even if combined according to a Dada sensibility. In a more limited

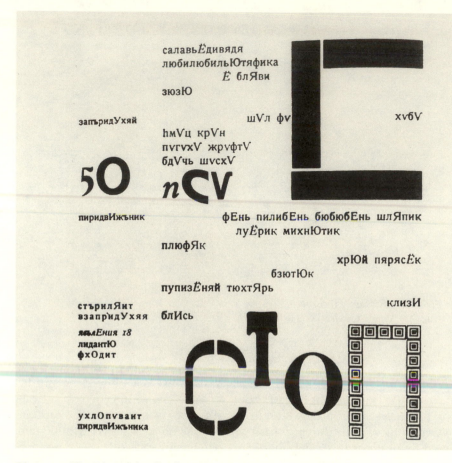

Figure 6.5 Ilia Zdanevich (Iliazd), Ledentu, *Paris, 1923*

but highly specific instance, Man Ray created "Major–Minor" in 1940, a "poem" consisting of schematic drawings of guitar chords on graph paper which have no other verbal message.

Expressive Visual Means: Typography, Calligraphy, Painting

Pieces whose visual features were neither iconic nor orchestral in nature made use of the visual effects of typography, calligraphy, painting, or collage in order to make works whose enactment is integral to their means. These are works that cannot be read according to any other convention— pictorial, literary, or musical. Such a treatment occurred in the pages of the short-lived vorticist publication *Blast* (London, 1914) whose display-face typography was meant to invoke an association with street handbills or posters of unions or workers' movements.[13] In the ransom-note typography used by Tristan Tzara in poems like "Boxe" or "Bulletin" (published in the pages of *Dada* in 1917 and 1918) the visual information of the typographic medium bears evidence of a social and cultural context which thus interpenetrates the poetic text. Traces of newspaper headlines, railway schedules, advertisements, and the like inflect Tzara's poetry with a quality of "found" language, whether produced mimetically or through actual appropriation. The effect of these is that the work is interlinked with a linguistic field, which is visually as well as verbally related to the larger domain of language use. In a performative sense, what is evidenced by such visual means is that poetic language is never a fully autonomous domain, never the isolated

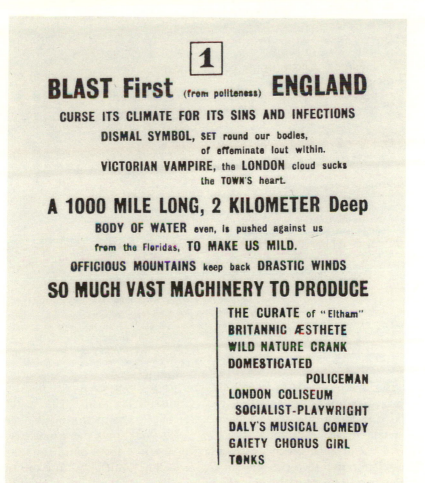

Figure 6.6 Wyndham Lewis, from Blast, *1914*

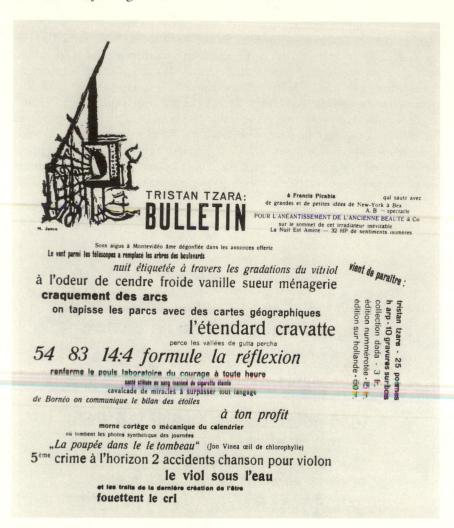

Figure 6.7 Tristan Tzara, "Bulletin," 1918

linguistic space outside of biography and history yearned for by the interpretive apparatus of, for instance, New Criticism. The visual value in these works does not reside in their invocation of a verbal performance—since any rendering of typographic style by a voice would be a mere mockery of style, a playful joke on the differences of one face from another—nor in their relation to a pictorial referent (there is none), but in the use of visual information as material in its own right. These are works that cannot be translated—either linguistically or typographically—without losing some essential value performed by the original work.

The same claim can be made for the works produced in the context of Italian Futurism by artists such as Giacomo Balla, Franceso Cangiullo, Carlo Carra, Fortunato Depero, Angelo Rognoni, Paolo Buzzi, and others—all of whom used the freedom offered by calligraphic or painterly means or compositional strategies available through the cut-and-paste techniques of collage. Circular poems, works of brilliant color, elaborate graphic spatialization and arrangement, changes of scale, typeface, size, and visual organization were conceived within the tenets of Marinetti's 1915 "Technical Manifesto of Futurist Literature." Freeing the word from its conventional constraints engaged these poets with a hybrid painterly poetics expressive of dynamic modernism in all its cacophonic visual form—reflecting the synaesthetic sensibility of Futurist poetry by engaging the visual means directly in the production of verbal works. In one Futurist poem after another the words are distributed to create an effect of movement and activity at odds with the conventional poetic page or traditional verse form.

The range of visual works within early-twentieth-century experimental poetics is not exhausted by this discussion, but the basic strategies according to which visual means were put at the service of poetry are fairly well covered by this enumeration of iconic, orchestral, and expressive works. The work of Hendrik Werkman, who in the 1920s created designs from typographic elements, extends this field, as do the painterly collages of the French cubists—but to the point where the term *poetry* seems to lose any useful specificity, however important it might be to consider the linguistic aspects of painterly practice in another framework. In modern poetry broadly considered—from the work of Ezra Pound and T. S. Eliot to Laura Riding, Gertrude Stein, e. e. cummings, William Carlos Williams, and others—the use of visual means within the conventions of verse form demonstrates an increased sensitivity to the possibilities for using spatial structure as an aspect of poetic expression in the modern period. The complexity and subtleties, as well as the huge scope, of a comprehensive discussion on such a topic is far outside my parameters here; see, however, the critical work of Susan Howe, Michael Davidson, Jerome McGann, Marjorie Perloff, and others, who have dealt extensively with these issues.[14]

There are also those idiosyncratic individuals for whom no suitable category can be articulated and whose contributions to visual poetics nonetheless are significant enough to require at least brief mention: Christian Morgenstern, whose "Fisches Nachtgesang" ("Fishes' Nightsong") of 1905, with its versified rows of dashes and brackets turned on their sides to resemble fish scales, displayed a resolution in form that exemplifies a performative visual poetics: there is no translation for a work whose integration of meaning and means is so well realized at the intersection of poetics and visuality. Vassily Kamensky created a major small opus, *Tango s korovami* (*Tango with Cows*) (Moscow, 1914), a work of what he termed ferro-concrete poetry. Produced as wild typographic innovations printed on wallpaper, it is, again, without significant precedent or imitators. Its typographic innovations have

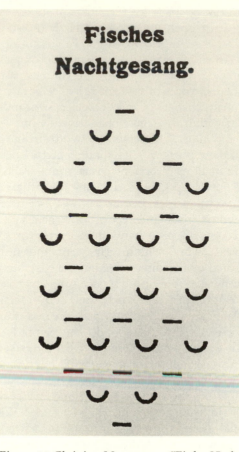

Figure 6.8 Christian Morgenstern, "Fisches Nachtge-sang," 1905

their echoes in the works of Dada poets, of Iliazd's *zaum* plays and various ephemeral works, and in certain instances of poetic typographics in the works of Vladimir Mayakovsky and Igor Terentiev from the same decade.[15] Finally, there are Francis Picabia's schematic mecanomorph works from the 1910s, which integrate suggestive fragments of visual form—usually indicated by a few sketchy lines showing a bit of screw threading, a hint of a gear, a mechanical post or joint—and words lettered into the design as a completion of its visual shape. The meaning of the words is in part related to their placement, their visual role of completing the image, which is in turn inflected by the texts, which cast its minimal forms into anthropomorphic and/or erotic frames of reference.

Surrealist writers and poets were considerably less interested in the vi-

Figure 6.9 Vassily Kamensky, Tango with Cows (Tango s korovami), *Moscow, 1914*

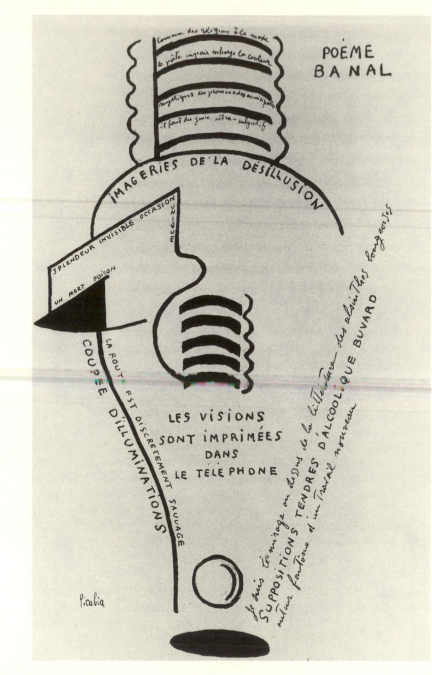

Figure 6.10 Francis Picabia, "Poème Banal," Paris, 1918

sual potential of language than their predecessors had been—and the association of certain kinds of conspicuous typographic experimentation with the earlier Dada and Futurist movements no doubt contributed to the Surrealist desire to differentiate the look of their publications from these earlier works. But there are exceptions: both Joan Miró and Max Ernst used visual and verbal means in expressive combination. Miró's paintings often contain poetic language rendered in a visually elaborate calligraphy. These are unique works, unrepeated elsewhere and gaining their full significance from the visual rendering—color, stroke, size, mass—as much as from the import of the language. Ernst's various collage experiments continued throughout his long career to blur the boundaries of visual/verbal distinctions in a manner consistent with that of the early Dada sensibility—also sustained across the full span of the work of Kurt Schwitters and Raoul Hausmann. But it is perhaps a single small work by Louis Aragon, which, for all its visual mutability (capacity to be reset in various typefaces without loss of meaning), contains the most succinct expression of the surrealist attitude towards the visual components of language. Titled "Suicide," Aragon's poem of the early 1920s consists of the letters of the alphabet spelled out in sequence.[16] It is the letters, not the sounds, of language that Aragon is condemning and being condemned by. The finitude and infinite possibility of the limited set indicates a dead-end for Surrealist engagement with visual poetics, a turning away from the typographics and collage manipulations of Dada and Futurist poets. The poem can read as a work about language in a general sense, but the fact that it is that it is the letters, those fundamental atomic particles of visual langauge that are the means by that the poem spells out its message, cannot be ignored.

Poetry of Unknown Words: *A Moment of Historical Reckoning*

In 1949 Iliazd published an anthology of experimental poetry from the early part of the twentieth century. Titled *Poésie de mots inconnus* (*Poetry of Unknown Words*), the volume contained works by twenty-one individuals, many of them canonical figures within the early avant-garde, such as Raoul Hausmann, Tristan Tzara, Igor Terentiev, Velimir Khlebnikov, Hugo Ball, Kurt Schwitters, and Pierre Albert-Birot.[17] It is the first attempt to put this work into anthologized form as a historical record. The anthology had been prompted by a series of contentious exchanges between Iliazd and the newly formulated Lettrist group whose originator and major spokesman, Isidore Isou, had stridently refused to acknowledge the existence of any precedents for his work. Appearing on the Paris scene in the years immediately following the end of the Second World War, the Romanian Isou had issued exaggerated and inflammatory statements claiming the originality of his Lettrist precepts. Iliazd had a double commitment to the recent history of experimental poetry—as a writer and as a printer/publisher—both of which he brought into play in this work.

Poésie de mots inconnus is both a recapitulation and a terminus point. It is a gauntlet thrown down against the possibility of amnesia, of historical erasure, eclipse, and forgetting, but it also marks, by its bid to establish a historical record, an exhaustion of certain possibilities, their passing into history and out of practice. Iliazd was uniquely qualified to create such an anthology: he had personally known almost all of the figures whose work he presented, he had participated in and witnessed firsthand the evolution of experimental poetics in Futurist and Dada circles in Russia and Europe, and he had a relentless drive toward establishing an accurate historical record of the achievements of his peers and contemporaries. That the Lettrist Isou wished to ignore that history and easily could have, given its relative invisibility at mid-century, is symptomatic of the status of radical poetic experimentation. Iliazd's project was conceived at a crucial moment of transformation from early avant-garde activity to what has to be characterized as the neo-avant-garde. By the late 1940s, the earlier impulses of radical experimentation had become exhausted without becoming canonized and the latter-day extensions of poetic innovation were proceeding along lines that depended upon and reworked earlier activity without necessarily referencing it in any explicit way. Iliazd's anthology served to fix a set of canonical references for ongoing experiment within a twentieth-century framework. The obvious paradox is that the concept of experiment and innovation was never supposed to fix itself into a tradition—but to have the prodigious output of experimentalism ignored served as an impetus for Iliazd to overcome his reservations in that regard.

The distinct visual character in which Iliazd cast each poem and its accompanying image (produced by a group of artists of equally canonical stature, including Matisse, Chagall, Arp, Braque, Picasso, Metzinger, Giacometti), gives these pieces a format that was not necessarily an aspect of the author's original work. The visual performances of works in this volume are the result of Iliazd's work as designer, printer, anthologizer—they are editorial recastings of each poem. Page by page this anthology is varied, innovative, and visually distinct: but the vision is, in its own way, as standardized as that of a Norton anthology—imposed as an editorial prerogative in the name of foregrounding and preserving the individual features of the works. Iliazd used a single typeface throughout, a sans-serif face called Baton, which was to his eye a neutral face, basically modern in style. It is in the format of each work that their distinctions were given graphic emphasis by Iliazd. He considered the format of each poem individually, overprinting and interlining red and black lines in order to create visual effects, shaping text blocks on the page, making patterns of columns of type, letters, words, and so on—some of which was meant to reinforce sound values, some of which was primarily a matter of visual expression. The one exception to this treatment is a work by Hausmann, a well-known typographic Dada piece from 1918. This single exception is useful because it allows for a discussion of the contrast that this one piece offers to the rest of the anthology.

Visual Performativity: Hausmann's "Original"

The idea of visual performativity derives from the conviction that there is a form of poetry that inheres in visual means that cannot be reproduced in another visual format without destroying the work or radically altering its signification producing qualities. One must distinguish between the idea of a "treatment"—that is, a rendering in visual form that inflects a particular work—and the idea of a visuality of form that is original with and integral to a particular work. The bulk of the poems in Iliazd's anthology have been subjected to a treatment, they have been rendered—sympathetically, but according to Iliazd's inclination, just as in any other kind of performance. The effect is no different in essence from that of a reading or a musician's specific enactment of a scored work. The treatment gives an expressive inflection to the poems, but never becomes an integral feature of the works— it is not a necessary and significant aspect of each piece from its inception and creation. This treatment is an aspect of all on-the-page performances of poetic works: from the violences rendered through standardization in anthologies to the misrepresentations of poetic manuscript in print form to the careful and judicious selection of typeface or format in the presentation of a poet's work and so forth.

But the work that Hausmann presents and which Iliazd then represents is one in which visual performativity is original to the work's conception and execution, thus making it a primary aspect of the poetic expression rather than an inflection. The poem is a reprint of a 1918 broadside that contained two lines of letters printed from headline-sized wood type. The impression in the original is somewhat uneven, the result of different pressure exerted by worn type as it comes into contact with the inking rollers and with the sheet of paper over the surface of either a platen or an impression cylinder on the printing press. The poem is comprised of two lines of lowercase letters: "fmsbwtözäu / pggiv-..?mü." The type is a slab-serif of the sort developed in the nineteenth century for advertising use in broadsides, handbills, and posters, meant to attract attention through visual novelty. Though no longer a novelty by 1918, the face has a distinct identity as an advertising face: it was associated with publicity and commercial venues rather than with literary modes of expression. As is the case with many Dada works, this poem bears distinct traces of a public and even commercial linguistic frame of reference.

In making the transformation from the original image to the anthologized version, Iliazd chose to recast the poem in the lowercase letters of the Baton face he was using in majuscule for the rest of the book. This decision allowed Hausmann's piece to occupy a conspicuous place within the anthol-

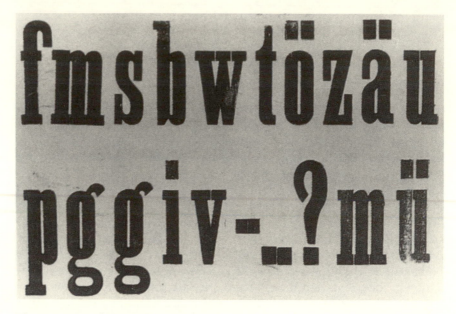

Figure 6.11 Raoul Hausmann, "fmsbwtözäu," 1918

ogy. Every other poem in the collection was accompanied by an image, sometimes by the same author/artist, and most frequently by an artist selected to complement the work. Hausmann's page has no other image— it contains a second poem, "Cauchemar" ("Nightmare"), a sound work from the late 1930s (it bears the date 1938–1946 on the page). But the re-printed "fmsb . . . " holds the place of an image, it in fact *is* an image in its status within the anthology as a whole. The recasting in new type was perhaps in part an expedient, since finding the original wood or making a metal plate from an image of the poster would have had technical and logis-tical difficulties (though it should be noted that since every other image in this anthology has its own technical history and that the anthology com-prises a survey of printing possibilities from linoleum block to woodcut to etching, lithography, and engraving, technical challenges were clearly not a factor in Iliazd's decision about the Hausmann). More likely, Iliazd found the visual effect of these large-scale letters effective and got satisfaction from the fact that they closely resembled the original printed version while dif-fering from it sufficiently to provide a typographic connection to his an-thology.

In setting Hausmann's piece in its respectful version of the original, Iliazd quotes the original visual instantiation of a work that exemplifies the complexity of Hausmann's approach to poetic experiment: the often blurred line between visual and verbal aspects of expression. The piece has no evi-dent linguistic value, but it does have an expressive effect—one that is

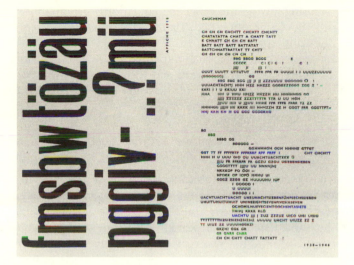

Figure 6.12 Raoul Hausmann's "fmsbwtözäu," reset in Poésie des mots inconnus, *edited and designed by Ilia Zdanevich (Iliazd), 1949*

equally available whether "read" or "heard." In a famous self-portrait collage of 1923, *ABCD,* Hausmann pictured his face surrounded by fragments of type, collaged visuals, his name, the word *Merz* and other obviously Dadaesque elements. Clenched between his teeth are the first four letters of the alphabet (in Bodoni majuscules) and from them emanates a stream of cosmic dust. Hausmann's use of the letters—which are quintessentially visual signs, not vocal ones—as the image of speech, of language produced in and by the mouth—conflates the two domains of the visual and verbal. The confusion that Hausmann allowed into his work seems like a self-conscious engagement with this apparent ambiguity and Iliazd's re-presentation of "fmsb . . ." as an "image" in his *Poésie* anthology shifts the balance toward the visuality of this work, its dependence upon visual effects for expressive impact, rather than its expectation of a vocal rendition.

An investigation of visual poetics could be developed simply by following the work of Iliazd—from his early *zaum* typographic work of the 1910s and 20s to the book projects that occupied him until his death in 1975. In each of these works, early or late, Iliazd created with the idea of the letter, the page, and the book as visual forms in their entirety. Whether turning letters on their sides, as in *Le Courtisan grotesque* (*The Grotesque Courtesan*),[18] where this gesture is meant to call attention to the verbal puns in the original text of the seventeenth-century author, Adrian de Monluc, or shaping the words to echo the compositional vectors in Hausmann's woodcuts, as in *Poèmes et bois* (*Poems and Woodcuts*), or disposing letters into a graceful drift down the vertical axis of the page in Paul Eluard's *Un Soupçon*

(*A Hint*), or using any of the other manipulations of typography he used in creating the books he published, Iliazd was consistently attentive to the page as a theatrical space for the visual performance of the word. While Iliazd's work can easily support such a focused reading, his practice continued to be concerned with visual form and format, and in the decades after mid-century, this is only one aspect of the wider field of visual performances on the poetic page.

Visual Formalisms: Lettrism and Concretism

Theoretical considerations and critical precepts about the ways in which visuality functioned as an aspect of poetics were explicitly articulated by both Concrete poets and the Lettrists, the two most conspicuous nodes of visual poetics in the immediate postwar period. While one could argue that Marinetti's "Technical Manifesto" was equally prescriptive, his was never a theory of poetics per se—but rather a set of guidelines for bringing formal expression into line with a general Futurist aesthetics of speed and dynamism. Marinetti gave instructions for the transformation of visual outcome, not for the creation of poetry through visual performance. For both the Lettrists and Concretists, visuality was an integral aspect of poetic conceptualization. Both Concretism (narrowly defined here as that work which is explicitly associated with those poets who self-identified the term in either Brazilian or German/Swiss contexts) and Lettrism have to be seen as the final extension of modernism—with counterparts in the visual arts, in literature, and in literary and artistic criticism at mid-century.

Lettrism: The Illegible Sign

The major tenets of Isidore Isou's Lettrism were most fully realized in visual form by his associates and followers, such as Maurice Lemaître, Gabriel Pomerand, and Roland Sabatier.[19] Isou's precepts involved both a revamping of poetic conception and a megalomaniacal theory of literary history in which Lettrism was to serve as the fulcrum point for surpassing the entire Western tradition. Lettrism required the reduction of language to its atomistic particulars, letters, which were to function as the fundamental signifying units of a poetic form that was visual and verbal simultaneously (in later extensions, also olfactory, tactile, conceptual, and immaterial, in accord with Isou and Lemaître's critical claims of the moment). The visual signs used in Lettrist works were not merely letters in the pedestrian sense of the elements of the alphabetic system, but also included calligraphed marks, suggestive glyphic signs with esoteric meaning, personal hieroglyphic symbols, rebus-like poetic compositions using graphic elements that were in fact small schematic drawings—in short, a wide vocabulary of visual marks whose unifying feature was their graphic discreteness, their autonomy as signs.

Legibility was not the foremost feature of Lettrist works, quite the contrary, and for all that Isou was an able publicist, keenly aware of emergent forms of popular culture and culture industry activity in the 1950s, and though he modeled himself and his public persona on that of American rock stars, his aesthetic sensibility was avant-garde: esoteric, difficult, resistant to easy consumption. In fact, Lettrist work is fundamentally *illegible*, dependent on strategies of encoding, translation from one set of signs to another, or the creation of idiosyncratic sign systems. The contradictions of the movement are many, its inherent paradoxes stretched between the exaggerated claims mounted by Isou and the resistant difficulty of its realized works, but as a form of visual performance in the poetic vein, it exemplifies a curious terminus point for certain modern precepts. Chiefly, these are the aspirations for a formal visuality in which meaning is both pure and apparent, distilled and potent, reduced and available. The Lettrists aspired to the avant-garde agenda of radical transformation (with both social and aesthetic implications) through the remaking of the symbolic order of language at the level of the sign. Taking this literally, Isou attached an arcane, even kabalistic, value to the power of the individual mark: even the terms "atomistic" or "elemental" are words burdened with occult associations. Visual forms were the primary mode of poetic production in Lettrist work: but the illegible signs occluded meaning, retaining the fascination for the eye, trapping the viewer in dense mazes and fields of marks articulated across surfaces (and also on objects, clothing, walls, etc.) in a perverse exaggeration of modern form for form's sake, as in an example of a page from Lemaître's "Roman hypergraphique" ("Hypergraphic Novel").[20] There is no transcendence out of Lettrism except through a mystical leap of faith, and the formal beauty of the work stages a performance at the level of surface, but rarely at the level of meaning. Isou succeeded in his goal of pulverizing language, in destroying its capacity for communication or even expression, but the result is merely a termination rather than a point of departure for any further investigation of visual performativity.

Concretism: Reduction and Reference

Concrete poetry also extends modern precepts of avant-garde radicality and formal innovation, but with very different consequences from those of the Lettrists. While Lettrism becomes closed into its visual forms, unable to move beyond the sign to meaning (almost unable to fix a relation between the manifest signifier of the glyph and a conceptual signified value), Concrete poetry attempts to unite these aspects of the sign according to reductive principles that forged meaning through visual, material facticity, as a performed presencing of meaning in the formal work. Rarely has such intense concentration been put on integating the visual form and the meaning of a work. Signifier and signified are to be as isomorphic as possible— that is, to be as close in their form/meaning connection as they can be

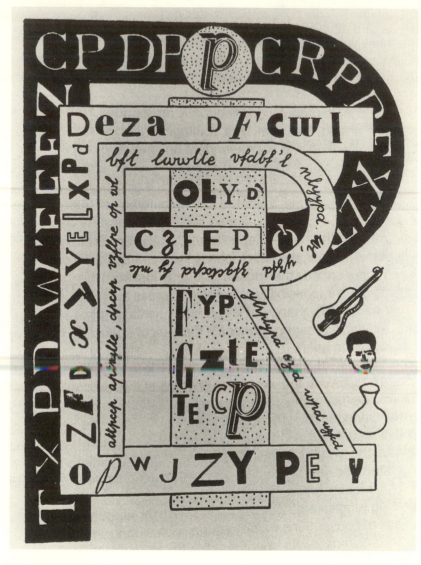

Figure 6.13 Maurice Lemaître, "Roman hypergraphique," Canailles, Paris, 1964

within the limits of visual and verbal modes of expression. If Lettrist work took the modern formal investigation of the visual properties of the sign to one extreme—to its resonant impenetrability and irreducibility to anything but its presence as visual form—then Concretism took modern form to its other extreme—to a search for reductive certainty in which visual enactment was to be the same as verbal signification. Eugen Gomringer's canonical work, "Silencio" ("Silence") from 1954, in which a grid is comprised entirely of columns repeating this word in order to describe a space at its center—the space of silence as the place without language—exemplifies this unity. Poetic form makes meaning through a fusion of visual and verbal means.[21]

The rigorously articulated precepts of Concretism that emerge in several distinct geographical and cultural sites in the post-1945 period make its initial character relatively easy to describe—and its visual means relatively easy to characterize. In two major centers of activity, in Germany and in Brazil, poets working simultaneously and originally without knowledge or contact with each others' work, arrived at a concept of Concrete poetics. Neither group was without a corollary interest in sound poetry, and as in so many instances in twentieth-century art, the engagement with radical innovation led to the exploration of many avenues of experiment simultaneously. The Concretism of the Brazilian Noigandres group derived in part from the work of Ezra Pound and his interest in the condensed image of the poem as an ideograph: word/image/idea all conflated into a single unit of poetic expression. Working within the modern literary tradition, Augusto and Haroldo de Campos and Decio Pignatari also reflected an awareness of the density of visual/verbal materials that were offered in contemporary life in the form of advertising signs, commercial and public language in daily urban experience and media exposure, as in Pignatari's oft-cited "Bebe coca-cola" (1957). These elements were largely repressed in Lettrist work as well as in some other forms of visual experimentalism in which the language is imagistic and descriptive rather than suggestive of cultural context. In Concrete poetry, visual performance *is* the work; though in many cases a verbal performance is linked to the visual form, it does not use the work as a score but rather attempts a synesthetic parallel rendering in the other medium. A striking instance of such work is Augusto de Campos's *Poemobiles*, a book in which each turning contains a folded and cut element on which there is

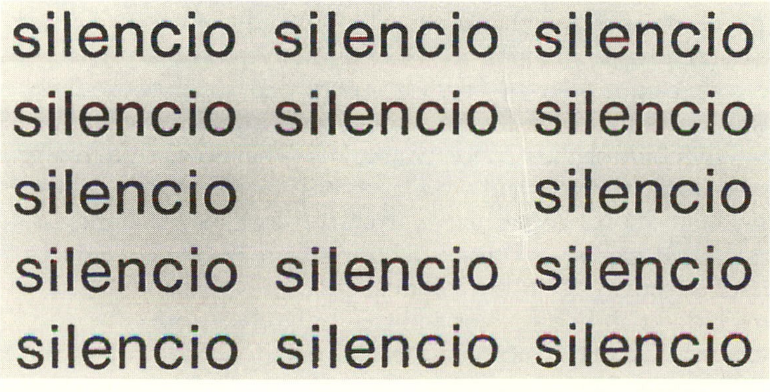

Figure 6.14 Eugen Gomringer, "Silencio," 1954

printed a word that changes, as the book opens, to reveal a second word.[22] The interlocking of the words and the dynamic movement within the pages *is* the dramatic mobility of the poems—the works don't merely refer to or thematically invoke the concept.

The German/Swiss Concretists such as Eugen Gomringer and Max Bense extended certain features of formal visual modernism, specifically those articulated in the work and writings of Max Bill, into a poetics of self-sufficient formalism with its emphasis on purity of means. While this is obviously related to the work of the Brazilians, its conceptual field is more tightly focused, and its premise of belief more clearly focused on making meaning begin and end in the visual performance of the work rather than resonate with a larger and more esoteric referential field (as is the case with the work of the Brazilians). The bounded space of the page as a self-sufficient field for production of meaning is frequently evident as a feature of Gomringer's work, as in "Silencio," mentioned above. The most conspicuous feature of Concretism is its conviction that the visual form of the work can and does anchor its meaning in the visual performance on the page, and that the integration of structure and linguistic value are so complete that they cannot be separated even for the sake of analysis, let alone be "translated" into another form. While other visual poets from the 1960s onward would reinvest in iconic and figural work (John Furnival, for example), in collage practices (Nanni Balestrini, Eugenio Maccini), or in structural format as expressive means (Emmett Williams, Adriano Spatola), these Brazilian and European Concrete poets were clearly extending modern poetics from both Anglo-American traditions and European symbolism into an abstract poetic performance in which meaning was not reducible to an image but was utterly integral with its visual form.

Reconceptualization of Visual Performance as Process

But the most significant transformation in the integration of visual means with poetic composition that occurred after mid-century is the shift from attention to *form* to attention to *process* and *concept* as the primary force of poetic composition. For all of their variety and sophistication, the visual poems of early- to mid-twentieth century were conceived with form as the primary endpoint of their conceptualization. This holds true to a great extent even in the sketches and working notes for the works—which exhibit strong compositional arrangements from the start, whether they are iconic images, scored works, or collages whose formal resolution displays a high degree of sensitivity to such traditional concerns as balance, mass, rhythm, patterns of light and dark, color and weight, and so forth.

But two directions emerge in the later decades of the twentieth century that differentiate themselves in fundamental ways from this modernist, formal sensibility. The first is an emphasis on concept, on idea, as the primary way to motivate the visual outcome of a work and the second is the notion of composition as process. These two are intimately related, since in both cases the form of a work is a direct result of the act of making. It is the making, the performance of the work, that becomes the visual/verbal manifestation of the piece. This basis in concept and process is the foundation of much literary and artistic activity from the 1960s onward. This work initiated under the influence of John Cage, Charles Olson, and Marcel Duchamp, and is manifest in the work of contemporary figures such as Henri Chopin and Bernard Heidsieck, Italian sound-performance poets, and American, European, and Japanese poets involved with the intermedia activities associated with Fluxus and so forth. In such work light and sound displays, photographic manipulations, and all manner of work in which performance is process, demonstrate that composition is procedural, and the recorded trace of the activity makes a poetic composition. Raymond Hains's poems reflected in rippled surfaces and rephotographed; Hansjorg Mayer's progressive "poems" of overprinted letters in his *alphabetenquadratbuch;* and Jackson Mac Low's carefully constructed poems as potential performance scores, such as the "Gatha" series, are all 1960s examples of this shift in sensibility.[23]

While it may be a generalization, this assertion nonetheless explains the differences between those works that continue the aesthetics of early-twentieth-century compositions and those later twentieth-century works that participate in a more process-based sensibility. This is a distinction between a formalist modern poetics in which visuality is confidently and self-consciously present on the page, and a late-century poetics in which visual means are a record of activity and evidence of something having occurred and/or a basis for a performance in which the making of the work is really new and specific in each instance (as in the case of Mac Low). The difference between reading Apollinaire's "Il pleut" and a Mac Low "Gatha" is the difference between the performance of a fixed script and a performance of an open-structure script—the first reading can only be a treatment, an inflection, while the second actually requires an act of making a work anew each time. Even where the works appear on the page as their final destination and are not meant as the basis of a live performance, a similar contrast exists. One has only to think of the wandering lines of Ana Hatherly's elegant poetic structures, interweaving as she writes them across a sheet like so many genealogical threads knotting and unknotting in the production of the work, and contrast it to the organized spaces of Huelsenbeck, Janco, and Tzara's orchestrated simultaneous poem for this distinction to become vividly evident. Hatherly's "História da poesia: poeta chama poeta" (1989) has a form that could not be made to "fit" a set of verbal elements—its organic form is testimonial evidence of its making—it displays its own history as process in the final outcome.

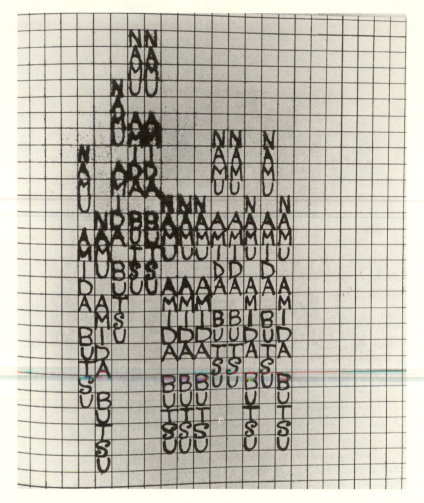

Figure 6.15 Jackson MacLow, "2nd Gatha," from "The 21 Nams Amida Butsu Gathas," 1961

The work of late-twentieth-century poets for whom visual performance is integral to their work divides along these lines—into those who continue the formalist investigations of an earlier modern aesthetic and those for whom the processes of composition structure the work as it comes into being in a performance on the page. One could even stress this distinction through a contrast of phrase as "the work performed" versus the "work in performance," in which the emphasis in the first case is on arriving at form as instantiation and enactment of the poetic work and in the second case is on performing a work within visual means that are always coming into form through the process of poetic composition itself. In the first group one

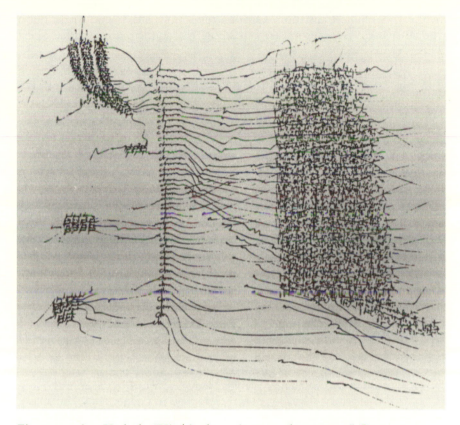

Figure 6.16 Ana Hatherly, "História da poesia: poeta chama poeta," Concreta experimental visual poesia portuguesa 1959–89, *1989*

might find such figures as Ian Hamilton Finlay, certain works by Ilse and Pierre Garnier, and Oyvind Fahlström, while the bulk of well-known names of more recent decades would belong to the second, no matter how diverse their poetic enterprise is in other respects: Emmett Williams, John Furnival, Carl Andre, Steve McCaffery, George Brecht, Alison Knowles, Brion Gysin, Bernard Heidsieck, and so on.[24]

The visual properties of a written work carry value, whether that value is directly translatable into linguistic or semantic equivalents or not. This is the effect of expressive means, the optically perceptible information of material form whose impact varies from insignificantly incidental (merely bearing some trace of the historical circumstances of production) to manifestly integral to the work (the very stuff of the piece itself, inseparable from every aspect of its poetic function). Such materiality is never an excess, never a surplus, never an addition to the work. It is the performative instantiation of the work, its condition of being as a thing, a piece. Each successful treatment (typographic translation, version) reinscribes any poetic work, but a work that uses visual means as its material makes these an essential aspect of its very existence as a poem.

Whether the work on the page is meant for performance—a rendition in vocal presentation—or whether the page is conceived of as the site of the performance of the work, the nature of visual performativity remains the same: an instance of expressive means creating effect without direct connection to the presence of the artist, a performance in which the performer is the visual form. Part of the fascination of hearing poetry read resides in the resonant presence of the poet, the sense of auratic selfhood, of an apparent and apprehendable person in the work, which is available for the audience as an aspect of the piece. One looks at the poet, or listens to the timbre and the somatic aspects of the voice, trying to extract from its particulars the compelling quality of the poet's presence. The visual mode of performance replaces that particular satisfaction with another—the possibility of staring at the word, the work, and elucidating from it an effective value which may not be containable within the linguistic parameters of meaning production and yet cannot be conceived of without them. There is a presencing and a performance, but it is not the poet or reader that offers an object of scopic fascination, but the poem—with all of its visually performative features.

NOTES

1. *Poésure et peintrie,* exhibition catalog (Marseilles: Musées de Marseilles, 1993).

2. Herbert Spencer, *Pioneers of Modern Typography* (London: Lund Humphrey, 1969), and Johanna Drucker, *The Visible Word* (Chicago: University of Chicago Press, 1994).

3. Jerome McGann, *Black Riders* (Princeton: Princeton University Press, 1993).

4. Guillaume Apollinaire, *Calligrammes* (Paris: Mercure de France, 1918). e. e. cummings, *Complete Poems 1904–1962,* edited by George J. Firmage (New York: Liveright, 1991).

5. Timothy Mathews, *Reading Apollinaire* (Manchester: Manchester University Press, 1987), Willard Bohn, *The Aesthetics of Visual Poetry* (Cambridge: Cambridge University Press, 1986), and David Seaman, *Concrete Poetry in France* (Ann Arbor: UMI Research Press, 1981).

6. Giovanni Lista, *Futurisme* (Paris: L'Age d'homme, 1973).

7. Both were published in Marinetti's *Les Mots en liberté futuristes* (Milan: Edizioni Futuriste de Poesia, 1919).

8. *Iliazd,* exhibition catalog (Paris: Musée National d'Art Moderne, 1978).

9. Vladimir Markov, *Russian Futurism* (Berkeley: University of California Press, 1964).

10. Ilia Zdanevich, *Janko, King of the Albanians* (Tiflis: 41 Degrees, 1916).

11. Ilia Zdanevich, *Ledentu as Beacon* (Paris: 41 Degrees, 1923).

12. Kurt Schwitters, *Ursonate* (Hannover: Merzverlag, 1932); there is also a Wergo CD version of this (Mainz, 1993).

13. Marjorie Perloff, *The Futurist Moment* (Chicago: University of Chicago Press, 1986).

14. Susan Howe, *My Emily Dickinson* (Berkeley: North Atlantic Books, 1985); Michael Davidson, "Le Texte materialisé dans la poésie anglo-américaine," *Poésure et peintrie*, pp. 218–27; "Palimtexts: Postmodern Poetry and the Material Text," *Genre*, vol. 20 (fall–winter 1987), pp. 307–28; Maggie Gilchrist, "Des ailes d'ange, une queue de souris, une dose de vitupération et la concrétisation de la poésie anglo-saxonne," *Poésure et peintrie* pp. 228–37; Jerome McGann, *Black Riders;* Marjorie Perloff, *Radical Artifice* (Chicago: University of Chicago Press, 1991).

15. Gerald Janacek, *The Look of Russian Literature* (Princeton: Princeton University Press, 1984), and Susan Compton, *World Backwards: Russian Futurist Books, 1912–1916* (London: British Museum, 1978).

16. Louis Aragon, *Le Mouvement perpétuel* (Paris: Gallimard, 1925).

17. Ilia Zdanevich, ed., *Poetry of Unknown Words* (Paris: 41 Degrees, 1949).

18. Adrian de Monluc, *Le Courtisan grotesque* (Paris: 41 Degrees, 1974); Raoul Hausmann, *Poèmes et bois* (Paris: 41 Degrees, 1961); Paul Eluard's *Un Soupçon* (Paris: 41 Degrees, 1965).

19. Jean-Paul Curtay, *Letterism and Hypergraphics* (New York: Franklin Furnace, 1985).

20. Maurice Lemaître, "Roman hypergraphique," *Canailles* (Paris: Centre de Creativité, 1964).

21. Eugen Gomringer, "Silencio," in Mary Ellen Solt, *Concrete Poetry: A World View* (Bloomington: Indiana University Press; London: Hispanic Arts, 1968).

22. Augusto de Campos and Julio Plaza, *Poemobiles* (São Paolo: Brasiliense, 1984).

23. Emmett Williams, *An Anthology of Concrete Poetry* (New York: Something Else Press, 1967); Stephan Bann, *Concrete Poetry, an International Anthology* (London: Magazine Editions, 1967).

24. See Caroline Bayard, *New Poetics in Canada and Quebec: From Concretism to Post-Modernism* (Toronto: University of Toronto Press, 1989) on the Canadian poets; Eric Vos, ed., *Experimental—Visual—Concrete: Avant-Garde Poetry since the 1960s*, Avant Garde Critical Studies (Amsterdam: Rodopi, 1997).

7

Voice in Extremis

STEVE McCAFFERY

There is no such thing as a neutral voice, a voice
without desire, a voice that does not desire me.
If there was, it would be an experience of absolute terror.

RÉGIS DURAND

[The] rigor of performance [is] engaged with what
memory wants to forget.

HERBERT BLAU

The ear, observes Michel de Certeau, "is the delicate skin caressed or irritated by sound: an erogenous zone, exacerbated, so to speak, by the interdictions which banish from language and good manners, coarseness, vulgarity and finally passions."[1] How then to define the ear's most intimate lover—the voice? Régis Durand demonstrates the volatility of voice as a cultural and psychoanalytic concept positioned between reality and representation, and functioning as both a metaphorical support of pure time and a physical production.[2] Writing comes into being through the midwifery of fingers and a trained competence with encoded incisions. But in order to reach Certeau's erogenous zone, human sound, like human birth, must pass from a cavity through a hole dilated under pressure. Indeed, "voice" is an inadequate term to describe the full workings of this organ concept, and Certeau's definition of it as "a sign of the body that comes and speaks" factors out the complex buccal and respiratory labor essential to its functioning, and thus proves insufficient.[3] Voice is a polis of mouth, lips, teeth, tongue, tonsils, palette, breath, rhythm, timbre, and sound. Less a component than a production of a materiopneumatic assemblage of interacting bone, liquid, cartilage, and tissue. Enjoying such complexity even a single voice resonates as a simultaneity of corporeal, acoustic events; the consequence of energy and respiratory force in flight through fixed cavities and adjustable tensors.

The twentieth century presents two distinct scenarios for the voice in poetry. One is a primal identity, culturally empowered to define the property of person. This is a phenomenological voice that serves in its self-evidence as the unquestionable guarantee of presence—when heard and understood through its communication of intelligible sounds this voice is named conscience.[4] The other scenario—renegade and heterological—requires the voice's primary drive to be persistently away from presence. This second is a thanatic voice triply destined to lines of flight and escape, to the expenditure of pulsional intensities, and to its own dispersal in sounds between body and language. Aspects of this second scenario are traced in this paper as the *adventure* of voice from the rebellious and jubilant pyrotechnics of early modernism, through its bigamous encounter with two graphisms, to its failure in the 1970s to establish the poem as community.

Barthes is responsible for introducing into theories of the voice the concept of granularity. Rhapsodizing on the paralinguistic effects of that vocal modification, as an amorous entwining of timbre and language whose aim, we are assured, "is not the clarity of messages," but the blissful search for "pulsional incidents, the language lined with flesh, a text where we can hear the grain of the throat, the patina of consonants, the voluptuousness of vowels, a whole carnal stereophony: the articulation of the body, of the tongue, not that of meaning, of language."[5] Despite Barthes's consummate rhetoric, this attempt to emancipate voice from code succeeds no further than a repositioning of the existing relationship. Language, signification, and code are certainly corporealized—Barthes is emphatic in this claim—yet voice, empowered by this embodiment, is still not freed from language. A voice outside of language? Blanchot offers a tremulous hint of such a siting in what he terms the "neutral" voice; a voice in intransigent nonidentification with a self.[6]

Let us trace a similar dynamic in that protracted cultural irregularity, the twentieth-century sound poem, emerging in the late nineteenth and early twentieth centuries as an uncompromising effort at abstraction; its primary goal being the liberation and promotion of the phonetic and sub-phonetic features of language to the state of a *materia prima* for creative, subversive endeavours.[7] Mike Weaver describes the modus operandi of this poetry as that of "the figure (sound) [rising] off the ground (silence) producing a configuration of filled time against emptied time."[8] This emphasis on the sound poem's temporality had already been emphasized by the Dada poet Raoul Hausmann when claiming his own "optophonetic" poetry to be "an act consisting of respiratory and auditive combinations, firmly tied to a unit of duration."[9]

Hugo Ball's *Lautgedichte* or poetry without words possessed a more mantic base. "In these phonetic poems," claims Ball, "we totally renounce the language that journalism has abused and corrupted. We must return to the innermost alchemy of the word, we must even give up the word too, to keep poetry for its last and holiest refuge."[10] Ball celebrates these aspirations realized in a journal entry for 18 June 1916. "We have now driven the plasticity of the word to the point where it can scarcely be equalled. We achieved this at the expense of the rational, logically constructed sentence . . . We have loaded the word with strengths and energies that helped us to rediscover the evangelical concept of the 'word' (logos) as a magical complex image" (Ball, 68). These desires are, to say the least, paradoxical: a quest through a "poetry *without* words" in order to obtain the word's innermost alchemy. However, Ball's interior verbal transmutations do approximate those undertakings of linguistic delirium noted by Foucault in Brisset—"to restore words to the noises that gave birth to words, and to reanimate the gestures, assaults and violences of which words stand as the now silent blazons."[11]

In their experimental *zaum* or "transrational language," the Russian Futurists Khlebnikov and Kruchenykh grant a similar autonomous value to sound—an independence endorsed and scientifically scrutinized by the Russian Formalists. Yet even a cursory glance at their theoretical statements and manifestos makes it clear that the voice's emancipation is at most a coincidental achievement and not *zaum*'s central concern. Markov suggests that much *zaum* was written as a conscious imitation of foreign linguistic sounds,[12] a claim endorsed by Kruchenykh when he describes his own *proto zaum* texts as verbal constructs whose words "do not have a definite meaning" (quoted in Markov, 44). The target of Kruchenykh's attack is not the word as such but the word's semantic and grammatical subordination to meaning.

For all their subversive accomplishments, Dada and Futurist sound poems fail to escape an ultimate organization by the signifier. Ball's verse without words, for instance, is testimony to the omnipresent possibility, in cacophony and gibberish, of language returning in either recognizable words or a comprehensible "syntax" suggestive of an unknown language. The xenoglossic evocations in Ball's and Kruchenykh's poems conjure up a sense of texts whose meanings are inherent, but defiant of comprehension. The consequence to vocality is that voice retains its quality as ontologic presence with the mandate to communicate at least a semantic suggestion. To link Ball's poetry without words and *zaum* to cross-cultural glossolalia or to the Jewish automatic speech known as "maggidism" is thus a natural temptation. For speaking in tongues, *zaum*, and the Dada sound poem commonly retain the simulacra of a semiosis.

Certeau describes the experience of such heteroglossia as "voices" haunting a plurality of boundaries and interstices. "The voice moves, in effect, in a space between the body and language, but only in a moment of passage from one to the other and as if *in* their weakest difference . . . The body, which is a thickening and an obfuscation of phonemes, is not yet the death of language. The articulation of signifiers is stirred up and effaced; there remains nonetheless the vocal modulation, almost lost but not absorbed in the tremors of the body; a strange interval, where the voice emits a speech lacking 'truths', and where proximity is a presence without possession" (Certeau, 230). Certeau's formulation of voice as the prime constituent of a breach in normal signification differs significantly from the one advanced by Derrida who—in the now famous critique of Rousseau's theory of speech—detects the marked privileging of speech over writing with the former authenticating presence and marking the closest proximity to the signified (Derrida, 11).

Despite their celebration of non-sense and attendant consecration of orality, Dada and Futurism did not provoke a disavowal of the written. On the contrary, the legacy left by both is one of conspiratorial innovations realized through a bigamous relation with both sound and the written mark—its heritage, a condition of voice that can best be described (to borrow a category from Gertrude Stein) as a "dependent independence." One of the undeniable achievements of Dada and Futurist poetics is their decisive advancement of poetry's graphic notation. Ball's frequently reprinted "Karawana" employs a variety of typefaces in its first printed form, and Hausmann's optophonetic poetry achieves a notational precision that he himself likens to musical notation—a score for repeating the poem's vocalized entailments of intonation, volume, and pitch.[13]

Graphic and sonic innovation go similarly hand in hand in Futurist practice. It is less the liberation of the voice than a successful application of advanced typography that allows Marinetti in his *parole in libertà* (words in freedom) "to treat words like torpedoes and to hurl them forth at all speeds: at the velocity of stars, clouds, aeroplanes, trains, waves, explosives, molecules, atoms."[14] And Marinetti is not an isolated case. Francesco Canguillo's "Piedigrotta" and "Caffè concerto, alfabeto a sorpresa" are stupendous, unprecedented typographic tours de force. But despite its verbal deformations *parole in libertà* still commits the performing voice to a textual dependency—a confinement clearly hinted at in Marinetti's comments on his own poem "Zang-tumb-tumb" where "the strident onomatopoeia *ssiii*, which reproduces the whistle of a tugboat on the Meuse, is followed by the muffled *fiiii fiiii* coming from the other bank. These two onomatopoeias have enabled me to dispense with a description of the breadth of the river which is thus measured by contrasting the consonants *s* and *f*" (quoted in Clough, 50). In its dominant goal—a mimophonic representation of ambient technology and powers by means of predominantly martial and industrial onomatopoeia—the most lasting accomplishment of *parole in libertà* is a graphic system of notation for sonic rhythms and forces—in other words an efficient score for voice.[15]

Language, be it sonorized, pulverized, deracinated, plasticized, lacerated, or transrationalized by this collective avant-garde still resists an ultimate demolition. Voice, as a consequence, remains subordinated to the dictates of a graphism, the resultant poetry remaining an *ars dictandi,* that learned Scholastic expertise in the speaking of a written text.

The final move away from the written to a full orality begins in the early 1950s with four young French writers: François Dufrêne, the Situationist Gil J. Wolman, Jean-Louis Brau, and Henri Chopin: collectively known as the Ultralettristes.[16] In the late 1940s the pioneers of Lettrisme, Isadore Isou, and Maurice Lemaître, opted for the letter over the word as the basic unit of their poetic composition. The break with the word (which in Dada, *zaum,* and *parole in libertà* succeeded no further than its plasticization and deformation) was finally accomplished. Celebrating the lettristic impulse amidst the debris of the word, they developed in their works both visual and auditory innovations.[17] The seeds of Ultralettrisme were already nascent in this parent movement. Isou's New Letteric Alphabet reascribes to alphabetic characters nonphonetic values and paralinguistic features: A = hard inhalation; B = exhalation; O = coughing, clearing the throat; P = a clicking of the tongue. Fulfilling the demands for Lyotard's "theatre of energies,"[18] Dufrêne's *cri-rhythmes,* Wolman's *mégapneumes,* and the *instrumentations verbales* of Brau are all morphological transformations in extremis. Less texts than sonic performances the ultralettristic poems comprise a high-energy expulsion of inarticulate sounds, cries, and grunts.[19] In linguistic parlance ultralettristic performance emancipates non- and subphonomatic material from the necessity of primary articulation, and as a category of sound poetry explores—at its maximum level of intensity—the area of human expression David Crystal terms paralanguage, "a kind of bridge between non-linguistic forms of communicative behaviour and the traditionally central areas of 'verbal' linguistic study—grammar, . . . vocabulary, and pronunciation."[20]

Breton insists on a discernment between the work of art as a "happening" and the work of art as a "ribbon" of repetitions, preconceptions, and anticipations. However, it was Apollinaire in "The New Spirit and the Poets" who reminded poetry that its greatest resource was surprise.[21] The ultralettristic performance is such a surprise happening. Neither a preconception nor a sedimented terminal signification, it registers—like pleasure—as a pure affect, reconfiguring performance not as a validation of authorial presence (there is no author) but as a profoundly destabilizing force, removing the poem from familiar semantic and orthographic certainties.[22] Poet Bob Cobbing describes the *cri-rhythmes* as utilizing "the utmost variety of utterances, extended cries, shrieks, ululations, purrs, yaups and cluckings; the apparently uncontrollable controlled into a spontaneously shaped performance."[23] Due to the abolition of any normative meaning in this poetry, the distance between poet-performer and audience becomes radically altered from its standard configurations. The functional separation that derives from a traditional transit model of communication (with a message sent across a textual or auditory space to a receiver) no longer obtains. Rather than validating their creators' presence as an immediate emotional "truth, ultralettristic performances destabilize all ontological grounding and free the productions from both semantic and orthographic hegemony."[24]

The auditory reception of these performances, first presented in 1950 under the category of "Prelinguism," is described colorfully by Arrigo Lora-Totina. The sonic expulsions "strike the ear as brutally as a material in the pure state of incandescence, a brute, heavy, physical substance still fresh from the flesh that has expelled it, impregnated with the weight and the electricity of the tissue of the cells that has created it, a torid place of existential incubation" (Lora-Totina, 33). The sense evoked is of Barthes's vocal granulation pushed beyond all connection to language, as vocal emissions without meaning whose closest proximity is to a "death of language."

A profound and obvious commitment is evident in Ultralettriste improvisation to the release of primary and libido-genetic processes via spontaneous voicing. Writing in 1963 Raoul Vaneigem extolls the revolutionary potential of spontaneity as a vital component of radical subjectivity. "Spontaneity is the true mode of being of individual creativity, creativity's initial, immaculate form, unpolluted at the source and as yet unthreatened by the mechanisms of co-optation."[25] One might be tempted to regard this description of vocal Evian water as an attractive agenda for poetic praxis, but what guarantees the emergence of unconscious drives in automaticity or spontaneity?[26] If Kristeva's formulations are correct and a semiotic interruption of instinctual drives is always present in the sociolectal, symbolic order, then the loss of conscious control within the spontaneous act of voicing will always emerge as symptomatic of a double disposition and cannot fail to index a dialectic of drives.[27] Barthes, however, cautions against such optimistic determinism, alleging automatism "is not rooted at all in the 'spontaneous,' the 'savage,' the 'pure,' the 'profound,' the 'subversive,' but originates on the contrary from the 'strictly coded.' "[28] "The 'spontaneity' which people normally talk to us about is the height of convention. It is that reified language which we find ready-made within ourselves, immediately at our disposal, when we do in fact want to speak 'spontaneously.' "[29] Lora-Totina admits to similar misgivings about Ultralettriste performances concluding that "divorced from the common language, repetition rapidly and inevitably generated boredom, for, when it comes to the point, inarticulate expression, like sex, does not have an infinity of ways of conjugation, in fact it is extremely limited" (Lora-Totina, 33–34). We should also recall the austere warning offered by Althusser "that every 'spontaneous' language is an ideological language, the vehicle of an ideology."[30]

Whether from premonition of this subsequent criticism, or developing their own misgivings, the Ultralettristes quickly modified their performances into multimedia events. Early in their history a technological turn occurred toward the use of human sound as a primary material for technological modification. Lora-Totino describes these works as embroideries of "primitive and indistinct material with rhythm, superimpositions, accelerations, . . . creating veritable ballets of expectoration, cascades of little noises and disagreeable noises" (Lora-Totino, 34).[31] Paralanguage in such manifestations merges with concrete music, as a component in a complex instrumentation of speed, timbre, volume, and quantity. If Charles Olson saw advanced and untapped possibilities offered to poetic notation by the typewriter, then Wolman, Dufrêne, Brau, and Chopin see equally lucrative potential offered to Prelinguism by the tape recorder. It would be straining genealogy to argue that these later Ultralettriste tape recorder productions comprise merely an extension into acoustics of the treated text—indeed, the intransigent difference between media here is absolute. Clearly they signal a return to a graphism, arrested and repeatable, but most crucially, through their recovery of human expenditure as a new vocabulary for secondary orality, they signalize a revised poetical economy. The tape enhancements of the Ultralettristes are the culmination of the romantic subject in the unfolding (via technological prostheses) of its insular "lyric" interiority. Unquestionably the conceptual base of the spontaneous voice is radically altered. Impromptu ephemera become recoverable, redeployable as combinatorial and distortable material in a complex, textural composition. If the *cri-rhythme* and *megapneume* fall within the purlieu of Bataille's general economy as acts of expenditure,[32] these later poems—the products of recovery, preservation, and modification—announce the extreme limit of the voice in a powerful alterity, a cacophonous amplification, pulverized into a microparticularized Other, the experience of which is more of an extra than a paralinguistic phenomenon. If such is the fate of voice, it is the sound poem's ironic destiny not to escape repetition but to enter it and give itself over to the fixity of digital imprint. For with the seductive advent of the tape recorder, technology offered Prelinguism a secondary orality capable of transforming its acoustic ephemerality into the electro-acoustic data of the Foucauldian archive.

In the 1970s the body emerged as both a conceptual and actual preoccupation in art and performance. We might cite as its most memorable examples the Dionysian enactments of Herman Nitsch complete with dripping animal carcasses and blood-splattered stage; the self-mutilations of the Vienna Aktion group that culminated in Swartzkogler's self-castration; the extreme physical submissions of Gina Pane or Chris Burden; and Linda Montano's self-application of acupuncture needles to her face in "Mitchell's Death." The ambient theories of the times were to be found in "Anti-Oedipus," "Libidinal Economy," and "Revolution in Poetic Language," each offering libidinal templates by which to reformulate a theory of the body as process, or becoming.[33] Out of this convulsive context appeared a species of collective, improvised sound performance that might be dubbed "paleotechnic," its practitioners largely Canadian (*The Four Horsemen:* Rafael Barreto-Rivera, Paul Dutton, Steve McCaffery, and bp Nichol) and British (*Konkrete Canticle:* Bob Cobbing, Paula Claire, Bill Griffiths, as well as *Jgigigig:* Chris Cheek, Clive Fencott, Lawrence Upton).[34] Via such ensembles, sound poetry reappeared as a practice of outlay and dispossession. In Canada especially there was a wholesale rejection of technological enhancement and manipulation of the voice.[35] Inspired neither by a purism nor a primitivism, a collective human group emerged, highly conscious of the pressures from both its ambient cultural theories and radical psychopolitics—schizoculture—to rethink the body, poem, and community through formulations of assemblage, movement, and intensities.[36] Consciously developing (in part) from Tzara's famous dictum that "thought is made in the mouth," the paleotechnic sound poetry of the 1970s was formulated around two primary desires: to create a poetry of spontaneous affect predicated on a paradigm of unrepeatablity (this was the antitechnological component) and to reformulate the "poem" as a manifestation of unpremeditated and ephemeral community.[37] Conceptually speaking, these readings pushed ontology toward polis, addressing the accidental configuration of two intermeshed ensembles—performers and audience—as an urgent issue of community.

There is a Greek term—*hyponoia* (the underneath sense)—that aptly describes the telos of those performance-presentations. What was absorbed from Marx and Freud—at a minimum—is the basal illusion of appearances. Beneath the envisaged performance of sonic outlay was a required loss of self in the region of spontaneous enactment. We might figure here a body-before-self as the negative presence operative in the paleotechnic sound poem. Breton had spoken earlier of his own desire to experience what lay beneath appearances as an uninterrupted quest (Breton, 106). Conceived as a function of movement and evanescence these collective spontaneities claimed the status of phonocentrism's heterological dimension and dynamic. Such vocal performances do not index or supplement stability; they function through overdeterminations of rhythm and energy as the conduit for a loss. Falling under the primary conceptual governance of expenditure rather than orality, voice in these occasions—no longer a guarantee of a conscious self—precipitates a maximum rupture in any signifying system.[38] Replacing the traditional author is a complex machinic assemblage generating performances that take the form of pulsional escapes from meaning and being, their release effected by a community of agents/"poets" functioning as a complex interrelation of transistors.[39] An assemblage is to be understood as an "increase in the dimensions of a multiplicity that necessarily changes in nature as it expands its connections."[40] The variant machinic assemblage is bifocal. "One side . . . faces the strata, which doubtless makes it a kind of organism, or signifying totality, or determination attributable to a subject; it also has a side facing a body without organs, which is continually dismantling the organism, causing asignifying particles or pure intensities to pass or circulate" (Deleuze and Guattari, 4). We should not lose sight of the intense corporeality of this machinic assemblage, which I have insisted on calling a community. But can such assemblage be reconciled to a concept of community? As a community-in-process yes, it can be constantly positioned in that double estrangement between a signifying social organic called "the group" and that totality's self-diremption in a performed expenditure by numerous bodies in occasion—a performance "without organs."

In the distinction offered by Romanticism between *ergon* and *energeia* paleotechnic sound poetry, like its Ultralettriste precursors, sided unequivocably with the latter term of being-in-action, and the unqualified valorization of energy clearly links the paleotechnic sound performance with Olsonian notions of Projective Verse. With their depreciation of textuality and a stress upon high-energy emission, the sound improvisations of the 1970s entailed a forceful decanting—though not a rejection—of Olson's basic theories. The poem's source in both cases is physiological "down through the workings of [the poet's] throat to that place where breath comes from, where breath has its beginnings, where drama has to come from, where the coincidence is, all act springs."[41] Defining energy in "The Gate and the Center," Olson grants it a cosmologic status: "The proposition is a simple one (and the more easily understood now that we have been shocked at what we did not know nature's energies capable of, generally): energy is larger than man, but therefore, if he taps it as it is in himself, his uses of himself are EXTENSIBLE in human directions & degree not recently granted."[42] There is a substantive difference in application, however, that must be remarked. In Olson's biopoetics the imperative project is to embed energy in a sonographism by means of a precise written placement of energy within the imprinted syllable. The syllable is to Olson what onomatopoiea is to Marinetti: a threshold in biomaterial language where the paralinguistic enters graphic stability. The significant disagreement of the paleotechnic sound poem with Olson's Projective Verse thus centers on the issue of how and where that energy manifested. In retention and recall through the binding fixity of a printed text? Or in the anasemantic expenditure of performance?

The fundamental break made by this paleotechnic assertion from the prelinguism of the Ultralettristes is in rethinking the poem as a spontaneous community—what Pierre Mabille might term an *egregore*.[43] Its basal renunciation was the antisocial antilyricism of individual composition, replete, in the case of the later Chopin and Dufrêne, with its technologically generated autoaffective nuncupations. The paleotechnic poem was conceived as a communal performance at its outset. Such improvisational activities, involving simultaneity and a resultant indeterminate texturality in its realization, are complicated when manifesting in a group context.[44] Herbert Blau illuminates a crucial consequence of improvisation when insisting on "a critical gap between repression and pretense, the construction of an appearance and, more or less overdetermined, the appearance of indeterminacy."[45] Opening up the poem to such overdeterminations and indeterminacies of performed community was paleotechnicism's prime commitment.

I have described the intense corporeality of sound performance as a machinic assemblage of body and voice in the transmission and retransmission of asignifying, nonrepeatable energies, in a collectivity without preparation.[46] But is such a poetry of pure outlay even thinkable? Jean Barrot has claimed that "all activity is symbolic," creating simultaneously a product and a vision of the world.[47] If symbolic impedimenta are unavoidable, then how do we assess this species of performance? Theorized through Bataille, the sound poem takes on the defining dynamic of inevitable vocal excess spilling over from a libidinal, phonorhythmic dispositif of evanescent expenditures and meaningless outlays. If it does achieve such a sovereign negativity then the sound poem is truly deserving of the title of literature's *part maudite* — a heterological expulsion from the scriptural regime of Logos. But can voice ever escape a minimum signification? Barrot evidently thinks not and if Durand's claim is true that "[t]here is no such thing as a neutral voice, a voice without desire, a voice that does not desire me" (Durand, 103) then a poetry of pure expenditure is unachievable and we can look back wistfully at these attempts at libidinal assemblage—these struggles to emancipate a praxis of voice from the presidential mandate to mean—and acknowledge their failure in legacy. Sought after (and unattained) was the poem as exemplary community—ephemeral and symbolic—whose manifestation might take the place of the conventional poetry reading and its attendant ideology of appearance. A community was aimed at that would take existence paradoxically outside of language. Perhaps the closest theoretic formulation of such a group is Giorgio Agamben's concept of the "Coming Comunity"— a community that lays no claims to identity or belonging in which "the coming being is whatever being."[48]

Do we then write off the Paleotechnic as yet another failed utopia in poetry? The precise realization of a body-in-process unavoidably involves an absolute decommissioning of the body politic—and a scream can never be a social contract. In his discussions of the differences between interjectional and propositional speech functions, Ernst Cassirer declares propositional speech as unique to humans, configuring the world for us in permanent, stable forms "with fixed and constant qualities."[49] As an interjectional poesis, the sound poem renounces this unique attribute. Breaking with Cassirer's "Propositional Man"—at the historic moment Foucault proclaims the death of man—this hesitant poetics of negative presence faltered at its inability to specify the exact purpose of its energetic expulsion. Was the performance of expenditure merely recovered into the spectacular society that Debord isolated and analyzed (in 1967)?[50] Or can it be explained through the patinated rhetoric of the 1960s as an after-effect of Ultralettrisme, whose dubious accomplishment was a failed radicality of the subject? From the plethora of statements available I choose the following for its domestication of heterology into a community of hope: "If thought is really to find a basis in lived experience, it has to be free. The way to achieve this is to think *other* in terms of *the same*. As you make yourself, imagine another self who will make you one day in it turn. Such is my conception of spontaneity: the highest possible self-consciousness which is still inseparable from the self and the world" (Vaneigem, 150).

The extreme mission for poetry from Artaud to the performative enactments of the 1970s was neither expenditure nor spontaneity per se but rather the killing of speech in its capitalistic embodiments. This death of speech—it should be qualified—entailed a theft of silence within sound. To paraphrase a thought of Valéry's that captures with beauty and accuracy the circularity of this mission: a scream escapes from pain. Out of this accident a poem is made, with an explanation round about it. In this context the scream acquires a role, a function. As was the case with Pascal's thought: "I had a thought. I have forgotten it. In its place I write that I've forgotten it."[51]

NOTES

1. Jeremy Ahearne, *Michel de Certeau: Interpretation and Its Other* (Stanford: Stanford University Press, 1995), p. 140.

2. Régis Durand, "The Disposition of the Voice," in *Performance in Postmodern Culture,* ed. Michel Benamou and Charles Caramello (Madison: Coda Press, 1977), pp. 99–110.

3. Michel de Certeau, *The Writing of History,* tr. Tom Conley (New York: Columbia University Press, 1988), p. 341.

4. "The voice is heard (understood)—that undoubtedly is what is called conscience—closest to the self as the absolute effacement of the signifier: pure auto-affection that necessarily has the form of time and which does not borrow from outside of itself, in the world or in 'reality,' any accessory signifier, any substance of expression foreign to its own spontaneity." Jacques Derrida, *Of Grammatology,* tr. Gayatri Chakravorty Spivak (Baltimore: Johns Hopkins University Press, 1976), p. 20.

5. Roland Barthes, *The Pleasure of the Text,* tr. Richard Miller (New York: Hill and Wang, 1975), pp. 66–67.

6. For a full discussion of the "neutral" voice see Maurice Blanchot, *L'Entretien infini* (Paris: Gallimard, 1969), esp. p. 564.

7. "Fascination with the abstract is an instance of *jouissance* proper . . . The abstract does not act through a simulacrum-effect, but by means of the organization of its material alone . . . [T]he libidinal *dispositif* is noticeable in every abstraction, and in particular of the theatrical kind, in that it thwarts the client's transference onto a simulated object, onto a reference." Jean-François Lyotard, *Libidinal Economy,* tr. Iain Hamilton Grant (Bloomington: Indiana University Press, 1993), pp. 245–46. We might note in passing that the Futurist Depero named his version of onomatopoeic paroxysm "verbalizzazione astratta" (abstract verbalization).

8. Mike Weaver, "Concrete Poetry," *Lugano Review,* nos. 5/6 (1966), p. 101.

9. Quoted in Hans Richter, *Dada Art and Anti-art,* tr. David Britt (New York: Abrams, 1965), p. 121.

10. Hugo Ball, *Flight out of Time: A Dada Diary,* tr. Ann Raimes (New York: Viking Press, 1974), p. 71. For an informative and entertaining description of Dada performance see Annabelle Henkin Meltzer, "The Dada Actor and Performance Theory," in *The Art of Performance: A Critical Anthology,* ed. Gregory Batcock and Robert Nickas (New York: E. P. Dutton, 1984), pp. 37–55. A more detailed, contextualized, and comparative discussion can be found in J. H. Matthews, *Theatre in Dada and Surrealism* (Syracuse: Syracuse University Press, 1974).

11. Gilles Deleuze, *Foucault,* tr. Sean Hand (Minneapolis: University of Minnesota Press, 1988), p. 149n.

12. Vladimir Markov, *Russian Futurism: A History* (London: MacGibbon & Kee, 1969), p. 20. Although the invention of *zaum* (a contraction of the longer phrase *zaumnyj jazyk* meaning "transrational") is usually credited to Kruchenykh, Serge Fauchereau proposes Elena Guro (1877–1913) as its inventor, citing the opening of her poem "Finland" as the primal *zaum* (Serge Fauchereau, *Moscow, 1900–1930* [London: Alpine, 1988], p. 129.) In his own more parsimonious assessment Markov claims Guro's to be "a minor contribution [made] inconspicuously, subtly, and with feminine gentleness" [!] via a single neologism—*shuyat*—inserted in the same poem (Markov, p. 19). Fauchereau, who attributes the invention to Guro's interest in children's language, counting rhymes and lullabies, does not cite Markov's example but quotes the poem in full with its arguably "transrational" opening : "Lula, lola, lala lu / Lisa, lola, lula-li." For details on Guro's life and work see Markov especially pp. 14–23. Kruchenykh himself claimed that *zaum* originated in the glossolalia practiced by Sishkov, a religious mystic and flagellant of the Khlysty sect (see Markov, 202).

13. Writing in the *Courrier Dada* Hausmann describes the optophonetic poem and procaims its historical significance. "In order to express these elements [i.e. respiratory and auditive combinations] typographically . . . I had used letters of varying sizes and thicknesses which thus took on the character of musical notation. Thus the optophonetic poem was born. The optophonetic and the phonetic poem are the first step towards totally non-representational, abstract poetry" (quoted in Richter, 121).

14. Quoted in Rosa Trillo Clough, *Futurism: The Story of a Modern Art Movement: A New Appraisal* (New York: Philosophical Library, 1961), p. 52.

15. Existing recordings of Marinetti's own readings of *parole in libertà* are convincing proof that in his enactments of voice he never aspired beyond a stentorian declamation. He can be heard reading "La Batagglia di Adrianopoli" on *Futurism & Dada Reviewed,* produced by James Neiss (Brussels: Sub Rosa CD, 1988). This valuable CD also contains live performances by Cocteau, Schwitters, and Apollinaire.

16. Arrigo Lora-Totina postulates a four-stage evolution in the movement of the written text into a full orality. First is the read text: "the poem is written, its author reading it aloud seeks to give it a different dimension (in this case the author's interpretation is just one of many that are possible, whether declaimed or merely recreated mentally)." Second is the spoken text, in which graphic and acoustic versions are of equal value, wherein "the sonic element may determine a different disposition of the written text, the declamation becomes an independent creation" (Lora-Totina, "What Is Sound Poetry?" in *Futura Poesia Sonora: Critical Historical Anthology of Sound Poetry,* ed. Arrigo Lora-Totino [Milan: Memoria Spa, 1978], p. 8). Third is the spoken composition, in which the written composition functions as a score initiating a declaimed event where "every sound of the mouth is admissable, rediscovery of onomatopoeia, creation of neologism, use of techniques of vocal instrumentation" (8). The final stage is sonic composition: a free improvisation either in performance or directly onto recording equipment but without premeditation or revision and without the aid of written or visual texts.

In a brief commentary on the Ultralettristes, Lora-Totina cites a precursor in the Italian Futurist Canguillo who performed an "Interventio di pernacchie" (Intervention of Raspberries) at the Spovieri gallery in 1914 (33).

17. Isou announced a system of metagraphics, or postwriting, aspects of which were resistant to any oral approximation. The component characters in this writing were a mixture of elements from non-Roman alphabets, invented, imaginary signs and ideograms. For a full exposition of metagraphics see Isadore Isou, *Les Champs de force de la peinture lettriste* (Paris: Avant-Garde, 1964). Isou's "New Letteric Alphabet" and important "Manifesto of Lettriste Poetry" are contained in his *Introduction à une nouvelle poésie et une nouvelle musique* (Paris: Gallimard, 1947). Isou's Lettrisme was quickly parodied as "bird-song" in an anonymous entry under "Expression" in the *Encyclopedia Da Costa*, published in the fall of 1947. This ephemeral publication is now generally available in *Encyclopaedia Acephalica*, tr. Iain White (London: Atlas Press, 1955), pp. 107–56.

18. See Jean-François Lyotard, "The Tooth, the Palm," *Sub-Stance*, vol. 15 (1977), pp. 105–10.

19. The Ultralettristes are not without their Enlightenment precursors. As early as 1714 the Abbé Fénelon proposed a type of theater without language in section 6 of his *Lettre à l'académie*, arguing that language be replaced by gestures and predenotative cries. This occasioned a reply from du Bos focusing on the difficulty of tragic composition composed solely of cries. For a detailed discussion see Wladyslaw Folkierski, *Entre le classicisme et le romantisme* (Paris, 1925), p. 175.

20. David Crystal, "Paralinguistics," in *The Body as a Medium of Expression*, ed. Jonathan Benthall and Ted Polhemus (New York: E. P. Dutton, 1975), p. 162.

21. André Breton, *Conversations: The Autobiography of Surrealism*, tr. Mark Polizzotti (New York: Paragon House, 1993), p. 199.

22. We owe to Levinas a primary insight into the ground of the groundlessness of pleasure. Pleasure is affect and as such derides the category *being*. John Llewelyn summarizes the nature of Levinasian pleasure as a pure dynamic of affect. "If pleasure is to augur escape from being then the categories of being cannot apply to it. It cannot be a state of being. This is why pleasure is an affect. It is affective rather than effective because affectivity is recalcitrant to the categories of activity or will and of being and of thought." John Llewelyn, *The Genealogy of Ethics: Emmanuel Levinas* (London: Routledge, 1995), p. 17.

23. Quoted in *Text-Sound Texts*, ed. Richard Kostelanetz (New York: William Morrow, 1980), p. 20.

24. The great disservice of the conventional poetry reading is surely to have fostered illusions of presence via a purportedly essential corporeal connection to a written text sufficient to restore the author to her work in a fetishized reunification. Celia Zukofsky records her husband's feelings on the otiosity of the poetry reading and its disagreeable requirement of authorial presence. "Why can't they read my poetry themselves? Why do I have to read it for them?" (Celia Zukofsky, "1927–1972" in *Paideuma*, vol. 7, no. 3 [1978], p. 372). Ron Sukenick advances his own misgivings, pointing to several negative implications. "A reading puts emphasis on the performance, not the poem. / Some good poets are bad readers. / Some bad poets are good readers. If the essence of poetry is its performance in public, why not hire trained actors for readings?" (Ron Sukenick, "Against Readings," in *The Poetry Reading: A Contemporary Compendium on Language & Performance*, ed. Stephen Vincent and Ellen Zweig (San Francisco: Momo's Press, 1981), p. 317. Both Zukofsky and Sukenick demonstrate a keen awareness of the threat to writing by a reading's demand for a restored and necessary athleticism or elocutionary expertise. Their disagreements, however, refer to what might be roughly classified as "the

spoken word" and fail to address that other confluence of the performative and poetic: the text-sound poem. Prior to both Sukenick and Zukofsky, Hugo Ball expressed his own disquietude around the shortcomings of poetry readings. "Nowhere are the weaknesses of a poem revealed as much as in a public reading. One thing is certain: art is joyful only as long as it has richness and life. Reciting aloud has become the touchstone of the quality of the poem for me, and I have learned (from the stage) to what extent today's literature is worked out as a problem at a desk and is made for the spectacles of the collector instead of for the ears of living human beings" (Ball, 54). Ball's reservations confess a different motivation than Zukofsky's and Sukenick's. Indeed, they seem to spring from a strikingly polar conviction. Ball's implication is clear: the written poem alone is an inert configuration of signs requiring the corporeal supplement and oral vitality of the poet in real-time action to realize its destiny.

25. Raoul Vaneigem, *The Revolution of Everyday Life,* tr. Donald Nicholson-Smith (London: Left Bank Books, 1983), p. 149.

26. Guattari and Deleuze offer an innovative notion of the unconscious as a productive force, not—as in Freud's case—a primal scene of repeated complexual enactments. "The unconscious is not a theatre but a factory." Félix Guattari, *Chaosophy* (New York: Semiotext(e), 1995), p. 75.

27. In an obvious updating of Nietzsche's famous agonistic binary of Apollo and Dionysus, Kristeva proposes a double disposition in all language toward two antinomial orders: symbolic and semiotic. The *symbolic* specifies that inclination within the linguistic subject toward naming, predication, order, and the communal linguistic apparatus of its sociolect. The *semiotic,* in contrast, is a disposition to asserting instinctual and prelinguistic drives as a propulsion *through* language. Interpreted through Kristeva's theory the sound poem, in so far as it abolishes the symbolic, involves a consequential privileging of the semiotic as far as the abolition of the symbolic.

28. Roland Barthes, *The Grain of the Voice: Interviews, 1962–1980,* tr. Linda Coverdale (New York: Hill and Wang, 1985), p. 244.

29. Roland Barthes, *Writer Sollers,* tr. Philip Tody (Minneapolis: University of Minnesota Press, 1987), p. 55.

30. Louis Althusser, *Lenin and Philosophy and Other Essays,* tr. Ben Brewster (London: New Left Books, 1971), p. 207.

31. A prescient awareness of the possibility of sonic declamations for use in radio broadcast was a constant factor in the work of the Futurist Fafa (Vittorio Osvaldo Tommasini), whose poetry Marinetti lauds in ebullient Futurist terminology. "Sport is entering triumphantly into poetry, enhancing its elasticity, its heroic leaps, its tireless dynamism. We have finally emerged from the mephitic atmosphere of libraries. The muscular surge and the roar of engines impose new rhythmic laws and prepare us for the great aeropoetry" (quoted in Lora-Totina, 16). Among Fafa's deviant and varied accomplishments Marinetti lists "[r]adio poems with transoceanic wave-jumps to revenge himself for his short-sightedness" (in Lora-Totina, 16).

32. In Bataille's own words, "The general economy deals with the essential problem of the use of wealth. It underlies the fact that an excess is produced that, by definition, cannot be employed in a utilitarian manner. Excess energy can only be lost, without the least concern for a goal or objective, and, therefore, without any meaning" ([O.C.V. 215–16] quoted in Michèlle H. Richman, *Reading George Bataille Beyond the Gift* (Baltimore: Johns Hopkins University Press, 1982), p. 70).

33. Gilles Deleuze and Félix Guattari, *Anti-Oedipus: Capitalism and Schizophrenia,* vol. 1, tr. Robert Hurley, Mark Seem, and Helen R. Lane (New York: Viking Press, 1977); Jean-François Lyotard, *Libidinal Economy,* Julia Kristeva, *Revolution in Poetic Language,* tr. Margaret Waller (New York: Columbia University Press, 1984). All three titles were originally published in 1974 and Lyotard's book is an acknowledged response to *Anti-Oedipus.*

34. It is frequently argued that twentieth-century sound poetry has been a development of two opposing dispositions: the scientific and the primitive. Beneath this binary are two separate interests: one, an embrace of technology as a positive alliance with the human voice; the other an eschewal of all forms of technological contact. Regarding the first interest, the voice is treated as a material point for departure; for the second it is a still not fully fathomed phenomenon in its basic libidinal-acoustic state. Ellen Zweig offers a peacefully coexistent version of this bifurcation: "Sound poetry explores the human voice as human. Sound poets take apart language to see how it works . . . The poet becomes close to the animal, close to the child. Sound poetry explores the voice as other. Sound poets record and manipulate the voice . . . They cut the voice into pieces, reverse it, change its speed, make it digital. The voice becomes electronic, a strange machine whining toward communication with other planets." Ellen Zweig, "Sound Poetry: An Introduction" in *The Poetry Reading.*

35. For a rationale of this rejection see Steve McCaffery, "Discussion . . . Genesis . . . Continuity: Some Reflections on the Current Work of the Four Horsemen," in *Text-Sound Texts,* ed. Richard Kostelanetz (New York: William Morrow, 1980), pp. 277–99.

36. If we concur with Freud, however, that the unconscious is our oldest mental faculty, then we might confidently theorize improvisation as a species of primitivism—as an ur performance.

37. René Viénet reproduces graffiti painted by the Marxist-Pessimist Youth during the French student occupation movement of May 1968, which reads, "A bas le sommaire vive l'ephémère" (Down with abstraction long live the ephemeral) (René Viénet, *Enragés and Situationists in the Occupation Movement, France, May '68,* [no tr. specified] [New York: Autonomedia, 1992], p. 75). Viénet's book first appeared in French in 1968. I mention it to hint at the uneasy alliance across time between the abstractionist proclivities of Dada and the spontaneous ephemerality in which the group sound poem of the 1970s was figured.

38. Both Self and Identity, predicated upon static genesis, are strategic concepts in the arrest of becoming. Their ideological function is to halt or at least decelerate the flow of intensities producing, when successful, a mineralization of processual ontology.

39. The machinic rather than existing in opposition to the human organism, homologizes its very rhythms: the regular repetition of pulse and heartbeat is repeated in the regulated movements of cogs.

40. Gilles Deleuze and Félix Guattari, *A Thousand Plateaus,* tr. Brian Massumi (Minneapolis: University of Minnesota Press, 1987), p. 8.

41. Quoted in *Concerning Concrete Poetry,* ed. Bob Cobbing and Peter Mayer (London: Writers Forum, 1978), p. 24. In what amounts to a staggering ecumenical defense of breath William James conflates mentation and human respiration. "I am as confident as I am of anything that, in myself, the stream of thinking (which I recognize emphatically as a phenomenon) is only a careless name for what, when

scrutinized, reveals itself to consist chiefly of the stream of my breathing. The 'I think' which Kant said must be able to accompany all my objects, is the 'I breathe' which actually does accompany them." After this strident, anti-Cartesian stance James continues and revises Bergson's stream of consciousness as a respiratory stream. "There are other internal facts beside breathing . . . and these increase the assets of 'consciousness,' so far as the latter is subject to immediate perception; but breath, which was ever the original of 'spirit,' breath moving outward between the glottis and the nostrils, is, I am persuaded the essence of which philosophers have constructed the entity known to them as consciousness." Quoted in Don Byrd, *The Poetics of the Common Knowledge* (Albany: State University of New York Press, 1994), p. 35.

42. Charles Olson, *Human Universe and Other Essays,* ed. Donald Allen (San Francisco: Auerhahn Society, 1965), p. 22. "The Gate and the Center" first appeared in 1952; coincidentally at the height of French prelinguism.

43. *Egregore,* " 'a collective psychic being' driven by a life of its own." Quoted in Breton, 95.

44. The collective reading-performance was not a novel phenomenon. Henri-Martin Barzun's "chants simultanés" were performed in 1912 and Pierre Albert-Birot's experiments in multivocity, published in *Sic* between 1916 and 1919, include a "Promethean Poem" and "Blue Crayon" for four and three voices respectively. Among the Futurists, Giacomo Balla scored an "onomatopoeic noise canzone for typewriter" scored for twelve simultaneous voices.

45. Herbert Blau, *To All Appearances: Ideology and Performance* (New York: Routledge, 1992), p. 4.

46. An unacknowledged influence on the Canadian paleotechnic sound poem is Gertrude Stein's credo that there is no repetition, that each reiteration of an identical within a series registers with a slight variation in emotional insistence. Stein argues against the very notion of a neutral voice, an argument repeated in Durand. There is a pertinence in Stein's assertion to Derrida's own metaconceptual notion of *différance* as difference and deferral—as if Stein anticipates this notion and transfers it from the grammatologic to the emotive plane.

47. Jean Barrot, *What Is Situationism: Critique of the Situationist International* (London: Unpopular Books, 1987), p. 11.

48. Giorgio Agamben, *The Coming Community,* tr. Michael Hardt (Minneapolis: University of Minnesota Press, 1993), p. 1.

49. Ernst Cassirer, *Symbol, Myth, and Culture: Essays and Lectures of Ernst Cassirer, 1935–1945,* ed. Donald P. Verene (New Haven: Yale University Press, 1979), p. 150.

50. Guy Debord, *Society of the Spectacle* (Detroit: Black & Red Press, 1983) [no tr. specified].

51. This final passage is a deliberate détournement of a beautiful thought of Paul Valéry's. "A blob of ink falls from my pain. Out of this accident I make a face, with a drawing round about it. In this context the blot acquires a role, a function. As was the case with Pascal's Thought: 'I had a thought. I have forgotten it. In its place I write that I've forgotten it.' Paul Valéry, *Analects,* Bollingen Series 95, no. 14, tr. Stuart Gilbert (Princeton: Princeton University Press, 1980), p. 278.

8

Toward a Poetics of Polyphony and Translatability

DENNIS TEDLOCK

> can you tell us which direction we are taking
> caz we waan no whé paat we guen;
>   bisétuna nasú busini halía badúa lañ;
> queremos saber nuestra dirección
>   whé paat we guen . . .
>
> LUKE E. RAMIREZ

*I*f a poem is supposed to consist of exactly the right words and no others, then there are multiple worlds in which poems are never quite finished, never quite closed. In some of these worlds poets use writing, but there is nothing about writing, in and of itself, that requires a text to be fixed for all times and places. Writing, like speaking, is a performance.

If poetics is supposed to belong to the interior of language, as opposed to the exterior realm of referentiality, then there are multiple worlds in which being a verbal artist means pursuing a dual career in poetics and semantics. This does not mean bringing words and their objects into ever closer alignment, but rather playing on the differences. The sounding of different voices does not require putting multiple poets on the same bill, but takes place in the poem at hand. If the poem is written there may be multiple graphic moves in the same text, and these need not be in synchrony with the voices.

If literature means the world of letters, Greco-Roman alphabetic letters, then the poets of these other worlds are not producers of literature. Some of them do use the alphabet, but not necessarily for the purposes intended by lettered invaders and evangelists. For those looking outward from the inside of the Greco-Roman heritage, composing verse with its rhymes blanked, its meter freed, and its breaths notated is not quite enough to open the boundaries between worlds. There is still this recurring desire to close in on exactly the right words. For other poets in other worlds, paraphrase has never been a heresy and translation has never been treasonous.

In geographical terms, alternative poetries completely surround the world of letters and are practiced in the very precincts of its culture capitals. The examples presented here happen to come from speakers and writers of Mayan languages, who number well over six million today. Their homelands lie in Guatemala, El Salvador, Honduras, Belize, and Mexico, and they also have communities in south Florida, Houston, Los Angeles, and the San Francisco Bay Area. The earliest evidence for poetry in their world is a brief text on the back of a jade plaque, written in the Mayan script.[1] Included is a date, with the number of the year given as 3483. For those of us who come from within the world of letters that was 320 A.D., before there was any such thing as English literature.

An excellent introduction to Mayan poetics may be found in a sixteenth-century work known as Popol Vuh or "Council Book," from the highlands of Guatemala.[2] It is written in the Mayan language known as Quiché or *K'iche'*, but in the letters of the Roman alphabet. The authors chose letters in the aftermath of the European invasion, when books written in the Mayan script were subject to being confiscated and burned. They give their lessons in poetics in the course of telling the story of how the gods prepared the world for human beings, and how human beings built towns and kingdoms. Their lessons take the form of examples, but instead of quoting poems by famous authors they offer hypothetical poems of the kinds humans might have performed at different stages in their condition as poets.

From the very beginning the gods wanted to make beings who could speak to them, but their expectations were only partly linguistic. Yes, they did want beings who could put the adjective *ch'ipa* (newborn) in front of the noun *kaqulja* (thunderbolt) and say *ch'ipa kaqulja,* referring to a fulgurite (a glassy stone formed where lightning strikes the ground). And yes, they wanted beings who could combine the stem *tz'aq-* (make) with the suffix *-ol* (-er) and say *tz'aqol* (maker). But their expectations were also poetic. They didn't yearn to hear complete sentences so much as they wanted to hear phrases or words in parallel pairs, such as *ch'ipa kaqulja, raxa kaqulja,* "newborn thunderbolt, sudden thunderbolt," and *tz'aqol, b'itol,* "maker, modeler." When they made the beings that became today's animals and tried to teach them to speak this way, each species made a different sound. Worse yet, a given species simply repeated its cry, as if to say something like *tz'aqol, tz'aqol* instead of *tz'aqol, b'itol*. Some animals, especially birds, received their names from their cries. The whippoorwill, which says *xpurpuweq, xpurpuweq,* is now called *purpuweq*. The laughing falcon, which says *wak ko, wak ko,* is called *wak*.

The whippoorwill can index its own presence with its call, but it can neither name the laughing falcon nor pretend to be one. For Mayans, it is only in this compartmentalized, subhuman domain that wordlike sounds can stay in tidy, isomorphic relationships with their meanings. Once *purpu-weq* and *wak* become words in a real language, a poet who names the *purpu-weq* may also call it *chajal tikon,* "guardian of the plants." Instead of naming the *wak* straight out, the poet may say *jun nima tz'ikin, ri wak ub'i,* "a large bird, the laughing falcon by name." Europeans once imagined a time, lasting from Eden until Babel, when humans spoke a single, original language composed of words that were intrinsically and unambiguously tied to distinct objects. For Mayans this would be a world before language, and certainly a world before poetry.

After four tries the gods succeed at making real humans, four of them. When they ask these four to talk about themselves, they get a poem in reply. It opens as shown below, with a monostich followed by a distich whose lines are parallel in both syntax and meaning:

Qitzij chik,	Truly now,
kamul k'amo,	double thanks,
oxmul k'amo,	triple thanks,

The pairing of words or phrases is by far the commonest gesture in parallel verse, whether it be Mayan or Chinese or else from the ancient Middle East. Equally widespread is the use of a monostich to provide a frame, as in this example, or to mark internal transitions.[3] The gods would have been perfectly happy with a composition that followed the first distich with a succession of other distichs of similar construction, but they had unwittingly created poets who were more than versifiers. Even the distich has a twist to it, playing off form against meaning by pairing "double" with "triple." The poem continues with a tristich that has a playful turbulence in its syntax, with each line structured slightly differently from the others. Then comes a tetrastich, the rarest of the forms employed so far, but its unusual length is compensated by the uniformity of its syntax:

mixojwinaqirik	we've been formed
mi pu xojchi'nik,	and we have mouths,
xojwachinik,	we have faces,
kojch'awik,	we speak,
kojta'onik,	we listen,
kojb'isonik,	we wonder,
kojsilab'ik,	we move,

In verse of this kind groups of parallel lines can be isometrical, as in the case of the four-syllable lines that make up the distich, but they can just as

well be heterometrical, as in the case of the lines of six, five, and four syllables that make up the tristich. In the passage as a whole, lines range from
three syllables (in the monostich and the first line of the tetrastich) to twice
that number (in the first line of the tristich). There are rhythms here, but
they are temporary rhythms created by temporary alignments of syntax and
therefore of meaning. There are rhymes as well, in the broad sense of recurring combinations of consonants and vowels, but again they are aligned
with syntax and meaning. The effect is to foreground the parts of parallel
lines that do *not* rhyme, which is to say, the morphemes or words that
change from one line to the next without changing their position within
the line. In the distich, everything rhymes except for the morphemes *ka-*
and *ox-*, equivalent to "dou-" and "tri-" in the translation. In the tetrastich,
the repetition of the morphemes *k-* (incomplete aspect), *-oj-* (first-person
plural), and *-ik* (clause-final verb ending) places the emphasis on the contrasting verb stems they enclose.

The first sentence uttered by the first human beings is not yet over, and
as it continues they add a few more poetic moves to the ones they've tried
already. In syntactic terms their next line is a monostich, contrasting in
structure with the lines that immediately precede and follow it, but in semantic terms it forms a tristich with the syntactic distich that follows it,
creating a momentary tension between form and meaning:

utz kaqana'o,	our thinking is good,
xketamaj naj naqaj	we have the knowledge of the far and near
mi pu xqilo nim ch'utin	and we've seen the great and small
upa kaj,	in the sky,
upa ulew.	on the earth.

The first of the two distichs harbors a slight syntactic change of its own,
adding *mi* (perfect aspect) and *pu* (a conjunction) in front of the verb in the
second line, and each of its lines harbors a smaller-scale distich, composed of
naj nakaj (far near) in one and *nim ch'utin* (great small) in the other. The
latter line is the longest in the whole sentence, running to seven syllables,
but the first line of the final distich drops all the way back to three, returning to the shortness of the monostich that began the sentence.

Each of the poetic moves in this first of all human sentences can be
found elsewhere in Quiché and other Mayan poetry, whether ancient or
contemporary, but seldom are so many different moves employed in so
short a time. This is the performance of beings who have, for the moment,
complete understanding of everything in the world, and the utterance itself
is a poetic tour de force. The gods are alarmed by what they have wrought
and decide to cloud the vision of the first humans. After that "it was only
from close up that they could see what was there with any clarity," and

with this came a decline in their poetic abilities. Reduced to mortals who could only communicate with the gods from a distance, they began their first prayer as follows:

Aqaroq!	Alas!
at tz'aqol,	thou maker,
at b'itol,	thou modeler
kojawila',	look at us,
kojata',	listen to us,
mojasako,	don't let us fall,
mojapiskalij,	don't leave us aside,

After the opening monostich, consisting of a lament called out to unseen gods in the distance, comes an unbroken series of distichs that rolls on for many more lines beyond the ones quoted here. The first distich is isometrical, but the rest at least have the virtue of having unequal hemistichs.

After a long period of wandering in darkness, humans recover some of their lost understanding. They become dreamers and diviners, and they also learn how to use *ilob'al,* "instruments for seeing," such as crystals and books. At the same time they regain their former poetic skills, but unlike the first poets they don't squander all their best moves in just a few lines.

One of the effects of parallel verse is what the Sinologist James Hightower called "verbal polyphony."[4] This effect is prominent in Russian folk poetry, but M. M. Bakhtin left that out of consideration when he set up an antithesis between poetry, which he declared to be monological, and the dialogical or polyphonic discourse of the novel. Tracing dialogical effects all the way down to the scale of individual words, he noted that a given word exists in an environment of other words that could have been used with reference to the same object, and that these other words may come to the mind of the hearer or reader.[5] What happens in parallel verse is that one or more of these other words is actually given voice. Consider this distich from the opening of the Popol Vuh:

Waral xchqatz'ib'a wi
xchiqatikib'a wi Ojer Tzij.

Here we shall inscribe
we shall implant the Ancient Word.

By using the stem *tz'ib'-* in the first line, the authors refer to writing without venturing into figurative usage. But then, in the second line, they use the stem *tiki-,* which refers to planting—not in the sense of sowing seeds that will become something else, but in the sense of planting (or transplanting) something that is already a plant in its own right. That something is the Ancient Word, which the authors are transplanting from one book, written in the words and syllables of the Mayan script, into another book, written in the consonants and vowels of the Roman script. In both cases the signs in the graphic field are planted in rows.

The completion of a group of parallel lines that share a common object does not imply that all has been said that could be said about it. In other passages about writing, the authors of the Popol Vuh use other words they could have used here. For example, they might have added a phrase that included the word *retal,* "sign, mark, trace," which refers to a clue left behind by a past act, such as a footprint. Or they might have made use of *wuj,* literally "paper" but a metonym for "book." If they had been inscribing a wood or stone surface instead of paper, they might have invoked *k'ot* (carving), a stem they later pair with *tz'ib'* (writing) when referring to the scribal profession.

It could be argued that the choice the authors actually made in the passage quoted above, to pair planting with writing, ultimately clarifies what they are proposing to do. But the notion of planting serves this purpose only by way of a figurative detour that leaves a residue of additional meanings that would only complicate matters if we stopped to explore them. If we want parallel lines to bring their common object into focus with a minimum of complication, a better example is provided by passages in which the authors pair the word *poy,* which refers to dolls or manikins but doesn't tell us what they are made of, with *ajamche',* which refers to woodcarvings but doesn't tell us, by itself, that the woodcarvings in question are manikins. The Sinologist Peter Boodberg compared the effect of this kind of distich to stereoscopic vision,[6] a notion that has been picked up by various students of parallelism. But I think Jean-Jacques Rousseau came closer to the mark when he wrote, "The successive impressions of discourse, which strike a redoubled blow, produce a different feeling from that of the continuous presence of the same object, which can be taken in at a single glance."[7] It needs to be added that there is no moment at which the successive blows of discourse hammer out a complete object, but only a moment in the course of a performance at which writers or speakers either stop or move on to something else.

In some passages the writers of the Popol Vuh leave their "manikins, woodcarvings" behind right away, but in others they add such statements as *xewinaq wachinik, xewinaq tzijonik puch,* "They were human in looks, they were human in speech as well." It might be claimed that this distich clarifies the picture further, even beyond what the addition of "woodcarvings" did for "manikins," but it also has the potential for contradicting an image we had already formed and replacing it with a new (and still incomplete) image, or making us wonder whether someone is ventriloquizing the manikins, which now sound like puppets, and so on. Instead of being present continuously, the object never quite becomes identical with itself.

There are times when parallel words or phrases, instead of constructing an object out of its parts or aspects, converge on saying nearly the same thing about it. The example given below also happens to shed light on how contemporary speakers of Quiché construct the relationship between language and experience. It comes from a conversation in which Barbara Tedlock and myself were learning how to talk about dreams from Andrés Xiloj Peruch, a diviner. When we asked whether one could describe a *q'alaj wachik* (clear dream) as *kajuljutik* (shining or gleaming), he began with a charitable "yes" but then suggested a more acceptable statement:

> *Xulik pa ri saq*
> > *q'alaj ri wachik,*
>
> *kajuljutik,*
> *kachupchutik.*

> The dream came out bright
> > and clear,
>
> gleaming,
> glittering.

Thus he produced the word *saq,* "light, white, bright," to make a pair with a word from our question, *q'alaj,* which refers to clarity (as opposed to obscurity) and can be used to describe discourse. Then he took the onomatopoeic verb *kajuljutik,* whose reduplicated stem (*julju-*) gives it the character of a small-scale distich, and added a second verb with a reduplicated stem (*chupchu-*). Both verbs indicate some degree of fluctuation in the reception of this "bright and clear" dream, but with a slight difference. *Julju-* carries a sense of acuteness that includes the prickliness of spines and the piquancy of chili, while *chupchu-* is less fine-grained, evoking sensations that include the flickering of a candle and the splashing of water. The effect of the sentence as a whole is to raise the discontinuity of the "presence of the same object" to a high frequency. To paraphrase (and subvert) Charles Olson's version of the famous dictum of Edward Dahlberg, one perception immediately and directly leads to a separate perception of the same object.[8]

The convergence of meaning in Xiloj's statement is supported not only by vocabulary and syntax, but also by the assonance and alliteration that link *saq* with *q'alaj* and *kajuljutik* with *kachupchutik.* But there are other moments in which resonances of this kind are used to rhyme words that are parallel neither in syntax nor in meaning. The purpose is not to answer the demands of a rhyme scheme, but to make a pun. The Quiché term for punning is *sakb'al tzij,* "word dice." Winning combinations of words that share sounds create a sudden shift in meaning that is nevertheless appropriate to the matter at hand. Hearing such a shift provokes neither groans nor outright laughter, but a chuckle or "ah" or "hm" of recognition. Diviners often interpret the Quiché calendar by speaking the number and name of a given date and then giving its augury by playing on the name.[9] Here are three successive dates, each accompanied by two alternative auguries:

Wajxaqib' Tz'i', tz'iyalaj tzij.	Eight Dog, a jealous god.
(or)	(or)
Wajxaqib' Tz'i', katz'iyarik.	Eight Dog, it's all in a fog.
B'elejeb' B'atz', kab'atz'inik.	Nine Monkey, right on the money.
(or)	(or)
B'elejeb' B'atz', ri tz'onoj.	Nine Monkey, matrimony.
Lajuj E, ri utzilaj b'e, kalominaj b'e.	Ten Tooth, on the tried-and-true route.
(or)	(or)
Lajuj E, xasachom ub'e.	Ten Tooth, the wayward youth.

There are times when phrases that are properly parallel in their syntax and meaning nevertheless stand at a considerable distance from one another, opening up a whole range of distinct objects between them. The following example, from the Popol Vuh, evokes the powers of shamans:

Xa kinawal,
xa kipus xb'anataj wi.

Their genius alone
their sharpness alone got it done.

To possess *nawal* is to possess genius in the old sense of the word, adding the powers of a spirit familiar to one's own. A second power is *pus,* literally referring to the cutting open of sacrificial flesh but here understood as the ability to reveal, with a single stroke, something deeply hidden. As a pair these words imply a range of shamanic powers, not because they comprise two grand categories into which everything else fits but because they form a pair of complementary metonyms. The authors could have made a further power explicit by adding (for example) *xa kitzij,* "their words alone," but instead they chose to use this phrase elsewhere.

In Mayan languages, as in Chinese, complementary metonyms may be compressed into a single word. Here are some Quiché examples, hyphenated to show the locations of suppressed word boundaries; each is followed by a literal English rendering and an explanation:

cho-palo	lakesea	all pooled water, fresh or salt
kaj-ulew	skyearth	world, water included
q'ij-ik'	sunmoon	includes planets but not fixed stars
kej-tz'ikin	deerbird	animals of land and air
kar-tap	fishcrab	aquatic animals
nan-tat	motherfather	parents and all ancestors

Even when Mayans make long lists instead of stating a double metonymy, they seem to let some items that could be on the list remain implicit, as if resisting totalization. The authors of the Popol Vuh stop at either nine or thirteen generations when they list the predecessors of the current holders of noble titles, not because the historical total for any lineage was nine or thirteen, but because these numbers belong to a poetics of quantity, one that continues to be followed in present-day invocations of ancestors.[10] The names not mentioned in the Popol Vuh, though perhaps not all of them, can be found by consulting other sixteenth-century sources. There are several documents containing overlapping lists, no two of which are identical in their choices.

Proper names would seem to have at least the potential for bringing words and objects into stable, isomorphic relationships, but they are not exempt from the poetics of saying things in more than one way. Mayan speakers and writers are fond of undoing the "proper name effect," which, to quote Peggy Kamuf's translation of Claude Lévesque's quotation of Jacques Derrida, is manifested by "any signified whose signifier cannot vary nor let itself be translated into another signifier without loss of meaning," which is to say without the loss of one-on-one referentiality.[11] When the authors of the Popol Vuh invoke a proper name that might seem foreign or otherwise opaque to their readers, they often gloss it instead of allowing it to remain in isolation. In telling an animal tale they introduce one of the characters by writing, *Tumusul u b'i, ri xpeq,* or "Tamazul is his name, the toad." Thus they treat their version of *tamazulin,* the ordinary Nahuatl (Aztec) term for a toad, as a proper name, but then demystify this name by supplying *xpeq,* the ordinary Quiché term for the same animal. In the course of telling how the name of the god Hacauitz came to be given to a mountain, they produce the following pair of phrases:

> *Mana pa k'echelaj xk'oje wi Jakawitz,*
> *xa saqi juyub' xewax wi Jakawitz.*

> Hacauitz didn't stay in the forest,
> Hacauitz was hidden instead on a bald mountain.

Here they show their knowledge of Chol, a Mayan language in which *jaka witz* is literally "stripped mountain," a condition described by *saqi juyub',* "bare (or plain) mountain," in Quiché. The effect they create is something like that of disturbing the properness of the name Chicago, which comes from an Algonkian language, by remarking, "Chicago was founded in a place where wild garlic once grew."

Another way Mayans dispel the properness of names is to multiply them. This is not simply a matter of using both a name and a surname (Robert and Creeley), but it does resemble the cases of a name and nickname (Robert and Bob) or a name and an epithet (Buffalo and Nickel City). What remains different is that a single proper name, unless it forms part of a list of persons or places that parallel one another, is likely to be denied self-sufficiency. Instead of replacing some other name, a nickname or epithet is invoked alongside it, as if to say "Robert Bob" or "Buffalo Nickel City." An eighth-century picture of a Mayan noblewoman at the site of Yaxchilán, in Chiapas, is captioned as follows: [12]

Na Ba'te'el,	Mother Warrior,
Wak Chan Ahaw,	Sixth Sky Sovereign,
Na Ik' Ahaw,	Mother Wind Sovereign,
Na Bakab	Mother Cornerpost

The use of the Mother and/or Sovereign titles with each of the four names equalizes them, making it impossible to tell the difference between primary names and secondary epithets (if indeed there is any). The caption for another picture of the same woman utilizes some of the same words and adds others:

Na Ch'ul,	Mother Goddess,
Na Wak Tun,	Mother Sixth Stone,
Na Ik' Ahaw,	Mother Wind Sovereign,
Na Bakab,	Mother Cornerpost,
Chik'in Chak Te'	Sunset Red Tree

For the original writers and readers of these captions, the multiple names may have evoked discontinuous aspects of this woman's history, personality, or powers. In other words, the effect would have been different from that of the continuous presence of the "same" person.

Whether parallel words or phrases refer to the same (although intermittently present) object, or else point to objects other than the particular ones they name, they constantly work against the notion that an isomorphism between words and their objects could actually be realized. To paraphrase (and invert) Charles Olson's version of the famous dictum of Robert Creeley, this is a poetics in which form is *always other* than an extension of content. [13]

A parallel poetics stands opposed to the philosophical or scientific project of developing an object language whose meanings have been shorn of all synonymy and polysemy. At the same time it stands opposed to the literary project of protecting poems against the "heresy of paraphrase" by treating them as if they were Scripture, composed of precisely the right words and no others. To paraphrase (and invert) Charles Bernstein's rephrasing of the orthodox position of I. A. Richards and/or Cleanth Brooks, a parallel poetics is one in which a poem *not* said in any other way is not a poem in the first place. [14]

In a poetics that always stands ready, once something has been said, to find other ways to say it, there can be no fetishization of verbatim quotation, which lies at the very heart of the Western commodification of words. In the Mayan case not even writing, whether in the Mayan script or the

Roman alphabet, carries with it a need for exact quotation. When Mayan authors cite previous texts, and even when they cite earlier passages in the same text, they unfailingly construct paraphrases. Such is the case at the site of Palenque, in Chiapas, where three eighth-century temples contain texts that tell a long story whose episodes are partly different and partly over-lapped from one temple to the next. Among the events are the formation of the present world by the gods and the deeds of kings who claim divine inspiration, but the text is not what we would call Scripture. In the overlap-ping episodes not a single sentence is repeated verbatim from one temple to another. Smaller-scale examples of paraphrase occur in the dialogues among characters in the Popol Vuh. When spoken messages are sent through third parties, the words that are quoted as having been sent and those that are quoted as having been delivered never match one another verbatim. This is true even in an episode in which the senders are described as having messen-gers who "repeated their words, in just the same order." Here are before and after versions of a sentence from the message:

> *Chikik'am k'u uloq ri kichoqonisan.*
> So they must bring along their sports gear.

> *Chik'am uloq ri ronojel ketz'ab'al.*
> He must bring along all their gaming equipment.

It would have been easy for the authors to match the quotations letter for letter, since they occur on the same page, but they didn't bother. The two sentences are at least parallel, or put together "in the same order," and they share a focus on sports equipment.

Our own notions of accurate quotation have been shaped, in part, by print technology, which finds its purest expression in the exact reproduction of Scripture and other canonized texts. The technology of sound recording is a further chapter in the same grand story of representation, but it pro-duces a surplus of aural information that causes problems for text-based researchers who turn their attention to recorded speech. Folklorists have a way of making "oral formulaic composition" sound like a primitive prede-cessor of typesetting, providing a partial remedy for the crisis of memory that supposedly afflicts the members of oral cultures. Linguists have a way of making "performance" sound as though it were an optional addition to a standard software package, one that would otherwise print out a perfectly normal text. Meanwhile, in the poetics of parallelism, variation is not some-thing that waits for a later performance of the same poem, but is required for the production of this poem, or any poem, in the first place.

Translation caused anxiety long before the current critique of represen-tations, especially the translation of poetry. Roman Jakobson pointed the way to a new construction of this problem, suggesting that the process of rewording might be called *intra*lingual translation.[15] Here we may add that within parallel verse, not only in theory but in practice, the further step to *inter*lingual translation may take place, with words from two different languages dividing an object between them. In the simplest case the passage from one parallel phrase to the next entails the replacement of a single word with its near-equivalent in another language.

The epigram to this essay changes languages by whole phrases, passing from standard English to Belizean Creole to Garífuna (an Amerindian language spoken by Belizean blacks whose ancestors learned it on St. Vincent) to Spanish and then back to Creole, ironically bypassing the indigenous language of Belize (Mopán Maya).[16] In the macaronic verse of medieval Europe, the changes took place between Latin and the local vernacular. Quiché writers of the sixteenth century sometimes paired words from Nahuatl (the language of the Aztecs) with Quiché equivalents. In the Popol Vuh two terms for a royal house or lineage, *chinamit* (from Nahuatl *chinamitl*) and *nimja* (Quiché), are paired in *e oxib' chinamit, oxib' puch nimja,* which might be translated as "those of the three casas grandes and three great houses." In contemporary discourse Spanish has taken the place of Nahuatl, as in this double question from a story told by Vicente de León Abac of Momostenango: *Jasa ri kab'anoq chech? De que consiste?* This is something like saying, "What could be happening to them? Was ist das?"

Here we have entered a realm in which the popular notion of an enmity between poetry and translation does not apply. To quote Robert Frost's famous phrasing of this notion, as remembered by Edwin Honig in conversation with Octavio Paz, "Poetry is what gets lost in translation."[17] As Andrew Schelling remembers this exchange, Paz countered Honig by paraphrasing Frost, saying, "Poetry is what is translated." To take this statement a step further and paraphrase it for purposes of the present discussion, poetry *is* translation.

Frost's notion is an ethnocentric one, rooted in a poetic tradition that has devoted much of its energy to manipulating linguistic sounds at a level below that of words and syntax, which is to say below the level of segments that have already begun to carry meaning. This is the level that is most resistant to translation—unless we do as Louis Zukofsky did, finding English meanings to fit the sounds of Catullus. But in a tradition that does its main work above the phonetic level, translation is one of the principal means by which poems are constructed in the first place. Translation into a further language at a later date, like nonverbatim quotation at a later date, then becomes a continuation of a process already under way in the poem itself.

Keeping parallel phrases parallel solves one kind of translation problem but raises others, among them the question of graphic representation. To speak of "parallel lines" is to speak the language of alphabetic writing even before the letters are arranged in lines on a page. For well over a thousand years, Mayan poetry was written in a graphic code that looks quite different from the one in which the texts quoted so far have been cast. In his *Mayan Letters,* Olson first suggested that "the glyphs were the alphabet of [Mayan] books," which "puts the whole thing back into the spoken language." Four days later he wrote, "A Maya glyph is more pertinent to our purposes than anything else," because "these people . . . had forms which unfolded directly from content."[18] Taken together, these statements project the dream of a writing system that is transparent to language and the world at one and the same time. As it turns out the signs of Mayan writing do notate linguistic sounds, but they do not constitute an alphabet. And, though some signs do take their forms from objects in the world, they rarely mean what they look like.

Instead of notating consonants and vowels, Mayan signs go by syllables and whole words. And where an alphabet constitutes a closed code, fixed at a small number of signs that are (ideally) isomorphic with the sounds they notate, Mayan signs (like Egyptian and Chinese signs) are abundant, providing multiple ways of spelling any given syllable or word. This kind of script is reader-friendly in its own particular ways, permitting the annotation of a word sign with a syllabic hint as to its pronunciation, or permitting a reader to recall a forgotten sign or learn a new one by comparing two different spellings in places where the text would seem to demand the same word. It is also writer-friendly, presenting choices that are more than a matter of calligraphy or typography. Here we need a new term or two, perhaps *polygraphy* or *diagraphism*. Just as a Mayan poem reminds the hearer that different words can be used with reference to the same object, so a Mayan text reminds the reader that different signs can be used for the same syllables or words.

When a Mayan sign appears to be iconic, its object, if we want to get on with the reading of the text, is usually a sound rather than the thing it

pictures. In this pair of signs , written by a poet/scribe of the fifteenth century, the upper one is the profiled head of a *mut,* a kind of partridge. But here it is meant to be read as the syllable *mu,* and below it is a sign for *ka,* read as the sound of *k* alone in this position, where it completes the word *muk,* "herald" or "augur." Now it happens that the bird called *mut* is an augur, a giver of signs or omens, and that its name serves as a metonym for omens in general, which may be why the poet chose this particular way of spelling *muk.* It also happens that the same poet used the word *mut* in the other half of the same distich in which *muk* appears, but

chose to spell it with this pair of signs: . The upper element stands for *mu* and the lower one for *ti,* here read as the *t* sound that completes the word *mut.* As in the case of two lines of verse that are parallel semantically but not syntactically, the result is a tension between form and meaning.

These examples of Mayan spelling have been extracted from larger characters or glyphs, which often include more than two signs apiece. The signs that make up a glyph are clustered in a rectangular space and account for at least one complete word. The glyphs themselves are arranged in double columns, with each pair of glyphs read from left to right and each pair of columns read from top to bottom. With such a format it would have been easy for Mayan poets to create graphic displays of the structure of parallel verse, bringing variable syllable counts into line by packing more signs into some glyphs than others. In books the minimal text consists of four glyphs, one pair beneath the other. Even the quarter-inch glyphs used in books sometimes contain as many as six syllables, so four glyphs could have been composed in such a way as to spell out two full distichs, one beneath the other. A more legible text could have been produced by giving each half of a distich a whole line (two glyphs) to itself. What the scribes did instead, more often than not, was to devote most of the available space to the first part of a distich and then resort to ellipsis for the second part. The following text (the source of the signs discussed above) is from an almanac that tracks the changing relationship between the moon goddess and the fixed stars. It concerns moon rises preceded by the appearance of the Macaw constellation (the Big Dipper):[19]

Mo'o	*yox mut*
The Scarlet Macaw	is the third sign of
Sak Che'l,	*u muk.*
the Arc of Light,	her herald.

A priest-shaman reading aloud from this text in the presence of a client would have had the option of expanding upon "her herald" to fill out the second hemistich, saying some or all of "[the Scarlet Macaw] is the [third] herald of [the Arc of Light]." A further option might have been the substitution of alternative names, such as *Wuk Ek'* (Seven Stars) for "Scarlet Macaw," or *Pal Ú* (Young Moon) for "Arc of Light."

In longer texts Mayan scribes created a sustained counterpoint between poetic structure and visual organization. At the scale of a whole composition they sometimes divided a text covering two major topics into two blocks of writing with an equal number of glyphs, but always with the transition between the two topics offset from the visual boundary in the text. The boundary was as likely to fall in the middle of a sentence as anywhere else, as in the case of the excerpt below.[20] It opens the second half of a text that is divided into right and left halves by a picture. The first pair of phrases, "on 2 Kib 14 Mol" (a two-part date on the Mayan calendar), corresponds to two glyphs written side by side, but a similar pair appearing later, "3 Kaban 15 Mol," is split between two lines. The distich "Sun-Eye

Sky Jaguar, Holy Lord of Egrets" is written with paired glyphs the first time it appears, but the same two glyphs are split between lines the second time. The double name of the temple where the inscription is located, "Thunderbolt Sun-Eye" and "Feathered Jaguar," is carried by paired glyphs (with "temple" appended to the second), but the two glyphs that give the double name of a portion of the Milky Way, "Hollow Tree" and "Sky Granary," are divided between lines. Moreover, "Hollow Tree" is in the right half of a glyph whose left half, "It happened at," starts a new sentence in the middle of a line. The tristichs in this passage—"Mirror, Thunderbolt, Sustainer of Dreams" and "Sixth Sky Thunderbolt, three Jaguar Thunderbolts, Holy Lady of Egrets"—could have been squared up by spelling out their Mayan equivalents with even numbers of glyphs, but in both cases the scribe chose to highlight their oddness rather than conceal it, using exactly three glyphs.

Though the pairing of glyphs in ancient Mayan texts cross-cuts the structures of Mayan verse, it still keeps verse in visual play at least part of the time. In this respect it stands between the graphic practices of ancient Mesopotamia and Egypt, where a text in verse looks the same as any other, and those of ancient Greece and Rome, where verse was written in lines that mirrored its structure. In the beginning, Greco-Roman lines were those of isometric verse, and the lines of various European poetries have followed suit for most of their history. In purely graphic terms, such verse has a curious kinship with prose. When Greeks and Romans wrote prose, they strove for a justified right margin and broke words wherever necessary. When they wrote verse they left the right margin just ragged enough to call attention to the achievement of a near-match between the organization of discourse and the organization of the graphic field. The addition of end rhymes made this achievement still more visible. Against this background the contemporary move to verse that is not only blank (note the visual metaphor) but also free of isometric schemes created a deficit in the visual display of poetic artifice. Olson, as if seeking to compensate for this, wanted the poet to use typography "to indicate exactly the breath, the pauses, the suspensions even of syllables, the juxtapositions of parts of phrases, which he intends."[21] His project comes very close to reversing a long-standing Western subordination of voice and ear to the scanning eye, but he reaches for the voice without letting go of the notion that the poem said in some other way is not the poem. To get the poet's intentions right, he tells us, we must repeat not only the words but the breaths, pauses, and suspensions as well.

As we have seen, Mayan poets who used the Mayan script chose to treat the graphic field and parallel verse as semi-independent systems rather than forcing one to mirror the other. When they adopted the Roman alphabet they chose to put everything they wrote (except for a few lists) into a prose format with occasional paragraph breaks. Some of our own poets—Gertrude Stein and Lyn Hejinian, for example—have also chosen to use a

. . . on 2 Kib   14 Mol

they rejoined   their umbilical cord,

the divine triplets: Mirror,

Thunderbolt,   Sustainer of Dreams.

On the day   3 Kaban

15 Mol   he walked around

Thunderbolt Sun-Eye   Feathered Jaguar Temple,

the home of   those who fast:

Sun-Eye Sky Jaguar,   Holy Lord of Egrets.

On the third day   he summons the ghost of

the namesake of Lady Sky,   a wise woman,

from the cut in his tongue;   he takes the white crown of

his holiness: Sun-Eye Sky Jaguar,

Holy Lord of Egrets.   It happened at Hollow Tree,

Sky Granary,   the invocation of

Sixth Sky Thunderbolt,   three Jaguar Thunderbolts,

Holy Lady of Egrets.   4 and 6 score days . . .

From the tablet in the Temple of the Foliated Cross at Palenque in Chiapas, Mexico. The reading order is left to right and top to bottom. The date 2 Kib 14 Mol fell on 18 July 690, when Sun-Eye Sky Jaguar was Holy Lord of Egrets (the king who ruled from Palenque). The Divine Triplets or three Jaguar Thunderbolts (Mars, Jupiter, and Saturn) had all met up with Sixth Sky Thunderbolt (Antares) at the foot of Hollow Tree or Sky Granary (the part of the Milky Way that currently stood on the southwest horizon at midnight). On 3 Kaban 15 Mol (19 July) the triplets were joined by their mother, Lady Sky or Holy Lady of Egrets (the moon). Sun-Eye Sky Jaguar then called up the ghost of her namesake, a former queen of Palenque and his own grandmother.

prose format for parallel phrasing. The five lines of Quiché prose illustrated below come from the manuscript of an ancient play known as *Rab'inal Achi,* "Man of Rabinal," or *Xajoj Tun,* "Dance of the Trumpet":[22]

chin tzatana cu uvach chin metzetzeh-
tah. chinhiquiquehtah chupam unimal.
tzaɛ. unimal goxtun chigahpa' chigah-
xugutal xatanima retalil nugamic nu-
tzachic varal chuxmut. gah. chuxmut.

Demonstrating the verse in such texts for the European eye requires reorganizing them into parallel lines, as I have done for the Popol Vuh excerpts already presented. Scanning the present text (and modernizing its sixteenth-century orthography) yields the following results:

chinsata na k'u uwach,	and I have yet to show her face,
chinmesesejtaj,	I would dance her round and round,
chinjikikijtaj,	I would dance her on and on,
chupam unimal tz'aq,	inside the great fortress,
unimal k'oxtun,	the great walls,
chi kaj pa,	in all four directions,
chi kaj xukutal,	in all four corners,
xata nima retalil nukamik,	just to mark the greatness of my death,
nusachik,	my disappearance,
waral chuxmut kaj,	here at the navel of the sky,
chuxmut	at the navel of

As they were written on a page, these lines happen to begin halfway through a distich (the first half translates as "I have yet to show her mouth") and end in the midst of a hemistich (which ends with "the earth"). The scanned version appears to rescue the poetry from the prose, but there remains the problem of how to voice it. Taking our own verse tradition as a guide, we might end each hemistich by lowering our pitch (as indicated by the commas) and then pausing. Or we could modify this approach by saving our pauses for the transition between one full distich and the next, which would put our combination of pitches and pauses directly in the service of the hierarchical structure created by the scanning eye. But that is not the way these words are performed by an actor.

Just as the phrasing of Mayan glyphs interacts with the structure of verse without being reduced to a mere instrument of scansion, so does the phrasing created by Mayan pitches and pauses. Pitch contours and pauses also interact with one another, but without being mere functions of one another.[23] The punctuation and line breaks in Emily Dickinson's manuscripts make it plain that she understood the polysystemic nature of spoken phrasing quite well, and the simplifications carried out by the editors of older printed versions testify to the dominance of eye over ear in mainstream Western poetics. In the case of the Mayan play, the art of speaking the parts has been passed along orally, in company with the manuscript. José León Coloch, the present director and producer of the play, coaches the actors by reading their parts aloud. When he speaks the passage under discussion here it comes out as shown below. Each dash indicates a slight rise, each new flush-left line is preceded by an unmistakably deliberate pause, and the final period indicates a sentence-ending drop in intonation:

> and I have yet to show her face—
> I would dance her round and round—
> I would dance her on and on—
> inside the great fortress—
> the great walls—
> in all four directions—
> in all four corners—
> just to mark the greatness of—
> my death—my disappearance—here at the navel of the sky—at the navel
>   of the earth.

Thus hemistich boundaries are marked in the same way as distich boundaries. The tension created by the pauses at these boundaries, instead of being softened by a slight fall in pitch that would signal the completion of a phrase or clause (but not a sentence) in ordinary conversation, is heightened by a slight rise that emphasizes incompleteness. A slightly steeper rise would imply a question, signaling that the hearer should complete the pitch contour by providing an answer with a terminal drop (as we do in English). In other words, each successive line is poised on the edge of a question-and-answer dialogue, but the second half of a distich is not allowed to sound like an answer to the question raised by the first half. These quasi-questions go on piling up until the tension reaches its high point with the line "just to mark the greatness of—," where syntactical incompleteness (or enjambment) reaches its high point and the completion of a hemistich is withheld until the next line. The phrases in that line continue to be marked off by rises, but the elimination of pauses lessens the suspense and a sentence-terminal fall (marked by a period) releases it. At the largest scale, this passage might be said to raise a list of questions for which the long last line provides an answer.

Like the director of the Rabinal play, Quiché poets who specialize in the performance of prayers treat verse phrasing, intonational phrasing, and pause phrasing as three semi-independent systems. In this excerpt from the opening of a prayer spoken by Esteban Ajxup of Momostenango, the commas indicate slight drops in pitch, in contrast to the slight rise indicated (as above) by a dash:

> *Sacha la numak komon nan—*
> *komon waq remaj,*
> *komon waq tik'aj,*
> *komon chuch, komon qajaw,*
> *komon ajchak, komon ajpatan, komon ajbara, komon ajpunto, komon ajtz'ite,*
>   *komon ajwaraje,*
> *uk'amik, uchokik, wa chak, wa patan, chikiwa ri nan, chikiwa ri tat,*

> Pardon my trespass all mothers—
> all six generations,
> all six jarsfull,
> all matriarchs, all patriarchs,
> all workers, all servers, all mixers, all pointers, all counters of seeds, all
>   readers of cards,
> who received, who entered, this work, this service, before the mothers,
>   before the fathers,

Here the opening monostich has been created by means of ellipsis; it could have been followed by some or all of "pardon my trespass all fathers." Next comes a distich whose delivery as two separate lines, each of them ended with a slight drop in pitch, marks it off from what comes before and after. The next distich is run on as a single line, which again sets it off (but in a different way). There follows a further acceleration, with two very long lines in succession. They are parallel in the sense that each consists of three distichs, and in the sense that they are identical in their pitch and pause phrasing, but there is a tension between them at the level of syntax. The first one reiterates a single grammatical pattern six times, while the second moves through three different patterns, repeating each one twice. As in the case of performances of the Rabinal play, there is no moment in Ajxup's performances at which a sustained pattern of pitches and pauses falls into lock step with scansion.

Following Bakhtin, we could try to see the complexity of Mayan poetry as the result of a conflict between centripital forces in language, which are supposed to produce formal and authoritative discourse, and centrifugal forces, which are supposed to open language to its changing contexts and foment new kinds of discourse.[24] But this is a profoundly Western way of stating the problem. Available to speakers of any language are multiple systems for phrasing utterances, including syntax, semantics, intonation, and pausing. Available to writers (even within the limits of a keyboard) is a variety of signs, of which some are highly conventional and particulate while others are iconic and may stand for whole words. There is nothing intrinsic to any one of these various spoken and written codes, not even the alphabet itself, that demands the reduction of all or any of the others to its own terms. Bringing multiple codes into agreement with one another is not a matter of poetics as such, but of centralized authority. It is no accident that Mayans, who never formed a conquest state and have kept their distance from European versions of the state right down to the current morning news, do not bend their poetic energies to making systems stack.

Lastly, a poem written by Humberto Ak'abal of Momostenango.[25] By means of an animal metaphor he evokes the recent Guatemalan civil war, with its helicopter gun ships and clandestine cemeteries. But instead of extending his chosen metaphor into a systematic allegory, he runs it up against the fact that animals are without language, thus evoking the story told in the Popol Vuh:

K'uch:	Buzzard:
kaxa re kaminaq,	box for the dead,
muqub'al karapapik,	grave on the wing,
xawi karaj kaweqaj	but you're not burdened
ri ub'i ri kaminaq.	with the names of the dead.

NOTES

1. For a detailed account of this artifact, which is known as the Leyden Plaque after its present location in the Netherlands, see Floyd G. Lounsbury, "The Ancient Writing of Middle America," in *The Origins of Writing,* ed. Wayne M. Senner (Lincoln: University of Nebraska Press, 1989), pp. 205–8.

2. This and other textual excerpts from the Popol Vuh or *Popol Wuj* are given in the official orthography of the Academia de las Lenguas Mayas de Guatemala and include emendations of the manuscript. For a complete translation see Dennis Tedlock, *Popol Vuh: The Mayan Book of the Dawn of Life,* rev. ed. (New York: Simon & Schuster, 1996).

3. See Roman Jakobson, *Language in Literature,* ed. Krystyna Pomorska and Stephen Rudy (Cambridge, Mass.: Harvard University Press, 1987), p. 156.

4. Cited in a 1959 source not available to me by Roman Jakobson, in Jakobson, 172. He relies heavily on Hightower when discussing parallelism in Russian poetry.

5. M. M. Bakhtin, *The Dialogic Imagination,* tr. C. Emerson and M. Holquist (Austin: University of Texas Press, 1981), pp. 68–82.

6. Peter Boodberg, "Cedules from a Berkeley Workshop in Asiatic Philology," in *Selected Works of Peter A. Boodberg,* comp. Alvin P. Cohen (Berkeley: University of California Press, 1979), p. 184.

7. Jean-Jacques Rousseau, "Essay on the Origin of Languages," in *On the Origin of Language,* tr. by John H. Moran (New York: Frederick Ungar, 1966), p. 8.

8. See Charles Olson, *Selected Writings,* ed. Robert Creeley (New York: New Directions, 1966), p. 17. Olson's version of Dahlberg's statement, which Olson

means to keep the poet moving fast rather than lingering, is "ONE PERCEPTION MUST IMMEDIATELY AND DIRECTLY LEAD TO A FURTHER PERCEPTION."

9. For more on this see Barbara Tedlock, *Time and the Highland Maya,* rev. ed. (Albuquerque: University of New Mexico Press, 1992), chap. 5.

10. Dennis Tedlock, 56, 194–97.

11. Claude Lévesque, Introduction to "Roundtable on Translation," in *The Ear of the Other: Otobiography, Transference, Translation,* ed. by Christie V. McDonald (New York: Schocken, 1985), p. 93.

12. The two pictures and captions discussed here are on lintels 41 and 38, illustrated and glossed in Carolyn E. Tate, *Yaxchilan: The Design of a Maya Ceremonial City* (Austin: University of Texas Press, 1992), pp. 177–78, 250–51, 277–78. The translations are mine.

13. Olson, 16. His version of Creeley's statement is "FORM IS NEVER MORE THAN AN EXTENSION OF CONTENT."

14. Bernstein's formulation, "The problem is that the poem said in any other way is not the poem," may be found in his *A Poetics* (Cambridge, Mass.: Harvard University Press, 1992), p. 16.

15. Jakobson, 429.

16. The epigram is from the end of a longer poem in Luke E. Ramirez, *The Poems I Write* (Belize: Belizean Heritage Foundation, 1990), p. 17. The ellipsis is in the original.

17. Edwin Honig, *The Poet's Other Voice: Conversations on Literary Translation,* ed. Edwin Honig (Amherst: University of Massachusetts Press, 1985), p. 154.

18. Olson, 108, 113.

19. The hieroglyphic text, in Yucatec Maya, is from p. 16c of the Dresden Codex, which is reproduced in full in J. Eric S. Thompson, *A Commentary on the Dresden Codex* (Philadelphia: American Philosophical Society, 1972). The alphabetic transcription is a revised version of the one given in Charles A. Hofling, "The Morphosyntactic Basis of Discourse Structure in Glyphic Text in the Dresden Codex," in *Word and Image in Maya Culture: Explorations in Language, Writing, and Representation,* ed. William F. Hanks and Don S. Rice (Salt Lake City: University of Utah Press, 1989), p. 61. The translation is mine.

20. For a detailed discussion of this text, see Linda Schele, *XVI Maya Hieroglyphic Workshop at Texas* (Austin: Department of Art and Art History, University of Texas, 1992), pp. 169–74. My departures from her views are minor at the level of the phonetic values she assigns to the glyphs but considerable at the level of translation and interpretation. In separating the incomplete and complete aspects of verbs (rendered here as present and past tenses) I follow Stephen D. Houston, "The Shifting Now: Aspect, Deixis, and Narrative in Classic Maya Texts," *American Anthropologist,* vol. 98, pp. 291–305 (1997).

21. Olson, 22.

22. From Miguel Pérez, "Rabinal achi vepu xahoh tun," p. 57. Manuscript dated 1913, copy in the Latin American Library, Tulane University. This is the most recent in a series of copies made over a period of centuries in the town of Rabinal.

23. For a linguistic discussion of the contrasts among different kinds of phrasing, see Anthony C. Woodbury, "Rhetorical Structure in a Central Alaskan Yupik Eskimo Traditional Narrative," in *Native American Discourse: Poetics and Rhetoric,* ed. Joel Sherzer and Anthony C. Woodbury (Cambridge: Cambridge University Press, 1987), pp. 176–239.

24. Bakhtin, 272–73.

25. Humberto Ak'abal, *El animalero,* Colección Poesía Guatemalteca 5 (Guate-mala: Ministerio de Cultura y Deportes, 1990), p. 14; translation mine. An extended discussion of contemporary Mayan poetics is included in Enrique Sam Colop, "Maya Poetics," Ph.D. diss., State University of New York at Buffalo (1994).

9

Speech Effects
The Talk as a Genre

BOB PERELMAN

*T*alk has its charm, evanescent but persistent.

Driving in Philadelphia July 19, 1996, I heard a few minutes of funk singer George Clinton being interviewed on National Public Radio by Terry Gross. It was an "archive" Fresh Air program from 1992—or was it '94?—now being rebroadcast in conjunction with the release of Clinton's new CD, *The Awesome Power of a Fully Operational Mother Ship*. Or was the original broadcast timed to promote *Mother Ship* (*Mothership!*), and the repeat presentation timed to promote some new release whose existence and therefore whose name I'm not sure of? Talk is evanescent, especially when it comes from a more or less unfamiliar quarter.

Clinton spoke of his early involvement with the Parliaments. Other Motown groups—the Temptations, Gladys Knight and the Pips—had tightly organized choreography and costumes. Body size was important: the Temptations were each exactly six feet tall. The Parliaments, on the other hand, were all sizes; it wasn't easy to keep shirts ironed and ties clean; in their dance routines they weren't as tight as the Pips or the Temptations. After a certain point, attempts at patching together some kind of uniformity were abandoned and "We threw down the suit and wore the bag."

Transcribed from memory now, those words look blander and odder than they did at the time, when they conveyed real charm—funking around on stage in a garment bag, rather than aspiring to the machined, upwardly mobile libido of the Temptations in their matched suits. Clinton's own vocal routines seemed quite rehearsed. He'd clearly given these kinds of interviews many times before; he knew the questions and the answers and knew that an audience who considered him famous would appreciate hearing some casual inside information, even if it didn't come from all that far inside. Commodified it may have been, however, the routine of his speech was a pleasure; after all, commodities do provide enjoyment to the receiver.

Clinton was master of his own social trajectory and projections, and this mastery was audible in his speech, amused and amusing, entrepreneurial but laid-back.

In the following considerations of the poet's public talk as a genre, I would like to keep the potential charm of talk in mind. Talk is the most mixed of media: social, bodily, clichéd, spontaneous, conflictual, identificatory. But the tone and rhythm of culturally perspicacious speech make for an effective token of the possibility of individual agency, however local, within the densely conflicted institutional grids of the contemporary socialscape. Print and the hierarchies of publishing and circulation are territories where social contentions are as densely coded as anywhere: the evanescent charms of talk are difficult to discern in printed speech. Nevertheless, here, in print, I want to remind readers of those possibilities.

I

My investigation of the talk as genre is grounded in reconsideration of the San Francisco Talk Series and the collections of talks I edited in the early eighties, *Talks* (*Hills* 6/7) and *Writing/Talks*.[1] The books exist as independent critical documents; however, they also can be read as a partial record of the Talk Series that I curated in the Bay Area in the late seventies and early eighties and as part of the history of the construction of the language-writing group—though it remains a contentious issue how much of a group phenomenon language writing is.[2] Some of the talks are sites where influential notions were first presented: Ron Silliman's "The New Sentence"; Lyn Hejinian's "The Rejection of Closure," though in each case it is the modified, identically titled essay that is almost always cited, not the talk. It makes sense that the talk, as a form for criticism, would seem sketchier than an essay. But the form of the talk contains possibilities that are not explored elsewhere by the ranges of language-writing practice—specifically dramatic and rhetorical effects that depend on narrative and an unambiguous notion of person, and thus seem to go against the grain of much of that practice.

Before turning to the Bay Area language-writing talks, I want to mention some antecedent figures from the context of the New American Poetry—specifically David Antin, Allen Ginsberg, and Jack Kerouac—and some related forms. The talk is very much a middling genre. Made out of speech but often later constituted by writing, the talk's amorphous territory is bounded by poetry readings, performance art, teaching and other academic procedures, interviews, and entertainment. Its form is multiplex, existing as both performance and transcription. It can focus around one speaker, a few, or a group; it can be an act of criticism or an art performance; it can connote professionalism or antiprofessional spontaneity. As a recording of mixed-group intention, it lacks the focus that acts of writing

have, whether these arise from authorial decision or preestablished procedures. But a different level of intention is created by the fact that a talk has
been recorded, transcribed, and published. This elevation of the speakers'
words pushes the talk closer to the interview, where we reproduce George
Clinton's words because they're George Clinton's.

But such a syndrome, though it can be ascribed to curiosity, an unex-
ceptional reaction to the hierarchies of renown, can rub the democratic,
self-fashioning assumptions of intellectuals the wrong way. Pushing the adjectives slightly, it could be called sycophantic, prurient. The increasing popularity of the interview in academic contexts has been decried by David
Simpson as arising from "anxiety or insecurity about professionalism":

> To disavow the labor of the article or book for the immediacy of the inter-
> view is of course to put one on a footing with the rock stars and movie
> stars whose expressive norm in our culture is already that same interview,
> or printed conversation. But it is also access to presence and to voice, to
> the very things that Derrida told us long ago we were too much in love
> with . . . To *write* the transcript of *speech* . . . is thus to have it both ways,
> to be available for posterity without any sacrifice to the pleasures and/or
> illusions of full presence.[3]

The ethical nuances of this are clear enough. Having it both ways and dis-
avowing labor are not compliments. Talk is a morally deficient, degraded
substitute for the written word and is given the old Calvinist brushoff:
they're lazy; they just don't want to *write!*

Academic interviews may be proliferating, but the written dimension
remains primary. An academic talk is most often simply an individual pronouncing written words. The prestige of this speaker varies from academic
star to nervous job candidate. In both cases the audience will be there because of the words on paper, but depending on the status of the speaker,
judgment will arise from different sources. Posture, accent, timbre, ward-
robe, ability to inhabit and inflect the written phrases will add interest if
the speaker is a star; but if the speaker is a job candidate these paraverbal
factors can contribute as much to the eventual judgment rendered as the
words themselves. The star's words circulate as writing, with live speech or
the simulated speech of the presentation or interview a side issue of human
interest; in contrast, the candidate's words, even though written, are speech
aspiring, eventually, to the status of writing.

The situation is different in poetry, with an increasing number of scenes
where the spoken is the primary mode—poetry slams, the Nuyorican Café,
sound poetry, performance art. And amongst page poets, the poet's voice
has, since the sixties, been valorized across a wide range of aesthetics from
Charles Olson and Allen Ginsberg, who make breath a key element of composition, to the workshop notion of voice. But this quite mixed chorus
praising sound ultimately reads from a printed score. Whether the voice is
pronouncing spoken word art or a double sestina, the words have almost
always been organized prior to the performance.

David Antin's talk poems reverse this priority, originating as improvised speech. "what am i doing here" (1973), the initial poem in his first
book of talk pieces, is a twenty-page transcript of a spoken improvisation
that covers a range of loosely interlocking subjects and stories: writing versus talking; an acquaintance who dated a man who turned out to have a
tattooed penis; Antin letting a very paranoid friend borrow his car; a discussion of scientific terminology from an antifoundational viewpoint. The deliberate casualness of the segues lasts on through to the end, which, though
earlier themes are remembered, is not a climactic summing up of previous
themes. This seeming casualness comes from a notion of compositional
rigor:

> as a poet i was getting extremely tired of   what i considered an unnatu-
> ral language act   going into a closet   so to speak   sitting in
> front of a typewriter   because anything is possible sitting in front of
> a typewriter and   nothing is necessary   a closet is no place to
> address anybody[4]

In the standard regimes of writing there is a time lag between production and reception of words. By making speech the site of creation, Antin
is attempting to make the two times coincide. His transcription imitates
this immediacy: he avoids capitals, punctuation, apostrophes, flush left and
right margins, and uses spaces to mimic the pauses between his phrases.
The features of writing have been reduced to spaced clumps of lowercase
letters aiming to designate nothing more than sonic immediacy.

Aiming at unmediated sound, however, does not eliminate questions
about social context. Antin's typography has a second target: it attacks normative prose and the authority of conventionalized discourse. The battle
involves tangled issues, as can be seen from the blurb on the back cover. I
want to display—quote is not quite the right verb—a large portion of it
here:

> For the past few years the poet and art critic David Antin has been per-
> forming spontaneous "talk poems" . . . "I see my talking pieces," says
> Antin, "as philosophical inquiries to which I try to bring the resources of
> language, not only my own language, but natural language in its natural
> setting, or one of its natural settings—talk. I've been a poet, critic, linguist,
> and engineer, and though this knowledge informs the book, it is not the
> work of a professional.
>
> "*Talking at the Boundaries*," he continues, "asks questions about life,
> about art, about the nature of experience . . . All of the pieces in it be-
> gan—like most talk—as improvisations on particular occasions in particular
> places . . . as an improvisation is not in 'prose,' which is an image of the
> authority of 'right thinking' conveyed primarily through 'right printing'—
> justified margins, conventional punctuation, and regularized spelling—this
> book has been printed without recourse to such appeals . . . Shakespeare's
> father's name is recorded in eighty-three different spellings . . . he himself
> spelled it four different ways in his own will."

The title of the book is a bit Shaxperean, since it changes depending on where one looks: on the front cover and the top of the back, it is *talking at the boundaries;* the Library of Congress publication data gives it as *Talking at the boundaries;* but inside the blurb, inside the quotation marks that designate Antin's own words, the typography is the most normative: *Talking at the Boundaries.* These variations seem the product of contemporary print bureaucracies rather than any echo of free-wheeling Elizabethan attitudes toward the written word: a lowercase title acquiring an initial capital from the Library of Congress and a second capital from an editor at New Directions following the dictates of the style manuals.

The words appear in quotes and the phrase that introduces the quotation is "says Antin." But the words are clearly appropriate for a blurb, and it seems likely they were never spoken but written to be inserted into the blurb prose. It is a rather blunt irony that these words claiming the necessity of typographic freedom for speech are writing set into justified blocks of prose, with their appearance in quotation marks merely designating that they are Antin's intellectual property, rather than his speech.

In both the above excerpts Antin calls talk natural: it is "natural language in its natural setting"; temporally separated writing is "an unnatural language act." But speech does not exist in a pure state of nature: issues of property and prestige frame and occupy the phrasal pulse of the talk pieces. For each piece, Antin writes an introduction that uses the same format as the talk poems themselves, with the addition of italics. The preface to the first talk in the book, "what am i doing here," begins like this:

> *this poem-talk was improvised at the san francisco poetry center on the   occasion of a joint reading by jerome rothenberg and myself in april 1973   we had each been asked by kathy fraser to provide some sort of statement about our   own work to provide something of a context for the audience and for kathys introduction   i had suggested that i had always had mixed feelings about   being considered a poet   "if robert lowell is a poet i dont want to be a poet   if robert frost was a poet i dont want to be a poet   if socrates was a poet ill consider it"*
> (1)

While Antin may expect the typography to connote simplicity of language in its natural setting, the setting here is institutional: venue and names are mentioned: the San Francisco Poetry Center, Kathleen Fraser, Jerome Rothenberg. Each introduction begins like this, mentioning a particular professional venue: *"the philadelphia art museum and moore college were cooperating on a series of talks set up loosely to coincide with the duchamp retrospective"*; *"i had to stop in new york to talk to people at the acquavella gallery who were putting on a matisse show"*; *"i was tired of riding on planes so i decided to take the bus to south bend where i was going to be talking at notre dame"* (25, 51, 87).

Antin's use of quotation marks around the Lowell-Frost-Socrates statement in the first introduction seems anomalous. In general, he uses lowercase letters even to the point of courting awkwardness: "*ill*" is more easily read as an adjective than as the contraction of "*i will*," so that "*if socrates was a poet ill consider it*" suggests "ill-considered." Does Antin allow the quotation marks to interrupt the lowercase regime in the blurb because he needs to specify speech acts? But while the subsequent speech act of his talk "what am i doing here?" takes up the next twenty pages, the phrase "*if robert lowell is a poet i don't want to be a poet*" was not spoken in the course of the talk. It was, he writes, a "statement" provided to the audience. Though it's in quotation marks, it's doubtful it was spoken before the reading. Poets almost always begin with a remark or two before reading; but how would a talk-poet draw the line between introductory patter and the performance itself?

I'm chasing the ontology of this phrase because it is one of the most memorable statements in the book. With all the straightforwardness of speech, Antin is kicking Frost, the dead king, and Lowell, the current king (as of 1973), out of the realm of poetry. It is not pure speech that is doing this, however, but situated speech, speech requiring the addition of quotation marks, which are not sonic at all, but markers of intellectual property. With his talk poems, Antin is proposing a reconfiguration of the literary field; the quoted sentence announces and recognizes it, and thus is nearly as important as the subsequent talk-poems. It is more than a real-time phrase uttered to a real-time audience; it is a social-literary act.

Margreta De Grazia has shown that quotation marks used to have precisely the opposite valence as today: in Elizabethan times they designated cultural commonplaces, which would be marked amid blocks of print so that the phrases by Aristotle, Augustine, etc., could be copied into commonplace books. Our current usage arose along with the entire panoply of rights of the individual. From the abolition of torture in state trials to the Fifth Amendment and the acceptance of intellectual property, the words of the individual were deemed inviolably specific; quotation marks defend them from being taken over by the state or by other individuals.[5]

In the blurb for *talking at the boundaries,* Antin said/wrote that the pieces arose "as improvisations on particular occasions in particular places." When he gave a talk in the Talk Series in 1978 at 80 Langton Street in San Francisco, the particular place completely changed the nature of his talk. Rather than an Antin monolog, it became a talk with a great deal of audience participation, to the distress of some who felt that Antin's artistic property was not being respected. Issues of power and literary genealogy were clearly relevant. It was five years after Antin began to do talk pieces; *talking at the boundaries* had just been published by New Directions; the Talk Series had been going for two years; Antin was the one of the first speakers from outside the Bay Area scene and had the most literary capital.

He arrived late, having gotten stuck in a Bay Bridge traffic jam, and, as organizer, I introduced him with a minimal comment—something like, "Here's David Antin." In hindsight, some mention of his monologic procedures and the polylog ambience of the Talk Series would have been in order. But the clash that followed was lit up more luridly by my laissez-faire naïveté. His talk, "Figures of Speech and Figures of Thought," began by developing different themes: classical Greek notions of metaphor, harmony, and negotiation; a long story about a coed who became anorexic; and a consideration of metaphor—anorexia as athleticism? anorexia as disease? But this cluster of themes was ultimately overshadowed by the verbal choreography between Antin and the audience.[6] He never finished the anorexic's story as he and the audience became embroiled in a discussion about the talk form and the usefulness or impropriety of audience participation; and in fact the talk was never transcribed.

In a number of places he invited this participation. He singled out some audience members with extended mention: he opened the talk by mentioning Ron Silliman's tape recorder: "Now that Ron's recorder is working we're capable of doing it." He asked George Lakoff if Lakoff's new book was going to be about metaphor. He would react to laughter by extending an amusing riff. He spoke of an uncle also named David Antin, then contrasted name to definition by comparing the sentence "I wonder if Ron Silliman will be here tonight?" with "I wonder if there will be a Ron Silliman here tonight?" While initially he held the floor absolutely, such nods to the audience gradually encouraged comments and suggestions to which he responded increasingly, so that after an hour Silliman, Lakoff, Tom Mandel, and I were asking questions and illustrating points with extended comments. Near the end of the piece, Antin and Silliman had a long dialog about the form of the talk, with Silliman, in a comment that in hindsight anticipated the clash to come, suggested that Antin was not interested in innovation and was perhaps courting catastrophe to move forward. Antin replied that the formal catastrophe in the arts of discourse had occurred near the end of the eighteenth century when a fixed sense of the group being addressed disappeared.

The discussion had been amiably intellectual to this point; but the issue of group incoherence and a small version of rhetorical catastrophe began to materialize when one man said that he had felt very uncomfortable with the last hour's interruptions or conversation. He said that he couldn't see Antin's interlocutors, who were all sitting in the front row; and that Antin's work needed to be uninterrupted to succeed. Antin was responding to this concern when he was interrupted by his wife, Eleanor Antin, who said that she had come to hear art and felt violated by the interruptions. "We're all prisoners of five guys. Is that what these things are? Everybody comes to hear these five guys?" Mandel refused to accept her characterization of the talks. Silliman said that both forms of talk—Antin's monolog and the Talk Series polylog—were valid and that the audience was witnessing a transition from one form to another. David Antin said that he had expected the interruptions and that he had been trying to find out how much negotiation was possible. The discussion grew crowded and loud; the tape recorder did not pick it all up.

> *Eleanor Antin:* You're facing them, David [the interlocutors in the front row]. Even for the young men here as well as for the women it's an extremely macho situation in which we are here, and you are looking at their faces; they're talking to you.
> *David Antin:* [unintelligible—possibly suggesting Eleanor was free to leave]
> *Eleanor Antin:* Oh come on! Where can I go? I came in the wagon; I can't go anywhere [laughter] [much unintelligible, overlapping conversation] . . . I experienced it that way because they have more strength than we do. They talk louder; and I can't see their faces; and they're in the front, and I personally came for something else. I came to hear David Antin do an art work. And it was stopped before it even started, as it happens, he was in the middle of a rather horrific story about a young woman who died. And the story was just—poof! Everyone interrupted it and it just ended.

This was followed by discussion about the physical space: the pillars blocking views, the difference between the front and the back rows. Eleanor Antin dismissed this more neutral material. Her comment switched pronouns in midstream, goint from public to personal: "I felt violated, literally. Look, I came up here with him. He's willing to improvise his way, it's OK with him, but *I know that you thought you were going to do an art work here. I know you did.*"

There was more discussion; senses of endings and compromise were offered; Antin said he was interested specifically in "the conditions that exist here . . . I'm sorry, I don't feel violated" [laughter]. Eventually people stood up, continuing to talk, but the tape recorders were shut off.

This is only an extremely fragmentary transcription-description of a two-hour event that would translate to something on the order of sixty to eighty pages of print. I'm pointing to one charged section near the end. But this was not just a collision between Antin's oral-based art and several poets involved with language writing. Gender played a large role. There were less conflictual novelistic ironies: the status of the narrative—who knew the story and who didn't; Eleanor Antin revealing its conclusion in the course of a complaint that her husband was interrupted; husband and wife arguing over who was violated when he was interrupted. Eleanor Antin's accusation that the Talk Series regulars had wrecked her husband's art inverts complaints that Antin's talk-pieces had no art.[7] Yet from the perspective of the regulars they were certainly art, and perhaps were, from that seventies antinarrative perspective, too artful.[8]

Where, and when, did the art occur? In the performance, on the page, or in the longer-term, diffuse space of the literary field? In that larger perspective Antin's redefinition of poetry would be confirmed by every new talk piece performed, published, referred to, imitated, challenged, attended to. The negotiation he hoped for at the Langton Street talk was just one item in a larger, scattered series of negotiations. This essay is, partially, another item in that series.

2

When he champions speech as the site of art, transcription is for Antin a necessary evil; in his insistence on lowercase minimal typography he privileges a more or less poetic look, somewhat cummingsesque, set against the normativities of prose. Jack Kerouac's transcription of conversation between himself and Neal Cassady (Cody) in *Visions of Cody* demonstrates how transcription can create art out of speech that was not originally conceived of as art in the slightest. Antin's talk pieces use print to present speech as the essence of poetry; Kerouac's transcriptions find writing in the midst of speech.

Here is a small moment. The subject is a letter from Cody's father. Jack wants to hear it aloud; Cody insists on their reading it. They're talking about what they're reading; we're reading their talk, and behind it, getting glimpses of the somewhat bathetic letter of the father.

JACK. Let's hear his—because his—

CODY. Yeah but I want you to *read* it. Yeah that's what I'm tryin to say . . . it's real crazy . . . See, here's the way he writes. You can always—he can't write on a straight line, see, and he's very slowly, carefully like a child, see . . .

JACK. (*reading*) Diana Pomeray

CODY. Lookit . . . D.O. Arlington . . . *a-i-r*—

JACK. What does *D.O.* mean?

CODY. I don't know

JACK. *Do?*

CODY. Lookit, Airlington, see it's really north but he doesn't know, see

JACK. How to write an *n?*

CODY. I guess *n*—well, he does that but he might have, misunderstood, but here Airlington, *a-i-r-l-i-n-g* . . . Airlington

JACK. Nappan who's that? That's the—

CODY. That's their name, yeah, care of Cody Pomeray, that's his address for the last fifteen years, it's Green on Market, see—

JACK. Market Street Denver (*because of Frisco*)

CODY. Yeah . . . this letter. He usually only writes one page, he never puts any date or anything, see? "My dear"—see how he does it? (*laughing*) . . . "son and daurter" . . . *d-a-u-r-t-e-r*—

JACK. Daurter

CODY. "Received—"

JACK. *R-e-c-d*!!

CODY. Yeah, he does that right. "Your most welcome" without an *e* (*laughs*) "and was . . . your most welcome . . . and was" (*laughs*) dig him, see?, that's formal, see, according to *him*. He's writing a nice, you know, liter-ary—(*both laughing*)[9]

Kerouac transcribes four nights' conversation—ending with a radio blaring a midnight sermon to an empty room. The conversations are a very dope-laden affair; their content is amusing at times while at others "you had to have been there." But the transcription itself, as Allen Ginsberg points out in his introduction to the book, is wonderfully artful and always inter-esting. Ginsberg claims significance for the transcripts for various reasons:

1) Vocal familiar friendly teahead life had never been transcribed . . .
2) Despite monotony, the gaps and changes . . . are dramatic.
3) It leads somewhere, like life.
4) It's interesting if you want the characters' reality.
5) It's real.
6) It's art because at that point in the progress of Jack's art he began transcribing *first* thoughts of true mind in American speech. (viii)

"First thought best thought" has of course become Ginsberg's poetic credo; he almost always presents the truth-making spontaneity of the mind in tan-dem with the breath and the voice as the essential instruments a poet needs to cultivate and obey. And his assertion that transcribing the tapes trans-formed Kerouac's writing seems very plausible: the thoroughness of the transcript required relentless, even attention to, and affection for, every par-ticular in the temporal stream, qualities that differentiate Kerouac's writing from almost everyone else's. His spiritual élan arose from that evenness. But it seems a hazy assertion of Edenic virtue to say that what Jack and Cody *said* was a "first thought." To me, the transcript reveals the difficulties of speech ("Yeah that's what I'm tryin to say"), the varying rhythms of attention, and the patient, almost comic receptivity of careful transcription and punctuation. At times each speaker is responding to what the other said, or to what the other said two speeches back, or to the father's letter. The rhythm of attention between the two speakers is quick, diffuse, darting, with the most elemental questions erupting out of nowhere—"How to write an *n?*"—and being answered by the wisdom of banal repetition—"I guess *n.*" Misspelling and abbreviations turn into words: air, do. The provinces of speech and writing are interlaced as Jack and Cody critique the insufficient writing of Cody's father in their own insufficient speech—and yet the transcribing mind of Kerouac feels exemplary. "*R-e-c-d*!!" is equally fascinating as speech and as transcription. It shows the abbreviation Jack marveled at, "Recd," while at the same time Kerouac the transcriber uses quotes, hyphens, italics, and a double exclamation mark very knowingly to capture the pitying enthusiasm of Jack the speaker who spells out, letter by letter, the automatized, bathetic-noble attempt of Cody's father to be "literary." And then the book's hero, Cody, manifests his father's naïveté about writing by simply agreeing, "Yeah he got that right."

The transcription is what makes this interesting. It is not "first thought best thought"; it is novelistic, reanimating the past and adding a present perspective. Spelling out the speech accurately makes it public, but the transcription is also intimate. In the sentence "Market Street Denver (*because of Frisco*)" the phrase in italics is added to explain—to whom? the world?—why Kerouac specified Denver when Cody would of course know it. There are Market Streets in both cities, but Denver functions for Kerouac as locus of a Golden Age of Cody's adolescence, where cars were stolen, sex was ubiquitous, inconsequential, and momentous. Even though Kerouac transcribed these tapes almost immediately—he and Cody discuss a transcribed moment from one night on the following night[10]—by being transcribed the conversations are placed in the past. Kerouac uses the alphabet along with all normative resources of punctuation to preserve this past. This complex act, which governs the rest of his writing, is not "first thought best thought," it is more like rememoration: one-time life disappears into writing.

3

The Bay Area talks were oriented toward the present and the future: the participants were attempting to construct a plural poetics in public. Talking out these writing values was at times clarifying, at times diffuse. The written talk that remains casts a dramatic, novelistic light on these thrashings-out. The variance between these dimensions and the poetics discussed keeps the talks in an undefined space. Their specific forms differ: some were protoacademic essays; some were performance pieces; some were group discussions of poetics centered around an initial speaker with the audience chiming in, interrupting, suggesting detours, wrestling over control of terms and of the verbal arena—as the Antin talk illustrates.[11] The methods of transcription differ as well. Of the talks I chose to print, most were edited "for clarity," which involved pruning at various levels. What I tried to leave in was a structure that was at some moments obvious but at others seemed detectable below the verbal surface or among the words: a dramatic negotiation of poetic value, acted out by author-speakers projecting various versions of a poetic space. To reveal this—and of course to some extent such a subterranean structure is an idealized projection—I removed words at all levels. "Ums" and "ahs" were deleted. Sentences were sharpened—"And—or it's, incredible affection . . . in a vacuum" becoming "Incredible affection . . . in a vacuum." Some sentences, digressions, interchanges were removed. And, while every talk contained conversation, either throughout or at the end, some of the final conversations were not printed. In those cases, a reader's sense that the words were a speech act must become tenuous. "The New Sentence" (1979), for example, begins with the name of the speaker, Ron Silliman, printed in bold followed by a colon followed by the words of the talk; twenty-seven pages later the final word of the piece, even though it is followed by the date of the talk in italics, seems to conclude an essay, not a talk. And the reference to writing becomes even more pronounced in this case because Silliman wanted that final word, "PERIOD," printed in caps to suggest that the whole performance be thought of as one gigantic sentence.

If Silliman's talk is more written than spoken, Lyn Hejinian's "The Rejection of Closure" (1983)—the talk not the essay of the same name presents a case in which the talk format contains linguistic moments that can only occur as written speech. And in this case that means including material that embodies openness in very direct ways. Where the essay ends conclusively—"While failing in the attempt to match the world, we discover structure, distinction, the integrity and separateness of things"[12]—the talk ends with a more comically graphic depiction of openness:

> *Hejinian:* . . . And then, also, a whole other day could be spent talking about what the relationship of language is to desire, and how libidinous is speech, and all of that, which I've been thinking about a lot, especially after that panel discussion at Intersection, hearing people talk about how they felt about talking. And it really seemed like there was a connection, which I hadn't thought about before, but the more I think about it the more . . . [tape ends] (*Writing/Talks*, 291)

At another point in the conversation, Benjamin Friedlander says, "Think of a Bach score. It's closure made as finite and compact as possible. There's no single reading, there's nothing you can take out of it, it's all there" (289). But in fact, Friedlander may have been talking about a "box score," which is also closure with open possibilities of reading. At this point, he doesn't remember which it was. The tape is ambiguous.

A third possibility is the transcription of all noise. Steve Benson, in his "Views of Communist China" (1977), transcribed every identifiable noise during his performance piece. The performance, which needs to be remembered when reading the piece, involved layers of defamiliarization. Benson moved much of his furniture and personal effects into my wife's and my loft and acted as if the audience was in his apartment. A second layer of defamiliarization: he framed this tour by some dramatic recitation of material taken from an article on Communist China. At the beginning and end of the piece he was "Master Ch'en" discussing his very oppressed early years, his pride at making his own radio, his fealty to the Party. In the middle he was Steve Benson conducting a tour of "his apartment" and at times his libido and his writing practice. The familiar household stuff of a writer's apartment—books, mirrors, posters—and how all those objects might provoke real writing sparked a long intimate discussion. Here is a sample moment:

> *Steve Benson:* [. . .] the Pollock I wound up finally putting on its *side,* and—
> *Bob Perelman:* Why? Just . .
> *Benson:* I've got, well, for a long time I—
> *Perelman:* To knock a chip off its shoulder or something?
> [laughter in group]
> *Benson:* I had seen it regular for so long, and it was always just like an object, it was never like an all-over painting or it was never really an experience, it was too small, and it was too much, sort of, *over* there against the wall, kind of . . so . .
> *Dorothy Phillips:*—a piece of paper?
> *Benson:* Yeah.
> *Phillips:* How do you put a piece of paper on its side. I just, can't—
> *Benson:* Oh, I meant, like, well . . it's a horizontal composition, right? [laughter in group] So I put it up as a vertical composition.
> *Perelman:*—sticking up from the wall . . like a shelf, you mean.
> *Francie Shaw:* That's a great idea.
> *Benson:* The Delacroix . . that, I mean, that was always just like a problem. It was like, here's this really frenzied white horse, and I sort of respected it or admired it but more just as an idea.
> *Barrett Watten:* Do you have an overall strategy that's more uh, solid and compelling than any strategy having to do with any particular object?
> *David Highsmith:* That's like asking him what he does for a living.
> [laughter in group]
> *Two voices:* What *do* you do for a living? (*Hills,* 95–96)

Shklovsky's account of his discovery of defamiliarization—one day after years of ignoring a tobacconist's sign, he sees it set sideways and is shocked into vivid perception by the change—is possibly all-too-familiar to many. Here it is reinvented, by happenstance. And then, by being misunderstood, it becomes truly unfamiliar.

The talks were not always sites of misunderstandings; at times there were straightforward conflicts. In Charles Bernstein's talk, "Characteriza-

tion" (1983), a rather far-reaching argument developed between him and
Barrett Watten. At stake, implicitly, were conflicting definitions of the language movement: Watten arguing for a constructivist model deriving from
the Russian formalists and Bernstein for a permanently uncontainable textuality.[13]

The piece begins with Bernstein quoting a sententious elegy to an ad
executive—"The real giants have always been poets / men who jumped
from facts / into the realm of imagination and ideas. / / He elevated advertising to high art / and our jobs to a profession. / / He made a difference."

> *Charles Bernstein:* . . . I've always objected, actually, to the character-
> ization of myself as a poet, much because of the way they have "He was a
> *poet* . . ." This idea of the poet being singled out. In fact, I've noticed
> recently that poster for "Jim Morrison, an American poet." . . . It's as if
> you want to say that Zukofsky is a great American poet, you would say
> that he is a "great American musician" . . .
>
> *Michael Palmer:* It's interesting, too, that when Zukofsky is character-
> ized as such, to distinguish that kind of "great American poet" from "the
> great American poets," let's say like Robert Frost, who people actually
> know about, it's then followed parenthetically by "a poet's poet" . . . it's
> at once "poet squared" but also "poet diminished."[14]
>
> *Bernstein:* You see this in respect to some American playwrights want-
> ing to say that what they're doing is opera. Robert Wilson, in *Letter to
> Queen Victoria,* which he called an opera,—it was, to me, one of the best
> pieces of theater I've ever seen. But it had to be called an opera because it
> was so good.
>
> *Ron Silliman:* There was a review in last Sunday's paper: "A 3–D
> movie good enough to be 2–D." [laughter]
>
> *Barrett Watten:* You better look out or you might start doing a perfor-
> mance piece, Charles. [laughter] (*Writing/Talks,* 8–10)

The issue of professionalism that David Simpson identified as one of the
causes of so much printed talk by academics is certainly on the table here.
Recall that Antin, too, disclaimed the profession of poet;[15] and that Watten
asking Benson about an "overall strategy" was instantly perceived as asking
about his profession, drawing a burst of nervous laughter. In Bernstein's
talk, the initial jokes are genial, but the discomfort with the job description
of "poet" cuts a number of ways. No one wants ad executives to claim
poetic, high-art status and at the same time to boast of their professionalism; but no one can quite imagine what it would be like to claim the title
of poet without the irony needed to beat the executives back from poetry's
imagined social spaces.

Later in the talk, arguments over how to define the poet's activity become much more heated. I had asked Bernstein to do a close reading of a
few lines of his poem "Standing Target." In the course of his response he
cited some lines from another poem, "Part Quake" (*Islets/Irritations*): "They
ridicule revolutionary theory / and sneer that having a correct / position is

sectarian." It is difficult to read these lines as expressing Bernstein's own position in any simple way if one has read much of his work. He immediately qualifies the unambiguous denotation, mentioning the dangers of Stalinism, on the one hand, the problem of having no position vis-à-vis material historical situations, on the other. Criticizing Deleuze and Guattari's romanticization of deterritorialized flows, he goes on as follows:

> *Bernstein:* And that's why I disagree with the way language is characterized within French structuralist thought from Saussure to Derrida, in which language is thought to be divided in a polarity between the signifier and the signified, as two different things, and that the relation between the sound and the mental image is arbitrary . . .
>
> *Watten:* But that's two different meanings at two different times. When Saussure wanted to talk about the arbitrariness of the sign what he meant was that it was not mystic. He was trying to get rid of undue concern with etymology in 19th-century linguistics, and that's exactly what that means, and it doesn't mean *anything else.* I wish somebody would put it on a billboard someplace . . .
>
> *Bernstein:* Criticism insofar as it's provisional sets up terms. And those things do have value within their context, but when they get reified . . . then you have this monster . . . Saussure has to attack etymology by proposing his things, just as I could be forced into attacking those things because of the monster that gets created from that.
>
> It seems to me that criticism, rather than trying to establish fixed things . . . in its best exists at a provisional level, and that provisional quality doesn't need to be masked. But the wrinkle in it is that that masking has social power . . .
>
> *Watten:* Okay, Charles, I really think you should purge your vocabulary of phrases like "structural linguistics from Saussure to Derrida."
>
> *Bernstein:* I should purge my . . . ?
>
> *Watten:* You shouldn't allow yourself to say that. And that would be the answer to the whole thing. I mean, if you know better . . .
>
> *Kit Robinson:* Why can't he say that? (17–19)

Watten's verb, "purge," takes Bernstein's lines, "They ridicule revolutionary theory / and sneer that having a correct / position is sectarian" unironically; Watten is claiming that editing—vocabulary purges—is necessary, but of course "purge" has been used in harsher contexts. Robinson's protesting question, made in the name of freedom of speech, is a resonant one, and doesn't have an easy answer. Watten's reply, "Because it's not only a provisional construction, but it's an illusory and unexamined construction that you in fact know better of. And so in fact you can *do* better," challenges all laissez-faire celebrations of the present.

The talks lie between two soundbites of the contemporary critical scene: Richard Rorty's praise of liberal "conversation" on the one hand; and on the other the slogan of radical textuality and the dethroned subject, Michel Foucault's "What matter who's speaking?" In their opposite ways, both these moments even out the field of utterance, either into a transpersonal grid, or a democratic town meeting. The talks can be read as offering a useful supplement or roadblock to these too-regular solutions. They acted out in public space a dialogic dimension of poetry that usually remains private, in letters, comments after readings, lifted eyebrows, pointed silences. In supplementing the monologic voice of poetry, the talks opened a precarious space between dominant voices and democracy, auratic performance and group participation. While I think this space remains useful, it was not utopic: men talked more easily than women; different degrees of educational capital made for an uneven floor. A number of writers who attended the talks spoke (afterward, off the record) of being "terrified" to speak.

NOTES

1. *Talks* (*Hills* 6/7), ed. Bob Perelman (San Francisco: n.p., 1980), and *Writing/Talks,* ed. Bob Perelman (Carbondale: Southern Illinois University Press, 1985).

2. I discuss this at length in *The Marginalization of Poetry: Language Writing and Literary History* (Princeton: Princeton University Press, 1996). See the second chapter especially.

3. David Simpson, *The Academic Postmodern and the Rule of Literature* (Chicago: University of Chicago Press, 1995), pp. 69–70.

4. David Antin, *Talking at the Boundaries* (New York: New Directions, 1976), p. 56.

5. Margreta De Grazia, "Sanctioning Voice: Quotation Marks, the Abolition of Torture, and the Fifth Amendment," *Cardozo Arts & Entertainment Law Journal,* vol. 10, no. 2 (1992).

6. See Ellen Zweig's article for more discussion. "Where Is the Piece? An Account of a Talk by David Antin," in *The Poetry Reading: A Contemporary Compendium on Language and Performance,* ed. Stephen Vincent and Ellen Zweig (San Francisco: Momo's Press, 1981), pp. 174–86.

7. See Robert Kroetsch's objections to Antin in the correspondence between him, Antin, and William Spanos in *Boundary 2,* vol. 3, no. 3 (spring 1975), pp. 595–652.

8. Antin's comments from a recent letter to me (November 10, 1996) are germane: "I knew the neo-formalist concerns of most of the language group, as well as what I would call the political modernism of notions of a writerly resistance to a coercive, institutionally controlled 'readerly' language, etc., which took the form of hostility to 'narrative' and 'representation' and intermittently to the idea of 'referentiality.' Since I came out of a very similar modernist (experimentalist) background and had moreover a doctoral education in just such modernist derived linguistics as inspired many of the language poets, I was curious to examine what I was looking for in 'narrative' in spite of my own history."

9. Jack Kerouac, *Visions of Cody,* intro. Allen Ginsberg (New York: McGraw-Hill, 1972), p. 171.

10. It is a fascinating moment. Kerouac has added "(*demurely downward look*)" as a description of Cody who is talking about his inability to "get it down"—to write. Kerouac can, of course, get it down: does that make him more masculine than the suddenly "demure" Cody? Cody senses something like this, since he objects to the description of himself he reads the following night. Michael Davidson dis-

cusses this passage in *The San Francisco Renaissance: Poetics and Community at Mid-Century* (Cambridge: Cambridge University Press, 1989), pp. 73–76.

11. Ron Silliman's description: "Poets model the discussion / portion of a talk after the territorial behavior / of male elephant seals, each striving / to be the dominant alpha bull." In *What* (Great Barrington, Mass.: The Figures, 1988), p. 112.

12. Lyn Hejinian, "The Rejection of Closure," in *Poetics Journal,* vol. 4 (May 1984), p. 143.

13. I have outlined this issue from another angle in *The Marginalization of Poetry,* where I discuss the differing implications of the titles of the magazines each was involved in editing: Watten and *This;* Bernstein and $L=A=N=G=U=A=G=E$ (see *Marginalization,* 19–20).

14. Guy Davenport has called Zukofsky a "poet's poet's poet." Guy Davenport, *The Geography of the Imagination* (San Francisco: North Point Press, 1981), p. 107.

15. To cite the blurb: "I've been a poet, critic, linguist, and engineer, and though this knowledge informs the book, it is not the work of a professional."

IO

Sound Reading

PETER QUARTERMAIN

> So I go to these readings and that old singsong starts in—half
> rapt, half-assed—Thank God for the shining exceptions, the
> formed intensities.
>
> DAVID BROMIGE, "Voice // Voicing // Voices"

> Strength of vocables: to bind.
>
> EDMOND JABÈS, A Foreigner Carrying in
the Crook of His Arm a Tiny Book

I want to consider in general terms the vexing question of whether it is
possible to read a poem aloud badly—and of course, its corollary, whether
(and under what conditions) it might be possible to read a poem aloud
well. On the face of it this looks pretty absurd, since we've all been to
lifeless readings of leaden parlour-poetry, or have walked out of mumbled
(or shouted) performances by drunken readers more attentive to their
friends in the audience than to the inept words they are attempting to read.[1]
If, as Charles Bernstein suggested in a slightly different context, "a poetic
reading can be given to any piece of writing" (his emphasis),[2] then, plainly,
so can an *un*poetic. Clearly, the question of what "poetic" and "unpoetic"
might mean is crucial, though it remains unstated throughout my discussion, partly because of its great complexity. It is deeply intertwined with
the notion of readerly competence, and that notion is under scrutiny, implicitly more often than explicitly, pretty well throughout what follows.

I shall not explicitly consider obviously "bad" readings of the kind I've
mentioned at all, though it seems to me that the terms *good* and *bad* are
notoriously up for grabs, and a moment's reflection will suggest that readings of this sort are perhaps most appropriately to be considered as primarily social rather than "aesthetic" or "literary" occasions. And I want to sim-

plify my discussion by excluding from detailed consideration such (possibly lesser) extremes of apparent readerly incompetence as those of first-year university English courses and the like, where (sometimes) an embarrassed youngster reads aloud to her or his more or less inattentive peers a poem s/he's never seen before. It may be that such a performance, with its social ineptitudes and attendant miseries, does not constitute a "reading" at all, for it is frequently hesitant and confused, marked by stumblings, mispronunciations, stutterings, and mumblings—or it is delivered at breakneck pace and metronomic regularity with scarcely a pause for breath and scarcely any inflection whatsoever. But anyone who has heard John Cage reading "Mureau," with its attendant inaudibilities and sudden clarities (as the poem moves into and out of various articulations), or has heard Tom Raworth's mercurial gallop through a poem like the highly political "Survival"[3] will perhaps suspend judgment. Raworth said after his 1991 reading of part of that sequence in Vancouver that he takes the poems at speed because that's the only way he can get through them to make sense to the ear and voice; read slowly with the eye, certainly, they present an almost baffling opacity, which seems designed to defeat any attempt at intelligible inflected expressive voicing as speech.

For the moment, however, it is convenient to think of these as special cases, though we should caution ourselves, too, that the sort of reading that is learned in high school and university English courses is also a special case. Or rather, a series of special cases, since it is plain to everyone who has undergone the process that reading practices and performances vary widely from teacher to teacher and room to room as teachers privilege their expert reading. It is equally evident, though, that experienced readers have learned to take the poem slowly and/or repeatedly, paying attention to each word as it combines with others into the sentence, heeding each word as it unfolds to the ear, balancing the play of speech patterns with or against prosodic patterns, following the syntax as the resonances of the work draw forth. What I'm saying, I need hardly add, makes it pretty clear that what I have in mind are more or less conventional poems, not necessarily rhyming or metrical, but certainly recognizable as poems by pretty well any reader, written within a clearly identifiable and familiar poetic tradition. Such poems as a rule have a long history of interpretation, and enjoy what can be loosely referred to as canonical status.

Poetry readings, of course, take place in a great variety of conditions, and the contingencies attendant upon the occasion affect the reading performance itself. It is one thing to hear a text for the first time (and be obliged to cultivate your aural memory), and another to be able to follow that text with the eye (because you bought the poet's new book on your way into the reading). Texts that are familiar to the audience might well be heard in a more critical frame than would texts that are completely new to the hearers, perhaps because the recital of a familiar poem, as well as the reading occasion itself, affords a kind of comfort food for the spirit. This certainly seems to have been the case at Dylan Thomas's lucrative public readings in the 1950s, though unquestionably the cult of his personality also helped pack the crowded halls, as did his slight Welsh lilt, which lent the music of his recitation an exotic air. And it is true that, once you've heard Thomas reading, his Welsh voice flavors the sound of all of his poems. His readings were very much a Public Occasion and enjoyed a ceremonial and even ritual status. That flavor leaches over into some of his recordings (notably his readings of Shakespeare and Webster).[4] As a public reader, Thomas was enormously influential, setting a standard for mellifluous expressiveness that could famously lull the hearer along on the wings of poesy, and it is instructive to compare his readings with those of his chief disciple and imitator, Theodore Marcuse.[5]

Marcuse, a professional actor, emphasized the expressive while keeping an eye (if that is the right word) on the mellifluous, and it is hard indeed to see why his readings were at all popular. His performances of Keats and Shelley (to crowded performance halls) are blatantly virtuoso. It is extremely difficult to describe his performance of Keats's "Ode to a Nightingale" at all: the drawn-out vowels and the highly nasalized consonants of the opening, lingering especially (I think for as long as a second) on the *mbn* of "numbness," presage what is to come: exaggerated and dramatic expressiveness. Marcuse's articulation of "Fade far away and quite forget," for instance, is to my ear more appropriate to a performance of King Lear's most histrionic speeches: a somewhat high-pitched diminuendo through the first three of those words, so that by the time he reaches the word "away" his voice has faded to the lower limit of audibility; it is followed by a quite rapidly rising crescendo which climaxes in the last syllable (almost a shout) of "forget." To put it bluntly, Marcuse's reading is tediously funny (I cannot even attempt a description of his performance of Shelley's "Ode to the West Wind"). His reading is, I think, almost unhearable, and affords this listener at least little instruction and some unintended pleasure. As a virtuoso performance it draws our attention to the performer and his skilled range of voice and expression, rather than to the poem—in this, I think, it is representative of many actors' readings, as well as of readings by imitators of Thomas's luxuriant style. Thomas's own style, however, has a long tradition: "There is a *chaunt* in the recitation both of Coleridge and Wordsworth," William Hazlitt recorded in 1823, "which acts as a spell upon the hearer, and disarms the judgment."[6] But fashions of reading change.

Another difficulty is much more perplexing. When Marcuse lingers on a syllable, or prolongs a consonant, our ear is so caught up in the sound itself (an almost two-second sibilant, for instance) that we tend to lose the syntax and the sense. Which is to say, we lose track of what presumably the reading is all about: the narrative/discursive thrust that this reading of Keats's "Ode" is presumably trying to bring forth. Such apparent inconsistency should not be dismissed out of hand, however, as symptomatic of "badness." In the first place, for me to do so is to claim that my own historically flavored response is exempt from historical contingency: fashions of reading and recital change, sometimes quite rapidly. In the second, to anyone familiar with them, Marcuse might well seem a forerunner, however unwitting, of the pataphysical performances of the Four Horsemen or the sound poetry of bill bissett, just as he might equally perhaps be seen as an unconscious follower of Hugo Ball or Velimir Khlebnikov. Similar effects are achieved, on occasion, by readers with a strong ("foreign") accent; hearing them, we find ourselves responding to the nonsyntactic and nonsemantic qualities of the language, and even on rare occasions feeling as though we have stepped outside our own language, and are viewing it as a foreign tongue.

This might suggest that a poem, then, would best be read in the dialect of its maker. But Wordsworth's Cumberland dialect rhymed *water* with *chatter, July* with *duly,* and according to Hazlitt he talked "with a mixture of clear gushing accents in his voice, a deep guttural intonation, and a strong tincture of the northern *burr,* like the crust on wine" (118). What would an audience expecting the *koiné* make of him, puzzling out the words as it well might need to? Audience expectation (and for that matter, I suppose, audience "competence") does to some extent determine the success and the nature of a performance. Marcuse and Thomas both read in a more or less standard *koiné* unlikely to offend the ear—Marcuse, cis-Atlantic American; Thomas, educated Anglo-Welsh—and this in turn might suggest that a poem might best be read in the dialect of its audience. That's a very tall order, though, for a public reading. Most of us manage our vowels with consistency and precision (or so we suppose), but each of us manages them differently, and if we move into an unfamiliar dialect region we may find (as a result of our listening) that our vowels begin to slide all over the place. The instabilities and inconstancies of pronunciation vexed Spenser and Harvey in their correspondence, and the sound of the vowel slides as it dopplers through time. "I compose by the tone-leading of vowels," Robert Duncan wrote; "the vowels are notes of a scale, in which breaths move, but these soundings of spirit upon which the form of the poem depends are not constant. They are the least lasting sounds in our language; even in my lifetime, the sound of my vowels alters. There is no strict vowel standard."[7] How, then, read well? Dialect, inflection of sentence pattern: the perplexing variables. Markers of class, of economic and educational status, and of race. To insist on—or even expect—any sort of uniformity is to privilege one reading community over another, is to make the sort of reading we learn in high school and university English courses the universal, transcendent case, rather than the special case it actually is.

Douglas Oliver has suggested that poems, where there is an "absolute agreement" between different readers in a given dialect group about "the semantic, emotional and syntactical interpretation," have "an ineffable 'neutral' tune" that is "fairly standard across many performances."[8] I find this somewhat imponderable, since (as Oliver's "absolute" recognizes) it boils down to a reading group of one; plainly no such "agreement" is possible, and the hypothesized tune is, as Oliver says, "unattainable" (x). This is partly because, as Deleuze and Guattari have famously pointed out, "[t]here exists no ideal 'competent' speaker-hearer of language, any more than there exists a homogenous linguistic community."[9] But it also has to do with the nature of sound itself. Tape recordings have confirmed the intuition that no two readings of a poem are ever exactly the same; sound is the least constant part of the poem, the least durable, and possibly the most elusive. The visual habit of print has taught even professional readers to ignore by and large the momentary nature of close hearing, caught in the instant as it is, and to forget that each time we read the poem it sounds itself differently in that voice we all (except perhaps those of us born deaf)[10] have in our heads.

But the more any of us reads a given poem, silently or aloud, the more established becomes an inward notional neutral tune that persists from reading to reading, familiar but elusive in its fine detail. There is a wide and inevitable disparity between how we hear the poem when we read it silently, and how we sound it, saying it aloud; the poem performed in the head is an imagined poem in the world of sound. This may be why, when we voice the poem, we can never match what we breathe to what we think we heard. The inner speaking we hear as we read is not the voice we hear when we outwardly speak, and the noises we make when we read a poem aloud are never the noises we think the poem makes. But the difference between our internal reading and our oral performance will vary from poem to poem, and also from occasion to occasion. Maybe the variation has to do with the familiarity of the poem, or the fixity of our interpretation, or the frequency of our performance.

The difficulty in voicing the poem, though it has something to do with our understanding of the work, may also have to do with a kind of tentative polyvocality, a simultaneity of possible tones and interpretations, possible (at least in a gestural sort of way) inside the head but impossible of public performance—a kind of undecidable music or tune. The eye moves so much faster than even the inward voice and ear that by the time we begin inwardly to "hear" a speech segment we've already considered a number of alternative voicings in light of what is to come. Some poets deliberately surprise the mind by exploiting undecidability of voice, as in the Janus-headed "near" of:

> the whole pageantry
>
> of the year was
> awake tingling
> near
>
> the edge of the sea[11]

That "near" is an odd sort of voiced noncommittal crux in the unorthodox syntax/sound of Williams's poem. Temporal in relation to the words before it, and spatial in relation to those following, "near" obliges the reader of the poem radically to rebalance the rhythm- and intonation-pattern the sentence seems to demand, and the voice necessarily flattens out into a curious and unanticipated music.

But the rhythm is a problem. Since Williams's poem is unpunctuated, and the syntax rather unorthodox, some readers provide their own punctuation to clarify their voicing of the poem. The poem seems in such cases to resolve into three or four sentences, but their boundaries are undecidable, and a variety of punctuations is possible. Sentence breaks affect intonation: they are usually signaled by a falling pitch. For ease of discussion, I write the poem out as prose:

> According to Brueghel, when Icarus fell it was spring. A farmer was ploughing his field, the whole pageantry of the year was awake, tingling. Near the edge of the sea, concerned with itself, sweating in the sun that melted the wings' wax, unsignificantly, off the coast, there was a splash quite unnoticed. This was Icarus drowning.

An obvious alternative is to open the poem with a principal clause introducing a lyric catalogue: "According to Brueghel, when Icarus fell it was spring: a farmer . . ." Clauses introducing a list usually signal the start of that list by rising in pitch—a voicing, then, in complete contrast to the closing fall of an opening sentence.

Punctuation has a strong rhetorical function, and by reducing the range of voicing possibilities, it makes this subtle and complex poem (despite the interesting syntax of the third putative sentence) pretty banal; it decides what Williams left undecidable, porous, and fluid, and it fixes a narrative meaning. In the process it tells the voice what to do, how to intone. When we look at the poem as Williams wrote it, without punctuation, we see that it is actually unvoicable in any completely satisfactory way: the polyvocality, the simultaneity of possible tones, rhythms, and interpretations, is available only to the inner ear, and cannot be spoken. One might therefore conclude that it is impossible to read this poem well aloud. Certainly, it cannot be voiced as "ordinary" speech.

It may be that Williams's poem presents such difficulties because there is not a long history of its interpretation, and because it has not been absorbed into the culture the way well-established canonical works have. It may even be that in three or four hundred years' time a tradition may have grown of repunctuating and modernizing twentieth-century texts along the lines accorded the texts of Wyatt or of Shakespeare. In Shakespeare's case, editorial practice has over the past three centuries focused upon deciding what Shakespeare (or his printers) left undecidable (and, perhaps, well-nigh unvoicable). The third quatrain (lines 9–12) of sonnet 129, "Th' expence of Spirit in a waste of shame" (and especially its final two lines), is a famous instance of what I am calling voiced noncommittal crux:

Made In pursut and in possession so,
Had, hauing, and in quest, to haue extreame,
A blisse in proofe and proud and very wo,
Before a ioy proposd behind a dreame,
                    (version of 1609)

Editors since Lintott in 1709[12] have assiduously recast and repunctuated
this text, in most cases agreeing with Booth's 1977 version, which is as follows:

Mad in pursuit, and in possession so,
Had, having, and in quest to have, extreme,
A bliss in proof, and proved, a very woe,
Before, a joy proposed, behind, a dreame.[13]

The impulse behind this editorial activity is akin to that behind the late-
twentieth-century practice of tape-recording poets reading their own
poems: to provide an authoritative and authentic register of the poem's
sound—how it *should* be said in order to keep the meaning straight. Such
practice congeals an interpretation and defines a voicing that, as Laura Riding and Robert Graves argued, severely limits available responses to the
poem, in effect closing it down.[14] It is arguable, perhaps, that *all* readings
of the repunctuated sonnet 129 are "bad," and that *no* "good" reading of
the 1609 version is possible. Whether or no, the punctuated version of line
12 (the last line quoted) completely forfeits the tenuous polyvocality of the
1609 version and establishes an orthodoxy that necessarily determines the
criteria by which to determine the quality of a reading.

   Not all canonical poems, however, have suffered this fate. Donne's first
Holy Sonnet offers a much more complex instance of voiced noncommittal
crux, because the poem has a long history of canonical recognition and
interpretation, and because we know what we do of the circumstances of
its author and its composition. "Misvoicings," though possible, are dismissed as eccentric, unimportant, and "bad." The crux is in the opening
line, indeed in the first four words:

Thou hast made me, And shall thy worke decay?
Repaire me now, for now mine end doth haste,
I runne to death, and death meets me as fast,
And all my pleasures are like yesterday;
I dare not move my dimme eyes any way,   5
Despaire behind, and death before doth cast
Such terrour, and my feeble breath doth waste
By sinne in it, which it t'wards hell doth weigh;
Onely thou art above, and when towards thee
By thy leave I can looke, I rise againe   10
But our old subtle foe so tempteth me,
That not one houre my selfe I can sustaine;
Thy Grace may wing me to prevent his art,
And thou like Adamant draw mine iron heart.

What's interesting about this poem is its emphatic vehemence, which Donne achieves through a high count of monosyllables, dense consonant clusters (especially but not only in the opening line), a prosodic variety that ranges from the iambic almost-doggerel jingle of line 4 to the paired ana-pests opening line 10, and his characteristic measure of adjacent strong stresses (speech stress overriding the perhaps anticipated weak syllable char-acteristic of strict iambic pattern). The poem's strict control of pace, indeed, emphasizes the quantitative rather than the accentual elements of the sound, and draws us to pay attention to the duration of the syllable as much as (if not more than) to the stress. Consequently, we tend to process the utter-ance one word at a time rather than in our more habitual speech clusters.

The first four words, "Thou hast made me," set the whole poem up. How they are said determines how the rest of the first line shall be said—it's a matter of tone—and how the first line is said determines our under-standing (the meaning) of the whole poem. Meaning, after all, determines tone; tone determines quantity; quantity is (usually, in English) a function of stress. When I was a schoolboy we used to bait our teachers by saying "good morning" sexily, angrily, comically, obsequiously, scornfully, and so on; everyone knows how to pack the most trite expression with strong and malapropos feeling. Change the stress, and you change the quantity; change the quantity, and you change the tone; change the tone, and you change the meaning.

So how voice those first four words? My own rather conventional and orthodox ear bids me to take them slowly, delivering them with more or less equal duration but by no means in a monotone. This severely slows down a line that is already slowed by the density of its consonant clusters (*st/m; d/m; ll/th; k/d*), and almost completely overrides what iambic impera-tive the line seems at first glance to have, yielding a sound that is very close indeed to one word at a time (I italicize the long syllables):

> *Thou hast made me,* And *shall thy worke* de*cay?*

I'm talking duration here, rather than accent, though clearly there is a rela-tionship between the two, and I must add right away that I'm not at all sure that I can satisfactorily *say* the poem this way, it gets too rodomontade (I'm not at all sure that I can sound this poem in any other way either). But my inward ear—what Don Wellman once called "a speaking within hearing"[15]—tells me this is how the line should sound; those first four words are a voiced noncommittal crux. This is not simply because of the poem's curiously *meditative* vehemence, but because almost any other distri-bution of durational (quantitative) stress radically alters the speaker's atti-tude towards "Thou," and quite possibly eliminates the meditative note al-together. Put primary stress on "Thou" and "thy" and the speaker might be blackmailing the Lord—I'm not sure Donne is incapable of such an attitude, but the unorthodoxy or inappropriateness of such a reading gives me pause. So does that of other readings, distributions of stress and duration, which by turns make the speaker sniveling and whining, truculent, self-regarding, or scornful, and my difficulties arise from what I know of the circumstances of the poem's author and its composition.

My assumption here is not that my ear is "correct," or even that it's a representative index of any heard emotional register other than my own; my voicing of this poem is quite possibly very eccentric. The semiotics of tone in ordinary and even in highly structured formal speech is notoriously uncertain: the fearful voice can be heard as resentful; the shy but friendly as aloof and ironic. Weeping is sometimes mistaken for laughter.[16] Donne's poem and its various readings demonstrate in a quite obvious and dramatic way that tone is a matter of quantity is a matter of meaning, and confirm— were confirmation necessary—that there can be no ideal "competent" hearer of language any more than there can be such a speaker; to some extent each of us speaks a foreign tongue. Some, more foreign than others, perhaps. Students, inexperienced readers coming across the poem in a footnoted textbook in a classroom setting, have much to contend with: "knowing" that they had better understand the poem "correctly" they find themselves confronted with their ignorance, and bullied by it. It affects the way they say the poem. Teachers, (presumably) experienced readers, bring to the poem their knowledge of the canon, of Donne's place in it, and of other of Donne's poems. They find themselves confronted with their knowledge, and possibly bullied by it. It affects the way they say the poem.

It would be an exaggeration to say that Donne's (or even perhaps any) poem needs to be protected from the reader's knowledge, but the modern-ist practice of "make it new" led some poets to court an unpredictability designed to undermine the presuppositions and expectations that accom-pany any experienced reader's knowledge of poetry generally. Yet they al-most invariably sought to control the sound. William Carlos Williams, pretty well throughout his career, sought a notation-system that would ade-quately register the sound of the poem as he heard it, was at one stage strongly attracted by Sidney Lanier's notions of musical notation, and for much of the time (but especially in the 1920s and 30s) tinkered with the shape of the poem on the page with aural as well as visual considerations in mind.[17] A slavish obedience to line break, however, has led many an inexperienced reader (to the bored dismay of the listener) to intone each line as if it were a complete sentence, and many a younger poet—following perhaps his or her reading of Olson's *Projective Verse*—to recite a poem in "that old singsong" that David Bromige complained about, "half rapt, half-assed."[18]

The poet's determination in this century to control the sound of the poem notationally was no doubt largely responsible for the enthusiastic and widespread recourse to electronic recording once the technology became available. With the advent of cheap tape recording, what Doris Sommer has called "the readerly will to appropriate a writer's position"[19] could turn to the poet's own reading for clarification and enlightenment, and the poet's own voice gains the status of Authentic Source. The listener can feel that he or she is now in touch with the genuine and originary poetic voice. However, such pursuit of the authentic (which I have elsewhere called the archaeological fallacy) [20] gives rise to some very real problems, not least because it establishes some readings as normative, and suggests that a "good" reading is timelessly stable, transcendent.[21] Thus the 1962 liner notes to the Caedmon record of Dylan Thomas reading Shakespeare and Webster comments, "All who have written of Dylan Thomas's recordings agree that the voice holds the absolute key to the works." [22] What would a late-twentieth-century audience make of Keats's cockney, I wonder?

On the evidence of tape recordings, for instance, the opening of Louis Zukofsky's "So That Even a Lover" should properly be read

> Little wrists,
> Is your content
> My sight or hold . . .

since that is invariably Zukofsky's voicing.[23] Zukofsky had one of the finest ears in the business, and in this poem—as in so many of his short lyrics— he is working for the tune. This does not mean, however, that a reading that substitutes "cóntent" for "contént" is inept, or even inappropriately jars the tune: that "hold" in the third line suggests Zukofsky's awareness of that pun and its resonance in this context. No reading can be definitive, either reading opens up the poem.

That tiny voiced noncommittal crux becomes, in the practice of a poet like Robert Grenier, a basic compositional tool. His fairly early poem "Warm," for instance,[24] exploits undecidability and is extremely difficult if not impossible to voice at all satisfactorily. The poem is designed, I think, not to be heard, but to be read with the eye. It's a very deceptive piece of writing, for it comes trippingly and easily off the tongue, it makes a very pleasing noise. But voicing the poem closes down its play of indeterminacies.

> WARM
> Bones in the child
> child in the womb
> womb in her
> body in
> bed in the room
>
> room in the house
> house in the
> plain
> moon
> drifts
>
> blackness
> because we have
> drawn curtains

It reads like a series of notations, hastily jotted down. It works so strongly for the eye that it is difficult to imagine any satisfactory reading aloud, save *possibly* to an audience that has the text before it. The use of line break (is the "womb in *her*," for instance, or "in her *body*"?); the extreme recurrence of "in" (which appears in lines 2–9 and line 14—i.e., nine times in this fourteen-line poem); the shifts or ambiguities in the parts of speech (is "drifts" a noun or a verb?); that "have" of line 13 (does it signify possession, or tense?); are the curtains open or shut? But it also reads—especially at the beginning—like a nursery rhyme, and it invites the voice to sing, or at least chant. The poem is, then, a really quite dense play of possibilities, the possibilities afforded by the eye playing with and against those afforded by the ear. A Zukofsky trick, maybe. Or Donne's. Or Shakespeare's.

Unsayability, in the sense I have been discussing, is a central feature of a great number of poems, of this and of earlier centuries. How curious, and how interesting, that Shelley's punctuation is so problematic. How important it was in the eighteenth century to pin Shakespeare's noise down. The attraction of firm punctuation is the attraction of the clear voice, which is in turn the attraction of the authentic and the sure: certainty is transcendent. But the unsayable casts doubt on the reader's/hearer's capacity to *know*, all uncertainty removed, without (and I borrow my phrasing from Doris Sommer) "allowing incapacity to float into the comforting, unmanageable mists of ambiguity" (264). The unsayable cripples masterful understanding by holding on to an inexplicable and perdurable residue. Its cultivation has important ethical and political implications, for it leaves us uncompromisingly face to face with the unknowable and different. It is the allure of the unsayable that has led so many poets to a courtship of the unpredictable, because the unpredictable disconcerts: Lyn Hejinian, Barrett Watten, Susan Howe, Robin Blaser, Rae Armantrout, Bruce Andrews; the extravagance of Robert Duncan, the economy of Lorine Niedecker. As Howe cogently and vividly has instructed and reminded us in *My Emily Dickinson* and elsewhere,[25] the last half of this century especially has been the age of the stammering poet, groping for words, stuttering in quest of articulation, refusing the preset certainties of pattern. The stammerings of Billy Budd and the astonishing hesitancies of Emily Dickinson plumb us in the undecidability of language as it moves through us. They have become representative voices of the last half-century, along with Olson, say, especially in his emphysemic breathing through his poems. Or Jackson Mac Low, and his use of random or indeterminate procedures. Or Kathleen Fraser, and her incorporation of error into her text. And dozens upon dozens of others.

The voiced noncommittal crux is the voice of coming-to-speech, that moment on the threshhold of speech where syntax as we have been taught it is thrown over as we come to words, as words come to us. As we move to utterance, the mind and the body cast for and negotiate possibilities, overriding if only momentarily the rhetoric of socially differentiated understanding, with nothing quite adequate to the exact event, never exactly sayable. Robert Grenier, in his well-known 1971 essay "On Speech," put it this way:

> what now I want, at least, is the word way back in the head that is the thought or feeling forming out of the 'vast' silence/noise of consciousness experiencing world *all the time* . . . I want writing what *is* thought/where feeling is/*words are born*.[26]

Where words are born. A century and a half ago Whitman said of the American poet, in one of those extravaganza flourishes that informed and directed him, possessed him and *thought* him through his 1855 *Preface* that "Mississippi with annual freshets and changing chutes, Missouri and Columbia and Ohio and Saint Lawrence with the falls and beautiful masculine Hudson, do not embouchure where they spend themselves more than they embouchure into him"—and they stutter out again, disjointed inarticulate freshets of lists, fragments and piled clauses, heap upon heap of them. Almost, if not completely, unsayable. Voiced, tentative, noncommittal cruxes. Which make poems poems, whatever their ideological stripe. Good reading, bad reading: neither is wholly possible; either might bring us to the threshold of speech. Strength of vocables: to bind.

NOTES

1. I have in mind the kind of reading described by Jonathan Williams in "Take the Number 78 Bus to Helicon," in *The Magpie's Bagpipe: Selected Essays,* ed. Thomas Meyer (San Francisco: North Point, 1982), pp. 127–30, or by Paul Metcalf: "[I]ncredibly bad. Stoned out of his mind, mumbling inaudibly, chain-smoking throughout the reading, begging drinks, ignoring all of us save for an occasional leer . . . I'm told he grosses something like 90 thou a year for this sort of performance" (quoted by Jonathan Williams, " 'Anyway, All I Ever Wanted to Be Was a Poet,' Said Leon Uris, with a Smile, as We Strode Together into the Vomitorium . . . ," *Magpie's Bagpipe,* p. 74).

2. Charles Bernstein, "Artifice of Absorption," in *A Poetics* (Cambridge: Harvard University Press, 1992), p. 9.

3. John Cage, "Mureau," *M: Writings '62–'72* (Middletown, Conn.: Wesleyan University Press, 1973), pp. 35–56; Cage's reading of part of "Mureau" at St. Mark's Church, New York, 1 January 1975, is on the LP *Biting off the Tongue of a Corpse* (Giorno Poetry Systems Records GPS005); Tom Raworth, "Survival," *West Coast Line,* vol. 7 (spring 1992), pp. 7–14; *Survival* (Cambridge: Equipage, 1994). Raworth read "Survival" at the Kootenay School of Writing, Vancouver, in fall 1991.

4. *Dylan Thomas Reading from William Shakespeare's "King Lear" and John Webster's "The Duchess of Malfi"* (Caedmon TC1158).

5. *Keats and Shelley read by Theodore Marcuse* (Lexington 7505). Lexington Records was a division of Educational Audio Visual Inc., New York.

6. William Hazlitt, "My First Acquaintance with Poets," *The Complete Works of William Hazlitt,* ed. P. P Howe, vol. 17, *Uncollected Essays* (London: Dent, 1933), p. 118. The essay first appeared in Leigh Hunt's *The Liberal,* vol. 3 (1823).

7. Robert Duncan, "The Truth and Life of Myth," *Fictive Certainties* (New York: New Directions, 1985), p. 50.

8. Douglas Oliver, *Poetry and Narrative in Performance* (New York: St. Martin's, 1989), p. x.

9. Gilles Deleuze and Félix Guattari, "Rhizome," *Ideology and Consciousness,* vol. 8 (spring 1981), p. 53.

10. For a preliminary discussion of the speech perception of those born deaf, see Ivan Fónagy, *La Métaphore en phonétique,* Studia Phonetica 17 (Ottawa: Didier, 1979), pp. 111–20.

11. William Carlos Williams, "Landscape with the Fall of Icarus," in *The Collected Poems,* vol. 2, 1939–1962, ed. Christopher MacGowan (New York: New Directions 1988), p. 386.

12. Bernard Lintott's was the first "responsibly edited" reprint of the *Sonnets* (Stephen Booth, *Shakespeare's Sonnets, Edited with Analytic Commentary* [New Haven: Yale University Press, 1977], p. 543); further and more scholarly editions appeared in 1766 (one edited by George Steevens, another by Edward Capell); and in 1780 (as part of Edmond Malone's great annotated edition of the complete works).

13. Booth, III. Among those accepting the 1609 punctuation is John Dover Wilson, who remarks that "as [Martin] Seymour-Smith insists, to impose a modern punctuation on the *Sonnets* would indubitably lead to misrepresentation" (*The Works of Shakespeare,* ed. John Dover Wilson, vol. 36, *The Sonnets* [Cambridge: Cambridge University Press, 1966], p. cxxiv).

14. Laura Riding and Robert Graves, "William Shakespeare and E. E. Cummings," *A Survey of Modernist Poetry* (London: Heinemann, 1927). For a vigorous contrary view, see Booth, 441–52.

15. Don Wellman, "Preface," *Oars,* no. 6/7, *Voicing* (1989), p. 1.

16. The semiotics of tone is extremely complicated, and is inextricably compounded with the question of whether (all? some? of) language is motivated rather than arbitrary. The notion that the meaning of tone is universal attracted a number of modernist writers: Basil Bunting, for instance, was not alone in his belief that "it is perfectly possible to delight an audience by reading poetry of sufficient quality in a language it does not know" ("The Poet's Point of View," *Three Essays,* ed. Richard Caddel [Durham, England: Basil Bunting Poetry Centre, 1994], p. 34). Bunting's practice of reading Goethe and Hafez to students in North American classrooms (at, for example, the University of British Columbia in 1970) has kinship with Zukofsky's adoption of transliteration as a compositional principle in his and Celia Zukofsky's translation of *Catullus* (London: Cape-Goliard, 1969), and elsewhere. The literature on the semiotics of tone is vast. I owe much to excellent discussions in David Appelbaum, *Voice* (Albany: State University of New York Press, 1990); Ivan Fónagy, *La Vive voix: essais de psycho-phonétique* (Paris: Payot, 1983); Roman Jakobson and Linda Waugh, *The Sound Shape of Language* (Bloomington: Indiana University Press, 1979); Reuven Tsur, *Toward a Theory of Cognitive Poetics* (Amsterdam: North-Holland, 1992); and—also by Tsur—*What Makes Sound Patterns Expressive? The Poetic Mode of Speech Perception* (Durham, N.C.: Duke University Press, 1992).

17. "Some Simple Measures in the American Idiom and the Variable Foot"—and especially the "Exercise in Timing" (*Collected Poems,* vol. 2, pp. 418–23)—confirm Williams's use of line break as a semantic, syntactic, and above all rhythmic control, though his recordings—most of them made after his stroke—don't usually follow the line breaks.

18. David Bromige, untitled contribution to "Voice // Voicing // Voices. A Forum on the Theme of Voicing," *O.ars* 6/7 *Voicing* (1989), p. 26.

19. Doris Sommer, "Textual Conquests: On Readerly Competence and 'Minority' Literature," in *The Uses of Literary History*, ed. Marshall Brown (Durham, N.C.: Duke University Press, 1995), p. 260. This is an extremely useful discussion, to which I owe a great deal; at one or two points in my essay my own phrasing echoes hers.

20. Peter Quartermain, *Disjunctive Poetics: From Gertrude Stein and Louis Zukofsky to Susan Howe* (New York: Cambridge University Press, 1992), pp. 124–25.

21. For a brilliant discussion of the hubristic aspects of the archaeological fallacy as it relates to the "authentic" performance of music, see Richard Taruskin, *Text and Act: Essays on Music and Performance* (New York: Oxford University Press, 1995). In the introduction (14), Taruskin quotes the following from the article on "Performing Practice" in the *New Grove Dictionary of Music and Musicians* (14:370): "The principle that the performers should be allowed some scope to 'interpret' the notation subjectively has been challenged successfully for the first time . . . with the advent of recordings and electronic means of fixing a composition in its definitive form once and for all."

22. The liner notes list five further LP recordings of Thomas reading his own work, plus a two-disk set of *Under Milk Wood* (Caedmon TC 2005), and add: "At no former time in history has a poet's own voice been treasured and familiar in so many thousands of homes."

23. Louis Zukofsky, *Complete Short Poetry* (Baltimore: Johns Hopkins University Press, 1991), p. 114. The Harry Ransom Humanities Research Center, at the University of Texas at Austin, has what may well be a complete collection of Zukofsky's taped readings.

24. Robert Grenier, "Warm," *Series: Poems, 1967–71* ([Oakland] This, 1978), p. 17; also *In The American Tree*, ed. Ron Silliman (Orono, Me.: National Poetry Foundation, 1986), p. 6.

25. Susan Howe, *My Emily Dickinson* (Berkeley: North Atlantic, 1985); *The Birth-mark: Unsettling the Wilderness in American Literary History* (Hanover, N.H.: Wesleyan University Press, 1993).

26. Robert Grenier, "On Speech," *This,* vol. 1, no. 1 (winter 1971), n.p.; also in *In the American Tree,* 496–97.

PART III

Close Hearings/ Historical Settings

II

Understanding the Sound
of Not Understanding

JED RASULA

Consider the familiar distinction between listening and hearing: to hear is physiological accident, while to listen is psychological posture culturally disposed. To listen is an act of attunement—to which a precise analogy is tuning in a radio station, locating that space along the spectrum with the least noise, the greatest clarity of sound, what's called "definition." But there's a flaw in the analogy. To tune in a radio signal is to ultimately arrive at a recumbent state, in which the static interference is banished and one can hear the broadcast without having to pay so much attention. So let's augment the model by suggesting that the signal is coming through loud and clear but the radio is in a car, and you're driving away from the transmitter while listening to a ball game. In fact, it might be said that you begin by merely *hearing* the game—since you don't have to put any effort into it—but after four or five innings you're exiting the domain of the broadcast signal and so you start *listening* to it. Listening is then your only recourse in a regime of noise. A paradox finally occurs here too, when you begin to realize that the static has reached parity with the signal, and that you are yourself the source of much of what you understand to be happening "out there." As the static momentarily abates you hear a cheering crowd, excited by one of two probabilities: the home team has either homered or batted in a runner. But the noise of the crowd soon blends back into static and the result is more or less consigned to the scope of your imagination. To "listen" in this fashion tends toward a compensatory or prosthetic conclusion. We'd hardly call it listening of course, let alone close listening, if the channel reception was impeccable and yet you somehow ended up concluding that the Dodgers beat the Phillies 7 to 6 when in fact it was the Blue Jays 8 to 1 over the Yankees. To hear is to simply receive and register what's given; to listen is to correct and displace it.

To listen is to simultaneously attend to what is present and what is absent, like Wallace Stevens's snowman, to "nothing that is not there and the nothing that is." On the face of it, the challenge of a symposium on close listening entails a readmission of the oral. The historical provocation is clear enough: several decades into the ontological readjustment sponsored by Derrida, purporting to wage holy war on logocentrism, it now appears necessary to reaffirm a certain oral plenitude so as to offset the glamour of intertextual materialism. But to leave it at that is to acquiesce in the most banal and predictable of intellectual fashions, conceding priority to the binary schematism that alternates competing paradigms in predictable rotation over the firepit of professional advancement. The challenge of close listening is not merely compensatory, however; it is not a corrective to the graphic textualism of Language Poetry (signaled, in Ron Silliman's defining anthology, by the prominence of Bob Grenier's emphatic declaration "I HATE SPEECH"), nor a return to the breath notations of projective verse. It is (or may be) instead a belated recognition of a stubbornly social fact, which is the persistence and, now, even the increasing popularity of poetry readings, where "reading" (that alphabetic term) is coded to mean oral recitation.

The public poetry reading is a phenomenon of variable historical significance, but apart from the rare instances of post-Nobel adulation, the occasion is not one in which people gather to attend, with a sense of public moment, to the "voice" of their time. The poetry reading, in other words, does not intersect with political oratory, or with the ceremony of public occasion. In fact, a poet who rhetorically assumes such a posture now seems an anachronism, an atavistic remnant of some humanitarian forum in which the debate of weighty issues by cultured dignitaries is invested with a political cachet no longer viable in the age of the sound bite and the computer byte. The moment marking this lapse is suggested by Eric Griffiths as 1883, when Gladstone and Tennyson made a public appearance together. "This moment at Kirkwall, the poet mute and the politician eloquent, is an emblematic moment in the history of the decline of the bardic, it marks an emancipation of political speech from the curacy of literary sensibility, an emancipation which has proceeded, and proceeds, apace."[1]

By 1883 (although the specific year doesn't matter) Thomas Edison had chanted "Mary had a little lamb" into a microphone conducting the sound to an aluminum foil cylinder. He was already entertaining the remedial possibility of offering up Dickens novels in recorded versions for the benefit of those too tired to read them, or indisposed for whatever reason. Edison soon switched to wax as the medium for his recording cylinders, and in 1890 his agent, Colonel Gouraud, prevailed upon certain public figures in England to deposit their voices for posterity in the new medium, Browning and Tennyson among them. These recordings mark a watershed in the history of poetry. Dim as Tennyson's voice now sounds (in the acoustic equivalent of photocopies of photocopies, in which the ratio of grain to image exponentially increases), it is still possible to make out the cadence and the bardic resolve. It is as if the poet laureate—like the aged Ulysses he had prophesied in his own youthful poem, setting out on new adventures in his twilight years—were clinging by sheer oral tenacity to the magic of the voice machine. The ferocity still audible in the recording looms out of the past as a proprioceptive angst, a profoundly somatic intuition that a limit is at hand, a frontier crossed.

That border is as obvious as the Berlin Wall yet little noted. But think of it: the existence of audio-recording media divides humanity into two clans, those with voices and those without. This fact has long since penetrated the history of music; but readers and students of poetry have been relatively heedless. On one side of this unalterable divide we have Yeats, Eliot, Pound, H. D., Williams, Frost, Stevens, Auden, Moore, and an ever expanding cavalcade of poets preserved reading or performing their work. On the chill nether side are those huddled together as in an infernal setting Dante might have devised, the Circle of Poets Whose Voices are Silenced; and to list *these* would be to summon the legions of generations of those who signify "poetry." An appalling thought, unless you're so sanguinely resigned to graphism as to dismiss the thought of poets' voices as logocentric nostalgia.

Foremost among Thomas Edison's expectations was that the phonograph and the poet's voice would be mutual beneficiaries. The voice of the poet was to be a cornerstone in the triple alliance of phonography, neurology, and spiritualism, conducted under the imaginal auspices of the city of the dead.[2] In a postmortem rehearsal that defines the precinct of a poetic Necropolis, Robert Browning's friends gather to hear the dead poet's voice reanimated from wax cylinder recorded by George Gouraud in April 1889. Partway into his recitation Browning stops apologetically, unable to remember his own lines. "I am exceedingly sorry that I can't remember my own verses: but one thing that I shall remember all my life is the astonishing sensation produced by your wonderful invention."[3] The uncanny alliance registered by the survival of the voice endows memory with a funereal commemoration that even Plato had not suspected when he denounced writing as a blight on memory. If writing—as aid to memory—impairs even as it benefits, orality too has its liability, acceding to the sheer flow of words as they occur, swept along by a pace that may or may not be coincident with understanding.

Tennyson was also captured by Gouraud vocalizing his poems.[4] One of them is "Northern Farmer," notable for its assiduous annotation of dialect.

Seeä'd her todaäy goä by—Saäint's-daay—they was ringing the bells.
She's abeauty thou thinks—an' soä is scoors o' gells,
Them as 'as munny an' all—wot's a beauty?—the flower as blaws.
But proputty, proputty sticks, an' proputty, proputty graws.[5]

Tennyson's manner of reading aloud commonly struck people as oracular, chanted not spoken, an incantation not a recital. His preferred device was the vowel drone. In the account of one contemporary who heard him read

"Ode on the Death of the Duke of Wellington" in 1884, "he lengthened out the vowel *a* in the words 'great' and 'lamentation' till the words seemed as if they had been spelt 'greaat' and 'lamentaation,' and . . . he rolled out and lengthened the open oes in the words 'To the nooise of the moourning of a mighty naation.' "[6]

Reflecting in old age on his distant boyhood, Ford Madox Ford recalled an atmosphere of numbing pomposity whenever his parents' poet friends came over to the house and declaimed their verse: "Mournfully, then, up and down the stone staircases, there would flow two hollow sounds. For, in those days, it was the habit of all poets and poetesses to read aloud upon every possible occasion, and whenever they read aloud to employ an imitation of the voice invented by the late Lord Tennyson, and known, in those days, as the *ore rotundo*—'with the round mouth mouthing out their hollow o's and a's.' "[7] The oracular declamatory style, however, is not merely the antiquarian baggage of Victoriana, but a persistent feature of the poetry-reading voice. It may even be the voice-over of a particular metrical tradition insinuated into the very notion of what the cadence of poetry is—a "standard currency, a guaranteed emotional tender insured against inflation" as Walter J. Ong puts it.[8] Assessing this tradition as the particular legacy of Spenser, Ong notes that "In this bright and shining world of a successful Newtonian physics, a Cartesian mathematical solvent for all reality, and a naïve materialism, there is something which inevitably gave body to a 'continuous literary decorum.' Like the decimal measurement systems, Spenserian smoothness represented great achievement to the enlightened mind" (152). By "smoothness" Ong specifies "the quiet throbbing of the smooth alternating-stress verse he [Spenser] perfected" (151).

A further endowment, and an implicit subtext of the English verse tradition—at least since the imperial cadences of *Paradise Lost*—was Virgilian Latin; and Latin, as an increasingly dead language by the late nineteenth century, was the language of narcosis (as Leopold Bloom notices in the Lotos Eaters chapter of *Ulysses* when he peeks inside a Catholic church). The ensemble of sound elements is barely recuperated to the semantic dimension in Gerard Manley Hopkins, Jesuit priest, inviting a hypothetical if unlikely alliance with the "Lautgedichte" or sound poems pioneered by the Dadaists. The explicitly ceremonial and liturgical aura surrounding Hugo Ball's initial presentations of *Lautgedichte* at Cabaret Voltaire in Zurich serves as a reminder of the spirit of sanctification discernible in the Tennysonian oration as well. In the recitation of poetry, the liturgical style stresses (often unwittingly) an alliance between the high sublime and the sound poem, disclosing both as exercises in orality as *not understanding*. The incantatory mode, then, legislates between the bardic posture of superior wisdom and a less privileged endowment, which is that of the stupefied or narcotically enchanted believer. This latter position is bequeathed to any latecomer to a tradition, in effect consigning nearly the whole contingent of poets and readers alike to the insecurity and bewilderment of belatedness, a dilemma given simply with the defamiliarizing anaesthetic of old cadences persisting in the present.[9] Hearing stress and pitch as ventriloquial imperatives, bulletins from the ward bosses of prosodic heritage, we glean the uncanny thought that understanding encompasses rather than clarifies (as does explanation, in the common hermeneutic distinction),[10] and that within its circumscribed territory there are dark areas, zones that exceed what "understanding" normally signifies.

Accentuation of stress and pitch is a normal prerogative of oral performance that can readily become a characteristic feature of a poet's delivery, as in Ezra Pound's nasal drawl, which doesn't lend emphasis to the text so much as amalgamate it to innuendo. This manner is most effective in a poem of social satire like "Moeurs Contemporaines," in which the poet intones the opening four lines in one continuous breath, with lingering stresses, and in a steadily falling tonal drone. It is a memorable demonstration of the collapse of air out of a pair of human lungs, dazzlingly coordinated to lavish its physical decrescendo on the satirical target:

> Mr. Hecatomb Styrax, the owner of a large estate and of large muscles,
> A 'blue' and a climber of mountains, has married at the age of 28,
> He being at that age a virgin,
> The term 'virgo' being made male in mediaeval latinity . . .[11]

Interestingly, Pound's locution has drawn on another feature of medieval latinity, which is the plainchant. If the nasal wryness marks this passage in recording as satirical, the liturgical ebb and flow of a voice in devotional transport to its phonological base rings through loud and clear. Certain words are sufficiently elongated that they might well be assigned notes on a musical staff.[12] What is most notable here is not the "musicality" of Pound's performance—at least not insofar as that quality is associated with lyric transport—but his incorporation of musical tonality into a speech cadence. Music, in other words, is held in strict abeyance to the sonority of the voice, a voice that emphatically retains its conversational register. Pound achieves a paradoxical delivery in which the listener seems privy to gossip while attending evensong.

Other features of Pound's characteristic reading style are the rolled *r*s and a semitone hum (less nasalized when the subject is not satirical); but this is by no means unique to Pound. It is strikingly similar to the way Yeats reads "The Lake Isle of Innisfree," which, in turn, is in the "ore rotundo" mode of Tennyson. This triple alliance of Tennyson-Yeats-Pound would be unthinkable were it not for the existence of recorded readings by all three, which clearly delineate a manner of recitation that may begin with the poet laureate, but seems increasingly to have ended with Pound. Zukofsky's famously "musical" *ear* is deeply insinuated into his deft balancing of phrasal registers, but the undertone (even in so potentially abstract a text as his Catullan homophonics) is securely bound to a conversational speaking voice—as T. S. Eliot thought it must ("The music of poetry . . . must be a music latent in the common speech of its time").[13] The sound dimension released in, and inhabited by, poetry need not aspire solely to the condition of music. Or, to be precise, "music" is a variable term which, with regard to poetry, is like the X in an algebraic equation.

Music, it is assumed, is a vocal sonority that impresses the ear as "poetic." But is it the voice that is sonorous, or the poem?—and how to tell the difference? Might it be that this phantom quality marks the conjunction—like a sidereal eclipse—of sound and sense, of the sensed and the senseless? In Michael Taussig's exposition of somatic particularities in South American native/colonizer encounters—a realm somewhere "between the real and the really made-up"[14]—a tantalizing image is given of nineteenth-century ethnographers and others taking phonographs into the jungle. For Taussig, this was a practical exercise meant to glamorize a new mode of mechanical reproduction just as it had become slightly too familiar. In the jungle, the mimetic faculty is reinstalled "as mystery in the art of mechanical reproduction, reinvigorating the primitivism implicit in technology's wildest dreams, therewith creating a surfeit of mimetic power" (208). The image of the RCA dog, ear alert at the bell of the horn, registers the command of mimetic surfeit. Is the development of sound in late-nineteenth- and early-twentieth-century poetry a comparable exercise in mimetic superfluity? Do the indulgences of sound in Swinburne or Hopkins, like the sheer somatic vocalizations of Hugo Ball or Kurt Schwitters, exuberantly insist on scraping away a veneer of chatter in order to arrive at the pulse and heave of language itself, thoroughly cleansed of its human shadows?

Sidney Lanier's 1880 *Science of English Verse* opens with an "Investigation of Sound as Artistic Material"; and the very first definition of verse he offers is that "when formal poetry, or verse . . . is repeated aloud, it impresses itself upon the ear as verse only by means of certain relations existing among its component words considered purely as sounds, without reference to their associated ideas."[15] As a practical demonstration, Lanier proposes "the simple experiment of substituting for the words of a formal poem any other words which preserve the accentuation, alliteration, and rhyme, but which convey no ideas to the mind,—words of some foreign language not understood by the experimenter being the most effective for this purpose." This exercise is strikingly suggestive of the homophonic translations of Louis Zukofsky (of Catullus), Ernst Jandl (Wordsworth), and David Melnick (Homer). These recent poetic exercises admit a certain measure of semantic recuperation, of course, so that the estrangement of the borrowed soundscape is *internalized* to English (or German in Jandl) where it ventriloquizes a different semantic dimension. Lanier's experiment is more radical in its affirmation that "all ideas may be abolished out of a poem without disturbing its effect upon the ear as verse" (21). Needless to say, Lanier doesn't envision anything like sound poetry as such, largely because the allure of musicality proves irresistible. In his case, the attraction is literal not metaphorical.

Logocentrism prevails in Lanier's vision of written poetry as prelude to sound: "Print and writing are systems of notation for the tone-colors of the human speaking-voice" (52). And his classification of sounds into the four "particulars" of duration, intensity, pitch, and tone color is familiar enough from traditional prosody (24). So it is no surprise to find him extolling the musical virtues of the voice. "The human voice is practically a reed-instrument of the hautboy class, the vocal chords being the two thin vibrating reeds, and the mouth and throat (the buccal cavity) constituting the tube" (31). But for Lanier, verse is not dignified by comparison with music; the comparison is made in order to prove the superiority of the voice. Music lacks any system for tone color, he declares: tone color in music is, instead, "indicated by stating the instrument upon which the strain is to be played" (53). Whereas "in this capacity of varying the tone-color of sounds made on the same instrument the human speaking-voice is very wonderful, and excels all other instruments" (52).

Lanier's advocacy, in writing, of the somatic primacy of poetic voice, is another contribution to that extensive field Ong calls "rhetorical culture . . . in which, even after the development of writing, the pristine oral-aural modes of knowledge storage and retrieval still dominate noetic activity."[16] "It is paradoxical and thought provoking," he adds, "that rhetoric was one of the first fields of knowledge worked up as a formal art with the aid of writing, for rhetoric means primarily oratory or public speaking" (*Interfaces*, 215). For Lanier, obviously, the poetic text is a storage and retrieval system for activating the voice. But his account of the "science" of verse is not prescriptive. Unlike a host of predecessors,[17] Lanier resists anything along the lines of an elocutionary guide to the performance of poems. Being oriented to production, not reproduction, he posits a phonotextual dimension in which "each sense has not only what is ordinarily called its physical province, but also its corresponding imaginative province"; in which "the imagination of the ear" does not refer to sound waves producing an "actual vibratory impact upon the tympanum immediately preceding the perception, but [to] indirect causes (such as the characters of print and writing) which in any way amount to practical equivalents of such impact" (22). Alphabetic characters are indirect causes transposing sound in a relay, not originating instigators of sound. Having set aside the awkward problem of rhetorical culture—specifically the performative aspect ("delivery" being one of the five parts of classical rhetoric)—under the sheltering trope of anatomically specific fields of imagination, Lanier is free to bypass the obligations of the elocutionary handbook and assign this phantom quintessence of sound directly to poetry as such, even if it is predominately *written*: "although the great majority of formal poems in modern times are perceived by the mind through the original agency of the eye, the relations indicated by the term 'verse' are still relations between sounds" (23). To so define verse is to reaffirm a pure nonsemantic materialism of the text.

Despite the radical implications of some of Lanier's suggestions, in his own poetry as in nearly all Victorian versifying, "sound" is still in retainer to a sensibility mired in a soporifically melodious sense of rhythm. But the *sound* of "sense" is compromised by these very same principles which, like Victorian furniture, are so ample as to defeat the practicalities they are designed to serve. As critics have observed about Swinburne, for instance, the sound dimension of his verse is so melodiously narcotic as to anaesthetize the semantic message. In fact, whether intentionally or not, Swinburne turns out to have short-circuited the sentiments of versified piety so fondly routinized by his contemporaries, leaving a body of work in which the sound of not understanding is implicitly all there is to be understood of the poems. To consider an equally "musical" poet like Hopkins is to discern another level of practice closer to the nonsense disposition of his contemporaries Lewis Carroll and Edward Lear than to the ear-stuffing sonorities of German symphonic music or the chamber bagatelles of the French belle epoch.

Here is Gerard Manley Hopkins encountering his own verse in that heightened frame of mind, defamiliarization—by which I mean not only Shklovsky's sense in which literature is that which *roughs up* convention and violates expectation, but also Kandinsky's experience coming into his studio and seeing one of his canvases leaning upside down and through that momentary *mis*recognition finding the path he would take into abstraction; ". . . when, on somebody returning to me the *Eurydice*, I opened and read some lines, reading, as one commonly reads whether prose or verse, with the eyes, so to say, only, it struck me aghast with a kind of raw nakedness and unmitigated violence I was unprepared for: but take breath and read it with ears, as I always wish to be read, and my verse becomes all right."[18] At this point Hopkins is reversing Lanier's sense that "that is the best description which makes the ear an eye" (22). Hopkins's glimpse of his own writing discloses a horrible disfiguration, denuded words reduced to graphic marks, sucked clean of the inbreathed *logos* of vocality. Hopkins's vision *[sic]* is keenly attuned to sound, and he is insistent on oral priority when discussing poetry. Of "Spelt from Sibyl's Leaves" he urged Robert Bridges to "remember what applies to all my verse, that it is . . . made for performance . . . loud, leisurely, poetical (not rhetorical) recitation, with long rests, long dwells on the rhyme and other marked syllables, and so on. This sonnet shd. be almost sung . . ."[19] Hopkins set more than two dozen lyrics to music, and "The Leaden Echo and the Golden Echo" was intended as a choral hymn for his uncompleted play *St. Winefred's Well*.[20] He would appear, then, to be among those for whom poetry aspires to the condition of music.

The journals tell another story. Here is a symptomatic passage, from July 22, 1873:

Very hot, though the wind, which was south, dappled very sweetly on one's face and when I came out I seemed to put it on like a gown as a man puts on the shadow he walks into and hoods or hats himself with the shelter of a roof, a penthouse, or a copse of trees, I mean it rippled and fluttered like light linen, one could feel the folds and braids of it—and indeed a floating flag is like wind visible and what weeds are in a current; it gives it thew and fires it and bloods it in.—Thunderstorm in the evening, first booming in gong-sounds, as at Aosta, as if high up and so not re-echoed from the hills; the lightning very slender and nimble and as if playing very near . . . Flashes lacing two clouds above or the cloud and the earth started upon the eyes in live veins of rincing or riddling liquid white, inched and jagged as if it were the shivering of a bright riband string which had once been kept bound round a blade and danced back into its pleatings. Several strong thrills of light followed the flash but a grey smother of darkness blotted the eyes if they had seen the fork, also dull furry thickened scapes of it were left in them. (*Journals,* 233–34)

This extraordinary evocation offers a minute registration of the tactile quality of the muggy day and the visual excitement of its lightning conclusion; but what's notable is how little attention Hopkins pays to sound. This passage is typical of his journals in general, which might just as well have been penned by a deaf man. The visual acuity on the other hand is astoundingly precise: "I took a last look at the breakers," he notes a few weeks after the thunderstorm, "wanting to make out how the comb is morselled so fine into string and tassel . . . I saw big smooth flinty waves, carved and scuppled in shallow grooves . . . the crests I saw ravelled up by the wind into the air in arching whips and straps of glassy spray and higher broken into clouds of white and blown away. Under the curl shone a bright juice of beautiful green. The foam exploding and smouldering under water makes a chrysoprase green" (235–36).[21] Soundless underwater explosions incite the poet's eye, all the sonority being reserved for the elastic resonance of his (written) English applied to the mute scene ("arching whips and straps of glassy spray" and "foam exploding and smouldering under water" could be inserted untouched into his poems). This inattention to observable sound seems strange in a poet whose work is commonly accorded a supreme place among English ravishers of the ear.

Is it simply, as Michael Sprinker suggests, that in "Attempting to capture the presence of spoken language, Hopkins is compelled to proliferate systems of writing"?[22] Sprinker elaborates on the subject of Hopkins's famously speech-oriented sprung rhythm: "Sprung rhythm is natural and yet it must be marked, something that the reader would fall into merely by speaking but nevertheless so elusive that he would miss it if it were not indicated by a system of notation. Hopkins recognizes the antinomy of speech and writing and attempts to overcome it, but his device for reproducing the 'natural rhythm of speech' produces yet another system of writing" (74–75). Hopkins's graphic provocations are so fecund as to have proliferated beyond the grave. He has been more fortunate than Emily Dickinson in having editors willing to experiment with his diacritical notations; but those notations have proven prodigiously undecidable. The Hopkins of Norman MacKenzie's 1990 Oxford English Texts edition has a strikingly different appearance from earlier compilations, and the editorial choices can be conveniently compared with the bewildering tapestry of orthographic possibilities tested out by the poet himself.[23] The extent and skill of Hopkins's draughtsmanship in the notebooks reinforces the sense that this was a poet of the keenest eye. Bearing that in mind, it is revealing to consider his blazoning of verses with dozens of diacritical markings as visual supplement rather than aural cue. There are numerous instances in his poetry in which the stress indicators fall at unlikely places, where stresses bunch up inside a line (sprung rhythm being a method of indicating contractions and expansions *internal* to the metrical measure, as if all metrics were part of an exfoliating continuum like fractals). To study the notebooks is to sense a man overmastered by a *vision* of his poems even as he purports to be merely notating them as speech.

Hopkins's visionary gleam is compounded on and harbored in a romance of sound as grit, phonemic incident as testament. Hence his famous definition of poetry as compelling notice of language for its own sake: "Poetry is speech framed for contemplation of the mind by the way of hearing or speech framed to be heard for its own sake and interest even over and above its interest of meaning. Some matter and meaning is essential to it but only as an element necessary to support and employ the shape which is contemplated for its own sake. (Poetry is in fact speech only employed to carry the inscape of speech for the inscape's sake . . .)" (*Journals*, 289). This may be the most cited of all Hopkins's pronouncements, and generally taken to sanction a subordination of sense to rhapsodic oral delivery. But he goes on to carefully distinguish a work "composed without meaning" (nonsense verse and choruses) as insufficient to stand as poetry on its own but only as part of a poem. "But if it has a meaning and is meant to be heard for its own sake it will be poetry if you take poetry to be a kind of composition and not the virtue or success or excellence of that kind, as eloquence is the virtue of oratory and not oratory only and beauty the virtue of inscape and not inscape only" (289). It is difficult to gain purchase here without special understanding of the word "composition." The sense apparently intended (not to mention the word itself) invites comparison with Gertrude Stein. For Hopkins, *poetry* is not an honorary term indicating excellence in versecraft; poetry is rather a *composition* meant to be heard for its own sake—that is, *not* as an instance of—or conduit to—something else. That "something else" may be an aesthetic or rhetorical effect (excellence of achievement) or it may be a message or meaning (efficiency of communication), but these do not constitute a "composition" about which one might take an interest for its own *sake*. Sprinker draws attention to the unique sense the word "sake" has for Hopkins. In a letter, the poet indicates "It is the *sake* of 'for the sake of,' *forsake, namesake, keepsake*. I mean by it the being a thing has outside itself, as a voice by its echo, a face by its reflection, a body by its shadow . . . something distinctive, marked, specifically or individually speaking, as for a voice and echo clearness; for a reflected image light, brightness."[24] To attain a being outside oneself is the literal meaning of the word *ecstasy*—to stand outside, beyond, to be set apart. Hopkins's association of this distinction with the sound of the voice and with the patina or brightness of reflected light suggests that kind of radiance associated with devotional intensity and ecstatic transport, the peace that passeth understanding. The vocalization of a poem, especially a poem "meant to be heard for its own sake," is one in which the acoustic dimension literally marks the limits of understanding. In the ecstasy of orality, the poem stands apart; its sense no longer aligned with *under*standing but with that profound stutter which is so often the character of Hopkins's syllabic anatomy. It stands aside or gets out from under. As there is an inscape and instress, so there is also an outside that exceeds understanding; and this outside is the voiced poem: words ecstatically exempted from graphic retainer. But in this condition of being *beside themselves,* words are also sites of paranoia—another way of being beside—an anxiety marking the speech/writing opposition

At times, in Hopkins, the visual emphasis on voicing induces a near-nonsense stress pattern.

And the córn is córded and shóulders its shéaf,
The ear in milk, lush the sash,
And crúsh-sílk póppies aflásh,
The blóod-gúsh bláde-gásh
Fláme-rásh rúdréd
Búd shélling or bróad-shéd
Tátter-tángled and díngle-a-dánglèd
Dándy-húng dáinty héad

(Poetical Works, 132)

Dimly made out through the crackle of accentuation is the perspective of the woodlark of the poem's title, looking down at wheat and corn fields and spotting poppies in bloom. As indicated by the stress marks, this passage, if read aloud, would be a nearly continuous staccato, the effect of which is to obliterate the sense of the words as they snap along the string of oral firecrackers. In the end there is an abortive discrepancy between sound and sense here, which may be why Hopkins chose not to finalize this draft. In this fragment, the diacritical marks almost seem like divine sparks, beneath which the accidentals which are words have been summoned into momentary existence (but not quite for their own "sake").

Other poems are more pragmatically expressive. In "God's Grandeur" the treading generations literally inhabit the prosodic feet in the triple "have trod" of line five; a triplicate vision expanded in the next line with *seared,* *bleared,* and *smeared* and enhanced by *smudge* and *smell* in the following line, all of it looped through the uncharacteristically insistent end rhymes (foil/oil/toil/soil, and God/rod/trod/shod). This acoustic carnival sets the turmoil of a human scene to which the saving grace of the last stanza is contrasted. There the "dearest freshness" of nature "is never spent"—such riotous sibillance of the opening stanza being a contrasting illustration of human expenditure. The poem closes in what is a veritable hush, a cleansed ensemble of rounded vowels and soothingly shaded consonants that suggest nothing so much as the cooing of doves deep in the rafters of a barn:

> morning, at the brown brink eastward, springs—
> Because the Holy Ghost óver the bent
> World broods with warm breast and with ah! bright wings. (139)

"Stress" as a feature of prosody is absorbed by Hopkins into the metaphysical drama of *instress,* which Norman MacKenzie aptly calls "the selving force within a being."[25] In scansion, then, one might observe that the stresses are where the poem achieves its being, the pattern of marks that "selve" it. Stress is salvation. This salve of selving is agonized in the opening of "The Leaden Echo":

> How to kéep—is there ány any, is there none such, nowhere known
>   some, bow or brooch or braid or brace, láce, latch or catch or key to
>   keep
> Back beauty, keep it, beauty, beauty, béauty, . . . from vanishing away?
>   (169)

The echo effect named by the title is immediately rendered in the double "any," minutely discriminated by the stress, as if the very sign of self is precisely that diacritical flick, or flicker. The stress is not to be confused with emphasis or with any verbal pressure; Hopkins's stresses are not alternatives to italics. The stresses are like thorns on Christ's brow: they *ride* the words like pricks of numinous incident, summoning one after another into a transpositive dimension of redemption through individuation. In the mode of mortification the stress is indicated in a kind of encasing, in the famous "Not, I'll not, carrion comfort, Despair . . ." with its memorable concluding parenthetic emphasis: "I wretch lay wrestling with (my God!) my God" (183). In "Spelt from Sibyl's Leaves" the fatal "Disremembering, dismémbering" marks that riven condition which Rilke memorably names as "zwiespalt"—split as spilt, figured by Hopkins here in the two spools on which are punned a silent waxing, waning, and winding:

> . . . Óur tale, O óur oracle! | Lét life, wáned, ah lét life wind
> Off hér once skéined stained véined variety | upon, áll on twó spools;
>   párt, pen, páck
> Now her áll in twó flocks, twó folds—bláck, white; | right, wrong;
>   réckon but, réck but, mind
> But thése two; wáre of a wórld where bút these | twó tell, éach off
>   the óther; of a ráck
> Where, selfwrung, selfstrung, sheathe- and shelterless, | thóughts agaínst
>   thoughts in groans grind. (191)

The oracular impact of the sybilline leaves is comparable to the method of prophecy given in the parable, where the leaves (like pages of an unbound book) blow away in throngs, suggestive of a masterscript now literally cast to the winds. The immense variety of things, descended to the dichotomous zone of black/white (words on a page) and right/wrong (deeds inscribed in the heart), signify ceaselessly the sundered being stuck on the spit or rack of self-division, where self *is* division, its stress an agony that only the providence of a savior can properly scan as "instress." To live at all, for Hopkins, is to commit to that act of faith entailed in the submission of one's speech to the graphic (ominously explicit) indications of a text. To live the Christian life is to incarnate in oneself the scriptures—that is to say, the wrack of marks, the (w)reck of signs.[26]

In Hopkins the sounds of the world are harbored in the poems, almost as in exile, where their potential release is paradoxically hemmed in by the thicket of diacritical cues for their enunciation. It is a paradox commonly found in attempts to annotate particularities of speech. In the Dorset poems of William Barnes, for example, the hazard of dialect impinges heavily on the phrasal and lexical dimension:

> Good Meäster Collins heärd woone day
> A man a-talkèn, that did zay
> It woulden answer to be kind,
> He thought, to vo'k o' grov'lèn mind,
> Vor they would only teäke it wrong,
> That you be weak an' they be strong.[27]

While it is admittedly easier to transpose this rather than, say, the Scots poems of Hugh McDiarmid into common English, the specific inflexions of the dialect are invariably mutilated by being forced through a substrate of standard English orthography as through a funnel. Barnes's own view of the relation between speech and writing is straightforward: "Speech is the speaking or bewording of thoughts," he says. "Speech is of breath-sounds with sundry breathings, hard or mild, and breath-pennings, which become words."[28] But to take Barnes's lines above as breath-pennings that become words is to admit that the speech they precipitate may bear little or no resemblance to Dorset dialect in the reading of someone from North America. The varieties of spoken English being what they are, and the vagaries of English spelling favoring no particular pronunciation, a poem written in "proper" English will neatly deliver itself up to whatever accent and idiomatic expressions the reader brings to it. In that light, Barnes's poems may be seen not as cues for pronunciation but as standard English marked for the readerly ear of the man who wrote it: "teäke" and "vo'k" signal the putting of standard English into receivership, as it were—the protective custody of one who, like Barnes or Hardy or Tennyson or even Hopkins, agonized about English as the site of a struggle between homogeneity and heterogeneity. Despite a few exercises in dialect like "Northern

Farmer," Tennyson shied away from trying to particularize speech patterns in his orthography, although he did seem receptive to William Allingham's suggestion "that he might put on record a code for pronouncing his own poetry, with symbolised examples, and he seemed to think this might be done."[29] But it wasn't. The problem may have been that, in Thomas Hardy's estimation, "if a writer attempts to exhibit on paper the precise accents of a rustic speaker he disturbs the proper balance of a true representation by unduly insisting upon the grotesque element." As Eric Griffiths goes on to remark, "Semi-phonetic spelling does indeed make it look as if speakers with regional accents mispronounce because it subordinates their speech to the norms of correct orthography" (83). Writing may prove exceptionally unconducive to the aspirations of logocentrism. In this light, the familiar deconstructionist critique (that writing, the ontological regime of logocentric orality, is fallen supplementarity) takes on another character when we reformulate the logocentric position: if writing is merely the representation of speech, then whose speech and in what accent? By what right or on what basis does writing neutralize or efface the prodigious variety of speech patterns? In popular synopses of deconstruction there is a tacit conflict between the One of logocentrism and the Many of textuality; but to introduce the claims of actual speech into the equation is to confront a reversal of perspective, in which it is writing that violates diversity and inaugurates the monodrama of identity as a thwart to elocutionary difference. It is of particular interest, then, that the very advantages claimed by deconstruction on behalf of writing—its marks, spacings, and so on—are most insistently produced in these efforts to make writing *speak,* to register the truth of a vocal *deviation* in or by means of a ballet of signs.

Anyone who has seen *My Fair Lady* will recall its sense of English as an Alpine summit from which a large portion of the native speaking population is in danger of slipping. Linguistics professor Henry Higgins could well have hazed the Cockney lass Liza Doolittle with this passage from Browning's "The Flight of the Duchess" as yet another in his series of intimidating tongue-twisting phonological exercises:

> I could favour you with sundry touches
> Of the paint-smutches with which the Duchess
> Heightened the mellowness of her cheek's yellowness
> (To get on faster) until at last her
> Cheek grew to be one master-plaster
> Of mucus and fucus from mere use of ceruse:
> In short, she grew from scalp to udder
> Just the object to make you shudder.
>
> (Quoted in Frye, xiv)

This is versification of a sort more familiar from novelties like "Six Septembers Susan swelters, / Six sharp seasons' snow supplied; / Susan's satin sofa shelters / Six small Slocums side by side."[30] Such works are exercises in sibilants, fricatives, and other phonemic contours. But there is an entire zone of written matter courting comparable labyrinths and straits of vocalization—namely, in elocution manuals, rhetoric and public speaking primers. "Abracadabra, babe, babble, baptism, bauble, beblot, bedaub, beef, bepeppered, beverage, biblical, biped, blubber, brabble, bribe, bobbin, bubble, bump, hubbub, probable";[31] "ith iss ith, ith ish ith, iss ith iss, iss ish iss, ish iss ish, ish ith ish" and "ip it, ip ik, it ik, it ip, ik it, ik ip."[32] These examples mark another site of the convergence of poetry and vocalization, writing and speech, in the work of Alexander Melville Bell, professor of vocal physiology at Edinburgh University, and author of some of the most influential manuals of oratory and elocution in the nineteenth century.[33]

The unique soundscape of Victorian poetics is illuminated by comparison with the contemporary vocal exercises of Bell. Under "Syllabic Quantity" in Bell's *Elocutionary Manual* are found such prosodically enticing word clusters as "help, felt, elk, tent, lamp, dreamt, bank" and "alps, bolts, belch, bulks, prints, inch, imps, tempts, thanks" (examples of "Breath Articulations," 64, 65); "leave, bathe, ease, rouge" and "bulbs, builds, bilge, rhumbs, lands, finds, fringe" ("Voice Articulations," 65); and "act, tact, sect, erect, strict, hacked, shocked, ducked, poked, looked, walked, ached, leaked, liked, cactus, lacteal, affected, lecture, picture, dictate, instructive, octave, doctor" ("Mixed Articulations" utilizing what Bell calls "Breath Obstructives" such as *pt* and *kt,* 65). Bell's books bristle with catalogues like this, stockpiles of atomic particulars from which flexible and confident oratory is to be formed. Speech for Bell is a mechanical activity elevated by the elusive quality of "feeling." "There is a Vocal Logic; a Rhetoric of Inflection; a Poetry of Modulation; a Commentator's explanatoriness of Tone" (111). A remedial function is supposed for many of the uses to which his books may be put (cure of stammering and other speech impediments, clarity of normal articulation); and one manual culminates in a compendium of "difficult sequences" for practice, ranging from the vocally challenging if ludic ("Robert loudly rebuked Richard, who ran lustily roaring round the lobby," "Pull the poor fool out of the full pool") to the homiletic tags of Victorian masscultural sentiment ("Vice oft wears variegated velvet, while virtue walks in vulgar velveteen").[34]

Bell's relevance to poetry is different now than what it was in his own time. As a proponent of well-tuned "vocal physiology," Bell was concerned of course that recitations of poetry be unencumbered by avoidable defects of pronunciation and phrasing. To this end he conspicuously printed many poems in prose so as to break readers' habitual overstressing of line ends. Byron's "Address to the Ocean," given this treatment, loses the visual dimension that might otherwise provoke too jingling a reading: "There is a pleasure in the pathless woods; there is a rapture on the lonely shore; there is society, where none intrudes—by the deep Sea,—and music in its roar."[35]

In his note "On the Reading of Verse," Bell advises the reader that "Verse, or metrical composition, consists of sense in connection with the music of rhythm, or the consonance of syllables. The reader's business is to express the sense—by uniting or separating words exactly as in reading prose" (28). Prose sense prevails over metrical nonsense—this is the gist of Bell's message. "If any want of harmony exist, the poet is in fault." Bell's method may be counted as one of the broader cultural influences contributing to the eventual rise of free verse. The printing of poems as prose is offered "as a mode of obviating the too rhythmical delivery which is often associated with metrically printed LINES; and as an assistance to the habitual use of pauses and tones in strict accordance with the SENSE" (139). If line ends unduly suggest pauses, abolishing them forces the reader to seek intratextual cues consonant with the sense (that is, thought and feeling combined) for the ebb and flow of vocalization.

Like Hopkins (albeit less concerned with poetry as such) Bell devised methods of indicating stress and inflection; and as in the case of sprung rhythm with its professed adherence to the exigencies of speech, Bell's marks are designed to admit the local variables that arise beneath metrical patterns, constituting a phonemic domain of effective delivery. A chart outlining the "Gamut of Inflexions" prepares the reader to comprehend annotation indicating a sarcastic enunciation of "One murder makes a villain: Millions a hero" (21).

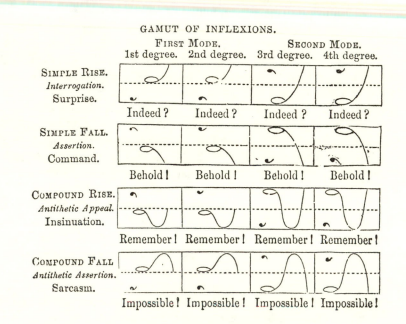

Figure 11.1 From Bell, Bell's Standard Elocutionist, *20*

In his *Elocutionary Manual* these inflexional marks are combined with a repertoire of others indicating modulation, force, time, and expression:

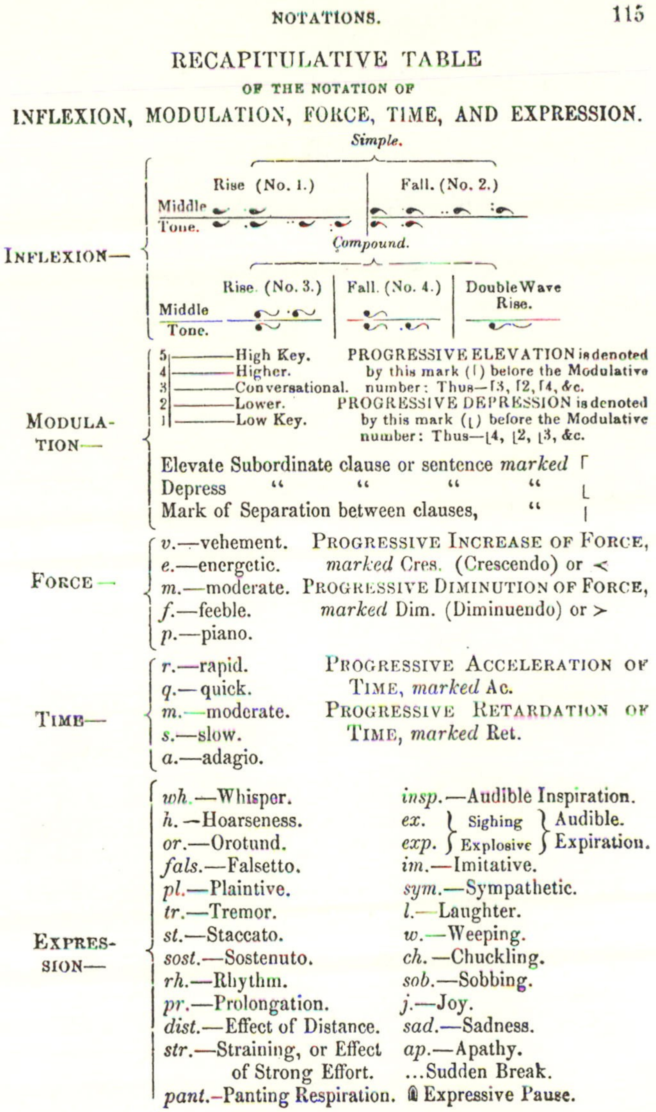
NOTATIONS. 115

RECAPITULATIVE TABLE
OF THE NOTATION OF
INFLEXION, MODULATION, FORCE, TIME, AND EXPRESSION.

INFLEXION—
Simple.
Rise (No. 1.) | Fall. (No. 2.)
Middle Tone.
Compound.
Rise. (No. 3.) | Fall. (No. 4.) | Double Wave Rise.
Middle Tone.

MODULATION—
5 High Key.
4 Higher.
3 Conversational.
2 Lower.
1 Low Key.
PROGRESSIVE ELEVATION is denoted by this mark (⌈) before the Modulative number: Thus—⌈3, ⌈2, ⌈4, &c.
PROGRESSIVE DEPRESSION is denoted by this mark (⌊) before the Modulative number: Thus—⌊4, ⌊2, ⌊3, &c.
Elevate Subordinate clause or sentence *marked* ⌈
Depress " " " " ⌊
Mark of Separation between clauses, " |

FORCE—
v.—vehement.
e.—energetic.
m.—moderate.
f.—feeble.
p.—piano.
PROGRESSIVE INCREASE OF FORCE, *marked* Cres. (Crescendo) or <
PROGRESSIVE DIMINUTION OF FORCE, *marked* Dim. (Diminuendo) or >

TIME—
r.—rapid.
q.—quick.
m.—moderate.
s.—slow.
a.—adagio.
PROGRESSIVE ACCELERATION OF TIME, *marked* Ac.
PROGRESSIVE RETARDATION OF TIME, *marked* Ret.

EXPRESSION—
wh.—Whisper.
h.—Hoarseness.
or.—Orotund.
fals.—Falsetto.
pl.—Plaintive.
tr.—Tremor.
st.—Staccato.
sost.—Sostenuto.
rh.—Rhythm.
pr.—Prolongation.
dist.—Effect of Distance.
str.—Straining, or Effect of Strong Effort.
pant.—Panting Respiration.
insp.—Audible Inspiration.
ex. Sighing Audible
exp. Explosive Expiration.
im.—Imitative.
sym.—Sympathetic.
l.—Laughter.
w.—Weeping.
ch.—Chuckling.
sob.—Sobbing.
j.—Joy.
sad.—Sadness.
ap.—Apathy.
...Sudden Break.
Expressive Pause.

Figure 11.2 From Bell, The Elocutionary Manual, *115*

As applied to lines from Coleridge, the result is a text fully anatomized for recitation:

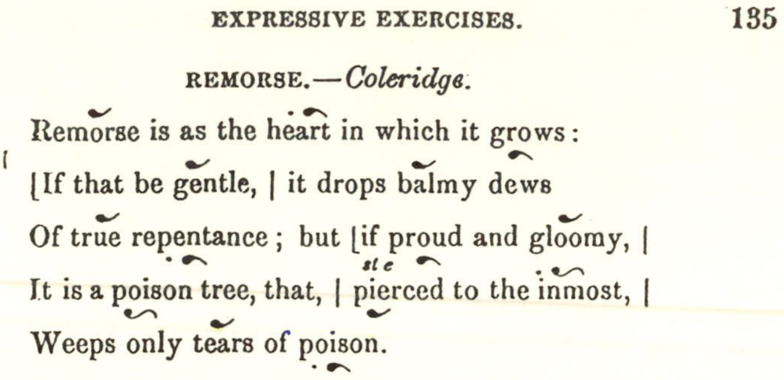

EXPRESSIVE EXERCISES.   **135**

REMORSE.—*Coleridge.*

Remorse is as the heart in which it grows :

[If that be gentle, | it drops balmy dews

Of true repentance ; but [if proud and gloomy, |

It is a poison tree, that, | pierced to the inmost, |

Weeps only tears of poison.

Figure 11.3 From Bell, The Elocutionary Manual, *135*

Bell's catalogue of diacritical marks rivals that of Joshua Steele's "rational prosody" of 1775.

Such a system of physiological indictators was to become Bell's major ambition in the development of "visible speech," an orthography devised with strict attention to the vocal organs, the letters of which may be applied as readily to any language and even to acoustic sounds as such, like the noise of sawing wood:

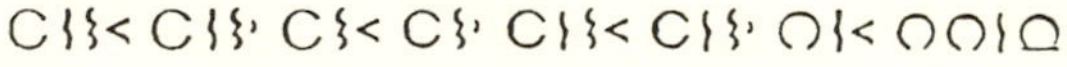

C}}< C}}⸲ C}< C}⸲ C}}< C}}⸲ O}< OO}O⸱

Figure 11.4 From Bell, Visible Speech, *65*

Nor does Bell refrain from "spelling" the sounds of suppressed chuckling, a hiccough, nausea, clearing the throat, a soft hem, a "baby's scolding," sipping, sniffing, spitting, and even kissing. His earlier efforts on behalf of precise articulation reveal certain thresholds on the border of visible speech, moments in which a different order of representation abruptly seizes the phonic dimension and reduces it to silence in the face of the visual challenge of its orthography. Having numbered the vowel sounds in *The Elocutionary Manual* (36), Bell then offers orthoepic exercises keyed to the numerals. An uncredited poem, "The Law of Love," is abruptly lifted out of the bric-à-brac of Victoriana and given a futurist look *avant la lettre:*

II. THE LAW OF LOVE.

P$^{11\cdot8}$r f$^{11\cdot8}$rth th^2 $^{10\cdot1}$], p$^{11\cdot8}$r b^{12}]dl^2 f$^{11\cdot8}$rth ; ^{2}t w^{2}l n^{10}t f^3] ^{9}nt^{2}l
Th$^{7\cdot13}$ f^3]^{4}st v^{4}s^{4}lz t^{13} pr^{12}v$^{7\cdot1}$d wh^{2}tch ^{2}t m^3 l$^{7\cdot8}$rdzhl^2 f^2].
B^{9}t th^{4}n, wh^{4}n s^{9}tch $^{7\cdot8}$r f$^{7\cdot13}$nd n^{12} m$^{11\cdot8}$r, th^{12} fl$^{12\cdot2}$ng br^{10}d ^{5}nd fr^1.
T^{2}l th^{4}n, ^{5}nd n^{9}r^{2}sht fr^{10}m ^{10}n h$^{7\cdot1}$, ^{2}t str^{3}tw^3 st^{7}ntsht w^{2}l b^1.
D^{2}g ch^{5}n^{4}lz f^{10}r th^2 str^{1}mz ^{9}v L^{9}v, wh$^{4\cdot8}$r th^3 m^3 br^{10}dl^2 r^{9}n :—
^{5}nd L^{9}v h^{5}z ^{12}v^{8}rfl$^{12\cdot2}$ng str^{1}mz, t^{13} f^2] th^{4}m ^{4}v^{8}r^2 w^{9}n.—
B^{9}t ^{2}f, ^{5}t ^{4}n^2 t$^{7\cdot1}$m, th$^{7\cdot13}$ s^{1}s s^{9}tsh tsh^{5}n^{4}lz t^{13} pr^{12}v$^{7\cdot1}$d,
Th^2 v^{4}r^2 f$^{7\cdot13}$nts ^{9}v L^{9}v, f^{10}r th^1 w^{2}l s^{13}n b^1 p$^{7\cdot8}$rtsht ^{5}nd dr$^{7\cdot1}$d.
F^{10}r w^1 m^{9}st sh$^{4\cdot8}$r, ^{2}f w^1 w^{13}d k^{1}p, th^{5}t g^{13}d th^{2}ng fr^{10}m ^{6}b^{9}v.
S^{1}s^{2}ng t^{13} g^{2}v, w^1 s^{1}s t^{13} h^{5}v ; s^{9}tsh ^{2}z th^2 L^{10} ^{9}v L^{9}v.

Figure 11.5 From Bell, The Elocutionary Manual, *52*

Other exercises in varying inflection begin to sound like Gertrude Stein's manner of composition as recomposing the virtual present: "He reads correctly. He reads correctly. He reads correctly. He reads correctly when he likes. He reads correctly when he likes. He reads correctly when he likes to pay attention" (*Bell's Standard Elocution,* 37). And finally, a memorable feature of Bell's elocutionary challenges is his "Literal Exercises" in which, as the title indicates, "breath articulations" and "voice articulations" are confined to letters themselves in a piece that forecasts such purely abstract works as Alexei Kruchenykh's "Heights (Universal Language)" or Kurt Schwitters' "Sonata in Urlauten":

```
b d     d b     b d b     d b d     b d d b     d b b d
b g     g b     b g b     g b g     b g g b     g b b g
d g     g d     d g d     g d g     d g g d     g d d g
b d g   b g d   d b g     d g b     g b d       g d b
b v     v b     b v b     v b v     b v v b     v b b v
b w     w b     b w b     w b w     b w w b     w b b w
b v w   b w v   v b w     v w b     w b v       w v b
                            (Principles of Speech, 249)
```

"We can be deeply stirred by hearing the recitation of a poem in a language of which we understand no word; but if we are then told that the poem is gibberish and has no meaning, we shall consider that we have been deluded—this was no poem, it was merely an imitation of instrumental music" (Eliot, 30). But if, as Stevens writes in "Man Carrying Thing," [36] "The poem must resist the intelligence / Almost successfully," isn't the lineage unwittingly promoted by the elocutionary exercises of Bell and rendered in explicitly poetic choreography by Schwitters and Kruchenykh the very one that finally gives us to understand the sound of not understanding?

What is known as "sound poetry" presages a sound exceeding the boundaries of "poetic diction" or "musicality." But what is this sound? And what do we know when we know it or hear when we hear it?

In Foucault's influential account: "The idea that, when we destroy words, what is left is neither mere noise nor arbitrary, pure elements, but other words, which, when pulverized in turn, will set free still other words—this idea is at once the negative of all the modern science of languages and the myth in which we now transcribe the most obscure and the most real powers of language." Furthermore, "it is because [language] has never ceased to speak within itself, because it is penetrated as far as we can reach within it by inexhaustible values, that we can speak within it in that endless murmur in which literature is born."[37] This "immense rustling of denominations that are overlying one another, contracting into one another, hiding one another, and yet preserving themselves" is nothing less than that "rustle of language" that transported Roland Barthes to reveries of textual joy, to which has since accrued that unsavory status of intertextual bliss flickering on the pyre of the immolated author. Foucault's is the definitive, if not the first, declaration of language as industrious beyond the recuperative installations of the familiar governing body of the logos. He salvages "literature" as the categorical name for a field of exceptions to any law, a field subordinated to the covenant sanctioned by a ludic undertow that language exerts on discourse, "a murmur of analogies rising from things" even prior to denomination, in an "articulated patterning of representations" (119). "If language exists, it is because below the level of identities and differences there is the foundation provided by continuities, resemblances, repetitions, and natural criss-crossings . . . Discourse dissipates the murmur, but without it it could not speak" (120).

The Foucauldian murmur, the "raw being" of language in its primary emission, is a prediscursive locus of what others too have come to associate with literature.[38] In Foucault's concise formula: "In the modern age, literature is that which compensates for (and not that which confirms) the signifying function of language" (44). Two responses or ways of enacting this compensation might be made (though Foucault himself is not so explicit): in one, which we can call conservative, the signifying seditiousness of language (that it signifies *as such* without agency) is compensated for by affirming innate meaning in the world or in human institutions. Language might be slippery, but the enduring values are pre- or extralinguistic (this is the struggle of Eliot's *Four Quartets*). The work of literature is, as it was for Eliot, to master unruly dependent classes of signifying particles. In the radical alternative, the compensatory move is less obvious but no less impassioned: whether in the Dada sound poem with its liturgical accompaniment, or the surrealist sleeping fits, automatic writing, and the game of Exquisite Corpse, the subterranean rumble of language as such is enthusiastically affirmed as value—presocial, unconscious, indigent, subversive, a *flânerie* of sounds and graphic particles. In either case the dynamic is compensatory: a powerful configuring agency (language) requires subordination to another order (ethical, religious, political); or a powerful configuring agency (the discursive norms of a given society) is resisted by confiscating the raw material of its collective will (prediscursive language) and celebrating its sleek transcendent (animalistic/angelic) glamour.

This "raw being" of language, like Bataille's unrecuperable remainder, conspicuously provokes its compensatory labor of formalization through the medium of literature. "An excrescence, an excess, a surplus, a bonus — one which literature, as opposed to other forms of writing, is slow to give up, and thus slows reading to reinstate."[39] Garrett Stewart's intricate *Reading Voices* follows Foucault in its adherence to language as primary resistance, reservoir of presocial plasticity. "The reigning ideology in any period may be one of containment, but the material base itself is always insurgent," Stewart writes, affirming a credo shared with Thomas Vogler and Jerome McGann, among others. "This insurgency is what, in and of itself, we call literary" (64). The formula is attractive but too tidy: the material base equals revolt, sedition; and literature is the name of this condition. Fortunately, Stewart's purpose in *Reading Voices* is not to insist on the redemptive cacophony of the phonemic dimension but to chart (and celebrate) its seepage and overflow, "the league and leak of acoustic matter delegated from word to word" (27). As we have already seen in Bell's elocutionary exercises, the "natural criss-crossings" Foucault establishes as prediscursive foundation of language — those intramural segmentations of phonemes and graphemes — does not begin to resemble literature until literature invites it to do so at the Cabaret Voltaire.

Stewart's method of phonotextual reading follows the transsegmental drift of phonemic particles along the signifying chain. The protagonists are the familiar ones from Foucault: discourse and language, or "the errand of meaning versus the errancy and hazard of signifying" (27).[40] The term Stewart uses for this encounter is *style,* that loose but suggestive indicator of a writer's mastery of unruly words. Initiating a renewed attention to the receding — and at this point seemingly anachronistic — problem of "style" is promising, inasmuch as it assigns "genius" to the inborn initiative of language itself. For Stewart, then, style is "the continuously returning *challenge* of sound to sense" and "the continuous possibility of regression" (25, 24). A question arises: is style the helpless (hapless?) remainder of artistic will? — marking that zone in which artistic sapience concedes inspiration to the material dimension of the medium? At what point is *style* the sufficient term for what Duchamp does with a shovel? When stylistic resources are conceded to the initiative of the medium and the insurgency of the signifying hazard, then style has passed out of the domain of heroic exemplarity, divorced itself from the creative labor of craft and apparently forsaken all claim to genius. But of course "genius" names the animating spirit, the inspiring (in-breathed) force that is said to give voice to the poet from Hesiod to the present, precipitating a dual allegiance to chance and will, serendipity and assertion. By insisting on the poetic initiative of the phonotext, Stewart reasserts the lineaments of creative benediction, staking a claim for the sublexical foundation of literariness.[41] In drawing attention away from the tropological contours within words, and *to* the precarious and provisional edges *between* words (on which Anne Carson meditates in *Eros the Bittersweet*),[42] phonotextual reading rediscovers something like Kristeva's maternal *chora,* or the semiotic fundament prior to the militarization of syntax (as Cage understood it in his own radical turn to linguistic particulate in *Empty Words*), not a pregnant silence but a pregnant spaciousness: "Blanks represent hiatus, not void, a secret source in nature mated to a waiting hollow in the mind, a source imagined yet again as fecund, reverberant, eternally renewed" (87). The blank space is not merely an element in a graphic code, in which it would reliably signify silence. The prospect of an alignment, however momentary, in which blank and silence achieve a reciprocal signification, incites a dream (and drama) of emblematic union, balance, harmony. For that reason it's important to insist on a similar reciprocity between poetry and language, in which the latter is not the broader category from which poetry emerges as a specific practice, but the site of an ancient *agon* between rivals.

Roman Jakobson defines the poetic as "not a supplementation of discourse with rhetorical adornment but a total re-evaluation of the discourse and of all its components whatsoever." Michael Sprinker goes on to summarize: "Poetry is not merely the obedient and subservient offspring of ordinary language, but its Oedipal rival. Language is always already poetry" (23). Language so ordained—as the poetic function *par excellence* prior to the appearance of poetry—is quite familiar from Emerson's "fossil poetry"; and before Emerson's geological sanction, it is consistently rehearsed in Romanticism (and before that, Hellenic pastoral) as the primordial sound of wind and water and trees.[43] The Aeolian harp is a prosthetic alternate to the human voice; another and more recent model is the digital sampler, synthesizing a voice from bit-mapped data. To say, then, that language is already poetry is to open the door to a radical consideration that the poet is an extraneous, parasitical supplement to the poem. It is to apprehend the poet as a byproduct of the occasion, or as a technician facilitating a broadcast (as in Jack Spicer's poet-as-radio hypothesis). Of course, the legacy of the Muses is a traditional way of making the point that inspiration is self-effacement; and that poetry is either unreliable speech or an opportunistic realization of the duplicity of language. Such pairs as writing/speech and reason/rhetoric are themselves duplicitous; that is, they are double structures that incite fantasies of resolution. Insofar as "poetry" names a challenge to both speech and writing, by oscillating between them it keeps both in play, ventilating the circumstances of their appearance and the occasions of their recognition.

Recently there has been a flight from or an evasion of sound, particularly the sounds that would awaken an understanding of that *not-understanding* which is so consistently bound up with poetry's heritage. Contemporary (or post-Vietnam) American poetry has developed a laconic, speech-oriented vocalization, wary of the narcotic blur of panegyric intonation and liturgical recitative. This idiomatic plainness reflects a semantic penury, a "commonsense" appeal encoded thematically to vindicate those who have felt threatened by the archaic claims of a presentient soundworld, the "raw being" of language; those for whom the *sound* of "plain speech" reassuringly disavows the need to glance below the surface of words. The measured sanity of the pedestrian reading voice certifies the semantic stability of words on the page by means of its vocal autoregulation. But this normative voice veils a cavalcade of anxieties: fear of the common analogy of poetry with song (why does it have to be written down if it's a song?— and how does writing preserve melody?); fear of the religious implications of the liturgical drone (that poets do in some sense aspire to hypnagogic authority, but poetry is too idiosyncratic and impractical a means to assert such authority); and fear of writing (the urge to vocalization being a faint-hearted assertion that the poem cannot be properly compared with other forms of writing because it harbors a declamatory potential that sets it apart). To *listen* to the varieties of modern poetry reading is to encounter a version of poets' fear of poetry as such, or a fear of what poetry might become if words wander too far off the page, and meanings drift apart from the words. Should it sound good, or should sound guide?

The point is not to advocate any return to the vitamin supplement of pure sound. Nothing is to be gained by countering the laconic talk-poetry style of workshop free verse with Dada dissidence. But it is equally presumptuous to think of sound poetry as a radical challenge safely quarantined at the far end of the century. Sound and sight work in concord in poetry, and discord is a medium of concordances yet to be recognized. As long as there is a repertoire of sounds on the one hand, and an alphabet on the other, any resolution is a forced settlement, compounding a security deposit invested in a proscription of sound from sense. When sound and sense come together the sound renders "sense" senseless, or precariously sensed by being overcharged, as if everything that signified profoundly needed to be profoundly sensuous as well. Everyday speech is happily exempted from such an aspiration, but poetry (despite the American embrace of "low mimetic realism" and its workshop vernacular) is not.

The complex union of sense and sound, seeing and hearing, in Ronald Johnson's *Ark,* dramatizes the way homophonic transsegmentals are a driving principle behind the poem.[44] The sections of *Ark* are titled "Beams"; and in concert with the poem's own tendencies to reconfigure minutiae of an atomic accord, *beam* invites a breakdown to the rudimentary verb forms *be* and *am*. When Beam 8 begins "Line eye us. / Web stir us" it is only in an acoustic register that we pick up the subtext, Johnson's homage to those anatomists of the constituent particles of plants and words, Linnaeus and Webster. Elsewhere in Beam 8, phonetics poses a seemingly visual pun as an acoustic challenge: "wind Os wind Os," repeated four times to make a foursquare visual emblem, forces in its repetitions a semantic challenge—is "wind" always noun, or is it sometimes (half the time, preserving symmetry?) verb? In a poem that adamantly budges its way forward by the most minute lettrism ("Linkings, inklings") transegmental drift is openly courted and becomes a modus operandi: "sensings" yielding "SENSE *sings*." The "f lux f lux" of Beam 13, like the "no where / now here" configuration in Beam 29, forces a collaborative discord involving the ear that doesn't quite see what the eye never says. (Beams 4 and 7 are reveries on eye and ear.) "Y is space. X, time" (Beam 28): *Ark* is a space-time constructivist performance (or performative construction); its musics are pictures, its images oddly *resound*, like the diagrams of cell division in Beam 25 illustrating the pun "prosper / O / cell".

The time-space equation indicates a meeting, not a resolution—conjunction, not conclusion—and *Ark* is a poem most instructive about the resources of a poetry not strictly beholden to logocentric speech fantasies (though its vernaculars are precise), nor to the graphic materialism of concrete poetry (from which Johnson so nimbly draws). So I feel it as inseparable from the sound texture of *Ark* that its one wordless Beam (number 18)—a full print of a right hand, reduced somewhat to fit the page—nevertheless resounded for me in my daughter's voice expressing her gratified glee, at age four, putting her hand to the print and finding it an exact fit. *That* sound could only happen once: the sound of a nonreader's understanding vocalized in spiraling joy from a "text" that offered itself at a very precise moment in time as the mark of, a marking of, time. To submit to the material current of unfamiliarity in a text (which includes the oral sounding) is to apprehend the animation that is poetry. The rush of felt alignment is where seeing and hearing become attunement to a dimension of the inscrutable: this is not a debility of understanding, but an indication that experience moves so forcefully *before* understanding that to some extent understanding is already committed to mirroring (reflecting on and resounding) this excitement; this gasp of gratified fit, the way the words of a poem you didn't write can suddenly and surprisingly fit into your speaking voice like a firm-clenched glove on the hand. When you really let a poem occupy you like that, in rhetorico-proprioceptive-acoustic pulsation, vocalizing line upon line, the poem accumulating a sheen, a reptile glamour, the husk of your familiar speaking voice shed . . . : when you let that happen (or more often find it happening), you discover why poetry is famous for its delinking of pleasure from understanding. And further, you know precisely how its (phonic) materialism registers a *sound* of not understanding. In time, the poem *is* that sound. To understand the resistance, the obduracy of the material, is to submit to a fund (a fundement) of bafflement. It *is* in a sense to "know"—but as knowing moans. And memorably seems to mean.

NOTES

For their useful comments on a draft of this essay, I want to thank Charles Bernstein, Tracy Ware, Glen Willmott, and Stephen Pender. I also want to thank Mel Wiebe and Chris Keep for providing me with elusive recordings of Tennyson.

1. Eric Griffiths, *The Printed Voice of Victorian Poetry* (Oxford: Clarendon Press, 1989), p. 79.

2. See Kahn, "Death in Light of the Phonograph," in *Wireless Imagination: Sound, Radio, and the Avant-Garde,* ed. Douglas Kahn and Gregory Whitehead (Cambridge: MIT Press, 1992), pp. 69–103.

3. *The Times* (December 13, 1890), quoted in Ronald W. Clark, *Edison: The Man Who Made the Future* (New York: Putnam, 1977), p. 164.

4. On May 15, 1890, Tennyson was recorded reading "Come into the garden, Maud" *(Maud* XXII), "The Charge of the Light Brigade," "The Heavy Brigade," "Blow, Bugle, Blow," "Ask Me No More," "Northern Farmer—New Style," and parts of "Boadicea" and "The Wellington Ode"—"giving magnificent readings in a voice of amazing power," writes his grandson, "in spite of having to speak into a tube under such unfamiliar conditions." Charles Tennyson, *Alfred Tennyson* (New York: Macmillan, 1949), p. 519.

5. *The Poems of Tennyson,* ed. Christopher Ricks, rev. ed., vol. 2 (London: Longman, 1987), p. 689. The Lincolnshire dialect of Tennyson's notation is not far from that which elocutionist Alexander Melville Bell specifies in certain vowels as a Scotticism, particularly "nation" pronounced as "nehtion" where the long *a* becomes a diphthong *(The Elocutionary Manual* [London: Hamilton, Adams (1859)], p. 44). More on Bell follows below.

6. H. D. Rawnsley, quoted in Donald S. Hair, *Tennyson's Language* (Toronto: University of Toronto Press, 1991), pp. 64–65. Northrop Frye observes (but without specific reference to Tennyson): "The chanting of verse tends to give it a hieratic quality, removing it from the language of common speech, and it thereby increases the exhilaration of poetry, bringing it nearer to the sphere of the heroic. In drama this stylizing of speech takes the form of declamation, which is also appropriate to heroic themes. Declamation is also a feature of rhetoric and oratory, where again we can see literary analogues of musical elements: oratory, for instance, resembles music and differs from ordinary speech in its use of patterns of repetition" ("Introduction: Lexis and Melos," in *Sound and Poetry,* ed. Frye [New York: Columbia University Press, 1957], p. xxv).

7. Ford Madox Hueffer, *Memories and Impressions: A Study in Atmospheres* (New York: Harper, 1911), p. 110. He adds ruefully that "The effect of this voice heard from outside a door was to a young child particularly awful. It went on and on, suggesting the muffled baying of a large hound that is permanently dissatisfied with the world."

8. Walter J. Ong, "Sprung Rhythm and English Tradition," in *Hopkins: A Collection of Critical Essays,* ed. Geoffrey Hartman (Englewood Cliffs, N.J.: Prentice-Hall, 1966), p. 151.

9. The mundane persistence of moribund cadence has a far more pervasive and devastating impact on generations of "latecomer" poets than the more glamorous

scenario of Harold Bloom's psychodrama of influence anxiety. Bloom's fascinating work, being fixated on tropes, bypasses consideration of the sound domain of poetry altogether.

10. To encompass through understanding rather than objectify through explanation—this is the promise of hermeneutics, with its explicit assent to historicity and the contingency of the interpretive act. From his large book on Freud, *De l'interpretation,* to the present, Paul Ricoeur has pursued a dialectic of understanding and explanation, immanence and contingency, singularity and plurality. In a prospectus of his concerns there is a long but cogent recapitulation: "I am fighting on two fronts: on the one hand, I cannot accept the irrationalism of immediate understanding, conceived as an extension to the domain of texts of the empathy by which a subject puts himself in the place of a foreign consciousness in a situation of face-to-face intensity. This undue extension maintains the romantic illusion of a direct link of congeniality between the two subjectivities implied by the work, that of the author and that of the reader. However, I am equally unable to accept a rationalistic explanation which would extend to the text the structural analysis of sign systems that are characteristic not of discourse but of language as such. This equally undue extension gives rise to the positivist illusion of a textual objectivity closed in upon itself and wholly independent of the subjectivity of both author and reader. To these two one-sided attitudes, I have opposed the dialectic of understanding and explanation. By understanding I mean the ability to take up again within oneself the work of structuring that is performed by the text, and by explanation the second-order operation grafted onto this understanding which consists in bringing to light the codes underlying this work of structuring that is carried through in company with the reader. This combat on two separate fronts against a reduction of understanding to empathy and a reduction of explanation to an abstract combinatory system, leads me to define interpretation by this very dialectic of understanding and explanation at the level of the 'sense' immanent to the text" ("On Interpretation," tr. Kathleen McLaughlin, in *Philosophy in France Today,* ed. Alan Montefiore [Cambridge University Press], pp. 194–95). In the case of the poet reading—that is to say, vocalizing—the balance of terms so carefully elaborated by Ricoeur is upset. In particular, that quantum he calls empathy is heavily invested in the "abstract combinatory system" constituted by the phonemic materiality of the text. The traditional combination of prosody, rhetoric, elocution, grammar, and phonetics is implicitly proximate to the poet's reading. What's more, the poet reading his or her own work has an ambiguous relation to the "empathy" that Ricoeur protests as conflated with understanding. The poet, given to *understand* her own poem by virtue of a confluence of traditions of authorial priority and sheer mechanical familiarity, is more likely to seek an empathetic encounter with the gradually revealed undertone and intertext, the sound shape of the language in performance, rather than with the all too familiar semantic dimension.

11. Ezra Pound, *Collected Shorter Poems,* 2nd ed. (London: Faber & Faber, 1968), p. 196.

12. This was Joshua Steele's practice in his *Prosodia Rationalis* (London, 1775).

13. T. S. Eliot, *On Poetry and Poets* (London: Faber & Faber, 1957), p. 31.

14. Michael Taussig, *Mimesis and Alterity: A Particular History of the Senses* (New York: Routledge, 1993), p. xvii.

15. Sidney Lanier, *The Science of English Verse* (New York: Scribner, 1880), p. 21.

16. Walter J. Ong, S.J., *Interfaces of the Word: Studies in the Evolution of Consciousness and Culture* (Ithaca: Cornell University Press, 1977), p. 214.

17. See for example John Herries, *The Elements of Speech* (1773), John Walker, *Elements of Elocution* (1806), Gilbert Austin, *Chironomia; or, a Treatise on Rhetorical Delivery* (1806), James Rush, *The Philosophy of the Human Voice* (1827), all influential figures in elocution and rhetoric. For an overview, see Eugene Bahn and Margaret L. Bahn, *A History of Oral Interpretation* (Minneapolis: Burgess, 1970).

18. Gerard Manley Hopkins, quoted in Gerald Bruns, *Inventions: Writing, Textuality, and Understanding in Literary History* (New Haven: Yale University Press, 1982), p. 138.

19. G. M. Hopkins, December 11, 1886, in *The Poetical Works of Gerard Manley Hopkins*, ed. Norman H. MacKenzie (Oxford: Clarendon Press, 1992), p. 472.

20. For a list of Hopkins's musical compositions, see *The Journals and Papers of Gerard Manley Hopkins*, ed. Humphry House, completed by Graham Storey (London: Oxford University Press, 1959), pp. 464–65.

21. Hopkins appears to have been refining his observations of hydraulic action at this period. Journal entries of the previous year, 1872, are comparably meticulous: "The shores are swimming and the eyes have before them a region of milky surf but it is hard for them to unpack the huddling and gnarls of the water and follow out the shapes and the sequence of the running: I catch however the looped or forked wisp made by every big pebble the backwater runs over" (223); "The overflow of the last wave came in from either side tilting up the channel and met halfway, each with its own moustache. When the wave ran very high it would brim over on the sloping shelf below me and move smoothly and steadily along it like the palm of a hand along a table drawing off the dust" (225). Again, the world seems eerily silent amidst the tumult of breaking and reforming waves.

22. Michael Sprinker, *"A Counterpoint of Dissonance": The Aesthetics and Poetry of Gerard Manley Hopkins* (Baltimore: Johns Hopkins University Press, 1980), p. 76.

23. For Hopkins's copious attempts to achieve a satisfactory orthography, see *The Early Poetic Manuscripts and Note-Books of Gerard Manley Hopkins, in Facsimile*, ed. Norman H. MacKenzie (New York: Garland, 1989) and *The Later Poetic Manuscripts of Gerard Manley Hopkins, in Facsimile*, ed. Norman H. MacKenzie (New York: Garland, 1991).

24. Hopkins, *Letters*, vol. 1, p. 83; quoted in Sprinker, 62, n. 31.

25. Norman H. MacKenzie, *A Reader's Guide to Gerard Manley Hopkins* (Ithaca: Cornell University Press, 1981), p. 234.

26. J. Hillis Miller locates a tension between Hopkins's religious beliefs and his poetics, describing it in the now classic idiom of lapsarian poststructuralism. "The center around which Hopkins' linguistic speculations revolve, the unsettling intuition that they approach and withdraw from, is the exact opposite of his theological insight. It is the notion that there is no primal word, that the divisions of language have always already occurred as soon as there is language at all. If this is so, there is no word for the Word, only displaced metaphors of it" *(The Linguistic Moment, from Wordsworth to Stevens* [Princeton: Princeton University Press, 1985], p. 261). Miller's sketch discloses a logical contradiction that it is the avowed purpose of religious faith to overcome. It might be more accurate to say that Hopkins's faith in original unity was fractured by the seditious proliferation of words; but that would be untenable, given his fascination with etymology (the science of more deriving from

less) and his own polylinguality (he wrote poems in English, Welsh, Latin, and Greek). Actually, Miller's revelation of a "linguistic moment" itself expresses dismay at lapsed unity. What's striking about this lament (and a tide of similar pronouncements long since constituting a North American academic litany) is that it assumes so direct (and unwarranted) a link between the linguistic subject (the speaker of a language) and God. It repeats a suspicion well documented by Umberto Eco in *In Search of the Perfect Language* that words are counterfeit coins not redeemable against the gold currency of the divine Logos. Such a view admits of only two responses: that of self-abnegation (my speech is tainted, so I choose silence or else amplify the taint in abusive self-mortification), or else the gnostic solution, which is to identify oneself with a deity fallen away from the divine security of his own emanation.

27. William Barnes, "Kindness," in *Selected Poems of William Barnes, 1800–1886,* ed. Geoffrey Grigson (London: Routledge & Kegan Paul, 1950), p. 207.

28. William Barnes, *An Outline of English Speech-Craft* (London: C. Kegan Paul, 1878), p. 1.

29. William Allingham, quoted in Griffiths, 83.

30. Source unknown, quoted from memory.

31. A. Melville Bell, *The Principles of Speech and Vocal Physiology* (London: Hamilton Adams, [1863]), p. 166.

32. Bell, *The Elocutionary Manual,* 66.

33. Melville was Alexander Graham's father. The son's invention of the telephone was an explicit extension of his father's "visible speech" as a prosthetic aid to those with communication disabilities. The senior Bell's scheme for an oral script was presented in *Visible Speech* (London: Simkin, Marshall & Co., 1867).

34. Alexander Melville Bell, *The Principles of Speech and Vocal Physiology,* new ed. (London: Hamilton, Adams [1863]), pp. 252–54.

35. Alexander Melville Bell, *Bell's Standard Elocutionist,* new ed. (London: Simpkin, Marshall, n.d.), p. 163.

36. Wallace Stevens, *The Palm at the End of the Mind,* ed. Holly Stevens (New York: Knopf, 1971), p. 281.

37. Michel Foucault, *The Order of Things* (New York: Pantheon, 1970), p. 103.

38. Saussure glimpsed this internal rustling in his work on anagrams in Saturnian verse, driven by the suspicion that the names of Roman deities were furtively inscribed in poems. But were these phrasal mannequins deliberately implanted by the poets? Were they unwitting corroborations of divine guidance? Were they even there at all? To sustain awareness of these variables simultaneously is a paranoid act, like suspecting the person you're talking to is conveying a clandestine insult in the phonetic patterns of his syllables. (The paranoiac is made known not by entertaining this possibility, but by failing to consider a corollary: if my interlocutor is going to all the trouble of double-coding his speech, why have I been singled out to be the target of this immense labor? The profile common to paranoiacs is exemplified by the implacable assurance with which Judge Schreber asserts that everything in the universe happens with reference to him.) For a large portfolio of such speculations, see *Imagining Language,* ed. Jed Rasula and Steve McCaffery (Cambridge: MIT Press, 1998).

39. Garrett Stewart, *Reading Voices: Literature and the Phonotext* (Berkeley: University of California Press, 1990), p. 19.

40. The dualism launched in this hypothetical encounter, however, doesn't give sufficient credit to the continual *overlap* of these two forces in normal speech. An

entire acoustic landscape might be credibly summoned just by noting the phonemic preferences of proper names (*Bruno* and *Hepzibah* are not just "archaic" but, in our current soundscape, more threatening labels to append to a newborn than, say, the lambent-sounding *Sarah* or the stalwart *Robert*).

41. Stewart brandishes "phonotext" as a blazon against the psychodynamic model of satanic defiance theorized in Bloom's "anxiety of influence." It's not so much that the *agon* is removed, but reallocated to a different level of efficacy. It might be taken as proof of Bloom's own intimidating priority, or equally as proof of Stewart's audacious indifference as "ephebe," that Bloom is not mentioned in *Reading Voices*.

42. Anne Carson, *Eros the Bittersweet* (Princeton: Princeton University Press, 1986).

43. John Hollander's history of prosodic misconstrual in English verse tradition, "The Poem in the Ear," concludes with a somewhat euphoric affirmation that "we all still dwell in the Romantic world of the ear, in which the song of birds is more like poetry than a Beethoven string quartet"—a region of "the ear's larger, undomesticated vastnesses . . . in which real poetry, rather than cultivated verse, is to be found, the realm of all the [?] human and natural utterance, from cries of pain to shouts of discovery: the sounds of language and of the wind in trees." *Vision and Resonance: Two Senses of Poetic Form* (New York: Oxford University Press, 1975), p. 43.

44. The first section of *Ark*, "The Foundations," appeared in 1980. The complete *Ark* was published in 1996 by Living Batch Press (Albuquerque).

12

The Contemporary
Poetry Reading

PETER MIDDLETON

A person stands alone in front of an audience, holding a text and speaking in an odd voice, too regular to be conversation, too intimate and too lacking in orotundity to be a speech or a lecture, too rough and personal to be theater. The speaker is making no attempt to conceal the text. Signs of auditory effort in the audience are momentarily lost in occasional laughter, tense silences, sighs and even cries of encouragement. Sometimes the reader uses a different, more public voice and refers to what is being read, or to some other information of apparent interest. No one talks to the reader. No one proposes a second take. No one reflexively discusses the ritual itself. It is "a particularly 'mute' form of activity . . . designed to do what it does without bringing what it is doing across the threshold of discourse or systematic thinking."[1] This ritual is an ordinary poetry reading of the kind that has become widespread in the past forty years, and is therefore so familiar to most readers of contemporary poetry that its strangeness requires an alienating description in order to be visible at all. Listeners and poets have had almost nothing to say about this phenomenon despite its importance for financing and fostering their careers, assisting the distribution of their poetry, and even shaping its very forms. Public readings seem to belong to those "background expectancies" of poetry that are "recognizable and intelligible as the appearances-of-familiar-events," and about which a participant "is at a loss to tell us specifically of what the expectancies consist."[2] What could be more natural than people interested in poetry gathering together and singling out someone to present a low-budget demonstration of the full emotional and sonic effects of their poetry so that dedicated readers can comprehend the author's intentions to the full? The apparent indifference to explanation may also be simply the result of a commonplace assumption that nothing remarkable happens to the poetry itself at these events, that meaning stays fundamentally unchanged.

This elective mutism should be questioned. It could be that poets and audiences just put up with readings that don't in themselves mean much. There isn't much to say about an obviously successful way of publicizing poetry, and audiences at least enjoy seeing the poets live, seeing their faces, shapes, clothes, and mannerisms. Surely this is too cynical. Many poetry readings since the Beat poets read at the Six Gallery have radiated a belief in poetry's revolutionary cultural power. Perhaps too much self-analysis might destroy this confident radicalism by revealing that what appears to be an entirely new venture at the limits of representation has a long embarassing ancestry. Calling attention to the manipulation of powerful collective effects might also make the poetry seem parasitic on other political struggles, and at best a vehicle for social bonding. When a feminist poet claims that "poetry readings are an integral part of the contemporary feminist movement, and these acts of art . . . not only reflect, but forward, women's political struggle," and cites Judy Grahn saying that "we used poetry to help energize women and speak to women's needs," the risk with such openness would seem to be that such an assessment might lead to the conclusion that the poetry could be jettisoned altogether, and "communitas" built more directly in other ways,[3] despite the author's claim that poetry is a necessary art that projects possible social change. Maybe poets and audiences share a desire to believe in some collective magic and don't want to look too closely at the hidden compartments and trick wires by which the illusions are created. The persistent interest amongst those who do discuss oral poetics, in shamanism, bardic lineages, mysterious energies, and transformations might make one think so. Maybe Victor Turner's conviction that "performance is often a critique, direct or veiled, of the social life it grows out of, an evaluation (with lively possibilities of rejection) of the way society handles history," applies to poetry readings, and their critique works best when veiled with a silence about aims.[4]

Poets certainly become uneasy when they do occasionally reflect on poetry readings. Michel Deguy is bothered by the "technical conditions involved, the possible staging of an 'act,'" and prefers to separate out the poem from the "festival moment, the regulated, preconceived moment of a vociferal act, itself operating within the field of a whole complex of technological apparatus . . . the microphone, the recording session, the sound conditions for the audience on a given evening."[5] Donald Justice called poetry readings "a kind of vaudeville," and as another poet points out, "writers have become well known not because of the value of their work, but because they're good performers" using "methods of delivery and gimmickry that owe more to show-biz than to literature."[6] Maybe the whole thing is a con. John Glassco recalls a large poetry reading organized by the League in Toronto in 1968, where the "showmen" and the "mindless diatribe" were "the sensation of the evening." He complains about the "naive listener's belief that he is getting 'closer' to a poem by hearing it from the poet himself," and the way that "not only is one listening to *him* more than to what he is saying but, as part of a crowd, one is not so much having an esthetic experience as participating in a communal one." Performance degrades cognitive apprehension of poems because "the educated *inward* ear can do more with the rhythms, vowels, syncopations and stresses of any poem than the amateur human voice can hope to do."[7] As a result the performance movement may have irreparably weakened poetry. Donald Hall reports an unnamed poet complaining that "the poetry reading has ruined a generation once promising, because in pursuit of platform success poets wrote simplistic poems; no poem that is decently or humanly complex, he said, can reach an audience of twenty-year-olds at one sitting."[8] These are important criticisms, and few poets and critics have tried to answer them. Even Frederick Stern, in a careful, introspective analysis of his own experience of poetry readings, feels compelled to conclude that that "the act of 'speaking,' while it may affect our apperception of the poem, does not change its meaning in any fundamental way."[9] He doesn't share Glassco's dislike of readings because he values the celebration of the poet and community that can take place, although he is careful to distinguish between the "formal" reading and "festivals." "To put living voice and flesh together with text," to momentarily dispel the anonymity of silent reading, and to affirm the importance of poetry, are the real achievements of poetry readings." Revealingly, he admits that when listening to William Everson read despite an advanced case of Parkinson's disease, he eventually ignores the poetry altogether and simply watches the man. His bodily courage is the real performance.

These reservations are admittedly mostly from conservative voices, and likely to be dismissed by those for whom performance itself is a value, because it draws on the performativity of identity, and makes an open display of the processual dimension of art. If a poem is "energy transferred from where the poet got it . . . by way of the poem itself to, all the way over to, the reader," this dynamics would seem likely to be most fully realized in the interactive performance of poetry.[10] If as Robert Creeley says of Louis Zukofsky, "all that is, as whatever has spoken it, may occur as it is, each time it is spoken" and "there is nothing which anything so existent is 'about,' " then poetry is performance.[11] Robert Kelly says that the sections of *The Loom* emerged from the energy of a first line that produced the ensuing "Recital" (using a word for performance that had entirely different connotations before the Second World War).[12] Douglas Oliver deliberately uses the word "performance" instead of the word "reading," saying "when I talk about poetry as a poet, as an artist and not as a critic, I always focus upon peformance of poems: artistically that's where the action is, where the possibilities begin."[13] He disarmingly admits that when he reads a poem like Dryden's "Absalom and Achitophel" to himself, he is performing it so intensely that he becomes aware of how truthful and honest he is being as he does so, and is made aware that some of its scorn for the Earl of Shaftesbury could be directed at his own dissenting politics. Such reading is an event because performance is necessarily an embodiment of the poem in time and space. Current performance writers stress the importance of the unique location in history, space, and interaction for the significance of the poem, a condition that is paramount in performance. Steve Benson summarizes this very thoroughly: "Within the generic context of 'poetry readings' and 'talks,' I hope that my performances, involving improvisatory oral generation of texts, intermedia real-time relations, site-specific engagements of circumstances proper to the social and physical properties of the event setting, dramatic inflections of the presentation, and interpersonal collaborations with other writers, have called attention to a performance as a constructive, constitutive act, over and above its representation of previously determined plans."[14] Such general use of the term *performance* to describe the actions of poetry has powerful but unexamined support from the use of the word in current theories of sexuality and identity, as well as theories of deconstruction.[15] When Judith Butler uses the term *performance,* she, like Douglas Oliver, is using certain features of performance as the ground for what is effectively a form of analogy. "The forming, crafting, bearing, circulation, signification of that sexed body will not be a set of actions performed in compliance with the law; on the contrary, they will be a set of actions mobilized by the law, the citational accumulation and dissimulation of the law that produces material effects, the lived necessity of those effects as well as the lived contestation of that necessity."[16] Such a formulation could be reapplied to the performance of the identity of a poem, as a dialectic of interpretation and reinvention, since, according to Butler, identity is constructed through a process of active reiteration and citation of discursive elements. Her theory uses the mobility of this rhetoric to claim that drag performances are also allegorical performances of "*the sign* of gender" (Butler, 237). Cultural theory is part of an even wider appropriation of this rhetoric of performance in philosophy, where its use ranges from Lyotard's pejorative use to describe the functionalism of expertise to the free interpretations of Austin's theory of performatives in speech acts by deconstruction. Actual poetry performance can therefore assume a much wider significance for the participants than the actual texts might indicate, and in particular, as Butler's hypothesis shows, can be read as if it were a performance of the affirmation or transgression of foundational social structures.

So what is that person doing reading aloud from a text (or iconoclastically improvising without) to a patient audience? Do readings change the meaning of poems in fundamental ways? I shall try to answer these questions by discussing the significance of the improvised venues and presence of the author, before going into more detail about the history of reading aloud, verse speaking, sound symbolism, and finally the intersubjectivity of poetry readings. This will show that there is much more semantic activity in a poetry reading than the dogmas of literary theory would allow. It will also show that the silence about poetry readings from the poets themselves probably arises from an uneasy relation to a long history of verse speaking that promoted itself as a reconciliation of art and science. The apparent failure of the elocution movement reflects badly on similar unacknowledged ambitions in today's poetry readings, where a similar reunification of art, politics, and knowledge is also attempted.

One question still bothers me. Where is the politics in this analysis? For years in the late seventies and early eighties this political question met every literary analysis offered by young theorists, not as rejection but as a reminder of the importance of what we were doing. Yes, I want to reply, there is a politics here, a demonstration that readings are part of the public network that is a poem, and the recognition of this long interaction is an important political step. But the question still bothers me. I am writing this after returning from a long weekend at a conference in New Hampshire on avant-garde poetry, missing those people with texts who stood out there in the middle of wires, mikes, and abandoned lecterns, missing the communitas of such a large gathering of people with common interests. During the fifteen-hour daily schedule there wasn't much chance to see the country. Fortunately the buildings abutted the pine woodland so closely that nature was always close to culture, and the building itself pretended to be just a more highly evolved pine tree. Back here in the lifeworld I miss that intensity badly. Is poetry possible here at all? Maybe poetry readings are even more essential than I thought. Now I must rewrite a lecture on *Wuthering Heights,* draft a letter to a sick student, find a way to work on a current poem, finish unpacking my new office, reconnect the E-mail, silently read the poems of the poets I listened to. Instead my mind wanders back to my first poetry reading. It was held in the meeting hall of the local Labour Party in Cheltenham, a town so conservative that socialist politics seemed highly abstract. The room where we sat on splayed and creaky folding chairs smelled of polish, dust, and the dried sweat of claustrophobic meetings. It strikes me now that we were inventing our own version of an avant-garde culture, which most of us had never witnessed, as if poetry readings were already a part of the cultural language. A tape of Steve McCaffery reading in New Hampshire is playing as I write this, and I am listening out for a passage illustrating the way a poem's meaning at a performance becomes contingent on the very constitution of an audience. He seems to be saying through the not-quite-Dolby-scrubbed hiss that it's called "No One's Listening," and I measure my own responses with the laughter for such epigrams as this: "Paul de Man as the Al Gore of deconstruction."[17] Some of the lines are heavily overdetermined for the event. Members of the audience appear in the poem in lines like the one saying something like—"Barrett Watten sit down Isaac Newton is about to speak"—and I wonder what is going on with this. Will Barrett, should he, could he, respond, should we others think some private message in the line, is it about private messages, and spiral on. Another of the poets programmed his laptop to read a poem straight into the microphone, rather like a latter-day Jacques de Vaucanson (the great eighteenth-century inventor of machines that imitated people and animals, and the theme of a poem by John Ashbery discussed later in this essay). If I had recorded the computer voice, his machine would have spoken directly to my machine, almost missing out the middle stuff. Wherever the politics are they are in this middle stuff. That was an author speaking.

Gillian Rose takes the spatial metaphor of the middle as her governing trope in her study of the difficulty of ethics in modern society:

> Whereas post-modernity remains dualistic and pits its others against domination, the broken middle is triune. It will investigate the breaks between universal, particular and singular, in individuals and institutions. Reconfigurations of this trinity, nevertheless, pervade our common sense as oppositions: between inner morality and outer legality, individual autonomy and general heteronomy, active cognition and imposed norm. Made anxious by such inscrutable disjunctions, we invariably attempt to mend them . . . with *love,* forced or fantasized into the state.[18]

Her brilliant investigation of the damaged modern understanding of ethics leads her into a discussion of authorship, and its paradoxes of authority and pseudonymity, which she argues are the only means for avoiding the arrogation of the authority that ethical philosophers are questioning. In her discussion of three Jewish women philosophers, Rahel Varnhagen, Rosa Luxemburg, and Hannah Arendt, she suggests that their greatness emerges from just this commitment to a performative authorship. "They neither opt to abandon political universality, even though it is demonstrably spurious; nor to resolve its inconsistency and antinomy in any ethical immediacy of love: 'community,' 'nation,' 'race,' 'religion' or 'gender.' Remaining within the agon of authorship they cultivate aporetic universalism, restless affirmation and undermining of political form and political action, which never loses sight of the continuing mutual corruption of the state and civil society." One sign of their commitment is that they recognize that the politics of the " 'middle,' conceived now as 'social' and as 'civil' in the sense of sociability or civility . . . involves indirect communication, not 'ideal speech situation' or ideal communication" (Rose, 155). This subtle and complex argument offers a clue to the politics of the poetry reading. The ambitions of the poetry reading to place its art within a community of listeners should not be collapsed into either a moment when a work independent of the collective process is handed over in speech, nor as a moment of collective shared understanding that "reads" the work within its own encompassing discursivity. Rose points us to the need to consider the poem outside any ideal beginning or end, and to recognize its large ethical ambitions in performance. The middle ground between objectified poem and its interpretation is a field of flawed ethical and semantic ambitions where the agon of authorship waits.

The Presence of the Author

"A spectre is haunting poetry readings. The 'dead author,' risen from the text again and trailing the rags of the intentional fallacy, claims to be the originating subject from which poetry is issuing, right in front of your eyes."[19] This is how I described the seemingly regressive *presence* of an *author* in an age of deconstruction for audiences, some of whom at least know their Barthes and Derrida. It ought to be suprising that an author is still the cynosure of every contemporary poetry reading, usually uttering the words of a written text as if every single one bore the indelible mark of their composer. This fixed element might appear to depend upon beliefs about authorship well past their sell-by date. Is this a ritual to reestablish the authority of authorship in the face of its downsizing by the academic industry, or is the performance of authorship not an attempt to resist this delayering after all, but tacitly working for different collective ends? The socialist specter hints that authorship may be a radical force in this shifty, untheorized practice.

Two possible answers to these questions seem fairly obvious because they apply to most acts of reading aloud in public, even when the reader is not the author. Many institutions and intimate situations require texts to be read to an audience, whether of conference delegates, churchgoers, or children at occasions where the contingent relations of place, people, and history mould the actual reading. The reader in turn uses these elements to produce a multidimensional commentary on what is read, through tones of voice, asides, and physical gestures. Such a medium is a highly flexible signifying vehicle for the affective and cognitive information presented alongside the reading itself, adding further semantic tracks to the performance. It is almost always informative to hear a lecture read aloud, although no substitute for reading it silently at another time. In particular the listener is made aware of the illocutionary force of the utterances in ways that cannot always be signaled by written linguistic markers. While speaking the words aloud a reader temporarily owns them, whatever their origin, and they then become words to which the reader lends a life. This is because the ordinary act of speaking in conversation is assumed in our culture to be a reliable index of the individuality of the speaker. Reading aloud relies heavily upon this axiom. However ironic or sceptical the tone of delivery, the words uttered are momentarily given a life context, as if the reader were showing what it means for a life to say these words. The physical presence of the speaker acts as their warrant for their relevance to a specific body, point of view, and history. Such effects are obviously greatly amplified when the speaker is the author, when the moment of reading acts as a figure of an imaginary moment of composition. This radiant core then illuminates the attendant interactive commentary and gives energy to the implicit acts of asseveration. The reader of poetry performs authorship. To say this is to say something very different from Denise Levertov, who argues that a poet can't really spoil the reading of a poem by adding personality to it because the poet's personality and the personality emulsified in the poem are the same, so that "his voice will clarify, not distort."[20] For her there is a kind of authoriality inherent in the poem and the poet already, just as ideology would have it that there is a gender already inside us according to Butler's critique. Levertov's misleading assumption may derive in part from the contemporary fascination with metapoetic displays of authorship, from Robert Duncan's "sometimes I am permitted to return to a meadow," to Ron Silliman's iterative references to the pen in *Tjanting*, which both effectively question any simple egoistic derivation of intent.

Authorship fascinates poets and audiences because the author is the subjective crossroads for the enormously complex transactions of institutional legitimation in the contemporary world. Unremitting efforts go into maintaining the authority of specialized knowledges and the rights of individuals to be its authors, critics, and revisionists. Poets cannot claim that the authority, truth, and pertinence of their work is directly dependent upon such existing institutional networks, and instead they have to generate this platform from within the work and its distribution, adding any authority they can from their standing as a poet. When poets do plug into the standard networks of scientific knowledge, the result is a reminder of the idiosyncrasy of poetic articulation. J. H. Prynne printed a list of scholarly endnotes referring to learned journals and books on the page following his poem "Aristeas, in Seven Years" without any heading, so that they read as a further stage in the poem and their status is unclear.[21] The notes tell the reader where to look for more information but they don't validate the poem nor allow the poem to emerge as a corrective, extending critique of this existing body of historical knowledge. Instead the poem unsettles the authorizations it negotiates. *Brixton Fractals,* Allen Fisher's narrative series set in the south London of Blake and the Greater London Council, finishes with a "bibliography" of 123 items that runs to several pages.[22] These listings extend the range of the poems and certainly repay investigation but they cannot lend the kind of authority to the poems that even the citations to a humanities essay like this one will provide, as the preface admits: "A *bibliography* has been added as a Resources in the back of the book, and has been kept as simple as possible to emphasise some of the indirect perception involved in making *Brixton Fractals*. This is not intended as an itinerary for suggested further reading, or a listing to give authority to the text. It is to thank those who have taken part in the perception and memory that has made the text, and to keep open the opportunity to hear them" (Fisher, 4). In both cases the status of information, whether the dates for the invasion of the Scythians, or the possibility of "phases between nematic and smectic parallelisms" (Fisher, 69) of an ice sheet, does not have a direct dependence upon the accepted value of these facts, which may change with scholarly and scientific developments. It is not enough to shrug and say like the Wife of Bath, "Experience, though noon auctoritee / Were in this world, is right ynogh for me."[23] Poets like Prynne and Fisher recognize that they have to find some way of staking a claim to be heard, and the more their work moves in the wider public and scientific sphere, the more there is a problem. That poetry readings stage this difficulty is recognized by Lisa Robertson's amusing strategy for outlining her sources in *XEclogue.* She defines the relation between poem and authority in a manner that echoes Fisher's gesture of gratitude, and avoids any implicit claim to borrow scientific codes, by saying that "XEclogue has had many houseguests" and then naming various writers and performers as people who "taught me the necessity of women's tactical intervention in the official genres."[24] This strategy redefines the structure of authority in terms of relationship, and reminds me of the problem faced by the fictionalized figure of Bill Clinton in *Primary Colors,* who can only campaign by meeting people and empathizing with them, because he has no public credibility. He is fine in New Hampshire, where he can shake everybody's hand personally, and even spends a whole day in the mall doing just that, but in the vast state of Colorado he is lost because he can't politick live. Yet meeting people individually still powers his campaigning very effectively. We should not underestimate the power of live performance to establish authority even in a world where bureaucracies manage knowledge and foxy mass media exclude response from their reading spaces.

The Reading Space

Most avant-garde poetry readings take place in borrowed spaces—pubs, bars, lecture rooms, art galleries, halls, and theaters where the readers stumble over stage sets, talk above the noise of drinkers returning from the bar, or try to figure out how best to use a PA system installed for other purposes. Readers are rarely as proficient as actors at articulating the words, and often suprised by their tongue and larynx into misstarts, repetitions, and sinusoidal amplitude. Unplanned sound, material objects that insist upon other social purposes, obtrusive failures of attention, and an insistent temporariness, are common features of readings. The result can seem a deficit that might achieve finer results through better funding, organization, and audience behavior. The persistence of these momentary ascendancies of poetry in an everyday world that threatens at every instant to flood back in and reclaim the space for its everyday function suggests another possibility. Perhaps these intruders are really participants. The contemporary poetry reading is an art deeply marked by the age of consumption. Its grating, nonsemiotic aural intrusions, and the irrelevant signs of other occupancies, become stage villains in the dramatic appearance of poetry's temporary rule over the everyday world in which it is marginal. The hissing background is a constant reminder that readers and audience have taken hold of a space defined by the dominant culture and, as Michel de Certeau explains, have "diverted it without leaving it."[25] These visual and sonic incursions may

also have another more liminal effect. The insistence of these fricative im-
perfections can help create an awareness of the space in which the performance is occurring, in an experience of what John Cage calls "an utter emptiness" in which "each sound is unique . . . and is not informed / about
European history and theory," and "one can see anything can be in it, is,
as / a matter of fact, in it."[26] Many contemporary poets consciously strive
to extend the semantic repertoire of their performances, and this wide troublesome frame around the actual performance helps cue the audience's attention constantly to possible extensions of the field of significant action.
Avant-garde poets are aware, like Carolee Schneeman, that the space of the
event itself induces recognition. She recalls the traditional dancer's tense
witholding of spatial response in terms that also describe the situation of
the reading: "Space was anchored in their bodies, space was where they felt
their spines. They didn't realize a radiator behind them equaled their mass,
asserted verticals against their legs. I want a dance where a body moves as
part of its environment; where the dancer says Yes to environment incorporating or says No transforming it . . . where that choice is visual as a dancer
is Visual Element moving in actual real specific dimensions."[27] Poetry readings add an aural choice, yet it has to be admitted that space is still an
uneasy participant in the poetry reading, because most readings only faintly
acknowledge the location as any more than a vehicle for the generation of
spoken language. The extempore poet of the unanswerable talk, David
Antin, can ask "what am i doing here?" in his performance at the San Francisco State Poetry Center and have it be a question specific to a time and
location.[28] Most poetry is read from an existing text, or at least emerges
from the kind of preplan that Steve Benson referred to, and its relation
with the audience produces what Schneeman calls a "projective space" generated from within the person, an abstract space similar to that used in the
theater, but much more raggedly, so that the actual site constantly shows
through the rips in the fabric of the reading. Virtual space and material
space jostle uneasily as the poems are read, and this unstable coexistence
forms part of allegorical counterpart to the dramatization of a fundamental
instability between writing and speech center-stage of the reading.

The Silent History of Reading

What is the history of poetry readings? The conventional view seems to be
that the proliferation of readings since the 1950s is an entirely new response
to the long established constriction of poetry diagnosed by Charles Olson:
"What we have suffered from, is manuscript, press, the removal of verse
from its producer and its reproducer, the voice, a removal by one, by two
removes from its place of origin *and* its destination."[29] Poetry readings of
the kind offered by universities for several decades were much too "podium
oriented," too formal and too closely linked to the lecture format to offer

any opportunity to radically enact the wider possibilities for poetry.[30] Poets took poetry readings out of the universities into diverse urban venues where they could mingle with other arts, politics, and forms of leisure, stimulated by widely reported events like Dylan Thomas's tour and readings by Beat writers. Expectations of performance have been written into poems composed in a context characterized by an extraordinary and increasing amount of activity and interest in the public reading of poetry. George Economou's evaluation of the reading series he helped organize in New York, at which he and other poets read medieval poetry to a jazz accompaniment, typifies the accepted history. "It was," he says, "to my knowledge, the first time that translations of medieval European poems and original Middle English lyrics were read with jazz accompaniment, that a group of poets was concerned with the problems of preparing for performance the work of old and, in some cases, anonymous poets rather than their own" (Economou, 656). A widespread resistance to any claims for tradition led these poets to acknowledge only Dada and the oral poetics of nonliterate societies as precursors, and as George Quasha makes clear, Dada's influence was felt to be only indirect, even on a poet like Jackson Mac Low. To appeal to Dada, says Quasha, "does not help us to enter the necessary relation to the text either as written or as performed, since it draws us away from a *radical particularity:* the freedom of the performer and audience to originate an unknown state of attention or to enter an 'anarchistic' social relationship through language."[31] Poets who gave this any thought at all linked their oral practice to preliterate cultures where poetry was performed as an ordinary part of the culture's business, and elided modern history altogether. Jerome Rothenberg's remarkable work on oral poetics led him to a curious denial of the pertinence of recent history altogether: "The Renaissance is over or it begins again with us. Yet the origins we seek—the frame that bounds our past, that's set against an open-ended future—are no longer Greek, nor even Indo-European, but take in all times and places."[32] In his interview with William Spanos he more explicitly sidelines the recent past by invoking a "*mainstream* of poetry that goes back to the old tribes & has been carried forward by the great subterranean culture."[33] The contemporary poetry reading seems to stand clear of history altogether in a thoroughly modern fashion.

In fact, poetry readings emerge from a long history of the oral performance of written texts, which reaches back through the Renaissance and medieval cultures to the classical world. Until the advent of the new forms of leisure after the First World War, ordinary experience for almost everyone, whether rich or poor, included participation in groups listening to texts read aloud. The reading aloud itself was not merely taken for granted either. Many rigorous forms of pedagogy under a range of nomenclatures from rhetoric to elocution have taught people how to read texts aloud, including poetry. Only in the decades immediately prior to the emergence of the contemporary poetry reading did this training really falter, for reasons

I shall examine in a moment. So that when Quasha says that "there has *always* been more oral than written poetry," and that "there is clearly a gain in seeing both oral and literate in the same transcultural and synchronic context—as *synchronicity* rather than literary history," he is accurately describing a history that his other statements seem to belie. Silent reading and reading aloud have been part of a single economy of reading throughout history. The difficulty for poets wanting to extend the poetics of orality has been that the shift from oral to written culture is usually portrayed as a gradual, irreversible change from reading aloud to silent reading, one that happened gradually over centuries until its completion in the Renaissance, and eventually led to the utter ascendancy of print at least four centuries ago. It is a history with no place for the poetic virtues of orality, which assumes that such change is inevitable since silent reading is wholly preferable to the cumbersome demands of reading aloud to a group, and only took so long to develop because of illiteracy, the scarcity of texts, and a general lack of privacy. Recently there have been signs that historians of writing and reading are finding evidence that supports the idea that orality and literacy are much more interdependent than has hitherto been supposed, and poets have become less inclined to polarize orality and literacy in such value-laden terms. The intense preoccupation with the history of texts, language, speech, and writing in recent French thought has overthrown many unexamined prejudices, although some of these ideas have themselves created new dogmas about writing and communication.

The history of reading is still full of puzzles. We know much less about the extent and emergence of silent reading than we might wish, and we still don't know enough about the complex social conditions and consequences of oral reading. Scholars dispute when literacy emerged in ancient Greece, and whether Chaucer wrote his poetry for oral performance. Suprisingly little information has been collated about reading aloud even in the last century, despite innumerable references to domestic practice and its importance. Henry James attributed his interest in the dramatic possibilities of fiction to the experience of listening to Dickens read aloud. Even contemporary poets occasionally offer glimpses of the continuing importance of reading aloud, as Susan Howe does in remarking that it was hearing poems read aloud as a child that stimulated a habit of thinking within patterns of rhythmic phrasing.[34] Two important conclusions emerge from recent research into this history of oral reading for the understanding of the sudden explosion of poetry readings in the past half century. One is extremely obvious.

All the essays on contemporary poetry readings stress, with varying degrees of approval, that the poetry reading "brings together an audience which wishes to participate in consuming poetry with others who also wish to do so, to acknowledge poetry, and to feel part of a community,"[35] and in doing so they are recognizing what readers have always known. Reading aloud is a form of sociality. When Augustine recalled his mentor Ambrose in his *Confessions,* he particularly remembered the bishop's ability to read silently, but instead of seeing the future he saw someone resting from social contact: "We wondered if he read silently perhaps to protect himself in case he had a hearer interested and intent on the matter, to whom he might have to expound the text being read if it contained difficulties, or who might wish to debate some difficult questions . . . Whatever motive he had for his habit, this man had a good reason for what he did."[36] You needed a good reason, a good excuse, to read silently. A historian of medieval reading habits, Joyce Coleman, cites Robert Manning saying that he wrote his history of Britain

> For to haf solace and gamen
> In felawschip when thai sitt samen.[37]

Chaucer offers a satirical self-portrait of himself as a silent reader in *The House of Fame* as a "heremyte" who sits "dumb as any stoon," implying that this is a peculiar and unsociable activity for his contemporaries. By the mid-sixteenth century, reading was becoming much more private, especially amongst the cultural elite, for whom it often represented a desirable form of withdrawal from the demands of the world, yet reading aloud remained a widespread means of sustaining sociality. The historian of books and reading, Roger Chartier, who believes that "reading is always a practice embodied in acts, spaces, and habits," cites a very moving account of a man on military service between 1635 and 1642 who dragged around with him nearly a whole cartload of books to share with his fellow soldiers. One of them, Henri Campion, explained in his memoirs how reading them sustained his friendship with fellow officers: "l'un de nous lisait haut quelque bon livre, dont nous examinions les plus beaux passages, pour apprendre à bien vivre et à bien mourir, selon la morale, qui était notre principale étude" ("One of us would read some good book aloud. We would examine its most beautiful passages with the intent of learning how to live well and likewise to die in accordance with moral science, which was the chief object of our study").[38] For Samuel Pepys, reading aloud was part of other social activities, whether an attempt at flirtation with a strange woman in a coach, or part of his relationship with his wife, or simply an early equivalent of listening to the radio by using his servant to read to him. Reading aloud was deeply embedded in ordinary social relations of every kind, from court to the domestic world.

The vicissitudes of a lost poem by James Boswell underline how embedded in everyday life, and how interconnected writing, silent reading, and reading aloud really were. In his London journal for 5 January 1763, he records how he sent a poem (since lost) to his friend Lord Eglinton, saying, "You know we have often disputed whether or not I am a poet. I have sent you an ode. Lord Elibank thought it good. I think so too."[39] Eglinton writes back the same day with a wonderfully ambiguous response: "I like your ode much. There was no need of that to convince me you had genius.

I wish I was sure of your judgement of men and things." Eglinton interprets the poem as a display of intelligence, as if that is what a poem is ordinarily for. That evening Boswell goes to Lord Eglinton's and joins a group of clever men who talk about a whole range of things upon which he has no judgment to make at all. Suddenly Lord Eglinton produces the poem claiming that he has just discovered it in his pocket where it has lain for such a long time he doesn't recall the author. One of the other guests takes the paper and reads the poem aloud, and then criticizes it, especially for the very lines that Boswell is most proud of. At the end of the evening Eglinton takes him aside, and says, "I hope we are very good friends," in case the young man has misinterpreted events. On the way home Boswell projected his sense of having been robbed of his poetic dignity onto a fear of street robbery, and "determined against suppers" for the sake of his health. This little game is Eglinton's answer to Boswell's original question, partly to avoid a direct written response that might wound his friend, but largely because reading aloud and the resultant discussion are an ordinary form of criticism. Subterfuge helps to displace any formality attendant on an author reading a poem in public, as well as shielding the young man from exposure.

In the nineteenth century, performance became more and more formalized in public settings. Alongside the nearly universal domestic readings of poems and novels, there was a new interest in public readings by actresses like Fanny Kemble and writers like Dickens. Working-class men organized themselves into groups to read aloud in public, notably in the "penny Readings," meetings where the audience would each pay a penny to hear selected audience members read aloud from texts that tended to the comic or the emotional, so that any impetus toward self-improvement behind these reading groups was kept in check by the desire for entertainment. Factory workers might pay someone to read aloud to them, from a book or newspaper,[40] while they worked, and in the coffeehouses, which commonly had libraries attached, people would often read aloud to a group. Local clubs and reading circles existed everywhere and made singing, reciting, and lecturing a part of the entertainment they provided to people looking for a mix of education and fun. These clubs persisted into the early twentieth century.

A comparison of two clubs inaugurated in the same year, 1916, both successful on the terms they set themselves, and both carrying on this long tradition of clubs organized around participant performance, summarizes the consequence of these changes. In October 1916 William Carlos Williams helped form the Polytopics Club in Rutherford, New Jersey, where he practiced as a doctor.[41] Its members, twelve couples whose husbands worked as lawyers, doctors, and businessmen, wore tuxedos to their fortnightly meetings at which they often had an outside speaker, as well as discussion, reading aloud, music, and singing. In March 1921 Williams read to them from *Kora in Hell,* and the secretary afterward noted that the usually calm discussion became unusually heated. It was too much for Williams's wife, who pointed out to him that the audience had laughed at the wrong things and made him promise not to read his poems to them again. Even a profession and a dinner jacket were not enough to make modernism palatable for oral performance. The incomprehension and laughter that greeted *Kora in Hell* became the marker of a sociable antisociality, which another club started that year began to aim for. The Cabaret Voltaire is usually treated as if it were a world away from the bourgeois suburbs of places like Rutherford, yet what often goes unnoticed in accounts of its Dada performances is that alongside the radical verse and the simultaneous readings were readings of Rimbaud and Apollinaire, Russian poetry, and music that was recognizably music. The radical material emerged from and counterpointed the more familiar activities. Moreover the Cabaret Voltaire was a hybrid, part club, part café, and part music hall. One historian of the influence of popular performance on modern art argues that it was music hall that most influenced the artists, because it was so modern, or as Marinetti said, had "no tradition, no masters and no dogma."[42] The Polytopics Club was tame by comparison and took place on the boundary between private and public spheres, yet some of its entertainments sound close to cabaret. In the thirties there were plays, some written by Williams, in one of which he wore shaving cream on his face and his wife wore mud, and they played husband and wife. Another play was set in a Paris café, as if aspiring to some of the ambience of a Cabaret Voltaire.

The disappointing reception of *Kora in Hell* showed that a reading circle could not provide the kind of relation with his readers that a modernist poet needed. Some new kind of performance space was needed. In 1919 Williams went to Chicago for several days at a time when he was feeling exhausted by his medical work and family life, to give a talk and a reading to an audience that included Carl Sandburg and Ben Hecht, and feeling reinvented as a poet he was emboldened to sleep with a woman who was the assistant editor of *Poetry*. A few weeks later he wrote to Harriet Monroe, the editor of *Poetry,* and half apologized for his behavior, saying, "I had never in my life before had an opportunity to be just a poet, the one thing I want to be. I was, to the vulgar eye at least, a poet! I was at least as near to being a poet as I had ever been and it was as if new bones had been put into me" (Mariani, 160). It took the emergent college-reading platform to provide the social energy he needed to sustain himself as a modern poet. A revealing comment by a young woman interviewed by the Lynds for their follow-up study of "Middletown" confirms Williams's sense that reading aloud in everyday groups was increasingly unviable for modernist writing: "My mother belongs to a little group who are reading together such things as Hart Crane, e. e. Cummings, Gertrude Stein, and Vincent Sheean. They steer clear of most of the poets tinged with economic radicalism, but are well read on the symbolists. Yet I don't think they derive a great amount of personal satisfaction from their reading."[43] The Lynds's research confirms that reading aloud disappeared rapidly after the First World War in the face of new forms of public entertainment, more educational opportunities, mass journalism, and the automobile. "Middletown" in the 1890s loved reading circles, yet by the twenties they had almost disappeared. "No longer do a Young Ladies' Reading Circle, a Christian Literary Society (of fifty), a Literary League, a Literary Home Circle, A Literary Fireside Club meet weekly or bi-weekly as in 1890, nor are reading circles formed in various sections of the city, nor does a group of young women meet to discuss the classics."[44] The diverse cultural effects created by public oral reading were increasingly segmented into more specialized leisure pursuits, eventually including the contemporary poetry reading.

A second less easily comprehended element of this history of oral reading is the relation between the different forms of understanding active in silent and audible reading. Medieval authors and readers were, according to Joyce Coleman, part of a performance economy that worked "synchronically to shape a mutually satisfying performance text and diachronically to create a shared vernacular of vocabulary and significance (126)." A man like the medieval miller Menocchio merged oral and written culture together, as Carlo Ginzburg's rhetorical question indicates: "To what extent did the prevalently oral culture of those readers interject itself in the use of the text, modifying it, reworking it, perhaps to the point of changing its very essence?"[45] Reading aloud and the ensuing conversation were integral parts of the text, in a way that Ginzburg insists is utterly different to that of a modern "educated reader." But is it? Recently a strange debate has broken out amongst Chaucer scholars about the value of reading Chaucer's poetry aloud in a supposedly authentic pronunciation. One line of argument against it is that the poetry is too complex to be assimilated aurally, and deliberately uses ambiguities that are ruined by a speaker's choice between them[46] Alan Gaylord makes a comment that is of particular relevance for understanding the economy of the poetry reading: "[O]ne *says* the verse in order to find those places that *will not be said;* which is to say, performance is a propaedeutics to contemplation."[47] This contemporary academic can only imagine the interjections and modifications in terms of the social sphere he knows best, the academy, but in effect he is admitting that the different forms of reading together still constitute an economy of reception.

Scholars working on the emergence of writing and reading in ancient Greece provide useful insight into the interdependence of reading aloud and silent reading, because this highly articulate and self-analytic culture only slowly embraced reading, perhaps not until the end of the fifth century B.C. Most reading was done by specialists, the scribes and others who recorded information and read aloud to the rest, and so people were acutely aware of the implications of this relation. Jesper Svenbro believes that reading felt invasive to these Greeks because they imagined that to read was to lend one's voice and become "the instrument necessary for the text to be realized"[48] in what they sometimes understood as an almost sexual penetration of the self. Inscriptions on the base of early funerary monuments are often written in the first person ("Eumares set me up as a monument" or "I am the memorial of Glaukos" [Svenbro, 30]) but this did not imply that they believed that the statues had an inner being of some kind, simply that the writing would remain mute until a passerby lent it a voice and read it aloud. Such inscriptions therefore anticipate and control a reader's relation to the text. A memorial verse for a man called Mnesitheos uses two different words for reading and both refer to it as a vocal act, not as an act of semiotic decoding, as we might expect. One of these, the verb *ananémesthai,* which means literally "to distribute," and was used ordinarily to mean "to read and recite," is used in this context to ask the passerby to distribute the memorial verse by reading it aloud, and in doing so to distribute the meaning to him or herself (Svenbro, 48–52). "The reading aloud is a part of the text, an integral part of it" (Svenbro, 45). Reading aloud was often left to slaves, because during reading it was felt that someone else's words took possession of a passive reader, like a male lover approaching a boy, and so was given to people whose self-integrity did not matter. Svenbro even claims that "pederasty was one of the models the Greeks used in order to think about writing and reading" (Svenbro, 198). This ethnography of reading in a very different culture to the contemporary world suggests two lines of enquiry into the poetry reading. It shows that a culture may try to comprehend reading according to dominant forms of affective relationship, and suggests that for Greek culture at least, silent reading would have been incomplete reading, not because its acoustic properties were left idle, but because the distributive power of the writing would remain inactive.

I think that some limited evidence of uneasiness about poetry readings evident in the biographies of writers whose careers either spanned the decades between the demise of the reading clubs and the emergence of contemporary readings, or began during that phase, supports Svenbro's speculation about the projection of dominant forms of desire into acts of reading. Some very obviously male ego anxieties were generated by the situations in which these poets sometimes found themselves. Williams became a regular on the college circuit but often experienced a degree of alienation. "It makes me weary for some instructor at Columbia to come up to me after a reading and ask why I put a certain verse in the form which I put it in."[49] After a reading at New York University in 1949 when he had read one or two confessional pieces that he had not intended to, he told the friend who had arranged the reading that he felt like he had been "talking into a felt mattress." Confessing in public felt as if you have pulled "back your foreskin (if you have one) in public" (Mariani, 589). The containment of castration anxiety within the possibly anti-Semitic reference, suggests how threatening reading could become. Williams was usually more sanguine about readings, and never shared Wallace Stevens's chronic hatred, expressed in a letter refusing to read at the Museum of Modern Art in 1943. "I am not a troubadour and I think the public reading of poetry is something particularly ghastly."[50] This is a trope which the next generation would actually find quite congenial, as Economou's account showed. Charles Olson seems to have imagined that readings were like formal political speeches in their defining impact, if Tom Clark is to be believed. Robert Duncan told Tom Clark that Olson had to be reassured before a reading in San Francisco that this was not a definitive performance: "'Charles, you're just reading your poetry among friends, it won't have to last four days,'" Duncan told Olson.[51] I wonder if Duncan also meant that the reading's impact was not intended to be a policy pronouncement intended to last "for days." These three stories all remind us that the contemporary poetry reading has had to develop its own social relations.

What we can conclude from this history is that written poetry has always been read aloud by both authors and readers, long before the advent of the contemporary poetry reading, which is now such a dominant feature of poetic practice. The contemporary poetry reading is an attempt to reintroduce features of the reading economy that have been lost, just as the growth of fan conferences for genre writing, especially science fiction, obviously results from the desire of readers to take an active part in the shaping of the texts themselves, as well as a desire for that sociability mediated by texts which was such a distinctive feature of earlier forms of reading. The precise nature of that loss can only be grasped if the poetry reading is placed in another history that has shaped it, the history of public speaking. Sometimes called rhetoric, sometimes elocution, oral reading, even orthophony, the training of public speaking with written texts including poetry, is the missing part of the story of poetry readings. When George Economou said that he and his fellow poets were the first to read aloud the medieval poets, he was forgetting the work of the verse speakers of the early twentieth century. Writing as late as 1951 on "The Audible Reading of Poetry," Yvor Winters felt the need to begin with a disclaimer: "My title may seem to have in it something of the jargon of the modern Educationalist"—but by the sixties most poets (Denise Levertov is an interesting exception, although she is entirely dismissive of what she remembers of prewar public verse speaking)[52] seem to have forgotten entirely the importance attached to public verse speaking by teachers and social reformers over the past two centuries.[53]

Verse Speaking

The Popular Elocutionist and Reciter comprising Practical Hints on Public Reading and Reciting and An extensive collection of speeches, dramatic scenes, dialogues, soliloquies, readings and recitations selected from The Best Authors Past and Present with Original hints on elocution by J. E. Carpenter, published in 1906, devotes an entire chapter to "readings in poetry," and anticipates many features of the contemporary poetry reading. Poetry rectitation is a problem he blames on the intersubjective demands that easily exceed an ordinary reciter's powers.

> There are many excellent readers of prose who entirely fail to distinguish the equable and harmonious flow of sound which distinguishes poetry from ordinary unmeasured composition . . . Unless the author be thoroughly appreciated and his intention, not only expressed but implied, mastered, the natural emotions (and consequently the proper inflexions and varieties of voice) cannot possibly arise, and, if not, how can they be expressed save by a studied, stilted, and artificial style? It is, perhaps, not saying too much to aver that only a poet can read poetry properly: at any rate only those who are perfectly imbued with the poetic feeling can do so. Given all these qualifications, and action, voice, and gesture will follow naturally and spontaneously; the electric fire will flash from the speaker to his audience, enthusiasm will be kindled, and a result that only true genius can achieve will be accomplished. The great secret in reading poetry is to exercise the art that conceals art, or rather the art that seems to heighten and improve nature and to subdue it, so that it is never apparent that the speaker is delivering the words of others. To the hearers it should be as though the speaker were giving the utterances of his own heart, and his own brain, an impulsive and involuntary outpouring excited by existing and surrounding circumstances.[54]

This forgotten advice bears repeating because it encapsulates beliefs that are still active in poetry readings today, even though no one links them with elocution, and the author is almost always the reader (as if audiences have decided that only the poet who composed the lines is capable of sufficient "poetic feeling" to do justice to the work). Many poets read as if they were uttering the lines for the first time in "an impulsive and involuntary outpouring," and try hard to make that electric fire flash in what Olson called the "energy-discharge" of the poem (Olson, 52). This continuity between 1906 and the present is no accident. Poetry readings draw upon a long history of training and practice of formal oral performance whose history is ignored, as much because such analysis as Carpenter's makes too explicit the artifice behind the spontaneity, as because elocution is now hopelessly associated with training in correct pronunciation of the kind needed by aspirant middle-class children, or actors needing to improve the projection of their voice. In Carpenter's time it had far more ambitious aims than these. Its history helps explain both the implicit agendas of contemporary poetry readings and why it has become so difficult to justify the claim that the semantic repertoire of the poem is significantly extended by oral performance.

Rhetoric was a part of the training of an educated young man from the time of Socrates until the Renaissance. It simultaneously provided the necessary basis for participation in public life, where effective public speaking was essential, and a training in the varieties of argument. We have no modern counterpart because we divide our knowledge, politics, and arts very differently into specialisms. Rhetoric's organization of thought helped shape education, and provided the means to comprehend writing, speech, and language. The oration largely took the place that the essay does today in our educational system. Performance, which included everything from voice and emotional influence to the structures of reception, was integral to logic, and the consequence was that actual voice production was usually, in Aristotle's words, "not regarded as an elevated subject of inquiry."[55] All this changed at the end of the seventeenth century, once logical argument was prized away from its association with certain features of rhetoric, notably the studied use of tropes as a means of making ideas persuasive and accessible. The Royal Society advocated a plain style for scientific writing, and the arts of persuasion were treated as at best ornaments, and at worst, distortions of good, well-argued evidential prose. In all this ferment the actual business of delivery seems to have gone uncriticized by the reformers, and perhaps for that reason eighteenth-century critics began to talk about it with a new zeal, as if the lack of criticism proved its continuing validity (Howell, 153). It seems likely, too, that this very continuity enabled its proponents to imagine that a training in oral rhetorical performance would somehow recreate a bond between ethics and cognition that had been lost to the public sphere. Thomas Sheridan, father of the playwright Richard Sheridan, justifies the importance of a training in elocution on the grounds that without it "how many well instructed minds, and honest hearts, furnished with the means, and most ardent inclination to serve their country, have sat still in silent indignation, where her interests were nearly concerned, for want of a practised tongue to disclose what passed in their minds."[56] He internalizes an imaginary unity of moral purpose, argumentative accuracy and clarity and represents its public absence by this muteness, which he wishfully attributes to a fault in the engineering of voice. He is therefore able to assume that the existence of what has disappeared from the public sphere continues in a series of lost private worlds.

The continuing interest in elocution, as it came to be known, depended upon a conjunction of such elevated ambitions with much more pragmatic, self-interested concerns. Young people from the upper classes needed to be able to read aloud reasonably well because this was one of the cultural accomplishments that distinguished a young person, along with music, singing, dancing, and drawing. Speaking well became the sign of good breeding, and this added to its importance for those aspirants less sure of their class position. Books and teachers of speaking aloud became very popular, and they used both prose and poetry as material. According to Mary Robb, two theories of elocution came to dominate the field. One emerged directly from the Enlightenment commitment to scientific rules and method, and was promulgated in such books as James Rush's *The Philosophy of the Human Voice,* and later in Alexander Melville Bell's *The Principles of Elocution* (he was the father of the inventor). The creation of a physics of the voice is captured in this passage from Bell: "Expression may be defined as the *Effective Expres-*

sion of Thought and Sentiment by Speech, Intonation, and Gesture. Speech is wholly conventional in its expressiveness, and mechanical in its processes. Intonation and gesture constitute a Natural Language, which may be used either independently of, or as assistant to, speech . . . The student of Elocution, then, should be made acquainted with the instrument of Speech *as an instrument,* that all its parts may be under his control, as the stops, the keys, the pedals, and the bellows are subject to the organist."[57] It is not hard to see that this could lead to a mechanical artificial style of speaking and would lead to a reaction away to a more natural approach. Aided by the growth of psychology, elocution gradually shifted the emphasis away from physiology to the mind behind the voice. It became possible to claim that sound was a systematic vehicle of expression: "[P]articular sounds or elements are uniformly used to express particular emotions . . . tone-colour is the avenue along which the emotion passes in its progress from within outward, or from the poet to his hearer. The mere fact is expressed by the words; the emotion is expressed by the various qualities of the voice."[58] It is a kind of urtheory of sound symbolism limited by the way the adjective "uniformly" reveals that this is a prestructural theory of language, and goes too far in assuming that sounds themselves form a fixed code of affects. Nevertheless, Clark's emphasis on emotion points the way forward to the emerging "naturalist" school of elocution, which argued that voice production depended upon aesthetic and interpretative criteria and could not be reduced to a system of rules.

A final flowering of elocution took place in the twentieth century, and found many suprising supporters early in the century. In his commencement address at Bryn Mawr in 1905, Henry James recommended a diligent study of good speaking to the graduating class, as if this were the most effective means to engage in social reform he could imagine for these young women. His argument, although more sophisticated than Sheridan's, still assumes that clarity of articulation will facilitate the communication upon which society rests: "[A]ll life comes back to the question of our relations with each other. These relations are made possible, are registered, are verily constituted, by our speech, and are successful (to repeat my word) in proportion as our speech is worthy of its great human and social functions; is developed, delicate, flexible, rich—an adequate, accomplished fact. The more it suggests and expresses the more we live by it—the more it promotes and enhances life . . . it is very largely by saying, all the while, that we live and play our parts."[59] The same aspirations that animated Sheridan are still evident here, and they similarly lead to the seeming bathos of a call for better pronunciation. James was not alone in his convictions. The leading teacher of speech in Britain in the first decades of this century, Elsie Fogerty, founded the Central School of Speech Training and Dramatic Art in London the following year, 1906, and a few years later also helped found the new medical field of speech therapy. Fogerty trained several generations of actors and speakers of verse, teaching them that written words were the record of "audible movements translated by visible signs."[60] Like earlier elocutionists she believed that "the knowledge and practice of written speech in all its mental and physical forms represents for us the lifework of prophet, poet, and philosopher, of thinker and fool alike,"[61] and in her textbooks, as in her teaching, brought together an extraordinary synthesis of Bergson, anthropology, physiology, linguistics, and aesthetics under the rubric of rhythm. She may have been influenced, like John Masefield, by the style of W. B. Yeats, whose oral reading, according to Masefield, "put great (many thought too great) yet always subtle insistence upon the rhythm; it dwelt upon the vowels and the beats. In Lyric it tended ever towards what seemed like Indian singing; in other measures, towards an almost fierce *recitativo*."[62] Later still in the twenties she collaborated with John Masefield, Marjorie Gullan, and others in the development of public displays and competitions in verse speaking.

This final fling of the elocution movement in Britain led to some extraordinary attempts to recreate the performance of verse. Masefield founded a verse-speaking competition in Oxford in 1923 and later helped found the English Verse-Speaking Association in 1929. His aim was to sweep away the artificiality that had resulted from methods of teaching elocution that "had concentrated on acquiring an equipment of tricks and recipes for delivery that should fulfil their every requirement," failing to recognize that "the sound of a poem is part of its meaning, and needs a vocal cultivation for its revealing that shall be as exacting as a great singer's, and as undemonstrative as the singer's often is demonstrative."[63] In his autobiography he recalls ironically that in his youth popular stage reciters of verse were "at their best in works dealing with the murderous, the mad, and the drunken" (Masefield, 132). He strongly supported the work of Fogerty and Gullan, whose pupils aimed for "natural voice habits" in all their work, some of which even included choral verse speaking, surely one of the most peculiar developments in verse speaking. Several of these choirs were formed in the twenties and thirties, and practiced a kind of speaking in unison, not, as one might imagine, aiming for clever part harmonies as in the singing of a madrigal.

In America voice training was now widely taught in higher education, according to Mary Robb, but was undergoing a rapid transformation signaled by the way the terminology changed. The Emerson College of Oratory became the Emerson College of Liberal Arts in 1936, and the word "elocution" was used more and more rarely. College catalogues for 1929–1931 listed over two thousand courses in oral practice, but the favored term now was "interpretation," and increasingly these courses were being tied to specialisms, notably linguistics and drama. Academics could still claim, like Clarence T. Simon in an essay called "Appreciation in Reading," that "muscles, nerves, glands, all do their part in our reaction to literature . . . it is this 'doing something' which is the appreciation," but increasingly the passage from glands to literary criticism was Balkanized by incommensurable and noncommunicating sciences and arts.[64] It seems reasonable to assume that the young Charles Olson was trained in these traditions as a successful school debater, and then drew on these unacknowledged sources in his "Projective Verse" essay, which is why the continuities mentioned earlier can be found.

The history of elocution and verse speaking is a history of an attempt to restore a diremption of cognition, ethics, and art that developed during the Enlightenment, and a futile attempt because "pronuntiatio" always meant much more than the mere shaping of vocal sounds by the face. The deliberate amnesia about the importance of the elocution movement for shaping our current experience of verse speaking in the contemporary poetry reading probably derives from the unwillingness to recognize this failure for what it is. Certainly the primitivism of much discussion of oral poetics would confirm this, because it so evidently represents a similar aspiration for imagined pre-Enlightenment unities.

Sound Symbolism

When William Carlos Williams gave his poetry reading in Chicago in 1919, Carl Sandburg was sitting in the audience. Sandburg was much better known than Williams (who did not even appear in Louis Untermeyer's anthology of American poetry published in 1921, which included Sandburg, Lindsay, Pound, H. D., Eliot, and Stevens among nearly a hundred others). Sandburg was a popular performer of his poetry, and had developed a style of verse that would make the most of his performance skills. The result was a poetry that "uses a high percentage of obstruents to portray his rough messages."[65] *Smoke and Steel,* published the following year, celebrated industry and labour with lines full of these phonetic obstacles: "Pittsburg, Youngstown, Gary—they make their steel with men."[66] The route to success was the prominent use of sound symbolism, the use of the sound of words to intensify the meaning of what he wrote, and which therefore worked especially well in performance.

Poetry readings are often justified as opportunities to hear the poem uttered by the reader who understands its sounding best. Even if sound had no semantic value, performance would enable listeners to grasp the full beauty of the verbal music. If, however, sound does also have a semantic value, then performance is given an added justification, and this does seem to be the current belief amongst contemporary linguists. Linguists now accept that some sounds used in the production of words do carry meaning that is in addition to the lexically generated meaning of the word. Some sound patterns appear nearly universal, others exist across groups of languages, and some are local to a specific language, and they range from the involuntary bodily expression to the most conventional and metalinguistic forms. Despite some intensive research, the consequences of these features of language are not entirely clear, especially for global theories of language of the kind employed in literary theory. Saussure's model of language assumes that sound is fundamentally arbitrary, a mere vehicle for indicating the differences between words, lacking any positive significance of its own. Linguists like Roman Jakobson and Linda Waugh argue that we would be better advised to drop the idea of arbitrariness, and talk instead of degrees of conventionality and iconicity. The link between meaning (not reference) and sound is conventional, but the sound itself may also have formed an associative network with other words that share the same sounds, and so may share semantic links as well. The words *glitter, glisten, glow, glimmer* for example, all use the phonestheme *gl* associated with an indistinct light (Hinton et al., 5). The study of sound symbolism is rapidly becoming a technical field that requires more detailed treatment than is possible here, so I shall not try to outline the linguistics further. Instead I shall assume these findings and consider their implications.

Poets are likely to be unsurprised by this work, but as J. H. Prynne recently pointed out, literary theory's reliance on the Saussurean paradigm leaves the critic with no wider framework for what is almost universally practiced by readers and writers of poetry, the use of sound as bearer of significance.[67] The concept of sound symbolism has not yet had time to influence literary theory, and so the linguistics does not help us resolve several key issues concerning the poetry reading. One possibility is that poetry readings are spaces in which readers can improve their attentiveness to this area of the semantic repertoire. Waugh herself notes that "Some language users are poets, while others are deaf to the music of language" (Waugh, 75), and this analogic use of poetry to describe a high level of competence suggests that the poetry reading can plausibly be considered in this manner.

What linguists are not usually able to help us with is the degree to which fine shades of sound symbolism are at work in a poem, and how performance might transpose it. Should, for example, a reader encountering the phonestheme *gl* in the word *glad* in a poem try to hear traces of light symbolism in the word? The answer probably depends upon the context, yet in actual examples the relevance is hard to gauge. The following is taken from Maggie O'Sullivan's "Hill Figures" from the recent anthology *Out of Everywhere: Linguistically Innovative Poetry by Women in North America and the U.K.*:

Skull—
  alarge, Oth
        Twisted
        merry-go
        superates,
        congregates,
         rolled-a-run
          lettering[68]

"Oth" could be an obsolete form of *oath* or *otter,* it could be a segment of *Goth, other, troth,* or it could echo the sound of words like *loathe.* It can therefore be pronounced in several different ways, and be linked to several associational networks, allowing an imprecision of pronunciation that performance cannot replicate. The phonestheme *gr* in the word "congregates" is a particularly strong one, with associations of unpleasantness, complaint, and unwanted rubbing (Waugh, 77), yet the pertinence of this iconicity is deliberately unclear, although the tone of this poem about the poisoning of outdoor freedoms does seem to encourage a reader to hear such a semantic trace. Performance could linger with a growl or quickly open out into the following vowel, without resolving the question, unless one grants the author's pronunciation an absolute authority. Take another instance from the same anthology. When Deanna Ferguson writes "Had I seen square when / eyeball suture teethed with / cankorous proclivity" (O'Sullivan, 131) in the poem "It's Bad for You," should we hear an active phonestheme in the "sq" with echoes of the crushing in *squash, squelch, squeeze?* We can say with more confidence that the replacement of *seethed* by "teethed" brings the teeth more actively into use to make the *th* sound and gives the awkward adjective (with verbal overtones) more bite.

These examples might seem to confirm the importance of sound without quite solving our problem, because oral reading could actually diminish these semantically productive indeterminacies by forcing a choice of pronunciation and emphasis on the reader. The silent reader's inner theater might after all be the best place for a full rendition of the poem. There are two reasons why this is not the case. The first is that it is a mistake to think of silent reading and performance as exclusive alternatives. They jointly contribute to the reading of a poem, and may well both sometimes be necessary for unskilled readers, as a mixed set of critical readings of a poem by Maggie O'Sullivan demonstrates.

What happens when readers have only read a text on the page that is also written with performance in mind as part of its promulgation? In one issue of the magazine *Responses,* a series of reader surveys consisting of unrevised written responses to specific poems edited by Steven Pereira and Anthony Rollinson, O'Sullivan's "Giant Yellow" was published alongside a series of extremely revealing attempts to discuss or reject it.[69] There are eleven of these, and all but the last are only half a page long. Comments by readers of this poem who had never heard her perform nor encountered her work suggest that without witnessing her performance the work's imagined readership can be hard to discern. Some of the readers were defeated by its neologisms, insistent sound patterns and lack of integrating syntax. They are "made to feel uncomfortable," the poem "creates ignorance," it is like listening to a foreign language or just white noise. Some are even more abusive, calling it verbal butchery, vomit, or that most awful term of abuse, an "academic exercise." Other respondents seem to have read a different poem. These respondents are ready to praise the work, and it is noticeable that these poets, who have all been part of the London scene for years, immediately summon up a picture of the poet herself performing the poetry aloud. For them, the author's vocal performance is now inscribed within the text. One poet summons up "striking if not conventionally beautiful dark Irish features" which are "transformed, transfused with beauty as she reads unhurriedly." Another poet contrasts the "permanent disruption" on the page with the "elusive meanings" heard in the air by the "mental ear." Lawrence Upton has strongly internalized an image of the poet reading: "Maggie O'Sullivan has a remarkable reading voice—and manner, her manner is quite compelling though friendly and supportive, drawing in audience (they who hear)—which is warm, resonant and *not* colloquial, *not* casual but *causal*." One way of contrasting these positive readings with the other hostile ones is to say that the others have not heard O'Sullivan, so that instead of hearing her voice inscribed within the poem, they can only experience disorientation and nausea. A dissenter says perceptively, "I have no knowledge to sustain me," and shows how unpleasant this feels by spewing forth images of an abattoir, of eating offal, excrement, blood. To a reader who knows the writer, this respondent's comment that "through this carnage runs a blond" shows how easily readers project their own mistaken images of the writer into the act of the poem. The seventh respondent allows primary process to take over, and figures the poem as vomit and masturbation before saying that the poem "shits all over the reader." This litany of abjection, of images of the expulsion of taboo bodily substances, is evoked by the belief that the poem is a deliberate act of contempt for "dull bastards." The reader feels that the poem denies the patrimony of its readers, making them illegitimate as well as illiterate, because it fails to involve the reader, and instead "forces the reader into the position of spectator," which only a "sick" poem would do. Exclusion from a relation to the poem's performance produces these extreme reactions, in which by imagining the poem as a kind of bodily evacuation, the critic abjects it her/himself, throwing it violently away from attention. This reader is actually reading attentively, noting the performative style and the importance of sound, but is then unable to process the information and explodes, rather like the early Dada audiences, in a violent rejection. Although one of the readers unfamiliar with O'Sullivan's poetry does guess hesitantly that it "could be a poem for voices," even this is not enough to be part of the implicate readership.

The inner theater is an insufficient sound chamber, not just because of the limits of imagination's ear, as Adorno points out, but for another reason too.[70] The relation between speech and writing is much more disjunct than the metaphor of the inner theater implies, and indeed such metaphors actually mislead to some extent. Linguistics is not always as helpful as it might seem, and it is worth remembering that one reason for the decline of the elocution movement was that research into pronunciation like that of James Rush and Alexander Bell became the preserve of linguists for whom issues of performance and rhetoric were largely irrelevant. It is therefore significant that a recent article by David R. Olson argues that linguistics has habitually allowed itself to overvalue the insights of writing in all areas of investigation. Writing develops alongside speech, rather than as a means of directly recording something already comprehended: "writing systems provide the concepts and categories of thinking about the structure of speech rather than the reverse. Awareness of linguistic structure is a product of a writing system not a precondition for its development."[71] Writing goes through a two-stage process. It is developed to augment memory and facilitate communication, and then because it is "'read' [provides] a model for language and thought" (David Olson, 2). Olson speculates that writing systems like the Greek alphabet developed because of the need to use an existing script designed for one spoken language to represent another, and in the process of transformation the written system became more flexible and comprehensive. We still live within this process of development, and need to recognize that many features of speech remain unrepresented, or only imperfectly so, by our writing, simply because "a script is not initially or primarily an attempt at a complete linguistic representation." These ideas suggest that poets are like the users of the old Semitic sign system trying to accommodate it to spoken Greek (the accepted story of how the Greek alphabet was created) trying to utilize an imperfect set of written signs to indicate aural complexities that then compel new forms of recognition of links between thought and language. As Gaylord says about reading Chaucer aloud, but for somewhat different reasons, "[O]ne *says* the verse in order to find those places that *will not be said*" (Gaylord, 107), not only because of the use of the indeterminacy of writing's representation of sound, but also for the saying that is not yet writable.

Sound symbolism is resolutely linguistic. Sound itself is a bodily experience, and most sound in the world is extralinguistic, a continual vibration of the air by all the movements in the plenum. Dennis Lee describes an experience of sound that so permeates him it is not strictly heard at all: "Most of my life as a writer is spent listening into a cadence which is a kind of taut cascade, a luminous tumble. If I withdraw from immediate contact with things around me I can sense it churning, flickering, dancing, locating things in more shapely relation to one another without robbing them of themselves . . . I speak of 'hearing' cadence, but in fact I am baffled by how to describe it. There is no auditory sensation."[72] Poetry readings, as we saw earlier, position the sound of the poem on this sound stage quite deliberately, if somewhat unconsciously. One way of interpreting this is to say that all the sounds audible at a reading are part of a world of sound that the minds of the audience then scan in search of meaning. According to the cognitive linguist Reuven Tsur, our minds process language-bearing sound in an automatic manner. When we hear a sound, our minds make a decision whether to treat it as speech or pure sound, and once it has been processed as speech, we find it hard to recall the sounds out of which the linguistic units were made. We direct our attention away from the sound to the muscular movements that create the sound and from there to the phoneme itself: "We seem to be tuned, normally, to the nonspeech mode; but as soon as the incoming stream of sounds gives the slightest indication that it may be carrying linguistic information, we automatically switch to the speech mode."[73] These processing modes are not hermetically sealed, so some crosstalk occurs, and at times "some tone colour from the processing in the nonspeech mode faintly enters consciousness" (Tsur, 18), but this will vary according to many factors, especially the tone structure of the pho- neme and the way the speaker delivers it. A slow, punctuated delivery will be much richer in this acoustic information than one delivered at ordinary speed (although a very rapid delivery will start to produce a breakdown of the reception ability and also create semantic effects that link with the larger semantic units). The acoustic structure of the particular verbal sounds will determine how readily the neural system can exit speech mode. A front vowel with its formants widely spaced across the frequency spectrum is more likely to enable such switching than a back vowel that has a tighter less distinguishable structure (Tsur, 23). Writing that uses neologisms, non- sense words, partial segments of words, and syntactic disjuncture is likely to encourage an uneasy oscillation in a listener's mind between the "auditory and the phonetic modes of listening" (Tsur, 73) during a performance. Tsur claims that when some of the "rich precategorical sensory information" is noticed by listeners to poetry they interpret this nonlinguistic acoustical awareness as part of the mystery of sound (Tsur, 47).

The problem with Tsur's theory is that it still isolates sound too much from the wider social practice in which the making of sound as language is taking place. Roland Barthes's homage to old-fashioned singers shows what is missing in Tsur's account, and perhaps this is because the singer he singles out for special praise was obviously influenced by the elocution movement. In his essay "The Grain of the Voice," Barthes praised singers like Panzera, whose body itself seemed audible in the performance. According to Barthes, Panzera advocated something quite different to an emphasis on clear enun- ciation, especially of consonants, because he thought the consonants should be "patinated" or made to seem worn, in the way consonants are in actual use, showing "the wear of a language that had been living, functioning, and working for ages past."[74] Obviously romanticizing Russian singers, he says that one can hear in their performance something of their entire cultural matrix, "something which is the cantor's body, brought to your ears in one and the same movement from deep down in the cavities, the muscles, the membranes, the cartilages, and from deep down in the Slavonic language, as though a single skin lined the inner flesh of the performer and the music he sings" (181). The acoustic dance of language in performance stems from the roots of culture, the deeper, least articulated fields, tradition at its most unconscious. One can interpret this claim, using the insights of sound sym- bolism and cognitivist poetics, to mean that in a performance in which the corporeality of the voice glints through the semantic delivery, this apprehensible sound carries with it a culturally informed patterning derived partly from culturally determined habits of body, which when merged with the culturally formed iconicities of sound at the linguistic level, carry a cultural significance beyond the individual. It can do so also because of the intersubjectivity of the event of performance itself, which Barthes elides.

For many artists and philosophers, music has symbolized an art that evades the limits of representation. Albrecht Wellmer cites Adorno's belief that music was the lost counterpart to philosophy in a form that many poets would endorse in preference to cognitive analysis, even if they might hesitate about some of the implicit claims about music's direct line to the absolute. Wellmer argues that, for Adorno, "the language of music and discursive language appear as the separated halves of 'true language.'"[75] Such claims derive in part from Dada. Hugo Ball justified the Dada experiments with sound poetry in very different terms to Tzara's antibourgeois polemics, arguing that the Dada performers "should withdraw into the innermost alchemy of the word, and even surrender the word, in this way conserving for poetry its most sacred domain."[76] Richard Huelsenbeck reports that Kandinsky wanted to stop "darkening" the purity of the human voice with meaning. A contemporary philosopher, David Appelbaum, in a wonderful account of the voice, echoes such sentiments today: "With the great gift of speech, an unknown something is stolen from voice."[77] These poets and thinkers are saying something similar to David Olson. The activity of speech, language, is a phenomenon about which we theorize, develop linguistics, philosophy, technologies of analysis, but which like all phenomena, is not thereby exhausted or fully explained by our current practice of knowledge. Much is still unknown, perhaps unknowable, not because it is transcendent, but because actuality necessarily exceeds understanding.[78] Language opens onto the unknown, and performance is one direction into it.

Intersubjectivity and the Circulation of Poetry

The Poetry Society's 1987 pamphlet on how to promote poetry offers strong advice to novice organizers of poetry events about audiences. Treat them well! "A warm, crowded space is preferable to a cold, half-empty hall," the would-be organizer is told, and then given strict numerical guidelines on the number of minutes a poet should read for: "The importance of these timings cannot be over-emphasised: listening to poetry requires great concentration; an audience still eager for more will return, a bored audience never."[79] The relation between the audience and the poet is at the heart of the event, yet at first sight seems to be merely a matter of such managerial pragmatics, not the space in which the poem's meaning is negotiated and possibly extended. The eager audience may be suffused with empathy for the poet and interest in the work, but have they really extended their comprehension of the work itself? Like the inscription from ancient Greece, the poet has distributed the poem to the audience, but what does it mean to say that this is an integral part of the poem itself? For some readers O'Sullivan's poetry seems to require oral performance as well as silent reading, but this doesn't prove that the meaning of a particular poem is actually extended or transfigured by performance. To do that it is necessary to take seriously the Poetry Society's advice and think of the audience.

Audience and poet collaborate in the performance of the poem. The audience is not simply a collection of autonomous individuals whose auditions of the poem are entirely independent. During performance the audience is formed by the event, and creates an intersubjective network, which can then become an element in the poem itself. Intersubjectivity is only partially available as an instrument for the poet to play, and is an ever-changing, turbulent process that can overwhelm or ignore the poet, yet it is far from passive. Both the author poet and the listening audience are performances. The audience effectively stages its own reception, allowing the poet to script its semantic adventures as participant witnesses. All this takes place beyond an individual will and largely beyond a simple recording process. What we can do is to consider the metaperformative strategies in a particular poem read at a particular venue and speculate on the kinds of intersubjective formation that might be at work.

Intersubjectivity can be too ready to join in and empathize, and some poetries exploit this, notably the poetry of John Ashbery. He read with Denise Levertov at the 1985 Cambridge Poetry Festival, to a large respectful audience in the Cambridge Union debating hall. The venue was a strong reminder of undergraduate political debate, and the polished wooden paneling and seating evoked a feeling of permanence at odds with the event, and even more with Ashbery's preoccupation with the evanescence of experience. He looked a little frail beside Denise Levertov, and his poems sounded almost evasive compared with her firm self-assertions. On the BBC broadcast recording of his reading of "Vaucanson" from *April Galleons* his voice is quiet, very slightly elegiac, unemphatic.[80] There is no hint of chant or rhythmic pulse, just the clear enunciation of a man speaking in a reflective manner, about some unidentified writer who feels "relaxed and singular," and mistrusts the mood, convinced that he ought to be striving for understanding.

Vaucanson was an eighteenth-century inventor, most famous for his automatic duck that could eat, drink, and even excrete, but he was also, like his contemporaries, fascinated by the challenge of designing a machine that could speak recognizable words.[81] Such a machine would demonstrate the power of Enlightenment science. It would also have represented a challenge to its beliefs in the relation between the voice and reason. Ashbery uses the title allegorically, as if a useful adjective to describe the plight of a poet. His poem enables the audience to perform itself with a set of cues that work almost as stage directions, and then turns an unflattering mirror on its alleged self-indulgence toward both self-knowledge and art. From the start

Ashbery's presence offers a contrast to the scene depicted by the poem, a poet writing in a gray room, not a poet standing, talking, in a debating chamber. The first two lines are descriptive, but the third enacts a metadiscursive change of state: "But no one, of course, ever trusts these moods." Phrases like "of course," so ready in conversation, are rarely used in poetry, and commonly red-lined by editors and teachers, because they are redundant appeals by someone who is not sure enough of the argument to present it directly and falls back on an appeal to a putative consensus that it would supposedly be absurd to question, so the audience's complicity in this judgment is both taken for granted and made uneasy. This third line's direct proposition is given the full weight of the poet's authority by his presence, and brings the audience in on the wider argument, because presumably they too will want to affirm that they don't trust "these moods," and require "understanding" as well. We have been set up by the performance to demand understanding, and it follows that we even want to understand this poem, this very demand for understanding. Then the poem goes on to a larger proposition, which is offered as an apparent explanation of this will to knowledge:

> We are creatures, therefore we walk and talk
> And people come up to us, or listen
> And then move away

This is offered as if it were an explanation of why the writer in the gray room, and readers of the poem, and indeed people in general, all want to understand the relations among people, ideas, and things. In the recording, Ashbery pauses for longer after "creatures" than he does for the stanza breaks, allowing this word maximum air time to push listeners into a momentary contemplation of its resonance with the near homonyms "creators" and "created," as well as the implications of this fact. Standing there in front of his audience he models a bare account of human life as no more than a series of utterances and motions, colliding and rebounding. He himself is surely one of these creatures and we, the audience, "listen and then move away," figuratively through inattention or resistance, and literally by leaving at the end. The poem performed in this manner neatly places the audience in a narrative of its own making, making a prediction whose accuracy will soon be proven and therefore confirm the conclusions of the poem itself.

The poem then builds further on this foundation. Having taken over the broad outlines of the event with its proleptic narrative, it proceeds to imagine its relation to the space: "Music fills the spaces / Where figures are pulled to the edges, / And it can only say something." This admission of weakness, its inability to do more than "say something," is deceptive, as if more were somehow possible, and invites listeners to switch off all hermeneutic functions at once. It is deceptive because "saying something" is all that the poem can apparently do, and is usually taken to be an achievement. To say something is to say something worth hearing. The result is a kind of throwaway irony, as if all communication were a waste of time, and at the same time, as if it were boasting by understatement, in the way people say "it was nothing" when praised for their actions. Ashbery's line "it can only say something" also reverses Freud's dictum "where id was there shall ego be." Has the "it" finally found a voice in the person of the performer?

The final section invites the audience who have abandoned hope of understanding and hearing "something" said, to indulge in imaginary bodily sensations, of sun on one's shoulders, and thinking "good thoughts," only to reveal immediately that this would be self-deception. It is the sun which is doing the writing, "completing its trilogy," not the writer, poet, or listener. Enjoying the exalted mood leads immediately to absence, even of life, for if "life must be back there," someone is dead, or at least lacking in vitality. The listener who has been completely wrong-footed is offered a refuge in childishness, the whole performance to be ended in pretence, like a play, "by ringing down the curtain." The listeners in the poem, with whom the audience is encouraged to identify, would think that it had ended perfectly, wouldn't even notice, because they would not feel the guilt, dismay, or tragedy they ought to, "only the warm sunlight / That slides easily down shoulders / To the soft, melting heart." Thus the poem ends up enacting in an imaginary register its own staging and climax, and is able to underline this imaginary work it demands of the audience by the contrast with the absence of actual curtain and staging at the reading. Its allusion to the stage here, and the organization of performance by such external devices as the curtain, which functions as a period to the sentence of the drama, reflexively stages the adventures of the argument.

This authorial prestidigitation and the intersubjective coaxing into imagined moods, allows "Vaucanson" to gain a new dimension when performed in public. The identity of the poet in the gray room, who may or may not be Ashbery, because he may be referring to himself in the third person, or someone else, or a generic poet, becomes a question that the performance develops into a debate about the value of the activity itself. Perhaps being singular in the room rather than plural in the performance space is not the value it seems, or perhaps the testimony of the performance is biased. It surely depends on the work done in such rooms. "Vaucanson" anticipates performance and incorporates previous experiences of public reading while it stages an intersubjective melodrama in which the audience is constantly caught trying to indulge feelings it should not. It is a poem whose semantic range is extended by peformance, and when read silently, gestures at this absent occasion of its possible realizations. Much of this would escape most listeners who had never heard the poem, but typically the poem is then broadcast on the radio, remains in the memory, and is reread silently from a book, so that it becomes something larger than any single reading.

Poetry readings are part of the long biography of poems, part of the distribution from poet to readers, and readers to readers, which takes place through silent reading, memory, active analysis, discussion, performance, publication, and all the many processes whereby thoughts, feelings and knowledges circulate. The poem (like all texts) is a multidimensional entity, not reducible to one act of reading, one set of marks on one page, nor one poetry reading. J. Hillis Miller half-perceives this feature of texts when he says that once written, "the book is detached from its author and wanders here and there by itself in the world, having such unpredictable effects as it does have when it is read or misread, and even when it is not read at all,"[82] but this whimsical image of the wandering book is misleadingly singular. A much better image is that offered by Bruno Latour for the "quasi-object" or extended network that forms around a feature of the physical world, like the laser or gravity, so that an object, a social tie, a discourse and Being are all somehow intertwined. "This liaison of the four repertoires [i.e., material world, social world, discourse, Being] in the same networks . . . allows us to construct a dwelling large enough to house the Middle Kingdom, the authentic common home of the nonmodern world as well as its Constitution."[83] It exists in multiple locales at once, and has simultaneous receptions that develop both in and out of synch. Michael Davidson's distinction between Language Writers and the New American Poets, works with a distinction that, although it still somewhat reifies language, indicates how poetry has been working implicitly with such understanding: "Whereas gesture for the generation of Olson and Ginsberg implied single expressive moments, recorded spontaneously on the page and realized in the oral performance, for writers of a more recent generation gesture refers to the interactive, social web in which language exists."[84] And I would add, the poem itself. Instead of thinking of the poem as something that moves around being variously interpreted, read aloud, published in different forms, and generally provoking distinct interpretations, we might be better to think of it all as a large heteroclite entity, that mixes texts, people, performances, memories, and other possible affines, in a process that engages many people, perhaps only briefly, over a long period of time, whose outcomes are usually hard to see, and which has no clear boundaries, not the page, the reading, the critical study.[85] Then it is possible to say firmly that the poetry reading does change the meaning of the text because the poem is the totality of the field of these elements in time and space. That is its possible politics, its middle, which it shares with all texts, and which some contemporary poetries, especially the avant-gardes, have investigated with great care, persistence, and intelligence.

Conclusion

I will conclude with a statement I made in my earlier study of the theoretical issues raised by the practice of poetry readings, because it still summarizes the key points as best as I am able:

Performance is a moment when social interaction can study and celebrate itself and the poet is given significant new materials with which to extend the signifying field of the poem. Authorship and intersubjectivity collaborate with the implicit allegorisation of poetry's potential and actual place in everyday life. The unstable balance between the mimicry of expressive utterance that occurs when a poet reads a poem as if it were only then being spoken for the first time, and the self-alienation of reading a text written at another time as if by another self, offers a wide field of social and semantic significance for active poetic construction. The dramatisation of the moments at which subjectivity is generated in the relations between a speaker and an audience opens into a qualitatively different effect. The presentation of the poetry in a public space to an audience which is constituted by that performance for the time of the reading enables the poem to constitute a virtual public space which is, if not utopian, certainly proleptic of possible social change, as a part of its production of meaning. Part of what the poem means is what it means as an event in which individual identity is set alongside the group identification of an audience. Poetry readings foreground the ordinary processes whereby meanings are produced within linguistic negotiations between speakers in a textual culture, by balancing on the knife-edge boundary between two signifying media, sound and writing, at the moment of reception. Reading is made aware of itself as an activity organised by and within communities, and calling for a locally civic virtue. Poetry's oral stage is not therefore a childish regression to a mere babble of sound, because oral performance actually makes possible an extended semantic repertoire in which poetry fulfils more of its potentialities. Staging, authorship, sound and intersubjectivity, are constitutive elements of a poetry reading which are revealed as elements of reading itself, and reveal how much all reading, silent as well as public, depends on the network of hermeneutic communicative interactions within which we live. The different senses of the word "reading" turn out to be more than superficially related. Poems by contemporary poets use these resources projectively just as composers anticipate performances in their scores, because these are the conditions of contemporary reception. Readings are only the most salient form of oral circulation for their texts however, and even poets who never read their work in public still produce work for a culture which is not simply engaged in the direct interpretation of written texts as if they were mute objects waiting for a fairy tale reader to awaken them to life. Texts are already active projects, already on their way through an endlessly reconstitutive pattern of linguistic transactions which momentarily sustain meaning.

Who *was* that person at the front of this essay? What *is* the poem doing there? What does reading *do* to such people and poems? What happened in the middle?

NOTES

I would like to thank Charles Bernstein, Kathryn Burlinson, Cris Cheek, Allen Fisher, Ivan Gaskell, Gary Geddes, Robert Hampson, Peter Nichols, Denise Riley, for various kinds of assistance, and the organizers of "The Recovery of the Public World" conference in honor of Robin Blaser for the opportunity to try out an earlier version.

1. Catherine Bell, *Ritual Theory, Ritual Practice* (New York: Oxford University Press, 1992), p. 93.

2. These quotations are taken from Harold Garfinkel, *Studies in Ethnomethodology* (Cambridge [England]: Polity Press, 1984), p. 37. Garfinkel is talking about a typical "member of a society" rather than poets.

3. Katharyn Howd Machan, "Breath into Fire: Feminism and Poetry Readings," *Mid-American Review,* vol. 12, no. 2 (1992), pp. 120, 123.

4. Victor Turner, *The Anthropology of Performance* (New York: Performing Arts Journal Publication, 1986), p.22

5. Michel Deguy, interview with Gavronsky, in Serge Gavronsky *Towards a New Poetics: Contemporary Writing in France* (Berkeley: University of California Press, 1994), p. 71.

6. David Wojahn, "A Kind of Vaudeville: Appraising the Age of the Poetry Reading," *New England Review and Bread Loaf Quarterly,* vol. 8, no. 2 (1985), p. 268.

7. John Glassco, "A Real Good Noise: The Poet as Performer," in *The Insecurity of Art: Essays on Poetics,* ed. Ken Novies and Peter Van Toorn (Montreal: Véhicule Press, 1982), pp. 57–58.

8. Donald Hall, "The Poetry Reading: Public Performance/Private Art," *American Scholar,* vol. 54 (1985), p. 74.

9. Frederick C. Stern, "The Formal Poetry Reading," *The Drama Review,* vol. 35, no. 3 (fall 1991), pp. 77, 82.

10. Charles Olson, "Projective Verse," in *Selected Writings of Charles Olson,* ed. Robert Creeley (New York: New Directions, 1966), p. 16

11. Robert Creeley, "Louis Zukofsky: *All: The Collected Short Poems, 1923–1958,*" in *The Collected Essays of Robert Creeley* (Berkeley: University of California Press, 1989), p. 55.

12. Cited in Clayton Eshleman, *Antiphonal Swing: Selected Prose, 1962/1987,* ed. Caryl Eshleman (New York: McPherson, 1989), p. 41.

13. Douglas Oliver, "Poetry's Subject," *PN Review,* vol. 21, no. 7 (1995), p. 52.

14. Steve Benson, introductory note to "The Birds," *Language Alive,* no. 2 (1996), n.p.

15. See for example Andrew Parker and Eve Kosofsky Sedgwick, eds., "Introduction: Performance and Performativity," *Performativity and Performance* (New York: Routledge, 1995), pp. 1–18.

16. Judith Butler, *Bodies That Matter: On the Discursive Limits of "Sex"* (New York: Routledge, 1993), p. 12.

17. Transcribed from a tape of Steve McCaffery reading at the Assembling Alternatives conference, Durham, New Hampshire, August 30, 1996.

18. Gillian Rose, *The Broken Middle: Out of Our Ancient Society* (Oxford: Blackwell, 1992), p. xii.

19. Peter Middleton, "Poetry's Oral Stage," in *Performance and Authenticity in the Arts,* ed. Ivan Gaskell and Salim Kemal (Cambridge: Cambridge University Press, in press).

20. Denise Levertov, "An Approach to Public Poetry Listenings," in *Light Up the Cave* (New York: New Directions, 1981), p. 53.

21. J. H. Prynne, *Aristeas* (London: Ferry Press, 1968), pp. 13–17.

22. Allen Fisher, *Brixton Fractals* (London: Aloes Books, 1985).

23. Geoffrey Chaucer, *Canterbury Tales,* ed. A. C. Cawley (London: Dent, 1958), p. 158.

24. Lisa Robertson, *XEclogue* (Vancouver: Tsunami, 1993), n.p.

25. Michel de Certeau, *The Practice of Everyday Life,* tr. Steven F. Rendell (Berkeley: University of California Press, 1984), p. 32.

26. John Cage, "45′ for a Speaker," *Silence* (London: Marion Boyars, 1968), p. 176.

27. Carolee Schneeman, *More Than Meat Joy: Complete Performance Works and Selected Writings,* ed. Bruce McPherson (New York: Documentext, 1979), p. 18.

28. David Antin, *talking at the boundaries* (New York: New Directions, 1976).

29. Charles Olson, *Human Universe and Other Essays,* ed. Donald Allen (New York: Grove Press, 1967), p. 52.

30. George Economou, "Some Notes towards Finding a View of the New Oral Poetry," *boundary 2: The Oral Impulse in Contemporary American Poetry,* vol. 3 (1985), p. 655.

31. George Quasha, "Dialogos: Between the Written and the Oral in Contemporary Poetry," *New Literary History,* vol. 8 (1977), p. 488.

32. Jerome Rothenberg, "New Models, New Visions: Some Notes toward a Poetics of Performance," *Pre-Faces and Other Writings* (New York: New Directions, 1981), p. 165.

33. This was part of the statement on the masthead of *Alcheringa* Rothenberg cites it in "From a Dialogue on Oral Poetry with William Spanos," *Pre-Faces,* p. 31.

34. Talking of her parents, she says, "they loved to read aloud and so do I." In Janet Ruth Fallon, "Speaking with Susan Howe," *The Difficulties: Susan Howe Issue,* ed. Tom Beckett, vol. 3, no. 2 (1989), p. 41.

35. Frederick Stern, "The Formal Poetry Reading," *The Drama Review,* vol. 35, no. 3 (1991), p. 83.

36. Saint Augustine, *Confessions,* ed. Henry Chadwick (Oxford: Oxford University Press, 1991), p. 93.

37. Joyce Coleman, "The Solace of Hearing: Medieval Views on the Reading Aloud of Literature," *Nordic Yearbook of Folklore,* vol. 46 (1990), p. 126.

38. Roger Chartier, "Leisure and Sociability: Reading Aloud in Early Modern Europe," in *Urban Life in the Renaissance,* ed. S. Zimmerman and S. Weissman (Newark: University of Delaware Press, 1989), p. 107.

39. James Boswell, *Boswell's London Journal,* ed. Frederick A. Pottle (London: Heinemann, 1950), pp. 124–29.

40. Louis James, *Fiction for the Working Man, 1830–1850* (London: Oxford University Press, 1963), p. 8.

41. This and the remainder of the biographical information is taken from Paul Mariani, *William Carlos Williams: A New World Naked* (New York: McGraw-Hill, 1981). These details are taken from p. 137.

42. Jeffrey Weiss, *The Popular Culture of Modern Art: Picasso, Duchamp, and Avant-Gardism* (New Haven: Yale University Press, 1994), p. 5.

43. Robert S. Lynd and Helen Merrell Lynd, *Middletown in Transition: A Study in Cultural Conflicts* (New York: Harcourt Brace Jovanovich, [1937] 1965), p. 282.

44. Robert S. Lynd and Helen Merrell Lynd, *Middletown: A Study in American Culture* (New York: Harcourt, Brace, 1929), p. 233.

45. Carlo Ginzburg, *The Cheese and the Worms: The Cosmos of a Sixteenth-Century Miller,* tr. John and Anne Tedeschi (London: Routledge & Kegan Paul, 1980), p. xxii.

46. Michael Murphy, "On Not Reading Chaucer Aloud," *Medievalia,* vol. 9 (1987), pp. 205–23.

47. Alan T. Gaylord, "Reading Chaucer: What's Allowed in 'Aloud'?" *Chaucer Yearbook,* vol. 1 (1992), p. 109.

48. Jesper Svenbro, *Phrasikleia: An Anthropology of Reading in Ancient Greece,* tr. Janet Lloyd (Ithaca: Cornell University Press, 1993), p. 46.

49. William Carlos Williams to Ronald Lane Latimer, February 25, 1935, selected letters, p. 152–53; Mariani, 369.

50. Joan Richardson, *Wallace Stevens: The Later Years, 1923–1955* (New York: William Morrow, 1988), p. 225.

51. Tom Clark, *Charles Olson: The Allegory of a Poet's Life* (New York: Norton, 1991), p. 263.

52. Levertov, 46.

53. Yvor Winters, "The Audible Reading of Poetry," *Hudson Review* vol. 4, no. 3 (1951), p. 433.

54. J. F. Carpenter, *The Popular Elocutionist and Reciter* (London and New York: Frederick Warne, 1906), p. 25.

55. Aristotle, *Rhetoric,* tr. W. Rhys Roberts, 1403b 37–38, cited in Wilbur Samuel Howell, *Eighteenth-Century British Logic and Rhetoric* (Princeton: Princeton University Press, 1971), p. 152.

56. Thomas Sheridan, *A Discourse Being Introductory to His Course of Lectures on Elocution and the English Language* (Los Angeles: William Andrews Clark Memorial Library, Augustan Reprint Society, [1759] 1969), p. 52.

57. Alexander Melville Bell, *The Principles of Elocution* (New York: Edgar S. Werner, 1887), pp. 6–8, cited in Mary Margaret Robb, *Oral Interpretation of Literature in American Colleges and Universities* (New York: H. W. Wilson, 1941), p. 157.

58. William B. Chamberlain and Solomon H. Clark, *Principles of Vocal Expression* (Chicago: Foresman Scott, 1897), p. 386, cited in Robb, 176.

59. Henry James, "The Question of Our Speech," in *The Question of Our Speech: The Lesson of Balzac: Two Lectures* (Boston: Houghton Mifflin, 1905), p. 21.

60. Elsie Fogerty, *The Speaking of English Verse* (London: J. M. Dent, 1923). Cited in Evelyn M. Sivier, "English Poets, Teachers, and Festivals in 'A Golden Age of Poetry Speaking,' 1920–1950" in *Performance of Literature in Historical Perspectives,* ed. David W. Thompson (Lanham, Md.: University Press of America, 1983), p. 296.

61. Elsie Fogerty, *Rhythm* (London: George Allen & Unwin, 1937), p. 73.

62. John Masefield, *So Long to Learn: Chapters of an Autobiography* (London: Heinemann, 1952), p. 130.

63. John Masefield, cited in Clive Sansome, "Verse Speaking Today," in *Speech in our Time,* ed. Clive Sansome (London: Hinrichsen, 1948), p. 138.

64. Cited in Robb, 199. Clarence T. Simon, "Appreciation in Reading," *Quarterly Journal of Speech,* vol. 16 (1930), p. 185.

65. Leanne Hinton, Johanna Nichols, and John Ohala, "Introduction: Sound-Symbolic Processes," in *Sound Symbolism,* ed. Leanne Hinton, Johanna Nichols, and John Ohala (Cambridge: Cambridge University Press, 1994), p. 12.

66. Carl Sandburg, "Smoke and Steel" in *Modern American Poetry,* ed. Louis Untermeyer (New York: Harcourt Brace and Company, 1921), p. 201.

67. J. H. Prynne, "Stars, Tigers and the Shape of Words," the William Mat-

thews Lectures delivered at Birkbeck College, London [available from Birkbeck College], 1992.

68. Maggie O'Sullivan, "Hill Figures," in *Out of Everywhere: Linguistically Innovative Poetry by Women in North America and the U.K.,* ed. Maggie O'Sullivan (London: Reality Street Editions, 1996), pp. 70–71.

69. "The Responses project originated as an exploration of the ways people apprehend literature; of the processes of continuation that an engagement with texts provides; of the relationships (negative and positive) between writer and reader. This is not an anthology of contemporary poetry, it is an investigation into the union or interaction of creation and response, though some of the contributors are among the best and most interesting writers of today." Statement at the beginning of the *Complete Responses,* ed. Steven Pereira and Anthony Rollinson, 1992. The Maggie O'Sullivan issue was number 6, published 1991.

70. T. W. Adorno, *Aesthetic Theory,* tr. C. Lenhardt (London: Routledge, 1984), p. 56.

71. David R. Olson, "How Writing Represents Speech," *Language and Communication,* vol. 13, no. 1 (1993), p. 2.

72. Dennis Lee, "Writing in Colonial Space," in *The Post-Colonial Studies Reader,* ed. Bill Ashcroft, Gareth Griffiths, and Helen Tiffin (London: Routledge, 1995), p. 397.

73. Reuven Tsur, *What Makes Sound Patterns Expressive: The Poetic Mode of Speech Perception* (Durham, N.C.: Duke University Press, 1992), p. 11.

74. Roland Barthes, "The Grain of the Voice," *Image/Music/Text* (London: Fontana, 1977).

75. Albrecht Wellmer, "Truth, Semblance, Reconciliation: Adorno's Aesthetic Redemption of Modernity," in *The Persistence of Modernity* (Cambridge: Polity Press, 1991), p. 7.

76. Hugo Ball, quoted in *The Dada Painters and Poets: An Anthology,* 2nd ed., ed. Robert Motherwell (Cambridge, Mass.: Harvard University Press, 1981), p. xxvi.

77. David Appelbaum, *Voice* (Albany: State University of New York Press, 1990), p. 85.

78. The best discussion of this is in Thomas Nagel, *The View from Nowhere* (Oxford: Oxford University Press, 1986).

79. Pamela Clunies-Ross, "Promoting Poetry Events," in *Poetry Live: British and Irish Poetry,* ed. John Medlin (London: Poetry Society, 1987), p. 30.

80. John Ashbery, *April Galleons* (Manchester, England: Carcanet, 1988), pp. 25–26.

81. See Thomas L. Hankins and Robert J. Silverman, *"Vox Mechanica:* The History of Speaking Machines," in *Instruments and the Imagination* (Princeton: Princeton University Press, 1994).

82. J. Hillis Miller, *The Ethics of Reading: Kant, de Man, Eliot, Trollope, James, and Benjamin* (New York: Columbia University Press, 1987), p. 106.

83. Bruno Latour, *We Have Never Been Modern,* tr. Catherine Porter (Hemel Hempstead, England: Harvester Wheatsheaf, 1993), p. 89.

84. Michael Davidson " 'Skewed by Design': From Act to Speech Act in Language-Writing," *fragmente,* no. 2 (1990), p. 45.

85. Jonathan Morse presents compelling examples of the temporality of texts, which support this hypothesis. See Jonathan Morse, *Word by Word: The Language of Memory* (Ithaca: Cornell University Press, 1990).

13

Neon Griot

The Functional Role of Poetry Readings in the Black Arts Movement

LORENZO THOMAS

I

the gift and ministry of Song
Have something in them so divinely sweet,
It can assuage the bitterness of wrong

HENRY WADSWORTH LONGFELLOW

Before the twentieth century the two most widely known African American poets were Frances Ellen Watkins Harper (1825–1911) and Paul Laurence Dunbar (1872–1906). Harper was an accomplished elocutionist and—as with Ralph Waldo Emerson—her programs were not what we would call "poetry readings" per se. Her audiences could expect an abolitionist or feminist speech accompanied by poems composed on appropriate topics. Harper's practice was aimed at the harmonious alignment of head and heart. However, unlike Emerson's "Self-Reliance" and other lyceum circuit lectures that are now classic texts of American literature, it is Harper's widely circulated *Poems on Miscellaneous Subjects* (first published in 1854 and revised and reprinted for several decades thereafter) that still commands attention. While much of her work, like the eloquent poem "The Slave Mother," resembled Harriet Beecher Stowe's campaign to persuade white Americans that slavery must be seen as intolerable, some of her writing was intended very specifically for African Americans. In a recent biography of Harper, Melba Joyce Boyd comments: "Because most black folks were illiterate or in the process of pursuing literacy, the invention of a characteristic voice was needed to carry Harper's message and to bridge the cultural distance between standard English and black dialect. Hence, *Sketches of Southern Life* [1872] was composed in the language of the people as reflected in the slave narrative of a newly literate woman with similar experiences and a familiar voice."[1] Harper, intending this book for use in adult literacy programs, employed standard spelling to avoid the "overapostrophied" conventions of dialect fiction, depending instead on word order and syntax that would "assure a folk pronunciation" of the poems (Boyd, 156).

In much the way that writing teachers know that students tend to write just as they speak, Boyd suggests that Harper felt beginning readers would benefit from a primer that, when actually read aloud, sounded like their own accustomed style of speech. Identifying this early attempt to demystify the mechanics of literacy leads Boyd to a more generalized statement about dialect that raises many questions: "The dialectics of dialect poetry operates within a cultural and a linguistic framework, and the nineteenth-century American writer who strove to authenticate indigenous speech had to abandon imperialist perceptions of the English language and consider the American language as a departure in cultural values and expression" (151–52). While Boyd imputes this view to Harper, many would also see it operative in Mark Twain's celebration of regional speech. It has also been suggested by Margaret Walker and others that a similar motive underlies the more apparently "entertaining" dialect poems of Paul Laurence Dunbar. While Boyd's understanding of Frances E. W. Harper's attempt at capturing the vernacular is contextualized by Boyd's own apprenticeship as a Black Arts Movement poet, it is not at all the sort of ahistorical reading that mars some recent postmodernist criticism. The point is that we cannot assume — even in nineteenth-century texts — that the use of dialect is necessarily humorous or intended to ridicule the people who speak it.

That one should tread upon this ground with care is suggested also by Paul H. Gray's investigation of the "poet-performer movement" that lasted from 1870 to 1930 and involved the careers of Will Carleton, Ella Wheeler Wilcox, James Whitcomb Riley, Vachel Lindsay, and others. This "movement," writes Gray, was self-consciously and deliberately "low-brow," seeking a following among neither the readers nor the writers of traditional poetry. Instead, it aimed unerringly at the *petite bourgeoisie* — farmers, merchants, salesmen, and housewives — people who claimed they hated poetry but flocked by the thousands to hear these poets perform and then bought their books by the millions.

Gray makes two important points about this movement that may, in fact, also tell us something about the popular arts in general. First, success "depended as much on the poet's ability to perform his work as to write it"; and, second, "the kind of poetry the movement produced *and* the poetic careers it shaped were remarkably homogeneous."[2]

It is important to understand what success meant in this context. Detroit newspaperman Will Carleton, for example, was earning almost $500 a week in 1871 for nightly readings of his dialect monologues in rhymed couplets; and in 1873 his collection *Farm Ballads* sold forty thousand copies. Carleton himself saw his work as a commodity and his success dependent upon "a keen sense of the public taste" and his ability to satisfy it (Gray, 2–3). Gray refuses to dismiss Carleton's position as merely crass, noting that one reason for his popularity was that Midwestern audiences "were amazed and delighted to discover through Carleton's verses that their own lives and region could be a fit topic for poetry" (4). Furthermore, Carleton's poems dealt with realistic incidents of American life. But while Carleton was able to offer rhymes on divorce, frustration in business, and destitution in old age (albeit with happy endings), his most successful competitors were less probing about society.

James Whitcomb Riley, for example, was master of a type of homespun sentimentality that owed some of its popularity to the fact that it could be easily copied. "The Old Swimmin'-Hole" (1883) became something of a classic:

> But the lost joy is past! Let your tears in sorrow roll
> Like the rain that ust to dapple up the old swimmin'-hole.[3]

Riley's poetry celebrates itself as pure nostalgia:

> The simple, soul-reposing glad belief in everything,—
> When life was like a story, holding neither sob nor sigh,
> In the golden olden glory of the days gone by.[4]

It is worth noting that Riley spent several years touring as a salesman with medicine shows and that his Hoosier dialect poems were published in the fictitious guise of unsolicited contributions from a rural subscriber. In a sense he took F. E. W. Harper's conceit in *Sketches of Southern Life* a step further. While her poems are written in a voice that seems as if it could be that of her protagonist Aunt Chloe, Riley's impersonation of his reader's voice extended to the reputed authorship of the poems themselves.[5]

In any case, Riley was the most widely read poet in the United States in the 1880s and his influence can readily be seen in the work of Paul Laurence Dunbar and others. Dunbar's publishers, for example, emulated Riley's habit of issuing collections in December to accommodate Christmas shoppers and, beginning with *Candle-Lightin' Time* (1902), Dunbar published several beautifully illustrated volumes clearly intended as gift books.[6] Whatever contemporary readers may think of their poetry, which is not comparable in skill or message to Emerson's or Mrs. Harper's, Will Carleton and James Whitcomb Riley were indeed consummate *performers* who— in an age before radio and television—utilized the skills of oratory and dramatic presentation to fashion evenings of satisfying entertainment that were advertised to the public as poetry readings (Gray, 9).

Dunbar's performances were of a quite different nature. Though he was opinionated and outspoken on social and political issues, Dunbar's readings were straightforward recitals of his poems—written in dialect and standard traditional stanzaic forms. Because he was a talented humorist, Dunbar's recitals were above all entertaining; but his was clearly always entertainment with a message. In choosing to write in dialect, Dunbar was certainly attempting to reach a large public. When he was growing up in the 1880s, Joel Chandler Harris's Uncle Remus books were best-sellers, and Negro dialect was also part of poet James Whitcomb Riley's popular repertoire. But those who thought Dunbar's dialect poems somehow glorified slavery days or the antebellum South were mistaken. His message, made explicit in his journalistic pieces, was a celebration of African American kinship and strong, moral families and communities. If the communal joy depicted in such poems had been possible for unsophisticated rural blacks, certainly Dunbar's audiences would be led to think that an educated, empowered people could do as well or better. Dunbar's was a double-coded message, but it said the same thing to everybody.

While Dunbar achieved fame with white audiences, he was beloved in the black community (with fraternal lodges and cultural organizations being named for him in his own lifetime). He was proud, also, that African American high school and college students earned funds for themselves and their school organizations by presenting recitals of his poems. Dunbar authored some eloquent and lasting protest poems such as "Sympathy" and "We Wear the Mask," but he was most often concerned with drawing attention to the minor hypocrisies of daily life, the moments when

> As you breathe some pretty sentence, though she hates you all the while,
> She is very apt to stun you with a made to order smile[7]

There is little doubt that such poems were suitable for the audiences—both black and white—and venues of Dunbar's national tours. It is not a negative criticism to conclude that Dunbar had not only made a careful study of the literary marketplace but that he knew his audience and understood the most effective way to communicate his message.

If his reception in Houston in 1932 is any indication, Langston Hughes's celebrity in the African American community was the equal of Dunbar's. Sponsored by the local YMCA and YWCA branches, Hughes's appearance was highly publicized for weeks in advance and the city's Pilgrim Auditorium attracted a capacity crowd. Audiences responded to Hughes's urbanity and handsomeness as much as to his poetry. After the reading, Carter Wesley editorialized in the Houston *Informer:* "There was a purposefulness about the man and his work that gave us the key to his success. He had been to Africa and to parts of the West Indies, where Negroes live. He went because he wanted to know the black man everywhere." "Perhaps," wrote reporter Bernice Johnson, "Langston Hughes cannot be called great now. He lacks that maturity, that ripening, that tolerance that comes with age. But he understands his people."[8]

Hughes understood what his audience wanted. Fashionable and debonair, employing a slightly sardonic tone, he read his poems with precise and elegant diction—even those written in the blues stanza form. His purpose was not to impersonate the unlettered, but to elevate their idiom to a plane where its poetic qualities would be recognized. While many of his poems are in his own male voice, the blues poems often present a female persona; and Hughes also wrote dramatic monologues with specific social types as speakers. Individually these poems resemble Robert Browning's "My Last Duchess," but together, as in the 1931 collection *The Negro Mother and Other Dramatic Recitations* (intended for the use of schoolchildren), they depict a cross-section of the African American community. Very few of these monologues, however, are as perfectly crafted as Hughes's memorable "Mother to Son" (1922). In all of his poetry, and in his performance style, the character and experience of his personae are revealed by the words Langston Hughes has chosen for them, not by a stage accent.

Poetry recitals provided Hughes with much of his income throughout his life and he never deviated from the mode he had established on his first national tour in 1932; nor would his audiences have allowed it. Recalling a visit Hughes made to Detroit in 1961, Woodie King Jr. noted that the poet was a genuine celebrity among ordinary people, "the factory workers, the car washers, the day workers, domestics, bartenders . . . They knew one of his poems or one of his short stories or one of his plays or some of Simple they had read in the Chicago *Defender*."[9] King and his circle of local artists (including Margaret Danner and Ron Milner) wanted to meet Hughes but worried that he might be too much a celebrity, that "the new mayor and the middle-class Negro doctors and lawyers [had] cornered him" (21). Of course, that wasn't the case; Hughes welcomed the young poets into his hotel suite as if that had been the real purpose of his visit.

In some ways, the showmanship has been damaging. To the extent that poetry readings have been perceived as entirely secondary to the existence of poems as printed texts, very little attention has been directed to possible impact of performance contexts on poetic composition. As Kristin M. Langellier has shown, even scholarship in the discipline of speech communication is only slowly beginning to concern itself with this question.[10] But literary critics who see themselves as activists for innovation sometimes claim more for the contemporary practice of the oral presentation of poetry than they should. Reporting on "the scene" in the early 1960s, art critic John Gruen was noticeably underwhelmed by the Monday night open poetry readings in New York's East Village: "At the Metro, located on Second Avenue at East Tenth Street, you sip coffee and are treated to hours of poetic verbiage, most of it of the therapeutic, pretentiously self-purging variety. As for performance there are very few nascent Dylan Thomases. Frequently they know not when to stop, and then an aura of impatience and frustration makes itself felt."[11] In his *Tales of Beatnik Glory,* Ed Sanders also wickedly lampooned the modes of staged solipsism likely to be exhibited on such evenings.[12] When these coffeehouse poetry readings first reemerged in the 1950s, however, the aura was much more electric.

II

> What we have suffered from, is manuscript, press, the removal of verse from its producer and its reproducer, the voice.
>
> CHARLES OLSON, *Projective Verse*

> And we were there, lost in the sound of a beat
>
> BOB KAUFMAN

What Werner Sollors has described as the "centrality" of African Americans in the avant-garde movement called the Beat Generation was partly metaphoric because the Beats had chosen to move to the margins of mainstream society and to adopt the aesthetic of African American music as the principle of their artistic efforts.[13] It was also true that the Beats were probably the first group of so-called white people who—past the age of puberty—actually knew some black people as individuals, equals, and sometimes even lovers. By the same token, young black people involved in the movement would have to be the most completely "integrated" African Americans of that era. To appreciate the historical context, one might recall that it was only in 1948 that the U.S. Army was integrated, following an executive order from President Harry Truman.

That the United States at mid-century should have produced poets who did not think of their work as "high art" is not surprising inasmuch as the notion can be traced to Emerson's rejection of European "cultivation" in favor of an indigenous and energetic American inventiveness. In the late 1940s, John A. Kouwenhoven pointed out that cinema and jazz—the twentieth-century artforms that most fascinated young poets—were both "products of the interaction of the vernacular and cultivated tradition," which are nonetheless perceived primarily as *vernacular forms* "suitable for mass participation and enjoyment and so universally acceptable."[14] African American poets, particularly because of their interest in jazz, found it easy to develop similar ideas. Indeed, Amiri Baraka has suggested that one of the goals of the Black Arts Movement was the creation of "a mass art."[15]

As far as the general public was concerned, the Beat Generation was Jack Kerouac, Allen Ginsberg, and the mediagenic Ted Joans. It is not negative criticism to say that Ted Joans's masterpiece was the creation of Ted Joans; after all, carefully orchestrated eccentricity in the pursuit of publicity is no vice. Joans was a welcome incarnation of an ancient Greenwich Village lineage and his genial rebellion perfectly suited the Eisenhower era—which is why his photo wound up in Life magazine. Joans's persona was something like Bobby Troup under ultraviolet light. Even so, he was ahead of his time because the rest of us didn't get black light until the sixties. Many of Joans's poems from the 1950s seem like material for standup comedy—lacking the manic quality of Hugh Romney or the subtlety of Dick Gregory—but a pretty good warm-up act (if anyone had been paying attention) for Richard Pryor. Though described by journalists as an apolitical movement, it is clear that demanding the freedom to pursue interracial relationships (including romances) was part of the Beat nonconformity—as can be seen in Joans's poetry and in Kerouac's little masterpiece *The Subterraneans* (1958).

The Beats were interested in restructuring the poetry reading as something other than a genteel diversion. In New York, with the help of a young lawyer named Ed Koch, they fought City Hall and won a campaign to exempt Greenwich Village coffeehouses from the city's post-Prohibition cabaret license law. Sure, poetry readings should be entertaining, but the poets argued that they were also "art." The energy and funds came from the coffeehouse owners, of course, but this successful crusade represents the full measure of Beat political activism in the 1950s.[16]

In California, recalling the Six Gallery reading in October 1955 where Allen Ginsberg first recited *Howl,* Kenneth Rexroth ecstatically reported, "What happened in San Francisco first and spread from there across the world was public poetry, the return of a tribal, preliterate relationship between poet and audience."[17] The Beat innovation was, perhaps, returning poetry to the bacchanalian atmosphere of saloons, coffeehouses, and low-rent Friday-night house parties. The mainstream press in the late 1950s titillated readers with accounts of poets disrobing and other notorious occurrences. Charles Bukowski—the last bonafide bum "poet"—turned this aspect of the Beat legend into a vaudeville act, appearing in saloons across the country in the late 1970s. At one such appearance in Tallahassee, the "poetry reading" degenerated into little more than Bukowski trading chug-a-lugs and insults with the fraternity boys who filled the ringside tables. Here, the relationship between poet and audience was decidedly subliterate.

But even genuine Beat poets sometimes had to participate in the poetry reading as "cultural event." When Ginsberg, Gregory Corso, and Peter Orlovsky gave a reading at Columbia University, Diana Trilling's review of the evening in *Partisan Review* might have had a greater impact than the reading itself. Trilling coyly admitted knowing Ginsberg only as a "troublesome student" from a decade earlier, but also managed to discern from his appearance on the platform where T. S. Eliot had stood "that Ginsberg had always desperately wanted to be respectable, or respected, like his teachers at Columbia." What Trilling's article demonstrates most profoundly is that audiences hear what they want to hear.[18]

One would hardly expect to find the decorum built into an Ivy League university auditorium in a jazz nightclub, but the idea of respectability pulled out of the hat by Diana Trilling was also quite strenuously pursued by Kenneth Rexroth in an *Esquire* article. On one hand, Rexroth stressed an antiacademic theme. "Jazz poetry reading," he declared, "puts poetry back in the entertainment business where it was with Homer and the troubadours. Even Victorian epics like *Idylls of the King* and *Evangeline* were written to be read to the whole family around the fire in the evening by papa—not, certainly, to be studied for their ambiguities by a seminar . . ." On the other hand, as a jazz poet himself, Rexroth wanted respect. "Rehearsals," he assured, "are pretty elaborate, far more finicky than the average band rehearsal." In fact, he noted with pride, "jazz poetry is an exacting, cooperative, precision effort, like mountaineering."[19] Despite such precision, Rexroth's week at the 5 Spot was nowhere near as memorable as Thelonious Monk's wordless and continually extended residency or July 1961's intricately spontaneous Eric Dolphy/Booker Little performances that yielded four LPs that still amaze even those who long ago memorized every note. As one critic put it, Rexroth "knocked out the poetry fans" but left jazz fans unimpressed.[20] One of the reasons might have been that there was jazz in the room, but not in his poems.

Perhaps the most influential experiment of this kind was Charles Mingus's 1960 recording *A Modern Symposium of Music and Poetry*. Despite the pretentious title, it was a well-realized and swinging piece of work. As Ross Russell wrote in *Jazz Review:* "The script for *Scenes in the City* was conceived and written by actor Lonne Elder in collaboration with Langston Hughes and is narrated by Melvin Stewart. It is a rambling, introspective monologue of a young man of the city, any city, whose thoughts and dreams have been influenced by jazz, and it is a skillful amalgam of Harlem vernacular, Tin Pan Alley references, and believable bits of everyday speech."[21] If Russell makes this seem a bit like an audio version of Hughes's *The Sweet Flypaper of Life* (1955), that is not at all inappropriate. What is most important about Elder's *Scenes in the City,* however, is that the narrative structure follows the logical collage of a jazz solo; and Mingus's musical setting brilliantly complements and underscores both the spoken cadences and the meaning of the monologue. Though this was an enormously influential work, most poets who later attempted to capture the mood of jazz or to work with musicians chose to employ a more declamatory style—even with similarly personal material.

Bob Kaufman is the exemplar of the Beat commitment to an oral poetry. Capable of extemporizing astonishing poems, he not only memorized his own compositions but was fond of reciting the works of Federico Garcia Lorca and other poets at length. Kaufman was an electrifying performer even in his declining years, as poet Kaye McDonough reported:

> The dynamite volcano is not extinct
> We heard you at Vesuvio's
> singing Hart Crane
> You blew America from your mouth
> and smiled your ancient vision
> round a shocked barroom[22]

There is a direct line between the Beat poets and the Black Arts Movement. Amiri Baraka—whose enduring stylistic influence on younger poets is matched only by John Ashbery's—was a key figure in both movements; and the document that expressed the poetic theory of both movements was Charles Olson's 1950 essay "Projective Verse," which Baraka resurrected from the pages of Rolf Fjelde's *Poetry New York* magazine and published in his Totem Press chapbook series in 1959. Speaking for the poets included in Donald Allen's *The New American Poetry, 1945–1960,* Baraka stated: "we want to go into a quantitative verse . . . the 'irregular foot' of Williams . . . the 'Projective Verse' of Olson. Accentual verse, the regular metric of rumbling iambics, is dry as slivers of sand."[23] By the end of the decade this view would also be seconded by young African American poets across the country.[24]

Because it mimics Ezra Pound's authoritarian tone, Olson's essay strikes many recent readers as windy and offensively "patriarchal"; but the widespread impact of Olson's ideas is undeniable. Since every young writer in the United States goes through an e. e. cummings period and a Carl Sandburg and/or Gertrude Stein phase, any perceived affinity between Olson's prosody and those models (even if mistaken) couldn't hurt. Certainly the most significant and unimpeachable idea in Olson's essay—essentially a reiteration of a point made in Pound's edition of Ernest Fenollosa's *The Chinese Written Character as a Medium for Poetry* (first published in 1936 and reprinted by Lawrence Ferlinghetti's City Lights in 1958)—declares that poetry is an act of *speech,* that its element is *breath,* and that *writing* it down is a skill. Simplistic as that statement may first appear, it was soon shown to have far-reaching philosophical and—as redefined by African American poets—political implications.

In 1964 Amiri Baraka, Steve Kent, Larry Neal, Askia Muhammad Touré, and several others established an arts center in a Harlem brownstone. The Black Arts Repertory Theatre/School (BARTS) collapsed in clouds of notoriety in less than a year, but by 1968 there was a nationwide network of similar theater groups, poetry workshops, and groups organized by musicians and visual artists. This Black Arts Movement embraced many divergent tendencies. Perhaps the one thing that all of its participants agreed on was that art was—and should be—a political act. In his 1968 essay "The Black Arts Movement," Larry Neal declared: "the political values inherent in the Black Power concept are now finding concrete expression in the aesthetics of Afro-American dramatists, poets, choreographers, musicians, and novelists. A main tenet of Black Power is the necessity for black people to define the world in their own terms. The black artist has made the same point in the context of aesthetics."[25]

It would simplify the literary historian's task if we could say that the theme of "separation" employed by Black Arts writers was, like the "newness" of the verse published in Harriet Monroe's *Poetry* magazine, merely a polemical conceit. It wasn't. In the case of Black Arts Movement activities, rhetoric often conformed to reality. Nor was this only the fault of the poets: even now, except for a sentence in the biographical note on Amiri Baraka, you probably won't find the Black Arts Movement mentioned in college texts that supposedly introduce students to twentieth-century American literature.

While the movement rejected mainstream America's ideology, deeming it inimical to black people, Black Arts poets maintained and developed the prosody they had acquired from Black Mountain and the Beats. Even this fact, however, tended to cause dismay and some anxiety in literary circles. Ted Berrigan recalled an afternoon at Frank O'Hara's apartment spent talking poetry and art world gossip. Suddenly another friend of O'Hara's bounded up the stairs and burst into the room, heart attack if you don't slow down written across his face.

"Amiri Baraka's on the radio," the man gasped, red with alarm, "and he's talking about killing white people!"

"Well," said Frank consolingly, "I don't think he will begin with you or me. Now sit down and have some wine."

Not everyone is blessed with Frank's gift for nonchalance and the efforts made by Baraka and others to distance themselves from the Beats and downtown avant-garde created resentments and hurt feelings in many relationships. Some suffered through strained or ruined friendships; a few welcomed hatred. Many succumbed to the bad American idea that mutual mistrust is the same thing as civility, that optimism is a sign of deviancy or brain damage. Dudley Randall summarized the inner turmoil of the era with remarkable objectivity. Black poets, he wrote in 1971, "have absorbed the techniques of the masters, have rejected them, and have gone in new directions. Perhaps this rejection had its roots in the [Civil Rights] movement of the fifties and sixties. When the poets saw the contorted faces of the mobs, saw officers of the law commit murder, and 'respectable' people scheme to break the law (there was no cry for law and order then), perhaps they asked themselves, Why should we seek to be integrated with such a society?"[26]

With self-anointed missionary fervor, Black Arts poets extended the venues for their performances beyond storefront theaters to neighborhood community centers, church basements, taverns, and to the streets. Not surprisingly, the dominant mode of the poetry that proved effective in such settings drew upon the rhetorical conventions of the black church, which is the matrix of African American culture. Exhortation and easily accessible satire, appropriate and time-honored techniques of streetcorner orators, also became a notable element of this poetry. While these are natural developments, it is also true that the idea that "Form is never more than an extension of content"[27] endured serious stress during the Black Arts Movement. As the poets moved toward the African American vernacular, it also became necessary to find ideological rationalizations for employing forms that came from the same black church the poets were otherwise fond of denouncing.

As Henry Louis Gates Jr. eloquently and succinctly puts it, "the Church is at once a culture and a black cultural event, a weekly unfolding of ritual and theater, oratory and spectacle, the most sublime music, and even dance."[28] Indeed, whether or not one is religious, the influence of the black church within the African American community is basic and unavoidable.

One can hear the rich, emphatic voice that distinguishes much Black Arts poetry in the speeches of Martin Luther King Jr. Listening to a sermon such as "I'm into Something I Can't Shake Loose" by W. C. Thomas Jr. of the Canaan Baptist Church in Dayton, Ohio—Paul Laurence Dunbar's hometown—allows one to experience the full power of the African American sermonic tradition.[29] What you hear is the speaking voice that trespasses into song; and an antiphonal interaction with the congregation that reveals the same structures that inform the early "collective improvisation" of New Orleans jazz, bebop, and the avant-garde jazz of the 1960s.

Among the factors that influenced the developmental direction of Black Arts poetry were (1) the model of African American music—particularly jazz; (2) an interest in finding and legitimizing an "authentic" African American vernacular speech; and (3) the material or physical context of Black Arts poetry readings. In her useful study of African American theatre, Genevieve Fabre has pointed out that in the work of poets such as Baraka, Sonia Sanchez, and Marvin X, "theatre and poetry exchange customary structures and images." Beyond the fact that the neighborhood Black Arts theaters were most usually the site of readings rather than fully staged dramatic productions, Fabre notes: "The dramatization drawn from poetry and the use of lyrical modes on the stage are evident in the public reading. Read aloud, poetry becomes theatre. Black theatre thus embraces both dramatic poems and 'pure' plays. Which form is used will be determined by the message the theatre wants to communicate."[30] Perhaps even more importantly, the poetry reading as a characteristic mode of *publication* reinforced poets' tendency to employ "dramatic" structures and direct first-person address. The apostrophic mode was made obsolete by the presence of an audience prepared (and encouraged) to play the role of "amen corner."

The link between poetry and drama was evident not only in the way some poets wrote plays—Baraka's *Dutchman* (1964) and Sanchez's *Sister Son/ji* (1969) were both composed in night-long bursts of creativity, not in actors' workshops and rehearsals—but also in commercially successful plays such as Ntozake Shange's *for colored girls who have considered suicide when the rainbow is enuf* (1976) and Melvin Van Peebles's *Ain't Supposed to Die a Natural Death* (1973), both of which are actually staged poetry readings, collections of dramatic monologues assigned for recitation to different "characters."

Just as Dunbar's poetic production was cannily and problematically divided between dialect poems and lyrics in standard English, so does Amiri Baraka's poetry occupy two modes: intensely personal lyrics and incisively political social comment. The persona of Baraka's lyrics, however, is always clearly in this world now and the result is that his poems have both a universal and social comment dimension as well. It is not surprising that Baraka brought something of his ideas —as expressed in his bifurcated poetic output—to the developing Black Arts aesthetic.

Baraka had expressed this idea in a different rhetorical style in 1970. "There is not such thing as Art and Politics, there is only life," he wrote. "If the artist is the raised consciousness, then all that he touches, all that impinges on his consciousness, must be raised. We must be the will of the race toward evolution. We must demand the spiritual by being spiritual. THE LARGEST WORK OF ART IS THE WORLD ITSELF."[31]

The practical application of such ideas was not quite as chimerical as some readers might expect. In a 1973 article on Miami's Theatre of Afro Arts (TAA)—one of more than 150 such organizations then in operation— Eddie Osborne stated that Black Arts activists understood that "art definitely is not the revolution": "The founders of the TAA acknowledged this fact from the start, but they were also aware that art could, nevertheless, play a decisive role in the revolution; that art was an excellent means of interpreting the black experience to the masses, while at the same time fostering the principles of work, struggle, and self-determination."[32]

Transforming the poetry reading from an event suited to a genteel parlor or even a rowdy bohemian artists' and models' night out was soon an important goal of the movement and was rationalized by the political thrust of the developing "Black Aesthetic." Readings in nontraditional venues were now invested with a strategic value and it is worth spending the effort to understand why.

The antibourgeois stance of the Black Arts Movement and its dismissal of the Harlem Renaissance as a failure was not merely an expression of generational revolt; it was also a carefully considered political position. In *The Negro Novel in America,* Robert A. Bone had stated: "The early novelists were loyal members of the middle-class who desired only equal rights within the status quo. The younger writers of the 1920's were the second generation of educated Negroes; they were the wayward sons of the rising middle-class."[33] Bone points out that "the parents of the Renaissance novelists were 55 per cent professionals and 45 per cent white collar" and concludes that Langston Hughes, Jean Toomer, and Countee Cullen "were rebelling against their fathers and their fathers' way of life" (412). At this point Bone invokes psychology, but it might have been even more appropriate to compare these writers to contemporaries who made similar decisions: Hart Crane, for example, or (in an interestingly subversive way) Wallace Stevens.

In New York, however, when Baraka and his group abandoned Greenwich Village for Harlem, they also rejected the bohemian option in favor of a unique position that, however quixotically, denied the notion of avantgarde marginality. In recalling the early activities of the Black Arts group, Baraka stated:

> But that one glorious summer of 1965, we did, even with all that internal warfare, bring advanced Black art to Harlem. We organized, as part of HARYOU/ACT, the nation's 1st anti-poverty program, a summer arts program called Operation Boot Strap (under the overall direction of Adam Clayton Powell's point cadre, Judge Livingston Wingate). For eight weeks, we brought Drama, Poetry, Painting, Music, Dance, night after night all across Harlem. We had a fleet of five trucks and stages created with banquet tables. And each night our five units would go out in playgrounds, street corners, vacant lots, play streets, parks, bringing Black Art directly to the people.[34]

Those days may not have been as halcyon as recalled here, but the artistic offerings were uncompromisingly avant-garde and surprisingly well received by the audiences.

If Langston Hughes's triumphal 1932 tour epitomizes the national impact of the Harlem Renaissance, then two events might indicate the scope of the Black Arts Movement. One of these was "Black Spirits: A Festival of New Black Poets." This well-attended three-day festival held at New York's New Federal Theatre in 1971 was produced by Woodie King Jr. and featured readings by a cross-section of Black Arts poets including Baraka, Ed Bullins, Mari Evans, the original Last Poets (reading together and individually), and many others. King also amplified the impact of the event by producing a record album, issued by a division of Motown Records, and an anthology published by the Vintage paperback imprint of Random House. The other event was a reading by Amiri Baraka at a community center in Newark on a cold Christmas Eve in 1966. That reading was attended by neighborhood residents—teenagers, women with small children, a number of senior citizens. It was a small crowd, but not disappointingly so; about the number of folks who regularly turn up at twelve-step meetings or county commissioner's hearings.[35] Both of these events were notable for the enthusiasm of the audiences and the huge New York poetry festival was actually only a media-visible manifestation of the many grassroots events like the Newark reading.

At the grassroots level the Black Arts Movement was a genuinely national movement. Chicago's Affro-Arts, housed in a refurbished movie theater, was directed by jazz musician Philip Cohran. A veteran of Sun Ra's Arkestra, Cohran was also connected to the avant-garde Association for the Advancement of Creative Musicians (AACM), whose performing unit was known as the Art Ensemble of Chicago. Among the young people who benefited from the Affro-Arts music workshops were Maurice White and others who later achieved popular success as Earth Wind & Fire—a band that, without issuing manifestos, subtly disseminated Black Arts ideas more widely.[36] In Brooklyn's Bedford-Stuyvesant neighborhood, a coffeehouse called The East often featured poet Yusuf Rahman and filled every evening of the week with concerts, plays, poetry readings, lectures on history, and community organizing on local political issues. The East also published a magazine called *Black News* and was a center for visual artists.

Located in two renovated movie theaters and a warehouse building, Houston's Black Arts Center was an artists collective and a school: Loretta Devine and Mikell Pinckney taught drama; at various times Rahsaan Connell Linson, Thomas Meloncon, Harvey King, and I taught creative writing or organized literary events. In addition to music and dance workshops there was also Robert Gossett—a dauntingly versatile art teacher who held an M.F.A. in painting, was an excellent woodcarver, and also a competent ceramicist. All of this was somehow held together by Lloyd Choice, Neva Deary, Robert Becnel, and Mickey Leland (who started out as a poet and later became a U.S. congressman). Houston's BAC was dependent on funding from antipoverty agencies and arts patronage resulting in a fragile, if not unwieldly, structure. As with similar groups in other southern cities, there was no real antagonism between the BAC and other local arts groups; while firm in its aesthetic philosophy, the Black Arts Center was simply another part of the city's cultural variety.

In Houston in the early 1970s, bars such as Sand Mountain and the Hard Thymes Soup Kitchen were venues for weekly poetry readings. These were extremely democratic events attended by a crowd that included a few settled Southern beatniks (folks who knew Jon and "Gypsy" Lou Webb and the old-school New Orleans bohemians), Poetry Society of Texas members, and kids who had missed the Summer of Love but were doing their damnedest to make up for it. Attending such an evening allowed one to hear a wide variety of oral presentation styles—and among the most riveting of these were the performances of African American poets such as Edgar Jones.

A teenager who wandered into Houston's Black Arts Center in the early 1970s, Jarbari Aziz Ra was interested in poetry and music. He left Texas on a basketball scholarship and found his vocation in Chicago's Organization of Black American Culture (OBAC) poetry workshops.

Jarbari Aziz Ra's "A Writer's Statement" self-reflexively touches on the idea of "taking the poem off the page" as well as issues of censorship, the social utility of art, and the function of poetry itself:

> unable to cry poems the broke
> have no time, no ears, only eyes which become weary to glitter
> seeing no merit in ink on poems i color black,
> so if obscene today is also absurd, then let these pulse-beats be
> hieroglyphic notes for your momma, i need not leave too many
> hostile reasons for tomorrow's Black world as they shall have more
> than enough, i will only tell them my words were Black Dancing Trees
> sprouting branches dancing skyward hope filled to touch God's face [37]

This poem perfectly demonstrates the method used in creating poems expressly designed for oral presentation. The poem's technique is, to use Ra's own terminology, hieroglyphic. It is analogous to a jazz solo: Ra's glossolalic rush of rhythm contains a bidialectical alternation of slang and archly formal English as a vehicle for allusions and phrases that invite several differing but simultanous interpretations. Like the musical ideas in an Eric Dolphy or John Coltrane solo—as likely to be Eastern motifs or snatches of Tin Pan Alley standards—the glissando of allusions slide one upon the other, "faster than a bible shooting blanks / from a preacher's machine gun mouth" (11–12), echoing the dozens and Langston Hughes, Joyce Kilmer and a motif that appears in Harlem Renaissance poems such as Waring Cuney's "No Images" and Gwendolyn Bennett's "To a Brown Girl." As his earlier references to the stereotypical preacher and to "casper the ghost" indicate, Jarbari Aziz Ra is concerned with managing audience response and is undoubtedly aware of both the accessibility and possible triteness of these allusions. Indeed, this performance may usefully illustrate Stephen E. Henderson's suggestion that—in the "New Black poetry" as in jazz—"the use of stock phrases, lines, and other elements is not limited . . . to Black folk song, but the practice is so widespread in Black song that it must be considered an important part of the process of composition."[38]

An instructive documentation of what some of these readings were like is provided by Stanley Crouch's *Ain't No Ambulances for No Nigguhs Tonight* (1972) issued as a long-playing record by Flying Dutchman, the label that also featured albums by many avant-garde jazz musicians. Recorded live on a college campus, most of the program consists of a lengthy and tendentious lecture on black history, didactically espousing the same Afrocentricity that Crouch now rails against on network television. The whole performance is actually an energetic call-and-response "teach-in" that includes Crouch's recitation of a few of his poems. By the standards of the period, Crouch's poems are respectable products though not outstanding, and his polemics were precisely what the age (and audience) demanded. During these years even James Brown would "interrupt" his concert to sit on the edge of the stage at the Apollo Theatre and rap for about ten minutes on self-esteem and civic responsibility; then he would spring to his feet and electric slide into "There Was a Time." It is telling, though, that the proportion of polemical prose to poetry in Crouch's performance is almost exactly the reverse of what one experienced at a reading by Sonia Sanchez or Amiri Baraka.

Crouch's revolutionary rap is, literally, all talk; and his performance should not be considered typical of all Black Arts poetry readings. Crouch has none of the ecstatic oracular sonority of Askia Muhammad Touré, none of the swooping lyrical invention of Kalamu ya Salaam, who does both words and music in his own voice in the manner of *a cappella* Delta blues.

In "Black Poetry—Where It's At" (1969) and other essays published in *Negro Digest* and widely discussed among poets, Carolyn Rodgers proposed new prosodic categories specific to black poetry. Her ideas were based on what Jerry W. Ward Jr. has called "culturally anchored SPEECH ACTS and Reader/Hearer Response."[39] This work was elaborated upon by Stephen E. Henderson in his *Understanding the New Black Poetry* (1973).

Henderson does not spend much time on the typographical strategies that poets devised, instead he attempts to carefully identify the vernacular rhetorical devices that became more central to their work as the poets began to depend more and more on oral presentation in the Black Arts Movement's ubiquitous and popular poetry readings.

To anyone familiar with Olson's *Projective Verse,* the text of Sonia Sanchez's "Queens of the Universe" functions precisely as a *score.* The poem, as printed, indicates exactly how Sanchez performed it and how it should be read:

```
Sisters.
          i saw it to
                         day. with
My own eyes.
               i mean like i
got on this bus
               this cracker wuz
driving saw him look/
                    sniff a certain
smell and
          turn his head in disgust.
sisters.
     that queen of sheba
                         perfume wuz
doooooooooing it.
                    strong/
                         blk/
                              smell that it
be. i mean
          it ain' t delicate/stuff
sisters.
     when you put it on
                    u be knowing it on.⁴⁰
```

Similarly, Johari Amini's text (justified left and right, set in lower case) instructs and allows the reader to reproduce her breathless, exasperated voice:

```
we will be no generashuns to cum for blks r
killing r.selves did u hear bros. did u hear the
killings did u hear the sounds of the killing
the raping of the urgency of r soil consuming
r own babies burned n the acid dri configura-
shuns of the cycles balancing did u hear. did u
hear. hear the sounds of the balancing &
checking off checking off erasing r existence⁴¹
```

A poem such as Askia Muhammad Touré's "Transcendental Vision: Indigo" indicates through typography a sense of how the poet intends it to sound and the typographical method employed is very similar to that proposed by Olson in his Projective Verse essay:

And
   there
      are
         Whirlwinds embodied
in
  the
    minds of
Visionary griots/singing:
             Tomorrow!
                Tomorrow!) Language of
transcendental passion-flame
          (spirit-tongue. Surreal
                Saint-
inflected solo) motivating warrior
          generations
venerating liberation
       in
primary language of
     forever.[42]

What Touré describes here is precisely the aesthetic goal of Black Arts music and poetry: an attempt to recreate in modern modes the ancestral role of the African *griots* who are poets, musicians, and dancers whose songs record genealogies and the cosmologies of societies such as the Wolof and Mandinka. It is worth noting that most of those who have listened to Touré read have compared his style of declamation to that of the traditional black Southern preachers who also inspired James Weldon Johnson's *God's Trombones* (1927), one of the true masterpieces of the Harlem Renaissance and a pioneering attempt to present African American vernacular speech using the techniques of modernist poetry.

    Similar connections are illumined by Ugo Rubeo's analysis of Etheridge Knight's style. Attempting to decipher precisely how Knight's use of orality works, Rubeo identifies the poet's employment of Biblical parataxis and folkloristic motifs in a manner that establishes a "double dialogue with past and present" working to reinforce African American folk traditions while also creating a "mutual, dialogical pattern of oral communication" with the audience present.[43] A similar process has been identified in the traditional style of African American preaching and, in a brilliant discussion of Johnson's *God's Trombones,* Dolan Hubbard has demonstrated the political implications of this type of speech performance:

> As the freestanding spokesperson in the community, the preacher was one of the few members of the African American community who was permitted by the politically powerful white community to be educated, self-determined, and successful. The preacher is the transformational agent who walks the critical tightrope between the sacred and the secular; his speech act (sermon) is the agent for historical location. As the tap root of black

American discourse, the sermon historicizes the experience of blacks in America. The sermon as agent provides a link between generations of black families and makes it possible for the culture of black America to be transmitted over time.[44]

It is clear that Hubbard is not merely referring to the *content* of the traditional black sermon but to the performance as well. What Touré refers to as "Saint- / inflected solo) motivating warrior / generations" is precisely the interwoven allusions of the traditional sermon that moves from Biblical events to current events as if they were all occuring in the same moment; which, indeed, they are in the preacher's performative act. African American artists did not need Bakhtinian terminology to understand any of this and the musicians that the Black Arts poets admired were skilled practitioners of this technique. The bands of Charles Mingus and Sun Ra—which included some of the most innovative soloists of the 1960s and 70s—frequently quoted or evoked earlier jazz styles ranging from Ferdinand "Jelly Roll" Morton to the Swing Era and Bebop. Mingus, in compositions titled "Folk Forms" and "Wednesday Night Prayer Meeting," also created advanced jazz based on the choral music of the black church.

One of the arguments for the African American writer's continuing interest in the folk tradition is concisely stated by Calvin C. Hernton in *The Sexual Mountain and Black Women Writers* (1990): "Because people talk and sing before they write, poetry is the protoplasm of all literature and culture, it is the blood of all life. The folk always produce, preserve and transmit an entire [culture] based on speech and song. The oral culture of the folk is the foundation from which all writing springs. Poetry is the primal human form, the instinctive response to human existence. The aesthetics and the concerns of the written literature are contained in the oral, nonliterate foundations of a people."[45] This perception was central to the Black Arts Movement and is, of course, entirely consistent with a Herderian strategy—also employed by Alain Locke during the 1920s Harlem Renaissance—based on the idea that celebrating the folk tradition would simultaneously build group solidarity and protect the artist from the aesthetic distractions of novelty.[46]

In other words, the Black Arts Movement's interest in African American vernacular was not a return to Dunbar's use of dialect. That poet, wrote William Stanley Braithwaite in 1925, "expressed a folk temperament but not a race soul. Dunbar was the end of a regime and not the beginning of a tradition."[47] What was at work, rather, was a continuation of Langston Hughes's modernist idiom and a similarly modernist determination to avoid the clumsy artifice of traditional "poetic diction." It was, in fact, the "race soul" that Black Arts poets were attempting to find and set singing.

The impulse toward what, in political terms, was called self-determination is evident in all aspects of this poetry. Linguist Geneva Smitherman notes that "it is in style, rather than in language *per se,* that the

cultural distinctiveness of the Black idiom can be located."[48] There were
many attempts to capture this distinctiveness in sound and on paper. For
example, writes Smitherman, "The phonological items employed by the poets represent their attempts to spell according to Black America's pronunciation." As with nineteenth-century attempts to write dialect, similarly ap-
proached without formal linguistic study, Smitherman judges this effort and
its orthographic renderings to have achieved "uneven success," but adds:
"we can certainly applaud their success in oral performance for here is where
the full range of Black intonation patterns, tonal qualities, and other aspects
of Black phonology in the poetry spring to life." Short of employing the
International Phonetic Alphabet (IPA) or the musical stave, the most efficient critical method of indicating these phonological features in written
discourse would be to discuss the *generic* modes most readily associated with
them; and this is precisely the approach taken by insightful critics such as
Smitherman, Carolyn Rodgers, and Stephen E. Henderson.

Citing traditional African American folk forms such as the dozens and
call-and-response, Smitherman concludes: "The linguistic/stylistic machin-
ery of this poetry is firmly located in the Black oral tradition, and the Black
poet of today is forging a new art form steeped in the uniqueness of Black
expressive style." This was certainly a reasonable claim at the time Smitherman composed her essay. Even if more modestly framed, it is still true: the
Black Arts Movement expanded the American poetic vocabulary, adding a
new set of useful and effective free verse options to those already available
in American English.

III

If you could hear it you would make music too.

GWENDOLYN BROOKS

Critics who have raised the issue of whether poetry so oral/performance-
oriented is properly represented in the literary canon offered to high school
and college students present a legitimate concern; but their approach to the
question often seems like special pleading.

It is a fact that sheet music is not a symphony; indeed, according to
the protocols of jazz and the practice of an artist such as James Brown, even
an audio recording of a "live" performance is not an adequate representation of their art—which is to be found only in the next concert.

We should also be careful about how we historicize such performance-
oriented art; and in this instance Dunbar's poem "The Party" provides a
useful pedagogical cue. While the narrator tells us you "ought to been"
there (Dunbar, *Complete Poems,* 86), what listeners are really enjoying is the
narrator's generous, delightful inventory and delicious recollection of what
went on there. The fun is in the present narrative, not the past event. We

all remember similar experiences. As kids, the schoolyard retelling of the Saturday matinee could often be as exciting as the movie itself had been. A kid who was really inventive not only told you the plot but impersonated the actors and simulated all the sound effects as well. There are some of us, perhaps overly nostalgic, who may argue that—for some movies—the schoolyard version is better than the director's cut.

What eventually we must confront is that different types of artistic reproduction can be called "poetry," and it is important to identify the different skills they require from both performer and audience. It is true, as Steven A. Athanases reports, that experiencing the voice and person of Gwendolyn Brooks allows one to fully grasp the artistry of her "Ballad of Pearlie Mae," yet he also notes that much the same effect can be achieved from a student's carefully prepared recitation of poems by Langston Hughes.[49] What this suggests, to use a technological metaphor, is that we should be concerned equally with the technical quality of both *recording* and *playback*.

In the tradition of Carl Sandburg and Vachel Lindsay, Gwendolyn Brooks prefers a style of recitation based on the premise that poetry transcends ordinary speech. Her reading style is musical and carefully paced with subtle emphasis, but it does not resemble the fervent prayer style of the black church. Though the intervallic relationships of her words are less fluid than singing or chanting, Brooks does not read her poems in the rhythm or timbre of everyday speech. The relationship of her poems to these other forms of utterance is like the relationship of Tai Chi Chuan (a sort of aerobic exercise in slow motion) to the ordinary movement of our limbs. At the podium Gwendolyn Brooks is herself the "teller" she asks for in "The Womanhood" (1949)—the voice that recounts the world's realities but does so in a tone that ultimately confirms:

Behold,
Love's true, and triumphs; and God's actual[50]

"The audiences for black poetry of the sixties and seventies were already conditioned to the style and delivery that the poets exploited," noted Stephen E. Henderson.[51] But while it became clear that, as Smitherman put it, "the people's lingo is the poet's lingo, too" (81), it may be suggested that the reason the poets chose to adopt the vernacular is multifaceted.

The poetry of the Black Arts Movement was shaped by the context of oral presentation because the highly politicized aesthetic devised by the poets decreed that it should be. Fully cognizant of the implications of this decision, the poets must ultimately be held responsible for their written texts as well as their performances. Either the poems on paper work or they don't—and if they don't, it is the poet's fault. To suggest, as some critics have, that the Black Arts poets—as an entire school—were necessarily inadequate in the written transcription of their own work is both inaccurate and insulting. The alphabetic conventions of recording poetry in English on paper are not imposed externally but have been subject to continuous revision by the poets themselves for centuries. As a result, the properly trained reader should be able to handle the typeset transcriptions of George Herbert and Johari Amini, Will Carleton and Haki R. Madhubuti, with equal facility.

All poetry is incomplete until it is read aloud. The idea that sophisticated readers can simulate this experience mentally is, of course, a longstanding article of faith that has been systematically assaulted by subsequent technological efforts to construct "virtual" realities. Nevertheless, the poem printed on the page is effective when it functions as a memorandum to excite the reader's recall of a previous performance, or serves as a score for future vocal reproduction. If the poet has done the job of preparing that alphabetic transcription well, she can be sure that the poem will live.

During a period when much American poetry seemed the limited province of writing workshop apprentices, or a type of specialized do-it-yourself psychotherapy, one indisputable fact is that the poetry of the Black Arts Movement was *popular.* It reached a visible and enthusiastic audience, even if the movement's leaders tended to exaggerate the proletarian profile of their mostly collegiate following. "Granted," Mance Williams wrote, "many of these radicalized college students came from grass-roots environments; but the degree to which they epitomized 'the people' is somewhat minimal."[52] If, however, one looks backward to consider the hopeful strivings of those audiences' foreparents, it is hard to imagine that Frances E. W. Harper, for one, would have had a problem with that.

NOTES

1. Melba Joyce Boyd, *Discarded Legacy: Politics and Poetics in the Life of Frances E. W. Harper, 1825–1911* (Detroit: Wayne State University Press, 1994), pp. 150–51.

2. Paul H. Gray, "Poet as Entertainer: Will Carleton, James Whitcomb Riley, and the Rise of the Poet-Performer Movement," *Literature in Performance,* vol. 5 (November 1984), p. 1.

3. James Whitcomb Riley, "The Old Swimmin' Hole," in *American Poetry: The Nineteenth Century,* vol. 2 (New York: Library of America, 1993), p. 471.

4. Riley, "The Days Gone By," in *American Poetry,* vol. 2, p. 472.

5. See *American Poetry,* vol. 2, pp. 911–12; and Russel Nye, *The Embarrassed Muse: The Popular Arts in America* (New York: Dial Press, 1970), pp. 116–19.

6. Paul Laurence Dunbar, *Candle-Lightin' Time,* illus. Hampton Institute Camera Club and Margaret Armstrong (Miami: Mnemosyne, 1969). This volume was originally published by Dodd, Mead in October 1901. Similar volumes included *When Malindy Sings,* issued November 1903; *Li'l Gal* in October 1904; *Howdy, Honey, Howdy* in October 1905; and *Joggin' Erlong* in October 1906. See also *Collected Poems* (New York: Dodd, Mead, 1976).

Originally published in 1907, Lida Keck Wiggins, *The Life and Works of Paul Laurence Dunbar* (New York: Kraus Reprint, 1971), pp. 80–97, provides a good description of Dunbar's touring schedule and its toll on his health. For a description of Dunbar's performance with a string orchestra at the Matthewson Hotel in Narragansett, New York on August 25, 1896, see Virginia Cunningham, *Paul Laurence Dunbar and His Song* (New York: Biblo & Tannen, 1969), p. 152.

7. Paul Laurence Dunbar, "The Made to Order Smile," in *Majors and Minors: Poems* (Toledo, Ohio: Hadley & Hadley, 1895), p. 126.

8. See "Famous Negro Poet to Appear in Big Recital Here," Houston *Informer,* April 2, 1932, p. 1; "Langston Hughes," Houston *Informer,* April 16, 1932, p. 2; and Bernice Johnson, "Langston Hughes Reads before A Large Audience," Houston *Informer,* April 16, 1932, p. 1.

9. Woodie King Jr., *Black Theatre Present Condition* (New York: National Black Theatre Touring Circuit, 1981), p. 21.

10. Kristin M. Langellier, "From Text to Social Context," in *Literature in Performance,* vol. 6 (April 1986), pp. 60–70. Langellier summarizes recent scholarship suggesting that "the performed text emerges in the context of performance as a dynamic relationship among the setting, participants, and the event itself. In this dynamic process of interpretation, a text acquires sociocultural dimensions beyond its formal features" (65). It should be made clear that an attempt to decipher "sociocultural dimensions *beyond* . . . formal features" of the poems or the poets' conscious aesthetic choices—and the ethnographic approach thus implied—is not the focus of the present essay.

11. John Gruen, *The New Bohemia* (Chicago: a cappella Books, 1990), p. 69.

12. Ed Sanders, *Tales of Beatnik Glory* (New York: Citadel Press, 1995), pp. 12–25.

13. See Werner Sollors, *Amiri Baraka/LeRoi Jones: The Quest for a "Populist Modernism"* (New York: Columbia University Press, 1978), pp. 47–48.

14. John A. Kouwenhoven, *The Arts in Modern American Civilization* (New York: W. W. Norton, 1967), p. 222.

15. Amiri Baraka, "The Black Arts Movement"; typescript of speech delivered at the National Black Arts Festival, Atlanta, Georgia, August 1994.

16. Fred W. McDarrah, ed., *Kerouac and Friends: A Beat Generation Album* (New York: William Morrow, 1985), pp. 286, 306–7.

17. Kenneth Rexroth, *American Poetry in the Twentieth Century* (New York: Herder & Herder, 1971), p. 141.

18. Diana Trilling, "The Other Night at Columbia: A Report from the Academy," in McDarrah, 145.

19. Kenneth Rexroth, "Jazz and Poetry," in McDarrah, 61–62.

20. Harry T. Moore, "Enter Beatniks: The Bohème of 1960," in *Garrets and Pretenders: A History of Bohemianism in America,* ed. Albert Parry (New York: Dover, 1960), p. 384.

21. Ross Russell, review of Charles Mingus, *A Modern Jazz Symposium of Music and Poetry* (Bethlehem BCP 6026), *Jazz Review,* vol. 3 (February 1960), p. 31.

22. Kaye McDonough, "Bob Kaufman Reading at Vesuvio's, 1973," *Umbra 5: Latin/Soul Anthology* (1974), p. 78.

23. Amiri Baraka, "How You Sound?," *The LeRoi Jones/Amiri Baraka Reader,* ed. William J. Harris (New York: Thunder's Mouth Press, 1991), p. 17.

24. See, for example, Don L. Lee [Haki Madhubuti], *"Black Writing,"* in *Journal of Black Poetry,* vol. 1 (fall–winter 1971), pp. 85–86.

25. Larry Neal, "The Black Arts Movement," *Visions of a Liberated Future: Black Arts Movement Writings,* ed. Michael Schwartz (New York: Thunder's Mouth Press,

1989), p. 62. The historical context for Neal's view is provided by Louis E. Lomax, *The Negro Revolt* (New York: Signet Books, 1963), see especially p. 78; and *Report of the National Advisory Commission on Civil Disorders,* intr. Tom Wicker (New York: Bantam Books, 1968). In an important chapter, the commission compared the economic upward mobility of European immigrants and urban African Americans and concluded that "segregation denied Negroes access to good jobs and the opportunity to leave the ghetto. For them, the future seemed to lead only to a dead end" (15). While certain cultural traits are cited as contributing factors to the relatively successful upward mobility of immigrant groups, there is no mention of anything to indicate African American cultural distinctiveness. It was precisely this vacant area that the explorations of the Black Arts Movement—through poetry, music, and the development of communal celebrations such as Kwanzaa (the external manifestation of a "Black value system")—were intended to fill, either by discovery or invention.

26. Dudley Randall, ed., *The Black Poets* (New York: Bantam Books, 1971), p. xxv.

27. Charles Olson quoting Robert Creeley in *Projective Verse* (New York: Totem, 1959).

28. Henry Louis Gates Jr., "The Church," *Come Sunday: Photographs by Thomas Roma* (New York: Museum of Modern Art, 1996), p. 7.

29. W. C. Thomas, *I'm into Something I Can't Turn Loose,* Jewel Records LPS 0050 (1970). In the 1960s the speeches of Reverend Martin Luther King Jr. made elements of the African American sermonic tradition familiar to most Americans.

30. Genevieve Fabre, *Drum Beats, Masks and Metaphor: Contemporary Afro-American Theatre,* tr. Melvin Dixon (Cambridge, Mass.: Harvard University Press, 1983), p. 66.

31. Amiri Baraka, "Black Nationalism vs. Pimp Art," *Rhythm,* vol. 1 (summer 1970), p. 11.

32. Eddie Osborne, "Miami's Theatre of Afro Arts," in *Black Creation,* no. 4 (summer 1973), p. 38.

33. Robert A. Bone, "The Background of the Negro Renaissance," in *Black History: A Reappraisal,* ed. Melvin Drimmer (Garden City, N.Y.: Anchor Books, 1968), p. 412.

34. Baraka, "The Black Arts Movement," pp. 6–7.

35. Lorenzo Thomas, "Baraka in Newark: Gathering the Spirits," in *Editor's Choice: Literature and Graphics from the U.S. Small Press, 1965–1977,* ed. Morty Sklar and Jim Mulac (Iowa City: The Spirit That Moves Us Press, 1980), pp. 344–45.

36. Clovis E. Semmes, "The Dialectics of Community Survival and the Community Artist: Phil Cohran and the Affro-Arts Theater," *Journal of Black Studies* 24 (June 1994), pp. 452–54, 458. In some ways Earth Wind & Fire's musical approach achieved the synthesis of rhythm and blues and avant-garde jazz that Black Arts Movement music critics had begun calling for in the late 1960s. Songs such as "Shining Star" and "Keep Your Head to the Sky" represent the positive (and sometimes numbingly didactic) community message that was *de rigueur* among grass-roots Black Arts organizations; and the iconography and costumes associated with the band served, as Paul Gilroy has perceived, "as an important means for communicating pan-African ideas in an inferential, populist manner." See Gilroy, *Small Acts: Thoughts on the Politics of Black Cultures* (London: Serpent's Tail Press, 1993), p. 241.

37. Jarbari Aziz Ra, "A Writer's Statement," in *The Vision* (Houston: Afronese Black Press, 1989), p. 22.

38. Stephen E. Henderson, "Cliché, Monotony, and Touchstone: Folksong Composition and the New Black Poetry," in *Black Southern Voices,* ed. John Oliver Killens and Jerry W. Ward Jr. (New York: Meridian Books, 1992), p. 534. See also Henderson, *Understanding the New Black Poetry* (New York: William Morrow, 1973).

39. Jerry W. Ward Jr., "Literacy and Criticism: The Example of Carolyn Rodgers," *Druvoices Revue,* vol. 4 (fall/spring 1994/95), p. 65.

40. Sonia Sanchez, "Queens of the Universe," in *Black Spirits: A Festival of New Black Poets in America,* ed. Woodie King Jr. (New York: Vintage Books, 1972), p. 186. Sanchez, Etheridge Knight, Amiri Baraka, and others can be seen and heard on the videotape anthology *Color: A Sampling of Contemporary African American Writers,* ed. Al Young (San Francisco: Poetry Center and American Poetry Archives, 1994).

41. Johari Amini, "Untitled (in commemoration of the blk/family)," in King, 4.

42. Askia M. Touré, "Transcendental Vision: Indigo," in *From the Pyramids to the Projects* (Trenton, N.J.: Africa World Press, 1990), p. 55.

43. Ugo Rubeo, "Voice as Lifesaver: Defining the Function of Orality in Etheridge Knight's Poetry," in *The Black Columbiad: Defining Moments in African American Literature and Culture,* ed. Werner Sollors and Maria Diedrich (Cambridge, Mass.: Harvard University Press, 1994), p. 278.

44. Dolan Hubbard, *The Sermon and the African American Literary Imagination* (Columbia: University of Missouri, 1994), p. 14.

45. Calvin C. Hernton, *The Sexual Mountain and Black Women Writers: Adventures in Sex, Literature, and Real Life* (New York: Anchor Books, 1990), p. 153.

46. Johann Gottfried von Herder's view that a national literature must be grounded in the characteristics of the folk was an influential thesis finding adherents in Ralph Waldo Emerson and Walt Whitman, and much discussed by African American writers during both the Harlem Renaissance and the Black Arts Movement. See, for example, Bernard W. Bell, *The Folk Roots of Contemporary Afro-American Poetry* (Detroit: Broadside Press, 1974), pp. 16–19. Bell's important, historically based critical comment—first published in *Negro Digest*—helped to invigorate discussion among the poets themselves concerning the use of folk elements.

Other examples of how Herder's views make an appearance in African American literature can be found in Richard Wright's "The Literature of the Negro in the United States" in *White Man, Listen!* (New York: Harper, 1957; reprinted by Harper Perennial, 1995) and Amiri Baraka's "The Myth of a Negro Literature" in *Home: Social Essays* (New York: William Morrow, 1966), as well as in the writings of Alain Locke in *The New Negro* (New York: Atheneum, 1992) that set the tone for aesthetic debate in the late 1920s.

47. William Stanley Braithwaite, "The Negro in American Literature," in *The New Negro,* p. 38.

48. Geneva Smitherman, "The Black Idiom and the New Black Poetry," *Black Creation,* no. 6 (1974–75), p. 86. Subsequent references are to this page.

49. Steven A. Athanases, "When Print Alone Fails Poetry: Performance as a Contingency of Literary Value," *Text and Performance Quarterly,* vol. 11 (April 1991), p. 118.

50. Gwendolyn Brooks, "The Womanhood," in *Selected Poems* (New York: Harper, 1963), p. 64.

51. Stephen E. Henderson, "Worrying the Line: Notes on Black American Poetry," in *The Line in Postmodern Poetry,* ed. Robert Frank and Henry Sayre (Urbana: University of Illinois, 1988), p. 63.

52. Mance Williams, *Black Theatre in the 1960s and 70s* (New York: Greenwood Press, 1985), p. 154.

14

Was That "Different," "Dissident" or "Dissonant"?

Poetry (n) the Public Spear: Slams, Open Readings, and Dissident Traditions

MARIA DAMON

Dis poetry is like a riddim dat drops
De tongue fires a riddim that shoots like shots
Dis poetry is designed fe rantin
Dance hall style, Big Mouth chanting,
Dis poetry nar put yu to sleep
Preaching follow me
Like yu is blind sheep,
Dis poetry is not Party Political
Not designed fe dose who are critical . . .

I've tried Shakespeare, respect due dere
But dis is de stuff I like.

BENJAMIN ZEPHANIAH, "Dis Poetry"

*B*ook chapters and academic essays, like this one, are a far less public form than open-mike readings and poetry slams, my subject here; so I'm operating in a different register of intimacy and disclosure from the poets and performers I'm writing about. I'm writing for an audience, but that audience comprises individual readers rather than a gathered crowd ready for aural pleasure (unless some book club or poetry seminar gathers to read this critical work aloud—now there's an unlikely experiment for you). In a more personalized vein of one-to-one interlocution, I offer the following vignettes of close and productive, if uncomfortable, mislistenings:

When I telephoned the sister of an important but neglected Beat poet about whom I was doing some research, she responded with some suspicion. I had heard that the now-dead poet's family of origin regarded him ambivalently–the "proverbial black sheep," as another aficionado of this poet put it, though she, like the poet and his family, was African American—so I tried to present my credentials. I was a scholar, I explained, writing a book on her brother as well as some others—"several different twentieth-century American poets" was my soon-to-be-revealed-as-unfortunate phrasing. "Did you say different, or dissident?" the sister queried icily. On a tip from a friendlier sister of the poet, I had called her at a hotel where her husband was being honored for service to the local diocese for administering nursing homes. "Because my brother was *not* dissident, you know." End of interview. I, the chastened white girl stopped in my tracks from projecting my noble-savage/resistant-organic-intellectual fantasies onto the son of a middle-class black Catholic family who grew up in a city where middle-class black Catholics were the (very respectable) majority, withdrew to lick my narcissistic wounds and to ponder (to theorize without letting too much shame get in the way) once again my role in trying to bring the methodological and ideological gains of cultural studies to bear on studies of American poetry: *It's my role to valorize dissidence—isn't it? Not as if I didn't no one else would—but there is so little scholarly attention to social dissidence in poetry. There's plenty of attention paid to an exclusionary Oedipal dissidence made famous by Harold Bloom—how up-and-coming white male poets create traditions counter to that of their forefathers, how the Beats rebelled against the New Critics/ Agrarians, who were in turn reacting against what they saw as unseemly politicization of literature that could only lead to aesthetic Stalinism, etc. There's lots on the rap controversy, whether it is or isn't "poetry" and what's at stake in the question; far less on poetry that is intended as poetry, but is also intended to stay outside the parameters of text-dependent institutions . . .*[1]

But dis is de stuff I like.

Several years later, at a party I was hosting, I put on a tape of music from the Solomon Islands collected by my father the itinerant head-measurer, a.k.a. the physical anthropologist. Though to my ears the pan-pipe and percussion orchestra was lovely, familiar, and evocative, a friend winced and asked to change the tape. "It's kinda . . . dissident," she said. My wounded ego took refuge in passive-aggressive academicism. "You mean dissonant, don't you?" She winced again, this time from having been publicly corrected.

But dis is de stuff I like.

These anecdotes are intended to throw into relief, perhaps through negative example, the significance of close listening and its relevance to the public arts of contemporary poetry. The intimacy implied by this book's title invites us to hear "dissident" and "dissonant" in "different," while preserving their nuances of difference/dissidence/dissonance; that is, we don't confuse the three words (and however many others there may be) but let them orbit around each other; we try on the range of misprisions available to us looking for the ones that unfold into the greatest creative and intellectual possibilities. The respect implied by this book's title permits us to hold all semantic/sonic resonant possibilities concurrently, our attentive apparatus flickering between them all with such lucid intensity as to create a kinetic web of energy that is its own possibility, its own "becoming-poetry." While the public arts I address here—slams, open mike readings—have been accused of sanctioning mediocrity—that is, doggerel: poetry which, for academicians like Northrop Frye are slighted as "incomplete" or, in Deleuzian terms, valorized as "becoming," they (open readings, slams) offer an important venue for grassroots poetic activity that rewrites the privatistic lyric scene into a site for public discourse.[2] "Intimacy," "respect" and "close listening" are precisely what, according to traditional academic critics (such as Harold Bloom, Helen Vendler, and so forth), is missing from populist-oriented performance poetry. But they're responding from a narrow conception of what poetry is: the highly crafted, aesthetic transmutation of private emotions into lapidary objects a select audience can, with much specialized training, learn to appreciate. (I must admit that other than Northrop Frye, the critics specifically named above have not addressed this issue formally, so far does it lie beyond the purview of what is considered appropriate matter for serious academic analysis; I use them as emblems of a certain critical hegemony and I hereby apologize for any disservice this does to their views, inviting them to take up the matter in future work to set the record straight.) It is assumed, both in traditional critical circles and also among the experimentalists I will turn to in more detail below, that poetry that reaches for a wider field of conversants or emphasizes values other than craft and subjectivity necessarily suffers a diminution in subtlety and sophistication—the "lowest common denominator" theory of mass-culture critique. However, this is a faulty assumption: professional poetry aficionados need to be retrained to listen differently (dissidently, dissonantly).

Nick Piombino writes eloquently in his essay in this volume of the close listening a psychotherapist/poet/critic needs to perform on elliptical texts: quiet or halting, self-effacing utterances in which silence or circumlocution bespeak shyness or fear, the erasure of trauma or the protection of its memory. I would like to claim the same level of attention for modes of expression generally stereotyped as public, "loud," or unsubtle. The "public sphere" (Jürgen Habermas's term), in which citizens congregate as putative equals in debate and discussion to develop public policy and ideas (again putatively) beneficial for an undifferentiated public good, is fraught with dissonant, dissident nuances. As the essays in Bruce Robbins's volume *The Phantom Public Sphere* amply demonstrate, the notion of putative equality in public debate where there is no economic or social equality is extremely problematic, as is the concept of THE (monolithic, unitary) public sphere.[3] The condescending gesture of bonhomie inscribed in the granting of "free speech" rights to disenfranchised groups by power blocs operates as a palliative to ward off, rather than enact, serious social change. As Walter Benjamin has pointed out, freedom of expression for the "masses" without political rights and economic justice—"aestheticizing politics"—is a characteristic of fascism.[4] If everyone's voice really got an equal hearing—that is, if the permission for free expression were truly accompanied by social and economic equality as well—the (multiple) public spheres would be "THE" Public's fear. The world of poetry slams and open-mike readings, while not directly politically interventionist, perhaps, creates a public sphere that is healthily contestatory. Moreover, the phrase in my title, "public spear," refers to the possibility of poetry as what Martiniquan poet Aimé Césaire would call a set of "miraculous weapons" in a guerrilla war for equality, freedom, and joy; it refers also to Spearhead, the name of a hip-hop/Spoken Word/funk band headed by Michael Franti, formerly of the Disposable Heroes of Hiphoprisy, whose lyrics urge their hearers to a wider social consciousness that includes celebration of intimate human relations, cultural specificity, movement, and sound.

The following, then, to put the matter in a somewhat crudely dialectical framework, are the two major critiques of "people's poetry" venues—slams, open-mike readings, the "spoken word" movement that includes rap and other highly vernacular verbal forms: from the "right," it's not "really poetry" because it is too public and aims too aggressively for mass appeal; from the "left," it's not public enough because it is *merely* poetry, a cultural expression everyone knows to be effete, impotent, and elitist. (One letter responding to Henry Louis Gates Jr.'s article in *The New Yorker,* on Spoken Word arts meeting rap, took the author to task for even suggesting that poetry might have emancipatory potential; the form, the respondent claimed, is a priori corrupted by its "high art" origins and connotations.)[5] Another, more seriously analytic critique from the "Left" is a paraphrase of Walter Benjamin's point—to repeat: populist/democratic venues are mere palliatives whose flamboyance and surface-level engagement threaten to divert us from the fact that most of the lives celebrated in this work (working-class, marginal, ethnically other, etc) are getting harder and harder, even while it becomes trendier and trendier to celebrate them. Far from pointing beyond themselves toward activism for just economic or social solutions, these expressions' existence is mistaken for a meaningful solution in and of itself. This critique draws a distinction between a cultural *politics* and *cultural* politics, the former being effective and the latter being diversionary, and may place slams/open mike on the latter side of the binary.

A third critique, which shares some elements of both camps (corresponding most nearly to what a Frankfurt school, Adornian critique of populist-poetry-as-mass-culture might look like), emerges from the perspective of the radical, "language"-oriented avant-garde, which has been described as the contemporary poetic movement that most directly confronts language as ideology. Its critique of these populist venues could be summarized in this way: since these developments in public poetry must perforce appeal to a low common denominator, public poetry tends toward a utilitarian, semantically overdetermined "message," in which language is commodified, subordinated, and consumed as either spectacle or propaganda ("false consciousness"), both of which are considered to be epiphenomenal to "real poetry." Since any true social revolution must include a revolution in how language is conceived of and engaged (language must be liberated from a strictly utilitarian role in public social life), these public events ultimately enact a reactionary populism rather than the emancipation of the People's Words that their proponents claim. This pessimistic reading of populist poetics shares with academic criticism a belief that ("THE") people, vulnerable to brainwashing by the commercial messages everywhere embedded in mass culture, don't know what's best for them: that, for example, "Fuck tha Police" is a less politically (because less syntactically) radical phrase than, say, "Lotion Bullwhip Giraffe" because the former echoes "Buy Guess Jeans," "Join the Army," or "Eat Your Spinach."[6] While it is quite true that populism is not necessarily progressive (musicologist Simon Frith has an essay wonderfully subtitled, "Defending Popular Culture from the Populists," in which he argues for taking seriously the category of the aesthetic—with the understanding that will mean different things to different consumers, producers, and creators—in popular culture studies), it is also true that the populace involved in slams and open-mike readings is, for the most part, not the populace involved in the Posse Comitatus or the Aryan Brotherhood.[7] On the contrary, if one can generalize, it tends to be a multi-ethnic crowd that covers the class spectrum and espouses a progressive, leftist view although it is not "party political"; the declaimed poetry tends to reflect these social locations, vernacular traditions, and ideological positions in gestural and vocal styles consonant therewith. The dismal forecast of political cooptation is not a logically inevitable outcome of the slam/open-mike phenomenon; at its best, the spirit of these open venues has more in common with Gran Fury/ACT UP's pragmatic and interventionist aesthetics than with unimaginative sloganeering.[8]

Moreover, in practical terms, a possible "language"-oriented critique seems to rely on a conception of "quality" that, while differing in criteria from those of traditional formalists, is no less narrow, in that it does not take seriously the criteria of the slammers themselves, which seem to be, *tout court,* a skilled congruence of content, performance, and performer. The general stereotype of the slam performance as promoting an in-your-face, bullying theatricalism, and of the slam poem as delivering a simplistic personal or political message, can certainly be validated by superficial observation, but it can also be countered by a broader and simultaneously closer attention to the same evidence. The following anecdote illustrates this phenomenon: when the Nuyorican Poets' Café tour came to Minneapolis in 1993, slams were held all over the Twin Cities for a month beforehand. By the time the big "slam open" took place (a semifinal before the "slam shut," at which winners would be chosen to perform with the Nuyoricans at the grand finale), a certain number of slam poets were already familiar to anyone who'd been following the events: among them were Pony Tail, who fared well at smaller slams but whose adulatory imitations of Miles Davis et al. cut no mustard with a more savvy crowd; Blac Q, a brilliant nineteen-year-old freshman at MacAlester College whose paeans to the 'hood rhymed "drama" and "bomber" (and it worked!); and Spam, a hard-edged working-class poet whose work addressed with sardonic humor his sordid and picturesque childhood in Austin, Minnesota, a blue-collar town dominated in every way by the Hormel Foods Spam factory. On that charged semifinal night, however, a man who runs a neighborhood drop-in center brought a group of hitherto unknowns that included some adolescents and a variety of adults, several of whom placed in the finals. One of these, a woman who seemed unused to reading for an audience, and certainly not used to the high theater that slam poetry can be, read a heavily rhymed, anapestic tetrameter poem—a prayer, more accurately—about living with alcoholism and codependency. The poem was honest, and the delivery unaffected, genuine, confident but not showy; her voice was unassuming but tenacious, and there was no body movement to speak of, no "acting out" of the content. It was a dignified if understated performance. A silence reigned for a short while after she read, then loud applause; she scored very high. However, at the finals, the "slam shut," she produced a poem approximating the slam stereotype—theatrical imitations of bullets from assault weapons, complaints about the condition of her neighborhood delivered with speed and anger that sounded (to my ears) pro forma—it was awkward, as if she were forcing herself to do something she felt was required of her. The piece sounded hastily written, under the pressure of meeting hitherto unexperienced expectations; it sounded, in fact, like the work of Blac Q, Pony Tail, and Spam, and of the man from the drop-in center who'd brought her (who had also participated in the competition). This time she didn't score high at all. While the newcomer had been inducted into something one could term a "slam culture" with a normative sound, the audience itself acted as corrective: "No, no, we like you for who you are, not for who you think we want you to be." Vague as it may sound, the criterion for slam success seems to be some kind of "realness"—authenticity at the physical/sonic and meta-physical/emotional-intellectual-spiritual levels. This is why close listening is crucial; you're not just listening for technique, or "original imagery," or raw emotion, but for some transmission/recognition of resonant difference (dissonant sameness? dissident affirmation? that old "defamiliarization" which depends on its relationship to the familiar?), a gestalt that effects a "felt change of consciousness" on the part of the listener.[9]

This "felt change" does not have to be occasioned only through radical alterity of syntax or style, which criterion, like any other, can itself become inflexible: when I showed a video of the woman reading the prayer about living with alcoholism at a poetics conference in Albany, the irritation and skepticism of the audience, largely comprised of students of the American avant-garde (the Charles Olson–Black Mountain legacy), was palpable. They couldn't, it seemed, enter into a world where terms like "codependency" and rhymes like "grace"/"place" (*pace* T. J. Jackson Lears) were taken seriously as poem-making material; the line between banality and profundity was absolute, and it was obvious to them which side of the line they were on, and which side the poet in question was on. The literary text, however, is only a small part of the picture of evaluating a poetic performance (and by performance I mean process in the larger sense; not just the event that takes place on stage, but the way poetry and poem-making performs in people's everyday lives). One of my favorite instances in which the seemingly banal is rendered profound is a scene in Elaine Holiman's documentary film *Chicks in White Satin*. Two female lovers, both upper-middle-class Jewish women, plan a traditional Jewish wedding in the face of parental consternation and misgiving. In the film's climax, the wedding itself, one bride gives the other a Hallmark card that, she avows, perfectly expresses her feelings. Weeping with joy, she reads the text aloud; it is a sentence to the effect that meeting you was like giving myself the present I always wanted. But the context and the sincerity of emotion dignify the trite lines and complicate the high camp that the film could be; the moment is both comical and moving. While the codependency poem was not comical, it was not bathetic either, as the audience response in Albany suggested.

Thus I would repeat to all critics, "right," "left" and "avant-garde," listen more closely—not only with more analytic vigilance, though that too—with more openness, respect for context, and intimacy, perhaps with what therapists-in-training are taught as "soft focusing listening," in which the overtones and undercurrents of the purported narrative can come to the fore. Listen more completely, not to this text but to the hypothetical CD that in spirit accompanies this printed volume.

Charles Bernstein has posed another issue, that of prosody and its relation to the politics of slam performance, thus: "The very oldtime iambic beat of rap and much slam poetry [is] inflected with a regularity that . . . has the same problem as the most hidebound metrical poetry that some would argue . . . is antithetical to poetic music."[10] Iambic and other tetrameters are generally considered to be balladic rhythm, and the ballad a populist form with premodern folk and vernacular roots. Some contemporary poets who experiment with vernacular have contrasted the hard-driving four-stressed-beat line with the more upwardly mobile and circumspect iambic pentameter, which has become established as the normative rhythm of the Anglophone lyric, and whose five-stressed-beat slows down and domesticates the brash insistence of tetrameter.[11] So the question is, "Whose poetic music?" Contemporary "spoken word" poet Reg E. Gaines's "Please Don't Take My Air Jordans," delivered in (roughly) anapestic tetrameter, combines traditional elements of ballad—social commentary tending toward the moralistic, heavy adherence to rhyme and meter, and a fairly straightforward narration of dramatic event; like many contemporary "authored" poems, though, it uses the first person rather than the third, often to great effect. In Gaines's poem, the first-person narrative of one boy who shoots another for his expensive and fashionable sneakers conveys eerily the dissociated consciousness of kids so socially traumatized that they cannot feel the emotions that would seem to fit their behavior.[12] By drawing on a prosodic convention traditionally associated with the "people," with public declamation, and with the expression of public opinion, Gaines uses verbal weapons from the populist arsenal to excoriate publicly, rather than, for example, an elegiac lyric to mourn privately, from a safe, top-down linguistic distance, the commercialism that leads kids to kill each other for the sake of fashion. His image for cultural and ethical undernourishment is, significantly, the valorizing of a silent spectacularization over auditory recognition: "I'm style / N smile / N lookin real mean // Cuz it ain't about be / N heard just be / N seen" (Gaines, liner notes); suggesting that being "heard," or listened to closely as a subject, would more authentically meet a kid's need for acknowledgment than would being gazed at as an object. His scathing dedication also uses simple rhyme to indict African American cultural icons who could be models for oppositional self-empowerment but who instead fall prey themselves to commercialism: "I'd like to kick this poem to Spike, and Mike, and to all the Black kids who have been killed over these $200 sneakers"[13] (both Spike Lee and Michael Jordan have appeared in advertisements for these products). As Bernstein has suggested, "the heavily-stressed poetic rhythm creates the 'public' space in which the social work can take place."[14] The social work is the critique of the capitalist practice of killing black kids for profit; the poem is, in fact, a rather Adornian critique of mass culture, though it uses extremely simple, accessible language and the structure of a well-told, suspenseful narrative. What Gaines accomplishes aesthetically is to combine a public form with a "private" voice (the poem is an internal monologue, a sort of minimalist psychological profile), to render that private voice almost autistic in its lack of affect (thus eviscerating the "lyric I" of its traditional power to communicate individual emotion), and yet by doing so to accuse not the narrator of the poem but the system that has cornered him.

Thus, open readings and their more highly orchestrated cousins poetry slams continue, at least in theory, a tradition of a public poetics oriented more toward direct intervention in and commentary on public affairs than toward the relatively recent (i.e., post-Romantic) inner-directed lyric tradition. Though the content of poems read at slams and open-mike readings can be just as privatistic as poems primarily produced for consumption through silent, individual readings-on-the-page, the fact of their public declamation in relatively democratized spaces—bars, clubs, etc.—suggests that they participate in poetic activity with roots in a collectivity not conventionally recognized as a prime origin of literary—particularly poetic—production. This public poetics deserves a "close listening" that differs from, on the one hand, the close reading we have been taught (since the 1940s at least) to associate with a proper reception of poetry, and on the other hand, from the "generalized" or master-narrativizing (instrumentalist) listening that current cultural studies—which is sympathetic to the popular registers of culture slams purport to reach, but not to poetry itself—brings to such phenomena. The dearth of scholarly literature on slams, open-mike readings, and the new "spoken word" recordings (a marketing term coined to dispel anxieties about "poetry") compared to the plethora of articles, books and chapters on rap, pop stars like Madonna, and MTV points to an absence I hope to redress.

Open Readings

"Open-mike readings" (sometimes spelled "mic," a contraction of "microphone") have been a familiar genre in American literary bohemian circles at least since the 1950s—the Beat era—and perhaps—in different forms—extending back to the Greenwich Village days of the 1930s when a lively leftist scene overlapped with intellectual and artistic circles. One important early paradigm, for example, was "Blabbermouth Night" at The Place, a club in San Francisco, in the late 1950s: one night a week anyone could take the floor and declaim not only "poetry" but any imaginative verbal display—but had to be willing to withstand the heckling and other spontaneous, unpolished feedback from a range of highly opinionated, poetry-literate, politically (anarcho-socialist, mainly) sophisticated, and expressively forthcoming audience members. It was intended to be a highly interactive, democratic scene, while still maintaining a rough—and temporary—distinction between the designated speaker, who took the stage, and "his" (usually) audience, who sat at the bar or at the club's tables with their drinks.[15]

　Contemporary open-mike readings take place in bars, nightclubs, coffeehouses, high school gyms, college lounges, auditoriums, and other public spaces traditionally designated for combinations of entertainment and informal, relatively unstructured community formation. In general there is a sign-up period before the reading; a finite number of people are permitted to read for a short period of time (five to ten minutes, depending on how many poets are to be featured), one to three poems max. Sometimes a venue will host a "featured poet" whose performance will be followed by an open reading; this format preserves a hierarchic distinction while still allowing "lesser known voices" their minutes in the limelight. The atmosphere is often celebratory and casual; the audience usually comprises a mixture of venue-habitués, friends of the readers, and a sprinkling of poetry aficionados. If the venue is particularly well known, such as the Nuyorican Poets' Café in Manhattan, which has an international reputation for presenting lively, multiethnic, high-quality performance poetry and poets, the quota of poetry fans may, of course, be higher. In the last five years or so, in response to the popularity of the "spoken word" movement, many cafés and bars in major cities now feature a once-a-month open reading. Quality and enthusiasm vary: at one such event in Minneapolis, a group of my undergraduate students attended only because part of the course work required their attendance at one "poetry event" during the quarter; there were so few readers signed up that, fearing they wouldn't be able to fulfill the assignment, they (having—coincidentally?—brought along their own work) took over and performed for each other. They loved it, and felt powerfully and communally connected to a previously distant, private art.

Poetry Slams

According to legend and common lore, "slams" as they've come to be institutionalized originated at the Green Mill bar in mid-1980s Chicago, a city traditionally known for its rought-and-ready, industrial-era (and strength) working-class spirit with a confrontational, no-frills edge to its cultural vibe: steak, lumber, gangsters, blues, with Carl Sandburg sprinkled on top singing hog-butchers of the world unite.[16] The poetry slam partakes of this atmosphere: it is a mock competition that structures and theatricalizes a noncompetitive, free-for-allish open reading into a combination of the gong show and Olympic gymnastic competitions. Like spelling bees or ballgame seasons, slams are long events since they work by process of elimination; in spite of their now institutionalized format (earlier this year, a national slam committee voted to enforce the strict three-minute rule; the one holdout for flexibility on this issue was Bob Holman of the Nuyorican Poets' Café in Manhattan), slams tend to have an amorphous feeling similar to open mike readings. Slams, however, were purposefully structured to counteract aggressively the atomized and apathetic ambience that infected the grass-roots poetry scene. They marshall audience participation, ensuring the poets that there will be an audience right through to the end of the reading (often open-mike readings are attended only by the reading poets and their friends; in the words of Marc Smith, "If you were the last poet signed up, you read to yourself," because each poet and his/her entourage of friends would leave directly after his/her three minutes was up).[17] Subject matter, performance style, poetic form and so forth vary widely (in theory, at least) from poet to poet within a single night's competition.

And while slams have inaugurated some folks into a recent understanding of poetry as a competitive sport (a concept which makes traditionalists uneasy, in spite of the arguably more cutthroat competition for publication opportunities, admission to M.F.A. programs, and university teaching positions that poisons the mainstream "creative writing" community), verbal competition has a respectable history in many oral traditions; most famous in the United States is the "dozens," an African American game of one-upmanship (literally: it is a male social activity) in which wittily insulting repartees (usually targeting the interlocutor's mother) fly fast and furious. The winner is the one who delivers the line that stumps the opponent. It is a public sport, intended for an audience's delight, and there are unspoken but understood rules of etiquette about crossing the line from humor to inappropriate invective. A related form of public pseudo-competition is the jazz musicians' "cutting contest," in which a group of musicians gather to take turns delivering bravura solo performances aimed at establishing the soloist as the "king of the cats." The competitive aspect of the enterprise, though "real" to the degree that it inspires high standards and puts the pressure on, is not accompanied by personal rancor and there is no serious shame attached to "losing"—participation, rather than victory, is the key element, though victory is not a negligible pay-off.

Black arts and artists are not afraid of contention, and an audience can learn much about community values and engagement with difference through participating in/witnessing contentious or competitive moments. In a recent review of the 1994 National Black Arts Festival, David Henderson sums up a public argument between Ishmael Reed and Amiri Baraka thus: "Neither wanted to be held in a polite respect thing . . . This was nothing new to them. They thoroughly enjoyed it,"[18] and notes that "one of the rare times [poet/critic Calvin Hernton] smiled at a literary event was when Baraka, [Playthell] Benjamin, then Amina Baraka and Barbara Christian had a good old-fashioned, intellectual, emotional *shout-out*" (Henderson, 147; his emphasis). In other words, strongly worded public disagreement, battles of wit and argumentation, are purposefully spectacular, on display as opportunities for community formation, education, entertainment, intellectual and artistic expression. Dissidence, dissonance, and difference are not punished but rather studied, celebrated, performed, and challenged in discursively productive ways.

Familiar also by now in mainstream popular culture is the bragging that is as integral a part of rap versifying as invocations to the muse or envois used to be in European epic and lyric traditions: in rap, the speaker boasts of both sexual and rhyming prowess with a glamorous air of outlawry ("I'm the lyrical Jesse James," says Hammer in my favorite example of street claims for lyrical machismo)[19] in ways that so to speak embed these two expressive economies in each other; the convention shrugs off, with admirably theatrical nonchalance, the Euro-inflected yoke of the mind/body split (or the word/body split) under which much page-based poetry labors. Poetic competition, moreover, is a typical feature of oral societies, from the legendary "contest of bards" in pre-literate Great Britain to contemporary gatherings of Ethiopian intelligensia (which is highly literate as well as oral): Amharic-language poet Solomon Deressa writes of his farewell feast in 1972, when the left the Ethiopian Broadcast Service for the University of Iowa's International Writers' Workshop—the high point of the evening was the competitive, improvised or delivered-from-memory poetic lines offered by the celebrants and set to music/sung by the paid musicians in attendance: "a poetry jam session, no less."[20]

Other traditions that have been subsumed into Euro-American culture also make good cases for the importance of public readings as foundational community events. In 1988, Daniel Boyarin delivered a talk (or the preferred academic term, "paper," which preference underscores that institution's penchant for the written over the spoken) on the traditional meanings of the term "reading" in Judaic culture. Haranguing an academic conference audience quite unused to such a style, Boyarin declaimed and enacted for us the notion that "to read," in Biblical times through the Rabbinic period, meant to publicly harangue, to read aloud for an audience—there was originally no association of the term "to read" with a private act of silent communication between a single reader and a page of text.[21] These public reading events, moreover, did not encompass the performance of the reader's private or individual "feelings," though those may have colored the delivery; the text was usually a document that combined religious and civic directives, or interpreted those issued in other tracts. Moshe Carmilly-Weinberger had also written of the way in which, during the Rabbinic period, religious scholars/community leaders distinguished between serious (Biblical) texts suitable for "public study," and texts they held in low esteem, like personal letters and the Apocrypha, which were more fit for the trivial pastime of private consumption.[22] Public utterance, in other words, indicated seriousness of purpose.

Interestingly, one of the groups of texts deemed unfit for serious (i.e., public) study and/or declamation by the rabbis was that set of epics known as the Homeric texts, which were of course themselves performance pieces. The fact of their being deemed unworthy as such by the Judaic rabbinate says more about how these religious leaders viewed them (as artifacts of a pantheistic Hellenism inhospitable to Hebraism) than it does about their actual function; that function, as Gregory Nagy has exhaustively demonstrated, was precisely a public, performative one that bound together, through a rapport established by skilled delivery, the oral poet/reciter with a clued-in and responsive audience, who, because of their familiarity with song culture, in turn authorized the singer's ("author" 's) performance.[23] The Homeric poets, and later, the troubadours of Mediterranean Europe, performed variations not on a set, written text considered the "original," but of songs which came into being through these improvised, demotic variants (Nagy, 10).[24] In other words, the written text was the last step, rather than the first one, in the process of song-making or poem-making, a process whose essence was movement (*"mouvance"* is the term he borrows from Paul Zumthor's study of oral poetry) and process itself.[25] Like the many versions of African American urban, rural, or prison ballads about the Signifying Monkey, the freaks' ball, or Staggerlee (Stackolee), these variants did not strive to match a prior ideal but provided the means for public display of invention and constant reinvention within convention. This performance-based poem-making process characterized oral cultures and demotic (vernacular) languages; as these cultures became print-based, the concept of a static text authored by one individual—text as private property for private consumption—came to have more prestige and to command more formal respect than the oral.

Modern(ist) glosses, however, provide a contrary set of values, with publicness indicating frivolousness—at best "raw energy" but qualitatively inferior work is assumed. One "covers up" the "weakness" of a poem or verbal artifact by a performance style; public reading is the surface that must be brushed aside for a more weighty "expert" assessment of a work's "true," i.e. "deep," value. As print culture's dominance abates in the swirling complexity of postmodernity, there has been a resurgence of serious attention to oral and performative literatures, with a concomitant imaginative refiguring of communities.[26]

This perhaps pedantic race through pre-print-capitalist history is ultimately not necessary to justify the continued presence of the demotic, of oral culture, of the reemergence, through technology such as television, video, and audio taping, radio, and the like—and the populist uses thereof, such as local public-access TV stations, the rapid dissemination of "pirated" audio-cassettes throughout low-income neighborhoods and populations, etc.—of a dynamic insistence on presence itself, and the waning hegemony of the written as mediator for the Great Unknowable that reveals Itself only in private, one-on-one séances.

Publication Issues

> Dis poetry is not afraid of going ina book
> But dis poetry need ears fe hear an eyes fe hav a look
>
> BENJAMIN ZEPHANIAH, "Dis Poetry"

The question of whether to publish arises for slammers and oral poets. Like Nagy's medieval *trouvères* ("discoverers") their work ends when something is definitively cast in print; and there's a reasonable desire to forestall closure on a creative process: invention and reinvention, improvisation, performance, competition, and other interactive modes. However, a substantial number of eminent slammers have published chapbooks or trade books, though they haven't gone through the traditional route of amassing a respectable roster of appearances in journals, submitting completed manuscripts for prizes or publication with small literary presses, etc. Paul Beatty's *Big Bank Take Little Bank*[27] came about because he won a slam: the prize on this particular occasion was publication of a book, rather than an honorific title. Tracie Morris and Edwin Torres, both brilliant performers, have self-published chapbooks apiece; Dana Bryant, Cyn Salach, and Marc Smith (the "founding father of Chicago slam") have each, after ten years of high-profile slam and performance activity, recently published one book of poems.[28] Morris felt that self-publication allowed her complete control over every aspect of production, from choosing paper and type design to commissioning cover art; it also demystified the publishing process for her, so that she's less likely to be bullied in later encounters with professional publishers; it was an important educational project for her.[29]

This attitude of self-empowerment through experience contrasts sharply and admirably with what I've seen in mainstream or academic "creative writing" circles, where self-publication is taken to be a kind of shameful last resort in a business in which success depends on recognizable badges of social approval bestowed from on high, such as having been one of three writers selected from a pool of hundreds by, for example, Coffee House Press or Farrar, Straus & Giroux. A do-it-yourself orientation also brings this poetry into further resonance (though "differently") with small presses, alternative poetry movements, and 'zines that may not be slam-based; many "experimental" artists and writers now securely employed in universities and assured of well-known and well-funded publishers spent the greater part of their poetic careers years publishing themselves and each other in similarly autonomous/anonymous circumstances. (Slammers and open mikers are now undergoing the same kind of pick-up from the mainstream; Paul Beatty's second book of poems came out from Viking/Penguin, and his novel from Houghton Mifflin.)[30] Tia Chucha Press, founded and operated by Chicago slammer Luis Rodriguez, publishes work from its own milieu, including an anthology, *Stray Bullets: A Celebration of Chicago Saloon Poetry,*[31] and books by individual slammers.

Moreover, some slammers, like Bryant and Morris (who has been active in the Black Rock Coalition), have recorded their work with music, and consider this medium at least as significant as print (contrast this to the mainstream poetry world: recently I was asked to delete a section on "Recorded Work" from a bibliography for an encyclopedia article on Allen Ginsberg, though oral performance has been one of Ginsberg's signature contributions to postwar American poetry). Willie Perdomo's book, *Where a Nickel Costs a Dime,* comes with a CD, and Maggie Estep and Reg E. Gaines have both issued wildly popular "spoken word" CDs before coming out with books.[32] And there are more published and recorded anthologies every day.[33]

Book publication represents a different venue, a different economy, a different audience from the dynamic, interactive immediacy of the bar or café scene. Publishing a book is not generally regarded either as a sell-out nor as a crowning achievement. The challenge of creating a poem that "works on the page as well as the stage" is considered a worthy one, though it is not fetishized as a way of proving that a poem "can stand on its own"— another reliquary phrase that still sometimes haunts the literary world from the other side of '68. (A recent, fairly insipid reading by a poet who experiments daringly with the visual possibilities of the page prompts me to wonder why the corresponding observation is not more frequently made: "It looks so good on the page, but it sure doesn't hold up in a live reading.") A useful way to think of the discrepancy between text and performance in the case of slam poets is to think of the text as a score for the performance; it points beyond itself to its embodiment in the poet's person: voice, body, animating gestural presence. Tracie Morris's "The Spot," which excoriates "superficial people everywhere" for wearing X-ornamented fashion accessories without truly understanding the depth of Malcolm's message and martyrdom (Morris, 40), or her "Project Princess," which celebrates in exuberant portraiture ("Multidimensional shrimp earrings / frame her cinnamon face / Crimson with a compliment if a / comment hits the right place" [Morris, 13]) young girls in the Brooklyn housing projects where she herself grew up, are both reasonably rich page-reading experiences. But the live performance is breathtaking, as Morris sings, imitates with startling accuracy the "scratch" effect of hip-hop music, gestures, repeats phrases many times over with different syllabic accentuation, and otherwise defamiliarizes through vocal pyrotechnics not only normative American English but her own already highly vernacular written text. In this way, a poetic performance becomes a "total experience" in the way we are used to thinking of drama, film, or live jazz, rather than a secondary-to-the-private-reading-act event by which we ascertain what a page-famous poet looks or sounds like.

Part of the desire to publish is, I would conjecture, a desire to not be perceived in limited and limiting ways as primitives, entertainers, or simply "hip-hop" artists. While the debt to black and other dissident/marginalized popular cultures is acknowledged wholeheartedly, poets like Paul Beatty and Tracie Morris feel ambivalent about being labeled, respectively, the "premier bard of hip-hop" and the "reigning queen of hip-hop poetry," as this kind of pigeonholing is, like all categorizing, confining and in the long run diminishing to a poet's own growth and her/his reception by others. Morris, for example, works in a jazz idiom as much as in a more contemporary/mass cultural hip-hop/rap idiom; significantly, she credits Carmen McRae as a primary influence. Beatty took an M.F.A. in creative writing at Brooklyn College, where he studied under Allen Ginsberg (this is his second M.A.: his first was in psychology at Boston College). His bios on book covers deliberately specify that he is from "West Los Angeles," not to disown a connection with black working-class expressive cultures, but to challenge the stereotypical perception that all African American writers who use the vernacular idiom come from "inner city" areas like South Central. Li-

Young Lee, now well-known in the mainstream lyric poetry world and not considered primarily a performance poet, appears in *Stray Bullets,* where his contributor's bio enumerates his poetry awards (Lamont and NYU's Delmore Schwartz Memorial). Hannah Weiner, a relatively reclusive poet who writes directly from clairvoyant experience, and who has ties to both "New York school" and "language" poets, has been a slam winner at the Nuyorican Poets' Café.

Likewise, while arguing for the literary seriousness of slam and open-mike activity, it is important to not romanticize or fetishize a kind of oral purity over a corrupt mainstream or a precious, solipsistic avant-garde. The boundaries, if they exist at all, are permeable. It is perhaps useful here to invoke Antonio Gramsci's formulation of "the organic intellectual" to argue that these poetries and this poetic activity merit not only a telos-driven exemplification of nonacademic literary activity but the closest possible listening at all registers of poetic reception. The "organic intellectual" is not only a working-class person with an intuitive gift for understanding his/her class situation and social circumstance, but a trained, professional intellectual who uses his/her learning for the benefit of the people. As we have seen, many of the poets discussed here are both, and as public intellectuals their persons and their poetic activity enact the erasure of the barrier between the street and the page, the workshop and the stage.

Dis is de stuff *I* like.

NOTES

For this essay's formation, thanks are due to Charles Bernstein, who patiently edited, argued, and clarified, as well as to Bob Holman, Bob Gale, Kurt Heinz, Joseph Zitt, Carolyn Holbrook, members of the Poetrix list for random commentary, and Joanna O'Connell for common reading. The two epigraphs in this essay are taken from Benjamin Zephaniah, "Dis Poetry," *City Psalms* (Newcastle upon Tyne: Bloodaxe Books, 1992), p. 12.

1. For more on the "rap controversy" (this rap controversy is not the matter of obscenity v. ethnic oral traditions, or the celebration of gang warfare and violence but that of rap's status as "poetry"), see Tricia Rose, *Black Noise: Rap Music and Black Culture in Contemporary America* (Middletown, Conn.: Wesleyan/New England University Press, 1994), in which Rose makes the point that rap is a technology and that to call it poetry is to diminish and sequester it; Tim Brennan, "Off the Gangsta Tip: A Rap Appreciation, or Forgetting about Los Angeles," *Critical Inquiry,* vol. 20 (summer 1994), pp. 663–93, which makes an appeal for "rap appreciation" at the aesthetic level (its political content having been, he claims, done to death) and includes a close reading of a rap lyric (683); Richard Shusterman and Tim Brennan, "Critical Response," *Critical Inquiry,* vol. 22 (autumn 1995), pp. 150–61, in which Richard Shusterman argues that Brennan misread his work on rap and Brennan responds; Henry Louis Gates Jr., "Sudden Def," *The New Yorker,* June 14, 1995, pp. 34–42, which treats the "rap meets spoken word" phenomenon at the S.O.B. nightclub in Manhattan, and which presupposes that rap and poetry/spoken

word are somehow different though resonant forms (distant cousins perhaps), whose meeting is to be met with a certain bemused if affectionate eyebrow-raising.

2. See Lucy B. Palache, "Doggerel," *Princeton Encyclopedia of Poetry and Poetics,* ed. Alex Preminger and T. V. F. Brogan (Princeton: Princeton University Press, 1993), p. 301, for Frye's formulation concerning the "unfinished creative process."

3. Bruce Robbins, ed., *The Phantom Public Sphere* (Minneapolis: University of Minnesota Press, 1993). See especially Nancy Fraser, "Rethinking the Public Sphere: A Contribution to the Critique of Actually Existing Democracy," pp. 1–32; and George Yudice, "For a Practical Aesthetics," pp. 209–33.

4. Walter Benjamin, "The Work of Art in the Age of Mechanical Reproduction," in *Illuminations,* tr. Harry Zohn (New York: Schocken Books, 1969), pp. 241–42.

5. Ian Belcher, letter, *The New Yorker,* July 31, 1995, p. 9.

6. N.W.A. (Niggaz With Attitude), "— — Tha Police," *Straight outta Compton* (Priority Records, 1988). Tan Lin, *Lotion Bullwhip Giraffe* (Los Angeles: Sun & Moon Press, 1996).

7. Simon Frith, "The Good, the Bad, and the Indifferent: Defending Popular Culture from the Populists," *Diacritics,* vol. 21, no. 4 (1991), pp. 102–55. Though primarily concerned with popular music, this article has much to offer the student of popular poetries and other literatures.

8. For good analyses of Gran Fury's artistic, pragmatic, interventionist sophistication, see the final chapter in Walter Kalaidjian, *American Culture between the Wars: Revisionary Modernism and Postmodern Critique* (New York: Columbia University Press, 1993), pp. 252–63, and Yudice.

9. The criterion of the "felt change of consciousness" for determining the poeticity of a verbal artifact comes from Owen Barfield, *Poetic Diction* (Middletown, Conn.: Wesleyan University Press, 1973), p. 48.

10. Charles Bernstein, email to author, July 16, 1996, p. 3. This is not Bernstein's position, but one he was paraphrasing for the sake of analysis.

11. Kamau Brathwaite, in his collected essays, *Roots* (Ann Arbor: University of Michigan Press, 1993), contrasts the poetic possibilities of standard English with those of the more African-inflected Caribbean vernacular (p. 265), for which he has coined the term "Nation Language," and speaks of calypso's ability to "break down the pentameter" (p. 271); Charles Bernstein has suggested the contrast with tetrameter's more populist history (email to author, 11 August 1996).

12. Reg E. Gaines, "Please Don't Take My Air Jordans," on *Please Don't Take My Air Jordans* (Polygram Records, 1994). For a similar discussion of contemporary uses of the ballad form to tell of young people's urban horrors, see Maria Damon, "Tell Them about Us," in *The Dark End of the Street: Margins in American Vanguard Poetry* (Minneapolis: University of Minnesota Press, 1993), p. 101; see also newspaper and electronic media coverage of the trials of the "Central Park jogger" 's assailants, which dwelled on their seeming indifference to the proceedings—they were judged to be indifferent because they were expressionless.

13. The dedication does not appear on the CD but is extemporized in Gaines's performance of the poem on MTV's *Spoken Word Unplugged* (MTV, 1993).

14. Charles Bernstein, email to author, August 11, 1996, p. 3.

15. For descriptions of Blabbermouth Night and of the Place, see Kevin Killian and Lew Ellingham, *Poet, Be Like God: A Biography of Jack Spicer* (forthcoming from Wesleyan University Press); and John D'Emilio, "The Movement and the Subcul-

ture Converge: San Francisco during the Early 1960s," in *Sexual Politics, Sexual Communities: The Making of a Homosexual Minority in the United States, 1940–1970* (Chicago: University of Chicago Press, 1983), pp. 176–95.

16. For a good history of slams, their Chicago origins, their spread across the country to San Francisco, Ann Arbor, Boston and die ganze weldt, see Kurt Heinz, "An Incomplete History of Slam." http://www.tezcat.com/~malachit/slam (1996).

17. Marc Smith, poetry performance, Bryant-Lake Bowl and Theatre, Minneapolis, August 14, 1996. See also Bob Gale, "A Man, a Plan, a Slam: Interview with Michael Brown," *Shout: Community Arts Newspaper for Poets, Storytellers and Performance Artists,* May 1, 1995 (http.//www.bitstream.net/london/may96/brown.html); and, for general interest, *Slam! The International Performance Poetry Newsletter* (available from 24 Arlington St., Medford, Mass. 02155).

18. David Henderson, "The National Black Arts Festival Review," *A Gathering of the Tribes* (winter/spring 1995–1996), p. 145.

19. D. Benites et al., "The Power," BMG Ariola Muenchen GmbH, 1990. Also produced by Snap (single version: Arista Cassette CAS-2013) from the forthcoming album *World Power.*

20. Solomon Deressa, "The Poem and Its Matrix," in *Silence Is Not Golden,* ed. Taddesse Adera and Ali Jimale Ahmed (Lawrenceville, N.J.: Red Sea Press, 1995), p. 181. This poem/essay explores the sense in which poetry, an important cultural and civic activity, is bound up with one's sense of national/ethnic identity, and the trauma (to the poem, to the poet, to poetry) suffered when that sense of identity is obliterated.

21. Daniel Boyarin, Literature and Anthropology Panel, MLA Convention, New Orleans, La., December 1988.

22. Moshe Carmilly-Weinberger, *Censorship and Freedom of Expression in Jewish History* (New York: Sepher-Hermon Press, Inc. with Yeshiva University Press, 1977), p. 14.

23. Gregory Nagy, *Poetry as Performance: Homer and Beyond* (New York: Cambridge University Press, 1996), p. 19.

24. Nagy quotes Bernard Cerquiglini to eloquent effect: "[M]edieval writing does not produce variants; it *is* variance."

25. Paul Zumthor, *Oral Poetry: An Introduction,* tr. Kathryn Murphy-Judy (Minneapolis: University of Minnesota Press, 1990). He uses the word *mouvance* in connection with performance on pp. 51, 203, and 205. Nagy discusses Zumthor's coinage on p. 11 of *Poetry as Performance.*

26 Benedict Anderson, *Imagined Communities* (1983; New York: Verso, 1991) posits a link between the rise of print capitalism and the emergence of the nation-state (the imagined community for which people give their lives), and the concomitant value of "nationalism."

27. Paul Beatty, *Big Bank Take Little Bank* (New York: Nuyorican Poets' Café Press, 1991).

28. Tracie Morris, *Chap-t-her Won: Some Poems by Tracie Morris* (Brooklyn: TM Ink, 1993); Edwin Torres, *I Hear Things People Haven't Really Said* (New York: Edwin Torres, 1991); Dana Bryant, *Song of the Siren* (New York: Boulevard Books, 1995); Cyn Salach, *Looking for a Soft Place to Land: Poems* (Chicago: Tia Chucha Press, 1996); Marc Smith, *Crowdpleaser* (Chicago: Collage Press), 1996.

29. Tracie Morris, conversation with author, December 1993.

30. Paul Beatty, *Joker Joker Deuce* (New York: Penguin Books, 1994); *The White Boy Shuffle* (Boston: Houghton Mifflin, 1996).

31. Ida Therese Jablanovec, Susan James, and José Chavez, eds., *Stray Bullets: A Celebration of Chicago Saloon Poetry* (Chicago: Tia Chucha Press, 1991).

32. Willie Perdomo, *Where a Nickel Costs a Dime* (New York: Norton, 1996); Maggie Estep, *No More Mr. Nice Girl* (Imago/NuYo Records, 1994).

33. A selective sampling: in addition to *Stray Bullets,* see *Aloud: Voices from the Nuyorican Poets' Café,* ed. Bob Holman and Miguel Algarin (New York: Henry Holt, 1994); *Revival: Spoken Word from Lollapalooza,* ed. Juliette Torrez, Liz Belile, Mud Baron, and Jennifer Joseph (San Francisco: Manic D Press, 1995); and *Nuyorican Symphony* (Imago/NuYo Records, 1994).

15

Local Vocals

Hawai'i's Pidgin Literature, Performance, and Postcoloniality

SUSAN M. SCHULTZ

*A*t the 1993 reading for Lois-Ann Yamanaka's book, *Saturday Night at the Pahala Theatre*, written almost exclusively in Hawaiian Creole English (usually called pidgin), I sat quietly while an audience of upward of three hundred people actively and warmly participated in her reading.[1] I had moved to Hawai'i from the mainland only three years before to take a job in the University of Hawai'i–Manoa's English department. When Yamanaka referred to details such as the "Japan pencil cases" used in school, the crowd roared its response. I felt puzzled. Every one of her details sparked astonishment and pleasure in her listeners; there was joy in simply naming these objects that had never found their way into poems before. The audience was participating to an extent that approaches performance theorist Richard Schechner's description of "social" drama, where spectators are performers. He opposes social drama to "aesthetic" dramas that separate audience from performer.[2] In this case, I was attending an aesthetic drama and almost everyone else was participating in a social one. Never had I felt such a sense of other people's community at a poetry reading; rarely had I felt so foreign in an American place.

To write in pidgin is to write in a language that has no standardized orthography; reading pidgin can be difficult even for native speakers who are unaccustomed to seeing pidgin words on the page and who sometimes remark with surprise on the spelling of words like "so-wa" (for "sore"). Linguist Suzanne Romaine writes: "Alterations to standard orthography of whatever kind are visual signals to the reader that something is significant. However, it isn't always obvious that each non-standard spelling represents some significant phonetic feature."[3] Much of what may look like standard

English in a book sounds like pidgin only when it's read aloud by a native speaker. This is, I think, a crucial point; while the standard English reader is able easily to assimilate written pidgin in the silence and privacy of her own reading, she cannot easily do so when she hears pidgin spoken by a native speaker.

In their 1987 essay, "What Is a Minor Literature?," Gilles Deleuze and Felix Guattari argue that in minor literatures, which they define as those created by minorities within major languages, *"[l]anguage stops being representative in order to now move toward its extremities or limits."*[4] Minor writers are those who "hate all languages of masters," and who assert that "what can be said in one language cannot be said in another." Minor writers produce work that is inevitably political and that takes on collective value. Pidgin is such a nonrepresentative language, loud, extreme, and in this ironic manner, minor. For the pidgin writer the English language does not stop being representative so much as it stops being "universal," a dangerous word that is too often used to denote "dominant" rather than truly multicultural. The moment of strongest resistance by the pidgin writer to the dominant language and its "major" literature comes, to my mind, when that writer performs his or her text, either in public or on tape. It is the *sound* of pidgin, the resonance of its shared cultural references rather than its presence on the page, which is most different from standard English. The audience's reaction to Yamanaka was due not to the fact that they were finally hearing her speak *her own words*, the operative dynamic at almost every poetry reading I've ever attended, but because they were hearing their own words in a language more often spoken than written: "This is the authority," writes Deleuze, "the autonomy of the stammerer, of him who has conquered the right to stammer, in opposition to the 'well-spoken' major."[5] This phrase, "the autonomy of the stammerer," puts me in mind of Susan Howe's eloquent quotation of Charles Olson, who wrote that in *Billy Budd,* "the stutter is the plot."[6] Yet Yamanaka's stutter is different from Howe's, not because they aren't both steeped in culture and history, which they are, but because Yamanaka's pidgin is a shared language, nonstandard because it has a separate syntax and vocabulary from the English that most Americans speak and especially because pidgin is mainly spoken, not written down. Where Susan Howe's voice (for example) rises from the written page, Yamanaka's seems to be transcribed on the page, as if it were an edited record of a previously composed text, or the score for a musical performance. Unlike David Antin, Yamanaka does not compose in concert, yet her language emerges out of an oral tradition that his work can only imitate.[7] Deleuze is most interested in the ways in which minor languages transform major ones; he sees "the minoritarian as a potential, creative and created, becoming."[8] While Yamanaka and other pidgin writers will likely have that effect—her recent appearance on the television series *The United States of Poetry* hints at the power of her words for an audience of nonpidgin speakers—I am most interested in the ways in which the performance of pidgin poetry, in public and on tape, has transformed Hawai'i's literature and to some extent its culture more generally.

There is only one poem in Yamanaka's book that contains more than a short phrase of standard English, namely "Tita: On Boyfriends."[9] What the brash pidgin speaker, Tita, does is to shift into what might be called standard American California Valley Girl English at a strategic point in her conversation with her friend (the much berated listener in/to this series of Tita poems). The rest of the book, made up of a series of dramatic monologues by young female speakers talking about their lives, is in flat-out pidgin. On the page, the poem is readily accessible to readers who are not native speakers of Hawaiian Creole English; Yamanaka's spelling of pidgin words often overlaps with standard English spelling. The drama of the language switch is far clearer when Yamanaka reads the poem out loud, shifting from pidgin to standard English and back again. The question I will pose is, why does Tita change languages? And, more importantly, what does this shift tell us about the relationship of pidgin speakers to the dominant language and culture that so briefly makes its appearance in this poem? Finally, why is it that Yamanaka's performance of the poem is so crucial to our understanding of it—and to the very different understanding of native pidgin speakers in Hawai'i?

The word "Tita" refers to a large woman with a loud voice, who is brash and often funny; she is a stock character in routines by such comedians as the late Rap Replinger and more recently by Frank DeLima.[10] Titas gain their authority through their voices; Yamanaka's Tita, who is a preteen, is all voice. But she also feels profoundly insecure about her Japanese-American identity in a culture saturated with the signs of mainland American dominance. She takes on the assumptions of the dominant culture even as she cloaks them in local talk, constructing a highly ambivalent identity for herself. Tita is, above all, a performer, and her sense of herself is highly performative. As Judith Butler defines performativity, "the 'I' only comes into being through being called, named, interpellated, to use the Althusserian term, and this discursive constitution takes place prior to the 'I'; it is the transitive invocation of the 'I.' "[11] In this poem Tita instructs her quiet (because, we imagine, silenced) audience in the wiles needed to ensnare a boyfriend. As I hope to show, she thus mimics the dominant culture's silencing of pidgin speakers. The following passage is crucial:

Richard wen' call me around 9:05 last night.
Nah, I talk *real* nice to him.
Tink I talk to him the way I talk to you?
You cannot let boys know your true self.
Here, this how I talk.
Hello, Richard. How are you?

Oh, I'm just fine. How's school?
My classes are just greeaat.
Oh, really. Uh-huh, uh-huh.
Oh, you're so funny.
Yes, me too, I love C and K.
Kalapana? Uh-huh, uh-huh.[12]

Tita's switch of languages is significant for many more reasons than that of explaining to her friend the way to get a date. Rather, it opens up a problem with historical, cultural, and economic ramifications to pidgin and standard English speakers since at least the end of the last century, through Hawai'i's admission to statehood in 1959 (it was the last state admitted to the union), and on to the present moment. As a scholar and teacher of American poetry in Hawai'i, these are issues that I face every semester. Tita's conscious change of language as she asks her friend about school reveals her to be a savvy sociologist; the shift from pidgin to standard is equally a shift from a "lower class" to a "higher class" language, and from what my students tell me is considered a less to a more feminine way of speaking. She is also switching from the local language to that of the "haole," or white outsider. It is thus a "speech *act*," rather than an act of unconscious speech, like that, say, of a native standard speaker who knows no pidgin. The speaker is acting *up*. At the moment that Tita makes this move, she causes standard English—even for the standard English speaker/listener—to become "nonabsorptive" (Charles Bernstein's term for language that is not easily assimilated to meaning),[13] just as pidgin is the "absorptive" speech of all the characters in Yamanaka's book, and in the milieu that she describes. Or, as the Martiniquan writer Edouard Glissant argues in a related context, she causes the dominant and creole languages to seem *opaque* to each other.[14] That this reversal of positions, pidgin becoming the dominant language, standard becoming downright unstandard, is painful (if liberating) for the pidgin writer is clearest in the last poem of the book, "Name Me Is," where a girl and her friend WillyJoe tattoo their names on each other: his on his back, hers on hers, as they literally bleed language. Here is Yamanaka's speaker's pidgin misprision of Rimbaud: "I IS. / Ain't *nobody* / tell me / otherwise" (140)— the last words of the poem and the book.[15] "I is" is for these speakers every bit as revolutionary as Rimbaud's bit of proleptic postmodernism, "I is another." And every bit as self-estranging, in the way that self-knowledge so often is.

Yamanaka's discussion of dating in "Tita: Boyfriends" is hardly egregious or unique. In a 1960 article, "Communication: A Problem of Island Youth," published in *Social Process in Hawaii*, Andrew W. Lind writes (remember that this was a year after statehood): "The widely recognized reticence of Island youth, particularly of Oriental ancestry, in speaking their minds in the presence of Haoles is in large part, so they themselves confess, a consequence of an unfounded fear that their expression may reflect a flavor of pidgin and hence of lower-class status."[16] He then quotes an unidentified "Japanese male" as saying "Youths have hesitated to date because of the lack of social confidence. I have been asked many times as to how to act, how to ask for a date, and even as to what to do or where they should go on a date, by my friends."[17]

This young Japanese male also tells Lind, "Oriental youths are afraid to speak up. These youths lack social ease, in that they feel that they will be laughed at every time they open their mouths. They feel that people will not accept them, and that a mistake will show their intelligence." Later, he adds that he has "seen youths actually perspire, while speaking."[18] (And which of us has not?) Stephen Sumida, whose *And the View from the Shore: Literary, Traditions of Hawai'i* (1991) is the first important study of Hawai'i literature, writes: "Hawaii's local people have been stereotyped as being silent or quiet, not merely reticent but deficient in verbal skills and therefore incapable of creating literature of any merit, much less a literary tradition."[19] In 1994 Suzanne Romaine quoted a writer who reported that her university writing teacher told her to write in her pidgin voice (an unusual event, mind you). Her response: "I cannot do it because I will be showing my ignorance to the whole class. I don't want them to think of me as stupid because of the way we talk everyone thought we were stupid . . . And then what happened is I found this kind of artistic freedom because I saw the history."[20]

Some historical background, of necessity streamlined and simplified. Pidgin developed as a "language of command" that allowed lunas, or foremen on the sugar and pineapple plantations of Hawai'i around the turn of the last century, to give orders to their workers.[21] Plantations, which were developed in the middle of the nineteenth century and owned by "mainland haoles," brought foreign labor to work the fields, much of it from Asian countries: Japan, China, Korea, and the Philippines. The language that developed was a mix of Hawaiian, English, and the workers' native languages; these days, the vocabulary is recognizable as English, but the sentence structure more resembles that of the Hawaiian language. This morning a woman said to me, "Cold the weather, ya?" The multiculturalism of Hawai'i's society, as well as its language, thus originated as part of a strategy of "divide and conquer" on the part of plantation owners. According to historian Ronald Takaki, "Though they imported workers as supplies, planters were conscious of the nationalities of their laborers. The employers were systematically developing an ethnically diverse labor force in order to create division among their workers and reinforce management control."[22] The extent to which the plantation system was stratified according to race and power structures is made comically clear by Milton Murayama in his novel, *All I Asking for Is My Body*, which was written in the late 1950s and published in the 1970s. The manager's house in the novel was located at the top of the hill, the Portuguese and Japanese *luna*'s lived slightly below the managers, and below them were the run-down houses of Filipinos. "Shit too was organized according to the plantation pyramid," the narrator comments, as those at the bottom of the pyramid lived closer to the sewage ditches than those at the top.[23]

Shit may not be so well organized in schools as it was on the plantations, but the linguist Charlene Sato writes that with the demise of the plantation system in Hawai'i, "the locus of language contact and change . . . has moved from the plantation to the schoolyard."[24] In 1924 an English standard school system was installed; children attended either a standard school or a nonstandard one. "Paradoxically," Sato writes, "the English Standard schools played a crucial role in the development of Hawaiian Creole English, simply because they helped maintain the distance between HCE speakers and English speakers for another twenty years."[25] The child, Lei, in Marie Hara's short story "Fourth Grade Ukus," fails to get into Lincoln English Standard School (ironic name, that, since Abraham Lincoln is such an emblem of equality), because she pronounces "the volcano" "Da BO-LO-CA-NO."[26] Ukus, or lice, which stigmatize the student who has them, are also metaphorically words, pidgin words.

A scene of instruction from Yamanaka's new novel, *Wild Meat and the Bully Burgers* (1996): Mr. Harvey, the English teacher, "says for the fiftieth time [is this number fifty significant, I wonder, since Hawai'i was the fiftieth state?] this year: *No one will want to give you a job. You sound uneducated. You will be looked down upon. You're speaking a low-class form of good Standard English. Continue, and you'll go nowhere in life . . . Speak Standard English. DO NOT speak pidgin. You will only be hurting yourselves.*'"[27] Public expressions mirror private ones; the father in Yamanaka's novel tells his daughter, shifting registers as he does: "'And you, you wanna be this, you wanna be that, you better learn how for talk like one haole like me. 'Yes, sir, I would really appreciate this job. What a spell of nice weather we're having here. Oh yes, sir, I am a hardworking individual . . . Yes, sir, uh-huh, I am quite capable of speaking the haole vernacular.'"[28] These are fictionalized examples of what might be termed a pidgin speaker's primal scene, that of being silenced by a standard English speaker and his ideology, invariably based on economics (as was, ironically enough, the very creation of pidgin). Many not-so-fictional characters have spouted the same line, however; in 1960, for example, Elizabeth Carr wrote, in *Social Process in Hawaii:* "This group [of pidgin speakers] rightly deserves our concern, pedagogically, for, with the changing face of the landscape under statehood [in 1959] . . . these dialect-speaking citizens will find jobs to their liking increasingly hard to obtain and hold."[29] Twenty-seven years later, during one of the periodic language wars in Hawai'i, a woman named Yoshie Bell wrote to the editor of the *Honolulu Advertiser:* "Pidgin English is as useless as weeds in the flower garden. Speaking English well is an essential part of finding a good job for any kids and making it in the future."[30] Hawai'i is hardly the only place where this ideology is spelled out so neatly. Glissant, writing about another kind of plantation system in the Caribbean, which engendered another creole, argues that, "According to traditional textbooks [and note that these are *books*] creole is a patois that is incapable of abstract thought and there-fore unable to convey 'knowledge.'"[31] But Glissant quarrels with the kind of knowledge represented by this argument: "We should state that, taken in this sense . . . abstraction is a presumption of Western thought, a presump-tion based on technological expertise and the means of dominating na-ture."[32]

Diane Kahanu has a short poem that is quicker to the point, called "Ho. Just Cause I Speak Pidgin No Mean I Dumb."[33]

Along with the repressive scene of instruction, there is also a revenge narrative. In the 1981 Hawai'i number of *Mana,* a journal published by the South Pacific Creative Arts Society, Leialoha Apo Perkins's "Manifesto for Pidgin English" tells the story of an English composition class taught by a Mr. Holmes, who "treat[s] a paper with a fury that looked like a literary orgasm" and who insists on "correct usage" of English.[34] We all know what that means. He meets his match, however, in a pidgin speaking student from the Big Island town of Miloli'i, which is contrasted to the "important" cities where Mr. Holmes has taught previously. When Holmes (whose name is an ironic pun on "home," I suspect) challenges this student's essay, the student—for once—talks back. What the student asserts is that he knows *more* than Mr. Holmes, by virtue of his having been forced to learn about a history that has nothing to do with him. "Dass w'at I mean. Dass yo' history, *man,* not mine. So I know moah, an' you less; but all da time, you tellin' me I know not'in' when w'at you mean iss I no can never know w'at you know because yo' stuff is all yo' own an' you no can learn mine—mine no count for you, but yo's have to count fo' me. Dass bull, Mistah Holmes. Dass real bull."[35] Among themselves, once the smoke has cleared, the local students agree that this was their best composition class ever.[36]

When Lois-Ann Yamanaka came to my class on island poets from the Caribbean and Hawai'i a couple of years ago, she spoke at length about instructors she'd had at the University of Hawai'i from the mainland who told her not to write in pidgin. One recent Visiting Distinguished Writer, for example, had told her that his English was better than hers. She was angry at these outsiders who told her how to write "well"; she was also angry when she told an interviewer on National Public Radio recently that James Michener's novel, *Hawaii,* portrayed Asians as "Asiatic beasts." The week after Yamanaka visited my class I noticed that the atmosphere was more highly charged than usual, and it *had* been charged almost from day one. After a moment of confusion, I realized that *I* was "the haole instruc-tor." Because I perceived then—and at other times—that my voice was sus-pect, I discovered that the best way to run the class was to set up discus-sions that would run largely without my direct input. Silencing myself became my mechanism of defense against the strong emotions that circu-lated that semester. From that point forward, I better understood the dy-namics of a sometimes angry silence.

But thirty years ago, the *lack* of a literature in pidgin seemed to many a valid argument against the language. In his 1960 *Social Process in Hawaii* piece, Andrew Lind asserts that pidgin's "limited vocabulary and modes of expression, as well as the virtual lack of any literature, give to this language a restricted sphere of usefulness."[37] A couple of sentences further on he ascribes the following characteristics to pidgin speakers: "Servility, illiteracy, and slovenliness are of its essence and Hawaii's claims to maturity appear to be controverted by its widespread use." Going back a few decades, Lind's language of maturity finds its echo in John Reinecke's important study of pidgin, written in the 1930s and republished by the University of Hawaii Press in 1969: "In some places the local dialect, under the influence of past or present nationalist or regionalist traditions, has come to be a cherished semi-literary form of speech to be used beside the standard speech." Its use in literature is unlikely, however, writes Reinecke, because "the local dialect wholly lacks prestige. Its only appearance has been in farce such as 'Confessions of Joe Manuel of the Raddio Patrol,' which appeared in the Saturday editions of the *Honolulu Star-Bulletin* between 1932 and 1933 . . . there will be no reason to use the dialect in writing, except for local color in fiction, in advertising [and] in foolery."[38]

"If there is no such thing as a Hawaii writer," asks the poet, Eric Chock, "how can you teach a Hawaii kid to write?"[39]

More recently (1993) Chock has said: "We in Hawaii are expected to believe that we are subordinate to the mainland. At best we are expected to believe that we are really no different here and can even be *like* the mainland if we try hard enough. We are asked to reject the feeling that Hawaii is special. And when we become numbed and lose the feeling, it then becomes possible to accept mainland history and mainland culture as our own."[40] His poem, "Tutu on da Curb," is an elegy for island culture, disappearing like a traditional Hawaiian woman behind a cloud of smoke from a passing bus:

> She squint and wiggle her nose
> at da heat
> and da thick stink fumes
> da bus driver just futted all over her.
> You can see her shrivel up
> and shrink little bit more.
> Bum bye, she going disappear
> from da curb
> foreva.[41]

In 1993 Darrell Lum, one of Hawai'i's best fiction writers in pidgin, told an interviewer: "We continue to deny the value of our language. Local literature is about validating a people. When you acknowledge a language, you acknowledge a people."[42] Marie Hara, Arnold Hiura, and Stephen

Sumida organized the Talk Story conference in 1978 which, along with the founding of Bamboo Ridge Press, launched a renaissance in local Asian American writing. According to Chock and Marie Hara, the talk story tradition began when plantation workers gathered in the fields for meals and talked about political, social, and cultural issues.[43] People talking story squatted on their haunches, low to the ground, and spoke softly, without moving, so that the authorities couldn't see them. The founding of unions early in the century, which brought together workers from different nationalities and ethnic backgrounds, came out of such moments of talking story—in pidgin. Chock thinks that Hawai'i's local literature is in "the high period of the talk story form," a form that is necessarily oral in its origins. He himself didn't think of writing poems in pidgin until he began talking (and I think it important that it's *talking*) about writing not with professors at the University of Hawai'i, where he was a master's student in the late 1970s, but with friends in the Talk Story group and the Bamboo Ridge Study Group, which was founded in the early 1980s. Talking about pidgin literature, at that point, still took place beyond the purview of the "authorities" who taught literature. *Talk Story: An Anthology of Hawaii's Local Writers,* published in 1978, contained no poems in pidgin, although some stories and plays contain pidgin dialogue.[44]

The young writer, R. Zamora Linmark, organized the reading for his novel, *Rolling the R's,* as a performance—complete with drag queens and other costumed characters—because he wanted to "pay homage" to the voices he grew up with.[45] As my colleague, Craig Howes, noted at a Local Literature Conference in 1994, most people first encounter local literature through performances, whether of Darrell Lum's plays or dramatized short stories, the popular rendering of fairy tales into pidgin by Lisa Matsumoto (including *Once upon One Nodda Time,* a translation of Shakespeare's *Twelfth Night,* and the recent *Compleat Works of Wllm Shkspr*).[46] The creation of Hawai'i's literature in pidgin is, above all, a collective effort.

"We say that a national literature emerges when a community whose collective existence is called into question tries to put together the reasons for its existence," writes Glissant, who also (unfortunately) comments that "Martinique is not a Polynesian island. This is, however, the belief of so many people who, given its reputation, would love to go there for pleasure."[47] He claims that the movement from orality to literature is coming full circle, that creoles will develop an *oraliture,* as Haitian writers call it. Where better to represent this than in performance or on tape, in a "secondary orality" (Walter J. Ong's phrase) that is truer to the oral discourse of pidgin than are words on a page?[48]

Edward Kamau Brathwaite famously advocates a "nation language," or one that leaves behind the pentameter for a rhythm closer to that actually used by Caribbean people. It is also a public language: "Reading is an isolated, individualistic expression. The oral tradition on the other hand demands not only the griot but the audience to complete the community: the noise and sounds that the maker makes are responded to by the audience and are returned to him."[49]

But when asked if he composes differently in pidgin than he does in standard English, Darrell Lum, however, said that no, when he is composing a story, he thinks of pidgin as a written language.[50]

Lois-Ann Yamanaka insisted on recording her tape twice. The first time, according to the writer, Rodney Morales, who was technical director for the recording, she said it didn't go well because she didn't move her hands.[51] "The oral . . . is inseparable from the movement of the body . . . Utterance depends on posture, and perhaps is limited by it."[52] Yamanaka's performances are remarkable for their physical and emotional intensity; as the performer/director Keith Kashiwada said to me, it's as if she were born not so much to write as to perform.

The oral poet, according to Paul Zumthor, unifies his or her community.[53] This is easy to see in work by Darrell Lum or Eric Chock, work that evokes a community united by values like family and Asian traditions carried on in the new world. Strange then that Yamanaka's construction of unity comes out of poems so occupied with violence; it is as if community is being formed around the sounds of community falling apart. Yamanaka's (and Linmark's) characters are people under siege, threatened by domestic violence, by self-hatred, by mainstream American pop culture.

"Late in the summer of 1987," wrote Charlene Sato in 1991, "Hawaii's Board of Education (BOE) formulated a policy on 'Standard English and Oral Communication,' a preliminary version of which mandated that 'Standard English' [would] be the mode of oral communication for students and staff in the classroom setting and all other school related settings except when the objectives cover[ed] native Hawaiian or foreign language instruction and practice."[54] Opposition to the policy was, for once, loud, and the policy was not passed. But pidgin is still censored, in practice if not by law. Yamanaka has been asked to give schools lists of the poems she wants to read to students; sometimes she's asked not to perform certain poems. I would argue that such censorship has at least as much to do with the poems' being in pidgin as it does with their containing four-letter words. The poems are profane, but Yamanaka has taken this language from the world the students know, not from outside of it. The poems' speakers are often racist, but the author distances herself from them. Yamanaka's characters use violent language to talk about violence: in her poem "Parts," which begins with a flourish of language so intense and seemingly innocuous that members of the audience start laughing (I've witnessed this at two public readings and in the classroom, when I've played the tape), a mother yells at her child:

What I told you
about digging your nose?

Who taught you that?
You going get
two slaps
I ever see you
doing that
in public again.
Good for you
your nose bleed
and I hope you get
so-wa stomach too
for eating that shit.[55]

The laughing always stops suddenly in the middle of the poem, as audience members realize that they are laughing at child abuse. The effect, again, is much greater when Yamanaka reads to a large audience than when her work is read off the page. Walter Ong asserts that "violence in oral art forms is also connected with the structure of orality itself. When all verbal communication must be by direct word of mouth, involved in the give-and-take dynamics of sound, interpersonal relations are kept high—both attractions and, even more, antagonisms."[56] Glissant certainly helps us again in this instance: "the traditional Creole text, folktale or song is striking in the graphic nature of its images."[57] More specifically, according to Rob Wilson, "Yamanaka's local Japanese identity is hardly one of purity or ethnic wholeness, but one of self-division, self-hatred even, which includes a longing to be othered into haole (white) pop cultural styles."[58] To say this out loud, however, brings shame upon the community at large. And it must be said out loud in pidgin. As Darrell Lum, now working toward a doctorate in education, remarks, educators still intensely resist pidgin.[59]

Many of Yamanaka's poems are *about* acts of censorship within a pidgin-speaking community against its own language practices, including the potent use of profanity. In "Lickens" we hear:

Ho boy, one time my small sista wen' say *fut*
which we no could say 'cause the word
us had for use was *poot*
and she got lickens with the green brush
which was mo so-wa than the fly swatter
but both was less so-wa than the iron hanger.[60]

In the next poem in the book, "Dead Dogs RIP," the family's dog, Wiki, participates in the censorship:

Wiki wen' bite my friend Claude
on his ass 'cause he said fuck
in our house. My sista told him
no say f-word around Wiki
but Claude start screaming *fuckfuckfuck*
in my sista's face for fun

and Wiki wen' rush his ass, for real.
But now Wiki dead.[61]

Glissant comments on standard French bumper stickers in Martinique that are creolized by adding or subtracting letters. In Hawai'i you see bumper stickers that read: "no blame me: I voted for Bu." Bu (full moniker, Bula'ia, fake Hawaiian for "bull liar"), who sports a chaotic yarn wig and blacked out front tooth, ran for governor in the last election as a protest candidate, although he didn't appear on the ballot. (My seventy-eight-year-old landlord voted for him.) He can now be seen on TV advertising for Pacific Nissan, which shows that there can be a fine line indeed between a language spoken as protest and that same language used as an advertising tool. The connection between pidgin and humor is doubtless older than Bu or even Rap Replinger, who became a local hero in the 1970s, but few are as acute at social commentary as was Replinger. In his "Room Service" skit, Replinger does the voices of a tourist asking for his meal and of the Tita who rather purposefully misunderstands, speaking in pidgin and substituting local food for the hamburger that he wants.[62] As Schechner argues, "Western thinkers have too often split ritual from entertainment privileging ritual over entertainment."[63] If Hawai'i's readings and tapes represent a kind of communal ritual of self-affirmation, they do so often through sheer laughter, even when that laughter turns quickly to pain.

Glissant writes, in his "Cross-Cultural Poetics": "One could imagine—this is, moreover, a movement that is emerging almost everywhere—a kind of revenge by oral languages over written ones, in the context of a global civilization of the nonwritten. Writing seems linked to the transcendental notion of the individual, which today is threatened by and giving way to a cross-cultural process."[64] Is Hawai'i's literature on tape an "oraliture," as Glissant terms the return of the oral to literature? Are Hawai'i's literary artists more like griots than like writers? Yes and no. Certainly, the act of writing in pidgin is an assertion of a kind of "nation language," albeit in a place where most people speak the standard national language, American English. Reading that writing onto a tape recovers the sense of pidgin as a spoken language, though at quite some remove. This is oral language that has been written and then reread to an audience that is either actual (at a reading) or abstract (if the listener is alone) or a bit of both (as in classroom use of the tapes). To record a speaking voice is to fix it as firmly in time as it is to transcribe that voice in writing. Yet this paradox, this image of voice (like the performance poet David Antin's "image of talking"), is strikingly appropriate.[65] For pidgin is, among other things, a language of resistance, of anger (in Yamanaka's case), of active nostalgia (in Chock's case), a language that resists the absorptive talons of a dominant language and culture. As Glissant writes: "the role of Creole in the world of the [Caribbean] plantations was that of defiance."[66] It is at once a language of colonialism and postcoloniality, a language by which plantation workers were branded by plantation owners and lunas, and at the same time the language through which these workers resisted the world outside of their "talk story" culture. At a time when American culture is only getting stronger in Hawai'i as it enters through radio and television waves, cable, and the new outlet malls that are springing up all over the island of Oahu, these taped voices alert their listeners to the dangers—and the curious pleasures—of assimilation. But the spokenness of local literature also inspires nonpidgin speakers in Hawai'i to learn the language. According to Keith Kashiwada, his friend, John Wat, learned pidgin in order to present the work of Eric Chock and other local writers in performance.

If Chock's and Yamanaka's poems are written in something like a "nation language" (though they lack any vision of a political "nation" separate from the United States), the poems themselves are hardly pure instances of talk story unmediated by literary notions disseminated by members of the dominant culture. For these are carefully crafted workshop poems; for example, Chock bases his poems on images, his use of images on T. S. Eliot's notion of the "objective correlative," and he keys his use of pidgin to the particular image at hand. Yamanaka creates ironic written distances between herself and her narrators, playing Mark Twain to Tita's Huck, foreshadows images and ideas, brings the poems' elements to neat (en)closures. They are not just the poets of Talk Story; they are also poets who've studied with mainland writers teaching at the University of Hawai'i-Manoa. These twin influences are responsible for hybrid works, at once radical and conservative in the context of the Talk Story culture and in that of the university culture.

Work in pidgin, therefore, is almost inevitably in dialogue with the language and ideology of the dominant culture. In "Tita: User," Tita argues that she hasn't stolen her friend's tapes:

> Eh—no act. I no mo your Donny Osmond 8-track.
> I hate *Down by the Lazy Riva*.
> And I no mo your Captain and Tenille tape either,
> so get off it. I so piss off right now
> I like buss all the tapes
> I *did* borrow from you.[67]

She then distinguishes between "stealing" and "borrowing":

> No get *wise*. No ac-cuse.
> 'Cause when you ac-cuse,
> you *act* like I *use*,
> and I no use, I borrow.

In any meeting of dominant and nondominant cultures the question of "using" and "borrowing" is crucial; the characters in Yamanaka's world "borrow" American pop culture and standard American English even as they are "used" by it. Their modes of resistance are often seen as self-destructive; as we have heard, the very act of speaking pidgin is still considered by many to be self-destructive in the face of a national job market and a school system that reflects—and enacts—mainland values. And yet there are now countertapes: contemporary Titas have not only the current avatars of Captain and Tennille and Percy Faith to borrow or use, but also the tapes of Lois-Ann Yamanaka, Eric Chock, and others. Now that there are Hawai'i writers and performers, to return to Chock's point, Hawai'i's children are becoming writers.

With the recent publication of Lois-Ann Yamanaka's first novel, *Wild Meat and the Bully Burgers,* on the mainland United States by Farrar, Straus & Giroux, Hawai'i's local literature has entered the mainstream, something that seemed impossible merely a decade ago. According to the poet Eric Chock, another major New York house told Darrell Lum about a decade ago that his work was "too provincial."[68] Signs of a mainland audience do predate the 1996 novel, however. Yamanaka's *Saturday Night at the Pahala Theatre* was the first book published by Honolulu's Bamboo Ridge Press, which was founded in 1978, to have blurbs on the back cover; none of these blurbs is by a local writer. They assert, by turns, that the poems are "universal" and that they "transcend place" (Faye Kicknosway); that Yamanaka "refuels the English language" (Jessica Hagedorn); that her writing is "raw and elegant" (Kimiko Hahn). Howard Junker, editor of the California-based journal ZYZZYVA, goes so far as to say that "Lois-Ann Yamanaka speaks a language we all know in our heart of hearts, but never see on the page." *Do* we all know this language? If we do, have we then denuded language of its immediate value as a carrier of culture (as Ngugi wa Thiongo would insist) and supplanted it with a metaphorical meaning that erases that function? How many of us can speak it? How many of us understand references like "Japan pencil cases" and "li hing mui"? The tapes that Bamboo Ridge Press has made of its authors since 1990 embody this paradox, that local literature is at once resistant to the dominant culture and is being rapidly assimilated into the multicultural lit biz. According to Darrell Lum, one of the founding editors of Bamboo Ridge, the audience for the tapes originally was thought to consist of mainland teachers who wanted to teach the texts in their classrooms but couldn't read the literature out loud. But the reception by local listeners is, as you may imagine, quite different.[69] Now, according to Eric Chock, another of Bamboo Ridge's founding editors, the tapes sell mainly in Hawai'i, and the best-selling tapes are those by Lum and Yamanaka, namely those with the most pidgin on them.[70] For Hawai'i listeners, the tapes reinforce a sense of community centered around the person of the writer/reader. They assert the importance of community (a central tenet of Lum's and Chock's definitions of "local") over that of individualism (or the eminently written American tradition of Ralph Waldo Emerson and Henry David Thoreau). But the fact that the tapes carry voices that are reading texts—even if those texts are written in a language that is almost always spoken—suggests that Hawai'i's literature is created out of a strategic reconstruction of the oral out of the written. Speakers of standard English, and almost all members of the University of Hawai'i English department, including myself, do not speak Yamanaka's language; I think that is precisely one of her points in writing pidgin. That I have been speaking about—if not for—her, is ironic, and in some manner troubling to me. And yet, if I do not speak Yamanaka's language, I certainly recognize its importance. It is out of a double sense of that recognition and that lack of it that I have talked out this essay.

NOTES

1. Lois-Ann Yamanaka, *Saturday Night at the Pahala Theatre* (Honolulu: Bamboo Ridge Press, 1993).

2. Richard Schechner, *Performance Theory* (New York: Routledge, 1988), p. 171.

3. Suzanne Romaine, "Hawaii Creole English as a Literary Language," *Language and Society*, vol. 23 (1994), p. 541.

4. Gilles Deleuze and Felix Guattari, "What Is a Minor Literature?" in *Out There: Marginalization and Contemporary Cultures*, ed. Russell Ferguson et al. (Cambridge: MIT Press, 1990): pp. 59–70.

5. "One Manifesto Less," in *The Deleuze Reader*, ed. Constantin V. Boundas (New York: Columbia University Press, 1993), p. 220.

6. Susan Howe, "Talisman Interview," in *The Birth-mark: unsettling the wilderness in American literary history* (Hanover, N.H.: Wesleyan University Press, 1993), pp. 180–81.

7. In "durations," David Antin talks/writes that he is interested in "that kind of performance in which the moment directs me which way to go." He speaks because spoken language is spontaneous, resembles the movement of thinking; Yamanaka speaks because her language belongs more to an oral culture than to a literate one. The irony is that Antin speaks first and transcribes second, while Yamanaka writes her work first and then performs it. See Antin, "durations," in *what it means to be avant-garde* (New York: New Directions, 1993), p. 65.

8. Deleuze, 150.

9. Yamanaka, *Saturday Night*, 41–43.

10. Rap Replinger, *Poi Dog with Crabs* (Mountain Apple Company, 1992).

11. Judith Butler, *Bodies That Matter: On the Discursive Limits of "Sex"* (New York: Routledge, 1993), p. 225.

12. Yamanaka, *Saturday Night*, 41.

13. Charles Bernstein, "Artifice of Absorption," in *A Poetics* (Cambridge, Mass.: Harvard University Press, 1993).

14. Edouard Glissant, *Caribbean Discourse: Selected Essays*, ed. and tr. J. Michael Dash (Charlottesville: University of Virginia Press, 1989), p. 133.

15. Yamanaka, *Saturday Night*, 140.

16. Andrew Lind, "Communication: A Problem of Island Youth," in *Social Process in Hawaii*, vol. 24 (1960), pp. 44–53.

17. Lind, 48.

18. Lind, 48.

19. Stephen Sumida, *And the View from the Shore: Literary Traditions of Hawai'i* (Seattle: University of Washington Press, 1991), p. 227.

20. Romaine, 544.

21. Lind, 44.

22. Ronald Takaki, *A Different Mirror: A History of Multicultural America* (Boston: Little, Brown, 1993): p. 252.

23. Milton Murayama, *All I Asking for Is My Body* (1977; Honolulu: University of Hawai'i Press, 1988), pp. 28–29.

24. Charlene Sato, "Linguistic Inequality in Hawaii: The Post-Creole Dilemma," in *Language of Inequality,* ed. N. Wolfson and J. Manes (Berlin: Mouton, 1985), pp. 255–72. I used a manuscript copy with different pagination.

25. Sato, 255–72.

26. Marie Hara, *Bananaheart* (Honolulu: Bamboo Ridge Press, 1995), p. 48.

27. Lois-Ann Yamanaka, *Wild Meat and the Bully Burgers* (New York: Farrar, Straus & Giroux, 1996), p. 9.

28. Yamanaka, *Wild Meat,* 148.

29. Elizabeth Carr, "A Recent Chapter in the Story of the English Language in Hawaii," in *Social Process in Hawaii,* vol. 24 (1960), pp. 54–62.

30. Yoshie Bell, "Letter to the Editor," *Honolulu Advertiser,* 28 September 1987.

31. Glissant, 182.

32. Glissant, 182.

33. Diane Kahanu, "Ho. Just Cause I Speak Pidgin No Mean I Dumb," in *The Best of Bamboo Ridge,* ed. Eric Chock and Darrell H. Y. Lum (Honolulu: Bamboo Ridge Press, 1986), p. 43.

34. Leialoha Apo Perkins, "Manifesto for Pidgin English," in *Mana: A South Pacific Journal of Language and Literature: Hawaii Edition,* ed. Richard Hamasaki and Wayne Westlake, vol. 6, no. 1 (1981).

35. Perkins, 5, 8.

36. Perkins, 12.

37. Lind, 45.

38. John Reinecke, *Language and Dialect in Hawaii: A Sociolinguistic History to 1935* (1934; Honolulu: University of Hawai'i Press, 1969), pp. 180–89.

39. Eric Chock, "On Local Literature," in *The Best of Bamboo Ridge,* 8.

40. Romaine, 534.

41. Eric Chock, *Last Days Here* (Honolulu: Bamboo Ridge Press, 1989), p. 63. Bamboo Ridge also published a tape of Chock reading from the book.

42. Romaine, 533.

43. Telephone interviews, April 1996.

44. Eric Chock et al., eds., *Talk Story: An Anthology of Hawaii's Local Writers* (Honolulu: Petronium Press/Talk Story, 1978).

45. From Linmark's M.A. exam.

46. Howes's "Fact One" about Hawai'i writing is that *"the audience for Hawaii writing will continue to grow at a faster rate than the number of its readers"* (54). Craig Howes, "Tradition, Literary History, and the Local Talent," in *Hawai'i Literature Conference: Reader's Guide* (Honolulu: privately distributed, March 12, 1994), p. 53.

47. Glissant, 104, 1.

48. Walter J. Ong, *Orality and Literacy: The Technologizing of the Word* (London: Routledge, 1982), p. 136.

49. Edward Kamau Brathwaite, "Nation Language," in *The Post-Colonial Studies Reader* ed. Bill Ashcroft, Gareth Griffiths, and Helen Tiffin (London: Routledge, 1995), p. 312.

50. Interview with Darnell Lum, April 1996.

51. Interview with Rodney Morales, April 1996.

52. Glissant, 122.

53. Paul Zumthor, *Oral Poetry: An Introduction*, tr. Kathryn Murphy-Judy (Minneapolis: University of Minnesota Press, 1990), pp. 13–31.

54. Sato, 653.

55. Yamanaka, *Saturday Night*, 68.

56. Ong, 45.

57. Glissant, 125.

58. Rob Wilson, "Bloody Mary Meets Lois-Ann Yamanaka: Imagining Hawaiian Locality from *South Pacific* to Bamboo Ridge," *Public Culture*, vol. 8 (1995), p. 146.

59. Interview with Darnell Lum, April 1996.

60. Yamanaka, *Saturday Night*, 88.

61. Yamanaka, *Saturday Night*, 88.

62. Replinger, "Room Service," on *Poi Dog*. Replinger's appeal is not exclusive to Hawai'i audiences. Australian audiences laughed when I presented an earlier version of this essay—and played the tape—in Hobart and Melbourne.

63. Schechner, 155.

64. Glissant, 126.

65. Antin: "what i want to do is bring an image of talking out of the air and onto the page." "the river," in *what it means to be avant-garde*, p. 124.

66. Glissant, 127.

67. Yamanaka, *Saturday Night*, 35.

68. Telephone interview with Eric Chock, April 1996.

69. Interview with Darrell Lum, April 1996.

70. Telephone interview with Chock, April 1996.

Who Speaks

Ventriloquism and the Self in the Poetry Reading

RON SILLIMAN

For Larry Eigner

Who speaks? The trash containers in the cafeteria of a firm for which I used to work were not freestanding but were set directly into the walls. In the bland, corporate pastels of the room, the containers were almost invisible. Such invisibility is important to a society that feels squeamish about its waste products, even if they are only napkins, styrofoam cups, and plastic spoons. Functionally, each trashcan, lined with a dark nonbiodegradable bag, hid behind a small locked door. The top portion of the door was a hinged panel through which to shove your garbage. On each panel appeared the words THANK YOU.

Who speaks? At one level, the words *thank you* in this context mean "put garbage here." At another, an anonymous architect might be expressing relief as well as gratitude: the social contract permits a high-order abstraction, enabling him or her, as well as ourselves, to dispose of garbage while barely acknowledging its presence.

The first of these two readings harks back to Jacques Lacan's revision of Ferdinand de Saussure's famous illustration of the linguistic sign,[1] replacing the linguist's drawing of a tree next to the word "arbor" with a drawing of two doors, labeled "ladies" and "gentlemen."[2] Lacan's point—and he himself calls the substitution a "low blow"—is that reference entails displacement. It would not take much to show how the use of *thank you* for "put garbage here" extends a parallel logic. None of these signs names what is deposited therein. Which is more repressed, a form that genders its act of denial into a double system of toilets, or a form such as *thank you,* which avoids mentioning even a grammatical subject?

My second reading is more ironic. Part of me likes the idea of the self-reflexive architect stepping forward out of the shadowless wall to address the audience, even if the image is less a Brechtian theater device and more along the lines of the mythic hag-in-the-woods emerging to warn the travelers. Unfortunately, the bulk of that building is pure architectural banality. I'm suspicious of my attempt to assign the architect's voice to these words.

The question remains, Who speaks? Like a lot of what Fred Jameson and Stanley Fish have taken to calling "postcontemporary life," the words *thank you* simply irrupt on a cafeteria wall, proposing an entire conversation—"put garbage here," "okay," "thank you"—through a single element. Even the subject of the sentence (*I* thank you, *we* thank you, *your coworkers* thank you, *the bosses* thank you, etc.) remains tacit, repressed.

The writing on the wall is like much (possibly even most) of the written language Americans consume today in that it presents no overt evidence of a subject. Street signs, underwear labels, the narratives on our boxes of cereal, the questions our computers ask of us—all share this linguistic stance of anonymity. The tone of an absent-but-neutral subject is so common among newspaper headlines that a publication that strays from the norm, such as the *Village Voice,* the *New York Post* or even the *National Enquirer,* is immediately marked as distinct, with mucho personality. (The *Voice's* headlines, for example, make much use of puns, jokes, alliteration, and allusion, while its roster of hot books, subtitled *Our Kind of Best-Sellers,* announces the presence of a subject by foregrounding the possessive. This style has sustained the *Voice* as an editorial persona through no end of editorial revolutions, counterrevolutions, and coups over the years—the substance beneath the style seems virtually irrelevant.)

Much (although not all)[3] of the anonymous commercial language of daily life is constructed around what Charles Bernstein calls the normative or plain style of grammar. This discourse of the social contract is writing in the purest Derridean sense—even in its most truncated forms, as on this wall, it insinuates a universe of order, a hierarchy made to appear natural. This writing even invades our speech through communications technology, such as voice mail or telephone banking.

Far from being incidental, the instrumental language of an absent subject has, in the past half century, created a pervasive tone. This constant, not-quite-subliminal static, like the irritating electronic hiss of a cheap tape deck, forms the ground against which we consume all "postcontemporary" experiences of discourse, spoken or written. Note the range of emotional reactions that this phenomenon triggers. Even as we find it difficult to resist the seductions of these passive-aggressive discourses, we aren't very fond of the experience. From professional jargons to street lingoes, people everywhere perpetually stylize their use of language. This is part of the compulsive creativity of being human. But, in an age where an absent-but-neutral subject saturates us and represses any dynamic of linguistic innovation, simple everyday stylizations of the word take on new qualities of social resistance.

While such resistance occurs throughout almost all forms of literature, it approaches an extreme form in print through the poem as confession of lived personal experience, the (mostly) free verse presentation of sincerity and authenticity that for several decades has been a staple of most of the creative writing programs in the United States. Nowhere is this more evident than when this mask appears not in print but *in person,* at dozens of the open-mike or poetry slam events that occur around the United States every day of the week. These are events to which writers as well as an audience come with relatively little in the way of an advance idea who will or will not be reading[4] and in which any reader who is not an established regular of the particular venue must confront an audience that will be entirely unfamiliar with many if not most formal and referential allusions that occur in any given text. In such circumstances, a text *as text* is reduced to its most basic features: perceptible surface characteristics, narrative or expository thread and a sense of "personality" that is inseparable from the presentation of the reader him- or herself. Given that so many other phenomena associated with the poem are lost in this context, what motivates the audience to attend?

Many formal features of the text are, if not absent, only barely audible in an oral presentation—for example, the shape of lines, stanzas, or paragraphs on the page. Even with experienced performance poets, the question of form often reduces to one of sound, as in the use of reiteration (one wants to call it *rhyme*) in the work of John Giorno. Other dimensions of the poem account for much of the success of this sort of intentionally ephemeral verse: a pure pleasure in highly contained narratives and expositions;[5] the presentation of personality itself *as an object;* and a sense of pleasure in the event itself as a narrative of risk developed over an evening, especially in the case of slams where the overriding question behind every performance is not *what is this text?* but *who will win?*[6]

The presentation of personality, of person as such, represents the particular element of all open readings, competitive or not, that separates this phenomenon from nearly all other like public performances in our society.[7] Unlike the event of a reading devoted entirely to a featured reader, especially if that is a person whose books are available and apt to be known to a large portion of the audience, where the focus might shift over to a question of "how does he or she relate to his/her text," there is no substantial separation in the open reading between the performer and the text performed. Unless the performer takes on an elaborate and identifiable persona—"I am a sunflower," "I am Aaron Burr"—the "I" of the text and the "I" of the person standing in front of the audience are peculiarly wedded. It is not so much that in the open reading that identity and agency are joined but rather that in this setting, beyond all others, there is a claim for an equivalence of the two. This is, I would argue, the power of the open reading. It is also its most troubling feature.

Identity and agency are noticeably mysterious in the phrase *thank you* written on the cafeteria wall. They are not absent so much as assumed. (Certainly the implied statement "put garbage here" invokes an entire social relation, although one situated ambiguously on the fulcrum between a request and a command.)[8] More importantly, these elements are unnamed.

Like the term *self,* identity and agency are concepts that have had a raucous history of late. All three are implicated in the tradition of Enlightenment humanism that has presented a large (and largely vulnerable) target to several varieties of poststructuralism. The question that would unite these terms—"Who speaks?"—is the first sentence in Roland Barthes's 1960 essay, "Authors and Writers."[9] Barthes's text distinguishes between the instrumental activity of intellectuals, whom he calls writers, and others—authors—whose work "intransitively" invokes the vast and infinitely receding horizon of Language, capital *L,* that structure which is neither vehicle nor instrument.

Thirty-eight years ago, when Barthes wrote "Authors and Writers," his text seemed a restatement of Clement Greenberg's distinction between the alleged autonomy of "high" art and the instrumentalism of kitsch. The distinction fueled Greenberg's conceptualization of modernism and, through his influence and alliances, a good deal of the Anglo-American New Criticism as well. Making this element of New Criticism safe for structuralism (as Barthes's project was generally conceived in 1960) represented little more than the importation of an Anglo-American category over to the work of continental theory, a reunification of elements from two traditions that traced their histories back to the work of the Russian Formalists.

Today, however, "Authors and Writers" points in a very different direction—toward Barthes's 1968 text, "The Death of the Author."[10] That text begins by quoting from Balzac's *Sarrasine*[11]—"This was woman herself, with her sudden fears, her irrational whims, her instinctive worries, her impetuous boldness, her fussings, and her delicious sensibility" (a description not of a woman, but of a castrato in drag)—and then asks, "Who is speaking thus?" Only now the horizon of language invoked in 1960 swallows the author whole:

> We know now that a text is not a line of words releasing a single 'theological' meaning (the 'message' of the Author-God) but a multi-dimensional space in which a variety of writings, none of them original, blend and clash. The text is a tissue of quotations drawn from the innumerable centres of culture . . . The writer can only imitate a gesture that is always anterior, never original. His only power is to mix writings, to counter the ones with the others, in such a way as never to rest on any one of them. Did he wish to *express himself,* he ought at least to know that the inner 'thing' he thinks to 'translate' is itself only a ready-formed dictionary, its words explainable only through other words.

Barthes subsumes a lot under that first verb phrase, "We know." It invokes both agency and identity. It also invokes a body of knowledge, pointing to the labor of others, such as Derrida, who dissect the naive assumptions underlying instrumental communication. When Barthes calls instrumentalism " 'theological' meaning," he suggests not only that it is teleological, governed by an ultimate cause, implying the hierarchies of narrative and exposition, but also that it must be taken on blind faith.

The distinction of Barthes's earlier essay no longer holds: instead of writers and authors, one pragmatic and instrumental, the other not, there are only authors—except that the structure of language itself deconstructs any sense we might have of the individual author as an empty vessel, a vehicle for the immanence of language. Except that language here always already dissolves in front of our eyes.

The phrase *We know* demonstrates the least attractive feature of post-structuralism as well, a double-coding that foregrounds the problematic dynamics of meaning while simultaneously performing an institutionally instrumental social operation, using the former to mask the latter. Barthes's operation, the ritual slaying of the author in the text, at first appears to apply to all modes of writing. He explicitly includes criticism:

> Once the Author is removed, the claim to decipher a text becomes quite futile. To give a text an Author is to impose a limit on that text, to furnish it with a final signified, to close the writing. Such a conception suits criticism very well, the latter then allotting itself the important task of discovering the Author . . . beneath the work: when the Author is found, the text is 'explained'—victory to the critic. Hence there is no surprise in the fact that, historically, the reign of the Author has also been that of the Critic, nor again in the fact that criticism (be it new) is today undermined along with the Author.

Except that, in this terrain of pure textuality, where "writing ceaselessly posits meaning ceaselessly to evaporate it," all that remains aspires to criticism, even if it is now criticism with a *différance*. Barthes's text ends metaphorically with the birth of the Reader, capital R, whose existence "must be at the cost of the death of the Author": "Thus is revealed the total existence of writing: a text is made of multiple meanings, drawn from many cultures and entering into mutual relations of dialogue, parody, contestation, but there is one place where this multiplicity is focused and that place is the reader, not, as was hitherto said, the author. The reader is the space on which all the quotations that make up a writing are inscribed without any of them being lost; a text's unity lies not in its origin but in its destination."

This sounds as though Barthes might be intending to include the reader as a participant in the creation of meaning, each work, each reading a collaboration of complex parties—and Barthes's essay and overall work has sometimes been taken as suggesting that larger, essentially liberationist connotation. I myself once made just that interpretation. But I should have read more carefully, because Barthes in the very next sentence robs the reader of any existence: "Yet this destination [the reader] cannot any longer be personal: the reader is without history, biography, psychology; he is simply that *someone* who holds together in a single field all the traces by which the written text is constituted." The idealized, absent author of the New Critical canon has here been replaced by an equally idealized, absent reader. All that remains are the reports of other readers—call them critics— whose texts endlessly read textuality itself, whose claim to authority lies precisely in the self-knowledge of their texts as infinitely deferred, deferring, acts. The valorized irony of this self-knowledge points directly back to the New Critics, for whom irony was the sublime literary effect.

The phenomena that have thus characterized the dark underbellies of poststructuralism (especially in the United States) and the so-called post- modern debate are already inscribed in Barthes's 1968 essay. The problema- tizing of the New Critical canon while resisting any dramatic opening or dispersal of that canon,[12] the continued marginalization of literary alterna- tives, the institutional hegemony of the critic-as-author and of criticism as the object of criticism—criticism for criticism's sake—are all implicit in Barthes's slaying of the author while idealizing the reader of a *text*.

Barthes's move is in this sense a power play, of criticism as social prac- tice on the legitimacy of the literary *text* within that space where they coin- cide, which just happens to be the university. (I am, for the moment, delib- erately avoiding speaking about the voiced public reading, especially the open reading, which occurs typically outside the university proper, even if it is only across the street.) Given this, perhaps it should not be a surprise that while postmodernism in the arts has been conducted largely, although not exclusively, outside of the academy, the postmodern debate has been largely conducted between different schools of professors who agree only that they too dislike it. Thus the characteristic strategy of the ambitious critic and anxious graduate student alike is not the opening of the canons, but rather the demonstration of a critical move upon some text(s) within the already established ensemble of official canons.[13]

All this flows from Barthes's not-quite-innocent two-word phrase, with its simple assertion first of identity and then of agency: *We know.*[14] Even if we decide that Barthes, the person, did not intend the crass institutional politics that would follow, the inherent double-bind appears inescapable: it is not possible for Barthes or anyone else to operate in a purely negative— or, we might say, critical—fashion. Any articulation must include those twin elements of positivity, identity and agency, that socially constitute the mo- ment of presence without which a signifier cannot exist. Let me put this another way: Roman Jakobson's six functions of language—contact, code, signifier, signified, addresser, addressee—those elements active in each lin- guistic act, come into play only at the moment of presence, however com- promised or partial that moment might be.[15] In Jakobson's vocabulary, the category *contact* is nothing less than presence itself. In "The Death of the

Author," Barthes shifts the weight of presence, as such, from the writer to the reader, only to dehistoricize the reader also, denying him or her even the possibility of presence.

But does presence itself disappear, deconstruct, or otherwise evaporate in such circumstances? Absolutely not. Like the ghost in the machine, presence persists in the signifier. Without it, the text is a tree falling in an empty forest. The signifier will not signify. Presence transforms latency into agency. Presence *is* power. It has the capacity to occupy space and fill time.

Once both author and reader have been stripped of "history, biography, psychology," how is it that this free-floating ectoplasm, presence, remains? The New Critics argued that what we experienced was the presence of a text. Close reading without interrogation of the author, the specific methodology of New Criticism, could only magnify and reify the signifier. In Barthes's vocabulary, the presence of the text dissolves, five years after "The Death of the Author," into *The Pleasure of the Text*. Poststructuralism reverses foreground and background with regards to surface issues, but at least here the deeper sum remains unchanged. For if the New Critics argued for the presence of the text, poststructuralism replaces this with a web of influences, echoes, contradictions, and inferences, a social realm that Barthes calls language. In the New Critical case, the signifier is a positive—indeed very nearly a solid—whose complexities point toward an intentionality and thus can be identified as irony. For the poststructuralists, the signifier becomes a negative: meaning lies precisely where intentionality fails. The signifier opens onto a yawning chasm of never-ending possible readings.[16] In both instances, the signifier is not simply represented as a carrier of presence, but indeed as presence itself. Both strategies grudgingly acknowledge that presence necessarily implies direction or valence—one points toward the author, the other toward the reader. Yet each strategy has predicated itself on ultimately dehistoricizing and delegitimating that site of presence. In both cases, the sole authority that remains in the text is the mediating presence of a critic. Who speaks? The critic speaks, but seldom with her or his own tongue.

As a social phenomenon, the reading appears to counter this equation. From the Thursday night open mike at the Pourhouse coffee house and art framing shop in Malvern, Pennsylvania, to Allen Ginsberg playing his harmonium to an SRO crowd in a large auditorium on the Stanford campus[17] to a Saturday afternoon at the Ear Inn in New York, where two readers confront an audience composed mostly of writers and readers whom they already know, the apparent absence at the reading, as such, is that of the critic. Apparent, because in each of these circumstances critical discourse hovers ghostlike around, if not at, the occasion. In the case of a Ginsberg, a Rich, a Bly or an Angelou, it is the audience that, from the perspective of the performer, proves (largely if not entirely) anonymous.[18] Events such as those at the Ear Inn propose that meaning is at least partly a function of community.[19] To the degree that open readings or slams are not composed primarily of "regulars"—and increasingly, many are—they propose a sort of mutual anonymity as the grounds for performance.[20] Who then speaks? And to whom?

If, out of all performance types, the "anonymous" reading most appears to counter the canonical one (and both the celebrity and community readings can be understood as different conceptions of what a canon might look like, who might inform it, and how an individual writer might "fit in"), the ghost of criticism nonetheless lingers in the machine. The canon we might say is channeled first of all through the host, literally the M.C., especially in any circumstance in which some or all of the readers have been invited. If there is a featured reader, the event occurs on two levels, one anointed and the other secular. A slam may displace this slightly by having a panel of judges. Even in those circumstances where the "winner" is chosen through direct audience participation, what occurs is precisely the process of segregation that drives the impulse of canonization. In determining a winner, the slam "names" that writer who in theory shall not be forgotten. Any anonymity is merely a precondition for the process of naming itself.

Imagine a reading in which true anonymity could occur: poets unknown to an audience read works for which no prior context is available, then depart. For example, an unannounced reading at a major urban intersection in the middle of the day, or at an underground transit stop. The audience would then be composed mostly of listeners who had not *intended* to be at a reading, who might have little idea what contemporary poetry is in any of its variants, and who could care less. What would this purely performative event *mean*?

At first, it sounds as if such a reading might arrive at that apotheosis Frank O'Hara hypothesized in his manifesto on Personism: "It puts the poem squarely between the poet and the person, Lucky Pierre style . . . The poem is at last between two persons instead of two pages." But the situation is really just the opposite. O'Hara's pair are known to one another as individuals—the text is flooded with the contexualities of a specific relationship, the antithesis of anonymity. O'Hara's poet can drop names knowing that each will invoke an entire realm of denotation and nuance.[21] If O'Hara's Personism offers the poem as love letter, a purely anonymous reading would be much closer to a different erotic event, that of anonymous sex. The physical body of the Other (poet *and* audient) is present, but purely as a signifier. The subjective experience of each participant is almost entirely solipsistic. The parsimony principle that constructs all meaning still operates, but now the person of the Other is reduced to a fantasy signifier. It is the listener who supplies the entire context about the poet. Far from being a tabula rasa of pure experience, the vocabulary available to the listener (even the most unlettered and disoriented of listeners) through which to contextualize the poet and the phonetext, and thus to derive meaning from the event, is that precisely of the canonic Other—even if here we must expand that concept from Vendler and Bloom (the critical canon) to include such disparate sources as *Readers Digest* or Louis Farrakhan.

Contrast the hollowed-out signifier of a poet on stage with the curious stasis of semiofficial canons in spite of the rapid succession of schools of critical interpretation within the academy. Even as these schools have rejected the container metaphor for language and literature, they have reserved the canonic text itself as prime vessel. Once incorporated into an institutional canon, the text becomes little more than a ventriloquist's dummy through which a babel of critical voices contend. And there is no such thing as a text that has not been positioned by reference to the existence of these canons. Rendered mute by the ventriloquists of criticism, canonic texts differ from the poet at the podium or the trash cans of my office cafeteria only in that it is someone else's garbage being shoved outward upon us all.

In the open or anonymous reading, the specter of criticism still haunts, faintly heard, perhaps unidentifiable. The accidental listener may imagine that, for instance, the reader on a street corner is something akin to a preacher with a weird sacred text. Or is simply a lunatic. Why not?

Thus far, I have been describing what might be spatialized as concentric circles, working from the outside in. At the horizon lies the absent-but-neutral subject within the discourses of social control, the gray languages of administration and commerce against which the gaudier tones of advertising and popular media come as an almost physical relief. Closer in, an ensemble of academic critical practices can be found that directly and indirectly affect the social history of texts (not to mention the well-being of writers and readers alike). Each layer impacts the poet, poem, listener, and reader. How else can we explain, for example, those elements of the slam that openly mimic the culture of professional wrestling?

Closer still to the text—that intersection between writing and reading, between reading silently and to others, around which we pose the question *Who speaks?*—we find the terrain of poetry itself in the form of other poems. One does not write a poem without a conception of poetry. Each poet, each reader or listener perpetually constructs a subjective or private canon about which she or he can, and rightly should, feel enormously partisan. This experience is not just the compilation of a bibliography, but rather is a fully nuanced narrative: the order in which you come upon the writings of others makes all the difference in the world. This narrative is also "always already" thoroughly infected by the specter of secondary discourse, the murmur of ventriloquism, the received idea. Here, reader and writer alike acquire, recognize, and express "history, biography, psychology," those elements through which identity becomes agency, and presence power.

Far too many discussions about the self in the poem fixate upon, and break down at, just this point. The tropes of self adopted and announced by the text are reasonably limited and could be broken into types, perhaps as a series of axes constructed around potential oppositions:

- *the announced self* of both autobiography and the mask of persona, plus some interesting mixed-breed versions, such as Olson's Maximus, *versus unannounced selves,* including the absent-but-neutral voice of omniscience and a host of unreliable narrative options (Ashbery might figure prominently here)
- *the monolithic self versus the polyvalent construction of conflicting selves,* including versions of the latter that superficially present themselves as the former to the reader
- *the self that is conscious of "history, biography, psychology,"* and posits it explicitly or implicitly behind each sentence or line in a work—a feature that much "language poetry" shares with writing that arises from new social movements, regardless of how much they may differ on other planes—*versus the self that suppresses this awareness* in order to posit it implicitly as a transcendent or universal dimension

No doubt there are other polarities as well. Even if it were possible to represent just these axes as a three-dimensional diagram, no two writers would inhabit the same position, even though they might well group into some interesting clusters. The poet-as-signifier of the open or anonymous reading is exactly the case in point: the individual presenter may well have a different idea about what she or he wants the audience to take away from the performance, but the format of the event itself imposes its own order, which, in the most literal sense of that poststructuralist hiccup, "always already" functions as a part of the work.

To the degree that any argument for a position here is just that—an argument for seeing the entire terrain as though one point within it is somehow uniquely privileged—each such statement seems to me problematic. Thus, while I *personally* agree with Bob Perelman that "the represented self . . . centered within a nest of moral, thematic, and metaphorical coherence," presenting a "prefabricated, conventional unity,"[22] suppresses much of what I consider to be most important about living in the real world, I explicitly want to reject proposing that my own solution to this quandary of the writer might be generalizable and of prescriptive value to others. Any solution to the problem of ventriloquism and the crisis of the self in the poem is not to be found by writing as I do. What does seem evident is that evading the question altogether represents an even worse alternative.

Consider the problem of projectivism. The solution proposed by Charles Olson, with its emphasis on the poem as a score for voice, suggests a theoretical justification for the open or anonymous reading's reification of the speaker:

> the HEAD, by way of the EAR, to the SYLLABLE
> the HEART, by way of the BREATH, to the LINE[23]

In the Olsonian world, the text substitutes for the body of the poet. The reader, in a sense that should recall what Barthes wrote about criticism in general, uses the poem to literally *read the poet*, who is the ultimate object of the reading:

> The irony is, from the machine has come one gain not yet sufficiently observed or used, but which leads directly on toward projective verse and its consequences. It is the advantage of the typewriter that, due to its rigidity and its space precisions, it can, for a poet, indicate exactly the breath, the pauses, the suspension even of syllables, the juxtapositions even of parts of phrases, which he intends. For the first time the poet has the stave and the bar a musician has had.[24]

Olson's answer to the challenge of Barthes—"when the Author is found, the text is 'explained'—victory to the critic"—is to substitute the physical presence of the poet for the social ensemble of effects (a kind of absence) the New Critics sought to erase and which the poststructuralists posed as *langue*. In focusing on the performative, Olson's goal is to use the poem as a vehicle to read "the dance of the intellect," the true object of the poem. The physiologic and textual idiosyncrasies of both performer and text are simultaneous signifiers aimed ultimately at a sensual conception of mind: "Is it not the PLAY of a mind we are after, is not that that shows whether a mind is there at all?" In the Olsonian hierarchy, it would seem that the best poem would be that which most reveals the identity of text, body, and mind. Agency is almost a transcendent force: pure will, that which moves the mind and thus creates a text written on and by the body.

In listening to a tape of Olson reading, what one notices is how often the reading itself accelerates, creating an auditory narrative subtext, one of increasing excitement and anticipation. Because the voiced enjambment at the end of each line functions as an engine to the speed of a text, one might expect the texts to move from long lines to shorter ones on the course of the page.[25] While there are some Olson texts that do follow this model— "The Kingfishers" or "As the Dead Prey upon Us"—they are not common. Not unlike listening to a reading of Louis Zukofsky and discovering that he pauses for breath at the end of every second line, Olson's text is a deceptive score at best.

That projectivist poets were not entirely ignorant of the problematics of equating the text with a presentation of the poet, as such, can be seen from the text of a poem such as "The Pattern" by Robert Creeley, which begins

As soon as
I speak, I
speaks. It

```
wants to
be free but
impassive lies

in the direction
of its
words.²⁶
```

Agency is foregrounded with a degree of irony Derrida might envy—its entanglements with the decentering of identity are explicit. The equation of agency with speech, embodied here within an act of writing, raises the question of presence in a manner reminiscent of poststructuralism. Indeed, the next sentence sounds very much like Derrida's conception of supplementarity:

```
Let

x equal x, x
also
equals x.
```

My own argument demonstrates the sort of critical ventriloquism I have just been questioning. Written in the 1960s, Creeley's poem predates the English publication of *Speech and Phenomena* (1973), and *Of Grammatology* (1974) by several years. All that can be deduced from these three short sentences is that the self projected in "The Pattern" is both announced and polyvalent. The term "impassive" is neither a true subject nor an absent one.

Other Creeley poems are equally explicit about the awareness of "history, biography, psychology" as active both within the reading and writing of the text. Creeley's point is my own: within the reading as well as with the printed text, the relation between agency and identity must be understood as interactive, fluid, negotiable. Nothing can be assumed. The contrast with the writing on my cafeteria wall could not be more absolute. This assertiveness, the poem as proposition—and Creeley's sense of form (line, stanza, enjambment, economy of vocabulary) is as much a part of this assertion as is the semantic statement—might be thought of as one side of the coin of self within the poem from the specific perspective of the poet, the other side being the subjective or private canon, with all of the implications for genre and interpretive sensibility that suggests.

Avant le slam, projectivism was American poetry's most aggressive argument for the text understood as a form of speech. No literary tendency did more to foreground the importance of the reading as the social and phenomenal center of the institution of poetry. From Robert Duncan's flirtation, circa 1970, with the idea of the line as a fixed temporal unit (up to and including a half-whispered count of three after every line), to Paul Blackburn's initiation of the contemporary poetry reading series at St. Marks Church, to the book-length transcription of Olson's reading at the

1965 Berkeley Poetry Conference,[27] the reading was elevated by Olson, his friends and heirs to a degree not matched until the arrival of the slam.

The test of projectivism's commitment to voice must be the poetry of Larry Eigner. Due to a birth injury, Eigner suffered a severe case of cerebral palsy that rendered speech difficult. Kept largely at home in Swampscott, Massachusetts, until he was over the age of fifty, Eigner's physical limitations and simple lack of practice talking to people outside of his immediate family made his speech all but unintelligible to any but the most experienced, dedicated, and careful listeners. Even though his contributor's notes and biographical data often mentioned the fact of his palsy, Eigner's difficulties were generally not understood by readers who had not met the person. When he began to "give readings" once he moved west, visual copies of the texts to be read had to be produced, either in photocopy or as overhead projections. In some instances, other readers voiced the work, with Eigner sitting alongside—Allen Ginsberg at some point did a voice-over for a film on Eigner.[28] But on the page, at least, particularly in the early books, Eigner's work appears superficially as a demonstration of projectivist method. Donald Allen even included Eigner amid the Black Mountain poets in *The New American Poetry,* although Eigner had never attended the school.

It is, I suppose, possible to construct an argument that Eigner's attraction to Olsonian devices arose from their ability to approximate for him what his own body could not do with ease by itself and that, in fact, his writing mimed speech because he *desired* speech. Eigner's first contact with the larger poetry scene occurred when he wrote to Cid Corman to complain about the declamatory (i.e., "unnatural") way Corman read texts on his Boston radio program in the early 1950s. Such an argument would represent ventriloquism at its most reductive: as it "explains" the poet, it fail to address what happens in the real world in that moment when Larry Eigner would sit in his wheelchair before an audience (at times up into the hundreds), text projected overhead or everyone rustling through the pages of a handout, roaring his peculiar garble of liquid consonants and growling vowels, calling this (without irony) verse.

Neither the spoken voice, nor the "I" that speaks graphemically on a sheet of paper, nor the body of the reader in front of an audience can ever truly *be* the self of the poem. What you or I or any other reader or listener might bring to the text, Eigner's or any other's, participates in that construction. If there is an imbalance in the power relation between author and audient, in that only one produces the signifying chain of the text, this dynamic is itself open to the admission to awareness and negotiation between these two roles. If, socially and historically, any poem is open to that critical appropriation I've called ventriloquism, it is because the *power of presence* (POP) triggers latent meaning. But it is ventriloquism that codes it.

So the "self" in the poem has very little to do with whether the text is autobiographical, adopts a persona, is dictated by Martians (as Jack Spicer suggested), or utilizes the language of ghosts or lions except insofar as whatever stance it takes proposes a relation between the poet, a real person with "history, biography, psychology," and the reader, no less real, no less encumbered by all this baggage. In poetry, the self is a relation between writer and reader that is triggered by what Jakobson called contact, the power of presence. There is no subject that is not, strictly speaking, inter-subjective.

No event invokes the power of presence like a reading. The performer literally POPs off the stage and *is* the page from which the words of the text emanate, if not actually from which the words themselves appear to have been inscribed. The reading, even the projectivist event at its most rigorous (Duncan whispering linebreak counts), seems particularly struc-tured to invite this sort of ventriloquism, the narrowing of multiple possi-bilities down into a single, narrow "interpretation." By their very nature, readings problematize multiplicity and ambiguity, simply by virtue of this supplement, the body and physical voice of the reader. Most seasoned lis-teners of poetry will have had the experience of going to hear a poet whose work, on the page, seems enticing, even exciting, only to discover that the actual writer turns out to be a completely repellent little toad. Readings beg the audience to focus the text into a single thread of meanings, constrained and conditioned by the presence of the writer. The reading is not so much a vessel as it is a funnel. In fact, one wants the opposite: maximum resis-tance, the irreducible opacity of a text.

Eigner, a poet who seldom used the word "I," showed how such resis-tance might be achieved. His readings exploded the myth of a simple, un-constructed voice. His texts demonstrate still that this was not merely a byproduct of his physical challenges. The following untitled piece comes from *air / the trees,* a collection whose title conspicuously is neither a com-plete sentence nor utterance:

> the twilight
> of rain
> felt
>
> the window
> vibrates
>
> candle
> flames
>
> no more light
>
> a passing
> truck

   dark
     fallen

   peacefully
     keeps on

     over
       the center[29]

Eigner composed hundreds of short untitled poems that appear at first glance to be lists. The first six of the eight stanzas here can each be read as an isolated detail. The presence of any person is kept to a minimum: something *feels* that "twilight of rain," but the image breaks off right at the moment when we would expect to learn *by whom*. Someone drives that passing truck, some agent has set that candle aflame. The vibration of the window and the flaming candle suggest an interior view, looking out. The sequence of images, from twilight to dark, etches the passage of time, while the sparseness of detail underscores a silence that is extraordinarily difficult to achieve as an effect in language. Yet what for me as a reader moves this text so powerfully beyond pure pastoral lyric is how it hinges, how it turns, upon an adverb of characterization: "dark / fallen // peacefully / keeps on . . ." Carrying an image over into a second stanza, the act of judgment implicit—but entirely visible—within this adverb focuses the presence of a perceiving "I" far more powerfully here than could any first person singular. This focus enables the image now to move into a third and final stanza, with its deliberately mysterious object: "over the center." Without once mentioning an explicit subject, Eigner presents us with an extraordinary self-portrait, a mind through the lens of the world itself. Whereas Wordsworth, crossing these same Alps in *The Prelude,* could only present the reader with a vicarious experience of seeing one's own unconscious reflected in nature, the phenomenological poetics of Larry Eigner offers us something much more direct. Identity and agency are here the drama of language and experience itself. Presence, because it is so complex, is not a given. The object of "over the center" is never revealed.

    Again, I am committing ventriloquism. As powerful and deep a lyric as Eigner's poem is, there are an almost infinite number of alternative frameworks through which it can be read and discussed. I have no reason to believe that Eigner himself would have placed the same weight upon the word "peacefully" as I have. Yet because, as a poet, I refuse to abandon the field of talking and writing about poems solely to critics with canonical agendas, I cannot fully escape the trap of capturing a complex reality and rendering it two-dimensionally as one stage in the structure of an argument. Nor am I any more disinterested in power than Roland Barthes or Paul de Man. The sole point on which I differ from them is in my personal desire to use power against power, to turn it toward its own dissipation. The reader, the listener in whom I'm interested, is real. The concept of an "audience" is nothing more than an accumulation, a statistical average. The author is equally real, even the author of the words *thank you* on a cafeteria wall.

Who speaks? Who listens? Who reads? What are the impacts of these actions on our lives and the lives of others? Because history, biography, and psychology can only be real—they constitute reality's discourse—there can be no single way to proceed in either the poem or the reading: the path between any two people can only be specific. By inserting their own presence into the text while aggressively denying those of author and reader alike, the ventriloquists of canonization have powerfully, and often malevolently, shaped the terrain of choices available to participants in the text. These ventriloquists are a specter still haunting poetry. Their ghosts inhabit the process of scoring, differentiating winners from losers, in a slam, even when the judges are consciously "antiacademic." Their ghosts I would argue inscribe even the innocent reader's projection of context onto the visual cues of an anonymous reader at an open reading.

I am aware that in arguing that there can be "no single way," I have also privileged the poetry and reading strategies of Larry Eigner. In his inability to articulate the most casual of conversations, Eigner in fact stripped away precisely those fictions of "the natural," leaving the negotiation between author, text, voice and listener openly complex and raw. If "voice" and "person" are social constructs, Eigner reminds us at all points, so also are "ear" and "eye," the vehicles through which brute signifiers are socialized into meaning. Other methods are available that can empower the producer and consumer into becoming conscious of the degrees to which any act, even of overt resistance, both consents to a social contract and is nonetheless also the passive victim of generations of reification. Steve Benson, Carla Harryman, Jackson Mac Low, Abigail Child, David Antin, and others have demonstrated ways in which the "nature" of reading is always also a "culture." In recognizing its borders and the scaffolding of agency within, a listener at a reading from time to time may yet have an opportunity to gain a glimpse of the "self."

NOTES

1. Ferdinand de Saussure, *Course in General Linguistics,* ed. Charles Bally and Albert Sechehaye in collaboration with Albert Reidlinger, tr. Wade Baskin (New York: McGraw-Hill, 1959), p. 65.

2. "The Agency of the Letter in the Unconscious or Reason Since Freud," in Jacques Lacan, *Écrits: A Selection,* tr. Alan Sheridan (New York: W. W. Norton, 1977), p. 151.

3. Advertisements, especially tag lines and slogans, are the most noteworthy exception, driven by a need to foreground themselves against the constant recessive chatter of all this other language. Often enough, however, such high-relief commercial discourse attempts to have it both ways, presenting a thoroughly stylized and visible personality while speaking either through the passive voice of a grammatically

absent subject ("The real thing—it's Coke!"), the command from an anonymous speaker ("Run for the border!") or the agentless assertion created through the suppressed verb of being ("Bell Atlantic, the heart of communications"). This last example raises the problem to a new level in using a widely recognizable voice, James Earl Jones's, to deliver its message. Bell upped the irony even further when it ran a series of television spots showing Jones autographing phone directories exactly like an author at a reading.

4. Such foreknowledge, or lack of it, ranges from almost no idea whatsoever at many open mike venues to a general sense of who might be there in the case of a significant slam in a city where the slam scene has been established for a few years, in which the audience can expect to see or hear some or all of the local poetry performance heavyweights mixed in with unpredictable unknowns.

5. In contrast to the highly formulaic and ritualized narratives available today in other public media, such as cinema, TV drama, and sitcoms, or the popular novel. The two elements that are most pronounced in the free-for-all open reading are a wide (and unpredictable) range of such tales and the degree of containment posed both by the form of the work itself and the setting. The power of this combination should not be underestimated.

6. As the web page for Bob Holman's *United States of Poetry* notes, "It's not a slam without winners and losers."

7. The anonymous narratives of struggle that characterize meetings of Alcoholics Anonymous and other substance recovery groups. The range of narratives in these settings is limited, and the focus decidedly not on the aesthetic or formal elements of presentation, but many of the other features of the open reading can be found in such group meetings.

8. As is so often the case in the manners of class. No one is more obsequious than the British lord to his servants.

9. In *Critical Essays,* tr. Richard Howard (Evanston: Northwestern University Press, 1972), pp. 143–50.

10. In *Image/Music/Text,* tr. Stephen Heath (New York: Hill and Wang, 1977), pp. 142–48.

11. Barthes was in the first year of the seminar that led to the exhaustive close reading of that work in *S/Z.*

12. The term *canon* is unavoidably problematic. I have not eased this any for the sake of argument here, using the word both in the singular and plural form. Alastair Fowler once identified six types of canonicity: potential, accessible, selective, official, personal, and critical (Wendell V. Harris, "Canonicity," *PMLA,* vol. 106, no. 1 [January 1991], pp. 110–21). In general, when I use the term here, I refer to what Fowler would call the critical canon—those works "that are repeatedly treated in critical articles and books," noting that with the rise of theory in the American academy over the past two decades, any distinctions between this, the official and Harris' "pedagogical" canons have narrowed considerably.

13. Thus, in spite of many books of poetry, his anthologies of talks and his formative role in the creation of poetry over the past quarter century, Bob Perelman, well into his forties, wrote his doctoral dissertation on four modernists, only one of whom was born in the twentieth century: *The Trouble with Genius: Reading Pound, Joyce, Stein and Zukofsky* (Berkeley: University of California Press, 1994).

14. The phrase lies in the original: "Nous savons maintenant qu'un text n'est

pas fait d'une ligne," in "La Mort de l'auteur," *Le bruissement de la lange: Essai critiques, IV* (Paris: Editions du Seuil, 1984), p. 65.

15. These are not precisely Jakobson's names for the categories, but rather the terms best suited for their application to the field of poetry. See "Towards Prose" in my collection *The New Sentence* (New York: Roof Books, 1987), especially pp. 98–104.

16. This turns in just a few short years into Jean-François Lyotard's concept of parology.

17. Let alone Ginsberg reading a poem at a Rolling Renaissance "Be-In" to an audience of 100,000 or at the start of a San Francisco Giants baseball game, or Maya Angelou reading in front of millions at President Clinton's inauguration.

18. One could argue that critical discourse is what brings so many listeners to the event, but it is noteworthy that in each of these readings (and virtually any equivalent "star" reading I could imagine), what characterizes the popularity of the writer is how he or she has transcended the critical institutions of poetry in North America. In every circumstance, some external social phenomenon has served to make this or that writer a *name*. This follows Fowler's distinction between accessible and critical canons. A secondary effect is that, if it is the audience here that is anonymous, many of its members will arrive at the event with only the most superficial understanding of the work of the poet, which they may or may not have read. While there is some tendency on the part of committed literary participants to presume that "celebrity" poetry is second-rate or somehow watered down, the reality is that the relation of complexity or value in the work to its reception is all but irrelevant. Ginsberg and Rich may be superb writers and Bly a ridiculous one, but that has little or nothing to do with the popularity of the work.

19. This is why such readings can be the most alienating settings for newcomers to a given scene, who feel (rightly) that everyone already knows everyone else.

20. There are of course "star" slam poets, such as Marc Smith, Whammo, Bob Holman, or Patricia Smith, even a celebrity circuit of slams. One could imagine the institutionalization of this process following its sporting metaphor all the way to National Poetry Slam (which did in fact take place in Portland, Oregon, in September 1996). Holman's *United States of Poetry* web site includes its own "Hall of Flame." The origins of the slam in the performance art of the 1970s (G. P. Skratz's Actualist Conventions in Berkeley, Tom Marioni's boxing matches as performance art, the poetry "championships" in Chicago and Bisbee, Arizona), with at least reference to other forms of performance contestation, places the slam in a continuum that would include streetcorner tap-dance contests, the Van Clyburn competition, Star Search, the Paralympics, and the Super Bowl.

21. "Personism: A Manifesto," in *The Collected Poems of Frank O'Hara,* ed. Donald Allen (New York: Knopf, 1971), p. 499.

22. Bob Perelman, "Language Writing and the Selves," presented at the MLA Annual Convention, Washington, D.C., Dec., 1989; ms., p. 3.

23. Charles Olson, "Projective Verse," in *Human Universe and Other Essays,* ed. Donald Allen (New York: Grove Press, 1967), p. 55

24. Olson, p. 57. Note Olson's claim that the machine "leads directly." Everything in Olson's world "leads directly." The concept of directness is an organizing paradigm for Olson.

25. It is probably possible to argue exactly the opposite position as well, that

the text ought to move from the short line toward longer ones—the difference really has to do with how one conceives of the pause at the line's end, as a space that slows the reading or a catching of the breath that would increase syncopation and propel the reading forward.

26. Robert Creeley, *The Collected Poems* (Berkeley: University of California Press, 1984), p. 294.

27. Transcribed and edited originally by Zoe Brown as a book for Coyote Press, and now available in a Ralph Maud transcription in *Muthologos,* vol. 1, ed. George Butterick (Bolinas: Four Seasons, 1978), pp. 97–156.

28. Thus when the University of California chose to celebrate Eigner's work, it did so in a monumentally textual fashion, placing one of his texts in gigantic letters on the outside of the University Art Museum and holding a reading that included a dozen other poets prior to having Larry conclude the event, reading some poems on his own.

29. Larry Eigner, *air / the trees* (Los Angeles: Black Sparrow Press, 1968), p. 42.

Audio Resources

COMPILED BY KENNETH SHERWOOD

Sources for Individual Tapes

Academy of American Poets — Audiotape Archives
The Audio Archives has produced some twenty single-author cassette recordings from the Academy's reading series.

> The Academy of American Poets
> Audio Archives
> 584 Broadway, Suite 1208
> New York, NY 10012
> http://www.poets.org/lit/boothfst.htm

Bamboo Ridge Press
Primarily a print publisher, Bamboo Ridge typically issues cassettes with its books.

> Bamboo Ridge Press
> P.O. Box 61781
> Honolulu, HI 96839-1781

Fylkingen
The classic sound poetry distributor maintains a select catalog of older recordings and continues to release spoken-word CDs.

> FYLKINGEN RECORDS
> Box 17044
> S-104 62
> Stockholm, Sweden
> Fax: 46(0)-669 38 68
> http://www.bahnhof.se/~fylkingen/records.html

HarperAudio — Caedmon
The classic source for spoken word recordings, Caedmon maintains a catalogue of some thirty poetry recordings read by modern poets, including

cummings, Frost, Eliot, Hughes, Thomas, Plath, Pound, Sexton, Stein, and Stevens. Of particular note is the *Caedmon Treasury of Modern Poets Reading Their Own Poetry,* an anthology of nineteen poets.

HarperCollins Publishers
P.O. Box 588
Scranton, PA 18512-0588
800-331-3761
http://www.harperaudio.com

Lannan Foundation Videos
A contemporary poet is featured in each of this series of videotaped readings and interviews.

Lannan Foundation
5401 McConnel Avenue
Los Angeles, CA 90066

LINEbreak
A public radio program of performances, and interviews by Charles Bernstein, with twenty-five poets, from Barbara Guest to Paul Auster, LINE-*break* was produced for the Poetics Program of the University at Buffalo. On the World Wide Web, free RealAudio and broadcast quality soundfiles of LINE*break* programs and additional spoken word pieces are accessible through the Sound Room of the Electronic Poetry Center. Archive cassettes are also available by mail from Small Press Distribution.

SPD
1341 Seventh Street
Berkeley, CA 94710-1407
800-869-7553
SPD@SPDBooks.org
http://wings.buffalo.edu/epc/sound

New Wilderness Audiographics
A range of sound studio projects by poets, performance artists, and conceptual composers, produced in the 1970s by Charlie Morrow; individual cassettes by Jerome Rothenberg, Hannah Weiner, Bernard Heidieck, Jackson Mac Low, Armand Schwerner, and others.

Frog Peak Music (distributor)
Box 1052
Lebanon, NH 03755
frogpeak@sover.net
http://www.sover.net/~frogpeak/

Pacifica Radio Archive
Not exclusively a poetry source, Pacifica does maintain searchable broadcast archives, including readings by poets like David Antin and Larry Eigner, in addition to various poets recorded by Susan Howe.

Pacifica Radio Archive
3729 Cahuenga Blvd. West
North Hollywood, CA 91604
http://www.pacifica.org/archive/
ppspacific@pacifica.org

Poetry Center, San Francisco State University
The Poetry Center maintains an extensive collection of audio and video recordings that are available for on-site use, rental, and purchase. Highlights
include the many videos documenting SFSU performances held exclusively
by the Poetry Center.

Poetry Center
San Francisco State University
1600 Holloway Avenue
San Francisco, CA 94132
http://www.sfsu.edu/~newlit

Poet's Audio Center
A new, online service of the nonprofit Watershed Foundation, Poet's Audio
Center includes 150 well-produced audio recordings of poets ranging from
T. S. Eliot to Kamau Brathwaite. Their listings also include audio antholog-
ies and many Caedmon recordings. The World Wide Web resource lists all
their in-print recordings and information about other sources.

Poet's Audio Center / Watershed Foundation
6925 Willow Street NW, Suite 201
Washington, DC 20012-2023.
poetapes@writer.org
http://www.writer.org/pac/pac01

Rhino Records
Rhino has several relevant releases: *In Their Own Voices: A Century of Recorded Poetry* (R272408 for CD and R472408 for cassette)—a four-CD compilation of Frost, Stein, Pound, Millay, cummings, Hughes, Thomas, Kerouac, Ginsberg. Also: *The Beat Generation* (four CDs), *Allen Ginsberg: Holy
Soul Jelly Roll—Poems and Songs (1949-1993)* (four CDs), *The Jack Kerouac
Collection* (four CDs), and *William Burroughs: Call Me Burroughs.*

Rhino Records
10635 Santa Monica Boulevard
Los Angeles, CA 90025

Underwhich Editions
Primarily a print publisher, Underwhich also supports contemporary sound
poetry.

Underwhich Editions
P.O. Box 262, Adelaide Street Station
Toronto, Ontario, Canada.

Select Audio Anthologies

Bobeobi Lautpoesie
This CD features sound poets from John Cage to Christian Prigent, many in German.
> Gertraud Scholz Verlag
> Wein bergstr.
> 11, D-90587
> Obermichelbach, Germany, LC 4794

Futurism and Dada Reviewed
This useful compilation CD includes rare performances by avant-garde modernist poets like Kurt Schwitters, Marcel Duchamp, and Tristan Tzara.
> Sub Rosa America
> 13330-A White Oak Circle
> Tampa, FL 33618

howls, raps & roars: recordings from the san francisco poetry renaissance (4FCD-4410-2)
This four-CD set, compiled by Ann Charters, features Lenny Bruce and Allen Ginberg and includes cuts from Rexroth, Corso, Wieners, Whalen, and others.
> Fantasy Records
> Tenth and Parker
> Berkeley, CA 94710

JazzSpeak: A Word Collection (NAR CD 054)
This compilation CD includes thirty tracks of poets from Amiri Baraka and Quincy Troupe to Wanda Coleman. Many of these recently recorded pieces include improvised musical background, making this a great introduction to the jazz poetry performance styles made popular in the 1960s.
> New Alliance Records
> P.O. Box 1
> Lawndale, CA 90260

Live at the Ear (CD)
Edited by Charles Bernstein, former curator of the Ear Inn reading series, this audio anthology includes the seminal work of thirteen poets asssociated with L=A=N=G=U=A=G=E Poetry. Also available from SPD.
> Elemenope Productions
> 7 Market Square #208
> Pittsburgh, PA 15222

The Norton Anthology of English Literature, 6th ed., *Audio Companion* (1996)
Edited by M. H. Abrams et al., includes Tennyson reading "The Charge of

the Light Brigade," plus Yeats, Sitwell, Auden, Thomas, along with recitations from Beowulf to Hopkins.

Nuyorican Symphony: Live at the Knitting Factory (KFWCD-138)
Edited by Miguel Algarin, this CD includes seventy minutes of solo and group performances with a performative flair for which the NuYorican Poet's Café has become famous.
> The Knitting Factory
> 74 Leonard Street
> New York, NY 10013

United States of Poetry (314 532 139-2)
Over thirty poets, from Amiri Baraka and Lou Reed to Czeslaw Milosz, are included on this eclectic CD aimed at the MTV generation. Information on the CD as well as audio clips are available on the World Wide Web. The PBS video of the same title is available from KQED Books and Video, (800) 647-3600.
> Mouth Almighty / Mercury Records
> 516 West 25th Street, Suite 306
> New York, NY 10001
> http://www.itvs.org/poetry

Vocal Neighborhoods
Edited by Larry Wendt, this CD sound poetry anthology and magazine includes Henri Chopin and Pauline Oliveros.
> Leonardo Music Journal, vol. 3
> MIT Press Journals
> 55 Hayward Street
> Cambridge, MA 02124

On-Site Use Collections

Archive for New Poetry, Mandeville Special Collections Library, University of California at San Diego
The archive includes over 1,100 audio recordings, most notably those made by Paul Blackburn.
> Mandeville Special Collections Library
> UCSD Libraries 0175S
> 9500 Gilman Drive
> La Jolla, CA 92093-0175
> spcoll@ucsd.edu

Poet's House
The largely print-oriented collection includes the Axe-Houghton Tape Archive, consisting of hundreds of recorded poetry events, which are available for on-site consultation.

Poet's House
72 Spring Street, 2nd Floor
New York, NY 10012
(212) 431-7920

Woodberry Poetry Room, Harvard University
Though primarily for on-site use, poetry audio cassettes are available if written copyright permission is obtained in advance is obtained from the author.
Woodberry Poetry Room, Lamont Library
Harvard College Library
Cambridge, MA 02138
(617) 495-2454

Multimedia Products

Little Magazine, vol. 21
This ambitious CD-ROM, edited by Christopher Funkhouser and Belle Gironda, features works by seventy-seven artists and sets them in diverse manners. While not exclusively presenting poets' audio, it gives valuable insight into poetry's increasing use of hybrid media for performance and publication.
The Little Magazine
Dept. of English
University at Albany
1400 Washington Ave.
Albany, NY 12222
litmag@cnsunix.albany.edu
http://www.albany.edu/~litmag

Poetry in Motion
This widely available multimedia CD-ROM (Voyager 1994), edited by Ron Mann, includes texts, images, and audio/video clips. Among others, Allen Ginsberg, Robert Creeley, Anne Waldman, and Ted Berrigan each read one poem aloud. The audio quality is necessarily inferior to standard cassette recordings, but each performance is presented alongside the corresponding text.
http://www.voyagerco.com/

Bibliography

Abram, David, *The Spell of the Sensuous* (New York: Pantheon, 1996)

Adorno, Theodor, *Quasi una fantasia,* tr. Rodney Livingstone (New York: Verso, 1994)

Antin, David, *Talking at the Boundaries* (New York: New Direction, 1976)

Applebaum, David, *Voice* (Albany: State University of New York Press, 1990)

Athanases, Steven A., "When Print Alone Fails Poetry: Performance as a Contingency of Literary Value," *Text and Performance Quarterly,* vol. 11 (April 1991)

Attali, Jacques, *Noise: The Political Economy of Music,* tr. Leila Conners and Nathan Gandels (Minneapolis: University of Minnesota Press, 1985)

Attridge, Derek, *Poetic Rhythm: An Introduction* (New York: Cambridge University Press, 1995)

———, *The Rhythms of English Poetry* (New York: Longman, 1982)

Austin, J. L., *How to Do Things with Words* (Cambridge, Mass.: Harvard University Press, 1962)

Aviram, Amittai, *Telling Rhythm* (Ann Arbor: University of Michigan Press, 1994)

Baker, Houston, *Blues, Ideology, and Afro-American Literature* (Chicago: University of Chicago Press, 1987)

Baraka, Imamu Amiri [LeRoi Jones], *Blues People: Negro Music in White America* (New York: William Morrow, 1963)

Barthes, Roland, "Listening," in *The Responsibility of Forms,* tr. Richard Howard (New York: Hill and Wang, 1985)

Bataille, Georges, *The Accursed Share,* vol. 1, tr. Robert Hurley (New York: Zone, 1988)

Bauman, Richard, ed., *Folklore, Cultural Performances, and Popular Entertainments* (New York: Oxford University Press, 1992)

———. *Verbal Art as Performance* (Rowley, Mass.: Newbury House, 1977)

Benamou, Michael, and Charles Caramello, eds. *Performance in Postmodern Culture* (Milwaukee: Center for Twentieth-Century Studies, University of Wisconsin–Milwaukee, 1977)

Benjamin, Walter, "Doctrine of the Similar," tr. Knut Tarnowski, *New German Critique,* no. 17 (1979)

Bernstein, Charles, "Applied Monk: Preliminary Notes," *Caliban,* no. 4 (1988)

———, "Words and Pictures," in *Content's Dream: Essays, 1975–1984* (Los Angeles: Sun & Moon Press, 1986)

Blau, Herbert, "Deep Throat: The Grail of the Voice," in *The Book, Spiritual Instrument,* ed. Jerome Rothenberg and David Guss, New Wilderness Letters, no. 11 (1982; rpt., New York: Granary Books, 1997)

———, *To All Appearances: Ideology and Performance* (New York: Routledge, 1992)

Brathwaite, Edward [Kamau], *History of the Voice: The Development of Nation Language in Anglophone Caribbean Poetry* (London: New Beacon Books, 1984)

Brogan, T. V. F., *English Versification, 1570–1980: A Reference Guide with a Global Appendix* (Baltimore: Johns Hopkins University Press, 1981)

———, "Sound," in *The New Princeton Encyclopedia of Poetry and Poetics,* ed. Alex Preminger and Brogan (Princeton: Princeton University Press, 1993)

Bunting, Basil, "The Poet's Point of View," in *Three Essays,* ed. Richard Caddel (Durham, England: Basil Bunting Center, 1994)

Byerly, Alison, "From Schoolroom to Stage: Reading Aloud and the Domestication of Victorian Theater," *Bucknell Review,* vol. 34, no. 2 (1990)

Chartier, Roger, *The Order of Books: Readers, Authors, and Libraries in Europe between the Fourteenth and Eighteenth Centuries,* tr. Lydia G. Cochrane (Cambridge, England: Polity Press, 1994)

cheek, cris, *Language Alive [writing for live action or developed through live action or directly related to live action],* nos. 1 and 2 (Lowstoft: Sound & Language, 1996)

Cobbing, Bob, and Peter Mayer, eds., *Concerning Concrete Poetry* (London: Writers Forum, 1978)

Coleman, Joyce, "The Solace of Hearing: Medieval Views on the Reading Aloud of Literature," *Nordic Yearbook of Folklore,* vol. 46 (1990)

Chopin, Henri, *Poésie sonore internationale* (Paris: Jean-Michel Place, 1979)

Croll, Morris, *Style, Rhetoric, and Rhythm: Essays* (Woodbridge, Conn.: Ox Bow Press, 1989)

Cusic, Don, *The Poet as Performer* (Lanham, Md.: University Press of America, 1991)

Cutten, George B., *Speaking with Tongues Historically and Psychologically Considered* (New Haven: Yale University Press, 1927)

De Certeau, Michel, *The Practice of Everyday Life,* tr. Steven F. Rendell (Berkeley: University of California Press, 1984)

Davidson, Michael, "Technologies of Presence: Orality and the Tapevoice of Contemporary Poetics" in *Ghostlier Demarcations: Modern Poetry and the Material Word* (Berkeley: University of California Press, 1997)

Debord, Guy, *Society of the Spectacle* (Cambridge: MIT Press, 1994)

Drucker, Johanna, *The Century of Artists' Books* (New York: Granary Books, 1996)

———, *The Visible Word: Experimental Typography and Modern Art, 1909–1923* (Chicago: University of Chicago Press, 1994)

Edwards, Viv, and Thomas J. Sienkewicz, *Oral Cultures Past and Present: Rappin' and Homer* (Oxford: Basil Blackwell, 1990)

Entralago, Pedro Laín, *The Therapy of the Word in Classical Antiquity,* tr. L. J. Rather and John M. Sharp (New Haven: Yale University Press, 1970)

Fogerty, Elsie, *The Speaking of English Verse* (London: J. M. Dent, 1923)

Foley, John Miles, *Oral Tradition in Literature: Interpretation in Context* (Columbia: University of Missouri Press, 1986)

Fónagy, Ivan, "La Métaphore en phonétique," *Studio Phonetica,* vol. 16 (Ottawa: Didier, 1979)

————, *La Vive voix: essais de psycho-phonétique,* preface by Roman Jakobson (Paris: Payot, 1991)

Frank, Robert, and Henry Sayre, eds., *The Line in Postmodern Poetry* (Urbana: University of Illinois Press, 1988)

Frye, Northrop, ed., *Sound and Poetry* (New York: Columbia University Press, 1957)

Gary, Paul H., "Poet as Entertainer: Will Carleton, James Whitcomb Riley, and the Rise of the Poet-Performer Movement," *Literature in Performance,* vol. 5 (November 1984)

Gaylord, Alan T., "Reading Chaucer: What's Allowed in 'Aloud'?" *Chaucer Yearbook,* vol. 1 (1992)

Gibson, James J., *The Senses Considered as Perceptual Systems* (Boston: Houghton Mifflin, 1966).

Glissant, Edouard, *Caribbean Discourse: Selected Essays,* tr. J. Michael Dash (Charlottesville: University of Virginia Press, 1989)

Goffman, Erving, *Frame Analysis: An Essay on the Organization of Experience* (Cambridge, Mass.: Harvard University Press, 1974)

Goodman, Felicitas D., *Speaking in Tongues: A Cross-Cultural Glossolalia* (Chicago: University of Chicago Press, 1972)

Goody, Jack, *The Interface between the Written and the Oral* (Cambridge: Cambridge University Press, 1987)

Hall, Donald, "The Poetry Reading: Public Performance/Private Art," *American Scholar,* vol. 54 (1985)

Hartman, Charles O., *Free Verse: An Essay on Prosody* (Princeton: Princeton University Press, 1980)

Higgins, Dick, *Pattern Poems: Guide to an Unknown Literature* (Albany: State University of New York Press, 1987)

Hinton, Leanne, Johanna Nichols, and John Ohala, "Introduction: Sound-Symbolic Processes," in Hinton, Nichols, and Ohala, eds., *Sound Symbolism* (Cambridge: Cambridge University Press, 1994)

Hogg, Richard, and C. B. McCully, *Metrical Phonology: A Coursebook* (Cambridge: Cambridge University Press, 1987)

Holder, Alan, *Rethinking Meter: A New Approach to the Verse Line* (Lewisburg, Pa.: Bucknell University Press, 1995)

Ihde, Don, *Listening and Voice: A Phenomenology of Sound* (Athens: Ohio University Press, 1976)

Jakobson, Roman, *Language in Literature* (Cambridge: Belknap Press, 1987)

Jakobson, R., and L. Waugh, *The Sound Shape of Language* (Brighton, England: Harvester Press, 1979)

Kahn, Douglas, and Gregory Whitehead, *Wireless Imagination* (Cambridge, Mass.: MIT Press, 1992)

Kostelanetz, Richard, ed., *Text-Sound Texts* (New York: William Morrow, 1980)

Kramer, Lawrence, *Music and Poetry: The Nineteenth Century and After* (Berkeley: University of California Press, 1984)

Langellier, Kristin M., "From Text to Social Context," *Literature in Performance,* vol. 6 (April 1986)

Lazer, Hank, "Poetry Readings and the Contemporary Canon," in *Opposing Poetries,* vol. 1: *Issues and Institutions* (Evanston, Ill.: Northwest University Press, 1996)

Levertov, Denise, "An Approach to Public Poetry Listenings," in *Light Up the Cave* (New York: New Directions, 1981)

Levin, David Michael, *The Listening Self: Personal Growth, Social Change and the Closure of Metaphysics* (London: Routledge, 1989)

McCaffery, Steve, *North of Intention: Critical Writings, 1973–1986* (New York: Roof, 1986)

McCaffery, Steve, and bp Nichol, eds., *Sound Poetry: A Catalogue for the Eleventh International Sound Poetry Festival, Toronto, Canada, October 14–21, 1978* (Toronto: Underwhich Editions, 1978)

McGann, Jerome, *Black Riders* (Princeton: Princeton University Press, 1993)

———, *The Textual Condition* (Princeton: Princeton University Press, 1991)

Machan, Katharyn Howd, "Breath into Fire: Feminism and Poetry Readings," *Mid-American Review,* vol. 12, no. 2 (1992)

Mackey, Nathaniel, *Discrepant Engagement: Dissonance, Cross-Culturality and Experimental Writing* (New York: Cambridge University Press, 1993)

Manguel, Alberto, *A History of Reading* (London: HarperCollins, 1996)

Markov, Vladimir, *Russian Futurism: A History* (Berkeley: University of California Press, 1968)

Merleau-Ponty, Maurice, *The Visible and the Invisible,* tr. Alphonso Lingus (Evanston, Ill.: Northwestern University Press, 1968)

Meschonnic, Henri, *Critique du rythme: anthropologie historique du language* (Lagrasse: Verdier, 1982)

Morris, Adelaide, ed., *Sound States: Acoustical Technologies and Modern and Postmodern Writing* (Chapel Hill: University of North Carolina, 1997)

Morrison, Mark, "Performing the Pure Voice: Elocution, Verse Recitation, and Modernist Poetry in Prewar London," *Modernism/Modernity,* vol. 3, no. 3 (1996)

Murphy, Michael, "On Not Reading Chaucer Aloud," *Medievalia,* vol. 9 (1987)

Nagy, Gregory, *Poetry as Performance: Homer and Beyond* (New York: Cambridge University Press, 1996)

Nielsen, Aldon L., *Black Chant: Languages of African-American Postmodernism* (New York: Cambridge University Press, 1996)

Oliver, Douglas, *Poetry and Narrative in Performance* (New York: Macmillan, 1989)

Olson, Charles: "Proprioception" and "Projective Verse" in *The Collected Prose of Charles Olson,* ed. Don Allen and Benjamin Friedlander (Berkeley: University of California Press, 1997)

Olson, David R., "How Writing Represents Speech," *Language and Communication,* vol. 13, no. 1 (1993)

O'Neill, Ynez Violé, *Speech and Speech Disorders in Western Thought before 1600* (Westport, Conn.: Greenwood Press, 1980)

Ong, Walter, *Orality and Literacy: The Technologizing of the Word* (New York: Methuen, 1982)

Parker, Andrew, and Eve Kosofsky Sedgwick, eds., *Performativity and Performance* (New York: Routledge, 1995)

Perloff, Marjorie, *The Futurist Moment: Avant-Garde, Avant-Guerre, and the Language of Rupture* (Chicago: University of Chicago Press, 1986)

———, *Rhyme and Meaning in the Poetry of Yeats* (The Hague: Mouton, 1970)

Piette, Adam, *Remembering and the Sound of Words: Mallarmé, Proust, Joyce, Beckett* (New York: Oxford University Press, 1966)

Prinz, Jessica, *Art Discourse/Discourse in Art* (New Brunswick: Rutgers University Press, 1991)

Prynne, J. H., "Stars, Tigers and the Shape of Words," William Mathews Lectures, delivered at Birkbeck College, London, 1992 (available from Birkbeck College)

Quasha, George, "Dialogos: Between the Written and the Oral in Contemporary Poetry," *New Literary History*, vol. 8 (1977)

Richter, Hans, *Dada Art and Anti-Art*, tr. David Britt (New York: Abrams, 1965)

Robb, Mary Margaret, *Oral Interpretation of Literature in American Colleges and Universities* (New York: H. W. Wilson, 1941)

Rodenberg, Patsy, *The Need for Words: Voice and the Text* (London: Methuen Drama, Reed Publishing, 1993)

Rothenberg, Jerome, *Pre-Faces and Other Writings* (New York: New Directions, 1981)

———, ed., *Technicians of the Sacred* (New York: Doubleday, 1969)

Rothenberg, Jerome, and David Guss, eds., *The Book, Spiritual Instrument* (1982; rpt., New York: Granary Books, 1997)

Rothenberg, Jerome, and Diane Rothenberg, eds., *Symposium of the Whole: A Range of Discourses toward an Ethnopoetics* (Berkeley: University of California, 1983)

Rubeo, Ugo, "Voice as Lifesaver: Defining the Function of Orality in Etheridge Knight's Poetry," in *The Black Columbiad: Defining Moments in African American Literature and Culture*, ed. Werner Sollors and Maria Diedrich (Cambridge, Mass.: Harvard University Press, 1994)

Sansome, Clive, "Verse Speaking Today," in *Speech in Our Time*, ed. Sansome (London: Hinrichsen, 1948)

Sayre, Henry, *The Object of Performance: The American Avant-Garde Since 1970* (Chicago: University of Chicago Press, 1989)

Schechner, Richard, *Essays on Performance Theory* (New York: Routledge, 1988)

Scholz, Christian, *Untersuchungen zur Geschichte und Typologie der Lautepoesie*, 3 vols. (Obermichelbach: Gertraud Scholz Verlag, 1989)

Schwitters, Kurt, *Poems, Performance Pieces, Proses, Plays, Poetics*, tr. Jerome Rothenberg and Pierre Joris (Philadelphia: Temple University Press, 1993)

Shaw, Mary Lewis, *Performance in the Texts of Mallarmé* (University Park: Pennsylvania State University Press, 1993)

Spanos, William, ed., "The Oral Impulse in Contemporary American Poetry," *boundary 2*, vol. 3, no. 3 (1975)

Stern, Frederick C., "The Formal Poetry Reading," *The Drama Review*, vol. 35, no. 3 (fall 1991)

Stewart, Garrett, *Reading Voices: Literature and the Phonotext* (Berkeley: University of California Press, 1990)

Strauss, Neil, ed., *Radiotext(e), Semioetext(e)* no. 6 [vol. 6, no. 1] (1993)

Svenbro, Jesper, *Phrasikleia: An Anthropology of Reading in Ancient Greece*, tr. Janet Lloyd (Ithaca: Cornell University Press, 1993)

Tedlock, Dennis, *The Spoken Word and the Work of Interpretation* (Philadelphia: University of Pennsylvania Press, 1983)

Thompson, David W., ed., *Performance of Literature in Historical Perspectives* (Lanham, Md.: University Press of America, 1983)

Tsur, Reuven, *Toward a Theory of Cognitive Poetics* (Amsterdam: North Holland, 1992)

———, *What Makes Sound Patterns Expressive?: The Poetic Mode of Speech Perception* (Durham, N.C.: Duke University Press, 1992)

Udall, E., "Attitudinal Meanings Conveyed by Intonation Contours," *Language and Speech,* vol. 3 (1960).

———, "Dimensions of Meaning in Intonation," in *Intonation: Selected Readings,* ed. D. Bolinger (London: Penguin, 1972)

Vincent, Stephen, and Ellen Zweig, eds. *The Poetry Reading: A Contemporary Compendium on Language and Performance* (San Francisco: Momo's Press, 1981)

Waugh, Linda, "Against Arbitrariness: Imitation and Motivation Revived, with Consequences for Textual Meaning," *diacritics,* vol. 23, no. 2 (1983)

Wellman, Don, ed., "Voice // Voicing // Voices: A Forum," *O.Ars,* vols. 6/7 (1989)

Welsh, Andrew, *Roots of Lyric: Primitive Poetry and Modern Poetics* (Princeton: Princeton University Press, 1978)

Wesling, Donald, *The Chances of Rhyme: Device and Modernity* (Berkeley: University of California Press, 1980)

Wimsatt, William K., "On the Relation of Rhyme to Reason," in *The Verbal Icon: Studies in the Meaning of Poetry* (Lexington: University of Kentucky Press, 1954)

Winn, James Anderson, *A History of the Relations between Poetry and Music* (New Haven: Yale University Press, 1981)

Winters, Yvor, "The Audible Reading of Poetry," in *The Function of Criticism* (Denver: A. Swallow, 1957)

Wittgenstein, Ludwig, *Philosophical Investigations,* tr. G. E. M. Anscombe (New York: Macmillan, 1968)

Ziegler, Alan, Larry Zirlin, and Harry Greenberg, eds., *Poets on Stage: The Some Symposium on Poetry Readings* (New York: Some/Release Press, 1978); simultaneously published as *Some,* no. 9